Chap 17.2

Summary Judgment

Purpose: enable early J where D has no hope of success ie defence is spurious.

Main use - in contract esp debt
Rare in - negligence esp road acc. (argue contrib neg)
Not applicable: defamation, malicious prosecution

Conditions for Ord 14 Application

a) D must have given notice of intention to defend
b) St of Claim must have been served on D, and
c) The affidavit in support of the application must comply c̄ reqts of Ord 14 Rule 2

When these considerations are satisfied P will have established a prima facie case + becomes entitled to judgment. Burden shifts to D to satisfy Ct why judgmt should not be given vs him.

Rule 2 re Affidavit:

- Application under r1 must be made by summons supported by an affidavit verifying the facts on which the claim, or the part of a claim is based +
- stating that in the deponent's belief there is no defence to that claim.
- Affidavit here may contain statements of info or belief c̄ the sources + grounds thereof.
- The summons, copy of affidavit in support + any exhibits referred to therein must be served on D not less than 10 clear days before the return day.

Effect of application

→ Extends time of service of the defence until after the hearing of the summons.

Method of Application

to District Judge by summons seeking summary judgment + supported by an affidavit which:
a) Verify facts of claim (repeat "contents of the statement of claim are true")
b) State deponent's belief: no defence to the claim.
~~If acting on~~ If sworn by someone acting on P's behalf:
c) Swear - authorised by P to make the affidavit.

Issue summons; orig affidavit c̄ D's Registry
↓ Notice: 10 clear days before hearing date
Serve copy of Summons + affid on Def
↓
Can oppose application: serve on applicant copy of affidavit:
Notice: 3 clear days before hearing date
ie put defence on oath (perjury)

CIVIL LITIGATION

If notice not complied c̄ → P can require adjournment or press ahead

Hearing of the Summons

After hearing argument DJ may make one of 4 orders:

1. Judgment for the Plaintiff
if there is no issue or Q that ought to be tried. Burden of proof on Def to show there is an issue. Judge can look behind D's affidavit for bona fides.
Test: is there an ARGUABLE issue which ought to be tried before a judge in open Ct.
ie is there a triable issue?
- Claim for liq amt →(DJ) final J for sum claimed + int + order for costs
- Claim for Unliq amt → J on liability only + adjourn Q of damages to future hearing (c̄ evid on quantum)

If D doesn't attend hearing: P reqd to prove service of the summons (c̄ affidavit).

2) Unconditional leave to Defend
When D raises a triable defence (Q of law or fact) ie matter proceeds to trial; application for SJ fails. D needs to give full particulars of defence.
- Counterclaims + 3rd P: if claim + CC related → P may be given judgment but subject to a stay of execution pending trial of the CC;
if not related → judgment for P c̄ costs s̄ any stay pending trial of CC.
- "Some other reason" for trial
No defence but given uncond leave to defend; where interest of some other person might be affected by SJ.

3) Conditional Leave to defend
-some defence but doubt good faith of def.
Condition: Re[illegible] Ct [illegible] of the [illegible] an [illegible] d be [illegible]

→ gives judgment under O14
That will afford a ground for an order for interim paymt in respect of action for debt (excluding costs) under Ord 29 r11 + 12.
-unless Ct gives unconditional leave to defend.

4) Dismissal of the Summons
If P's application is in bad faith ie knew of defence → P ordered to pay costs in any event (not "costs in the cause" as for other options) ie meet D's costs. Prudent to withdraw the summons if outcome of the hearing seems inevitable ie arguable defence/substantial factual dispute exists

Q: Should SJ be given?
Ans
1. What is a SJ
   - its purpose
   - criteria
2. Apply to facts
   I would apply to SJ ∵ of pro facts.....
   But I would not apply ∵ of con facts.....
Discuss specific advantages/dis to client eg
- Speedy conclusion
- Concern about D's fin lab (will ultimate judgment be unenforceable ∵ D has no assets vs which a judgment can be enforced?)
- Suspicion about defence -full enquiries made about complainant
3. Conclude
   Is there a real defence to the action? consider points re D's evidence

Q. There is a triable issue. Should leave to defend be conditional upon payment in of the sum claimed by P.?

Ans

1. Circs in which conditional leave will be granted
2. Arguments applying to these facts c̄ appropriate explanations

a) whether defence shadowy
b) would they really have left this serious complaint to one message c̄ a receptionist?
c) if they did phone, why not follow up "within the next week"? Why only when received writ?
d) X is not compelling expert - def's employee
e) Why not itemise/produce proof of this alleged counterclaim?
f) Concern about financial viability of def.

[rumours if not in affidavits can not be relied on at the hearing]

Q Leave to def is given. Usual directions as to pleadings discovery + insp of docs, exchange of expert evid & W statements & setting down. What further directions may the Ct consider making & why?

Ans

1. TF to the County Ct?
2. Split trial?
3. Retention, preservation & insp of the lorry?

Discuss why these would/not be appropriate

P must:
- verify facts on which claim to which application relates is based
- That deponent's belief that there is no defence (RSC Ord 14/2/4)

D must:
Show cause vs P's application by
- Technical objection: there was issue or Q in dispute which ought to be tried
  - or difficult pt of law } which ought to be tried
  - dispute as to facts }

or
- show that D has a good defence on the merits

or
- any other circs showing reasonable grounds for bona fide defence (RSC 14/3)

How to show cause?
- by evid: affidavits + exhibits
- oral argument on fact + law

[Can only argue what's in the affidavit]

Where Leave to defend is given
Ct gives Directions:
Pleadings if application before service of defence, D now reqd to serve defence
Discovery
Expert evid
W statements
Split Trial
Retention, Preservation, Insp of Prop
Setting down + mode of Trial

Argument by P for Payment re Terms of Leave to Defend

- At best defence is shadowy
  - not raised at the time
  - never put in writing until responding to writ/last before action (X weeks after difficulties)
  ↓
  lot vague + unspecific
- P has been kept out of a substantial sum of money for too long.
- P entitled to feel secure in knowledge that, if matter goes to trial, money will be there when their confident expectation of judgment is realised. → leave must be conditional.
- D has, in effect, obtained substantial credit by virtue of raising a shadowy defence.
- Wholly unjust to P to keep them out of money due & payable

(• Cosand result → if in affidavit)

D's Arguments

- There is a triable issue (s).
- Matters for expert evid at trial - to resolve
- Clear evid that P's perf of contract did not meet the particular purpose.
- Well defined losses & counter claim.
- If D wins, & if payment in is ordered under conditional leave - wholly unjust that D will have been deprived of its working capital for so long.
- If D wins, CC will exceed claim & P may be out of business.

Order 14 & Ord 29

P should combine application for Ord 14 c̄ application for an Interim Payment under Ord 29

Grounds on which an IP may be made are set out in Ord 29 r. 11. Particular ground of interest to P here is:
"that if the action proceeded to trial the applicant would obtain judgment for substantial damages vs the respondent..."

If an IP had been sought, P's affidavit would have to go on to support the contention that P would be likely to obtain substantial damages.

[If unconditional leave to def granted to D → IP will NOT be awarded]

IP may be awarded where an Ord for conditional leave to def. is given.

Advantage: IP is a payment to P. while conditional leave only involves a sum of money being paid into Court

Ramani Chelliah

CIVIL LITIGATION

Craig Osborne BA, MA (Econ), Solicitor

formerly Senior Lecturer at Manchester Metropolitan University
and Visiting Lecturer at the University of Hong Kong
and the Institute of Commerce, Singapore

Security for Costs

D can consider this under RSC Ord 23. Where there is significant doubt whether, should D be successful at trial, it will be able to recover costs fr P

First published in Great Britain 1993 by Blackstone Press Limited,
Aldine Place, London W12 8AA. Telephone 0181-740 2277

ISBN: 1 85431 649 4

British Library Cataloguing in Publication Data
A CIP catalogue record for this book is available from the British Library.

Second edition 1994
Third edition 1995
Fourth edition 1996
Fifth edition 1997

Typeset by Style Photosetting Limited, Mayfield, East Sussex
Printed by Ashford Colour Press, Gosport, Hampshire

CONTENTS

PREFACE

This book is intended to be a 'legal resource book' for the Legal Practice Course in civil litigation. It covers all aspects of the written standards produced by the Law Society for that course, but it is the writer's hope that it also goes well beyond them. It is intended to be a legal resource book in the fullest sense, being a full and self-contained treatment of all relevant aspects of mainstream civil litigation in High Court and county court. It includes not merely a description of relevant procedures, but a discussion of practical and tactical matters which commonly arise, together with a full treatment of the more academic aspects such as remedies for torts and breach of contract and the Limitation Acts. That is not, of course, to claim that students will not often benefit from referring direct to the original sources referred to in this text (e.g., statutes, case law and rules of court). In addition, there are chapters on the financing of civil litigation, the management of civil litigation practice and alternative dispute resolution.

I am very grateful to Blackstone Press for their help with the production of this work, in particular by the indulgence shown in allowing me to overshoot, by more than 50 per cent, the prima facie page limit which I was given. The benefits of that indulgence are that I have been able to deal in considerably more depth and detail with many of the important aspects of civil litigation than would otherwise have been the case.

Although the text deals with all mainstream aspects of litigation, I have, in particular, dealt with some aspects of personal injury actions in sufficient depth in the hope that this Guide will also be of use to students in the many institutions who offer personal injury litigation as a separate option on the Legal Practice Course. I also hope that the Guide will prove to be of use to students during their training contracts.

It is appropriate to explain three things about the text. Firstly, readers may inevitably wonder why, given the hugely increased jurisdiction and importance of the county court, so much of the text concentrates on the High Court with only two chapters describing the respective differences in county court procedure. The reason for this is that, in my opinion, it is easier to learn the High Court procedures first and then the county court variations rather than the other way round. The only important stages where there is a significant difference between High Court and county court procedure are at the initiation of proceedings, and at the directions stage. Apart from those differences there are many instances where the County Court Rules are the virtual equivalent of the corresponding High Court Rules and in every such case the notes in the County Court Practice simply indicate that the procedure in the county court is in all respects to follow that in the High Court. This is true in many instances including the practice on discovery, exchange of witness statements, disclosure of expert evidence, interrogatories and pleadings. Thus, for example, someone who has thoroughly studied the rules relating to discovery in the High Court need learn nothing more about them in order to be able to apply them correctly in the county court. In every instance the tactical and practical considerations are the same and thus the differences between county court and High Court are less important than usually supposed and this is my justification for the order of treatment.

A huge exception to this principle is of course the problem of automatic striking out in the county court for non-compliance with the basic rule that one has to set down an action within, in effect, 15 months of close of pleadings or the cause of action is lost altogether. That remarkable feature of county court litigation is strikingly different from the more leisurely pace of High Court procedure and clearly deserves to be singled out for special attention in practice given the huge amount of important recent case law on the problems caused by the automatic striking out rule. Some, but not all, of those problems were resolved in a series of decisions in the Court of Appeal just before Christmas 1995 reported in early 1996. Even those thorough guidelines did not lay all the problems to rest, however, and the Court of Appeal had to give further guidelines in a series of cases reported in *The Times* on 2 May 1997.

Secondly, in every text which purports to describe civil procedure, there will inevitably be differences of opinion about the running order. To follow an action strictly chronologically involves pursuing sidetracks at every given stage. For example, notwithstanding that judgment in default of intention to defend comes about immediately after service of a writ, and summary judgment not much later, to give a full description of those procedural features at that stage would seem to me to detract from the narrative coherence of the text and that is why I have grouped those topics together in a separate chapter 'Termination without Trial' and placed it after a description of the rest of civil procedure.

A third and more vexing question is the way in which evidence should be treated and I have condensed the most important aspects of civil procedure into a number of chapters which are set, approximately, in the middle of the text. I have attempted to integrate a discussion of the pure law of evidence with the procedural aspects where evidence is important, such as discovery, interrogatories, exchange of witness statements and the like, so as to lead in to a description of the general preparation for trial.

I have been able to integrate material on the Civil Evidence Act 1995 which is in effect in respect of all actions where directions for trial have not been given before 31 January 1997.

I am grateful to everyone who has written to me with suggestions about this book. The Legal Practice Review at the end of 1996 made some dramatic changes to some aspects of the legal practice course, but left litigation virtually untouched. Indeed the only real change was the removal of the compulsory tuition in the skill of negotiation. Although negotiation no longer needs to be taught or tested, the ability to negotiate is clearly an important part of the armoury of an effective litigator and I have therefore not removed the few passing references to negotiation where they appear in the text.

With regard to suggestions which I have received from teachers at a variety of institutions, I have attempted to accommodate several of these although in fact some were contradictory. The most substantial change is the incorporation, relatively briefly, of a section on Security for Costs, an increasingly important topic at least in commercial litigation which has given rise to a good deal of very recent case law and now appears, somewhat arbitrarily, in **Chapter 18**.

I am grateful to the Solicitors' Law Stationery Society Limited who by kind permission have permitted me to reproduce the forms of writ and summons demonstrated in the text; and to the Legal Aid Board for their kind permission to reproduce the Green Form and Key Card.

Finally, I would like to thank the staff of Blackstone Press for their unfailing enthusiasm for this series, and this particular text, and the series editor, Paula Doolan. I am pleased to say that I have been able to incorporate some minor amendments at proof stage with the effect that this book is believed to be up-to-date to June 1997.

Craig Osborne

TABLE OF CASES

TABLE OF STATUTES

European legislation

TABLE OF STATUTORY INSTRUMENTS

ONE

REMEDIES AND LIMITATION OF ACTIONS

This chapter will consider some aspects of the remedies available in tort and contract, in particular, the principles for the award of damages and interest on damages, and injunctions and interim injunctions. Finally, the chapter will deal briefly with the law on limitation of actions.

This chapter, more than any other, is intended to be a 'resource' in that it is a source for reference back at various other stages of the book. It could just as easily have featured as the last chapter of all. It features first simply because it contains material which a litigator must always bear in mind, namely, the remedies available to a client who has suffered a tort or breach of contract, and the important matter of the time limit within which any action must be brought.

The chapter is not recommended for reading through at one sitting to any save chronic insomniacs.

1.1 Damages in Tort

1.1.1 ASSESSMENT

Damages in tort are compensatory in nature and are designed to put the plaintiff into the position in which he would have been but for the tort being committed. Thus an injured plaintiff will receive a sum deemed to be sufficient to compensate him for the type of injury he has received in terms of loss of quality of life and pain and suffering, but he will also receive a sum for financial loss flowing from that injury. For example, if, at its most serious, the injury has totally disabled him from working again, the plaintiff will receive a sum deemed to be sufficient to compensate him for loss of income throughout his working life. As will be readily apparent, a very substantial element of informed guesswork will have to go into the assessment of damages in such cases.

In torts not involving personal injury, such as false imprisonment, malicious prosecution, defamation or nuisance, there may be little in the way of financial loss and a figure is fixed by the court deemed to be a fair sum for compensation for the injury to feelings, inconvenience or as the case may be. In the case of damaged property, there are two alternative modes of assessing damages, one being the cost of rectification of the problem, e.g. awarding a plaintiff whose vehicle has been damaged the amount needed to repair it; the other being the *diminution in value* basis, i.e. awarding the plaintiff a sum deemed to be the difference between the value of a chattel as damaged and its previous value. The case law is far from consistent as to which of the two bases for compensation will be awarded, though in many circumstances there will be no difference between the two.

It is appropriate to mention three further matters in connection with damages.

1.1.2 CONTRIBUTORY NEGLIGENCE

By virtue of *s. 1* of the *Law Reform (Contributory Negligence) Act 1945:*

> *Where any person suffers damage as the result partly of his own fault and partly of the fault of any other person or persons . . . damages recoverable in respect thereof shall be reduced to such extent as the court thinks just and equitable having regard to the claimant's share in the responsibility for the damage.*

The word 'fault' is defined in *s. 4* as:

> *negligence, breach of statutory duty or other act or omission which gives rise to a liability in tort or would, apart from this Act, give rise to the defence of contributory negligence.*

Contributory negligence therefore operates by way of reduction of damages. It must be remembered that contributory negligence may relate not only to fault in the *causation* of an accident, but may operate to reduce damages where the contributory fault merely aggravates the *amount of damage* suffered (e.g. failure to wear a seat belt). It is for a person raising an allegation of contributory negligence to prove it, and once established the reduction of damages will be by a round percentage or fraction, usually expressed as 25 per cent, one-third, 50 per cent, etc. It must be remembered that if there is a collision involving two vehicles and driver A is assessed as being contributorily negligent by 25 per cent in respect of causation of the accident, driver B will be contributorily negligent by 75 per cent. Thus each will recover some damages, and if driver B should prove to be much more seriously injured than driver A, then driver B may recover a larger sum in damages notwithstanding that the accident was primarily his fault.

1.1.3 MITIGATION

The plaintiff has a duty to mitigate damages. All that this requires in fact is that he must take all *reasonable* steps to do so. Thus, for example, a plaintiff who is injured so badly that he cannot return to his previous job is expected to take any job that he can reasonably take in order to mitigate his continuing loss of earnings. If expenses are incurred in order to be able to mitigate (such as the cost of retraining for some other career), then these may be recovered as damages.

In questions of mitigation the tests are not entirely clear. In principle there is a subjective test, i.e. was it reasonable for *this* plaintiff to have behaved as he did. This applies in the case of damage to property as well as to personal injury damages. Though the case law is unclear, it is probably for the defendant to prove that the plaintiff did *not* act reasonably to mitigate rather than for the plaintiff to prove that he did act reasonably.

Example P's vehicle is damaged by D and while it is being repaired he hires a comparable vehicle. Unfortunately, due to a strike in the manufacturer's factory, parts prove difficult to obtain for many weeks. D's insurers contend that P should have mitigated his loss by selling the vehicle in its unrepaired state and buying a replacement, rather than hiring at great expense over the period. Will the courts hold that P should have acted thus to mitigate his damages?

The answer from the case law is that the defendant's insurers' contention will be unsuccessful. P is only expected to act reasonably in the circumstances and, the defendant's negligence having caused him to face the dilemma, the defendant's insurers cannot claim that P should have had the benefit of extraordinary foresight about the strike. The fact that some other course might look better with hindsight is irrelevant. Much the same arises in situations where the plaintiff, until he receives the compensation monies, cannot mitigate by having a damaged chattel repaired and so must hire. The famous case of *Liesbosch Dredger* v *SS Edison* [1933] AC 449, holding to the contrary, is now rarely followed (see *Martindale* v *Duncan* [1973] 1 WLR 573; *Perry* v *Sidney Phillips & Son* [1982] 1 WLR 1297; *Mattocks* v *Mann* [1993] RTR 13).

1.1.4 EXEMPLARY DAMAGES

Exemplary damages are designed not to compensate the plaintiff but to punish the defendant, albeit that the plaintiff receives them. They can be awarded in three situations laid down in *Rookes* v *Barnard* [1964] AC 1129, namely:

(a) Where there has been oppressive or unconstitutional action by the servants of the government, which is taken to include civil servants, politicians, officers of a local authority and the police.

(b) Where the defendant's conduct has been calculated to make a profit which may well exceed the compensation payable to the plaintiff. This includes situations such as where a libel is calculated to obtain such publicity and extra sales that it will exceed any damages normally payable, or where a landlord harasses a tenant so that he leaves, thus freeing a property for sale on the open market.

(c) In cases where exemplary damages are expressly authorised by statute. Such statutes are not uncommon in the United States but there are few examples in the UK. One is the *Protection from Eviction Act 1977*.

1.2 Damages in Personal Injury Cases

As indicated earlier, there are two elements of such damages. The first element is an attempt to compensate the plaintiff for his injuries by awarding him a sum of money. This is usually expressed as a conventional award, an approximately similar figure being given in respect of similar injuries to the same part of the body, notwithstanding individual characteristics of any given plaintiff (see **1.2.2.2**). Secondly, there is recompense for provable financial loss. In a simple case this can be computed as an exact figure (e.g. a plaintiff who suffers minor injuries necessitating a month off work without pay for which he can be recompensed by the precise net amount of his loss). In more complex cases, however, especially where a plaintiff will never return to work, compensation is based on predictions of future loss which, notwithstanding a great deal of factual information and semi-scientific projections (e.g. actuarial tables demonstrating average longevity), often end up being relatively arbitrary assessments. It is important for this purpose to divide damages in a personal injuries case into two parts, namely *general damages* and *special damages*.

General damages are the compensatory amounts which have to be assessed by the court of trial; special damages are the specific amounts which represent provable actual financial loss to the plaintiff. In the plaintiff's pleading, that is in his statement of claim, he need only claim general damages by adding the words 'and the plaintiff claims damages' at the end of the pleading. While it is usual in the statement of claim to give particulars of the injuries suffered and to indicate any special factors which apply, for example the loss of career prospects, it is not necessary to put in the pleading an exhaustive list of the aspects of the plaintiff's life which have been affected by the injury he has suffered, nor to suggest in the pleading figures which are appropriate for each. Having said that it is not necessary to do so, it is in fact not uncommon to put this extra information in modern pleadings, e.g. for a plaintiff whose leg has been broken to indicate in the pleading itself that his life has been affected in so far as his mobility is concerned so that his favourite sporting hobbies are now impossible. Nonetheless, he does not attribute a specific sum to these, the assessment of damages for such amounts being carried out by the judge at trial after hearing oral evidence.

Special damages do have to be pleaded in the plaintiff's statement of claim, however. Moreover, as precise as possible a computation has to be given of the exact amounts which he is claiming. If accurate figures are given it may be that the plaintiff and defendant, however strenuously the action may be contested on liability, may be able to agree the basis of the computation to be used by the judge in the event of his finding liability established.

The above is a general indication of the difference between general and special damages. In personal injury litigation, however, it is now for the plaintiff to supply, when serving his first *pleading* – that is statement of claim in the High Court or particulars of claim in the County Court – a computation of special damages and of some elements of general damages, in particular future loss of earnings (see **1.2.2.4**).

1.2.1 SPECIAL DAMAGES

Special damages include actual loss incurred between the accident and the trial. Items of expense which are to be incurred *after* trial, even if the amount is known with precision, such as the amount it will take to adapt the plaintiff's house for wheelchair access and instal a lift, are not, as such, special damages because they arise in the future. Special damages in the main include things such as:

(a) Provable loss of earnings until trial.

(b) Damage to clothing, repairs to vehicles, hire of alternative transport.

(c) Extra travel costs occasioned by the accident, e.g. by the plaintiff having frequently to visit hospitals as an out patient, or by relatives having to visit him in hospital.

(d) Private medical or nursing treatment.

1.2.1.1 Loss of earnings

Loss of earnings in the period between the accident and the trial forms part of the special damages. It is not, of course, possible to plead these fully in the statement of claim which is likely to be served quite soon after the accident and thus many months, if not years, before the trial. However, it is necessary to compute the loss of earnings up to the date of service of the statement of claim, and these figures must then be updated and worked out again just before trial. Loss of earnings *after* the trial is part of the claim for general damages, and we shall come to this in due course.

The plaintiff may only claim what he has actually lost, that is his *net* loss. Accordingly, his tax and national insurance contributions must be deducted from his gross earnings. The usual method of computing loss of earnings is to obtain details from the plaintiff's employer of his actual gross and net earnings over a recent typical period, e.g. the 26 weeks up to the date of the accident (choosing such a long period to allow seasonal fluctuations or overtime variations to even themselves out to a true average). The figure for one week's average net loss of earnings is then used as a basis for computing his continuing loss of earnings. It is important to find out when writing to the employer whether there have been any increases in pay since the accident for which the plaintiff would have been eligible, or indeed whether any promotion opportunities have arisen for which the plaintiff would have been a likely candidate. So, to take a simple example, suppose the plaintiff is injured on 1 January 1997 and you wish to compute his loss of earnings on 20 May 1997, a period of 20 weeks. His employers provide information which tells you that his pre-accident weekly average net pay was £200 but on 12 March 1997 (i.e. after he had been absent for 10 weeks) employees in his category received a pay rise giving a further £20 net per week. It is therefore very simple to work out the 20 weeks' loss of earnings, namely:

10 weeks @ £200 = £2,000
10 weeks @ £220 = £2,200
£4,200

Clearly this is a simple example, and to work out the loss of earnings can be complex where you are dealing with a long period. It is this item in particular which needs to be updated if the plaintiff has not returned to work before trial.

1.2.1.2 The plaintiff's contract of employment

It is necessary to consider carefully the plaintiff's contract of employment. It may be that his employer pays him for certain periods while he is off sick, and the defendant benefits from this since it is only actual loss for which he is liable to compensate the plaintiff. Suppose that in the previous example the employer had a private scheme negotiated with the plaintiff's trade union whereby he paid all employees who were off work regardless of whether the cause was accident or sickness for a period of, say, 20 weeks and the plaintiff returned to work after 20 weeks. The plaintiff would have no claim for loss of earnings in that time. In this situation only the plaintiff's employer loses because he has paid for 20 weeks' work which he has not received. He has of course no cause of action against the defendant.

Some employers have a provision in the contract of employment which is no less generous to their employees but does provide a sensible means of ensuring that they are reimbursed by the defendant. The contract provides that the employer will make the employee an interest-free loan equivalent to the amount of his net earnings while he is off work for a certain specified period. If the cause of absence is merely sickness, or some accident in respect of which the plaintiff is not able to recover any damages from some other person (e.g. an accident caused by the employee's own negligence), then he will usually not be asked to repay this loan. If, however, the employee is able to recover damages from some third party, he is expected to include in his action a claim for loss of earnings and is then obliged to reimburse his employer.

1.2.1.3 Tax rebates

Because it is only loss of *net* earnings for which one can sue, credit must be given for any tax rebates received. This is because tax allowances are worked out over a whole year and the allowance is given in the form of a weekly amount set against weekly salary. A person is entitled to the whole tax allowance, however, even if he does not work for the whole year. Suppose, therefore that an individual has tax allowances equivalent to, say, £40 per week when spread over the whole year. He works for three months or so into the tax year and is injured in July. He does not work thereafter. Taking into account the £40 per week which has hitherto been credited to him as his allowance, he is credited now with the balance of the whole of his tax allowance for the year. When offset against his salary received for only three months, he will then clearly be entitled to a substantial tax rebate. This must be brought into account and deducted from his claim for loss of earnings.

1.2.1.4 Benefits received

The way in which compensation is affected by taking into account benefits received was radically changed with effect from 3 September 1990. The need for special provisions about this is obvious. For example, where a plaintiff is injured and thus not able to work and earn his usual salary, he will generally receive benefits of various kinds. If at the end of the case the plaintiff recovers in full for his loss of earnings, but without having the benefits which he has received taken into account, then there will be two losers – the defendant, who will have had to compensate the plaintiff for a loss which he has not in fact sustained (since he will have received the benefits which ought partially to offset his loss of earnings), and the state who will have paid out benefits to the plaintiff which will be irrecoverable. The new provisions attempt to rectify this apparent injustice.

Briefly, the new provisions, originally contained in the *Social Security Act 1989* and now in the *Social Security Administration Act 1992*, provide that, except in the case of certain exempt payments, in any case where a defendant (the *compensator*) is to pay damages for personal injury to a plaintiff (the *claimant*), whether in consequence of a judgment at the end of a trial, settlement or compromise during a case, or the procedure known as payment into court (described more fully at **16.1**) or otherwise, benefits received by the claimant must be taken into account. At present the following provisions apply wherever the amount which the claimant is to receive under the judgment or compromise is more than £2,500.

(a) When the solicitor for a plaintiff writes to the defendant notifying him of the claim which is to be made, the solicitor for the plaintiff should inform the defendant of the plaintiff's date of birth, national insurance number, address and the name and address of the plaintiff's employer. Thereupon the defendant must notify a body called the Compensation Recovery Unit (CRU) who are part of the Department of Social Security by forwarding to them a certain form. This form will be acknowledged and thereupon the CRU will maintain records of all relevant benefits claimed and paid in respect of the injury in question.

(b) When the compensator is ready to make an offer of payment to the claimant, he should apply to the CRU for what is called a Certificate of Total Benefit. This certificate will then be issued by the CRU and will show the amount of total benefits paid to the claimant in respect of that injury since it occurred. Moreover, details will be given of future payments over the next eight weeks after the date of the certificate, thus enabling the compensator to know with precision what amount of benefits will have been paid on any given date during that period.

(c) Thereafter, when the payment is made to the plaintiff, whether by way of court order or agreed compromise of the action, the appropriate amount of benefit must be deducted from it by the compensator and this amount must then be remitted to the CRU. By this procedure the government is reimbursed for the benefits paid out, and the plaintiff has no element of double compensation.

The types of benefit which are relevant for these purposes include the following:

(a) Family credit.

(b) Disablement benefit.

(c) Income support.

(d) Invalidity benefit.

(e) Mobility allowance.

(f) Severe disablement allowance.

(g) Sickness benefit.

(h) Statutory sick pay.

(i) 'Unemployment benefit'. This form of benefit may now be paid under a variety of different names under the Jobseekers Act 1995. They are all to be brought into account.

(j) Reduced earnings allowance; retirement allowance.

(k) Housing benefit.

(l) Disability working allowance.

(m) Disability living allowance.

(n) Incapacity benefit.

When negotiating settlements of claims, or advising a plaintiff about likely future compensation it is accordingly vital that a plaintiff's solicitor remembers to take into account the repayment of benefit element so that a plaintiff is not left with the mistaken belief that these payments will not be brought into account by way of deduction from his total compensation.

It is very important that one does not lose sight of this. A plaintiff who is the main breadwinner and is receiving a variety of the previously mentioned benefits may well be getting £200 per week or even more. Thus benefits may be running at more than £10,000 per year and this will have a dramatic effect on the net eventual amount of compensation. Recoupment of benefits by the state will be offset not only against loss of earnings but against any other heads of damages so that, for example, a poorly paid employee who is the main breadwinner and who is injured in an accident at work may receive substantially more in benefits than his loss of earnings claim would have been. Thus when the state recoups the benefits it will recoup the whole amount even if part of that amount comes out of the injured person's general damages claims for pain and suffering and loss of amenity. The injustice of this has been the subject of a good deal of protest and complaint. At the time of writing the apparent injustices caused by the benefit recoupment scheme were anyway subject to review and amending legislation was said to be under consideration. This procedure may well be accelerated by the result of the May 1997 General Election, but no specific proposals have been formulated.

More detail will be given at individual points later in the text as to the precise practical steps which need to be taken in respect of these provisions at various stages in the action. See in particular the topics of payment into court (at **16.1**) and interim payments (at **16.5**).

The above provisions apply wherever the amount of compensation exceeds £2,500. If the amount is less than £2,500, then the former law governs the position. This law had a certain logic of its own but was latterly considered anomalous. Put briefly, it provides that in cases involving compensation of less than £2,500, the plaintiff has to give the defendant credit for one-half of certain kinds of benefit, and the whole of other benefits, which are deducted from compensation. However, although offset from the compensation, the amounts in question are not passed on by the defendant to the state but are retained by the defendant. The rules in relation to these provisions were fairly complex, caused in part by the application of *s. 2(1)* of the *Law Reform (Personal Injuries) Act 1948* and in part by a wealth of case law. In short, the benefits of which one-half had to be deducted from a claim included sickness benefit, invalidity benefit, non-contributory invalidity pension, severe disablement allowance, injury benefit and disablement benefit. The kind of benefits which were deductible in full included statutory sick pay and unemployment benefit. A full explanation of these provisions is most unlikely to be of practical benefit and is thus beyond the scope of the present text.

1.2.1.5 Other amounts received due to the accident

It should be noted that certain monies received as a result of an accident are *not* deductible from damages, i.e. the defendant does not obtain the benefit of these payments:

(a) Any sums paid under private accident insurance. Even if these come about *factually* because of an accident, the *legal* cause is the plaintiff's own prudence in arranging to have personal accident insurance. It is therefore wrong for the defendant to get the benefit of this by having it offset against his liability.

(b) The results of public benevolence, e.g. public collection. Likewise, it would be wrong for the defendant to gain the benefit of this by having his liability to pay damages reduced.

(c) The result of private benevolence, e.g. gifts from friends or relatives.

(d) Redundancy payment. If, for example, a person is away from work because of disablement and during that time he is made redundant, then, unless the cause of the redundancy relates to his incapacity resulting from the accident (which is unlikely), no credit should accrue to the defendant.

(e) Pensions. If the plaintiff receives a pension as a result of his or her injuries, no deduction is made whether the pension was contributory or non-contributory (see *Smoker* v *London Fire and Civil Defence Authority* [1991] 2 AC 502). Nor are state retirement pensions deductible (*Hewson* v *Downs* [1981] QB 73).

(f) Other earnings. It should be noted that credit must be given for earnings obtained whilst off work due to incapacity if they would not otherwise have been earned.

Example The plaintiff is a games teacher who is injured and unable to work. His claim includes loss of earnings. Suppose, however, that his second subject is French and he is able to give some daytime tuition to private students. The amount of income earned from this must be offset against his claim for loss of earnings since he would not have earned it had he been at work. If, however, it had always been his practice to offer private tuition in his own time (i.e. in the evening) to obtain extra income, then since he would have earned the sums in any event he would not be obliged to give credit for them.

1.2.1.6 Maintenance at public expense

Section 5 of the *Administration of Justice Act 1982*, provides that any saving to an injured person which is attributable to his maintenance wholly or partly at public expense (i.e. in a National Health Service hospital) must be calculated and set off against any income lost as a result of the injuries. This is to be set off in fact against both loss of earnings incurred up to trial and loss thereafter, which forms part of general damages as we shall shortly see. In other words, where a plaintiff is fed and saves rent, rates, lighting and heating, etc., by being in hospital rather than at home, the amount saved should be calculated and brought into account.

The circumstances in which this will be applied vary very greatly from case to case. Suppose, for example, that the plaintiff is a single man living in a bedsitter. Whilst he will still have to pay rent on his bedsitter he is entirely relieved of the cost of lighting, heating and food, etc. while in hospital. The amount saved may be reasonably substantial and of the order of, say, £40 or £50 per week. If, however, the plaintiff is a family man living in a three-bedroomed house with his wife and children, then the amount saved in terms of rent and council tax will be nil since the house will still be needed as a family home, and the amount saved with regard to heating and lighting will also be negligible. The amount saved in regard to food likewise may not be substantial, the difference in cost between food for six people and food for five people not being nearly as great as the cost of food for one person alone.

This provision was designed to give the defendant some compensation where a plaintiff is in hospital for a lengthy period. In the case of the single man given above, if his stay in hospital lasted a few weeks, it is most unlikely that the defendants would bother to argue for or compute the amount saved. If the period of hospitalisation is more extensive, however, then it may be that in individual cases it will be worth agreeing figures, which will usually be done in round terms. There appears to be no need to refer to this item in the statement of claim. The defendant should be left to claim and argue for this if he is so minded.

1.2.1.7 Other losses

(a) *Repairs to vehicle*

Naturally the cost of repairs to a motor vehicle damaged in an accident and the cost of a hired car of a similar type can be claimed for the period when the vehicle is off the road awaiting repair. There is no restriction on the right to hire an alternative vehicle to cases where the car is needed for business use. If a plaintiff chooses not to hire a car for the intervening period he will be entitled to general damages for inconvenience caused by the necessity to walk, use public transport and the extra time which these things will take over the convenience of motoring. For the law relating to any claim by the defendant that the period of hire is excessive, see **1.1.3.1** above.

(b) *Damage to clothes and property damaged in the accident*

As there is no ready market for secondhand or damaged clothes, wrist watches, stereos, etc., it is usual to negotiate about these items. The value of such things is usually too small for there to be much case law, though points of principle of some difficulty may arise. For example, if the plaintiff's suit, which cost a substantial sum of money but is over a year old, is damaged, then clearly, since repair of suits is unlikely to be a viable option, an appropriate figure for recompense will be sought. This is unlikely to be the cost of a new suit, but on the other hand should be far more than the price which the suit would have fetched in an Oxfam shop. Generally it is possible to compromise on a sensible figure.

(c) *Other expenses*

Other, more unusual expenses might involve, for example, adapting a car for disabled driving, or even adapting a house for wheelchairs by installing a lift. When arguing for these more esoteric things one should look carefully at the picture in the round. Putting ramps in a house and installing a lift not only cost a great deal, but will also actually diminish the value of the property since a future owner, unless also disabled, is unlikely to consider that these are attractive extra features. If the plaintiff, for example, has to move from a house to a bungalow, then expenses in the nature of estate agent's commission, solicitors' fees and removal expenses should be claimed.

(d) *Medical expenses*

By *s. 2(4)* of the *Law Reform (Personal Injuries) Act 1948*, it is provided that a plaintiff is entitled to claim the cost of private medical treatment. This is so even if National Health Service treatment is readily available. The plaintiff thus has the right to his choice of specialist in hospital, and even if the plaintiff is not someone who would ever otherwise have had private medical treatment, he will be entitled to reclaim the cost of it. 'Medical treatment' includes not merely surgery but after care, including nursing and convalescence. If a spouse rather than a relative has given up work to nurse the injured plaintiff at home, then either a sum equivalent to the commercial cost of nursing care may be claimed, or alternatively the spouse's or relative's loss of earnings (in an extreme case including full loss of earnings for an interrupted or a forfeited career) may be claimed and will be treated as the damages of the plaintiff.

(e) *Expenses incurred by other persons*

By convention, even though expenses are actually incurred by other people rather than the plaintiff personally, if travelling expenses are incurred for the purpose of visiting the plaintiff these are allowable in the claim as against the defendant as if they were the plaintiff's own loss. Obviously there will be a test of basic reasonableness, so that for a very close relative to fly back from the other side of the world to visit an injured plaintiff the fares may be allowable, whereas the same would not be true of a distant relative who had never previously seen the plaintiff but suddenly was overwhelmed by the desire to be with him in his hour of need.

1.2.2 GENERAL DAMAGES

1.2.2.1 Pain and suffering

An amount is awarded to compensate the plaintiff for the pain and suffering which has been suffered, not only in the past, i.e. the agony of the accident itself and its immediate aftermath, but also that consequent upon any medical or surgical treatment. Compensation will take into account mental suffering and matters personal to the plaintiff which may increase that suffering. In addition, if the plaintiff's life expectancy has been reduced, the award for pain and suffering should take into account the plaintiff's knowledge of this. The award may also take into account less specific items such as embarrassment (e.g. consequent upon facial mutilation). The plaintiff's age and life expectancy may also be relevant if there is to be a substantial continuing period of pain and suffering. All necessary evidence on this must be produced (and should be put in detail in the plaintiff's statement for exchange with the defendant under *Ord. 38 r. 2A*, see **12.3**). Full medical evidence must be provided for the trial judge.

1.2.2.2 Loss of amenity

Loss of amenity damages are meant to compensate the plaintiff for the loss of quality or reduced enjoyment of life. Thus, for example, a plaintiff who has lost a leg, whatever his age, will clearly have the quality of his life considerably impaired in relation to his ordinary, everyday activities. Almost everything will be more uncomfortable and inconvenient, and many normal things that an individual might want to do will be impossible for him.

In general, relatively conventional awards are given so that a basic figure is fixed by reference to the nature of the injury, and this figure, the so-called 'tariff' for that type of injury, will not differ between individuals. There is some logic in this because, for example, although age is a subjective factor it may cut both ways. Thus an elderly man who is suddenly severely disabled by the loss of a leg may well be thought to have lost more in terms of quality of life for the few years remaining to him than a child; whereas the child, even though he may adjust better to disability, has to cope with disability over a longer period and may thus never be able to enjoy sporting and other activities of which the elderly man has had the advantage over most of his life.

Nonetheless, it is increasingly common now to stress individual and subjective factors in making a claim for loss of amenity. Thus if the plaintiff's hobby is, say, playing the violin, loss of a single finger may be a crucial impairment, whereas it may be of marginal consequence to the quality of life of others. Similarly, a leg injury will matter much more to someone whose hobbies were sporting than to someone who has a relatively sedentary life. It is important to call as much evidence as possible on these subjective matters to demonstrate to the judge that there is no element of exaggeration. Thus if it is claimed that the plaintiff's whole leisure time was given over to amateur sport, this should be demonstrated by calling evidence from other members of sports teams or clubs to which the plaintiff belongs.

The two sums for pain and suffering and loss of amenity are assessed together by the trial judge. The three most important sources are, first, a publication by the Judicial Studies Board, *Guidelines for the Assessment of General Damages in Personal Injury Cases* published by Blackstone Press, now in its third edition. This was published to assist judges to achieve consistency in awards for similar types of injuries. The book is brief (48 pages of text) but invaluable, although its brevity inevitably leaves room for argument since fairly broad brackets are given for each of the many possible types of injury. It is essential as a starting point, however, and is used by all judges. A very much weightier book is Kemp and Kemp, *Quantum of Damages*, a substantial loose-leaf work which contains a great deal of case law showing awards for various parts of the body. *Current Law* is also useful because it has a monthly section on quantum of damages, which keeps the reader very up to date although the reports of cases are brief. It must be stressed that even using these three texts together, there is still plenty of room for distinguishing cases and for argument to contend that a given set of facts indicates that a case should be at one end of the bracket rather than the other.

Quite apart from any other aspects which may cause uncertainty in quantifying a claim (such as doubts about loss of earnings and the like), as will be observed there is a huge scope for negotiation and argument on the heads of pain, suffering and loss of amenity. Moreover, in injuries of any seriousness there may be two, three or more different parts of the body affected by the injury and different brackets of award needing to be considered for each.

1.2.2.3 Loss of future earnings

This is the most difficult head of damages of all, and in a case of serious injury to a young plaintiff is likely to be by far the largest element of damages. From the basic assessment of loss of present net earnings previously explained (**1.2.1.1**), you may have to launch off into many speculative areas.

The court works on the basis of two figures known as *multiplier* and *multiplicand. Multiplicand* is the net annual loss that the plaintiff has suffered. If the plaintiff is likely to be able to return to work in the same job in a year or two, then no great problem is involved, but what if the plaintiff will not work for five years, or will never work again? Here there is great difficulty in picking the appropriate multiplicand. Suppose that the plaintiff is relatively young. Is it fair to take as his net loss of earnings the sum he is presently earning, when he might have had a glowing career before him with eventual promotion to the highest level? How can a figure be arrived at based on what a plaintiff of 23 earns and what the plaintiff might have earned at 60? Even in the case of apparently highly structured and stratified professions with annual increments such as, say, local government or the civil service, assessing this figure can be an enormously difficult task (in fact the matrix of increments and promotion in the civil service is extremely complex). If faced with more volatile professions such as entertainment or sport, the difficulties seem virtually insuperable.

Example Suppose that the plaintiff is a 17-year-old professional footballer who has suffered a foot injury and will never play again. The evidence is that the plaintiff, who was a youth international and is currently in the first team of a third division football club, was attracting great interest from several Premier League clubs, though none had actually made an offer for him. Are his damages to be assessed on the basis that he would have eventually become a Premier League professional with a top club, or even an England international, or even have received offers to go abroad to play in Italy? Moreover, what of the fact that the promise shown by very young footballers is often not maintained and that it is a short and injury-prone career likely to last less than 20 years? How is one to take into account the possibilities now open to the plaintiff in other fields? What is one to make of the fact that he would probably not have been a top-flight professional footballer much after his mid-thirties and therefore would have had a further 30-year career in some unknown field?

The same problems may apply to the learned professions. How does one compensate a barrister of 24 who has been in an accident and suffered brain damage such that he will never work again? To take his last annual earnings which may be very modest would clearly be unfair, but is he to be compensated on the basis that he would inevitably have become a Queen's Counsel earning at the highest level?

In deciding these questions all that can be done is to present all available evidence about the plaintiff's future career. Full statements need to be taken from present employers, any other persons who might have been interested in the plaintiff (such as professional scouts or managers of other football clubs in the above example, or the plaintiff's colleagues in chambers and judges before whom he had appeared in the example of a barrister). Whatever evidence is available will still provide a less than full picture for the trial judge, especially in the case of young plaintiffs where income could vary very greatly. In the case, for example, of an injured schoolboy, in assessing future loss of earnings the courts will have to have regard to school reports and other inconclusive evidence. All that can be said is that in fixing on this multiplicand judges will use their considerable experience and common sense. Employment consultants, who specialise in providing evidence of earnings and job availability related to locality and profession, may be extremely useful.

After fixing the multiplicand the judge then needs to select the *multiplier*. This represents the number of years for which the plaintiff is to be awarded his net annual loss of earnings (the multiplicand). Let us take an example. Suppose the plaintiff is 25 and is earning £10,000 net per year. In principle, if he is never to work again he has lost 40 working years until 65 (possibly longer if he was self-employed). On the face of it the computation is simple and he should receive an award of £400,000. That is fallacious, however. If the plaintiff did indeed receive £400,000 now, if invested sensibly that would yield an annual income of several times the £10,000 which has been lost. Accordingly a multiplier is fixed to take into account accelerated receipt and other contingencies such as early death, the risk of unemployment or injury from other sources. It must be remembered, moreover, that in the above example the fact that the plaintiff's present income was £10,000 net would not in itself necessarily provide the appropriate multiplicand either, and one would be attempting to persuade the court to fix a higher multiplicand if the plaintiff had good promotion prospects in his job.

Hitherto the maximum multiplier even for a very young plaintiff tended to be about 18. This was on the basis that such a gross lump sum, properly invested and allowing for certain assumptions about the rates of interest obtainable and the fall in the value of money, would produce an amount equivalent to the plaintiff's loss over his working lifetime. The figures arrived at have been criticised for some years as relatively unscientific and a Law Commission Report in 1994 proposed approaches based on more scientific actuarial evidence. For some years the Government Actuaries Department have published a set of tables known as the *Ogden Tables* which have given more precise data about longevity, interest rates, work patterns and the like. Despite the availability of these tables, courts were still reluctant to use them but *s. 10* of the *Civil Evidence Act 1995* provides that a court may have regard to the *Ogden Tables* in assessing multipliers. The effect of this will be that the previous maximum multiplier of 18 may be significantly uplifted, possibly to about 24 or 25 in appropriate cases.

The matter of multipliers, however, remains in a state of flux. *Section 1* of the *Damages Act 1996* empowers the Lord Chancellor to prescribe expected rates of return on damages and thus to affect the multiplier to be used in personal injury cases. Before such an order is made there is a consultation process to be undertaken and at the time of writing, the new Lord Chancellor, like his predecessor, has made no attempt to implement this section.

More importantly, in October 1996 a series of cases in the Court of Appeal, of which the lead case was *Wells* v *Wells* [1997] 1 All ER 673, reversing in each case rulings by somewhat adventurous judges at first instance, held that when assessing damages for anticipated future losses and expenses in personal injury cases, the court should fix the award on the assumption that the plaintiff will adopt a prudent investment strategy, including investing on the stock market. Because of returns on the stock market over the recent past, this would tend to argue for the system of multipliers to remain roughly as at present rather than the more pessimistic view (leading to larger awards) taken by the Ogden Tables. The result of the Court of Appeal's decision therefore was to pour a dose of cold water over the use of the Ogden Tables and in the light of that and the fact that *Wells* v *Wells* is being taken on appeal to the House of Lords, from whom a decision is unlikely before 1998, *s. 10* of the *Civil Evidence Act 1995* has not been brought into force. It will be necessary therefore to await the outcome of the House of Lords' decision in *Wells* v *Wells*; to see whether the Lord Chancellor decides to make any regulation under the *Damages Act 1996*; and then to see whether *s. 10* of the *1995 Act* is brought into force.

1.2.2.4 Other factors affecting claims for loss of future earnings

(a) *Plaintiff's life expectancy*

If the plaintiff would have been unlikely to live until the usual retirement age, that is a factor affecting future loss of earnings. However, where the life expectancy has been reduced as a result of the injury, then no reduction is made because to make such a reduction would be to allow the defendant to benefit from his tort.

(b) *Female plaintiffs*

Sometimes a lower multiplier may be applied to annual loss because of the possibility of an interrupted career in order to have children and raise a family. Nonetheless, this is an individual, matter and if a plaintiff is able to satisfy the court that she will never marry, e.g. if her religion requires chastity or she is a lesbian, then the court may not make any such deduction. In the normal case of an unmarried or young married woman there will be some reduction in the multiplier.

(c) *Ill health*

If the plaintiff had ill health before his injury and the defendants are able to show that he had lengthy periods off work or unemployed, then these will naturally be taken into account to the extent that it is reasonable to do so.

(d) *The plaintiff's employment*

Individual factors relating to the plaintiff's career can make a difference. Some jobs (e.g. in professional sport) have low retirement ages and the multiplier will be accordingly reduced. On the other hand, a self-employed plaintiff who may well have continued beyond retirement age may obtain a higher multiplier. It is always vital to bring firm evidence on these matters.

(e) *Inflation*

No adjustment is made for inflation. This is because high inflation is usually followed by higher interest rates, and therefore the lump sum, when sensibly invested, ought to bring in a higher return to compensate for inflation.

(f) *Maintenance at public expense*

It must not be forgotten that from loss of future earnings credit must be given for maintenance at the public expense under s. 5 of the *Administration of Justice Act 1982* (see **1.2.1.6**).

1.2.2.5 Risk on the labour market, or loss of earning capacity

(a) *The nature of the award*

This head of damages has long been recognised but was re-emphasised in the leading modern case of *Smith* v *Manchester Corporation* (1974) 17 KIR 1. The facts of that case provide a good example of the principle.

Mrs Smith was a cleaner employed by the defendants. Due to their negligence she suffered injury to her shoulder. This made her a considerably less efficient cleaner, but the defendants did undertake to keep her on and thus she had no apparent future loss of earnings. She did, however, receive a separate sum of money in compensation under this head. This was because, should she ever lose or give up her job (because she might wish to move to another part of the country, or find her present job or work mates uncongenial), she would be at risk on the labour market because she would be competing with fully fit cleaners. She had thus lost her freedom of mobility of labour in that, as she was now no longer such an efficient cleaner, she would be considerably more wary of moving jobs.

This award, often now called a *Smith* award, is appropriate in the following situations:

(i) Where the plaintiff has returned to his or her pre-accident employment with no net future loss but will some time in the future be at risk of early retirement or a less well paid job. See *Moeliker* v *Reyrolle & Co. Ltd* [1976] ICR 252.

(ii) Where the plaintiff is back in pre-accident employment and will not lose it, but nonetheless the injury may have damaged prospects of promotion, ability to advance career, or the chance of moving to better employment.

(iii) Where the plaintiff is handicapped on the labour market by the injury, e.g. where the plaintiff may have been unemployed at the time of accident and will now find work harder to obtain.

(iv) Where the plaintiff is too young to have yet entered the labour market.

(b) *Quantification of the award*

There is a table in Kemp and Kemp, para. 5-009, which is of some assistance. Judges nonetheless tend to pick a 'conventional' award which is often within the range of one to one and a half year's gross salary. Nonetheless, a higher sum can be appropriate where clear evidence is provided, e.g. *Foster* v *Tyne & Wear CC* [1986] 1 All ER 567, where a lump sum of five times annual net pay was approved.

(c) *Practical problems*

It is not uncommon for judges to fail to draw a clear distinction between damages for loss of earnings and damages for loss of earning capacity, but it must be borne in mind that in general, for the years involved, the two heads are normally alternative to each other. Nonetheless, there may be cases where an award under both heads is appropriate, e.g. where a plaintiff has not yet gone back to work but is expected to do so in the future, at which stage he may be handicapped on the labour market.

It should always be borne in mind that there may be a possibility of this element in the claim even where it is not immediately apparent. Suppose, for example, that the plaintiff, amongst other injuries, has suffered a head injury giving him an unpleasant and aggressive personality change. This may obviously be covered by the damages for pain and suffering and loss of amenity, and for loss of future earnings; but it also may attract an award under this head on the basis that if the plaintiff is to be a difficult and unpleasant colleague, there may be reasonable probability of fallings out at work and the possibility of periods of unemployment and changes of job consequent on this.

1.2.2.6 Loss of pension rights

Pension rights for an employee who will not return to work are an extremely difficult matter to compute and it is essential to employ a forensic accountant to assist. If a plaintiff has lost employment because of injury, or even if employment has been substantially interrupted, the plaintiff's own and his or her employer's contributions towards a retirement pension will be lost and the pension will be substantially reduced. This reduction must be taken into account by payment of a lump sum as part of the overall damages. In calculating this lump sum, which may well be received some decades before a pension would have been, account will be taken of the comparable pension that can be purchased with the lump sum now being made available.

1.2.2.7 Future expenses

If the plaintiff is likely to need to disburse specified future amounts, e.g. for future medical treatment, further adaptations of a car for disabled driving, moving house, a new wheelchair every five years, then these are quantified on an appropriate cost basis at present day values. In such cases the fact that the plaintiff receives the money now (e.g. for six purchases of wheelchairs over a lifetime at present cost) is discounted by the fact that the wheelchairs will have risen in price.

Recurring items such as future nursing care, the cost of a care regime generally, the cost of a housekeeper and, where appropriate, gardener, and the value of voluntary services are quantified on a multiplier/multiplicand basis giving the value at the date at the time of trial. The multiplier is unlikely to be the same as that applied to the annual loss of earnings because in principle the period will last until the plaintiff's death rather than just to the date of his retirement and therefore reference again to actuarial tables for longevity may be needed.

1.3 Interest on Damages in Tort

Once damages have been awarded by a court at trial, the sum so awarded automatically carries interest under the *Judgments Act 1838* at a prescribed rate (currently 8 per cent) until they are paid. Quite separately, however, by virtue of *s. 35A* of the *Supreme Court Act 1981* or *s. 69* of the *County Courts Act 1984*, either court has a discretion in every case to award interest on damages from the date when the cause of action arose to the date when judgment is given or earlier payment. The rate of interest chosen is within the court's discretion. In cases involving commercial loss, for example, in passing off or similar economic torts, the rate chosen may be a high one representing the cost to the plaintiff of interest on the financial loss caused to his business, especially if he has had to borrow money from a bank at a high rate in the light of the business difficulties caused to him by the defendant's action. In torts involving only injury to feelings, such as libel and malicious prosecution, there is usually no award of interest at all. In cases such as nuisance which may, for example, have involved physical injury to property as well as distress and inconvenience, the court may adopt different rates of interest on different aspects of the damages. We shall now turn to personal injury cases where there is a set of very specific rules provided by case law.

1.3.1 PERSONAL INJURY CASES

In personal injury cases these two sections respectively provide that in an action for damages for personal injuries or death where judgment is given for a sum which exceeds £200, the court *shall* award such damages unless the court is satisfied that there are special reasons to the contrary. Thus there is a presumption in favour of the award of interest on damages; indeed, from modern case law it is difficult to envisage circumstances in which interest would *not* be awarded, unless perhaps there had been wilful delay in the conduct of the case by the plaintiff. The prevailing rates are now specified in case law on the authority of *Wright* v *British Railways Board* [1983] 2 AC 773, and this case provides the following straightforward, if not entirely logical, rules.

(a) Interest is awarded on damages for pain and suffering and loss of amenities from the date of *service of the writ* to the date of trial. The current rate is 2 per cent per annum. This rate is low because damages are valued as at the date of trial and thus, as awards of damages constantly creep up, a plaintiff would obtain slightly more in, say, 1997 than he would have obtained in 1995 for the same injury.

(b) Damages for future loss carry no interest because the plaintiff has not yet lost or expended the money.

(c) Special damages carry interest which will be awarded at half the prevailing court Special Account rate from the *date of accident* to the date of trial. This Account rate is fixed from time to time by statutory instrument and can be found in the *Supreme Court Practice*, para. 6/2/12. It is the rate of interest on funds in court and at the time of writing is 8 per cent per annum. The reason for awarding interest at *half* the appropriate rate is that the majority of such claims will be for loss of earnings. Accordingly, the loss will have been incurred gradually over the whole period from accident to trial, but clearly it would be unfair on the defendant to award interest at a high rate on the whole amount. Thus by awarding it at half the rate rough and ready justice is done and a great deal of difficult calculation avoided, because the rate will in effect be equivalent to the award of interest at the full rate on the figure due at the half way point between accident and judgment.

The justification for that is thus easy to see. What is less easy to see, and indeed is quite arbitrary, is the reason why interest is usually only payable at half the Special Account rate on all other items which have been paid out in full, perhaps quite early in the period in respect of which the plaintiff has been out of pocket for a very considerable time (e.g. private medical treatment a few weeks after the accident). The court therefore does have a discretion to depart from the guidelines and, in exceptional cases, interest at the full rate, or indeed at some other commercial rate, may be allowed on the item in question from the date it was incurred. See *Dexter* v *Courtaulds* [1984] 1 WLR 372 and *Prokop* v *Department of Health and Social Security* [1985] CLY 1037. Where the items in question are reasonably substantial it is well worthwhile, therefore, producing a specific argument aimed at increasing the rate of interest. Surprisingly, defendants' insurers in negotiations quite often concede the interest element at higher rates on such items as car hire, repair or private medical treatment in recognition of the arbitrary nature of the prima facie rule.

1.3.2 INTEREST ON DAMAGES SUBJECT TO BENEFITS RECOUPMENT

Section 103 of the *Social Security Administration Act 1992* provides:

> *In assessing the amount of interest payable in respect of an award of damages, the amount of the award shall be treated as reduced by a sum equal to the amount of the relevant payment . . .*
>
> *(a) . . . if both special and general damages are awarded, any such reductions shall be treated as made first against the special damages and then, as respects any remaining balance, against the general damages.*

In other words, in substantial personal injury cases, when computing interest it must be borne in mind that the plaintiff will not obtain interest on those parts of special damages which will be paid over by the defendant to the CRU. The recoupment bites first into special damages and only thereafter on general damages. This must be remembered when preparing preliminary quantifications in negotiations or for trial.

1.4 Alternatives in Personal Injury Cases to Once and For All Settlement

In principle, in litigation of all kinds in England, the award of damages to a plaintiff is a 'once and for all' award. Thus if an injured plaintiff has received judgment on the basis that his condition has a certain prognosis and then finds to his dismay that his condition rapidly deteriorates thereafter, he cannot in principle appeal against the original judgment, nor go back to the original court to seek a further award. Nor is there any provision for the court to award damages in the form of amounts to be assessed periodically which can be adjusted in view of changes to the plaintiff's condition. It must be pointed out that, in any event, such a variable method of receiving damages might not favour the plaintiff. It is not uncommon that plaintiffs often improve beyond the hopes of the doctors who prepared the pessimistic prognoses, and a plaintiff who has had damages assessed on the basis that he may never work again will sometimes be able to return to some form of work and thus will have been substantially over-compensated. In such cases there is no possibility for the defendants to appeal or go back to the original trial judge either.

When settling a case on behalf of a plaintiff, or arguing for an award at trial, it is important, therefore, to have as clear a view as possible of his medical prognosis and future career prospects. It would thus generally be considered negligent to attempt to settle a case before it was clear that the plaintiff's medical condition had stabilised to the point where a reasonably firm prognosis was available. However, where there is a great measure of uncertainty despite the lapse of time since the accident, there are three options open to the plaintiff's solicitor. These are respectively:

(a) Structured settlements.

(b) Split trials.

(c) Provisional damages.

1.4.1 STRUCTURED SETTLEMENTS

Structured settlements are a recent invention. It must be stressed that the court itself has at present no power whatsoever to order a structured settlement, and if the case goes to trial then the judge must in essence make a 'once and for all' award. In complex cases, however, where the plaintiff's and the defendant's legal advisers have been able to reach agreement, in the recent past, settlements have been arrived at in structured settlement form, particularly in cases where plaintiffs will need a great deal of expensive medical and nursing care over the years to come. These settlements provide for payment of compensation in the form of periodical payments. Although the court of its own motion has no power to give judgment in this form, the court does have power to make a consent judgment incorporating an agreement between the parties for damages to be paid in this way, which is known as a '*Tomlin*' order. Indeed, if the plaintiff is a mental patient or a child, the court's approval to the agreement will be positively required.

The drafting of these settlements requires very specialist tax, pensions and insurance advice. In essence, the defendants usually pay to the plaintiff a substantial lump sum but also purchase an annuity index linked for protection against inflation. The settlement must be submitted for the agreement of the Inland Revenue so that they will accept the scheme as periodical payments of capital rather than income and thus income tax is avoided.

The drafting of structured settlement agreements has been very greatly assisted by provisions in the *Finance Act 1996* which have considerably simplified the law and provide positively that appropriate schemes are to be treated as periodical instalments of capital. This has also been assisted by the *Damages Act 1996* which provides that if the parties consent, the court may order damages to be paid as periodical payments and contains other detailed provisions concerning structured settlements.

Structured settlements do involve a consideration also of the recoupment regulations by virtue of the *Social Security Administration Act 1992*.

Because of the complexities of setting them up and the cost involved, notwithstanding that the latter is usually borne by the defendants as part of the agreement, it is probably not worthwhile for there to be a structured settlement unless a sum of about £250,000 is involved, although the writer is aware of one such case where the amount involved was only £80,000.

1.4.2 SPLIT TRIALS

There has for many years been provision in the *Rules of the Supreme Court* and *County Court Rules* (*RSC Ord. 33, r. 4; CCR Ord. 13, r. 2(2)(c)*) enabling a plaintiff to issue a summons asking the court for an order for *split trials*, that is separate trials of the issues of liability and quantum.

If this order is made cases can proceed swiftly to a trial of liability while the memories of the witnesses of fact are fresh, and without the added expense of calling expert evidence to court on matters relevant only to quantum, particularly medical matters. Where a plaintiff wins on liability he can then obtain a substantial interim payment on account of eventual damages (see **16.5**). If, on the other hand, the plaintiff loses on liability, a great deal of legal costs in obtaining medical and other evidence relevant only to quantum of damages and the lengthy part of the trial that would have been devoted to assessment of such damages will be totally avoided.

Applications for split trials have not hitherto been particularly common, and in a number of cases the reluctance of a plaintiff's advisers to take advantage of this useful procedural possibility has been criticised by the higher courts. It should be noted that there is now a specific provision requiring the court of its own motion to consider the possibility of split trials in all cases (*RSC Ord. 25, r. 3*). Unfortunately this provision relates to summons for directions, and as in routine personal injury cases there will be automatic directions (see **13.2**), the court may not be able to form any view about the desirability of split trials until the setting down stage (see **14.4**) is reached, by which time it is usually too late to be of much benefit.

The opportunity to apply for split trials is a very useful procedural provision. In a case where a defendant purports to be defending strongly merely to avoid an application for an interim payment matters can often usefully be brought to a head by an application immediately after issue of proceedings for split trials, which may sometimes have the effect of concentrating the defendant's mind wonderfully on the desirability of admitting liability and making a sensible interim payment.

1.4.3 PROVISIONAL DAMAGES

There are many kinds of cases where the plaintiff's prognosis is reasonably certain in every respect but one. The one which is uncertain may well cause a great deal of worry to a plaintiff and his legal advisers, however.

Let us take two common examples. After a bone or joint injury most plaintiffs make full recoveries. A small proportion of plaintiffs may, however, often in the distant future, contract osteoarthritis in the joint affected. This is a painful, and indeed crippling, condition but it is often impossible to predict with any certainty whether a given plaintiff will sustain this deterioration. Similarly, in accidents which have involved a bad concussion, statistically a small minority of plaintiffs develop epilepsy at some time in the distant future. The precise medical causes of this are unknown.

In either case, what may have appeared a relatively modest accident involving only a moderate level of damages will be seen in retrospect as having disastrous social and professional consequences. For example, if the plaintiff is a lorry driver who has apparently recovered completely from minor injuries involving concussion and has returned to work as a driver, and who then, in five years, developes epilepsy, one consequence of this will be that he will be forced to give up his driving licence and thus will have a substantial loss of future earnings. If settlement had been accepted on a 'once and for all' basis earlier, nothing more could be done for such a plaintiff. The solution to the problem, however, is to apply for *provisional damages*.

Provisional damages were introduced by *s. 32A* of the *Supreme Court Act 1981*, which provides:

> *This section applies to an action for damages for personal injuries in which there is proved or admitted to be a chance that at some definite or indefinite time in the future the injured person will . . . develop some serious disease or suffer some serious deterioration in his physical or mental condition.*

The relevant procedural rules are *RSC Ord. 37, r. 7* and *CCR Ord. 22, r. 6A*. The principles are now contained in the case of *Wilson* v *Ministry of Defence* [1991] 1 All ER 638. This case holds:

(a) That the risk of serious disease or deterioration must be measurable rather than speculative.

(b) The 'serious deterioration' must be something which is quite distinct and severable and beyond the ordinary deterioration that may be a normal part of the plaintiff's condition.

Where the plaintiff can come within these provisions, then the following is the consequence:

(a) The plaintiff must plead his claim for provisional damages in his statement of claim, though no great detail need be given.

(b) At trial he will obtain judgment as to liability and, if successful, go on to be given an award of damages which will be made on the assumption that his medical condition in relation to the determined matters will *not* deteriorate in the way feared.

(c) The court must specify the type of disease or deterioration which it has been assumed will *not* occur for the purposes of the foregoing award of damages; the court may then prescribe that if the disease or deterioration *does* later occur a further application to the court for damages may be made and further damages will then be assessed at the later hearing.

It must be borne in mind that this is a tactical option available to the plaintiff only and the defendant may not argue that a provisional award should be made.

It is always open as an alternative for a plaintiff to accept a so-called 'risk' award, i.e. a modest further award at trial to account for the risk of epilepsy etc. Should the plaintiff be in the lucky majority who do not then sustain epilepsy, the plaintiff will have received a little windfall. Should he be in the small minority who do contract epilepsy, he will prove to have been drastically under compensated.

1.5 Remedies for Breach of Contract

The right to monetary compensation will arise in a contract case where there has been a failure to perform, without proper excuse, one or more of the obligations contained in the contract. The innocent party may also have the right to rescind (i.e. terminate) the contract, or alternatively to affirm it, go on to perform his part, and claim damages.

1.5.1 DEBT ACTIONS

The simplest case of breach of contract is undoubtedly debt, where typically goods have been sold for a prescribed sum, there is no dispute whether or not the contract has been performed by the seller, but the purchaser does not pay the price. In such a case the action is a simple one for recovery of a liquidated sum from the defendant, and usually for interest on that sum computed from the date when payment was due.

1.5.2 OTHER CASES: DAMAGES

The principle of damages in contract is restitution. That is, to put the aggrieved party in the situation which he would have been but for breach of contract. This may involve repayment of the whole of the price or payment for diminution in value, e.g. where a disgruntled consumer has had to spend a sum of money to put right a purchased item, and perhaps to hire a replacement item during the period of repair. Such items are precisely quantifiable. It may well be, however, that a claim for breach of contract may involve *general* damages which have to be assessed by the court, e.g. for distress, inconvenience or even personal injuries. For example, if a newly purchased television set suddenly explodes causing a fire, which in its turn damages the plaintiff's house and injures one of his children. The house needs to be redecorated. Not only can the cost of the redecoration be recovered as special damages, but the personal injury claim and a further sum for distress and inconvenience can likewise be recovered.

The above is a fairly straightforward situation but it is obvious that the computation of damages can become nearly as complex as in the case of personal injuries. Thus damages may include:

(a) Loss of the bargain or expectation, e.g. where, had the contract been completed, the result would have had a certain benefit to the plaintiff.

(b) Wasted expenditure such as out of pocket expenses.

(c) Loss of profit, e.g. where the business use of goods or services contracted for is impaired as a result of the breach of contract such as where the contract was for hire.

Example P contracts with D for the hire of some earth-moving equipment so that he can carry out some improvements to his market garden before the profitable summer season opens. D fails to supply the equipment and it takes P an extra month to hire it elsewhere. In principle P can claim for the cost of hire over and above what the cost would have been from D, and for loss of profits should he be unable to open his market garden until a month later than would otherwise have been the case.

1.5.3 SPECIFIC PERFORMANCE

It may be that financial compensation is not enough for the plaintiff and some other remedy of an equitable nature is required. For a discussion of injunctions, see **1.7**. Specific performance is a discretionary remedy requiring a party to honour his contract to perform obligations. The effect of this order is therefore to put the parties literally in the position in which they would have been had the contract been performed, though if there has been some delay past the proper contractual date, damages may be awarded in addition to specific performance. Specific performance will usually be awarded only in the situation where damages would not be an adequate remedy. Thus in purely business or monetary contexts, since damages are usually adequate, specific performance will not be ordered.

The plaintiff has to demonstrate the individual qualities of the thing contracted for and the financial ineffectiveness of damages. Consequently, a contract for, say, the purchase of a common type of motor car is unlikely to be enforced by specific performance, whereas a contract for the purchase of a given house may be enforced by specific performance notwithstanding that it may be one of several on a housing estate all virtually indistinguishable. The individual nature of the decoration, garden layout, etc. will be sufficient to make the contract enforceable by specific performance.

1.5.4 OTHER CONSIDERATIONS

Damages may well be an adequate recompense, and the fact that it will be difficult to assess them does not necessarily mean that they are an inadequate remedy. The defendant's inability to pay rather than to perform the contract with the specific chattel may, however, be relevant. Regard should be had, on the question of adequacy of specific performance, to some of the material on injunctions which appears hereafter. In particular, specific performance is unlikely to be ordered of any contract requiring the performance of services where the court would have difficulty in supervising the adequacy of their performance. In addition, since the remedy is an equitable one, the court will usually have regard to general equitable principles.

Regard should finally be had to the other remedies available for breach of contract, in particular rescission, rectification and the special case of remedies for misrepresentation, which are beyond the scope of the present text but which are discussed in some detail in any main contract textbook.

1.6 Interest on Damages in Contract

In cases where a claim is made in respect of a debt or breach of contract, the question of interest arises in two situations:

1.6.1 WHERE INTEREST IS PAYABLE AS OF RIGHT UNDER THE CONTRACT

The contract may provide that unless the amount due is paid in full on a certain date, interest on the whole amount begins to run at a rate fixed by the contract. In this case interest arises as of right as part of the contract and damages for breach of contract will include interest at the contractually agreed rate. In such a case interest may run at a higher rate than a court would ever award (subject to the term not being set aside under the *Unfair Contract Terms Act 1977*), and may even run past the date of judgment until the date of payment in full following enforcement. Such cases therefore provide no difficulty.

1.6.2 INTEREST PAYABLE UNDER THE COURT'S DISCRETION

It will be recalled that under *s. 35A* of the *Supreme Court Act 1981* and *s. 69* of the *County Courts Act 1984*, the court has a discretion to award interest on the amount of which judgment is given on any debt or damages claimed. In the case of personal injuries there was a presumption in favour of the award of interest, but in the case of contract actions there is merely a provision that the court *may* award interest. However, established principles now usually require the court to award interest since justice demands it. The court will have decided in its judgment that the plaintiff ought to be put in the same position as he would have been in but for the breach of contract, and thus, since he will have been kept out of monies which should have been his since the cause of action arose, he ought to receive compensation in the form of an award of interest. The rate which the court will choose is not specified as such, though *s. 35A(5)* of the *1981 Act* provides:

> *. . . rules of court may provide for a rate of interest by reference to the rate specified in section 17 of the Judgments Act 1838 as that section has effect from time to time or by reference to a rate for which any other enactment provides.*

The reference to the 1838 Act is to the provision in that Act providing for interest on *judgment debts*. This is of course a different matter from interest on the *claim* itself until judgment. In the High Court, where judgment is given, interest continues to run until the sum is paid at a specified rate (currently 8 per cent per annum), and this is known as the *judgment debt* rate. The section merely adopts this rate as a convenient one, and the court will take that to be the appropriate rate unless there are special circumstances. The court will not adopt that rate in personal injury cases because of the case law principles previously mentioned (see **1.3.1**). Until April 1993, the judgment debt rate had been 15 per cent annum for many years. That seemed a very reasonable return given the prevailing rate of bank lending rates which had dropped consistently in the early 1990s. For that reason, the Lord Chancellor directed that the rate with effect from 1 April 1993 should be reduced to 8 per cent. That is much closer to the rate obtainable on ordinary bank and building society investments.

In any given case, however, it should be noted that this rate will be adopted unless either party can successfully argue to the contrary. It might, for example, be that the sum involved is a very large one which, if placed on the money market might have procured for the person who has been wrongfully deprived of it over the period a much higher return than 8 per cent per annum. Alternatively, a person may prove that because he has been kept out of his money he has had to have recourse to bank borrowing himself at a higher rate than 8 per cent, and that he should receive restitution for this precise amount which he has had to expend. Similarly, it is open to a defendant to argue that 8 per cent is too high a rate given the prevailing financial climate, although this argument would be unlikely to succeed at present. In the case of substantial sums it may be worth either party arguing the matter fully before the court rather than adopting the norm. The matter is within the court's discretion and the court will have regard in every case to the evidence adduced to it of the financial realities of the situation when fixing the rate.

In the County Court the same rate is usually adopted by analogy with High Court practice.

1.6.3 PLEADING INTEREST

The Rules of Court (*RSC Ord. 18, r. 8(4); CCR Ord. 6, r. 1A*) provide that a party who wishes to claim interest must plead his claim. If no claim for interest is pleaded, then unless leave to amend is given at the trial no interest can be awarded. (The way in which interest should be pleaded is more particularly described in the material on pleadings at **7.4.1.2**.) In a personal injury case it is sufficient to plead the claim to interest generally, since interest is not capable of exact calculation in view of the fact that unliquidated damages are being claimed. In a debt case the claim should be pleaded precisely where the right to interest arises under contract, giving details of the amount accrued due at the contractual rate up to the date of issue of proceedings, together with a daily rate thereafter. Similarly, if there is no contractual provision for interest but the plaintiff is willing to accept the judgment debt of 8 per cent, it is both convenient and tactically wise for interest to be claimed at that rate in the pleadings, for the computations to be made in the same way. This will enable the plaintiff to obtain interest should the case terminate before trial in one of the ways described below (**17.1**).

1.7 Injunctions in Tort and Contract Cases

The procedure for obtaining an injunction will be discussed at **7.8**. At this point it is necessary to discuss the nature of injunctions.

An injunction is an order of the court requiring some person to do, or refrain from doing, some act. Breach of an injunction is a contempt of court, the penalty for which may be committal to prison, or sequestration of assets. Injunctions are either:

(a) *prohibitory*, i.e. orders prohibiting or restraining a party from taking such steps as are named in the order (e.g. restraining further defamation, breach of copyright, continuation of a nuisance, etc.); or

(b) *mandatory*, i.e. orders compelling a party to take specified steps (e.g. to pull down a wall which has been wrongly erected across a right of way).

An injunction is a discretionary remedy and the usual equitable bars to its grant apply. However, the hurdles may not be as difficult to surmount as in the case of some other equitable remedy (e.g. an order of specific performance). It will often be appropriate, however, for the plaintiff to establish that damages alone would not be an adequate remedy.

1.7.1 TYPES OF INJUNCTION

1.7.1.1 Final or 'perpetual' injunctions

This is a remedy granted at trial after the substantive rights of the parties have been determined. The effect of such an injunction lasts until some specified date or, if no date is given, in perpetuity.

1.7.1.2 Interlocutory injunction

This is an order made at some stage of an action before trial the object of which is to prevent some abuse pending full trial. Applications for interlocutory injunctions may be made either:

(a) *ex parte* (i.e. without notice to the other party in a case of great urgency, or where some element of secrecy in the application is required); or

(b) *inter partes* (i.e. on notice to the other party by either summons or motion).

1.7.1.3 Interim injunctions

This term is often used loosely to mean the same as interlocutory injunctions, but strictly speaking an interim injunction is one granted *ex parte* on an interlocutory basis, usually only until it is possible for a full *inter partes* hearing to take place.

Interim injunctions are usually expressed to continue in force only temporarily, e.g. 'until 11.00 am on 1 October 1997 (or so soon thereafter as counsel may be heard) or until further order.'

1.7.1.4 *Quia timet* injunction

This is an order sought to prevent the commission of some legal wrong which has not yet occurred but is threatened (e.g. by one land owner to prevent a neighbour running a pop festival on his land for a weekend, which the first land owner contends will amount to an actionable nuisance). In such a case the plaintiff will have to prove a high probability of the breach occurring and the likelihood of substantial damage.

1.7.2 POSSIBLE ALTERNATIVES TO AN INJUNCTION

The court will often consider alternatives. In particular:

1.7.2.1 Declaration

It may be that since the court will assume that its declarations will be honoured, it will find that to grant a declaration will be sufficient without the necessity for an injunction. Plaintiffs will not usually find declarations to be such a satisfactory remedy because non-observance of a declaration does not amount to a contempt, but in some cases it may be sufficient for the parties to have an authoritative pronouncement as to whether the defendant's conduct did or does amount to a tort or breach of contract.

1.7.2.2 Specific performance

This is likely to be most appropriate in breach of contract for the sale of some unique item. As has been observed earlier, for example, non-performance of a contract to sell a house is usually enforced by specific performance, although in fact an injunction in the same terms could quite easily be given.

1.7.2.3 Undertaking

Where the defendant is willing to give an *undertaking* to the court, this is as satisfactory as an injunction, and indeed procedurally is preferable because there is then no need to incorporate it into a court order and it will remain enforceable by committal in the event of breach. It must be clearly understood that what is meant here by 'undertaking' is one given in the face of the court, and undertakings *between the parties* or their solicitors, unless incorporated in an appropriate order, would not suffice to ground an application for committal if dishonoured.

1.7.2.4 Other remedies

There are specific remedies in *Ord. 29, rr. 2–3* and *Ord. 29, r. 2A* for the detention, preservation, sampling and delivery up of goods, and it may be that in a given context these remedies are adequate to achieve the plaintiff's requirements.

1.7.3 THE PRINCIPLES FOR THE GRANT OF AN INJUNCTION

1.7.3.1 An injunction must support a legal right

An injunction can only be granted in support of a legal right which is capable of being established in the general law, thus:

(a) a plaintiff's failure to establish that he has a legal right will lead to his application being unsuccessful, e.g. *Gouriet* v *Union of Post Office Workers* [1978] AC 435;

(b) a person entitled to an injunction must be the person whose legal right has been or will be infringed (i.e. he must have *locus standi*);

(c) a local authority, however, can seek an injunction in its own name by virtue of *s. 222* of the *Local Government Act 1972*;

(d) the legal right infringed may be one in tort, contract, breach of trust or any other head of substantive English law. It can also include a right which can only be established by reference to the *Treaty of Rome*, e.g. *Article 86* which governs the duty not to abuse a dominant market position. Thus a person who contends that he will suffer by such abuse may obtain an injunction (*Garden Cottage Foods Ltd* v *Milk Marketing Board* [1984] AC 130).

1.7.3.2 Application of equitable principles

Since an injunction is an equitable remedy it is discretionary and thus the usual equitable principles apply, in particular:

(a) He who comes to equity must come with clean hands. See *Armstrong* v *Sheppard and Short Ltd* [1959] 2 QB 384; *Argyll* v *Argyll* [1967] Ch 302.

(b) Acquiescence may deprive the plaintiff of an injunctive remedy if:

   (i) he was aware he had a legal right; and

   (ii) was aware of the defendant's conduct; and

   (iii) it would be unjust and unconscionable after the plaintiff's delay for him now to be allowed to enforce his rights, e.g. where he had led the defendant to believe that there would be no objection to the defendant's conduct. See *Re Pauling's Settlement Trusts* [1964] Ch 303.

1.7.3.3 The power to award damages in lieu of an injunction

By s. 50 of the *Supreme Court Act 1981*, the court has a discretion to award damages in lieu of an injunction even though the plaintiff may have established a basic right to a remedy. Damages may be awarded instead of an injunction where:

(a) the injury to the plaintiff's right is small; and

(b) the injury is capable of being quantified in monetary terms; and

(c) the injury is one which can adequately be compensated by small money payment; and

(d) the case is one in which it would be oppressive to the defendant to grant an injunction (see *Shelfer* v *City of London Electric Lighting Co.* [1895] 1 Ch 287 confirmed in *Jaggard* v *Sawyer* [1995] 1 WLR 269).

It should further be noted that:

(a) Damages in lieu of an injunction are not limited to losses accrued up to the date of issue of proceedings. Damages can be awarded in respect of an injury which will continue, and the amount can be quantified once and for all by the court of trial according to *Miller* v *Jackson* [1977] QB 966 (although that case has subsequently been doubted in *Kennaway* v *Thompson* [1981] QB 88 by a different Court of Appeal which indicated that the approach appeared irreconcilable with *Shelfer's* case).

(b) It is usually inappropriate to award damages in lieu of an injunction in the following cases:

   (i) where the defendant is in breach of an express restrictive covenant (*Doherty* v *Allman* (1878) 3 App Cas 709); or

   (ii) the injury cannot fairly be compensated by money, or the defendant has acted in an oppressive or highhanded manner; or

   (iii) the defendant is wrongfully interfering with the plaintiff's property and clearly intends to continue to do so (though see *Miller* v *Jackson* above).

1.7.3.4 Scope of an injunction

It should be remembered that an injunction is a flexible remedy. It is not necessarily a case of all or nothing. The court may merely restrict the defendant's activities in some way rather than prohibiting them entirely (see, e.g., *Kennaway* v *Thompson* (above) where power boat racing on a lake adjacent to a plaintiff's house was restricted to certain weekends rather than banned entirely). It should also be noted that the court has powers to grant an injunction but to suspend its operation to give the defendant time to rectify matters or change his industrial practices, e.g. *Halsey* v *Esso Petroleum Co. Ltd* [1961] 1 WLR 683.

1.7.3.5 Actionable nuisances

It should be noted that in regard to actionable nuisances, no matter how much the apparent public interest may be in favour of the activity continuing, the public interest should not always prevail over the private interest in the grant of an injunction. See *Kennaway* v *Thompson* above, expressly disapproving Lord Denning's views to the contrary in *Miller* v *Jackson*. Also see *Pride of Derby & Derbyshire Angling Association Ltd* v *British Celanese Ltd* [1953] Ch 149.

1.7.3.6 Mandatory and *quia timet* injunctions

There are some additional principles especially applicable to mandatory and *quia timet* injunctions. These are:

(a) A mandatory injunction will not be granted if it is difficult or impossible to supervise its carrying out (*Ryan* v *Mutual Tontine Westminster Chambers Association* [1893] 1 Ch 116).

(b) No injunction will usually be granted if the effect is to order specific performance of a contract of employment or for personal services. It should be noted that there are significant exceptions to this principle in employment case law, in particular those involving 'public office holders' or where there are certain procedures specified by statute which must be put in force before a person can be dismissed from office.

(c) In relation to *quia timet* injunctions, the criteria are as follows by virtue of the leading case of *Redland Bricks Ltd* v *Morris* [1970] AC 652:

   (i) there must be a very strong possibility that grave damage will be caused in the future; and

   (ii) that damages will be an insufficient remedy; and

   (iii) the court must consider the cost to the defendant of preventing the apprehended wrong; and

   (iv) the injunction must be in terms which clearly indicate to the defendant what it is that he must do or refrain from doing.

1.7.4 INTERLOCUTORY INJUNCTIONS

Interlocutory injunctions may be either prohibitory, mandatory or *quia timet*. An interlocutory injunction is one given prior to trial and is intended to last until the trial itself or some earlier event. Such an injunction is intended to cure some abuse or prevent some act pending full trial. A plaintiff may apply for an interlocutory injunction at any stage, e.g. after summons for directions or after setting down for trial, but in the vast majority of cases application for an interlocutory injunction is made very early in a case, typically contemporaneously with the issue of the writ.

Although an interlocutory injunction is intended to be a temporary remedy, in the majority of cases the grant or refusal of the interlocutory injunction decides the outcome of the case and the matter never proceeds to trial, both parties accepting the outcome of the interlocutory injunction application as conclusive and thereafter negotiating settlement of other outstanding matters. This is because in most cases where an interlocutory injunction is sought, it will be considered vital for the preservation of the rights of one or other of the parties; and if the intended act is not restrained, the position of both parties will have changed materially by the time the action comes to trial. This is pre-eminently the case in actions such as for passing off, or in support of a restraint of trade covenant. It may indeed be possible to obtain a holding injunction in interlocutory proceedings which it is conceded will not be appropriate at the final trial (see *Fresh Fruit (Wales) Ltd* v *Halbert* (1991) *The Times*, 29 January 1991 (CA)). Lord Denning has indeed said (in *Fellowes* v *Fisher* [1976] QB 122) that '99 per cent of cases in which an interlocutory injunction is sought do not proceed to trial'. This is only a slight exaggeration.

1.7.4.1 The modern law

Few areas of procedural law have been the subject of as much practitioner and academic criticism as the law on interlocutory injunctions. Because the need for interlocutory injunctions may arise in a very wide range of kinds of proceedings, the rules relating to the grant or refusal of such injunctions may vary depending on the field of substantive law with which they are concerned. Most leading cases have to do with issues of infringement of intellectual property rights, defamation or employment law. For a recent first instance decision, which thoroughly reviews the law in an accessible form see *Series 5 Software Ltd* v *Clarke* [1996] FSR 273. This case usefully reviews the leading case, which is the House of Lords' decision in *American Cyanamid Ltd* v *Ethicon Ltd* [1975] AC 396. One of the difficulties with this leading case is that there is only one speech, that of Lord Diplock with which the other law lords concurred without contributing. An enormous amount of subsequent case law has been devoted to the question of whether the principles in the *American Cyanamid* case are of universal application or subject to exceptions and, if so, when and how. The test formulated in that case for the grant of an interlocutory injunction in most instances (see **1.7.4.2** for exceptions) is as follows:

(a) Is there a *serious question* to be tried? In other words, the claim should not be frivolous or vexatious (this is *not* the same as a requirement to establish a prima facie case).

(b) Would *damages be an adequate compensation* to the plaintiff for his interim loss pending trial and, if so, is the defendant in a position to pay them? If the answer is 'yes', an injunction should not be granted.

(c) If the answer to the above is 'no', the court must then investigate whether the plaintiff is able to give an *undertaking* adequately to compensate the defendant for any interim loss pending a trial if the interlocutory injunction is granted but at the eventual trial the courts finds the plaintiff was not entitled to the injunction (see further **1.7.4.3**). If the plaintiff is able to give such an undertaking effectively, there is a strong case for the interlocutory injunction, for no eventual injustice is likely to be caused.

(d) If there is doubt as to the adequacy of the respective positions with regard to damages, then the case depends on the *balance of convenience* generally. The test is whether it would cause greater hardship to grant or to refuse the injunction. If even this consideration is evenly balanced, then other factors may be taken into account, e.g.:

 (i) the desirability of maintaining the status quo in general (*Attorney-General* v *Guardian Newspapers Ltd* [1987] 1 WLR 1248);

 (ii) the strength of one party's case being apparently disproportionate to that of the other. One must always bear in mind, however, the difficulty of embarking upon an investigation resembling a trial of the action based on conflicting affidavits when evaluating the strength of the parties' cases;

 (iii) the effect on the general public (*Smith* v *ILEA* [1978] 1 WLR 411).

1.7.4.2 Exceptions to the *American Cyanamid* principle

The principle is said not to apply in the following kinds of case. In these cases something similar to the old law is applied. In the previous law there was what amounted to a mini trial on affidavit evidence, where the key test was whether the plaintiff could establish a prima facie case; whether he would be entitled to a final injunction at trial; and who was favoured by the balance of convenience. These tests will still usually be applied in the following types of case:

(a) Where no action for a final injunction is likely to reach trial because the timing and circumstances mean that the grant of the interlocutory injunction will be conclusive of the issue. Important examples of this are:

 (i) enforcement of covenants in restraint of trade (*Office Overload* v *Gunn* [1977] FSR 39; *Fellowes* v *Fisher* [1976] QB 122). It must be observed, however, that this approach is appropriate where the covenant in restraint of trade is clearly valid. If there is a serious dispute about the validity of the covenant, the *American Cyanamid* approach may be preferred;

(ii) passing off or similar commercial cases in appropriate circumstances;

(iii) defamation cases (*Herbage* v *Pressdram Ltd* [1984] 1 WLR 1160).

(b) Breach of confidence cases (*Woodward* v *Hutchins* [1977] 1 WLR 760 although on its facts this case might now be decided differently). See *Attorney-General* v *Guardian Newspapers Ltd* [1987] 1 WLR 1248.

(c) Where a statute prescribes an additional test to be followed, e.g. *Trade Union and Labour Relations (Consolidation) Act 1992, s. 221(2): '. . . the court shall, in exercising its discretion whether or not to grant the injunction, have regard to the likelihood of that party's succeeding at the trial of the action'*. According to the leading case on this (*NWL Ltd* v *Woods* [1979] 1 WLR 1294) the court must in this situation consider:

(i) whether there is a serious question to be tried;

(ii) the balance of convenience; and

(iii) the likelihood of establishing the statutory defence.

(d) Where neither side is interested in monetary compensation and the decision on an application for an interlocutory injunction will be equivalent to final judgment (e.g. whether the transmission of a broadcast or publication of an article should take place, the whole impact and value of which depends on the timing of the transmission or publication) a different approach is necessary. The court should assess the relative strength of the parties' cases in such an instance (*Cambridge Nutrition Ltd* v *BBC* [1990] 3 All ER 523).

1.7.4.3 The plaintiff's undertaking

In every case where an interlocutory injunction is sought the applicant will be required to give an undertaking to pay the defendant damages for any loss sustained by the defendant as a consequence of the interlocutory injunction if in the event the plaintiff fails to obtain a final injunction at trial. It should be noted:

(a) That the plaintiff must almost always demonstrate that he has the means to perform that undertaking in damages.

(b) However, in certain circumstances a legally aided plaintiff will not be denied an interlocutory injunction even if his undertaking will be of limited value (*Allen* v *Jambo Holdings Limited* [1980] 1 WLR 1252).

(c) In *Blue Town Investments Ltd* v *Higgs & Hill plc* [1990] 1 WLR 696, the plaintiffs' claim to a permanent injunction was struck out at an interlocutory stage because of their refusal to apply for an interlocutory injunction. They had refused to apply for the interlocutory injunction because of the danger of giving the undertaking in damages. This refusal to apply was considered almost an abuse of process. However doubt was cast on this result in the later case of *Oxy-Electric Ltd* v *Zainuddin* [1991] 1 WLR 115, where in somewhat similar circumstances the Court of Appeal doubted whether the court had had the jurisdiction to act as it did in the *Blue Town* case since the effect would be to restrict the availability of interlocutory injunctions to the wealthy.

(d) In an action by a local authority for an injunction to restrain breaches of a statute, the court has a discretion to grant an interlocutory injunction without requiring an undertaking in damages since in such an action the local authority is exercising the function of law enforcement (*Kirklees Metropolitan Borough Council* v *Wickes Building Supplies Ltd* [1993] AC 227).

(e) Where a local authority or the Crown applies for an interlocutory injunction, it will ordinarily be required to give such an undertaking in damages unless the action is one to enforce the law (*F Hoffmann-La-Roche AG* v *Secretary of State for Trade and Industry* [1975] AC 295).

Note also:

(f) Sometimes a defendant is willing to undertake to do, or refrain from doing something instead of there being an injunction. In such a case the plaintiff will usually have to enter a cross-undertaking as to damages just as in an injunction case.

(g) If at the end of the trial an injunction is refused so that the plaintiff must perform his undertaking, then an *enquiry as to damages* will be held. This will usually be referred to a Master or District Judge, although the trial judge himself may undertake the investigation. If the investigation as to the amount of damage sustained appears very complex, the matter may be referred to a Special Referee or the Official Referee. The defendant must rely on the outcome of this enquiry into damages and will not be permitted to issue a separate writ in respect of any loss which he had sustained.

The procedure for interlocutory injunctions is described at **7.8**.

1.8 Limitation of Actions

1.8.1 LIMITATION PERIODS

The rules on limitation of actions are laid down in the *Limitation Act 1980*, as amended, in particular by the *Latent Damage Act 1986*. The rules provide a series of different periods in respect of different causes of action. They must also be read in conjunction with a number of specific statutes which lay down shorter periods, in particular those involving international trade or travel. It should also be remembered that there is a variety of specific procedural rules applicable to individual types of action which lay down different periods – often very short periods – as, for example, under *RSC Ord. 53, r. 4*, by virtue of which an application for judicial review must be made within three months of the event complained of, and applications in respect of unfair dismissal for which an application must be lodged at the Central Office of Industrial Tribunals within three months of the event claimed to constitute unfair dismissal. Similarly, in some landlord and tenant matters, in particular applications for new business tenancies under the *Landlord and Tenant Act 1954, s. 24*, such an application must be lodged not less than two months nor later than four months after the landlord's notice of termination.

It must be remembered that limitation is a procedural defence. The court will not take a Limitation Act point of its own volition and the defence must be specifically pleaded by a party wishing to rely on it (*RSC Ord. 18, r. 8*).

The basic time limits are as follows:

(a) For all actions in contract – six years.

(b) For actions for recovery of land or for the recovery of money secured by a mortgage – 12 years.

(c) Actions by beneficiaries to recover trust property or in respect of breach of trust – six years.

(d) Actions in tort – six years.

(e) Actions under the *Defective Premises Act 1972* – six years from completion of the house (*Defective Premises Act 1972, s. 1(5)*).

1.8.2 MISCELLANEOUS EXCEPTIONS TO THE RULE

1.8.2.1 Defamation

Actions in respect of defamation must be brought within three years (*Limitation Act 1980, s. 4*), to be reduced to one year when the *Defamation Act 1996* is in force.

1.8.2.2 *Consumer Protection Act 1987*

Actions under the *Consumer Protection Act 1987* must normally be brought within three years of suffering the relevant damage, or within three years of acquiring the necessary knowledge of the facts to sue if later. However, there is an absolute cut off date of 10 years from the date the product was first put into circulation (*Consumer Protection Act 1987, s. 5(5)* and *sch. 1*). It must be borne in mind, however, that this relates only to actions in respect of the strict liability under the Act. If the actions in question also amount to negligence, then the more generous limitation period applies of three years from *date of knowledge*, even if that should be outside the 10-year period.

1.8.2.3 *Latent Damage Act 1986*

The *Latent Damage Act 1986* inserted a new *s. 14A* in the *Limitation Act 1980*. This applies to negligence actions other than for personal injuries. It has a particular application in claims relating to defective buildings but may also cover other kinds of claims, e.g. against solicitors for negligent drafting of documents. The practical scope of these provisions, which were viewed as of great importance at the time, has been reduced by the overruling of the former leading authority *Anns* v *Merton London Borough Council* [1978] AC 728 by the case of *Murphy* v *Brentwood District Council* [1991] 1 AC 398.

The Act provides for two alternative periods, which are respectively:

(a) six years from accrual of cause of action; and

(b) three years from the 'starting date'.

But note both these periods are subject to a final cut off period of 15 years.

(a) *Accrual*

Damage accrues when it is initially suffered. So in the case of an action against a solicitor for negligently drafting a will, the plaintiff's cause of action accrues when the will takes effect.

(b) *Starting date*

The period of three years runs from the earliest date on which the plaintiff was aware of the following:

(i) that the relevant damage was sufficiently serious to justify commencing proceedings;

(ii) that the damage was attributable to the negligence of the defendant; and

(iii) the defendant's identity.

The *Limitation Act 1980, s. 14B* provides a 15-year final cut off date for negligence actions, after which such actions shall not be brought even if the cause of action has not yet accrued or the starting date has not yet arrived. In this case the 15-year period runs from the actual act or omission constituting the negligence resulting in the plaintiff's damage (i.e. in the case of solicitors drafting a will negligently, from the date on which the will was drafted or executed).

1.8.3 PERSONAL INJURIES AND FATAL ACCIDENTS

The law on limitation periods for damages for personal injuries and fatal accidents is now contained in *ss. 11–14* of the 1980 Act as supplemented by *s. 33* of that Act, which gives the court a discretion to disregard the prima facie time limits.

The three-year period of limitation for personal injuries applies to:

> *any action for damages for negligence, nuisance or breach of duty (whether the duty exists by virtue of a contract or of provision made by or under a statute or independently of any contract or any such provision).*

It follows, therefore, that the reduced limitation period of three years applies in respect of the personal injuries caused by breach of contract just as much as to those caused in a road or factory accident. In *Stubbings* v *Webb* [1993] AC 498, it was held that where an action for personal injuries was based on *trespass* rather than negligence, the longer period of six years applied. This overruled the old authority of *Letang* v *Cooper* [1965] 1 QB 232.

The term 'personal injuries' is defined to include any disease and any impairment of a person's physical or mental condition (*Limitation Act 1980, s. 38(1)*). Whether distress and injury to feelings, where they do not amount to impairment of a mental condition in a defined medical sense, come within the Act is undecided.

In personal injury cases, time initially begins to run on the date of the cause of action in negligence. This is an easy enough matter in the case of a physical accident, but in the case of industrial diseases or industrial deafness, which may have occurred over decades early in a plaintiff's working life, considerable injustice would be caused by a strict three year cut off date. Accordingly, the limitation period of three years runs either from the date of the *cause of action* arising or from the date of the plaintiff's *knowledge* of the cause of action if later. If the plaintiff dies before that period expires, the period survives for the benefit of the estate and becomes three years from the date of death, or the date of knowledge of the personal representative (*s. 11(5)*).

1.8.3.1 What is knowledge?

The definition of 'knowledge' is provided in *s. 14* of the Act, and the relevant date is the date on which the plaintiff had knowledge of the following:

(a) That the injury in question was *significant*, that is to say, sufficiently serious to justify instituting proceedings for damages against a defendant who did not dispute liability and was able to satisfy a judgment. It is suggested that the level of intelligence of the plaintiff in considering these matters may be taken into account (*McCafferty* v *Metropolitan Police District Receiver* [1977] 1 WLR 1073) but a personal reason such as unwillingness to sue one's employer may not be taken into account (*Miller* v *London Electrical Manufacturing Co. Ltd* [1976] 2 Lloyd's Rep 284). That the plaintiff's level of intelligence in understanding the facts available to him would be taken into account was further confirmed in *Nash* v *Eli Lilly* [1993] 4 All ER 383 although whether a subjective test at all was appropriate was further doubted in *Forbes* v *Wandsworth Area Health Authority* (1996) *The Times*, 20 March 1996

(b) That the injury was *attributable* in whole or in part to the alleged wrongful act or omission. This means that the plaintiff must in essence know what the cause was of his injury. However, the fact that the plaintiff did not know that he had a cause of action as a point of law is not relevant (*Brooks* v *J & P Coates (UK) Ltd* [1984] 1 All ER 702). A subjective test for this part of the section was positively approved in *Spargo* v *North Essex District Health Authority, The Times*, 21 March 1997 CA where it was shown that the plaintiff had been clear in her own mind when she first consulted solicitors that there was a causal connection between her suffering and the mistaken medical diagnosis, concerning which she brought her claim.

(c) The identity of the defendant.

(d) If it is alleged that the act or omission was that of a person other than the defendant, the identity of that person and the additional facts supporting the bringing of an action against the defendant (i.e. if the plaintiff wishes to hold the defendant vicariously liable, time does not run until he identifies the relevant employee and ascertains that he was acting in the course of his employment).

Section 14(1) expressly states that knowledge that any acts or omissions did or did not as a matter of law involve negligence, nuisance or breach of duty is irrelevant. In other words, a plaintiff is deemed to know the legal significance of facts.

1.8.3.2 Constructive knowledge

The plaintiff's actual state of knowledge is not necessarily what matters. There is a deeming provision in *s. 14(3)* which states that for the purpose of the section a person's knowledge includes knowledge which he might reasonably have been expected to acquire:

(a) from facts observable or ascertainable by him; or

(b) from facts ascertainable by him with the help of medical or other appropriate expert advice which it is reasonable for him to seek.

Nonetheless, so long as he acts appropriately he is not prejudiced if the expert whom he consults fails to find ascertainable facts. It is important to note that this deeming provision relates only to *facts*. If a plaintiff obtains incorrect *legal advice* time will continue to run against him.

1.8.4 THE DISCRETION TO EXTEND THE LIMITATION PERIOD

1.8.4.1 Matters the court will take into account

In the case of damages for personal injury and death only, the court may still allow an action to proceed notwithstanding that the limitation period has expired (*Limitation Act 1980, s. 33*). The court has a discretion to extend the time limit if it considers it equitable to do so having regard to the degree to which the ordinary limitation periods would prejudice the plaintiff and to which any exercise of the power to extend the period would prejudice the defendant. The court must have regard to all the circumstances, including:

(a) the length of and the reasons for the delay on the part of the plaintiff;

(b) the effect of the delay on the cogency of the evidence in the case;

(c) the conduct of the defendant after the cause of action arose, including his response to any request by the plaintiff for information;

(d) the duration of any disability of the plaintiff arising after the cause of action;

(e) the extent to which the plaintiff acted promptly and reasonably once he knew of the facts which afforded him a cause of action;

(f) the steps taken by the plaintiff to obtain medical, legal or other expert advice and the nature of any such advice received.

This provision gives the court a very wide mandate indeed to enquire into all the surrounding circumstances concerning the apparent delay. Although all the factors must be weighed, a key question will be 'the effect of the delay on the cogency of the evidence in the case'. Thus if the case depends on eye-witness recollection, it may be more difficult for the plaintiff to have the period extended than if there is a wealth of evidence in documentary form, e.g. in the case of a factory accident where there may be prompt reports and statements made at the time, a conviction of the defendants for breach of regulations made under the *Health and Safety at Work Act 1974*.

It should also be noted that the plaintiff will have to waive his privilege and reveal the nature of the legal advice he asked for and received. The court will thereupon have regard to the question of whether the plaintiff acted reasonably promptly after he had the relevant advice. The fact that the plaintiff may have an excellent case against his solicitors in respect of negligent advice or delay is not necessarily relevant. It must be borne in mind that an action against one's solicitors may be less advantageous than an action against the defendant because, after all, those solicitors may have knowledge of the weaknesses of the plaintiff's original case.

1.8.4.2 The procedure

Where a plaintiff wishes to apply to the court to extend the limitation period there are two alternative procedures available. One is to apply, after the issue of a writ and service of statement of claim, and the defendant's service of a defence taking the *Limitation Act* point, for leave to continue the action. Such an application may be made to the Master or District Judge, and it then should be supported by affidavit describing fully the background of the case and other facts. Although Masters and District Judges have the power to decide the matter, sometimes application is made direct to a High Court judge because the matter will clearly be one of some importance and an appeal from the original decision might be likely whichever party succeeds. Thus this avoids one tier of the stages of appeal. Alternatively, and perhaps more commonly, the matter is left to be taken as a preliminary issue at trial. This is because it may be necessary to investigate a good deal of factual background, including 'the cogency of the evidence', which is best left until trial. Otherwise there is a risk of duplication, with a great deal of the court's time being taken up with repetition of issues. In addition, all the factors in the case may not become apparent until after the interlocutory procedures, in particular discovery of documents, have been carried out.

1.8.5 DISABILITY

Under the *Limitation Act 1980, s. 28*, time does not begin to run against a person *under a disability* until the expiry of the disability. In this context 'disability' means legal disability, and therefore that the potential plaintiff is either:

(a) an infant, i.e. a person under the age of 18; or

(b) a person of unsound mind, i.e. a person who by reason of mental disorder within the meaning of the *Mental Health Act 1983* is incapable of managing and administering his property and affairs.

Where a plaintiff suffers from a legal disability, the usual limitation period applicable to the kind of claim will begin to run at the cessation of that disability. Thus if a mental patient recovers so as to become capable of administering his affairs, time will start to run from that point; in the case of an infant time will start to run from his eighteenth birthday, though it must of course be borne in mind that in a personal injury case it may be the date of knowledge that is relevant rather than the date of the accident. Thus it may be the case that a plaintiff, injured when young, does not obtain the relevant knowledge of the circumstances of the accident, the identity of the potential defendant, etc., until well after his eighteenth birthday, in which case time will begin to run from then.

1.8.6 THE RELEVANT DATE FOR THE LIMITATION PERIOD

The action that must be taken within the limitation period is the *issue* of the writ, not its service. Similarly, in third party proceedings what matters is the date on which the third party notice is issued at court (*Limitation Act 1980, s. 35(1)(a)*).

TWO

LEGAL ADVICE AND ASSISTANCE, LEGAL AID AND COSTS

2.1 Financing Civil Litigation

2.1.1 INTRODUCTION

In this chapter we shall consider the crucial matter of the way in which a solicitor is remunerated in litigation work and the extent to which all or any part of the charges which a client incurs for litigation work may be recovered eventually from an opponent. We shall also consider how the grant of legal aid to one or other party may affect the general position. This chapter should be considered in conjunction with **Chapter 22** which deals with the question of 'taxation', the technical term for the process by which the court assesses solicitors' and barristers' fees where they cannot be agreed.

It is vital at the outset of a litigation matter to ensure that one's client has a clear picture of the various possible outcomes of the litigation in terms of costs. If a client comes to see a solicitor in connection with a non-contentious matter, then he is usually under no illusion that anyone will be paying the solicitor's fees except himself. Parties intent on embarking on litigation, however, often have misconceptions, e.g., a plaintiff who believes he has a very good case may well also believe that the solicitor whom he is about to consult will be happy to take it on without any immediate outlay by the client, and that in the end the solicitor will be paid by the losing opponent in full.

It is vital to disabuse a client of these or other misconceptions and immediately to establish a proper professional relationship with him (see further **2.1.6**). A solicitor's relationship with a client is governed primarily by the law of contract, in particular implied duties as to payment, and as to the exercise of proper professional competence. The law of tort may also be relevant, e.g. since breach of the implied term to use proper professional competence will also amount to the tort of negligence. It may sometimes be worthwhile framing actions against a negligent solicitor alternatively in tort and contract because the rules as to limitation, and remoteness and quantum of damages may be different. These obligations are also tempered by the rules of professional conduct, which often have a bearing on matters to do with how a solicitor may charge a client.

For the businesslike conduct of litigation it is usually essential to ensure that the source of finance is clearly established at the start. Substantial payments on account from the client are usually required, and in order to ensure that payments in advance continue throughout the course of the litigation so that the solicitor is always, so to speak, 'ahead' of his own bills in terms of the money he is holding, these payments will be topped up or repeated from time to time. When money on account of costs is received it will be paid into the firm's client account.

2.1.2 METHOD OF CHARGING

Fees for work in litigation matters are worked out on the basis of actual time spent in the conduct of the client's case. Thus time spent interviewing in the office, collecting evidence, whether inside or outside the office, researching the law, perusing documents, conducting negotiations with the opponent, and travelling to and attending court for interlocutory applications or the trial are all charged on an hourly basis.

The rates chargeable may depend upon the type of work, so that, for example, something which requires minimal mental input, such as driving from the office to court, may be charged at one rate, whereas something that requires a high degree of concentration and skill, such as perusing documents obtained on discovery or researching the law, will be charged at a different rate. Arguably this is not entirely logical, because time spent driving to court on a client's business is time that could have been spent on another client's business, possibly at a higher rate. Nonetheless, this method of charging is common. Likewise, firms will of course have different rates of charging depending on the level of the personnel involved on the case, so that a firm will be entitled to charge more for the time of a senior partner than for that of a junior employee, say a trainee solicitor, who is engaged on some of the more mundane tasks in a case. These basic charging rates, computed by the hour, may be adjusted further to take into account aspects of the case itself, as indicated in the next paragraph.

2.1.3 FACTORS OTHER THAN TIME WHEN DECIDING WHAT TO CHARGE

The matters to take into account when deciding what to charge include the following:

(a) the complexity of the item or of the cause or matter in which it arises, and the difficulty or novelty of the questions involved;

(b) the skill, specialised knowledge and responsibility required of, and the time and labour expended by, the solicitor;

(c) the number and importance of the documents (however brief) prepared or perused;

(d) the place and circumstances in which the business involved is transacted;

(e) the importance of the cause or matter to the clients;

(f) where money or property is involved, its amount or value.

Thus, for instance, if a matter is both weighty, in the sense of the amount of money involved, and urgent, perhaps because an injunction is immediately needed, so that two or three employees of the firm have to cancel their diary engagements on the day instructions are received to give all their attention to the urgent matter, then naturally a higher charge can be made than for a purely routine case. Most firms have a time recording system which ensures that every minute spent on a client's business is billed. In some cases the billing is done through time recording sheets which each fee earner has to fill in for the working day showing what time has been spent on which client's file. More sophisticated systems are available and permit a fee earner to key into a central accounts record the time spent on a case direct from his desk top.

2.1.4 INTERIM BILLING

Efficient firms prepare accounts for the client, usually on a quarterly basis, and thus send the client every three months an account of the work they have done in the preceding quarter. Once the bill has been delivered the firm is in principle entitled to transfer the money which they hold from their client account to the firm's office account (i.e. the money now becomes the firm's own money). If this exhausts the money being held, then further substantial payments on account should be sought. This continues until the end of the case.

By the end of the case a solicitor will ensure that he has been paid in full hitherto and has sufficient funds in hand for the most expensive part of all of the litigation, which is the trial itself. Thereafter (subject to any appeal) the solicitor can bring the matter to an end and send the final bill. If the client has been successful in the action, since the loser is indeed usually ordered to pay the bulk of the winner's costs in litigation, the solicitor will now have the task of setting about recovering as large a proportion of the costs as possible for the client.

2.1.5 DEFINITION OF 'COSTS'

It is important to note that the term 'costs' has two distinct meanings in litigation. In general speech the word 'costs' usually refers to the total of a solicitor's bill. However, this bill will in fact comprise three distinct elements. The first of these is the solicitor's firm's own fees for the only thing which the firm has to sell, namely its time and expertise. The correct term for these fees is 'profit costs' but confusingly the term 'costs' is sometimes used to mean simply this element.

The second element on the bill is money paid out by the solicitor in the conduct of litigation on the client's behalf. This will include such things as court fees, travelling and accommodation expenses if part of the work has to be carried out at some distance from the solicitor's office, counsel's fees, fees to expert witnesses for reports and attending at trial, etc. The term for these payments is 'disbursements'.

The third element is VAT on the whole of the profit costs and most of the disbursements (but not court fees).

The term 'costs' thus usually includes profit costs, disbursements and VAT.

2.1.6 RELATIONS WITH THE CLIENT

It is a vital part of running a successful litigation practice to ensure that one's clients are satisfied. This involves giving clients a full account of the progress of their case, and in particular trying to give an honest idea of how long a case will last. Nothing is more unsettling for a client than to have the impression that his case can be dealt with in a matter of weeks, only to find that it lasts some years because of procedural developments which are so familiar to the solicitor that he has overlooked the need to explain them to the client.

One part of keeping clients happy is to make the position as to costs very clear at the outset. Information must be given to the client about the firm's method of charging in terms of the hourly rate, and it must be made clear that there is no litigation matter in which an accurate estimate of the hours involved can be made, although some general idea may be possible. The basis of charging, and the practice of interim billing and of payment on account must be carefully explained to the client so that he knows precisely what outlay he is likely to have and at what intervals. It can, of course, be explained to the client that costs will normally 'follow the event', i.e. that a successful party will generally be able to recover costs from the loser, but that this is within the discretion of the court. (The client must also, of course, be warned that if he loses he will become liable for his opponent's costs as well as yours.) It must also be made clear that what can be recovered from the loser may very well not involve the whole of the costs in the case and that, anyway, there may be no guarantee that the loser is able to pay. The special rules applicable to litigation against legally aided persons should also be explained to the client where relevant.

2.1.7 CONDITIONAL FEE AGREEMENTS

The possibility of conditional fee agreements was introduced by the *Courts and Legal Services Act 1990, s. 58*. This provides for a form of contingency fee. Unlike in America, however, the contingency fee will not be an all or nothing arrangement but will be an enhanced fee dependent on victory in the case.

The lawfulness of this arrangement, which is intended at present to be restricted to personal injury, insolvency, and human rights cases depends on regulations made by the Lord Chancellor. The regulations have caused a great deal of controversy, having been already condemned by some of the higher judiciary as tending to distort the proper relationship between lawyer and client so that unscrupulous lawyers may be tempted to recommend settlement, or refuse settlement, as the case may be, out of self-interest. The Law Society have drafted a 'model form' of agreement providing for certain norms in the regulation of conditional fees between solicitor and client. In addition there are overriding principles of professional conduct which leave the situation unclear. It has, for example, been suggested that it might be wrong for a solicitor to suggest a conditional fee arrangement to a client in a case where success looks very probable. In other words, the scope of conditional fee agreements might well be limited to cases which are doubtful and where the solicitor may genuinely be taking a risk in exchange for his expenditure of time and effort.

The way in which 'conditional fees' works is that following an agreement between solicitor and client, where at the end of a case the client is successful, the solicitor will obtain any costs awarded against the losing opponent. A conditional fee agreement may be made to the effect that a further amount of up to 100 per cent of the costs obtained from the losing opponent may also be retained from the solicitor out of damages recovered. Thus, in the event of total success, he will recover double the amount of fees for the case that, but for this provision, he would have obtained. The converse is also obvious, that if the case is lost the solicitor may have expended a great deal of time and effort for nothing.

The original object was that clients who were above the legal aid limit but not wealthy enough to fund litigation themselves would be advantaged by this procedure. Likewise, clients who had been refused legal aid in difficult or test cases might also be able to find solicitors willing to take on the case on this basis. Barristers may also engage in conditional fee agreements.

A key element in such difficult cases would, of course, normally be that the plaintiff, whilst being unable to fund his own solicitor's fees, would also greatly fear losing and suffering a heavy costs order in the defendant's favour. With legal aid he would of course have had the protection of the *Legal Aid Act 1988, s. 17* (**2.3.3.1**) against this contingency. Fortunately the Law Society have managed to negotiate an insurance arrangement with an insurance company Accident Line Protect who will, for a single modest premium (currently £85) agree to indemnify plaintiffs against costs orders in favour of defendants.

It is fair to say that conditional fees are at a very early stage although many solicitors have triumphantly reported their first successes in the area. It is true that the huge majority of personal injury cases are won by the plaintiffs, and in such instances there may be little to fear. A bad run of results however, especially ones involving very heavy legal costs, would undoubtedly lead to Accident Line Protect re-considering the commercial viability of the cover they offer, at least at current premiums. The future of conditional fees for the moment remains unclear.

2.1.8 EXCEPTIONS TO THE GENERAL REGIME

What has been described at **2.1.6** is a useful practice in many cases. It is, however, subject to variation in any individual case. If a client has legal aid then a very different regime in relation to costs applies which we consider at **2.2**. Likewise, a great deal of litigation in personal injury matters is carried out for trade union members, the benefits of whose membership usually include free legal advice and assistance in work-related litigation. In those cases solicitors usually have direct arrangements with the trade union concerned, that the union member will not be charged anything during the progress of the case and that the trade union will pay costs in those cases which are lost; but in those cases which are won, the firm instructed will be content with whatever costs it can recover from the loser. This is an apparently unbusiness-like arrangement but it must be recalled that in such a case the trade union is supplying the firm chosen with a considerable bulk of usually high quality litigation work. Firms most of whose practice involves acting for trade unions, are usually perfectly satisfied with the arrangement, notwithstanding that large amounts of money may at any given time be outstanding as 'work in progress'.

In addition, many firms are instructed mainly by defendant insurance companies in road traffic or factory accident litigation. Those firms will also have other working arrangements with the insurance company, who may well be their main, or only, client. Since insurance companies are commercial organisations in a way which trade unions are not, those firms may also get a healthy diet of commercial/company work from the insurance company concerned. In addition, the advent of *legal expense insurance*, although the take up is modest at the time of writing, may well change the picture further. Companies which insure persons against the need to litigate are likely to have specific arrangements concerning the funding and running of that litigation with the firms whom they select to conduct it on their behalf.

It must also be remembered that solicitors always have discretion in these matters. If the potential litigant is a sufficiently old client or sufficiently trustworthy for the firm to conduct the litigation without demanding payment in advance, that may done in any individual case. It is still generally financially prudent to deliver interim bills, for obvious reasons.

Lastly if a client has legal aid then a very different regime in relation to costs applies which we now consider at **2.2**.

2.2 Legal Advice and Assistance and Legal Aid

At the time of writing the future of these schemes is uncertain. Following dramatic reductions in the number of persons eligible for legal aid, the previous Lord Chancellor wished to put legal aid on (an allegedly) more business-like footing. This has already started to some extent by the granting of 'legal aid franchises' to certain firms who can pass a very comprehensive inspection by the Legal Aid Board based on defined criteria to do not just with their competence as lawyers but with the quality of their internal administrative and managerial procedures for processing cases. Where firms have been awarded a franchise, they are freed from certain restrictions which apply to other firms, in particular in how they deal with their legal aid clients and the extent to which they need to report back to the Legal Aid Board for authority to continue acting, or take certain steps.

When originally instituted, the system of franchises was firmly stated to be 'non-exclusive', that is, that firms who did not wish to apply for franchises, or indeed having applied did not qualify for them, might still obtain legal aid for individual clients on the same basis as hitherto which is described below. At the time of writing this is, to some extent, under threat.

On any view however the present system is likely to continue for at least a further year, and thus it is the present system that is described below.

2.2.1 DUTY TO INFORM CLIENT OF LEGAL AID SCHEMES

It is both unprofessional and negligent for a solicitor to fail to advise a client of the existence of the legal aid schemes. Even if the solicitor's firm itself does not do legal aid work, a solicitor is still obliged to inform potential clients of the scheme so that they can consider whether to go elsewhere.

2.2.2 ADMINISTRATION OF LEGAL AID

Legal aid is administered by the Legal Aid Board under the provisions of the *Legal Aid Act 1988*. England and Wales is divided into a number of areas and each has an Area Director who is in charge of legal aid locally. There is also a substantial supporting clerical and administrative staff, many of whom have some legal training, to process the enormous number of legal aid applications received. Each area also has an Area Committee which consists of solicitors and barristers in private practice who are paid a small fee for attending the area office on a rota basis to decide various matters concerning legal aid, in particular appeals against its refusal.

Legal aid applications may be submitted to any area office but as a matter of convenience such applications are usually submitted to the office of the area where the solicitor practises.

We discuss legal aid proper at **2.2.4**, but first it is appropriate to describe the legal advice and assistance scheme, known generally as 'the Green Form scheme'.

2.2.3 THE GREEN FORM SCHEME

2.2.3.1 Scope

The Green Form Scheme permits a solicitor to give a client who qualifies under the scheme advice and assistance. Any person may obtain advice from a solicitor about any matter to which English law applies, with some few exceptions. In general the matter may be either contentious or non-contentious, and it may cover any work a solicitor may properly do for a client except *taking a step in proceedings* (see further below). The exceptions provide that advice and assistance in the making of a will are excluded in most cases unless the client is aged 70 or over, or in some other restrictive categories; similarly, advice and assistance in conveyancing services is in general excluded from the scheme.

With these exceptions, however, the advice and assistance given could cover such matters as conducting correspondence on behalf of a client; entering into negotiations on behalf of a client; drafting documents; interviewing witnesses; giving a client advice relating to future proceedings whether as a potential plaintiff or defendant, or even, when proceedings have already commenced, giving a client advice on how he may best continue with the proceedings.

The solicitor may not, however, take any *step in the proceedings* on behalf of the client. That is to say, the solicitor may not represent the client in the proceedings as such. There is one exception to this known as 'assistance by way of representation'. This is limited in civil proceedings (other than matrimonial proceedings) to cases where the court itself authorises any solicitor within the precincts of the court to represent a person who is appearing in the court. For example, suppose that a solicitor was attending an appointment for a client before a District Judge in chambers in the county court; suppose also that another litigant in person was to appear in an earlier case and some difficult point arose on which the registrar considered it desirable that the litigant in person should receive immediate legal advice. If the client qualified on means the District Judge could authorise the solicitor who was present in court on his own client's business to assist the unrepresented person at the hearing before him. This would be entirely as a matter of speed and convenience and would always be an alternative to adjourning the proceedings so that the unrepresented person might apply for legal aid proper.

As far as we are concerned, however, the use of the Green Form will be for the preliminaries of litigation, and particularly for preparing a case so that an application for legal aid proper can be made.

2.2.3.2 Eligibility under the Green Form scheme

The test for eligibility under the Green Form scheme is purely financial. There is no need for the solicitor to investigate the merits of the client's case, so the solicitor need not feel that the client has in any sense a winning case. For example, the Green Form could be used to assist a client who admitted liability for a debt to negotiate payments by instalments, or, if proceedings had already been commenced, to give the client advice as to how he could make application to the court to be allowed to pay by instalments.

The assessment of financial eligibility is carried out immediately the client sees the solicitor. On the assumption that the client is not obviously disqualified on the grounds of means there will then be an exact assessment of financial eligibility. The solicitor uses a 'key card' which enables him to take financial details from the client and to assess quickly whether the client qualifies. The key card is used to compute the client's net disposable income after deducting from his gross income tax, national insurance contributions and certain fixed allowances for dependants. No allowances are made for such outgoings as rent or mortgage repayments because the allowances for these are built into the other allowances. If the client's income and capital are then below a certain net disposable figure he qualifies for legal assistance without any contribution on his part. An applicant automatically qualifies on income if he is in receipt of income support, family credit or disability working allowance. He may still not qualify, however, notwithstanding that his only source of income is these benefits, if his capital exceeds the permitted maximum.

The Green Form and current key card are illustrated on pages 44 and 45.

2.2.3.3 Two hours' work limit

Under the scheme a solicitor is entitled to work for a client for a total of up to two hours in an ordinary case. Solicitors are paid for their work on a fixed hourly rate which is adjusted from time to time.

> **Example** Suppose that a client comes to see you for advice in connection with, say, some consumer problem. You take details of his income and the permitted deductions by way of tax, national insurance and the weekly allowances for his dependants shown on the Green Form key card. If having made that computation you find that his weekly disposable income is over £77 (the current limit), then he would not qualify for assistance on the Green Form. It would then be for him to pay for the time taken with the advice. If, however, his income was less than £77 and in addition his capital was also below the maximum permitted, you could go ahead and give up to two hours' advice under the Green Form scheme.

The basic limit of two hours' work may be exceeded in an appropriate case with the prior authority of the Legal Aid Board, which is obtained by applying on a prescribed form to the area office. In an appropriate case where full legal aid is not available (let us say a difficult matter involving advice about how a client should represent himself before an Immigration Adjudicator) substantial extensions may be obtained, perhaps up to several hundred pounds where the area office considers that the case merits it. However, if full legal aid is available (i.e. for ordinary proceedings in the County Court or High Court), it is unusual to have an extension granted because the area director is likely to insist that the client applies for full legal aid to cover further steps in the proceedings so that, as we shall see below, a full assessment of the merits of the client's case as well as of financial eligibility can be made.

The two hours' worth of fees can cover the solicitor's time as previously described, whether engaged in advice, correspondence or drafting. It can also cover disbursements. Thus, for example, if the matter is particularly complex the solicitor may obtain counsel's advice on behalf of the client. Equally the fees may be used to finance other kinds of disbursements, e.g. to write off to obtain a police report of an accident if this can be obtained within the maximum figure.

2.2.3.4 Claiming under the Green Form scheme

When the solicitor has completed his work under a Green Form and wishes to claim his costs, he simply fills in the back of the form indicating the time expended on the matter together with details of any other specific elements, e.g. the number of letters written or telephone calls made and any disbursements incurred, and makes a claim by sending this form into the area office of the Legal Aid Board. In fact the practice is to wait until a solicitor has a number of such forms to send in and to send them in batches of a dozen or so at a time. Payment will then be made by the Legal Aid Board.

So far as we are concerned the most important use of the Green Form will be for the preliminaries of litigation, and particularly for completing an application form for full legal aid. As will be seen, this involves considerably more than a mere statement of means.

2.2.4 LEGAL AID

The effect of legal aid is simply that a solicitor who acts for a legally aided person, who is known as 'an assisted person', is guaranteed that he will be paid, whatever the outcome of the case. The legal aid scheme applies in the High Court, county court, Court of Appeal and House of Lords (and some tribunals, though not, unfortunately, the industrial tribunal). It covers all forms of civil proceedings except defamation cases.

2.2.4.1 Procedure for applying for legal aid

Application is made on the appropriate form, which is usually completed by the solicitor whom it is proposed to instruct, often using the time available under the Green Form scheme (see **2.2.3.3**). The form is considerably more detailed than the Green Form scheme and requires a statement of means and a statement of the client's case. Legal aid is granted on two tests, namely financial eligibility and that the applicant can show that he has reasonable grounds for taking, or defending or being a party to proceedings. Unlike the case of the Green Form, therefore, a client must in general show that he has some prospect of winning the case. Legal aid is thus not generally available if a defendant admits liability but needs to make representations to the court about time to pay.

Despite this requirement – that it is usually essential for a client to show that he will win the case, at least on a balance of probabilities – it is by no means unusual for both parties in a case to receive legal aid. This is because each party is in essence obliged to submit only his own version of the facts in his legal aid application (although all relevant correspondence must be sent with the form). Thus each party may produce a version of the facts which favours himself. For this reason it is important to support an application by sending any documents which assist in showing that the applicant has a good case (e.g. a police accident report).

2.2.4.2 Legal aid and other sources of finance

Legal aid is not generally available to those who are entitled to obtain representation from some other sources. Thus legal aid would not be available to an insured defendant in a personal injuries case who is entitled to legal representation under the terms of his policy. Similarly, if a party has the right to financial assistance from his trade union or by virtue of legal expenses insurance, this must be indicated on the legal aid application form and legal aid will then not normally be granted.

2.2.4.3 Assessment of financial eligibility

When the application form is received at the legal aid area office, the part relating to means is detached and dealt with by the Legal Aid Assessment Office. There they make a calculation of the applicant's disposable income and capital. This is a rather more sophisticated process of assessment than the computation of eligibility under the Green Form scheme, and involves consideration not only of gross and net income and dependants but also of other allowances, e.g. for mortgage, rent and council tax, etc. If the client is already receiving benefits there need be no interview because the DSS will already have a file on the client, but otherwise the Assessment Office may call the person for interview and ask him to bring with him documentary proof of his means.

Financial eligibility will then be determined. If a party does not qualify on financial grounds then it does not matter how good his case is. Legal aid will be refused, at least until part of his means has been exhausted in the preliminary stages of the case. Unlike the case of Green Form assistance, a party may qualify either without paying a contribution, or be required to make a contribution. A contribution may be called for in one lump sum or instalments from capital, or in instalments from income.

The applicant will be notified of the maximum contribution required. Thus a client who is offered legal aid with a maximum contribution of, say, £1,000 should be advised about the meaning of this. It by no means follows that he will lose that sum, or any sum, provided he wins the case. It may be that the costs recoverable from the losing party will cover the whole of his costs, in which case all his contribution will be returned to him. If, however, he loses his case, then it is likely that the whole of the contribution will be lost.

2.2.4.4 Assessment of the merits of the application

After the DSS have concluded that a person is financially eligible for legal aid they notify that finding to the legal aid area office who then consider the application on its legal merits. The office will decide on the apparent merits on the basis of the information supplied, and there is no oral hearing. Usually applications are decided in a fairly liberal way on the presumption that the version put forward by the applicant is the truth.

Apart from the actual *merits* as such (i.e. the probability of winning), a further matter to consider is whether it is *reasonable* for the applicant to have public money risked or expended on legal representation. For example, if the matter concerns something that is relatively trivial, even though based on a clear legal right, then although the applicant may be able to establish the legal merits in his favour, legal aid may still be refused.

2.2.4.5 The grant of legal aid

If legal aid is granted it is not granted in general terms. A legal aid certificate does not say, for example, 'X is granted legal aid to take proceedings to obtain damages for personal injury'. It will name the person against whom proceedings are to be taken. One consequence of this is that if at a later stage it becomes apparent that there should be some additional or different defendant, application will need to be made to the area office to amend the legal aid certificate.

The certificate must be filed with the court when proceedings are commenced. Notice of the issue of the certificate must be given to all other parties in the case because the grant of legal aid has certain important tactical and practical consequences. Civil legal aid is not retrospective and does not cover work done before the issue of the certificate, and therefore it should always be applied for as soon as possible. A legal aid application currently takes (with some local variation) some six weeks to be considered.

Green Form

To be used by solicitors with NO franchise contract which covers the category of work into which this green form falls

GF 1 Key Card

LEGAL AID BOARD LEGAL AID ACT 1988

Legal aid account no: ______

Ref: ______

(Copy from extension authority before sending claim)

➤ **If you have a franchise contract covering the category of work into which this claim falls, complete form GF7.**

➤ **If you give advice and assistance about making a will you must submit form GF4 with your claim.**

➤ **You should keep a copy of the entire green form.**

Client's details

*Please use block capitals *Delete the one which does not apply* Male/Female*

Surname: ______ First names: ______

Address: ______

______ Postcode: ______

National Insurance No: [| | | |] Date of Birth: ______

Capital details

(give these details even if the client gets income support, income-based Jobseeker's Allowance, family credit or disability working allowance) A

How many dependants (partner, children or other relatives of his/her household) does the client have? ______

Give the total savings and other capital which the client has (and if relevant his or her partner)

Client: £ ______

Spouse (or person living as if a spouse of the client): £ ______

Total: £ ______

Income details

B

Does the client get Income Support, any income-based Jobseeker's Allowance, Family Credit or Disability Working Allowance?

☐ Yes: ignore the rest of this section ☐ No: give the total gross weekly income of

The client: £ ______

The client's spouse (or person living as if a spouse of the client): £ ______

Total: £ ______

Calculate the total allowable deductions: Income tax: £ ______ C

National Insurance contributions: £ ______ D

Spouse (or person living as if a spouse of the client): £ ______ E

Attendance allowance, disability living allowance, constant attendance allowance and any payment made out of the Social Fund: £ ______ F

Dependent children and other dependants:

Age	*Number*	
Under 11	______	£ ______
11 to 15	______	£ ______
16 to 17	______	£ ______
18 and over	______	£ ______

G

Less total deductions: £ ______

Total weekly disposable income: £ ______

Client's declaration

I confirm that:

- I am over the compulsory school-leaving age (or, if not, the solicitor is advising me under Regulation 14(2A) Legal Advice & Assistance Regulations 1989);
- I have/have not *(delete whichever one is not correct)* previously received help from a solicitor on this matter under the green form; and
- I understand that I might have to pay my solicitor's costs out of any property or money which is recovered or preserved for me.

As far as I am aware, the information on this page is correct. I understand that if I give false information I could be prosecuted.

Signed: ______ **Date:** ____/____/____

97/04/08

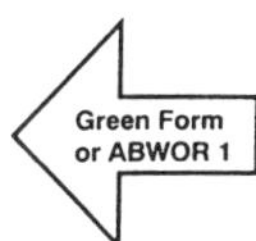

ENGLAND and WALES

Please see over for further explanatory notes.

GREEN FORM AND ABWOR KEY CARD (No. 29)

Effective from 7th April 1997

If you advise a client who returns to you for further advice on the same matter under a Green Form within 6 months of you submitting your claim for payment, fill in the client's details and the date of your claim only then strike through the rest of the front page. Set out your further claim on the back of the Green Form.

CAPITAL means the amount or value of every resource of a capital nature.

In computing Disposable Capital disregard

(i) the first £100,000 equity in the main or only dwelling in which the client resides, (see note 3(c)(i) overleaf) and

(ii) the value of the household furniture and effects, personal clothing and tools or implements of the client's trade and

(iii) the subject matter of the advice and assistance.

Maximum Disposable Capital for Financial Eligibility (dependant=partner, child or dependant relative)

Advice and Assistance*	ABWOR**
£1000-client with no dependants	£3000-client with no dependants
£1335-client with 1 dependant	£3335-client with 1 dependant
£1535-client with 2 dependants	£3535-client with 2 dependants

Add £100 for each additional dependant

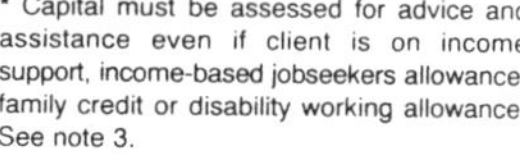
* Capital must be assessed for advice and assistance even if client is on income support, income-based jobseekers allowance, family credit or disability working allowance. See note 3.

** All capital is disregarded if client is on income support or income-based jobseekers allowance. See note 3.

INCOME means the total income from all sources which the client received or became entitled to during or in respect of the seven days up to and including the date of the application for advice and assistance.

The capital and weekly income of both partners must be taken into account unless:
(a) they have a contrary interest
(b) they live apart
(c) it is inequitable or impractical to aggregate their means

Some types of income are ignored. See note 3.

In computing Disposable Income deduct:-

(i) Income Tax

D

(ii) Contributions paid under the Social Security Acts 1975-88

These deductions also apply to the partner's income if there is aggregation.

E

(iii) £28 in respect of the client's partner (if living together) whether or not their means are aggregated. Where they are separated or divorced, the allowance will be the actual maintenance paid by the client in respect of the previous 7 days.

F

(iv) The following payments made under the Social Security Contributions and Benefits Act 1992:

- i) disability living allowance;
- ii) attendance allowance paid under section 64 or Schedule 8 paragraphs 4 or 7(2);
- iii) constant attendance allowance paid under section 104 and 105 as an increase to a disablement pension; or
- iv) any payment made out of the social fund.

v) £16.90 for each child under 11
For 11 year olds £24.75 if the child became 11 before 7th April 1997, otherwise £16.90. See opposite if applying after 1st September 1997.
£24.75 for each child aged 12-15
For 16 year olds £29.60 if the child became 16 before 7th April 1997, otherwise £24.75. See opposite if applying after 1st September 1997.
£29.60 for each child aged 17
For 18 year olds £38.90 only if the child became 18 before 7th April 1997, otherwise £29.60.
£38.90 for each dependant aged over 18 (but see opposite).

The rules for 11 and 16 year olds will change if applying on or after 1st September 1997. From that date for 11 year olds the allowance will be £24.75 only if child became 11 before 1st September 1997, otherwise it will be £16.90. Similarly for 16 year olds the allowance will be £29.60 only if child became 16 before 1st September 1997, otherwise it will be £24.75. These allowances apply to dependant children and relatives of the household of the ages specified. There is no allowance in relation to a foster child. At the time of printing the regulations providing for an allowance for dependants over 18 have not yet been finalised. Solicitors should check the Handbook or with the area office to confirm when the allowance will be payable.

vi) Back to work bonus under section 26 of the Jobseekers Act 1995.

vii) Payments under the Earnings Top up Scheme 1996.

viii) Payment under the Community Care Direct Payment Scheme.

Where the child or dependant relative is not a member of the household the allowance will be the actual maintenance paid by the client in respect of the previous 7 days.

Maximum Weekly Disposable Income for Financial Eligibility.
Advice and Assistance

Green Form advice and assistance is only available to people who get income support, income-based jobseekers allowance, family credit, disability working allowance or have not more than £77 a week disposable income (and who come within the maximum capital limit). They will pay no contribution.

ABWOR

Lower limit £69 a week (no contribution to pay)

Upper limit £166 a week (people with disposable income between the lower and upper limits will be liable to pay a **weekly** contribution (collected by the solicitor) from the date of the ABWOR approval to its withdrawal or the end of the proceedings.

The amount of weekly contribution is calculated as 1/3 of the weekly disposable income over £69.

Note

The Green Form must be signed by or on behalf of the client at the initial interview as soon as his/her eligibility has been determined except in the case of an authorised postal application or where a franchisee is exercising his or her powers.

2.2.4.6 Appeal against refusal to grant legal aid

If legal aid is refused on the ground of means then there is no appeal. If, however, it is refused on the question of merits, or as to whether it is reasonable to expend public money, then an appeal may be made to the Area Committee who will reconsider the matter. It is possible to have oral representation before the Area Committee but the Green Form scheme will not cover this, and therefore the client would have to pay a solicitor to represent him.

2.2.4.7 Conditional and unconditional certificates: scope

It ought to be remarked that once the legal aid certificate is granted it may be granted for the whole proceedings, i.e. it may be *unconditional*. Alternatively it may be *conditional*. A conditional certificate will authorise the solicitor to act for the client only up to a certain stage in the proceedings, after which the solicitor must report back to the area office to confirm that the solicitor is still optimistic about the prospect of success in the case.

Example Suppose that there is a dispute where it is reasonably apparent that the outcome can be more successfully predicted after the stage of discovery of documents (i.e. where each side is entitled to see the documents relevant to the case held by the other side). In such a case it may well be that the legal aid certificate when issued will be limited 'to all matters up to and including the discovery of documents'. After this stage, therefore, the solicitor will be obliged to report back to the Legal Aid Office to confirm that, in the light of the documents of which discovery has been obtained, he still regards the case as one which ought to be won. Other examples of limitations would be a limitation that legal aid is granted only to obtain counsel's opinion as to the likely outcome of the case, or up to the close of pleadings.

A solicitor must act within the scope of the legal aid certificate when granted. This does not mean, however, that he is limited merely to carrying out the bare procedure necessary to get the client's action to trial. In the course of acting for the client he may take all proper tactical steps. Legal aid may, for example, thus cover correspondence and negotiations between the parties, attempts to trace witnesses, the interviewing of witnesses and so on. It does not only cover the actual drafting of procedural documents or hearings before the court. Thus when one receives a legal aid certificate there is no obligation to issue proceedings straight away, or at all, and the certificate will cover work done on collecting evidence, preparation for and the conduct of negotiations which may lead to settlement without there being any proceedings.

Even if legal aid is unconditional it does not imply that the solicitor has *carte blanche* to spend any amount of money. The prior authority of the area office must be obtained for various steps, for instance instructing a Queen's Counsel in a case. It is advisable anyway to seek prior authority for taking any unusual steps, or steps which involve the incurring of large expenditure, e.g. obtaining a report from a particularly expensive expert witness. In such cases it is also vital to obtain the client's approval to the proposed step after giving a clear explanation of what is involved. This is because, as we shall see in **2.3.1**, even a winning client will be called upon to pay a part of his own costs and to reimburse the legal aid fund for such costs. Accordingly, even a legally aided client may well have an interest in the cost of the conduct of the case.

2.2.4.8 Amendment, revocation and discharge of legal aid certificates

(a) *Amendment*

A legal aid certificate can be *amended* in the course of proceedings. Application to amend is made by a letter to the area office, setting out the reason why amendment is required and any supporting documentation (e.g. counsel's advice about the matter). A typical amendment would be to add a second defendant where the need to do so emerged only after obtaining the first legal aid certificate during the course of proceedings. The amended certificate when received should be filed at court and notice of the nature of the amendment given to all other parties.

Clients are financially re-assessed from time to time as the limits for legal aid change, or indeed as their own income and outgoings change. Amendments may also, therefore, relate to the client's contribution. In this case, however, although the amended legal aid certificate must be filed with the court, no notice of the nature of the amendment need be given to the other parties. The other parties are not in any event made aware of the size of the client's contribution or whether he has to pay a contribution at all.

(b) *Revocation*

A certificate may be *revoked*. This implies that a client has in some way misled the legal aid authorities into granting legal aid. For example, if a client was subsequently discovered to have told a highly material lie about the merits of the case, or to have lied about his means. Where a certificate is revoked the effect is as if there had never been a grant of legal aid. The legally aided client's solicitor will be entitled to be paid by the legal aid fund for all work done up until the date of revocation, but the fact that the client is now deemed never to have had legal aid may be important in relation to his opponent's costs, as we shall see at **2.3.3.1**.

(c) *Discharge*

The *discharge* of a certificate may occur on the conclusion of all steps in the proceedings (which may include steps for enforcement of judgments in addition to the steps taken to obtain judgment). Certificates may also be discharged earlier. For example, a client whose means have risen above the legal aid limit may have his certificate discharged, as may a client who requires proceedings to be conducted in an unreasonable manner.

The effect is that the client has the protection of legal aid for tactical purposes (see below) whilst the certificate lasts – and of course his solicitor is entitled to be paid for the work done so far – but after discharge the client is no longer legally aided. This does not itself bring about the end of the case because the client is perfectly entitled to continue as a litigant in person, or indeed to pay another solicitor (or the same solicitor if the solicitor is willing to continue to act). This might be the case, for example, where the certificate was discharged on the ground of the client's means having risen above the legal aid limit due to a promotion or a legacy.

2.2.4.9 Professional conduct: the effect of legal aid on the solicitor-client relationship

In principle a legally aided client is in the same position as any other client on every matter except costs. Thus a solicitor owes the same duty to use his full expertise for such a client; owes the same duty of confidentiality to the client; has the same fiduciary duty in respect of any funds which come into his hands on the client's behalf, and so on. The solicitor is fully bound by the rules of professional practice, but with one important difference. This is due to the fact that the solicitor owes a duty to the legal aid fund in addition to those which he owes to the client, and this may sometimes lead to the solicitor being required to breach the basic principle of confidentiality about a client's affairs and report certain matters to the Legal Aid Board. This dual duty can be the source of some awkwardness in the relationship.

A common situation which arises is where a solicitor, perhaps well into the progress of the case, comes to the view that the client is now likely to lose that case, either because of new evidence which has arisen or perhaps because the client is now asking him to conduct the proceedings in an unreasonable way. Two examples are as follows:

Example 1 Suppose that as the litigation progresses and more evidence comes into the solicitor's hands, it becomes apparent that the client now has, say, only a 20 per cent chance of success in the action. The solicitor advises the client of this. However, the client, who has obtained legal aid with a nil contribution, stands to win a considerable amount of money if he is successful in the litigation. He may feel that since the litigation is costing him nothing, litigation with a 20 per cent chance of success is perfectly reasonable. He may instruct the solicitor to press on. At this stage the solicitor would have a duty to notify the Legal Aid Board of what had arisen. Whilst a client who stands to lose nothing and has a one in five chance of winning may feel it worth going on, the solicitor is obliged to advise the client as if he were 'a privately paying client of moderate means'. Accordingly, when the reasonable advice to discontinue the action in view of the slight chance of success is neglected, the matter should be reported to the Legal Aid Board who will in such a case inevitably discharge the legal aid certificate.

Example 2 Suppose in county court litigation for damages for personal injuries, counsel has advised that there is a serious risk that the plaintiff will lose outright and that the case on full liability is worth about £2,000 to £2,500. The defendants make an offer of £2,000 plus costs. The solicitor is of the very clear opinion that this must be accepted in view of the risk of losing outright, and in view of the fact that it is anyway within the bracket which counsel has advised. The client, however, refuses to accept the advice. If the client were privately paying then the solicitor would naturally continue and follow the client's instructions, the risk of the litigation being up to the client. In our example, however, the risks are partly the legal aid fund's since, if the client loses outright, the legal aid fund will have a substantial deficit for the solicitor's costs. Accordingly, the solicitor would be obliged, if he felt the client was unreasonable, to report the matter to the Legal Aid Board. This would again inevitably lead to the discharge of the legal aid certificate if the client maintained his refusal of the reasonable offer.

This aspect of acting for legally aided clients is an extremely difficult one in practice. Although in the examples previously given matters are fairly clear-cut, all solicitors could relate more borderline examples. For example, difficult clients who insist on interviews every week (or more frequently) despite the fact that the case has not progressed in the interim and there is really nothing to discuss, and thus that the time is merely wasted, possibly at the legal aid fund's eventual expense; and, indeed, cases where the solicitor becomes aware that the client has misled the legal aid authorities in relation to his means.

In such cases, reporting of suspicious circumstances or the client's unreasonable behaviour is a duty which the solicitor owes to the legal aid fund, and it will represent a permissible exception to the usual rule of confidentiality in relation to a client's affairs.

2.3 The Costs Consequences to the Client of Legal Aid

Where a client is legally aided the solicitor may not obtain money direct from that client in relation to that matter. (A solicitor may, of course, have an ordinary fee-paying arrangement with the same client in regard to some other matter, e.g. a client who wishes to move house whilst at the same time receiving legal aid for litigation.) Consequently, it is wrong for a solicitor to deliver a bill to a client in respect of a matter for which the client has legal aid. The solicitor will have his bill of costs assessed by the court by a procedure known as *taxation*, which we shall consider in due course at **22.3**. The solicitor will then be paid out of the legal aid fund the full amount of his costs. In addition, there will usually be an order that the loser will pay the winner's costs.

2.3.1 THE SUCCESSFUL LEGALLY AIDED PLAINTIFF

Let us assume that the litigation has been won for a legally aided plaintiff and the defendant is ordered to pay those costs. When those costs are recovered there will be a refund of a large proportion, and possibly all, of the costs incurred. The solicitor is then required to pass on those costs recovered from the losing party to reimburse the legal aid fund. If this happens so that the legal aid fund is wholly reimbursed for the costs and has no net outlay, then any contribution which the assisted person has had to make for the grant of legal aid will be refunded to him direct by the Legal Aid Board.

Suppose, however, the defendant is not ordered to pay the costs in full, or perhaps is ordered to pay the costs in full but becomes insolvent and is unable to pay them, so that the legal aid fund is put to some loss. In that situation the legal aid fund, under *s. 16* of the *Legal Aid Act 1988*, has a *statutory charge* over any money or property which the plaintiff has *recovered or preserved* in the litigation. Let us take two examples to demonstrate the operation of this charge:

> **Example 1** An assisted person who is a plaintiff in a debt case obtains judgment for £5,000. The legal aid fund has to pay his solicitors a sum of £1,000 for costs. The defendant is not ordered to pay all the costs but (because of various matters we shall consider subsequently) only to pay approximately two-thirds of them – say £650 which he pays. In this case the Legal Aid Board has suffered a net outlay of £350. It therefore has a charge on the £5,000 recovered and the plaintiff's solicitors must retain this sum until such time as all questions of costs are dealt with, or at least such proportion of the sum as will cover any question of costs. Accordingly, the plaintiff suffers a deduction from the damages he has received of £350, the amount of the difference between what the defendant has paid and what the Legal Aid Board has had to pay out to the plaintiff's solicitors.

> **Example 2** Suppose a legally aided plaintiff succeeds in an action for possession of land. Here no money for damages changes hands. In this situation (using the same figures) the Legal Aid Board's charge for the balance of the costs not recovered from the losing party attaches to the land itself as an equitable mortgage and will be registered as such. Accordingly, the successful party will have to redeem the charge as and when he is able, or when the land is sold, by payment of the £350.

It should be noted that the Legal Aid Board has no discretion to waive the charge even though its operation causes hardship. The examples given are relatively straightforward. As we shall see, however, when we come to consider one particular procedural tactic known as 'payment into court' (**16.1**), it may well be possible for a plaintiff to recover a substantial sum of money but not in the end to receive an order for costs against a defendant in respect of the whole case. Reference to the section on payment into court ought to be made for a full explanation of the costs consequences. It might well be, therefore, that a plaintiff recovers, say, £10,000 but is first ordered to pay part of his opponent's costs and, secondly, has to bear his own costs for a substantial part of the proceedings. The net effect of all this may well be that in such a case the Legal Aid Board's charge together with the opponent's order for costs eat up much of the amount in question. The interrelation of costs orders on payment into court and the operation of the Legal Aid Board's charge ought carefully to be explained to the client on any occasion where a payment into court is made. A more comprehensive example will be given later in the text at **16.1.12**.

2.3.2 THE SUCCESSFUL LEGALLY AIDED DEFENDANT

If a defendant is simply defending a claim for damages and wins, then at the end of the trial he will not, of course, be awarded any money in his own right. He will, however, be awarded costs from the plaintiff. His solicitor's costs will then be taxed by the court, and that amount will be paid by the legal aid fund. The amount claimed from the plaintiff will also be taxed, and this amount will often be a full indemnity for the costs which the defendant's solicitor has received from the legal aid fund. If the losing plaintiff is then able to pay the amount of costs awarded against him in full, the defendant's solicitor will reimburse the legal aid fund with the amount received. The Legal Aid Board will thus have suffered no net outlay on the case, and if the client has paid any contribution in respect of legal aid, it will be returned to him in full. If there is some shortfall between the amount which the Legal Aid Board has had to pay his solicitor and the amount recovered from the plaintiff, this will be deducted from the contribution, if any. If there is no contribution, or if the shortfall is greater than the contribution, then in a damages claim there is nothing on which the statutory charge can 'bite' and thus it will be of no effect.

On the other hand, if the defendant was defending litigation to do with title to land, then in the same circumstances the land in question would be 'property preserved' by the litigation. Accordingly, if there was a shortfall in such a case between the winning defendant's costs paid to his solicitor by the Legal Aid Board and those recovered from the losing plaintiff, the Legal Aid Board would have a charge on the land in question for the amount of the shortfall.

2.3.3 THE COSTS OF OPPONENTS OF LEGALLY AIDED PARTIES

2.3.3.1 *Legal Aid Act 1988, s. 17*

When a legally aided party is unsuccessful, it will not affect the amount which his own solicitor receives as remuneration. His solicitor will be paid by the Legal Aid Board on the basis previously described.

In principle, an unsuccessful legally aided party *could* be ordered to pay his opponent's costs. However, one must have regard in such a case to *s. 17* of the *Legal Aid Act 1988*. This section provides that where an assisted person is granted legal aid and loses, then:

> *(1) . . . an order for costs made against him with respect to any proceedings shall not exceed the amount (if any) which is a reasonable one for him to pay in regard to all the circumstances, including the financial resources of all the parties and their conduct in connection with the dispute.*

As is obvious, this is a very potent tactical advantage for an impecunious legally aided party. It means that in certain kinds of litigation it may well be uneconomic for his opponent even to contest the case, because his opponent will be unlikely to recover his legal costs even if he wins and the costs may be more than the amount claimed. For example, in county court litigation in respect of some relatively minor personal injury – say, a broken finger and two weeks' loss of earnings – a claim worth about £1,000 in value. Where the plaintiff is legally aided the effect of *s. 17* will be such that it is likely to cost the defendants more to defend the case, even successfully, than to make a reasonable offer early on to settle the claim.

Where under *s. 17* the court assess what amount it is reasonable for a legally aided party to pay, very often the court decides that it is not reasonable to require him to pay anything at all. Sometimes quite artificially (for there is no justification for this whatsoever under *s. 17*) the court limits his liability to his opponent to a sum equal to the amount that he has been ordered to pay by way of contribution to the legal aid fund for his own costs. Alternatively, the court often specifies a low, round sum figure, e.g. £100, or simply orders costs against the legally aided person but directs that they shall not be enforced without the leave of the court.

This form of order means that the winner will have to apply to the court for leave to enforce his costs order and face all the arguments under *s. 17* at the time he seeks to do it. Nonetheless, this form of order may occasionally have some advantages. If, for example, in, say, three years' time the legally aided person has obtained a good job and some assets, it may be worth advising a client who has obtained an award of costs in this form that some money could be risked on investigating the legally aided person's means in the medium future with a view to reapplying to the court for leave to enforce the award. The court is, of course, to have regard to the means of *all the parties*, and therefore the court may occasionally be persuaded to make a more generous order against a legally aided person if his opponent is also of modest means but just outside the legal aid eligibility limits.

Lastly, it should be noted that the court is given a mandate to examine the *conduct* of the parties under *s. 17*. If it therefore finds that the plaintiff has wholly fabricated his claim, and perhaps supported it by perjured evidence, then again the court may make a more drastic order than would normally be the case.

2.3.3.2 *Legal Aid Act 1988, s. 18*

Whilst highly advantageous tactically to the legally aided person, the effect of *s. 17* on his opponent is clearly capable of causing great hardship. A person of modest means who is not entitled to legal aid might well be put to great legal expense in defending proceedings brought by a legally aided plaintiff, have those proceedings determined entirely in his own favour, and then have to bear his own costs. There is therefore a provision which mitigates the full effect of *s. 17*. This is contained in *s. 18* of the *Legal Aid Act 1988*, and it provides that where proceedings are brought by a legally aided party against a person who does not have legal aid, the court can order payment of the defendant's costs out of the legal aid fund directly. It is important to note, however, that there is a number of conditions to be satisfied before this order can be made, namely:

(a) The plaintiff must have been legally aided and unsuccesful in the proceedings.

(b) The defendant must have been successful and not himself have been in receipt of legal aid.

(c) The court must first consider the personal liability of the legally aided party to pay any costs under *s. 17* of the Act.

(d) The court must be satisfied that it is *just and equitable* to make the order under *s. 18* in favour of the defendant.

(e) The court must (in proceedings at first instance) be satisfied that the defendant will suffer *severe financial hardship* unless the order is made.

It is important to note that *all* these conditions apply. The personal liability of the legally aided losing party must have been *considered* by the court, though it is irrelevant whether any order was or was not made. The words 'just and equitable' tend to mean that the successful defendant should have behaved reasonably throughout the case, including making any proper admissions, and should have won on the merits rather than on a technicality, such as a *Limitation Act* defence. The term 'severe financial hardship' it has been said (*Stewart* v *Stewart* [1974] 1 WLR 877), should be given a liberal interpretation so as to exclude only large companies, insured persons and the really wealthy. Even an apparently prosperous professional man may not be outside the words of the section given that his commitments and outgoings may well be commensurate with his income. The wealth of an applicant's spouse should only be taken into account to a limited extent (see *Adams* v *Riley* [1988] QB 372).

Where a defendant has been successful against a legally aided plaintiff, an application under *s. 18* is usually made at the conclusion of the trial. However, at that stage there will be nobody present to represent the Legal Aid Board who are the guardians of the legal aid fund. There are two possible courses of procedure, therefore. First, the court may adjourn the application to give the Legal Aid Board an opportunity to make representations to it. Where this happens, naturally the costs will be considerably increased. Alternatively, the court may make a provisional order which will be suspended to give the Legal Aid Board an opportunity to make representations at a later stage if it objects. If the Board does not object, or is unsuccessful in its later objection, then the order takes effect and the successful defendant will be paid his costs from the legal aid fund.

It should be noted that this latter provision applies only in proceedings at first instance. In proceedings before an appellate court, the court need only be satisfied that it is just and equitable to make provision for the costs of the successful party (whether plaintiff or defendant at first instance) out of the legal aid fund. In the recent past this provision has been widely construed so that the costs of even substantial companies, building societies, and a police force have been ordered to be paid out of the legal aid fund (see, e.g., *R* v *Greenwich London Borough Council, ex parte Lovelace (No. 2)* [1992] QB 155).

2.3.4 OTHER RELEVANT MATTERS WHERE ONE PARTY IS LEGALLY AIDED

The problems of *ss. 17* and *18* mentioned above should not lead one to conclude that it is always pointless to seek costs against a legally aided opponent. There are two particular further points to make:

2.3.4.1 Where a legally aided party fails to beat a payment into court

This topic is discussed in further detail at **16.1.12**. It should be noted that if a plaintiff fails to beat a payment into court but is awarded some money, then there is no reason why the usual order for costs ought not to be made.

2.3.4.2 Interlocutory stages

The costs of interlocutory stages in legal aid cases are sometimes passed over and go by default. There is no reason why this should be so. If, for example, a legally aided party, plaintiff or defendant, declines properly to supply further and better particulars of a defective pleading and application has to be made to the court for those particulars, the successful unassisted party should apply for costs in the usual way, e.g. 'defendant's costs in any event'. *Section 17* strictly should not apply at that time and the court should make whatever order it would otherwise have been inclined to make. Thus the non-legally aided party who has been the victim of unreasonable conduct at an interlocutory stage will receive the benefit of the costs awarded to him even if he loses the eventual litigation, because those costs can be offset against the legally aided person's final bill of costs for the interlocutory stages. See *Lockley* v *National Blood Transfusion Service* [1992] 1 WLR 492.

2.4 Interlocutory Costs

For the procedure on taxation of costs at the end of the case see **Chapter 22**. Some preliminary reference to that chapter is worthwhile at this stage, however, because the question of costs must be kept in view throughout the whole of the litigation process. One thing which it is appropriate to deal with at this point is the subject of interlocutory costs, i.e. the costs which may be ordered at the various stages of a case between issue of proceedings and trial. At the end of each interlocutory hearing it is important to ensure that some order for costs is made. Examples of common orders are as follows:

2.4.1 'COSTS IN THE CAUSE'

This is the most common form of order. It means in effect that whoever wins the eventual trial will also recover from his opponent the costs of that particular interlocutory application, including not merely the attendance at court for the application itself, which may have taken only a few minutes, but also the necessary preparation and drafting of documents for it. This order is appropriate in purely routine interlocutory applications which have progressed the case procedurally or the merit of which is unclear until the eventual outcome is known.

2.4.2 'PLAINTIFF'S (OR DEFENDANT'S) COSTS IN ANY EVENT'

This order is different from costs in the cause. It means that regardless of who succeeds at the trial, the named person will nevertheless recover the costs of this application. It inevitably implies some criticism of the conduct of the other party. It might, for example, be appropriate where the other party has refused to give further and better particulars of his pleading even though it is manifestly obvious that such ought to be given (see **7.5.1**).

2.4.3 'PLAINTIFF'S (OR DEFENDANT'S) COSTS IN THE CAUSE'

This is the midway stage between the first and the second orders. It implies a more modest criticism of the conduct adopted by the party who has lost the interlocutory application. An order in this form means that the successful party will obtain his costs of this stage if he wins at trial. But if he loses at trial, then although he will not get his costs of this stage neither will the opponent who does win at trial, whose slowness or inappropriate conduct has led to the necessity for this interlocutory stage.

2.4.4 'COSTS THROWN AWAY'

An order for costs in this form covers costs which have been wasted in some way due to the default of a party. An example is where a default judgment has been obtained by the plaintiff after the defendant, by some oversight, fails to return his acknowledgment of service to the court in time. If the defendant can show some merit in defending the case, or some excuse for having returned his acknowledgment of service late, he may be able to get the judgment set aside and be able to go on to defend, but will inevitably be ordered to pay the costs thrown away, i.e. the cost of the plaintiff having gone to the trouble of obtaining judgment in default and also of attending on the summons to oppose the application to set it aside.

2.4.5 'COSTS OF THE DAY'

This order involves costs which have been wasted by the necessity for an adjournment. They will be ordered to be paid by the party who has been responsible for the necessity for the adjournment.

2.4.6 'COSTS RESERVED'

In essence this means the same as costs in the cause (see **2.4.1**), so that the winner of the eventual trial will receive the costs of the interlocutory stage. The difference here is that the matter may be re-opened before the trial judge if the circumstances require it. Accordingly, if the eventual outcome of the trial makes the court take a quite different view of the appropriateness of an earlier procedural stage, the decision on the costs of that stage can be reviewed. If the matter is not re-opened at trial, or no different or further order is made, then the term mean precisely the same as costs in the cause.

2.5 Limits on Payments from the Legal Aid Fund

When conducting litigation for a client with the benefit of legal aid one would, naturally, hope to win the action. On winning his or her case a legally aided client would in effect be in no different a position from a person without legal aid because the court will usually order that the losing opponent must pay costs to be assessed by the process of taxation described in **Chapter 22**. As much as possible in the way of costs would be obtained from the opponent and any shortfall between the amount and the total fees which the legally aided person's solicitor was entitled to claim would be met by the Legal Aid Board. The Board would then recover its own outlay by a charge on the property recovered or preserved as explained in **2.3.1**.

However, this is subject to limits imposed by the *Legal Aid in Civil Proceedings (Remuneration) Regulations 1994* (SI 1994/228) which apply to any legal aid certificate granted after 25

February 1994. These regulations fix certain maximum hourly rates of charging, and specific figures for other items, where costs are to be paid only out of the legal aid fund (i.e., where they cannot be claimed from any other party). The schedule showing the rates of charging is set out in **Table 2.1**. It will be noted at item 3 in the schedule that a solicitor whose office is situated within legal aid area 1 (i.e., London) may claim a slightly higher rate for preparatory work.

Table 2.1 Standard rates of payment from the legal aid fund

	High Court	*County Court*
1. Routine letters out	£7.40 per item	£6.50 per item
2. Routine telephone calls	£4.10 per item	£3.60 per item
3. All other preparation work including any work which was reasonably done arising out of or incidental to the proceedings, interviews with client, witnesses, and other parties; obtaining evidence; preparation and consideration of, and dealing with, documents, negotiations and notices; dealing with letters written and received and telephone calls which are not routine.	£74.00 per hour (78.50 per hour where solicitor's office situated within legal aid area 1)	£65.00 per hour £69.00 per hour
4. Attending counsel in conference or at the trial or hearing of any summons or application at court, or other appointment.	£36.40 per hour	£32.00 per hour
5. Attending without counsel at the trial or hearing of any cause or the hearing of any summons or other application at court, or other appointment.	£74.00 per hour	£65.00 per hour
6. Travelling and waiting in connection with the above matters.	£32.70 per hour	£28.75 per hour

These are in essence the fixed rates, then, where costs are claimable only from the legal aid fund. They are not generous (for example £74 per hour for most High Court work). They may, however, be enhanced by an uplift taking into account the following matters:

(a) that the work was done with exceptional competence, skill or expertise;

(b) that the work was done with exceptional dispatch; or

(c) that the case involved exceptional circumstances or complexity.

Where any of those apply the taxing officer may allow the fees to be enhanced having regard to:

(a) the degree of responsibility accepted by the solicitor;

(b) the care, speed and economy with which the case was prepared;

(c) the novelty, weight and complexity of the case.

In county court cases the enhancement to the prescribed rate may be anything up to 100 per cent of the rate given; in High Court cases the enhancement may be anything up to 200 per cent of that rate.

We shall return to this topic and its interrelationship with costs obtainable from the opposite party in **22.3.2.1**.

THREE

MANAGING A CIVIL LITIGATION PRACTICE

To acquire mastery of civil procedure requires constant practice and constant effort in keeping up to date with the ceaselessly changing Rules of the Supreme Court, Practice Directions, Practice Notes, and changing practice of local courts. Civil litigation in particular generates an enormous amount of case law. *The Times* remains a particularly useful source for this, many cases on procedure only being reported there. Membership of the Association of Personal Injury Lawyers is essential if one is engaged in plaintiffs' personal injury litigation. Attendance at continuing education courses on civil litigation, even above the strict requirements of the Law Society, is also useful in order to ensure one is completely up to date. We discuss below some suggestions for acquiring and developing good practical working techniques in civil litigation matters; handling the paperwork; managing and accounting for time spent; and client care. We end with some practical suggestions for those starting out their careers in civil litigation practice.

3.1 Files

The file is the record of a client matter, and without the proper file it would be impossible to deal with most cases. Merely keeping a cardboard file with the papers within it is not by itself sufficient, however. For the efficient conduct of the action to which each file relates, the file must be logically arranged and properly maintained. A cardboard folder with an ill-assorted jumble of papers is unlikely to be a comprehensive record; letters may be filed out of sequence or lost and important documents such as pleadings, medical reports or original receipts may go astray amongst the copy correspondence. A good file keeps together relevant records so that once obtained and placed in the file, the same information does not have to be sought again elsewhere and can easily be found.

Each file should contain an information sheet at the beginning, containing, first, the essential details required by the office as a central record. This is sometimes obtained by the use of standard client questionnaires comprising the client's personal details; address; telephone number, method of contact and the like. The second part should provide for the insertion of additional useful information, such as the limitation period dates; time limits for service; hearing dates; availability of witnesses, etc. A correspondence file should be distinct from items of evidence and draft documents. In a civil case a further division of the file may be necessary into those documents which must be and those which need not be disclosed to your opponent. If the file becomes too bulky it should be divided into separate folders, preferably in such a way that when you are dealing with routine correspondence and telephone calls the file needed contains the current correspondence file only, with the addition of current draft documents. The use of ring binder files or box files with coloured dividers is often an essential aid to proper organisation. Proper management of the file will prevent the papers from becoming dog-eared and being mislaid, as well as being more convenient for instant access.

The importance of the diary and an effective reminder system is discussed in **3.2** below but any such system should be complemented by regular and systematic review of all the current files. It is essential that accurate records are kept of everything that happens in the file. This must include the date of and time spent on every attendance and the content of that attendance; every telephone call, together with an indication of what it was about; all the time spent considering the case, both before and after seeing the client (indicating briefly the nature of the discussion and any required follow-up action). Most of us have imperfect memories, and thus each item of work should be recorded separately as it is completed. The note should say exactly how long each item took and, if some special factor made it take longer than expected, why that was. This kind of note serves several purposes. Apart from being a useful reminder of just what was dealt with at the relevant stage, it may be of vital assistance in substantiating costs claimed from opponents or for justifying a bill to your own client. In addition, and all litigation lawyers have to face this, there will be cases that are lost. When you have a combination of a lost case and client with a difficult personality, it is the experience of every litigation lawyer sooner or later to face allegations that he conducted a case incompetently. The lawyer may therefore need to justify to the client, or to professional negligence insurers, just what he did when, and how, to defend such an allegation.

Information should therefore not be kept only in someone's head, however reliable their memory; files should be interchangeable and information kept in a uniform way within an office so that any person in the firm taking over the conduct of the case for any reason is able to tell from the file exactly what has happened to date. It must be borne in mind in litigation matters that problems may arise unexpectedly, and even someone who thoroughly briefs other members of the firm before going on his annual holiday may not have covered every conceivable contingency.

Keeping good memoranda on the file is also an aid to billing and provides the foundation of the claim to costs, as indicated earlier. Even if full time sheets are maintained, it is still necessary for memoranda to appear on the file as well. Indeed, by virtue of *Practice Direction (Taxation: Practice)* [1993] 1 WLR 12, there is a requirement that attendance notes filed in support of a bill on taxation must explain what was done as well as indicate the time taken.

3.2 Use of a Diary

The necessity for an office diary is obvious to ensure attendance at the right place at the right time and to avoid the requirement to be in two places at once. A diary should be more than a mere list of appointments, however. It can be both an essential safeguard and a weapon. It serves as a safeguard when used to note important time limits, not merely the Limitation Act date for the issue of proceedings but also other key dates, e.g. for service of pleadings. Missing time limits where time is of the essence is a frequent source of negligence actions against solicitors. In the conduct of civil litigation it can also be used to put pressure on an opponent, e.g. by noting forward each time limit which applies and then writing immediately or issuing the appropriate interlocutory application as soon as the opponent is in default. This is of vital assistance in negotiation tactics in the way explained later (**4.5.3**). This tactic will concentrate the mind of the defendant's solicitor considering a settlement, and ensure that this particular file remains constantly on the desk of your opponent. It will also reassure the client that something tangible is being done to move matters forward at every opportunity rather than simply drifting along without any sense of urgency. It must be remembered in litigation matters too, that the diary can prompt practical and tactical steps as well as steps involving the opponent. It may now take four or five months to obtain an appointment for an injured plaintiff to be seen by your chosen medico-legal specialist, and thus if the evidence needs to be constantly updated the need to book those appointments needs to be noted in the diary many months ahead.

Many solicitors use wall charts and information technology to supplement diaries, but whichever method is used it is essential that your secretary is briefed on the need to act as a further long stop in entering reminders and key dates.

3.3 Time Management

A further and important use of the diary is for managing a work load. Work on each matter should be planned and prioritised, with time allocated to it in the diary. It is always tempting to put off something which you find difficult or boring or time-consuming in favour of other, less important work. Most solicitors who have at some stage lapsed into bad practices are very aware of the temptation to deal with quick, satisfying matters that arrive on their desks, whilst worrying or difficult tasks are postponed, initially from day to day but eventually from week to week. One example which many civil litigators dislike is the task of computing special damages and the preparation of schedules in the appropriate form. The temptation to put this off is exacerbated if you know that your own files are in a mess and that finding and collating the necessary receipts, letters from employers and the like will in itself take some time. Most litigation lawyers would say, however, that however much they dislike this task, when they do eventually buckle down to it it always proves less difficult than feared. It should also be remembered that in cases of considerable complexity it is now increasingly common to have schedules of special damages and the like drafted either by forensic accountants or even as part of the tasks of counsel in preparing for trial.

When contributing to discussions about your own work load, whether as a new employee talking with the supervising partner, or eventually as a partner delegating work to others, it is always vital to have a general idea of how much of your working day is likely to be spent outside the office, to the obvious detriment of your ability to cope with a great deal of paper work. If you like to do your own advocacy in chambers, or possibly even at trial, then you will need backup staff to help cope with the more mundane aspects of civil litigation practice such as taking statements, drafting lists of documents and the like. Even if you do not go to court a great deal but have a practice which involves a lot of visiting, e.g., the site of factory accidents, or if you are a lawyer engaged in construction disputes and a great deal of your time is spent visiting buildings with expert witnesses, much the same applies. Civil litigation lawyers more than most others are thus often to be found organised into 'teams' or 'groups' for the proper sharing of big cases.

3.4 Use of Information Technology

Even if you have a mixed civil litigation practice comprising not only personal injury cases but a variety of other kinds, most civil claims necessitate the writing of similar letters at certain stages. Thus letters to employers, witnesses, the court office and opponents involve commonly used precedents. Such letters are often kept as drafts on word processor disks, with blank spaces for the insertion of the particulars relevant to the case. Use of standard letters and precedents keep the routine work to a minimum, leaving the solicitor and the secretary free to concentrate on the more important work. In the solicitor's case this involves concentrating on the decision-making aspects of the file and not on the routine administration. Precedents can likewise be used for lists of documents, common forms of summonses, writs and even pleadings where one has a practice which involves similar types of action, e.g. factory accidents or debt collecting.

Apart from these basic uses of information technology in civil litigation particularly, many larger firms have litigation support systems which, with the use of computers and word processors, assist in the back-up work for litigation. This may involve the employment of document analysts who assist fee-earners by organising documentation in those cases where there are vast amounts of it, e.g. pharmaceutical product claims or other major commercial actions. Data can be organised for quick analysis and retrieval and comparison purposes on custom-designed databases. Automation and office technology is thus an important component in case management in such cases. At present, however, the cost of such systems is prohibitive except for the larger firms, but inevitably their use will become more common.

3.5 Time Costing

3.5.1 THE NEED FOR TIME COSTING

Solicitors' charges cannot be based simply on the amount of time spent. We have already considered in **Chapter 2** some of the relevant factors governing the way in which a solicitor may charge clients, or eventually have part of his clients' bill paid by his opponent. It is important for a firm, in deciding how much to charge, to know how much it costs it to do the work in the first place. Time costing is not therefore a method of billing but a method of establishing what each fee earner needs to charge each hour to cover the true cost of running the firm, and what should be charged, therefore, on each matter to cover the cost of carrying out the work which has been done. How much will eventually be charged for each hour of the fee earner's time to the client is a quite different question. The extra element over and above what it costs to do the work in the first place represents the profit to the firm, i.e. the income of the partners. So time costing is used to establish the cost of running the firm, by which is meant keeping the firm open for each hour of the day.

3.5.2 METHOD OF CALCULATION

The method of calculation is to attribute to each fee earner the amount of his own salary plus other incidental expenses attributable to him (e.g. the employer's national insurance contribution and pension contribution), together with any support staff exclusively devoted to that fee earner (e.g. his own secretary) and then a due proportion of all the other expenses of the firm including rent, business rate, provision of office technology and salaries of every individual who does not directly earn fees for the firm. The effect is thus to produce an annual sum required to be earned by each fee earner as his notional share towards the true cost of running the office. Thus if, for example, the annual sum for an assistant solicitor, taking into account his own salary and the cost of other expenses attributable to him together with a contribution towards more general overheads, is, say, £55,000, an hourly expense rate for him can then be calculated.

The Law Society publish a booklet called *The Expense of Time* which demonstrates how this calculation should be made. That booklet suggests that it is fair to assume that most fee earners do 1,100 hours of chargeable work per year, taking into account weekends, holidays, sickness and, of course, the amount of time which fee earners must expend in some form of administration which is not directly billable to any given client. The rate applicable to the solicitor in the above example will thus be £50 per hour. £50 per hour, then, is what it costs the firm to provide his services to the client for that hour, and that forms the basic element of what the client is to be charged. To that figure has to be added whatever proportion the firm thinks appropriate in order to provide a reasonable rate of profit for the partners. Thus from the base of £50 per hour it is possible that the time of that assistant solicitor would in fact be billed at, say, £70 per hour, though the latter figure will depend in part on the various matters referred to in **Chapter 2** to do with, e.g., the urgency and complexity of the case, the amount involved and the responsibility.

3.5.3 TIME SHEETS

The *Expense of Time* exercise can only be effectively carried out if proper daily time sheets are maintained by individual fee earners. Information recorded on these time sheets will then be collated to calculate the amount of chargeable time spent on an individual client's file by all fee earners who have worked on it. The result will show what it has cost the firm for whatever work has been done on each separate matter.

Time records will show the length of time, though it is still essential to keep notes on the file showing how the time was spent, with an explanation of what was achieved in the time so as to help the costs draftsmen when the time comes to prepare the bill. If you know that you have spent 30 hours on a matter but can in fact justify only 10 of them, this will not be helpful in satisfying a Taxing Master or District Judge who considers your bill on taxation.

It is appropriate to mention that in certain cases which have come before the High Court where the Law Society's booklet *The Expense of Time* has been considered, the booklet's methodology has been severely criticised as unscientific. See, for example, *Johnson* v *Reed Corrugated Cases Ltd* [1992] 1 All ER 169. Nonetheless, it may be a useful first method for a firm to calculate its overhead rates.

3.6 Client Care

Many complaints about solicitors arise because the client feels, whether rightly or not, that his lawyer is not taking a sufficiently active and personal interest in the case. You may lose a client no matter how well you have dealt with his affairs unless he is kept fully informed and treated as an important member of the team working on his own case. This is the best way to establish sufficient rapport to enable the client to communicate his problems to you fully and for you to understand them at each stage of the case. You must, of course, remain sufficiently detached despite this closeness of contact to provide the objective and independent advice required. Few things are more embarrassing than litigating against an opposing solicitor who so identifies with his client's case that his emotions are involved and a most unprofessional atmosphere is created between the solicitors.

In connection with client care, as noted in **4.1.1**, rules of professional practice require that certain general information be given to clients and that every firm should operate a complaints handling procedure resolving problems with clients, by virtue of *Solicitors Practice Rule 15.*

3.7 Getting Early Experience

You can get an enormous amount out of a six-month period doing civil litigation during your training contract. It is vital to learn the nuts and bolts as quickly as possible and to achieve some mastery of costs and legal aid and advice at the outset, since the practicability and profitability of dealing with any individual case needs always to be considered. If, for example, you did not know that actions involving less than £3,000 go to arbitration and that very little would be recovered from your opponent by way of costs, you might be tempted to do a great deal of investigative work on a claim for a deserving client because, as is perfectly obvious, there may be as many factual and legal complexities in a case worth £2,999 as in one worth many times that amount. Clients with problems involving that kind of sum, however, must be informed that there is little prospect of getting costs of representation paid by their opponent, and therefore that any compensation obtained is likely to be subject to your charges.

Practice and procedure should then be mastered, including the details of legal aid financial limits, forms and personnel in the local office; the basic procedures in the preparation of service or process, from writs and summonses to final judgment and its enforcement; and time limits and the limitation periods.

Next you should familiarise yourself with the personnel, location and layout of the courts and registries in which you are most likely to be engaged. Every opportunity offered to engage in advocacy should be taken, however intimidating you may find it initially. It is to be hoped that you will initially be allowed to cut your teeth on relatively straightforward applications, e.g. uncontested directions hearings, in order to gain familiarity with the atmosphere and attitude of District Judges. Thereafter you should constantly attempt to accept challenges to do more and more complicated kinds of advocacy. This will help engender self-confidence and an insight into the behaviour of the more idiosyncratic District Judges.

Your own firm's practices and procedures in relation to file, case and time management should be noted, and you should abide by them scrupulously, unless of course it is possible for you to suggest improvements!

Lastly, you should never be afraid to ask for advice and help from your principal or someone else in the office, especially where you have doubts as to the professional propriety of any given course of action, particularly one which is being urged upon you by your client.

FOUR

PRE-ACTION AND GENERAL CONSIDERATIONS

We have already considered the financing of civil litigation and the important topic of case and file management. We shall now consider matters relevant to gathering evidence. Most of the early part of this chapter will be concerned with personal injury litigation but many of the points made are of general relevance to any kind of action. We shall then go on to consider specifically matters which one might need to consider in a contract or commercial case.

4.1 Personal Injury Litigation

The steps which we shall describe ought to be taken by a prudent solicitor before issuing a writ. That is not to say, of course, that some of those steps cannot be postponed until after issuing a writ, and if the plaintiff has consulted you in the last week of the limitation period they will almost all have to be postponed until after the issuing of the writ. However, it is as well to remember that a statement of claim will need to be served within a matter of at most a month after the writ has been served. Whilst a writ can be issued on the basis of relatively little information, reciting simply the date and place of the accident and the identity of the parties, the statement of claim is a full pleading of the plaintiff's case and contains all the factual allegations which he proposes to make; in addition, in a personal injury case, in principle a medical report and a worked computation of special damages must be served with the statement of claim. There is accordingly no point in getting matters off to a dynamic start by issuing and serving the writ on the day that instructions are received if subsequently you will have to ask the defendant's permission to serve the statement of claim late. The better practice is to collect all the evidence on every relevant matter, where the evidence is available, at the very outset of the case; to keep it in an organised and orderly manner, as described in the previous chapter on case management; and to give yourself the huge tactical advantage of ensuring that you are always on top of all the facts, and thus always in a position to dictate the pace at which the case will proceed. This necessarily involves the collection of as much evidence as possible at an early stage before court proceedings are set in motion.

Nonetheless, to suggest that all the following steps are essential, even in cases where they could be applicable, is a counsel of perfection. An example of this is that whilst a client really should never be told that he has a cast iron case on liability, there are many cases where the solicitor can make that judgment for himself. Thus if the client is a passenger in a vehicle which has been involved in a collision, then it is overwhelmingly probable that his solicitor will manage to establish negligence against one or other of the drivers involved. Likewise, where the facts are very obvious, e.g. where it is clear that unsafe working practices have led to a factory accident, or where the client is knocked down on a zebra crossing by a vehicle which is manifestly on the wrong side of the road at the time, a solicitor might well omit some of the following stages. It is always as well, however, to bear in mind that if liability is ultimately denied in a personal injury case it may prove awkward, and even impossible, to collect evidence on liability too late in the day. The solicitor should therefore be seeking the very earliest indication from the defendants that liability is not seriously in issue, whatever point they try to maintain by their pleadings, before omitting early steps, e.g., the collection of evidence from eye-witnesses while their memories are fresh. It should always be remembered that that work will be paid for in the end and that the client is entitled to a thorough professional service and not to have his solicitor cut corners, especially because of the pressure from an excessive workload.

In the following paragraphs we consider a number of important aspects of early work in personal injury cases and other routine litigation.

4.1.1 THE FIRST INTERVIEW WITH THE CLIENT

In some personal injury cases a solicitor may well be contacted within a few days of even a major accident, possibly by the anxious relatives of the victim. In other cases the victim does not begin to apply his mind to compensation until he has left hospital or is considerably recovered. In any event, at the first meeting the solicitor must commence to obtain some basic information in order to advise the client generally about his prospects; it should be remembered that the question of costs must be thoroughly discussed and the legal aid scheme explained.

4.1.1.1 *Practice Rule 15*

Rule 15 of the *Solicitors Practice Rules* requires that every solicitor should operate a complaints handling procedure which should ensure that clients are informed whom to approach in the event of any problem. This procedure need not be written but it is obviously preferable if it is documented in some way and the solicitor's firm has a formal procedure. The procedure must ensure that the nature of any complaint is investigated promptly and thoroughly. In addition, the client must be told the name and status of the person responsible for the day-to-day conduct of the matter and the principal responsible for its overall supervision. The client should be informed about the time scale involved in the case, including details of when his solicitor is likely to be in touch with him next; and the likely cost, and all other relevant matters as to how the cost will be met. Naturally, as the matter progresses the client should be regularly informed of all relevant aspects of it as they develop and of the progress made, and updated on the time scale for future action.

4.1.1.2 Legal aid

As noted above, it is unprofessional conduct not to explain the availability of legal aid, even if the solicitor himself does not take legal aid cases, so that the client has the option of going elsewhere. It may be that costs do not need to be discussed at all, as where the client is referred to a solicitor by his trade union. If an application for legal aid needs to be made, then sufficient evidence must be collected to support the application, but this will fall far short of the thoroughness with which evidence must be collected once the funding of the case is assured. On the assumption that these matters have been dealt with, a statement should then be taken from the client.

4.1.1.3 Taking statements

Techniques of taking clients' statements vary considerably. Clients are often poor at deciding what is relevant and what is irrelevant to their case, even on liability, still more on quantum. Even to describe how an accident happened on the road or the workings of factory machinery is very difficult for a lay person. It is sometimes a good idea to get the client to draw an approximate plan of a road junction and to use toy vehicles to enable him to show who did what, how and when. You should in due course visit the road junction for the purpose of taking photographs, and where necessary have professional plans prepared showing precise dimensions, angle, curvature and so on to check this early account. In the case of factory accidents involving complicated machinery, all that can be done at the early stage is to obtain as much information from the client as possible. An early inspection of the factory machinery will then be required, the procedure for which is described at **4.1.2.5** below.

When interviewing the client in a personal injury case, you should attempt to obtain as much information as possible, even if some of it seems of marginal relevance at the time. Because clients are not skilled at sifting the relevant from the irrelevant, it may appear that a good deal of time is wasted, but in fact, if you let a client talk on, sometimes the most crucial detail of all comes out, the importance of which had been unappreciated by the client. This is sometimes so on liability but is even more likely to be the case on quantum. By letting a client describe all the ways in which his life has been affected by the injury, extra elements of the claim can often emerge which would not have been discovered simply by taking questions on a formal questionnaire by reference to nature of lost earnings, bonuses, promotion opportunities, pension arrangements, perks and so on. The client's account of his whole life may be needed here, so that if, for example, it suddenly emerges that the client was a keen do-it-yourself enthusiast but has now been incapacitated so that he will never be able to do that again, a very worthwhile sum can be added to the claim for the cost of employing professional decorators, carpenters and the like over the rest of his lifetime. In industrial disease cases particularly, where the client may need to describe his whole work record going back perhaps some decades, the client should be encouraged to talk freely even if a great deal of irrelevance emerges.

The initial statement should begin with basic details, including full name, date of birth, address, telephone number, national insurance number, marital status, children, education where relevant, employer's name and address and any works reference.

The method of actually taking the statement varies. Many prefer to jot notes whilst the client is talking and then to dictate a full statement immediately after the client has left, sending it to him for him to make any necessary additions or amendments. In due course we shall consider the procedure by virtue of which in almost all cases witness statements, including those of the parties, have to be exchanged substantially in advance of trial under *Ord. 38, r. 2A* in the High Court and its county court equivalent *Ord. 20, r. 12A*. It is imperative that all the evidence which will go in that statement is obtained as soon as possible. However, the information in the statement now under discussion should not be confined to the things which it will be necessary or prudent to put in the statement for exchange. The client's initial proof of evidence should contain everything he can think of that seems relevant, including matters which will not be admissible in evidence and therefore will not appear in the formal statement for exchange under *Ord. 38, r. 2A*. For example, the client may wish to describe other incidents or bad practices at the factory concerned or put a good deal of opinion evidence in the statement, things which it will not strictly be proper to include in the formal statement for exchange. At this stage, however, you are collecting evidence not for the trial judge but for your own conduct of the case, and collecting this kind of information may provide useful lines of enquiry.

The statement should be signed by the client. This is not so that it can be used if the client should later die (because the statement would in fact be admissible anyway under the *Civil Evidence Act 1995*). The reason is to protect the solicitor himself. It is important in litigation more than in almost any other field of work (except perhaps those involving taxation) for a solicitor continually to keep proper records of advice given so as to protect himself against any later suggestion of negligence. For example, if at trial matters come out in a very different way from the client's version as put in the pleadings, and the client is put in difficulties in cross-examination, he may well allege that his own solicitor misinterpreted, or even distorted, his version of what occurred. Naturally one would not then use the proof of evidence to discredit the client at trial, but should any subsequent allegation of negligence in taking the statement be made, the signed copy will be useful. For the same reason it is best to send statements to the client at home to consider at leisure to avoid any suggestion that he simply signed what was put in front of him without reading it in the office.

4.1.1.4 Timescale

Apart from taking the client's own statement at first interview, it will be important to give him a rough timescale for future action indicating the stages at which you will wish to see him to review the case or to comment on evidence collected from other parties. In the early stages a fair degree of frequency of contact is often best. It reassures the client that early action is being taken on his case and can usually be justified on taxation of costs. The client should certainly be told that, except for the simplest case, it is unlikely that any progress towards settlement will be made in less than several months.

4.1.2 COLLECTING EVIDENCE ON LIABILITY

4.1.2.1 The police accident report

A copy of the police accident report book should usually be obtained if the police were involved at the scene. This report currently costs almost £50, and therefore, if advising the client under the Green Form, there will be little money left for covering other preliminary stages of interview and advice if this money is expended. The Chief Constable of the force in whose area the accident occurred should be contacted by letter, giving the date and place of the incident and sending the appropriate fee. In due course an extract from a police accident report book will be sent. In some places police forces are very slow to deal with this request. In any event, the accident report will not be sent until any criminal proceedings have been concluded, although at least insurance details will be sent if the rest of the report is not available.

The police accident report is an extremely useful source of information about a number of matters. It comprises at the very least the names and addresses of the people involved; the insurance particulars of any vehicles involved; witnesses' names and addresses and sometimes brief statements; details of vehicle damage; a plan or scale drawing prepared by a policeman at the scene showing the layout of any junction and the position of vehicles; and details of whether there has been a prosecution and its result. If the police consider that some aspect of the condition of a vehicle may have caused the accident there may be an examination at a police garage by a police vehicle examiner.

At the early stage of investigation this can save a good deal of leg work. It may be necessary to reinterview the witnesses, however, because the statements taken were principally for the purpose of establishing criminal liability against just one driver and the witnesses may not have been given a full opportunity to comment on the relative culpability of others involved in the incident, whom the police were not interested in charging. The statements are sometimes extremely brief.

4.1.2.2 Interviewing witnesses

The police accident report and the client's own account are likely to give details of witnesses. Witnesses should be interviewed at length in the same way as the client himself. Clearly they will have nothing to say relevant to quantum, and in a road accident case they may simply be describing an incident which took only a matter of seconds to happen and their proofs of evidence will not be long. In a factory accident case, however, it may be that the plaintiff's work mates are in a position to give a great deal of detail about matters which may become relevant in relation to a system of work at the factory, including descriptions of past incidents and so on.

Such witness statements should be taken in the long form at this stage, including matter which may be strictly inadmissible in evidence, though when the statements are prepared for service under *Ord. 38, r. 2A* they will need to be trimmed to the appropriate form and sent back to the witness for re-signing. It is always important to interview witnesses as soon as possible. As indicated above, some solicitors are inclined to cut corners at this stage since it may appear pointless to interview witnesses as to liability when liability seems overwhelmingly clear and it is believed that it will be conceded early in negotiations. Nonetheless, that approach can cause difficulties and it is far better to interview witnesses as soon as possible. No matter how dramatic an incident, witnesses's memories fade remarkably quickly. If the statement is not taken for some months it will be much vaguer – perhaps not on central matters, but on peripheral things such as the precise line taken by a vehicle, how close to the kerb it was, or how a relevant manoeuvre was started.

4.1.2.3 Inspecting the scene

If the accident occurred locally it is always worthwhile for the solicitor to go to see the layout of the road and to attempt to visualise how things must have occurred. A photograph should be taken, especially if there is any risk that the layout of the junction might be changed, e.g. by the introduction of a mini roundabout, or by the demolition of a building which may have obscured the view from one angle across a junction. It is often advisable to meet the client at the scene so that he can point out again just where the vehicles were on the road at the relevant time. Going back to the scene of the accident may also jog the client's memory about some vital detail. In due course, if the matter goes to trial a good plan of the junction will be required.

4.1.2.4 Road accident cases: examining the vehicle

If instructions are received early enough so that the defendant's vehicle is still in the state in which it was at the time of accident, then it may be worthwhile attempting to examine it. It may be, of course, that it is difficult to discover its whereabouts, although the police may be able to let you know this. This is because the initial letter to the defendant's insurance company often takes some weeks to receive attention. There is probably no rule of etiquette which prevents you telephoning the potential defendant directly at home and asking when the vehicle can be inspected. Some would consider this to be sharp practice, however. Nonetheless, a certain amount of speed is certainly going to be required since, unless the vehicle is a total write-off, the defendant will want to have it repaired as swiftly as possible.

If inspection is possible then a layman's inspection (i.e. by the solicitor personally) can at least show whether the tyres are in good condition, and perhaps whether the lights were working and the nature of any body work damage. It may be worth taking photographs of such damage. For example, if the plaintiff is a pedestrian knocked down by the defendant, it may subsequently be alleged that the plaintiff's claim is exaggerated and that there was only slight contact. If on an inspection of the vehicle it is discovered that there is a very substantial dent in the wing, this will be a vital piece of evidence. If on a preliminary inspection there is any suggestion that the condition of the vehicle in some way contributed to the happening of the accident (e.g. that it had been inadequately maintained), it may be desirable to have an expert witness present for this purpose. A consultant engineer may be able to ascertain problems with the braking or steering system which predated the accident.

4.1.2.5 Accidents at work

The collection of early evidence about this can be rather more difficult than in the case of road accidents. It may be difficult indeed to visualise the precise nature of the plaintiff's job. Of course, if a particular solicitor acts often in relation to accidents at the same factory, or for the same group of trade unionists or employees, technical terms will rapidly become second nature, but it can be difficult for a non-technically minded lawyer to visualise what is involved where a layman is describing some system involving flanges, pulleys, sprockets, bogies and the like. It can be a good idea to ask the client to draw the relevant piece of machinery, or, if he is back at work or has willing former workmates, to ask one of them to take a camera into work and photograph the relevant things. In due course a formal inspection of the site of the accident may be necessary. The client should be asked whether there have been any proposals made, whether in consequence of his accident or otherwise, the changes at the work place, e.g. in layout, fencing or replacement of obsolete machinery. If that is the case then very swift action may be needed to ensure that the nature and layout of the machinery or work process is recorded in some permanent form, e.g. by a video under the procedures for obtaining *pre-action inspection* mentioned below.

If you are instructed by a trade union on behalf of one of its members, it should be asked to cooperate in assisting with interviews with the shop steward or safety representatives. Even if you are not instructed by the trade union, those persons are likely to be perfectly willing to assist in relation to accidents to a workmate. Under the new health and safety regulations brought in with effect from January 1993, employers are required to carry out 'risk assessments' to examine every area of their premises and activities and to formulate plans for dealing with potential problems. A great deal of documentation must therefore inevitably be created by employers who comply with these important provisions and this naturally gives scope for demands to see such documents. An employer who has not carried out any of these exercises is clearly unlikely to be able to impress the court as having a safe system of work. There may be other documents which you will want to see in due course such as the records of proceedings of any safety committee or details of the notification of the accident to some other body, e.g. the local authority or the Health and Safety Executive. It is also worth writing to the Health and Safety Executive to ask whether it has looked into the circumstances of the accident and made records or taken photographs. It can also be asked whether it had ever visited the premises prior to the accident and what recommendations were made or notices served.

If the case seems to be one of urgency, the defendants or their insurers should be asked for immediate facilities for an inspection by a consulting engineer. They should in any event be asked to give an undertaking to preserve any piece of machinery or other relevant equipment *in situ* pending full inspection and trial. If there is non-cooperation it may be necessary to make an immediate application to the court for an order permitting inspection and videoing, and requiring the retention of property which may become a matter of evidence in subsequent proceedings under *Ord. 29, r. 7A* (see **4.1.4.2**).

4.1.2.6 Tripping cases

In the case of clients who have fallen on broken or uneven pavements the claim is usually to be made under *s. 41* of the *Highways Act 1980*. It may also be possible, or advisable, to join in whoever created the danger, e.g. the Electricity Company whose subterranean works nearby may have caused the problem.

In this case above all others it is vital to collect evidence before notifying the defendants of the problem. Whatever the funding problems that local authorities have in relation to their operations generally, they are notoriously swift, on the intimation of any claim in relation to a tripping accident, at getting their operatives round to knock the offending pavement flat or replace the broken stone. Cynical solicitors believe that their speed in this is so great that they must have a helicopter on standby, because often it is done on the very day that the complaint is received. This may, of course, be in the interest of preventing future accidents at the point, though many contend it is in the hope of destroying the evidence in case the solicitor notifying the claim has been sufficiently incompetent not to have taken a photograph or exact measurements of the precise location. Photographs should be taken of the 'trip' where paving stones have become raised or lowered from their neighbours, showing the precise measurement against a ruler. The client will have to attend with you at the time of taking the photographs in order to ensure that the paving stone is correctly identified.

4.1.2.7 Occupier's liability accidents

It is difficult to generalise about the procedures in occupier's liability accident cases. If, for example, the potential defendant is a neighbour or friend of the plaintiff, over whose frayed or badly laid stair carpet the plaintiff has tripped, perhaps with serious consequences, then often the plaintiff will be in something of a quandary. The plaintiff himself may be reluctant, even in the case of serious injuries, to sue his friend, relative or neighbour. The plaintiff's mind can be set at rest, however, that very often the ultimate compensating party will be an insurance company and that the plaintiff need feel no worse than in the case of his being a passenger in a friend's car and wishing to claim in those circumstances. Investigation of the insurance position should be made. Even if the potential defendant does not have a specific occupier's liability policy, compensation for this kind of accident is often included as a term of the insurance arranged by building society mortgagees. Only if the potential defendant is uninsured need the plaintiff then make the difficult decision of whether to seek proper compensation or not.

In collecting evidence in relation to such claims one must tread a difficult line. A solicitor should be reluctant to compromise the potential defendant too much by interviewing him and obtaining admissions because such conduct on the defendant's part may breach the terms of the policy so that his insurers are entitled to repudiate. In such cases it may be best simply to ask if the plaintiff can photograph the offending piece of carpet or floor and then intimate the claim direct to the insurance company before seeking formal facilities for inspection of the place in question.

In other kinds of occupier's liability cases, e.g. a fall on slippery floors or staircases in department stores, there is no need to feel such compunction about obtaining evidence. There would be no reason not to photograph the area in question, prepare plans and so on, including obtaining details of the type of any floor tiling so that an engineer may in due course advise.

4.1.2.8 Attending criminal proceedings or inquests

If acting for a potential plaintiff in civil proceedings arising out of a road traffic accident there will usually have been some consideration given to criminal prosecution. Criminal cases come to court very much more swiftly than civil cases, sometimes within a matter of weeks of the incident concerned. If funding has already been arranged for a case, it may be worthwhile to attend criminal proceedings. If your client has been charged along with the other party with careless driving or some other motoring offence, then you may well be there as an advocate anyway. In that situation it will obviously be desirable (although far from conclusive for civil purposes) to obtain the acquittal of your client. On the assumption, however, that your client is simply a victim, it can be equally important to see what happens in relation to the potential opponent. Naturally you have no *locus standi* to intervene in these proceedings and are simply an observer.

You will be able to obtain full details of the eventual outcome and should also take notes of evidence. The defendant is likely to be represented at the expense of his insurance company in most cases. It may be that some useful admission is made by the defendant in the course of the hearing which can be noted for future use. It may also be possible to save time by taking statements for the civil proceedings from prosecution witnesses who are waiting for the case to start. It can also be useful to observe the demeanour and apparent credibility of the defendant. If he appears shifty and evasive this is likely to be useful information should the civil proceedings be defended. For the precise usefulness of convictions and relevance of acquittals, see **7.4.1.4**.

If your clients are the personal representatives or dependants of a person who has been killed in an accident it can be vital to attend an inquest. An inquest is an inquiry into the cause of death in order to ascertain into which of the several categories of finding available to a coroner the case falls. The solicitor is not entitled as of right to cross-examine witnesses about how an incident occurred, nor to attempt to attribute civil liability. The coroner has the discretion to permit cross-examination and will usually allow this fairly liberally, although the cross-examination will not be in quite the same style as in an ordinary civil court. Nonetheless, it is often possible to obtain useful evidence and lines of enquiry, and equally to observe the demeanour of witnesses for future purposes.

4.1.2.9 Instructing experts

In some cases everything at trial will turn upon the nature and quality of expert evidence on liability. Experts on matters relevant to *quantum* need perhaps not be instructed quite so swiftly. It can, however, be vital to instruct an expert witness on matters relevant to liability at a very early stage. Chiefly for this purpose you will be considering instructing a consulting engineer to examine, say, a vehicle, factory machinery, the type of flooring in premises where a slipping accident occurred and so on. If there is open access to the item or area in question the defendant need not be consulted nor his permission obtained. If, however, it is a case of factory machinery, then the defendant will have to be asked for permission, and at the same time it is usual to seek an undertaking that the machinery will be preserved in its present state. If there is no positive response to this fairly swiftly, it may be necessary to apply to the court for inspection under *Ord. 29, r. 7A* the procedure for which is considered below at **4.1.4.2**.

In road traffic accidents the question of cause and effect is often easier to see. Nevertheless, specialist road traffic accident reconstruction experts may be useful and their employment, at least in big cases, is increasingly common. They are expert at reconstructing the precise angle of impact, distances, and speed.

Other experts who may be of use in establishing liability include consultant surveyors in cases involving bad building design or maintenance; and ergonomics experts in relation to such matters as work routines, work loads, and especially in repetitive strain injury cases.

4.1.3 COLLECTING EVIDENCE RELEVANT TO QUANTUM

We have already considered the question of quantum of damages generally in **1.2**. It may be that there is some element of each of those heads of damage in a client's claim. It is vital to begin collecting evidence on quantum at the earliest stage. At the outset one must tell the client to pass over, and keep carefully in future, all receipts for items connected with this claim no matter how trivial. For example, if a client needs to attend hospital as an out patient for many weeks, it will usually be considered reasonable for him to go by taxi if he is unable to drive, and receipts should be obtained for each excursion. Likewise, receipts should be obtained for such things as dry cleaning clothes after the accident, or for the purchase of replacement items, to say nothing of the larger disbursements such as car repair and car hire accounts.

If realistic negotiations with an insurance company can be opened early, then some idea of relevant figures will be needed in case settlement can be achieved even before the issue of proceedings. It may be that this is possible even in cases of serious injury, especially if there is no claim for future loss of earnings and an immediate and accurate prognosis is obtainable. In any event, for the good tactical reasons previously described, the plaintiff is likely to have an early monopoly of material relevant to quantum. If this is kept in a thorough, constantly updated and professional manner, the plaintiff's solicitor will be better informed at every stage than the defendant about key elements of the claim. This can often lead to a defendant admitting that he is in no position to challenge given items and conceding some, even whilst maintaining objection to others.

4.1.3.1 Obtaining medical evidence

Writing to the client's GP for a medical report on the plaintiff is of no use save in the case of the most minor accidents. Similarly, obtaining a report from the casualty officer at the hospital where the client was admitted is not of much use for the trial itself. However, in both cases they can provide vital information to the plaintiff's solicitor. You should always ensure that you obtain a copy of your client's GP's notes. Clients, even with highly meritorious cases, may often be tempted to over-egg the pudding and may claim, for example, that their favourite hobby was an active sport. If you have obtained the client's GP's notes and find that in the recent past there have been prolonged periods of incapacity due to backache, it is as well for you to know this so that the client can be gently discouraged from exaggerating the degree of his sporting enthusiasms. The defendants' solicitors, if they are competent, will certainly obtain copies of a plaintiff's GP's notes in due course, so it is better for you to obtain them before any exaggerated claims are made which may affect the client's credibility generally.

An early report is usually helpful. It may take some months to obtain an appointment with a suitable consultant and the steps to obtain this should be put in hand immediately. In most accident cases orthopaedic injuries will play at least some, and usually the major, part. A consultant should be instructed who has a substantial medico-legal practice. When instructing him, send a copy of the client's statement, although indicating that it is undesirable that any reference to the precise causation of the accident appears in the final form of the report. However, it is important for the specialist to know just what is said about how the accident occurred, because in giving a prognosis it can make a great deal of difference to know whether, for example, a broken ankle occurred because of an impact from the side by a vehicle, or, say, by falling. The orthopaedic specialist should be asked to recommend other specialisms which merit separate investigation. For example, it may not be clear whether some kinds of pain have an orthopaedic or a neurological origin. The consultant should be asked to give any prognosis that is possible at the time, and in particular to indicate at what interval it would be desirable to re-examine the plaintiff. If, as is common, there will be a delay of many months in obtaining this report, it is sometimes worthwhile to obtain a report from the hospital where the client has been treated and ask them to make any necessary recommendations for other specialists. It is often desirable to obtain a medical report early on from the hospital casualty department, even if a full medico-legal report will still be obtained later from the chosen specialist, because it is necessary to serve a medical report with the statement of claim. You are not, however, limited to relying on that report. When writing to the hospital it is important to give details of the date of admission and the client's hospital reference number.

A vexed question, to which differing answers are given even by very experienced practitioners, is whether it is desirable to instruct the consultant who is actually treating the client to provide reports for the purpose of litigation. In fact some consultants are reluctant to do this for their own patients, recognising that their views may not seem, or be, quite as objective as those of an independent specialist. Some plaintiff's solicitors contend, however, that if there is a difference of opinion between the plaintiff's specialist and the defendant's specialist and the plaintiff's specialist is actually treating him, that it would be very difficult for the judge to accept the defendant's specialist's opinion, i.e. implicitly to find that the plaintiff's specialist has been wrong in diagnosis or treatment. It is the writer's view, though, that it is generally best to instruct an independent specialist. Naturally copies of any other medical evidence, including the GP's notes, should be sent to the specialist, although often specialists prefer to obtain these themselves and perhaps to obtain more information direct from the GP.

When writing to the specialist with instructions it is vital to ask all proper questions which may touch on quantum of damages. Thus one should ask not simply about when the plaintiff will be able to return to work (he may have an entirely sedentary job) but, if it is the case, when the plaintiff will be fit to resume his hobby or sporting activities, as appropriate.

4.1.3.2 Writing to employers

When writing to employers the nature and complexity of the information required obviously depends upon the type of job and the severity of the injury. At the very least it is usual to send the employer a schedule of the previous 26 weeks before the accident for the employer to fill in, giving details of the client's gross and net earnings. Such a long period is usually chosen in order to obtain a true average in case of fluctuating bonuses or overtime.

In the letter it may be necessary to ask other more detailed questions. For example, if the injury is one of considerable severity and the plaintiff is unlikely to return to work for a long time, or ever, a great deal of help from the employers will be needed to build up a pattern of the plaintiff's career so as to maximise the claim. If the plaintiff is relatively young and has only just started out in his career, and this is perhaps his first job, then the information to be obtained from the employers may prove to be the most vital element in the case in maximising the damages. Thus questions should be asked about the client's prospects within the firm or in his profession generally; about what earning levels might have been achieved for an average person, and for an above average person at, say, five-yearly intervals for the rest of his working life; what assessments had been made by the personnel department as to the future prospects of the plaintiff; and if any formal assessments have been carried out (e.g. annually) the employer should be asked to provide copies of those. If the plaintiff may return to work questions must be asked about his status in the firm and loss of promotion opportunities; if he is viewed as a less valued employee because of the nature of his disability (e.g. he has lost a limb, or has been facially disfigured in a job where appearances are important) this information should also be obtained. A copy of the client's contract of employment should also be sought.

It may be necessary to supplement this letter with an interview in due course with the employer's personnel officer, or the plaintiff's immediate superior. If the employers are not also the defendants (e.g. in road accident cases) they are likely to take a positive and upbeat view of the plaintiff's prospects since they will have no interest in depressing the level of his claim. If, on the other hand, the employers are also the defendants (e.g. a factory accident) it may prove more difficult to obtain useful information. If there is no cooperation at all on these matters then one may end up having to collect evidence about the plaintiff's prospects from every other source that is available, e.g. work mates who may be willing to say that he was viewed as a high flier amongst his contemporaries, or from employment consultants or the various government agencies which are able to supply details of average earnings for many occupations at many stages of a career. This evidence will assist in fixing the *multiplicand* described in **1.2.2.3**. It must be remembered that this figure is not the plaintiff's *current* earnings but is a figure which takes into account his prospects.

4.1.3.3 The self-employed plaintiff

A good deal of work will need to be done here and inevitably a forensic accountant will in the end have to be consulted, as indeed he will normally have to be consulted in many cases involving substantial loss of earnings from whatever source. The accounts of the plaintiff's business will need to be perused and it is often best to have an independent accountant who has experience in giving evidence to do this rather than the firm which may have prepared the plaintiff's accounts. Underlying trends must be analysed to see whether the business was genuinely improving even though net profits may not have increased in the recent past. It should also be ascertained what extra benefits in non-taxable form the plaintiff was able to obtain by virtue of being self-employed, e.g. running what was in essence a private car on the firm, entertaining expenses and the like. These pieces of information can all be used in due course to maximise the claim.

4.1.3.4 Maximising benefits

Experienced personal injury lawyers treat it as part of their job to ensure that an injured plaintiff obtains all necessary benefits due to him, and in the case of those assisted by their trade union this may indeed include representation at the various benefits appeal tribunals which exist where an unsatisfactory initial assessment of benefit has been made. In due course, as we have seen, credit for these benefits will have to be given and they will in essence have to be repaid out of compensation to the Compensation Recovery Unit of the DSS. Nonetheless, it will assist the plaintiff's morale and standard of living to obtain as much as he can at present in the way of such benefits. The law, however, is that failure to claim such benefits is not treated as improper failure to mitigate damages (*Eley* v *Bedford* [1972] 1 QB 155).

4.1.4 APPLICATIONS TO THE COURT

We have so far considered the various ways of collecting evidence on liability and quantum *informally*, i.e. without the necessary to involve the court. We now consider two kinds of preliminary application to the court which may be useful in obtaining evidence at a very early stage, especially in cases where the evidence is vital to ascertain liability, or where there is any risk of the evidence being lost or destroyed.

Both the High Court and the county court have the power to make orders permitting a potential plaintiff (or any other party to a potential action although clearly it will be rare for a defendant to avail himself of these provisions) to obtain certain preliminary information concerning a proposed action. The two quite separate procedures are:

(a) application for pre-action discovery of a document; and

(b) application for pre-action inspection, etc., of things.

4.1.4.1 Application for pre-action discovery under *RSC Ord. 24, r. 7A* (Applied also in the county court by *s. 76* of the *County Courts Act 1984.*)

Under this rule a person who appears likely to be a party to a subsequent action *in respect of personal injuries or death* only can apply to the court for an order for discovery against any other person who is likely to be a party to that action.

Where a potential plaintiff therefore thinks that a potential defendant has some document in his possession and it is vitally important to him to see the content of that document before the action starts, then he may apply to the court for an order granting him sight of the document. The application is made by *originating summons* (called an *originating application* in the county court). An originating summons is merely a method of commencing proceedings in a case in which no writ has yet been issued. The form of the originating summons is prescribed in the *Rules of the Supreme Court, Appendix A, form 10* (reproduced in the *Supreme Court Practice*, vol. 2, para. 4). The originating summons is drafted so as to refer to the potential plaintiff as the applicant and the potential defendant as defendant. It must be supported by an affidavit which must be sworn by the potential plaintiff (or his solicitor) and contain the following details:

(a) The grounds on which it is alleged that the applicant and the party against whom the order is sought are likely to be parties to subsequent proceedings in a claim for personal injuries. In other words, the affidavit must briefly explain the background to the case and why it is alleged that the parties to the originating summons are likely to be parties to a future action for personal injuries.

(b) It must specify the documents in respect of which the order is sought and show why they are relevant to an issue arising in the potential claim for personal injuries and that the potential defendant has the documents.

At the hearing of the application the District Judge will mainly direct himself to one criterion, and that is whether sight of the document at this stage is so vital to the potential plaintiff that it will help him to decide whether or not to bring an action at all against the potential defendant. If, whilst interesting or relevant, it is not a document of this crucial importance, then the District Judge may very well decide that the plaintiff, if he has a prima facie case, should issue proceedings against the defendant and seek discovery and inspection of this document in the normal course of things at a later stage. A good example of a case where sight of the document may be essential to enable a potential plaintiff to decide whether or not to sue is perhaps a medical negligence case where he would like to see the hospital notes concerning his treatment. Complaints or accident reports about factory procedures would be another good example. It is difficult to think of an instance arising out of a road traffic case where sight of any document at such an early stage would in fact be so crucial. Perhaps one example might be where the plaintiff suspects that the defendant's vehicle had been inadequately maintained over a long period and that this directly caused the accident. If the vehicle was a commercial vehicle in respect of which there ought to be maintenance records kept, then he might conceivably ask for pre-action discovery under this provision. In the case of this, as in the case of almost every other application, it is as well to ask the proposed defendant whether voluntary discovery and inspection will be given without the need to apply to the court.

4.1.4.2 Pre-action inspection, etc., of a thing

This should be contrasted with the previous provision which relates to discovery and inspection of a *document*. Under the *Supreme Court Act 1981, s. 33(1)* and *RSC Ord. 29, r. 7A* (*CCR Ord. 13, r. 7*), the court has power to make an order providing for:

> *(a) the inspection, photographing, preservation, custody and detention of property which appears to the court to be property which may become the subject matter of subsequent proceedings in the [court] or as to which any question may arise in any such proceedings; and (b) the taking of samples of any such property . . . and the carrying out of any experiment on or with any such property.*

This provision applies to all types of action, not just to personal injury cases like the previous one. The procedure is identical to that under *Ord. 24, r. 7A*, that is application must be made by originating summons in the same form supported by an affidavit which, as before, sets out the background to the case explaining why the application is made and specifying the property in respect of which the order is sought and the nature of the order sought.

Under this provision, the court may make an order in relation to property which is the subject matter of the potential action. It might, for example, order that a certain thing whose title was in dispute be kept at a certain place pending the outcome of the action. However, the provision also applies to property 'as to which any question may arise', and thus may apply to some object which is a mere matter of evidence rather than the subject matter of the action. So, for example, in a road traffic accident, if the condition of a vehicle is alleged to have substantially contributed to the accident and the defendant's insurance company refuse to permit inspection of the vehicle before the writ is issued, then an application can be made under this provision. Likewise, if an action concerns, say, alleged lack of satisfactory quality of perishable goods application can be made under this provision for samples of the goods to be taken so that they can be inspected with a view to obtaining an expert report on whether or not they were of appropriate quality.

4.1.4.3 Application against non-parties

It is probably appropriate at this stage, before leaving the provisions of *RSC Ord. 24, r. 7A* and *Ord. 29, r. 7A* (and the county court equivalent), to mention that *after an action has been commenced* each provision can be used, in *personal injury cases* only, to obtain discovery of a document or inspection, etc., of a thing which is in the possession of a person who is not a party to the action. For example, suppose an employer who was not the defendant was dilatory or unhelpful about supplying details of earnings records for a plaintiff, or suppose the vehicle which caused an accident and which one wished to inspect was in the possession of a scrap yard. In either case the provisions of *Ord. 24, r. 7A* and *Ord. 29, r. 7A* can be used once an action has commenced to obtain discovery of documents in the one case and inspection of the object in the other case against persons who are not parties to the main action. See further **12.1.10**.

4.1.5 MOTOR INSURANCE

A plaintiff who suffers personal injuries in a road traffic accident can sue the defendant in the tort of negligence. The existence or absence of motor insurance makes no difference whatsoever to the actual procedure of an action under the *Rules of the Supreme Court*. It does, however, have enormous practical significance, particularly on the vital question of whether the plaintiff is going to receive any damages which he is awarded by the court. Plaintiffs are often very confused about their rights and or liabilities in relation to motor insurance. The position is much simpler than it may appear.

In the first case, if the plaintiff was a pedestrian at the time, matters are considerably simplified. His own insurance position is irrelevant, and even if he had a personal accident insurance policy which paid him an enormous sum it would not be taken into account in computing the damages due from the defendant. If the plaintiff was himself a driver at the time of the incident, then however clear cut liability seems he must be advised to notify his own insurers at once if he has not already done so, since there will inevitably be a term under the policy requiring him to do this within some fairly brief period. If some claim is subsequently brought against him the insurers will exercise the rights which they will have reserved under the policy to appoint their own choice of solicitors to represent him in the matter. It must be clearly understood that insurers are never themselves joined into the action as parties save in exceptional circumstances. The action is always brought against the motorist who is allegedly liable, though it is, of course, the insurers who will be paying any judgment awarded and in effect conducting the action. Insurance companies always employ one or two firms of solicitors in any given area, who handle all their personal injury litigation and whom they know to be competent and experienced in this field.

Assuming that for the moment no apparent question of your client's own liability in the accident arises, you need to consider certain technical matters to do with motor insurance. These are as follows:

4.1.5.1 'Road Traffic Act insurance'

Road Traffic Act insurance is the most basic insurance that can be obtained in respect of a motor vehicle. Such policies are actually quite rare and are often issued only (at correspondingly high premiums) to those drivers who are a very bad risk, e.g. drivers with recent drink driving convictions, so that no insurance company will sell them more extensive cover. Such a policy implies that the person insured is covered *only* in respect of those risks for which insurance is compulsory under *ss. 143* and *145* of the *Road Traffic Act 1988*. Under these sections it is an offence to use or permit the use of a vehicle on the road unless the driver is insured in respect of legal liability for the following three matters, namely:

(a) Personal injury or death to any other person.

(b) The cost of emergency hospital treatment.

(c) Damage to property (other than the insured vehicle itself and goods in it carried for hire or reward) up to a value of £250,000 in each claim.

Consequently, where the defendant has this kind of insurance a plaintiff will be covered for damages for personal injuries and loss of earnings, and for damage to his own property caused in the accident, e.g. to his motor car and its contents.

4.1.5.2 'Third party fire and theft'

This is a wider type of liability than the last. The person who has this kind of insurance cover will not only be covered for personal injury and damage to some other person's property, but, in addition, will be protected against theft of or fire damage to *his own* vehicle, so that if the vehicle is stolen and never recovered he will be paid the market value.

4.1.5.3 'Comprehensive insurance'

Under this type of cover an insured driver will be indemnified in respect of personal injury damage or property damage to any other person, and in addition will be covered in respect of damage to or loss of his own vehicle. This is so whether or not he was himself to blame for any incident in which his vehicle was damaged or destroyed. The premiums for this sort of cover are naturally considerably higher than for 'third party fire and theft' liability.

It must be clearly understood that the nature of the liability insured against is the negligence of the driver. Accordingly, the passengers in the vehicle of someone comprehensively insured who is to blame for an accident will, of course, be covered but he himself will not be. Therefore, a comprehensively insured motorist who is to blame for an accident and suffers personal injuries will have no claim against any insurance policy (unless he has a quite separate personal accident insurance policy) in respect of those personal injuries.

4.1.5.4 Subrogation

An insurance company which has paid a claim by the person insured (e.g. someone comprehensively insured who has had his vehicle damage paid for by his own insurance company) may exercise its rights of subrogation by using the insured person's name to bring proceedings against anyone else involved who is alleged to be negligent in the action. This right will be expressly reserved in the insurance policy.

4.1.5.5 'No claims bonus'

A no claims bonus is a discretionary bonus awarded by way of a discount on future premiums for years in which no claim has been brought under a policy of motor insurance. The bonus increases year by year, usually up to a maximum of about 65 per cent. After several years, therefore, this may be a very substantial benefit, typically reducing the annual premium for a policy from, say, £500 to £200. If any claim at all is brought against the policy the bonus is lost, even though the insured motorist was not himself to blame for the incident (for example, if his car was rammed by a hit and run driver who left the scene of the incident before he could be identified). It is possible to take out, for an additional premium, a type of policy where the no claims bonus is 'protected' so that the bonus is retained provided there is no more than, say, one claim within any two-year period.

4.1.5.6 'Excess' in comprehensive insurance

This involves the motorist agreeing to bear a so-called 'excess', i.e. the first part of any claim. This may be a small figure, such as £25 or £50, and will avoid the insurance company having to be bothered with very trivial claims, e.g. for scratches to paint work, loss of a wing mirror, etc. It may be that the insured can obtain a reduction on premium if he is willing to have an excess of a rather larger figure, e.g. £250. In many cases he would be well advised to agree to this, especially if his no claims bonus is anyway worth more to him than £250 a year. In that event he would not trouble the insurance company at all with a claim for minor accident damage up to this figure and his no claims bonus would be preserved. Should a claim be made involving a higher figure than this he would bear the first £250 of it which is the nature of the 'excess'.

4.1.5.7 'Knock for knock' agreement

If two vehicles which are both comprehensively insured are damaged in an accident, the insurance companies involved may well decide to each settle their own insured motorist's claim. They will do this if they have a pre-existing 'knock for knock', agreement as insurance companies often have. It saves them a good deal of time and trouble, and possibly litigation costs, in establishing the exact cause of an accident. Motor insurance companies doubtless consider that the matter is rather one of 'swings and roundabouts' i.e. that taking into account the saving on investigation and litigation costs over any given year they will lose nothing by the arrangement and may well gain.

The problem for a motorist who finds himself involved in this arrangement is that liability may seem perfectly clear. He would normally have expected his insurance company to have attempted to negotiate full settlement of his claim by the other insurance company but may now find matters settled to his disadvantage because he will immediately lose the amount of his excess and indeed his no claims bonus. In such a situation it will usually be worthwhile for the motorist who considers he was the innocent party in the incident to bring an action against the other motorist for his uninsured losses, i.e. the loss of his no claims bonus and excess. Since it is actually somewhat difficult to establish the amount of a no claims bonus, which may be cumulative over some years, it is probably better in such a case if the client takes legal advice in time, to advise him not to claim on his own insurance policy but to try and pay for the accident damage himself and meanwhile to bring proceedings against the other driver for the whole amount involved. Alternatively, if his own insurers have already paid, there is no reason why he should still not sue for the whole amount involved provided that if he is successful he then reimburses his own insurers with the amount which they have already paid him in settlement of the claim. They will then reinstate his no claims bonus. A knock for knock agreement between insurers naturally does not bind the insured person himself not to proceed in the way previously described.

Recently, knock for knock agreements have lost their popularity with some major motor insurers and such agreements are now rather fewer in number.

So far we have been concerned with a client's own insurance policy. It is now vital to consider problems to do with the opponent's insurance, or lack of it.

4.1.6 THE OPPONENT'S MOTOR INSURANCE POLICY

If a plaintiff obtains judgment against a defendant for personal injuries and consequential loss, the plaintiff may enforce that part of the judgment against the defendant's insurers even though the insurers themselves may have been entitled to avoid or cancel the defendant's policy, or indeed may already have done so. This is by virtue of *ss. 151* and *152* of the *Road Traffic Act 1988.*

It will be remembered that insurance contracts are contracts *uberrimae fidei,* i.e. of utmost good faith. A vital ingredient of this is that a person taking out an insurance policy must disclose all material matters to the insurer. Suppose that a person obtained a policy of motor insurance without disclosing to the insurers that he had previous accident claims against him, or driving convictions. Under the basic law of insurance the insurers, if they discover these matters, would be entitled to repudiate the policy and thus not to pay any claims on it. The effect of *ss. 151* and *152* of the *Road Traffic Act 1988* will generally be to stop the insurers repudiating, at least to the extent that they are obliged to compensate some other party for compulsorily insurable damages, i.e. the damages which must be insured under *ss. 143* and *145* of the Act (see **4.1.5.1**).

A plaintiff can use *s. 152* to ensure this payment if *before or within seven days* after the *commencement of proceedings* (i.e. the issue of the writ) he gave written notice of his intention to commence proceedings to the insurers. It is therefore important to remember in every case to give a potential defendant's insurers notice of intention to commence proceedings. In fact this can be done with the original letter before action provided the letter uses the words 'intend to commence proceedings'. That would apparently suffice to comply with *s. 152* and there is no need then for proceedings to be issued immediately or within any particular period. Ideally, the *s. 152* letter should be written as soon as the insurance details have been obtained from the police after an accident. You are then covered and can safely forget the matter. There is no need to refer to *s. 152* in the letter and no particular form of letter is prescribed. It should be borne in mind that if, having commenced proceedings, the need to add further defendants becomes apparent, it is prudent to write a *s. 152* letter in respect of each of them before the writ is amended to add the new defendants.

4.1.7 THE MOTOR INSURERS BUREAU

The Motor Insurers Bureau (MIB) is a body set up and financed by motor insurance companies. There are two distinct agreements made between the MIB and the former Ministry of Transport (now the Department of the Environment).

4.1.7.1 Uninsured drivers

Where it is apparent that a driver is uninsured, i.e. that there is no policy at all in force in relation to the motor vehicle in question (as compared to the position described in relation to *s. 152* of the *Road Traffic Act 1988* where there is such a policy but the insurance company had the right to repudiate it), then one might expect a plaintiff to be without a remedy, i.e., that whilst he could sue the uninsured motorist he might have considerable difficulty in enforcing any judgment obtained. The effect of the MIB agreement is to mitigate this problem.

Where a potential opponent is found to be uninsured, this should be brought to the attention of the MIB. They will then appoint a local insurance company to act as their agent for the purpose of negotiating the claim. Of course it must be proved that the uninsured driver was negligent. The mere fact that he was uninsured is not in itself grounds for bringing a claim. The insurance company appointed to negotiate on behalf of the MIB will have the power to settle matters without a writ being issued. However, if liability and compensation cannot be agreed, then a writ must be issued against the uninsured driver. In a MIB case notice of bringing proceedings must be given to the MIB within seven days following the commencement of proceedings, accompanied by a copy of the writ or summons. This notice and copy writ can be sent by fax.

The Motor Insurers Bureau is at 152 Silbury Boulevard, Central Milton Keynes MK9 1MB. Fax No: 01908 671660.

The MIB has the power to waive non-compliance with this requirement or late compliance, but one should not rely on such indulgence. The action then proceeds normally, except that the MIB has the right to be added as a party. More probably it will merely treat itself as if it was the insurance company of the uninsured driver and arrange for representation on his behalf. Naturally it can take any defences open to the uninsured person, or, e.g. make allegations of contributory negligence just as in the case of any other defendant. When judgment is obtained, if it remains unpaid by the defendant for seven days (as it presumably will be) the MIB will pay it and will also pay the normal taxed costs. The judgment must then be assigned to the MIB so that it is subrogated to the rights of the plaintiff and may attempt to recoup money it has paid out from the uninsured motorist. In fact it is rarely worth its while attempting to do this. In the nature of things, a person who did not have the means or inclination to insure his vehicle is unlikely to have substantial assets. It must be noted that the agreement applies only to those claims in respect of which insurance was compulsory under *ss. 143* and *145* of the *1988 Act* (see **4.1.5.1**).

4.1.7.2 Untraced drivers

A separate agreement applies in the case of untraced drivers (i.e. hit and run drivers). However, the agreement only applies in the case of personal injury and death claims. Here, of course, a writ cannot be issued at all against an unknown defendant. Accordingly there is no need to make application to the court at all, but the MIB must be notified within the usual limitation period, i.e. three years of the accident, by letter. It will then arrange for the case to be investigated and must be satisfied that the untraced driver was negligent and that the death or injury was not caused deliberately by him (i.e. that he did not use the motor vehicle as a weapon. If he did then any claim should be directed to the Criminal Injuries Compensation Board which compensates the victims of crimes of violence). The MIB then make an award on a voluntary basis, assessed in the same way as that in which a court would have assessed damages at common law, i.e. will include the usual items of pain, suffering, loss of amenity, loss of future earnings. However, damage to property is not recoverable, and thus a plaintiff cannot recover from the MIB if a hit and run driver collides with his parked car and makes off.

If the amount of the award is not agreed or the refusal to make any award is not accepted, there is an appeals procedure by way of arbitration by one of a panel of Queen's Counsel. There is also an accelerated procedure in the case of claims up to a total of £20,000 which allows the parties to settle the application without a full investigation. In this case there is no right of appeal.

Lastly, it should be noted that in the case of untraced drivers the MIB is under no obligation to pay legal costs. In fact the MIB pay a standard fee together with certain acceptable disbursements, in particular the cost of a police accident report and medical reports.

4.2 Contract and Commercial Cases

4.2.1 COLLECTING AND ASSESSING DOCUMENTATION

Naturally pre-action considerations in commercial cases are determined by the type of dispute, the nature of the parties and the things in dispute. It may sometimes be that such disputes depend just as much on factual evidence and even eye-witness accounts as a personal injury case, in which instance it would be important to collect evidence as previously described (see **4.1.2**).

The most common type of contract or commercial case is a straightforward debt-collecting action. In such a case it is important to ensure that all relevant documentation has been obtained from the client. Thus the written contract or terms of trade, if any, should be obtained and perused. It may sometimes be the case, for example, that a client's version of what his contractual terms are is not borne out by inspection of the documents themselves; a client's terms of trade may not have been updated for many years. This may be the time to persuade the client to let you redraft the documents or do other commercially based work for him. This kind of approach is somewhat pompously called 'client education' by the Law Society, but the opportunities it gives for marketing one's practice should not be overlooked. For example, a recent survey showed that fewer than half of all small and medium-sized businesses had written terms of trade requiring interest in the event of late payment of invoices. Indeed an astonishingly high proportion, over a third, were said to have no written terms of trade at all.

Even where there is a term of trade apparently importing interest in the event of late payment, you may be disappointed to find that the client has for some reason incorporated this into the form of invoice itself rather than the order form. In this instance, of course, as a simple matter of contract law, the term for interest will be of no effect since an invoice does not form part of the documents which create the contract.

4.2.2 ACTING FOR A PURCHASER

Naturally you may also be called upon to advise on the import of such documents from the opposing party's point of view, where a disgruntled purchaser may be sued for the price of the goods.

If instructed by the purchaser the action may be for a total refund of the purchase price, or for a refund of part of a price already paid to compensate for deficiencies for the goods supplied. It may well be that there are additional claims for damages for inconvenience, disappointment, distress, repairs, hire of replacements, and even for personal injuries caused by some defective article. In this kind of personal injury case it is by no means certain that an insurance company will be involved, thus, for example, where a defective appliance (say an electrical item) has been purchased from a small shop and the item has caused injuries, you may need to look further afield than the shop keeper to the protection afforded under the *Consumer Protection Act 1987* against the manufacturer or importer. In contract and commercial cases regard must always be had to ensuring that all proper defendants are brought into the action, especially with a view to seeing that the potential defendant has the ability to pay the damages and/or debt.

4.2.3 ENFORCEMENT OF JUDGMENT

The topic of enforcement of judgment is dealt with in detail in **Chapter 23**. It must always be borne in mind that there are only limited means of enforcing judgments. Thus a plaintiff who has obtained judgment in a debt case is often disgruntled to find that where the defendant fails to pay he can often do this with impunity and that there is, for example, no realistic possibility whatsoever of getting a person committed to prison for non-payment of a civil debt. It is vital to advise a client early on, therefore, that good money should not be thrown after bad in pursuing expensive litigation against someone who does not have the ability to pay a judgment when obtained. Money spent at an early stage on obtaining an enquiry agent's report into the financial status of a potential defendant, both in a debt case and in other forms of commercial disputes, may well be worthwhile. An essential part of protecting one's own position is thereafter to confirm in writing advice given to the client that there may be difficulties in enforcing judgment.

4.2.4 TIMESCALE

One feature of commercial contract disputes which is perhaps different from personal injury cases is the speed at which they proceed. If the client is intending to sue for a substantial debt he will want to progress as rapidly as possible. In personal injury cases there are likely to be all manner of necessary delays, in particular in the obtaining of medical evidence, waiting for the plaintiff's condition to stabilise, conducting negotiations, etc. Some kinds of commercial cases may need to be pursued at key stages with even more swiftness than a client requires in a debt collecting case, however. For example, we have considered above in the context of remedies the nature of interlocutory injunctions (see **1.7.4**). If a client consults a solicitor in connection with an urgent, business-related situation, the solicitor will have to ensure that he acts both swiftly and expertly because a procedural or evidential mistake made in this kind of litigation can have fatal consequences to the client's business position.

4.2.5 EVIDENCE AND INTERLOCUTORY INJUNCTIONS

When one needs to apply for an interlocutory injunction the basic position is that comprehensive evidence will have to be put forward on affidavit about the merits of a client's claim. The basic test to be satisfied is the *American Cyanamid* test referred to at **1.7.4.1** above. In order to ensure that all the various elements of this test are satisfied, the client and, if it is a business organisation, possibly several of the client's managerial personnel involved in the matter, will need to swear affidavits which are often very lengthy, setting out the background to the case, the present position and justifying the harm that is likely to be caused unless an injunction is granted. It may be that lines of enquiry will have to be pursued very urgently and commercial inquiry agents instructed to investigate such matters as, for example, attempts by former employees to poach contacts and customers, the misuse of trade secrets and the like. Statements will have to be obtained and rapidly put into the form of affidavits (see **7.7.2.2**). Counsel may need to be involved urgently at this stage, both in terms of ensuring his availability for a very early hearing and to see that he approves the contents of the affidavits. Conferences with counsel may need to be called involving the client, and it may be that whole days have to be set aside for this and all other work postponed.

It may be a vital matter also to ensure judge availability for an early application. In principle, an application for an interlocutory injunction should be made immediately after a writ has been issued and served, by summons to a High Court Judge in chambers in the Queen's Bench Division or by motion to a Chancery Judge in open court. However, applications may be made much more urgently than this, e.g. for an application for an injunction to be made even before a writ has been issued. In extreme cases it is possible to apply orally for an injunction without any documentation, and even to see a judge out of court hours for this purpose. Such applications are relatively rare save in specialised commercial work, however. Where injunctions are obtained by informal means they are usually limited in time (e.g. to last for only seven days) and thereafter the plaintiff must make a formal application for the injunction to be renewed with full documentation and on proper notice before it lapses.

4.2.6 EXPERTS' REPORTS

It may be that the nature of the action involves experts' reports just as much as a personal injury case might do. It may be, for example, that a consultant engineer is called upon to advise that a piece of machinery sold is inadequate for its purpose or has certain malfunctions which led to other undesirable consequences. Accountants may need to be employed, in particular to justify loss of profits or loss of earnings claims.

4.3 The Letter before Action

4.3.1 IN CONTRACT AND COMMERCIAL CASES

Having obtained sufficient information from a client, it is normal to start matters moving by writing a letter before action. In a debt case this is perfectly straightforward and will constitute a terse demand for the payment in full of the debt within a relatively brief period, on the basis that invoices and reminders from the client have presumably been ignored for some time. Such a letter should always insist that the amount is paid in full to the solicitor direct and specify a date upon which a writ will be issued if payment is not received. It is vital, to ensure credibility with the potential defendant, that if payment is not made proceedings are indeed issued on the day in question and that this is in no sense a bluff.

If the litigation is of some other kind, e.g. on behalf of a disgruntled purchaser seeking compensation in respect of a defective item, then no doubt some greater length of explanation is necessary in the letter detailing the defects complained of and making a demand for what it is that the client wants, e.g. return of the purchase price in full in exchange for the goods, or the cost of repairs necessary to make the goods of merchantable quality.

4.3.2 PERSONAL INJURY CASES

Styles of writing a letter before action in personal injury cases differ greatly. Some favour giving exhaustive details of the client's allegations about how the incident occurred, on the suggested basis that this letter may at some stage be put before the judge and it is as well to demonstrate consistency. Another advantage is that by making allegations in this form at least the defendants know precisely what it is that they should be investigating, especially with regard to a complex case such as injury occasioned by some industrial process. Others, however, favour writing as brief a letter as possible, giving no factual detail but merely stating that the plaintiff holds the defendant liable for the action and seeks compensation. The difficulty of this is that it inevitably attracts a request that the plaintiff's allegations be spelt out in full, so that they can be investigated properly.

It is suggested that generally a brief letter is the better choice. It can be written at a much earlier stage than one would dare to commit to paper what purports to be a full account of an incident. This is because it may take weeks or months to collect all necessary evidence on liability and then to discuss the evidence with the client to ensure that there are no apparent implausibilities, inconsistencies or hostages to fortune in the account given. If in general terms a piece of bad driving or an unsafe system of work is being alleged, then at least the ball can be set rolling for negotiation purposes and progressing the action generally, leaving it perhaps to verbal negotiations in which a client's account can be given on a without prejudice basis until pleadings are prepared and served.

In personal injury cases it is as well to write direct to the defendant, but if the identity of the insurance company is known and a satisfactory reference number is available, so that the insurance company can trace the policy and/or client, there is no reason not to write direct to the insurance company. This will then be sufficient to satisfy *ss. 151* and *152* of the *Road Traffic Act 1988* (see **4.1.6**). Letters should not in general solicit a reply direct from the potential defendant. Any reply, especially one admitting liability, may well compromise the validity of his insurance policy. The letter before action in personal injury cases should indicate that proceedings will be issued in due course concerning the incident and in some format invite the opening of negotiations. It may be possible, even in the most serious kind of case, to establish early on that liability is not in dispute thus saving a great deal of work in the collection and presentation of evidence relevant to liability. The letter before action should be an open letter and not one written 'without prejudice' (see below at **10.2.1.2**).

4.4 The Use of Counsel in Litigation

4.4.1 BARRISTERS

Until 1994 barristers enjoyed a monopoly of rights of audience in open court in the High Court and above. With effect from 1994, however, solicitors who have sufficient experience of advocacy in the tribunals in which solicitors have hitherto been able to appear may apply for a qualification entitling them to appear as advocates in the higher courts. For those with substantial judicial experience (e.g., as recorders or assistant recorders) or those who actually have advocacy experience before higher courts (e.g., in the case of some solicitors who formerly were barristers) the qualifications may be granted on their experience hitherto. For those not in this category there is a qualification procedure, involving passing demanding examinations on evidence and procedure and attendance at an approved advocacy training course. Despite this, for the foreseeable future, such solicitor advocates will be few in number and most firms of solicitors will be obliged to employ members of the Bar to conduct trials.

Because of the sums of money involved and because counsel are specialists in trial advocacy, whereas solicitors usually have more general practices, it is common to use counsel who will appear at trial to assist throughout the case. It is a somewhat overworked analogy but a reasonably accurate one to say that counsel's position *vis-à-vis* the solicitor corresponds approximately to that in medicine of a consultant and a general practitioner. The specific advantages are that counsel is usually free to concentrate his own mind on one case until he has completed the task associated with it. Solicitors, however, may well be running some hundreds of files at any one time, and in any given working day may have to apply their minds to some aspect of work in relation to 20, 30 or more of such files. Counsel may have many sets of instructions sitting on his shelves but he does not have to keep them continuously under review in the way that a solicitor does.

In essence counsel receives a set of instructions from a solicitor requesting him to do a certain task, some examples of which are described below. He then completes that task having done any necessary legal research, something which solicitors rarely have the time to do given their work load, and then returns the whole set of instructions together with his own completed work on the matter to the solicitor. He does not keep any running file on a case, nor indeed usually any copy of the piece of work he has himself done on the case. He does not follow it up or have direct contact with the client or witnesses, and it may be that the matter is settled and he never sees that set of instructions or that client's case again. On the other hand, the papers may be sent back to him for further work to be done on the case at intervals often several months apart. Thus counsel does not have the same kind of continuity of involvement as a solicitor does, which allows him to concentrate his mind on each task in hand and to retain a more objective and detached view of the legal problems affecting a client whom, unless the case is one of the small minority which comes to court or where there is a conference with the client, he may never see.

4.4.2 SOLICITORS

Solicitors do of course have rights of audience in all the lower courts including the county court (whose financial jurisdiction in tort and contract cases is now unlimited in amount) and in other courts where important civil matters are dealt with, in particular the industrial tribunal. Nonetheless, because of counsel's specialist expertise, in that he is engaged day to day in advocacy, it is usual to brief counsel in many of the courts where a solicitor does have right of audience. It is also, paradoxically, often cheaper for the client to have a specialist counsel represent him because a barrister's fees for a day in court may well be less than those of a solicitor would have been, because a solicitor has to charge in the main by the hour. When a barrister is briefed, in many cases there is no need for anyone from the solicitor's firm to accompany him. In other cases it is possible simply to send some junior member of the office staff to sit in with him in court. In more complex matters it may, of course, be necessary for a senior representative, or even several representatives of the solicitor's firm, to accompany counsel.

4.4.3 THE PARTICULAR USES OF COUNSEL

4.4.3.1 To give advice in writing

Both before and after proceedings are issued counsel may be asked to give advice in writing about such matters as *liability* (e.g. does he think the facts disclose a cause of action and does he think that the defendant is liable); *quantum of damages* (e.g. does he think on the facts that the offer put forward by the defendant is a reasonable one and should be accepted); *practical steps* (i.e. how does he think evidence should be collected and presented to maximise a claim in a large case); *procedural tactics* (e.g. does he think that an application for pre-action discovery or summary judgment would be likely to succeed on the basis of the facts as known); *evidence* (e.g. what witnesses need to be called to prove which part of a plaintiff's case and what documentary evidence needs to be brought to court and what procedural action needs to be taken).

To obtain counsel's advice on these kinds of matter one simply drafts a set of instructions to him. These are characteristically typed on 'brief paper' and folded in four to provide a brief in the bundle form, bound by pink ribbon, which is familiar. Within the brief are enclosed all material documents of any relevance, e.g. witness statements, police accident reports, computation of damages, etc. Then in the text of the brief a solicitor sets out his commentary on the matters involved. Increasingly, however, this rather archaic form of instructions is being abandoned in favour of including them in a much more user-friendly ring binder file where counsel will first receive at the front of the file the solicitor' s instructions, and thereafter the accompanying documents can be neatly and coherently supplied in an appropriate order separated by dividers. Subsequent sets of instructions in the same matter can then be added at the front. Papers in this format are much easier for counsel to work on without needing to manage unwieldy sets of documentation.

Many instructions to counsel are astonishingly brief. Often instructions say something like, 'Here are the instructions and counsel will see the nature of the problem'. Some, indeed, consider that instructions even in this form are unacceptably prolix. Instructions should, however, be thorough and professional. The first time he gets a set of instructions in relation to a case counsel will know nothing about the history of the matter, and he should be taken in narrative form through the background; there should be a commentary on each of the documents supplied; and if possible, the solicitor should summarise his own view of the law involved and give his own provisional views on the question on which he is seeking counsel's advice. The solicitor should then pose the questions on which counsel's advice is sought.

These papers are then delivered to counsel's chambers and in due course counsel will supply written advice in which he sets out his views on the questions put. Instructions should be full and self-contained in every case. Even if counsel has dealt with some aspect of the case before, it must be borne in mind that this may have been at intervals of many months and that in the interim counsel may have been involved in many scores of other similar cases, so his memory will need to be refreshed about this one.

4.4.3.2 To advise in conference

Sometimes the questions to be considered are so complex, or the position in the case at present so nebulous, that it is more satisfactory to have a so-called 'conference' with counsel in his chambers. 'Conference' is a somewhat grandiose term for an informal discussion about the case, but it is particularly useful in the early stages of complex or very large cases so that counsel may indicate to the solicitor what lines of approach he may recommend. Counsel's advice may indeed become as specific as recommending named expert witnesses, or the way in which an approach to a large loss of earnings claim should be formulated.

Instructions as previously described should still usually be drafted and sent to counsel, if possible well in advance of the conference so that he can do some preliminary research on the case and give it his mature consideration. Such conferences are often in the late afternoon after counsel has finished court for the day. It is not uncommon, especially in the later stages of litigation which it seems will go to trial, for the client to attend this conference. This is likely to be the first occasion on which a barrister, even if he has advised many times about a case as it went on, will have seen the client face to face. It is designed to give the client confidence in the barrister of the solicitor's choice. Conversely, however, it tends to increase the client's disappointment if the named barrister is unavailable for the trial itself, a problem with which all solicitors have to contend. In such a case, if the client had never seen his barrister it would presumably make little difference to him which barrister appeared at the trial. At such conferences counsel will often take the client through his version of events, sometimes in a fairly testing manner in order to see how he performs as a witness. This may well affect the ultimate advice that counsel gives. For example, if under searching questioning clear implausibilities or inconsistencies come out, or even if the client unfortunately has a shifty and evasive manner, the barrister may form the view that as he will make a poor witness some offer of compromise which has been put forward ought to be accepted.

Until 1995 the rules of etiquette of the Bar forbade barristers to meet witnesses of fact other than their clients before the trial, but they may now do so if necessary. They may, also, see expert witnesses in conference, and if there are difficult points of expert evidence it is increasingly common for there to be a round table meeting with the experts, the barrister and the solicitor to attempt to progress matters further. The object of this meeting is so that the expert witnesses are able to give the barrister all the necessary ammunition with which to cross-examine the opposing expert and to explain differences of opinion between themselves and the opposing expert. In substantial cases it is now not uncommon for conferences to take the form of negotiation meetings with the other side with both parties' solicitors, barristers and even experts present.

4.4.3.3 To draft pleadings

Counsel may be employed as a specialist draftsman in a number of fields. In non-contentious work counsel may draft, for example, trust deeds, partnership agreements or wills. In litigation counsel is generally used for drafting pleadings. Pleadings are a specialist art form, and whilst a solicitor may well draft simple endorsements on writs, usually drafting more complex pleadings such as statements of claim or defences in personal injury or commercial actions will be left to counsel. It may, of course, be that a solicitor does such a specialised form of work (e.g. deals only with factory accidents for trade union members who work in a particular type of factory) that he becomes very expert in the field and has an ample collection of precedents from previous cases. In such a case the solicitor may well feel able to draft the pleading himself. Nonetheless, this aspect demonstrates a useful background role for counsel which is that of longstop for professional negligence. Whilst the case law shows that in fact a solicitor is meant to bring his own independent scrutiny to every aspect of every case, and will still be negligent if relying on counsel's advice or drafting which was manifestly in error, it can be a useful backup if professional negligence is ever alleged for a solicitor to show that he instructed experienced counsel and reasonably relied on what counsel drafted or advised.

In instructing counsel to draft pleadings, it is particularly vital to send counsel all necessary papers and give him a full narrative of the matter. It is the drafting of pleadings which inevitably leads to delay in litigation. Although drafting a fairly straightforward pleading ought to take a barrister not much more than an hour, and often a lot less if he in his turn has ample precedents on which to draw, excessive work loads and typing difficulties in barristers' chambers may mean that the pleading and accompanying instructions are not returned within weeks, or even months, although the story of the solicitor who sent his set of instructions a birthday card to celebrate their being with the barrister for a year is doubtless apocryphal! One should ensure by means of a continuing relationship with the counsel of one's choice and his clerk that sets of instructions requiring the drafting of pleadings are returned promptly. It is the delay in getting pleadings returned that is likely to lead to a request for an extension of time in particular.

4.4.3.4 As advocate

(a) *In open court*

Subject to the exception indicated above, counsel has exclusive rights of audience in contested matters in High Court, Court of Appeal and House of Lords. It is usually considered preferable to brief counsel in the county court as well for the reasons previously outlined. We shall return to the question of the contents and preparation of a brief at a later stage (see **14.7.4.2**).

(b) *In interlocutory applications*

A solicitor has a right of audience in all interlocutory applications before a District Judge, or a Circuit Judge or a High Court Judge in chambers. A competent solicitor will usually appear in such applications even on matters of some substance, such as summary judgment or interim payment applications. The solicitor will have the whole file at his fingertips and will be experienced in such applications. There is hardly ever cross-examination of witnesses in such matters, as proceedings are on affidavit evidence alone, and the solicitor will be perfectly competent to deal with the law, practice and facts. If a solicitor is less experienced, or perhaps due to pressure of work unavailable for such hearings, it may be appropriate to brief counsel to attend on important interlocutory matters. It would not be normal to brief counsel on purely routine or procedural matters such as a summons for directions. The costs of counsel at an interlocutory application can be claimed if one is successful in the litigation, provided that the District Judge or Master has certified that the application was 'fit for counsel', i.e. of sufficient apparent complexity or substance that the employment of counsel is reasonable, and in such case the fees will be allowed and payable by the losing party.

4.4.4 COUNSEL'S CLERK AND THE ORGANISATION OF CHAMBERS

4.4.4.1 The organisation of chambers

The Bar is divided into two kinds of barrister – Queen's Counsel and junior counsel. Queen's Counsel comprise about 10 per cent of the practising Bar. They are practitioners of considerable seniority and eminence who in the main are used only in the most serious criminal trials and the most weighty civil litigation. Their fees are correspondingly higher. Queen's Counsel do not usually draft pleadings and their whole work is giving advice, in writing or orally (a conference with a Queen's Counsel is called a 'consultation'), and appearing as advocates. When appearing as advocates Queen's Counsel are often accompanied by junior counsel to assist them, although the rule which formerly required this in every case has been abrogated.

The remaining 90 per cent of barristers are known as the Junior Bar. Most junior barristers never become Queen's Counsel and remain junior barristers until they retire. They may undertake any work whatsoever, and a great deal of their time in civil cases is often given over to the drafting of pleadings.

Barristers are self-employed and may not practise in partnership. Nonetheless, they organise themselves into groups called 'sets of chambers' for the purpose of providing office accommodation economically and sharing of common facilities such as secretarial staff, telephones, fax machines and the like. In addition, each set of chambers will employ one or more clerks. Although they may not practise in partnership, and to some extent each member of a set of chambers is a business rival of his colleagues, most sets of chambers do develop a group ethos and a good deal of 'team spirit' and members will go to great lengths to assist each other with informal advice about difficult cases, which are sometimes discussed collectively, and senior members of chambers will go to great lengths to promote the careers of more junior members. Some chambers also develop considerable rivalries with other chambers.

4.4.4.2 The barristers' clerk

A barrister's clerk's relationship with his barristers is somewhat like that of a theatrical agent and his actor clients. That is, it is his function to keep his barristers fully employed, to negotiate fees for the work which they do, to ensure that they do not have two important cases coming up in different courts on the same day, and so on.

Barristers' clerks often feature high in the demonology of both solicitors and barristers. A great deal of socio-legal research has failed to discover much about the origins of barristers' clerks. Some contend that they spring, fully grown, and ready clad in Armani suits and Vidal Sasoon hairstyles, from dragons' teeth. The following propositions, however, are widely accepted:

(a) All barristers' clerks, in whatever part of the country they work, come from South London.

(b) Almost all barristers' clerks are called Trevor, Kevin, Graham or Bill.

(c) The entire English legal system is organised for the benefit of barristers' clerks.

Barristers' clerks often do not have any legal qualifications but come from some outside sphere of activity. Although barristers will claim that they 'employ' their clerks, in fact they 'employ' the clerk in much the same way in which a human being 'employs' his or her cat. That is to say that the contract takes the form of the human being offering to provide shelter, food, medical assistance, love and affection and in return the cat undertakes to do precisely what it wishes.

Barristers' clerks until recently were invariably remunerated by way of a percentage of the fee of each barrister in their chambers for each piece of work done, whether drafting pleadings, advising or advocacy. Typically this proportion was 10 per cent of the net fee, and thus it is easy to see that if a barristers' clerk was running a chambers of say some 25 barristers, his income being 10 per cent of each barrister's total fees was likely to exceed the income of all save the most successful, and possibly to exceed even his. Barristers' clerks exercise an inordinate power in chambers because although solicitors usually direct their work to a named barrister, in case of unavailability of that barrister the clerk is the ultimate distributor of such work (called 'returns'). The clerk thus has a considerable power to make or break a barrister's career, particularly in the early years where few barristers will receive work directed to them personally and will be reliant on work which senior members of chambers are unable to accommodate.

Where barristers' clerks come from or what they did before remain mysteries, but it is the writer's theory that they were usually engaged in some form of selling activity. Thus getting a job in chambers as a clerk is rather like becoming the Dalai Lama. Just as one day a simple peasant boy would be herding his yaks around the foothills of Tibet and the next day would be announced as the living God, so one day Trevor would be knocking out slightly imperfect kitchenware from a stall in Woolwich market and the next day he would become a barristers' clerk and be able to instruct some Queen's Counsel who earns £500,000 a year that he has to cancel his summer holidays because he, Trevor, is insistent that the Queen's Counsel should appear in Carlisle Crown Court for three weeks. This is some measure of the power of the barristers' clerk.

In trying to ensure that all the members of their chambers are as fully occupied as they can be, and thus maximising their own fee income, barristers' clerks will shamelessly manipulate the court lists to ensure that their most popular performers do not have competing engagements on the same day. It is in this sense that, whatever the requirements of justice, the solicitors or the litigants, the English legal system is run for the benefit of the barristers' clerks, who in the main determine in what order cases will come forward, whatever the requirements of the other more humble actors in the drama. If the clerk is unable to ensure that a given barrister does not have competing engagements he will re-allocate the work to some unoccupied junior member of chambers in the way previously described. In such a case, where a chosen barrister is unavailable for a trial, the solicitor is perfectly entitled to take the brief back and instruct a barrister from another chambers. In most cases, however, the solicitor prefers the matter to remain with another barrister from the same chambers, in the belief that the barrister originally instructed, who may well have done a good deal of preparatory work on the brief, will be more cooperative in coaching the late substitute in the problems involved than he would be for a member of another chambers. Remarkably, solicitors may often have a touching faith in the ability of a barristers' clerk to nominate an alleged expert in his chambers in the field of law in question. In describing the knowledge and talents of their 'stable', barristers' clerks develop an astonishing facility for hyperbole. **Table 4.1** sets out some examples of this, the left hand column giving the utterances of the barristers' clerk and the right hand column the true meaning.

Why do barristers employ clerks on this basis? No one really knows the answer. Barristers are often involved in giving hard-headed and highly complex business and financial advice to clients, but when it comes to organising their own diaries and work they seem to have a fit of the vapours like a maiden in a Victorian melodrama. Presumably they need to feel some security in the background and to be organised and ordered about in a way which they may not have experienced since nanny was tucking them up in bed and wiping the remnants of their little eggy soldiers out of their ears, and this is the function performed by their clerks, whom the Benson Report famously described as 'combining the functions of office administrator, accountant, business manager, agent, adviser and friend'.

Some chambers have in the recent past got away from the principle of remunerating their clerk on a commission basis. Increasingly, fixed salaries, possibly with a much more modest commission element as a bonus, are being employed. In addition, the more go-ahead chambers are employing so-called 'Practice Managers' who will often have formal accountancy or management qualifications and will be able to deal with the increasing complexity of a

Example 1	
'Yes of course Mr White is our expert on employment law. He is in the library at the moment researching the background to those papers which you sent in.'	Mr White is presently in the library desperately trying to find out whether the industrial tribunal sits with a jury and whether the Industrial Relations Act 1971 has been repealed.
Example 2	
'Yes Mr Brown is rapidly becoming our chambers' paperwork specialist.'	No one in their right mind would dream of letting Mr Brown appear in court.
Example 3	
'Mr Gray is very good on his feet and could probably squeeze it in.'	Mr Gray does not do any paper work because he cannot write English and has had no briefs for three months.
Example 4	
'Mr Black had a remarkably good result in an armed robbery case in the Old Bailey last week.'	Mr Black was involved in a dubious careless driving case in Rochdale magistrates' court last week.
Example 5	
'I am sorry I said that Mr Green was available – I was looking at the wrong page in his diary.'	Why didn't you say it was Legal Aid!
Example 6	
'Yes Miss Blue is very much our family law specialist.'	Miss Blue hates family law and wants to do intellectual property and patents but I know a sexual stereotype when I see one and she will do what she is given.
Example 7	
Same as example 6 substituting 'Mr Patel' and 'immigration.'	As above, substituting 'immigration' for 'family', 'racial' for 'sexual' and 'he' for 'she'.

Table 4.1 The secret language of barristers' clerks

barrister's life, involving, as it commonly does now, information technology systems, computerised accounts and so on. Such practice managers may often have marketing functions as well as purely administrative ones; for example, part of their job will be to keep the profile of the members of chambers high with solicitors and to explore new areas of legal work in which members of chambers can become specialists.

4.5 Negotiations

4.5.1 INTRODUCTION

The purpose of negotiations is to set in motion a process which will, one hopes, resolve a conflict or disagreement between the parties. In the case of a plaintiff it is hoped that the process of negotiation will lead to the early acceptance of liability and an offer of compensation at the best obtainable figure, or to some other remedy which is sought, such as an agreement to pull down a wall blocking a right of way, to avoid the necessity to go to trial to seek an injunction. In the case of a defendant, at its best one hopes the negotiation process will convince the plaintiff that he has no cause of action and that he will withdraw. Short of this, the defendant hopes to escape from the litigation as cheaply or successfully as possible by buying off the plaintiff's claim for considerably less than the maximum which the court might eventually order him to pay.

Negotiations in litigation are usually conducted on a 'without prejudice' basis so that the contents of letters, and what is said in face to face or telephone conversations, cannot be repeated to the court. This is because in the course of negotiations concessions, and even admissions, are often made for the sake of moving the negotiation process along, with each party reserving the right to withdraw those concessions or admissions should the case go to trial.

In the litigation process there may be no negotiation at all. It may become apparent to both sides at the very outset that the parties are completely in conflict and the matter can only be resolved by the court. Such cases would, however, be extremely rare. Where negotiation takes place it may be that there is no more than one single meeting or discussion in an attempt to achieve settlement; more commonly the negotiating process may go on from before a writ is even issued right through to, and during, the trial itself. It is by no means unknown for cases to be compromised part way through a trial, usually after the day's business has been concluded, by meetings between solicitors or counsel involved. Where that happens, in a sense there has been at least a partial failure of the negotiating process, the main aim of which should be to identify the terms on which an agreement can be achieved as early as possible in the interests of saving legal costs.

4.5.2 NEGOTIATION TECHNIQUES

There is a great deal of literature written about negotiations and the various tactics and techniques to be employed. Most of this literature is from the business field and in essence deals with techniques of salesmanship. These techniques are not to be scoffed at or ignored. In the non-contentious areas – as, for example, where the parties and their lawyers sit down to negotiate the terms upon which one company will merge with or acquire another; or where a potential tenant is negotiating for the terms of a business lease with a landlord; or even where an individual is in negotiation about the price of a house – these techniques have a part to play. The difference between those situations and litigation, however, is that in the end, in those situations, if the parties cannot agree there need be no falling out personally between them and they will simply walk away and probably never meet again. With litigation the crucial difference is that this is not possible. With litigation, if negotiation cannot achieve an outcome, the matter will go on and someone else, i.e. the court or arbitrator, will decide the rights of the parties. The sort of literature which suggests of negotiation that 'the aim is for both sides to feel good about the outcome: it is not a duel: there does not have to be a winner and a loser' has, perhaps, a limited application to the field of litigation. In the main it is not necessary for the parties to feel well disposed to each other by the end of the negotiations; probably in personal injury situations the plaintiff will never again have any contact with the defendant; even in other forms of litigation it is generally not a feature of the process to ensure that the parties remain happy in each other's company. There are, of course, exceptions to this; where businesses fall out about one particular past contract, it may be possible for them to commence litigation (or more commonly *arbitration*) whilst attempting to preserve their relationship for other contracts and the future. Negotiations in that context may need to be carried out in a somewhat different and more conciliatory manner than is the case in litigation generally.

4.5.2.1 The aggressive approach

Where you are acting for a plaintiff with a good prima facie case there are certain well-recognised techniques to ensure that you remain constantly in the driving seat. In general, an aggressive approach should be displayed from the outset. Care should be taken, however, to ensure that this never becomes personalised between the parties' solicitors, because even in the most bitterly contested litigation it is unnecessary to fall out with your opponent personally. This is not merely because the day may well come when, in another case, your opponent is acting for the plaintiff and himself in the driving seat, but simply because you may well get the best solution out of the litigation by courtesy allied to firmness. It is an obvious fact of human nature that if a solicitor feels that he is personally belittled and badly treated by his opponent, he is likely to try all the harder to 'get his own back' and may take every procedural or tactical point which can make life difficult for the person who has annoyed him.

4.5.2.2 Disparity of bargaining power

A feature often experienced when acting for plaintiffs, and not only in personal injury matters, is that there is often a great disparity of bargaining power between the parties. Thus if you are suing a local authority, a government department, or especially one of the recently privatised utilities, you are involved in litigation where the outcome may matter hardly at all to the defendant. Indeed, often the plaintiff's sense of frustration is measurably increased in such a case by the fact that the decision to resist his claim has manifestly been taken by a low-level employee, and the decision to support that employee's decision cavalierly undertaken simply because of the possibility of facing down the plaintiff to the point where he will have to risk significant sums to enforce his rights. This is pre-eminently the case where the litigation involves less than £3,000 and the plaintiff is unlikely to obtain a proper order for costs (see **21.9**). The most striking aspect of this disparity in bargaining power, however, is in personal injury litigation where often the plaintiff, a lone individual who may have been injured in circumstances which have had a traumatic effect on him personally, and in effect ruined his life in both personal and financial terms, is facing a multi-million pound insurance company so that the outcome of the litigation means everything to the plaintiff but will be a mere pin prick to the defendants.

This disparity in bargaining power can often be a crucial advantage for the defendant which it is the duty of the plaintiff's solicitor to counteract by doing everything in his power procedurally and tactically to obtain and keep the initiative.

Personalities of successful negotiators differ widely. Aggressive and truculent behaviour may sometimes prove successful, at least with opponents who are easily intimidated; likewise personal charm and courtesy may achieve much the same outcome. When acting for a plaintiff with a good case, however, matters of personality should take second place to the crucial feature in preparation for successful negotiation which is thorough groundwork.

4.5.3 PREPARING FOR NEGOTIATION

Nothing matters more than thorough preparation. When a solicitor is negotiating on behalf of a plaintiff, since he can dictate the timing of the start of the action and the speed at which it progresses, it is essential that he has all his material in scrupulous order. The law should have been thoroughly researched so that it can, if necessary, be cited in negotiations; and all evidence and documents should be thoroughly prepared, collated and to hand.

In principle good reports should be obtained before issue of proceedings from all relevant experts; receipts, vouchers and other necessary documents to prove every head of claim should always be to hand and kept in good order, and computations of quantum should be constantly updated so that at any discussion about the case the plaintiff's solicitor has at his fingertips the relevant items of detail and a good idea of what the case is worth to settle. Thereafter, a solicitor should ensure that he complies with every time limit in the Rules of the Supreme Court; serves writ and pleadings immediately they are due; completes automatic discovery fully and issues the summons for directions immediately, and thereafter moves swiftly to set down for trial.

Communications with the defendant's solicitor should be firm but always courteous. Keeping this kind of pressure on a defendant's solicitor, who customarily will have a very heavy workload, ensures that this particular file remains constantly on his desk and that it becomes a high priority in his working day to attempt to settle it, if possible. This will give you an edge over less aggressive solicitors who are content to wait weeks or months whilst the defendant's solicitor purports to take instructions from his insurance, or other, clients; awaits the return of his papers from counsel; or for one or other reason, genuine or not, seeks delay. It must be remembered that delay for defendants is more than a tactic; it is a way of life. A significant number of plaintiffs become deterred and abandon their claims or accept very low offers because of this delay. Moreover, money on unpaid damages continues earning interest at highly commercial rates for the defendant or its insurers. In personal injury cases particularly, the interest payable on damages, and even the extra costs occasioned during delay, may be insignificant compared to the value of these factors to defendants. Thus the pressure should always be kept on defendants procedurally by such manoeuvres as applications for a split trial (see **1.4.2**), applications for interim payments (see **16.5**) and the issue of any other appropriate summonses.

4.5.4 COMMENCING NEGOTIATIONS WITH INSURERS

In personal injury cases negotiations commonly start with the defendant's insurers, whether it be a road, factory, or occupier's liability accident. Insurers employ usually fairly competent claims staff who, whilst they may have no legal qualification, rapidly become expert in the law and practice relevant to personal injury litigation. These claims staff usually have a considerable incentive to see if the claim can be reasonably settled because, if it can, then sending the file to the insurance company's chosen solicitors is avoided with the consequent saving on costs since everything will have been dealt with in-house. If proceedings are issued, then insurance companies usually send the file immediately to their solicitors, although it may be possible to agree that the writ will be served for the sake of starting interest running, and that one would continue to negotiate direct with the insurers, making no other progress on the action for the time being. As indicated above, this may be an undesirable tactic. The best results are usually achieved from keeping the pressure on the defendant, his insurers, or their solicitors.

Solicitors' approaches to insurance companies vary. A renowned personal injury specialist once told the writer that he never negotiated with insurance companies but always issued proceedings immediately he was ready, because the only function of insurance companies was to delay and prevaricate. It is the writer's own experience, however, that in some kind of cases, at least with modest claims, a more reasonable offer may be obtained from an insurance company than from their solicitors, the tendency of the latter being naturally to be 'more Royalist than the King' in terms of negativity and aggression, at least in the early stages of claims.

The experience of insurance company representatives and their solicitors must tell them that a high proportion of personal injury claims are brought by inexperienced or incompetent solicitors. Thus delay by the insurance company will lead to no retaliation from such plaintiffs' solicitors who are reluctant to fight cases they hope to settle, often because of overwork or because they are not entirely sure of the proper practical or procedural steps which should be taken in the later stages of an action, however competent they may be to start one. Some solicitors do not have satisfactory office libraries and may not have access to Kemp and Kemp or to *Current Law*. It is the writer's experience as well that inadequate solicitors often use poor counsel, possibly so that they are not made to feel uncomfortable and their shortcomings are not exposed, and thus the plaintiff may end up with very mediocre advice throughout a case. It also seems that some insurance companies make a point of defending a certain proportion of actions to the death, no matter how hopeless their position may be, perhaps as an indication that they are not a 'soft touch' even in tough circumstances. You may therefore be involved in negotiations with insurance companies where there may be more behind their attitude than the present facts and they may be concerned, for example, to establish themselves as aggressive for the sake of their future relations with you personally.

4.5.5 NEGOTIATION WITH FREQUENT OPPONENTS

This may have its advantages, though the corresponding disadvantages often outweigh them. If you get on tolerably well on a personal basis with an insurance company representative, or with a defendant's insurer's solicitor, then some plaintiffs' cases may be facilitated. Should procedural cooperation be required, e.g. for unexpected adjournments or postponements, then they will usually give it on a *quid pro quo* basis; although then you will usually not be able to be quite as aggressive as you might have wished since you will have to extend reciprocal courtesies.

By convention, defendants visit the plaintiff's solicitor's offices to discuss cases. It may be that if the solicitor is engaged frequently in the same kind of litigation, e.g. road traffic accidents, several cases may be discussed at one meeting with the same opponent. The temptation must be resisted, however, to settle cases which really ought to be taken to trial just because of an amicable relationship with the opponent. A solicitor is not there to do personal favours for other solicitors; he is there to fight as hard as he can for the best outcome for each individual plaintiff. This does involve one awkward and rarely articulated feature, however. If a defendant's solicitor has a mainly amicable meeting and perhaps settles a big case for the proper figure with a frequent negotiating opponent, the plaintiff's solicitor may at the same meeting pass on to discussion of another file, and this time perhaps his client's case is very weak indeed. In the euphoria of achieving the large settlement, it is not uncommon for defendant's solicitors to offer at least 'nuisance value' or nominal amounts, even to plaintiffs with apparently hopeless cases. Thus the plaintiff's solicitor is in a sense achieving a particularly successful outcome for the client with the weak case on the basis of the warmth of his personal relationship with the insurance company representative or defendant solicitor. However, whilst 'setting the ground' for an amicable meeting which might lead to a reasonable offer on a hopeless case, the solicitor should ensure that he never compromises the true value of a claim of a client who has a good case.

The above is perhaps stating the obvious. A solicitor of integrity would never consciously accept global deals for three or four different clients. Unfortunately, where you do have a friendly relationship with your opposite number there may be more subtle ways in which concessions are made to a client's detriment. For example, where there are requests for procedural cooperation which may prejudice a client marginally or indirectly, e.g. that a few weeks, or months, delay be permitted because the defendant's witness has gone overseas or the specialist of their choice is unavailable. In some kinds of litigation you might be tempted to give this kind of modest concession as a professional courtesy, possibly implicitly in the hope of obtaining corresponding procedural concessions when you require them yourself. You must, however, always be aware of your own motivation in these cases. If you are able in principle to remain on top of a case from start to finish, complying with every procedural requirement and deadline, then you need never require favours from your opponents. However, there are few solicitors whose case loads permit them to take quite such a dogmatically 'holier than thou' attitude.

FIVE

JURISDICTION AND CHOICE OF COURT

5.1 The High Court

There are three divisions of the High Court, namely the Queen's Bench Division, the Chancery Division and the Family Division. The jurisdiction of the Family Division does not concern us. The jurisdiction of the Chancery Division and that of the Queen's Bench Division overlap to a small extent but in the main their work is quite different.

Proceedings are allocated to the Chancery Division by s. 61 of the *Supreme Court Act 1981* and *para. 1* of *sch. 1* to that Act. In particular, matters to do with mortgages; trusts; the administration of estates; bankruptcy; partnership; patents, trademarks and copyright; and the sale, exchange or partition of land are dealt with there. Whilst perhaps as recently as 15 years ago the daily work of the Chancery Division was seen as being dull, rarely involving interesting disputes of fact, since then it has, so to speak, spread its tentacles into a number of areas of purely commercial law work. This, together with the fact that proceedings for urgent interlocutory relief, in particular injunctions of various kinds, often form part of the day-to-day work has led to the situation where the Chancery Division now has a much higher profile. In this text, however, we shall be concerned mainly with the work of the Queen's Bench Division which deals with almost all cases brought in tort and contract.

The Queen's Bench Division of the High Court consists of the Central Office, that is the office of the High Court contained in the Royal Courts of Justice building in The Strand, London, and also the District Registries which are the offices of the High Court outside London. The personnel of the Queen's Bench Division with whom we are concerned are as follows.

5.1.1 MASTERS OF THE QUEEN'S BENCH DIVISION

These are the judicial officers who deal with almost all matters of an administrative or a judicial nature in a High Court action in the Central Office in London up to the stage of the trial itself. As we shall see, a writ is issued at court without the need to appear before a judge of any kind. It is simply an administrative act carried out at the court counter by paying a fee and producing the right number of copies of the relevant documents. Thereafter, in the Queen's Bench Division in principle, documents should be exchanged direct between the parties without the intervention of the court up to a certain point called 'the close of pleadings'. If, however, there is any dispute about the steps which the parties ought to be taking up to the stage of close of pleadings, or more commonly after that stage, one or other of the parties will make an application to a Master for a ruling on whatever procedural points have arisen. These applications are called 'interlocutory applications', and that term refers to anything that may arise from the commencement of an action up to the trial itself. With one important exception it is a Master who will decide such matters. Masters sit in a private room, with no public admitted, and do not wear wig or gown.

Examples of interlocutory applications would be: applications for leave to amend the writ; applications to renew the writ; application for further and better particulars of pleadings; application for summary judgment and so on. Each of these topics will be considered in detail in due course. A Master has jurisdiction to deal with all of such cases, no matter how large the amount of money involved or the importance of the case.

In some cases it is possible that an action may go from commencement to trial without there needing to be any interlocutory applications. Personal injury cases in particular are in this category, because there is a provision for so-called 'automatic directions' by virtue of which rules of court prescribe what the parties are to do at each relevant stage, and there is no need to apply to a Master for any rulings on those matters. It is, indeed, possible on other occasions for the parties to agree on the steps that should be taken between themselves to avoid the need for the cost and delay caused by applying for a ruling to a Master.

The only form of interlocutory relief with which we are concerned which will not be dealt with by a Master but by a High Court judge is an application for an injunction. Save in very limited circumstances – in particular, where an injunction is to be granted by agreement between the parties – a Master has no jurisdiction to grant an injunction.

5.1.2 DISTRICT JUDGES

District Judges are the equivalent of Queen's Bench Division Masters in the District Registries. The District Registries are the offices of the High Court outside London and there are about 100 of such registries in towns throughout England and Wales. A District Judge also has powers in relation to the work of the other two divisions of the High Court and will also deal with the assessment of bills of cost which in London is dealt with by a specialist Master called a Taxing Master. Thus the work of District Judges is somewhat less specialised than that of the Queen's Bench Division Masters.

5.1.3 HIGH COURT JUDGES

High Court Judges sit at the actual trial of cases in open court. In addition they hear some interlocutory applications as previously mentioned (e.g. applications for injunctions), and they are also the next tier in the appeals system from orders made by a Master or District Judge. Thus if a Master or District Judge has granted or refused some interlocutory application by one or other party, the aggrieved opposite party may appeal as of right to a High Court Judge sitting in chambers. For details see **26.1**.

5.1.4 THE RULES OF THE SUPREME COURT

Procedure in the High Court is governed by the Rules of the Supreme Court (RSC). These are reproduced with annotations in a book entitled *The Supreme Court Practice* which is commonly known as 'The White Book'. This contains the orders, rules, practice directions, precedents and prescribed forms, and explanatory notes and is published in three volumes.

The way to use the White Book is first to look up the subject matter of your enquiry in the index which is in volume 3. There will be a reference to the place in the text where more detail can be found. This reference will be in one of two forms. It will either consist of three numbers separated by oblique strokes, e.g. 6/2/21, or it will be a single number in square brackets, e.g. [316].

Example 1 Suppose you wished to look up some material on the question of what documents are privileged from production at the stage of procedure know as discovery. You would look in the index under 'Discovery' and would eventually find under the sub-heading 'Production' that the matter was dealt with at note 24/5/5. With this information you could turn to volume 1 of the 'White Book'. In that volume the text of each of the orders of the Supreme Court with the rules and sub rules is set out, and you would turn to the paragraph numbered (in the far right hand column of the page) 24/5/5. This note is an editorial note written by the Masters of the Queen's Bench Division who in the main edit the White Book, and appears after Ord. 24, r. 5 itself. It is to be found on p. 431 of volume 1. This briefly summarises the principle and cross-refers to three other places at which further research can be carried out a couple of pages further on from the main note. These in their turn cite leading cases and other authorities. Thus, where you need to research such a point, a clear trail is laid by this preliminary note.

Example 2 Suppose you wish to find the relevant form of order for dismissal of an action where the plaintiff had failed to appear at the hearing. You need to use a certain amount of ingenuity and persistence in the quest for such terms through the index, and it may be that this would be found under 'Failure to appear', 'Non-appearance' or 'Dismissal'. In the present case it is actually found under 'Dismissal' and the reference given is [260]. A square bracketed number like that refers to the second volume of the *Supreme Court Practice*. The reference is not to page numbers but to paragraph numbers, and the paragraph numbers are given in the far right hand column. Turning to the relevant paragraph number (which happens to be on page 78), you would see a precedent for the wording of an order to dismiss the action which could then be used in a suitably adapted form.

It is perhaps worth saying a word about the organisation of the second volume of the *Supreme Court Practice* which often causes confusion. In this volume the following material is set out:

(a) Various prescribed forms, practice forms and editorial forms drafted by the Queen's Bench or Chancery Masters.

(b) Various practice directions and tables given from time to time by Queen's Bench Masters, Chancery Division Practice Directions and Practice Direction tables.

(c) Court fees and stamps.

(d) Court funds office rules and practice, including extracts from relevant statutes, e.g. the *Supreme Court Act 1981*, the Court Funds Rules 1987, etc.

(e) Thereafter there are miscellaneous other sections (these are listed at pages ix–xii in the introductory pages of the second volume). They include amongst other things the full text of a number of relevant statues to do with civil litigation, in particular the *Supreme Court Act 1981*, the *County Courts Act 1984*, the *Civil Evidence Acts*, the *Legal Aid Act 1988*, the *Solicitors Act 1964*, the *Limitation Act 1980* and various *Trustee Acts*.

Whilst initially intimidating, in fact it becomes relatively easy to use the *Supreme Court Practice* after a short while provided the reader is willing to employ a certain amount of imagination and persistence in the use of the index in considering various alternative forms of title to the text that he wishes to find.

5.1.5 THE NATURE OF THE RULES OF THE SUPREME COURT

The *Rules of the Supreme Court* are set out in a number of Orders (currently 115 in number), most of them divided into a large number of rules and sub rules. Some of the longer orders, indeed, are sub-divided into dozens of rules. These rules govern procedure in the High Court, although the court also sometimes claims an 'inherent jurisdiction' to supplement or even replace the text of individual rules. Many of the rules seem to be expressed in fairly peremptory terms, e.g. they appear to instruct that the plaintiff shall at a certain stage take some particular step, usually within a given time limit. It is important to note that in fact failure to comply with the rules in almost all cases amounts merely to an irregularity which can be cured. The court in general recognises that its function is to assist the parties in obtaining justice and not to discipline the parties or their solicitors for their deficiencies in conducting litigation. Thus failure to take a step in the right way, with the correct document, or at the right time generally does not nullify the action itself or even the step taken. The court will almost always allow mistakes to be corrected, although the party who has gone astray, and may well have caused a waste of time and costs to his opponents, will inevitably be ordered to pay the costs wasted by a mistake or oversight (indeed, in many cases it is now the solicitor personally who is ordered to pay such costs).

There are many examples of provisions in the rules which are in fact generally overlooked or ignored. A common one is *Ord. 24, r. 2* which provides that after the close of pleadings each party shall attend to so-called 'automatic discovery' within 14 days. In fact few parties are prepared for this important stage so early in the case and often this is left by agreement, or even tacitly, for many months. Except in personal injury cases, there is a subsequent stage called a 'summons for direction' which in principle should also come about a month after close of pleadings but is commonly left for many months, and the matter of discovery is often left to that stage as well.

Another aspect of this is the fact that time limits given by the rules may usually be extended, either by written agreement between the parties or, if one party is not willing to agree to an extension of the given time limit, by application made to the court (that is to a Master in London or a District Judge outside London) by what is called a 'time summons' for an order extending the time. A very common example (to which we shall return) is that when the plaintiff's statement of claim is served on the defendant the latter has in principle only 14 days in which to serve his full defence to it. Many defendants are unable to do this within the time, especially if they need to have the document settled by counsel, and need to ask for an extension of time. If this is refused then the defendant will need to apply to the court for an order extending the time.

It must be understood, however, that not all rules of the High Court can be waived. There are exceptions where failure to comply with the relevant rule may have serious consequences. An example is the requirement that a writ must be served within four months of its being issued. Although an application can in fact be made to extend this period if good cause can be shown, and even to extend it retrospectively (for example, if the defendant has disappeared and cannot be traced), if the failure to serve was due to a mere oversight the court is unlikely to grant a renewal of the writ and the writ then lapses. That is not such a problem if the limitation period is still running because a second writ can be issued, although the solicitor will inevitably have to bear the costs (i.e. the wasted court fee) of his earlier mistake. If, however, the limitation period has also elapsed meanwhile it will not usually be possible to issue a second writ and the plaintiff's rights are thus substantially affected. Naturally, in such a case his remedy lies against his solicitor if the latter was negligent. There are some other examples of rules against whose breach no latitude is allowed. When dealing with important stages which require particular documentation, especially where time limits are involved, it is thus imperative carefully to analyse whether one's case falls within those situations where absolute adherence to the rule will be required, or is one of the purely procedural provisions where more latitude is allowed.

5.2 The County Court

The constitution of the county court is governed by the *County Courts Act 1984*. The county court now has no upper financial limit to its jurisdiction in matters involving tort and contract (see **5.3.2** below). There are rather more than 300 county courts in England and Wales. There is thus likely to be a registry of the county court in quite small towns in rural areas where there may be no District Registry of the High Court for many miles. In large towns, very often the same building is both the local District Registry of the High Court of Justice and the County Court Registry.

5.2.1 THE DISTRICT JUDGE

The equivalent of the High Court District Judge is called the County Court District Judge. Where the District Registry of the High Court and the county court do occupy the same building, then the same person is likely to be both District Judge of the High Court and District Judge of the county court. The jurisdiction of such a District Judge is to try any undefended case or any case where the sum involved is £5,000 or less; to conduct arbitrations and to try any other cases where all parties and the County Court Circuit Judge consent; and in addition the District Judge will deal with interlocutory applications in precisely the same way in which a District Judge of the High Court does.

When sitting as a District Judge of the county court the District Judge has wide powers to grant interlocutory and final injunctions even though a District Judge of the High Court may not.

5.2.2 CIRCUIT JUDGES

The judge who will hear trials in the county court is likely to be a Circuit Judge whose work will consist of alternatively trying county court actions on his circuit (i.e. local group of county courts) and periods in the Crown Court sitting in criminal cases. Applications for injunctions will be made to the County Court Judge, who also has an appellate function in relation to other interlocutory matters where an aggrieved party who is dissatisfied with a ruling by the District Judge may appeal as of right.

Circuit Judges are full-time judges but their work is often carried out in addition by recorders or assistant recorders (i.e. practising solicitors or barristers sitting part-time for a prescribed number of days a year on rota).

5.2.3 THE CHIEF CLERK OR 'COURT MANAGER'

The Chief Clerk is in charge of all administrative matters in a county court. In addition, although not himself a solicitor or barrister, or even necessarily having any form of legal qualification, the Chief Clerk increasingly has some minor judicial functions. In particular he deals with some matters to do with the rate of instalments by which a judgment debtor is required to pay judgments at a stage called a 'disposal' and also with attachments of earnings (see **23.2.5** below). Although most practitioners continue to refer to the 'Chief Clerk', in fact technically with effect from April 1997, the appropriate term is the 'Court Manager'.

5.2.4 THE BAILIFF

The High Court employs nobody for the purposes of service of process or enforcement of judgments. The High Court Under Sheriff may be called upon to help enforce judgments but he is not an employee of the High Court. Usually he is a solicitor in private practice who has been appointed Under Sheriff. In the county court, however, there is an officer called a bailiff who is employed for personal service of summonses and other applications and court orders; and for some of the steps in enforcing judgment particularly, by a so-called *warrant of execution* where the judgment debtor's goods are seized and sold at auction to realise the amount of the judgment (see **23.2.1.2**).

5.2.5 THE COUNTY COURT RULES

The *County Court Rules* (*CCR*) are contained in the *County Court Practice*, known as the 'Green Book'. This is still in one volume and is somewhat more difficult to use than the *Supreme Court Practice*. This is partly because in many cases the county court simply mirrors High Court procedure and the text of the rules does not fully set out what is to be done. Thus, although the time limit for taking certain steps is slightly different and the time at which certain steps may be taken is also different, the *CCR* often do not fully describe what is to be done but say merely that the procedure is as described in the corresponding *Rules of the Supreme Court* for a High Court case.

Increasingly of late there has been an attempt to bring the once very different systems of High Court and county court together. The principal points of difference from the corresponding High Court rules are the methods by which actions are commenced and defence is served; the existence of automatic directions in almost all cases in the county court; and the mechanism by which a case comes up for trial in the county court. In addition, the court has a more direct involvement in certain of the processes, particularly in the initiation of proceedings in the county court. Having said that, practical and tactical considerations vary hardly at all. Thus, in particular, the rules of evidence are exactly the same for both, and the procedure for serving Civil Evidence Act notices, notices to admit facts, discovery, the rules on contents of pleadings, the rules relating to expert evidence, and so on have only some slight differences in time limits.

5.3 Choice of Court

5.3.1 INTRODUCTION

There are two courts of first instance in civil proceedings, the High Court and the county court. Before 1 July 1991, the county court had a greatly restricted jurisdiction. In the most common type of case, actions in tort and contract, the maximum financial jurisdiction was £5,000. In equity and property matters that jurisdiction was £30,000. There were some cases in which statutes gave exclusive jurisdiction to the county court, for example in most actions under the *Consumer Credit Act 1974* and in some landlord and tenant cases. In addition, the county court chosen for the commencement of proceedings had to have some local connection with either the cause of action or the address of the defendant.

The High Court, on the other hand, had unlimited jurisdiction. That is to say that actions in the High Court could be commenced however small or large the amount involved. There did not need to be any local connection between the District Registry of the High Court chosen for issue of proceedings and the cause of action or the parties' addresses, although if there was in fact no local connection with the action the defendant may have been able to apply subsequently to transfer the action to a District Registry which did have such connections. Litigators, particularly plaintiffs' litigators, often saw substantial advantages in choosing the High Court for litigation rather than the county court even where an action was within the financial jurisdiction of the county court. In particular, speed and efficiency of early process, certain interlocutory procedures which were perceived as being more efficient in the High Court, and the methods of enforcement of judgment debt all made the High Court more attractive even if modest sums were involved.

In order to redistribute work from the High Court to the county court, a series of *Practice Directions* were made from 1988 requiring Masters or District Judges to consider transfer of High Court actions for trial in the county court at various stages of action. The effect of those *Practice Directions* was said to be that more than half of all High Court cases were being transferred for trial in the county court.

5.3.2 HIGH COURT AND COUNTY COURT JURISDICTION ORDER 1991

In July 1991, a new regime was introduced which transferred a great deal of routine litigation away from the High Court and into the county court from the commencement of the action, and not simply for trial. This enabled the High Court to concentrate on matters of greater complexity or substance. This redistribution is in the main effected by the *High Court and County Court Jurisdiction Order 1991* ('the Order').

Business is allocated between the courts at two different stages: (a) at the commencement of an action, which is dealt with by *Arts 4 and 5*; and (b) with regard to place of trial, which is dealt with by *Art. 7*. The Order requires that a claim be valued at certain stages of the action. It is thus important for a plaintiff to have in mind the value of his case, both at the outset and subsequently, because there are penalties, albeit limited ones, for commencing an action in the High Court which the court ultimately concludes should have been commenced in the county court.

There is no upper limit on the financial jurisdiction of the county court in cases in tort and contract. The upper limit on the court's equity jurisdiction for some purposes remains at £30,000. A separate rule (*CCR Ord. 4, r. 2*) provides that in default actions in tort and contract proceedings may be commenced in *any* county court and there is no longer any need for a connection between cause of action and the county court chosen. In the main, then, proceedings will be issued in the county court most convenient to the plaintiff's solicitor's office.

5.3.3 THE VALUE OF THE ACTION

The value of the action is dealt with in *Art. 9* of the *High Court and County Court Jurisdiction Order 1991*.

5.3.3.1 Value of an action for a sum of money

The value of an action for a sum of money, whether specified or not, is the amount which the plaintiff reasonably expects to recover. In a liquidated debt, damages or debt case, therefore, the valuation is obvious. In an unliquidated damages case, however, it will be for the plaintiff's advisers to consider carefully the likely bracket of damages. This valuation will only be of great moment, at the outset anyway, in a personal injury case for reasons set out below. In other kinds of case where unliquidated damages are sought, it will be for the plaintiff's legal advisers to consider in each case whether, having regard to the likely amount of damages, no doubt on their most optimistic view, the action should be commenced in the High Court because of the procedural advantages and also the sanction discussed at **5.3.5** below.

5.3.3.2 'The financial worth of the claim'

Where an action is for a specified relief other than money (such as an injunction or specific performance), then the test used is that the value is that equivalent to 'the financial worth of the claim'. There is no guidance as to what value can be put upon claims for non-monetary relief. A possible, though not inevitable, test is to ask what damages the court might award in lieu of the other remedies sought. So, for example, it will be recalled that under *s. 50* of the *Supreme Court Act 1981*, the court has the power to award damages in lieu of an injunction, although that power is subject to substantial restrictions under the principles in *Shelfer* v *City of London Electric Lighting Co.* [1895] 1 Ch 287. No doubt again it will be for the plaintiff's solicitors to put the highest reasonable value they can think of on the action. In non-personal injury cases a plaintiff's solicitor is not required to give a specific valuation at any stage, but merely, when called upon to do so, to state whether in his view the amount of the claim is worth less or more than £25,000 (see **13.1.5.2** below).

5.3.3.3 Matters to be disregarded in valuation

Where other remedies are sought in an action, such as unspecified further or other relief, or interest under statute, these, together with costs, are to be disregarded in the valuation of a claim. It should be noted, however, that interest *claimed under contract* is to be brought into account.

5.3.3.4 More than one plaintiff

If there is more than one plaintiff the value of the action consists of the aggregate of the expectations of all the plaintiffs. Thus, for example, three plaintiffs in the same motor car injured by the alleged negligence of the defendant, each of whose claims was for only moderate personal injury damages (say £20,000 or thereabouts each), could validly bring a joint action in the High Court because it is the total value of their claim that matters.

5.3.3.5 The financial assessment

In determining the value of an action the following are to be taken into account also:

(a) The amount of any debt which the plaintiff admits he owes to the defendant arising from the circumstances giving rise to the action (i.e. a true *set off*, see **6.1.3.2**). The effect of this is that the value of the action consists of the difference between the amount sought and the amount admitted due.

(b) No account is to be taken of *contributory negligence* when an action is valued unless that contributory negligence is admitted. Thus, in routine tort actions, unless the parties have agreed about respective proportionate liability and are litigating only about quantum, this is unlikely to affect the choice of place of *issue*. Naturally a plaintiff's solicitor will not wish to make any concessions on contributory negligence at the outset. It must be remembered, however, that most actions need to be valued twice – once at the outset (although this valuation does not need to be communicated to the court except in personal injury cases) and again in order to determine court of trial. It is perfectly possible, therefore, that by the latter stage, even in a personal injury case, contributory negligence will have been agreed between the parties.

(c) In cases of claims for *provisional damages* the value of the claim is taken to be that of the first award (i.e. the provisional damages) leaving out of account the possibility of a subsequent application for further damages.

(d) In *personal injury* cases it is the global gross value of the plaintiff's claim that matters, and the fact that money equivalent to benefits paid by the state must inevitably be deducted from damages under *s. 81* of the *Social Security Administration Act 1992* is left out of account.

(e) In personal injury cases *Art. 5* of the *1991 Order* is prescriptive. It provides that an action including a claim for personal injuries should be commenced in a county court unless the value of the action is £50,000 or more. Thus the only relevant criterion in personal injury claims is value, and it matters not that the action is particularly complex, or even a test case for hundreds of other plaintiffs, if it cannot truthfully be said at the outset that the value of the action is more than £50,000. In order to avoid any uncertainty as to the importance of this matter, a *Practice Direction (Personal Injuries Action: Endorsement on Writ)* [1991] 1 WLR 642 provides that a writ which includes a claim for personal injuries to be issued in the High Court must bear an endorsement in the following terms to be signed by the plaintiff's solicitor:

This writ includes a claim for personal injury but may be commenced in the High Court because the value of the action for the purposes of Article 5 of the High Court and County Court Jurisdiction Order 1991 exceeds £50,000.

When valuing a claim in personal injury cases it will thus be for a plaintiff's solicitor to give this certificate and to stand by the consequences of having given it in bad faith. It should be borne in mind, however, that what is being valued is the whole claim, and thus if, for example, there are personal injuries but also other damage, e.g. property or vehicle damage, the global value of the claim is what matters. So long as the certificate is given in good faith it is unlikely in fact that there will be much in the way of sanction if the figure of £50,000 is not eventually attained at trial. It would obviously be unfair, in personal injury cases more than any other, where brackets of awards may be subject to numerous variables and may be very wide, to compel a plaintiff's solicitor, under threat of personal sanction, to predict the outcome exactly. There are many personal injury cases where, if the writ is issued early, the bracket of damages cannot be fixed even within a band of, say, £20,000. A plaintiff's solicitor naturally will wish for negotiating purposes, in cases of any doubt whatsoever, to adopt the most pessimistic tenable view of the plaintiff's prognosis so as to be able in good faith to certify the action as fit for the High Court. It must be borne in mind anyway that if the valuation of the claim falls significantly later on in the light of new facts such as medical evidence, then provided that a plaintiff's solicitor applies for the action to be *tried* in the county court at the appropriate time, the court would be most unlikely to impose any sanction. One should have regard, however, to the wording of *s. 51* of the *Supreme Court Act 1981* which we consider at **5.3.5** below.

5.3.3.6 Later transfer

The value of an action is to be determined for the purposes of *Art. 5* as at the time when the action is commenced, and for the purposes of *Art. 7* at the time when the value is declared in accordance with Rules of Court. In other words, one article looks to valuation at the time of commencement in the case of personal injury actions, and the other to the decision as to court of trial. *Practice Direction (County Court: Transfer of Actions)* [1991] 1 WLR 643, provides procedures in respect of transfer of actions to the county court. It provides for certificates of value to be filed at various times when the court may be considering transfer. The certificate of value is in practice form FP 204 (obtainable from law stationers) and is to be lodged in the Central Office or the District Registry where the action is proceeding at certain stages when required by rules of court so that the court remains fully informed.

5.3.4 PLACE OF TRIAL

When making the decision as to place of trial, regard must be had to *Art. 7* of the Order. This provides in short that an action whose value is less than £25,000 shall be tried in the county court unless either the county court or High Court considers that the High Court ought to try the action by reference to the criteria described below. An action of which the value is £50,000 or more shall be tried in the High Court, unless the court, having regard to the said criteria, thinks that it ought to be tried in the county court. Between the figures of £25,000 and £50,000, the decision as to place of trial will depend entirely upon the relevant criteria. These are set out in *Art. 7(5)* and are as follows:

(a) 'The *financial substance* of the action including the value of any counterclaim'. This therefore indicates that the claim and counterclaim must be aggregated when considering the amount of money involved. In itself, however, value in money terms is not conclusive.

(b) Whether the action is *otherwise important*, e.g. whether it raises questions of importance to persons who are not parties or questions of general public interest'. A good example here would be a test case in group litigation, for example the *Benzodiazepine* litigation. This litigation concerns people who claim ill effects from addiction to tranquillisers of various kinds. It is very probable that many plaintiffs will not be able to certify that the amount of the claim in their case is over £50,000. Nonetheless, because the cases raise issues of considerable importance affecting many people, and because the first case to be tried as a test case may well involve issues on which hundreds of other cases depend, there is no doubt that the first case, however modest the claim, will be tried in the High Court. Similarly, questions involving points of general public interest, i.e. having a substantial public law element, will be tried in the High Court even if the amount involved in money terms is not great. (See also **5.3.6.3.**)

(c) 'The *complexity* of the facts, legal issues, remedies or procedures involved.' This criterion is very important. It is self-evident that points of law and evidence of as much difficulty can arise in a case worth £1,000 as in one worth a million times that amount. Whilst only one of the matters to be considered, it is nonetheless a criterion which might in appropriate circumstances make even a modest claim suitable for trial in the High Court, e.g. where a great deal of conflicting expert evidence is involved, or a novel or important point of law.

(d) 'Whether transfer is likely to result in a *more speedy* trial of the action (save that no transfer shall be made on the grounds of this sub-paragraph alone).' Whether in fact transfer *will* lead to a more speedy trial tends to be a local, and sometimes temporary, matter. In some parts of the country it is actually quicker to get a High Court trial date than a county court trial date for certain kinds of litigation at the time of writing.

The statement of value form PF 204 which has to be submitted to the Master or District Judge at relevant times, in particular at the summons for directions when setting down an action for trial, is not particularly informative. It simply requires the plaintiff to certify that the value is less or greater than £25,000 but does not require the plaintiff to give any more exact valuation. It allows the plaintiff to claim also that by reason of one or more of the criteria mentioned in *Art. 7(5)*, the case is suitable for determination in the High Court, but it does not require the plaintiff to explain the basis for this claim, and indeed there is no room on the form to indicate why it is said that the case should be tried in the High Court. The Practice Directions indicate that the Master or District Judge may, if he wishes, call the parties before him so that he may consider the matter of transfer if the case is one of any difficulty. At the summons for directions this will normally be one of the matters which will be considered.

5.3.5 THE SANCTION FOR WRONGLY STARTING IN THE HIGH COURT

By *s. 4(1)* of the *Courts and Legal Services Act 1990*, a new *s. 51* is substituted in the *Supreme Court Act 1981*. The new *s. 51(8)* and *(9)* provide:

(8) Where—

(a) a person has commenced proceedings in the High Court; but

(b) those proceedings should, in the opinion of the court, have been commenced in a County Court in accordance with any provision made under s. 1 of the Courts and Legal Services Act 1990 or by any other enactment,
the person responsible for determining the amount which is to be awarded to that person by way of costs shall have regard to those circumstances.

(9) Where, in complying with subsection (8), the responsible person reduces the amount which would otherwise be awarded to the person in question—

(a) the amount of that reduction shall not exceed 25 per cent; and

(b) *on any taxation of the costs payable by that person to his legal representative, regard shall be had to the amount of the reduction.*

This therefore provides a simple penalty which is as yet untested in case law. It should be noted that the penalty relates only to proceedings which have been *wrongly commenced* in the High Court. Proceedings which have been commenced in the County Court but wrongly transferred to the High Court do not fall within this provision. The effect of the subsections is that where the court at trial, or possibly the court at an earlier interlocutory application, considers that the plaintiff was wrong to commence in the High Court, a penalty by way of deduction of up to 25 per cent of *inter partes* costs may be imposed. It should be noted that this is not mandatory and the court may decide either to impose the penalty or not to impose it, or to impose a lesser deduction than 25 per cent of the gross costs, or to reduce or delete individual items in the winning party's bill up to that maximum. It is fairly clear that the provision is meant to be punitive, and there will be no need for the paying party necessarily to show prejudice, or even to show that the costs of the action have been increased by running it in the High Court. In the nature of things it is a penalty applicable only to plaintiffs, since the plaintiff has initial choice of venue.

It is still far from clear in what circumstances such orders will be made. Obviously a plaintiff whose solicitor wrongly certified that he expected to recover £50,000 in a personal injury case, would be unlikely to be penalised if there was only a modest shortfall on that amount, personal injury awards being notoriously unpredictable. Moreover, it will be appreciated that cases are to be reviewed at later stages, in particular at summons for directions (if any) or on setting down. There is thus a further opportunity for a case to be transferred for trial to the county court, and if a plaintiff properly took advantage of some change in circumstances to request that, it is unlikely that any sanction would be attached, although it must be remembered that the section relates in principle to where proceedings were *initiated*.

In cases other then personal injuries where a plaintiff may commence in either court without express restriction, the matter will be very much for the court's discretion. Given the greater speed and efficiency of early proceedings, the fact that judgment debts immediately carry interest and the perhaps more efficient methods of enforcing judgement by execution, it is anticipated that in debt-collecting matters many plaintiffs will still commence in the High Court even for quite modest amounts. If such cases do not terminate with default judgment or summary judgment, there will then be an opportunity to apply for transfer. Indeed, one of the occasions when a certificate of value must be lodged is where an application for summary judgment has been unsuccessful. It seems to the writer unlikely that the courts would usually be minded to impose any penalty under *s. 51(8)* in those circumstances, because few extra costs have been incurred and nobody's time has been wasted since an interlocutory application for summary judgment in the High Court would take just as long to be heard in the county court and often by the same person. There would thus seem to be no logical reason to impose the sanction.

In *Restick* v *Crickmore* [1994] 1 WLR 420 the Court of Appeal had to consider whether personal injury cases which had been wrongly started in the High Court, when the size of the claims dictated they should have been brought in the county court, should be struck out or merely transferred. Reversing the judges at first instance who had struck out the cases on the basis that the solicitors of the plaintiffs had brought them there improperly, the Court of Appeal held that the ordinary sanction for failure to comply with requirements as to jurisdiction would be in costs. Actions started in the wrong court were not necessarily 'frivolous, vexatious or an abuse of process' although exceptionally, if the action should plainly have been started in the county court and the High Court had been used, not due to a bona fide mistake but as an attempt to harass or intimidate a defendant, an action might then be struck out, especially if the defendant had already given a warning about the proper venue. Similarly where solicitors persistently started actions in the wrong court the ultimate sanction might be appropriate but in the cases under appeal the actions were transferred to the county court and allowed to proceed.

This is a useful indication of the way in which the court views irregularities in matters of commencement of proceedings and jurisdiction. It does not, in terms, however, give much indication of the way in which District Judges are likely to apply sanctions where modest actions, e.g. for contract debts, are started in the High Court.

Where the sanction is imposed, then the meaning of *s. 51(9)(b)* needs to be considered. This is not entirely clear. It provides that on any taxation of the costs payable by that person to his legal representative, 'regard shall be had to the amount of the reduction'. The meaning of this seems to be that a solicitor who wrongly commences proceedings in the High Court may not pass on to his client in his solicitor and own client bill, any costs which were reduced on the *inter partes* bill. The section, however, may not mean that at all. It may indeed mean the very opposite, i.e. that on a taxation of a solicitor and own client costs, regard *shall* be had to the amount of the reduction in the sense that the solicitor may have it reinstated, e.g. particularly where the client himself requested High Court proceedings. This latter reading seems unlikely but the drafting of the section is obscure.

Six years after the section came into force, there is at present no reported case on the meaning of the words. It may be that courts have never found the need to delve into the matter because sensible plaintiffs will ensure that cases, wherever they are started, are transferred down to the county court at an earlier stage, if that seems to be the appropriate court of trial.

5.3.6 OTHER FACTORS IN CHOICE OF COURT

5.3.6.1 Interest on judgments

In the High Court interest runs on judgment debts from the date judgment is given at the rate of 8 per cent per annum. This is therefore a valuable factor for a winning party, especially where a judgment may take some time to enforce, e.g. where a charging order is used. Judgment debts in the High Court carry interest no matter how small the amount involved. In the county court, however, judgment debts carry interest only where they are for more than £5,000. In addition there are other disadvantages, in particular the fact that whilst attempts are being made through the court to enforce the judgment by execution, garnishee, or attachment of earnings (see **23.1.2**) (and these may well last several weeks, or even months), interest lapses provided that any money is obtained from the judgment debtor by the enforcement procedure. There are ways of alleviating this problem, in particular by arranging to transfer the benefit of the county court judgment to the High Court for enforcement, when the judgment becomes subject to High Court rules as to interest which does not lapse whilst attempts are being made to enforce it. For further discussion of this topic, see **23.2.1.3**.

It should also be noted that where one proceeds to enforce a judgment by execution against goods, the High Court Sheriff must be used where the sum is £5,000 or more in whichever court the action has been proceeding hitherto; and the county court bailiff must be used where the sum is under £1,000 wherever the action has been proceeding hitherto. Only between those two figures is there any choice of method of execution, see **23.2**.

5.3.6.2 Specific remedies

By a separate statutory instrument, the *County Court Remedies Regulations 1991*, it is provided that the county court shall no longer have the power to award that form of interlocutory injunctive relief known as *Mareva* injunctions (which provide a power to freeze the assets of a potential defendant until the end of an action and enforcement of judgment); nor *Anton Piller* orders (which provide a power of search and seizure in certain kinds of cases). Where such orders are sought, application must be made to the High Court. Accordingly, it would be preferable to commence such actions in the High Court where that form of relief is likely to be needed.

If an action has already been commenced in a county court, application can be made to a High Court judge for that form of relief and any application made in the county court is deemed to include an application for transfer of the proceedings for that stage of the action. Thereafter the action will be retransferred to the county court.

The provision preventing application for *Mareva* injunctions or *Anton Piller* orders does not apply in matrimonial proceedings, nor for the purpose of making an order for the preservation, custody or detention of the very property which is the subject matter of the proceedings, nor in aid of an execution of a judgment or order already made in county court proceedings to preserve assets until execution can be levied.

5.3.6.3 Special types of action particularly suitable for the High Court

By virtue of *Practice Direction (County Court: Transfer of Actions)* [1991] 1 WLR 643, referred to at **5.3.3.6**, there is a specific indication that the following types of case, whether made by claim or counterclaim, may be considered important and therefore suitable for trial in the High Court:

(a) professional negligence;

(b) fatal accidents;

(c) fraud or undue influence;

(d) defamation;

(e) malicious prosecution or false imprisonment;

(f) claims against the police.

In these kinds of action, therefore, since it is possible that trial in the High Court will be ordered, it may be appropriate to issue in the High Court even if relatively modest sums appear to be claimed. Of course, in fatal accident cases, and claims against the police involving personal injuries, a claim can only be *started* in the High Court if the plaintiff's solicitor can certify, as previously indicated, that the claim is worth more than £50,000. In fact, despite this Practice Direction cases against the police very commonly remain in the county court if issued there.

Conversely, all defamation actions must be commenced in the High Court because the county court has no original jurisdiction although cases may be transferred there at a later stage (they rarely are in practice).

5.3.6.4 More general features in favour of the High Court

In a personal injury case there is little choice about place of issue unless the value appears to be greater than £50,000. If a case is worth more than £50,000, then it can be commenced in either the High Court or county court but all plaintiff solicitors would choose the High Court in such a case. If, despite a low value, some special feature arises after the action has been commenced, e.g. that there is a novel point of law, great difficulties of expert evidence etc., then application may be made to the District Judge for a transfer to the High Court. It is anticipated that such powers to transfer may be very sparingly used. In non-personal injury cases, however, the case can in principle commence in either court, bearing in mind that if it commences in the High Court the matter is likely to be reviewed anyway and may be transferred down, where appropriate, at a later stage. What, then, are the advantages generally of commencing in the High Court?

In favour of the High Court the following features are often said to apply:

(a) The plaintiff has far greater control over the early stages. The solicitor is responsible for the preparation and service of all documents. This is particularly relevant in a debt case where a solicitor may, if he wishes to proceed with expedition, issue and serve the writ on the same day. In the county court, despite provisions which permit the plaintiff to serve proceedings personally (*CCR Ord. 7, r. 10A*), the court almost always has some involvement in the process of preparing the documents to be served (see **20.7**). Similarly with applications at interlocutory stages, the county court has to be involved, and in many small county courts it is not possible for documents to be issued immediately over the counter; the county court staff will need to type up relevant notices, obtain details of the District Judge's diary and so on. In the High Court a solicitor can usually obtain the hearing date to be inserted in the summons which he has himself drafted at the time of issue.

(b) High Court process tends to look more impressive and even intimidating to an opponent, especially if he is a debtor. The documents bear a more impressive seal and are more peremptorily worded. A county court summons looks rather like some form of local government documentation, e.g. a demand for council tax. Moreover, the form of admission defence and counterclaim sent out with the county court summons is considered by many to be a virtual enticement to the debtor to think up some reason for prolonging the case. He is given in effect a questionnaire which he can complete quite easily, and if he does so successfully this may have the effect of bringing about many weeks or months delay in proceedings. Indeed, if he makes a partial admission in answer to the form there will then be a pre-trial review which will not be fixed until several weeks in the future. In the High Court a defendant must both complete the form of acknowledgment of service properly and follow this up with a defence within quite tight time limits. There is no form of instructions sent to tell him how to draft a defence, and an unrepresented litigant may well do so in such a defective way as to lead immediately to an application for summary judgment.

(c) In favour of the High Court is also the fact that enforcement is generally more efficient. This is pre-eminently so where the High Court Sheriff is involved rather than the county court bailiff, although this is now less of a problem given that county court judgments of over £1,000 may anyway be enforced by the High Court Sheriff.

(d) If it is hoped that the action will end short of trial, then it is actually swifter to take proceedings in the High Court. So, for example, if one hopes to obtain judgment in default of notice of intention to defend (*Ord. 13*) or summary judgment (*Ord. 14*) these will actually be swifter in the High Court than in the county court.

(e) In marginal cases, issuing in the High Court will simply persuade the opponent that you view the case more seriously than he had thought. It may make him think in High Court terms and put forward better offers of settlement. In marginal cases High Court judges tend to be more generous than county court judges (especially in personal injury actions), perhaps because they are used to thinking in terms of thousands of pounds rather than hundreds of pounds.

(f) If it becomes apparent that a case which involves a modest amount is to be seriously defended, contrary to the solicitor's initial hopes, then one can anyway apply to transfer a case which one has commenced in the High Court to the county court so little harm is done.

(g) Most solicitors would say that in general terms the High Court is more efficient than the county court. This is because, despite undertakings from the Lord Chancellor, county courts are often understaffed and overworked. There are often long delays in obtaining trial dates or dates for the hearing of an interlocutory application. Simply establishing contact by telephone to many county courts can be a difficult problem.

Features in favour of the county court

a) The first feature is the simple matter of geographical convenience. There are over 300 county courts, almost three times the number of District Registries of the High Court, and therefore in rural areas there is simply likely to be a more convenient county court. If one's solicitor's office is only a few hundred yards from the nearest county court, then clearly a great deal of time and costs can be saved in travelling alone. Some less busy county courts are set up in a 'group', however, and it often does not follow that there will be a District Judge in attendance every day, or a county court judge available more often than once a week. However, the county court office is open every day for the issue of proceedings.

(b) Some clients may prefer the lesser degree of formality usual in the county court, though this is not a reason which ought to persuade a lawyer.

(c) If so inclined, a solicitor who is keen to develop or use his advocacy skills has the professional satisfaction of being able to take a county court case all the way through to and including appearance in the trial himself. This is not possible in a High Court case unless the solicitor has obtained the Higher Courts Advocacy Qualification. This may be particularly worthwhile in rural areas where there is no local Bar and it may only be possible to obtain very junior counsel for modest cases. A client will often be much happier seeing his own solicitor represent him throughout where the solicitor is competent to do so.

Issue of Proceedings: Which Ct?
PI commence in CC unless > £50,000
Other proceedings → HC
Which Ct for Trial?
<£25,000 : CC unless "criteria" applied
>£50,000 : HC " "
£25,000 – £50,000 : depends on criteria
Decides choice of Ct
1. Complexity of case; remedy sought
2. Public interest
3. Speed of Trial
4. Financial substance

Small claims Ct for < £3000
or PI < £1,000
No award for costs

Then look at practical factors only if there is choice:
- Client choice – HC [illegible] more prestigious efficient
- Costs

Chap 6

Commencing a HC Action

Joinder of Parties + Causes of Action

Link together – cases involving 2 or more opposing parties or 2 or more causes of action

- **Joinder of Parties by P. s̄ leave**
  Where some common Q of law or fact arises in all the actions + all rights t. relief claims arise out of the same transaction.
  [D can't join parties; can only take 3rd P Proceedings]

- **Joinder of Causes of Action by P.**
  Where P has a number of causes of action (not nec. factually related) vs the same defendant. Parties must be claiming or liable in the same capacity re all causes of action.

- **Joinder of Causes of Action by D.**
  Where D has claims vs P → raise them in the same action as a COUNTERCLAIM:
  - Unrelated CC: cause of action may have arisen before or after P's cause of action / issue of writ – makes no difference.
  - Related CC = SET OFF
    - monetary cross claim
    - defence to claim by P → extinguish P's claim up to the extent of the set off
    - sum claimed must already be due at the date of commencement of P's action.

Costs Consequences of Joinder

Where P sues 2 Ds → 1 succeeded + 1 lost: Who meets costs of winning Def?:
- Where joinder was reasonable ~~Bullock~~ Sanderson Order Losing D pays. Most common; also where P is LA.
- Where joinder was unreasonable Bullock Order – P must pay + later recover fr other D.

WRITS

Form + Contents of the Writ

Completed by P's Sol.

- **General Endorsement**
  Concise statement of the nature of the claim made + relief / remedy reqd (damages); the cause of action + description of facts.
  Supplemented c̄ full Statement of Claim (SofC) served later c̄ details of facts on which cause of action is based + nature of the relief claimed

- **Special Endorsement**
  c̄ the SofC incl. computation for interest due for debt action.
  SofC brief enough t. be endorsed on the writ; avoid need for separate service of SofC later.

- **Fixed Costs Endorsement**
  fr White Book – Ord 62.
  Def. can extinguish all his liability by paymt claim in full + interest + fixed costs → within 14 days of receipt of writ. (won't fully cover P's Sol costs).

- **Endorsement as t. place where Cause of action arose**
  For debt P can allege CofA arose either in the place where contract was concluded, or if diff, place where paymt under contract was due t. be received (P's premises)
  → P can issue proceedings in the Dist Reg most convenient for him. D can't then have it transferred.

- **Endorsement of P's address for Service**
  Sol's office address + P's own address also given

Issue of the Writ

Attend personally at the District Reg (or post) with:
- Writ + enough copies (for Ct, P + each of the Ds)
- Writ fee – depends on sum claimed p117
- LA Cert if client is LA

[– if P under a disability: consent t. act + cert of no conflict]

One writ signed by Sol issuing it → stamped c̄ fee paid + kept at Ct.
Other 2 returned t. P → 1 stamped as 'original' to be retained
Ct Staff 1) enter action No at top of writ
2) Ct seal c̄ date of issue (relevant date for limitation period)

Duration + Renewal of Writ

- 4 mths fr date of issue (– 6 mths if served out of the jurisdiction)

Renewal – for a further period not exceeding 12 mths.
Application by affidavit stating reasons for non-service.

Service of the Writ (p118)

Send to each D (within 4 mths of issue)
- Sealed copy of writ c̄ SofC
- Ack. of Service Form
- Covering letter

- **Service on individuals**
  - Personal (effective at moment of S)
  - Postal, at own usual or last known address. Effected 7th day after post or inserted thro' letter box.
  - Nominated Sol, specifically appt to accept service for this transaction
    Serve: writ + orig. writ + A of S – return t. Ct
    endorse that he accepts service on behalf of D + return t. P's sol.

  If AofS in fact lodged, writ deemed t. have been properly served

- **Service on a Ltd Co**
  Post or leave at reg. office → effective immediately
  → "in the ord. course of post"
  1st class → 2nd working day after posting
  2nd class → 4th " "
  Any officer can complete + return AofS
  Thereafter must employ a Sol.

- **Service on Partnerships**
  - Personal or postal service on any P
  - Postal service t. principal place of business → 7th day after posting
  - Personal service at pr. place of bus on person managing business → effective immediately

  If Ps individually named on writ, should be served as individuals.

- **Service by Fax**
  Fax OK for all other docs but NOT for WRIT (needs physical delivery t. D. (RSC Ord 65 r 5)
  Provided:
  - all parties act by Sols
  - service by fax at business address of Sol of the party being served
  - Sol indicated in writing willingness to accept service by fax (eg headed paper c̄ fax No)
  - Copy of doc is also served by post at the same time.

SIX

COMMENCING A HIGH COURT ACTION

We shall now consider the early stages of a High Court action. The jurisdictional changes referred to in **Chapter 5** have had the effect of switching an enormous proportion of work from the High Court to the county court, at least in those cases which go on to trial. It follows therefore that the bulk of most solicitors' practices, at least outside major commercial litigation practices, will be in the county court rather than the High Court. All experienced practitioners would, however, concede that it is essential to have a thorough grasp of High Court procedure as a preliminary for approaching county court procedure for some of the reasons briefly referred to in the preface to this book. That is that practical, tactical and evidential features are exactly the same in both courts; and secondly that most, although not all, county court procedures exactly mirror their High Court equivalent and indeed in some cases the relevant county court rule merely says that the equivalent High Court practice 'shall apply' without even describing it (see, for example, *CCR Ord. 13, r. 7*). It is therefore the writer's opinion that it is easier to approach the county court after acquiring familiarity with High Court procedures. In the chapters hereafter which concentrate specially on the county court, great emphasis is placed on the features which are different from High Court procedures. The county court chapters are comprehensible on their own and readers whose courses commence with, or whose interests lie in, county court litigation could start with those chapters, **Chapters 20 and 21**.

6.1 Joinder of Parties and Causes of Action

6.1.1 INTRODUCTION

In straightforward litigation, comprising the majority of cases, there is no problem of choice of parties. There is only one potential plaintiff and only one potential defendant, e.g. in the common case where a pedestrian is knocked down by a motorist, or where an unpaid supplier of goods needs to sue his customer. However, not all situations are so simple. It may be that the pedestrian has been knocked down not as a result of the negligence of one driver only, but perhaps where two drivers have collided. Likewise, it may be that the unpaid supplier of goods who wishes to sue his customer has, in some dispute about the quality of the goods, been assaulted by the customer. The question of *joinder* concerns whether parties may link together and have heard at the same time either cases involving two or more opposing parties, or two or more causes of action which arise separately but which have some common factual connection thus making it convenient to litigate them at the same time.

The provisions of *RSC Ord. 15* must be studied in order to see what the possibilities are for getting the right people before the court at the right time, with the overall aim of convenience and saving costs. The rules in *Ord. 15* are largely *permissive*; they state what can be done, rather than what must be done, so that whilst a plaintiff may be able to join two causes of action, or to sue two defendants on the same writ, there is nothing which actually compels him to do so. If he thinks it more convenient in the circumstances of his case to issue separate writs in respect of each cause of action, or separate writs directed against each defendant, he may do so. Moreover, actions which a plaintiff himself takes by way of joinder are subject to a general power of review by the court under *Ord. 15, r. 5*.

6.1.2 JOINDER OF PARTIES

6.1.2.1 Joinder by the plaintiff without leave

Under *RSC Ord. 15, r. 4*:

> *two or more persons may be joined together in one action as plaintiffs or as defendants with the leave of the court or where—*
>
> (a) *if separate actions were brought by or against each of them, as the case may be, some common question of law or fact would arise in all the actions, and*
>
> (b) *all rights to relief claimed in the action . . . are in respect of or arise out of the same transaction or series of transactions.*

The meaning of this rule is that if, for example, one driver should leave the road and knock down several people standing in a bus queue, all the plaintiffs may combine together to issue just one writ against the driver because their actions arise out of the same facts. There is no obligation to do so, and in many cases it might be tactically or procedurally inconvenient. In that case, each could issue a separate writ.

Where there is more than one plaintiff on the same writ, all the plaintiffs must use the same solicitor and counsel and may not generally make allegations of fact which are inconsistent with each others' cases. Thus if all the persons in the bus queue happened to know each other, they might well combine to issue one writ. If, however, they were strangers, each might prefer to issue a separate writ using his own choice of solicitor and counsel.

Similarly, if the root cause of an accident seems to be the negligence of two or more drivers, e.g. in a large motorway pile up case where it may be impossible for an innocent person finally to judge which of several other drivers may have been to blame, a plaintiff, or several plaintiffs, can sue two or more defendants jointly or in the alternative on the same writ. Where there is more than one defendant, the defendants are entitled to their own individual choice of solicitors and counsel and there is no compulsion to use the same one. Indeed, since most defendants sued jointly or in the alternative have a conflict of interest with each other, in that it is often in their interests to blame their co-defendant, it would clearly be impossible for them all to have to use the same lawyers.

6.1.2.2 Joinder with leave

The opening words of *Ord. 15, r. 4(1)* allow joinder with leave of the court where the case is not within *para. (a)* or *(b)*. This would only rarely arise. The first two provisions allow joinder automatically by the plaintiff, who initially has the choice of parties, without needing to get the court's permission. If a case did not fit *para. (a)* or *(b)* of *Ord. 15, r. 4(1)*, then it is unlikely that the court would wish to grant leave because that rule envisages all the sensible situations where joining the parties together will save time and costs.

6.1.2.3 Joinder by the defendant

It is up to the plaintiff (or co-plaintiffs) who issues a writ to choose who the parties should be. A defendant cannot as such join any other party in to be a co-plaintiff with the present plaintiff, nor a co-defendant to himself. The only thing open to a defendant is to add another person to an action by bringing what are called *third party proceedings* against that person. How this is done and the effect of it will be considered in a later section on third party proceedings at **18.1**.

6.1.2.4 Joinder by other parties

In very limited circumstances, persons who have not been involved in the action may have the right to intervene and request that they be added as parties, usually as defendants. This is by virtue of *RSC Ord. 15, r. 6(2)*. A good example of the case where it might arise is where it is appropriate to join the MIB to an action because it wishes to participate and in its own right defend an action brought against an uninsured person.

6.1.3 JOINDER OF CAUSES OF ACTION

6.1.3.1 Joinder by the plaintiff

A plaintiff can claim relief for several causes of action in the same proceedings by virtue of *RSC Ord. 15, r. 1*:

(a) if the plaintiff claims and the defendant is alleged to be liable in the same capacity in respect of all causes of action or

(b) if the plaintiff claims or the defendant is alleged to be liable in the capacity of executor or administrator of an estate in respect of one or more of the causes of action and in his personal capacity but with reference to the same estate in respect of all the others or

(c) (in any other case) with the leave of the court.

This means that if a plaintiff has a number of causes of action against the same defendant, he may sue for them on the same writ even if there is no factual connection between them. Thus if a plaintiff has been libelled by a defendant and in meeting to discuss it the defendant then assaults the plaintiff, the plaintiff will be able to include both causes of action on the same writ. Whether it would be tactically wise to do so is quite another matter, and in the main it would not where the causes of action are very disparate, but the *right* to do so exists.

It is important to note that the parties must be claiming or liable *in the same capacity* in respect of all causes of action subject to (b) above. So, in general, if one was suing a person for one debt which he had personally incurred and for a debt which he owed as executor of an estate, two writs would have to be issued.

As in the case of joinder of parties, if the case does not fall within either of the previous provisions, there is the possibility of the court allowing joinder in an appropriate case, but since the provisions already described would permit joinder automatically in most mainstream instances there will be very few where it would be appropriate to ask the court to allow joinder outside the rule.

6.1.3.2 Joinder by the defendant — counterclaim

If a defendant has one or several claims against a plaintiff, he may raise them in the same action by way of a *counterclaim*. The nature of his action need not in any way be factually related to that on the plaintiff's writ which has been issued against him. Thus if a plaintiff was owed money by a defendant and at the meeting to discuss repayment the plaintiff slandered the defendant to some third party, the defendant could raise this separate cause of action by way of a counterclaim in the debt proceedings. In more complex cases a defendant may need to add other persons as *co-defendants to the counterclaim* with the present plaintiff, e.g. if the nature of the defendant's counterclaim is based on some action by a partnership firm in which the plaintiff is only one of the partners.

Counterclaims may exceed the amount of the plaintiff's claim or be less than it; and the cause of action may have arisen before the plaintiff's cause of action or after the issue of the writ – it makes no difference.

It is important to mention one further technical term in the same context, which is *'set off'*. A set off is a monetary crossclaim which is also a defence to the claim made by the plaintiff in the action. The distinction between counterclaim and set off is therefore obvious, since a mere counterclaim need have no reference to the plaintiff's cause of action. The effect of a set off is to extinguish the plaintiff's claim up to the extent of the set off.

Every set off can be pleaded as a counterclaim if the defendant so desires, and normally he should do so, but not every counterclaim can be pleaded as a set off. The distinction can be vital on the question of costs, because if the counterclaim has nothing to do with the plaintiff's claim, separate judgments will be given on each. If, however, the counterclaim is also a set off then any judgment will only be given for the balance between the two, if any. A good example is the case of *British Anzani (Felixstowe) Ltd* v *International Marine Management (UK) Ltd* [1980] QB 637. In this case the plaintiff landlord sued the tenant for arrears of rent. The defendant pleaded by way of set off a claim to damages for breach of the landlord's covenants to do repairs. The effect of the breaches had been to diminish the rental value of the land to the tenant and the court held this was a proper case for set off so that judgment was only given for the balance between the two figures. A further example is *s. 53(1)(e)* of the *Sale of Goods Act 1979*, which expressly provides that in an action for the price of goods, damages for breach of warranty of quality (e.g. the repair price) may be set off against the debt.

Lastly, it should be noted that in order to qualify as a set off, the sum claimed (whether the case involves a debt or unliquidated damages), must already be due at the date of commencement of the plaintiff's action.

6.1.3.3 Actions against estates

This difficult topic is dealt with further at **19.7**.

6.1.4 COSTS CONSEQUENCES OF JOINDER

It is inherent in any system of joinder that there is a possibility that parties may win and lose in different combinations. In practice the most important instance is where one or more plaintiffs sued two or more defendants and one of the defendants succeeded whilst the other lost. Where that happens the key issue is that of who is to meet the costs of the winning defendant. There are two possible outcomes:

(a) If the court decides that it was unreasonable, in his state of knowledge at the outset of the action, for the plaintiff to have joined the winning defendant to the action at all, it may order the costs of the winning defendant to be paid by the plaintiff.

(b) Where, however, the court considers that there appeared at the outset to the plaintiff to be some reasonable prospect of success against the defendant who in the end has been exonerated, then the court will usually order that, in effect, the losing defendant pays the costs of the winning defendant as well as the costs and damages due to the plaintiff.

The orders which may be made are:

(a) A *Bullock* order (*Bullock* v *London General Omnibus Co.* [1907] 1 KB 264). Under this form of order the plaintiff is ordered to pay the winning defendant's costs but is then allowed to add the amount of those costs to his own costs against the losing defendant and thus recover.

(b) A *Sanderson* order (*Sanderson* v *Blythe Theatre Co.* [1903] 2 KB 533). The losing defendant is ordered to pay the winning defendant's costs direct to him without the intervention of the plaintiff. In routine litigation, and especially where the plaintiff is legally aided or both defendants are insured, this form of order is much more convenient, allowing the attempt to negotiate costs and the subsequent taxation to be carried out direct between the interested parties.

The key issue in deciding what order to make is the reasonableness of the plaintiff's action in joining the parties at all. Thus where two motorists collide at a cross roads and one of the vehicles then mounts the pavement injuring the plaintiff, obviously the plaintiff will be reasonable in suing both in the alternative. Had he sued only one, say the driver of the vehicle which struck him, he might have discovered later that the accident was entirely the other driver's fault and it would then be too late to issue new proceedings and the first proceedings would have been fruitless. Therefore in that situation the court would undoubtedly conclude that the plaintiff had been reasonable to sue both drivers, and if one of them had been exonerated entirely, the losing driver's insurance company would have had to pay the costs of the winning defendant as well as those of the plaintiff. Suppose, however, that the plaintiff had decided, from an excess of caution, to join in the action the owner of another vehicle parked a few yards from the junction which, it might tenuously have been argued, could have contributed to the incident by obscuring the line of sight of one of the drivers going into the junction. That would have seemed such a baseless claim that there is no doubt that the costs of that defendant when he was exonerated would have been borne directly by the plaintiff.

6.1.5 SUMMARY

Joinder is not really a difficult topic in practice, although the rules appear complex. Although those rules *permit* actions to be commenced by co-plaintiffs, or actions to be commenced by one plaintiff concerning two causes of action, it is often tactically wiser and procedurally more convenient to issue separate writs. Such matters as compromise of the claim, acceptance of payments into court and so on are facilitated by this. This is certainly so in the case of co-plaintiffs unless they have a virtual identity of interest. Even in such cases a substantial saving in costs can anyway be effected by ensuring that interlocutory applications, and even the trial itself, proceed in such a way that all the plaintiffs are before the court at once even if the actions are not formally joined. This topic links with a related one of *consolidation*.

6.2 Consolidation

By *RSC Ord. 4, r. 9*, it is provided that:

Where two or more causes or matters are pending in the same division and it appears to the court—

(a) that some common question of law or fact arises in both or all of them, or

(b) that the rights to relief claimed therein are in respect of or arise out of the same transaction or series of transactions, or

(c) that for some other reason it is desirable to make an order under this paragraph,

the court may order those causes or matters to be consolidated on such terms as it thinks just or may order them to be tried at the same time, or one immediately after another or may order any of them to be stayed until after the determination of any other of them.

This rule therefore gives the court a discretion to consolidate actions to save costs and time, and is therefore generally similar to those in which parties have a choice of joinder under *RSC Ord. 15, r. 4.*

This rule can be of importance in multi-party cases, e.g. 'disaster' or pharmaceutical product liability claims. For example it allows the court to consolidate the actions up to the point where the issue as to liability is decided, giving the conduct of the action up to that point to one plaintiff's solicitor and leaving the actions separate on the issue of quantum of damage thereafter.

More commonly an order is made *staying* some actions pending the decision on the first action. However, there is no requirement on any party to accept the outcome of the test action under this procedure, which has been a crucial difference from equivalent American procedures where the result in the lead case is binding. In England, however, so-called 'class' actions (which ought really to be called 'group' actions) in disaster and pharmaceutical product liability cases cannot take place without the consent of all the parties. The defendant in particular will often be reluctant to accept the outcome of a test case as establishing liability, especially in pharmaceutical product claims where each plaintiff's claim on liability may have vital differences, for example the length of their exposure to the allegedly damaging product, the intervention of other possible causes, the plaintiff's conduct in relation to the matter, the applicability of the limitation period and the like.

6.3 Forms of Originating Process

6.3.1 ORIGINATING SUMMONSES

Proceedings may be commenced in the Queen's Bench Division of the High Court by a document called a 'writ of summons', usually referred to simply as a 'writ'. In the main we shall be considering actions begun by writ of summons. It is appropriate, though, to say a word about the other main form of commencing proceedings which is known as the 'originating summons'.

Originating summonses are used in certain specific kinds of action and the procedure is described in more detail in **Chapter 24**. Originating summonses have much greater use in Chancery Division actions but they may be used in Queen's Bench Division cases as well. In the main, although something of an over-generalisation, it is right to say that originating summonses are used for actions where there is no great dispute on the facts but which turn mainly on a point of law or construction of documents. They may also be used particularly where there is one short point to be taken which the court can dispose of quite briefly and for which the procedure involving pleadings and interlocutory stages common to writ actions might be superfluous.

We have considered two kinds of application made by originating summons already, i.e. for pre-action discovery under *RSC Ord. 24, r. 7A*, and pre-action inspection, detention, preservation etc. of an object under *RSC Ord. 29, r. 7A* (both of which have county court equivalents) (see **4.1.4.1** and **4.1.4.2**). In each of those cases the common feature was that there was one simple procedural point to be decided which made originating summons the appropriate method. A further instance which we consider in **19.8.7.2**, has to do with obtaining the court's consent to settle an action on behalf of an infant plaintiff before a writ has been issued.

In many cases the plaintiff has a choice of mode of action because, by *RSC Ord. 5, r. 4*: *'Proceedings may be begun either by writ or by originating summons as the plaintiff considers appropriate.'* However, *RSC Ord. 5, r. 2* provides:

> *. . . the following proceedings must, notwithstanding anything in rule 4, be begun by writ, that is to say, proceedings—*

(a) *in which a claim is made by the plaintiff for any relief or remedy for any tort, other than trespass to land;*

(b) *in which a claim made by the plaintiff is based on an allegation of fraud;*

(c) *in which a claim is made by the plaintiff for damages for breach of duty . . . where the damages claimed consist of or include damages in respect of the death of any person or in respect of personal injuries to any person or in respect of damage to any property;*

(d) *in which a claim is made by the plaintiff in respect of the infringement of a patent.*

The effect of these provisions is that almost all actions in tort are commenced by writ (and most must be) and so is the great majority of actions in contract.

6.3.2 WRITS

6.3.2.1 The form and contents of the writ

All writs must be in the form given in Appendix A to the *Rules of the Supreme Court* in the White Book, Vol. II. It is usual to purchase blank forms of writ from law stationers, although they may be held on a word processor. The problem with using a word processor is that the Royal Coat of Arms will then need to be impressed on the writ at court and this may cause some delay. For that reason most solicitors prepare writs on purchased blank forms.

The writ is usually in one or other of two different formats:

(a) a writ claiming *unliquidated damages* (e.g. in a personal injury case); and

(b) a writ claiming a *liquidated sum* (e.g. in a claim for a debt).

The forms of a writ are completed by the plaintiff's solicitor. Each writ must contain upon it in addition to the parties' names and the name and address of the solicitor issuing it, one of the two following endorsements:

(a) a concise statement of the nature of the claim made and the relief or remedy required (this is called the *general endorsement* and is used in a writ which claims damages); or

(b) an endorsement of the *statement of claim*. This form of writ is used in an action for a debt and the statement of claim will be brief enough to endorse actually on the writ, thus avoiding the need for a separate statement of claim to be served later. This is usually called a *specially endorsed* writ, although, strictly speaking, the rules no longer use that term. Where the statement of claim is endorsed on the writ there will normally be a computation of interest due if interest is to be claimed. We shall return to this topic in due course.

Where the *general endorsement* is used it is essential to state in it the remedy required, the cause of action and a very concise description of the facts. The general endorsement will be supplemented (if the action is defended) with a full statement of claim served later, in which the plaintiff will set out in considerably more detail the factual allegations on which he bases his cause of action and the nature of the relief claimed. The statement of claim can only allege causes of action which have been already referred to in the endorsement of the writ. Thus if, for example, a writ had been issued which only alleged negligence by the defendant and the plaintiff actually wished to allege both negligence and, say, nuisance or breach of a statutory duty, the writ would have to be amended so as to insert these additional causes of action before a statement of claim referring to them could be served.

6.3.2.2 The fixed costs endorsement

In writs which claim a liquidated sum, there is a so-called 'fixed costs endorsement' on the writ. This is already preprinted on the writ when the solicitor obtains it from the law stationers and he must complete it. The appropriate figure to claim as fixed costs is found in a table contained in the White Book as an appendix to *Ord. 62*. The effect of the fixed costs, endorsement and of the plaintiff pleading his claim for interest precisely is simply that the defendant in such a case who is minded to pay the amount claimed by the writ can extinguish all his liability by paying the claim in full together with the interest accrued to the date on which he wishes to pay and the figure for fixed costs. Provided this sum is paid within 14 days of receipt of the writ the defendant knows that he will not be liable for any further sums. In such a case a plaintiff will not be able to obtain an order that the defendant pay any other costs. Consequently, since this is the only sum for costs which can be recovered from the defendant, the plaintiff is going to have to bear some part of his solicitor's bill (unless there has been very little work indeed involved before the issue and service of the writ so that the amount of fixed costs does actually cover the whole of the solicitor's charges to his own client).

6.3.2.3 Endorsement as to place where cause of action arose

In the case of a writ issued from a District Registry, whether it is a specially endorsed writ or a generally endorsed writ, the plaintiff may complete the endorsement showing that the cause of action arose wholly or in part in the district of that District Registry. Completion of this endorsement prevents the defendant from applying in his acknowledgment of service to transfer the proceedings to the Central Office or another District Registry if this is the case.

Example Suppose the plaintiff lives in Newcastle and whilst crossing the street near his home he is knocked down by a vehicle driven by the defendant, who lives in Exeter. The plaintiff can endorse on this writ that the action arose wholly in Newcastle and issue his action in the Newcastle District Registry of the High Court. If he did not so endorse his writ the defendant would be able to apply, when he returned his acknowledgment of service to the court, for the action to be transferred to be heard at the District Registry most convenient to him in Exeter. Actually, on the facts of a case like this, the defendant would be most unlikely to succeed in his application because the court would conclude that the balance of convenience favoured having the action heard in Newcastle anyway, where the witnesses are likely to reside. However, endorsing the writ in such a way does prevent the defendant even making that application. In the case of a contract action, especially for a debt, it would be open to the plaintiff to allege that the cause of action arose either in the place where the contract was concluded, or, if different, the place where payment under the contract was due to be received. In this latter case, since the place where payment was due to be received is most likely to be the plaintiff's premises, this endorsement should ensure that the plaintiff is able to issue proceedings in the District Registry most convenient for him.

None of the above is to suggest that the advantage of issuing proceedings in the plaintiff's own local District Registry is that he is likely to obtain 'home town justice' or anything of that nature. It is simply a matter of the convenience of the plaintiff's solicitor. Naturally a solicitor prefers to attend at the court nearest his office. If plaintiff's solicitors are involved in an action which is proceeding in a court some miles away, they need to instruct a local firm of solicitors to act as their agents in attending court on interlocutory applications, and this is inevitably both more expensive for the party concerned and less satisfactory, since the agents are unlikely, however thoroughly they are briefed, to be as aware of all the facets of the case as the plaintiff's own solicitors.

6.3.2.4 Endorsement of plaintiff's address for service

An address for service must also be endorsed on every writ. This will either be the plaintiff's address if he is not employing a solicitor, or the solicitor's office address. The plaintiff's own address must also be given.

6.4 Issue of the Writ

6.4.1 METHOD

A writ can be issued by attending personally at the District Registry, or by posting the necessary documents to the Registry. It is more common to issue a writ in person if the solicitor is within easy reach of the District Registry concerned.

Two copies of the writ are prepared together with one copy for each defendant in the case, and therefore a minimum of three copies of the writ will be required. These are taken to the District Registry office together with the legal aid certificate if one has been issued and a cheque for the writ fee.

The fees on writs are increased from time to time and after a decade when the writ fee had only been subject to very modest increases, in January 1997 a wide ranging series of increases in court fees was introduced with the object of making the courts self-financing. In particular the fee on issue of a writ now depends upon the sum claimed and if unliquidated damages are sought, the Plaintiff's solicitor will be required to endorse the writ with a statement of the maximum amount of the claim. The rate of fees is now as follows:

(a)	where the claim is limited to £10,000 or less	£120
(b)	between £10,000 and £50,000	£150
(c)	between £50,000 and £100,000	£300
(d)	any sum over £100,000 or when no limit is specified	£500

The court staff check that the writ is formally in order. One of the forms must be signed by the solicitor issuing it. The signed copy is kept at court and is stamped with a note that the fee has been paid. The other two are returned to the plaintiff, one of which is stamped with the word 'original'. The plaintiff's solicitor should retain the 'original'. The court staff enter the action number at the top of the writ. The action number consists of the year of issue, the initial letter of the plaintiff's name and then a number which corresponds to the number of writs issued so far that year in that District Registry.

6.4.2 THE DATE OF THE COURT SEAL

On the front of the writ the court seal shows the date of issue of the writ and is the relevant date for the purpose of seeing whether the writ has been issued within the period allowed by the Limitation Acts.

6.5 Duration and Renewal of the Writ

6.5.1 DURATION

The writ has a life of four months from the date of issue unless leave to serve the writ out of the jurisdiction is required, in which case its validity is six months. Every effort should normally be made to serve the writ within the period of validity.

6.5.2 RENEWAL

If the writ is not served within the period of its validity the plaintiff may apply to the court for the writ to be renewed for a further period not exceeding 12 months. In principle, that application should be made before the writ expires, although in exceptional circumstances it may be made after it has already expired.

To apply for the writ to be renewed one must make application by affidavit (that is a sworn statement by the plaintiff's solicitor) indicating the reason for non-service. It is very important that a good reason be demonstrated for non-service of the writ. Examples of reasons which have been held to be sufficient on recent case law include:

(a) that the defendant is deliberately evading service.

(b) that there has been a clear agreement with the defendant's solicitors to extend the time for service (but note that mere *acquiescence* by the defendant's solicitors in the plaintiff's delay will not amount to such an agreement).

There is a great deal more case law recently demonstrating reasons which have been found *not* to be sufficient to enable the court to extend the writ, in particular:

(a) that legal aid is awaited;

(b) that it is difficult to trace a witness;

(c) mere oversight.

The affidavit explaining the reason is taken with the original writ and left at the court to be put before the Master or District Judge. There is no oral hearing and, of course, the potential defendant is not involved since he has not as yet been served with the proceedings. If the Master or District Judge thinks that the reason is sufficiently made out he will renew the writ for such period as he thinks appropriate to cope with the difficulty hitherto experienced in service. Thus if, for example, the reason why the writ has not been served is that there was an agreement with the defendant's solicitors to defer service, he is likely to renew it only for a period of seven days to allow the writ now to be served. If the reason was difficulty in tracing an evasive defendant, then he may allow several months.

If renewal is not granted, or one overlooks the period of four months, then the writ lapses. One may therefore need to issue a second writ, though naturally the costs involved in the first writ will then have to be borne by the plaintiff. There is no rule against issuing a second writ. If, however, the limitation period has meanwhile expired, whilst the second writ may still be *issued* the defendant will naturally rely in due course on the *Limitation Act* in his defence.

6.6 Service of the Writ

The sealed copy of the writ which has been brought away from court for service on the defendant, must be served on him together with an acknowledgement of service form. This is obtained from law stationers and completed by the solicitor in his own office. In addition, notice of legal aid must be served if the plaintiff is legally aided. This alerts the defendant to the practical consequences of having a legally aided opponent. (See **2.3.3.1**.)

6.6.1 SERVICE ON INDIVIDUALS

6.6.1.1 Personal service

Personal service means that the writ is actually delivered into the defendant's hands. Solicitors employ process servers to serve writs, and the fees of such process servers will generally be allowed on taxation of costs so that a solicitor suffers no loss. If a person refuses to take the writ, touching him with it and the accompanying documents will suffice. Until quite recently it was generally necessary to effect personal service, but now the need for personal service and the extreme indignities which can sometimes accompany it have been alleviated because of the second available method of service.

6.6.1.2 Postal service

The documents may be sent by ordinary first class post to the defendant at his usual or last known address, or may be put through the letter box at that address in a sealed envelope addressed to him. Service is presumed to be effected on the seventh day after the date on which the documents were posted to the defendant or inserted through the letter box.

This is now the common method of serving documents. One must be sure that one is bona fide posting them to the defendant's own address. It will not do merely to know, for example, that the defendant has some relative who lives at a certain address and to post the documents to him there. The reason for this is that if the acknowledgement of service is not returned to the court in time, the plaintiff may generally proceed to sign judgment in default (see later section on termination without trial at **17.1**). At this time the plaintiff's solicitor will need to swear an affidavit stating that the writ was validly served. One cannot in truth swear that a writ was properly served if it was sent to some address from which it was merely hoped that the person would collect it. It must be served at the defendant's own address.

Despite the provision for postal service there are some cases, particularly so-called debt-collecting cases, where solicitors still prefer to rely on personal service. This is because personal service is deemed to be effective at the moment of service so that seven days are saved, and also because it is common for defendants in debt cases to allege that documents were not received in the course of post; that they were not at home within the relevant weeks; that the dog ate the documents as soon as they came through the letter box, etc. In debt-collecting cases, where speed is often of some importance, solicitors generally prefer the greater certainty of personal service despite the increased expense.

6.6.1.3 Service on a nominated solicitor

A writ is deemed to be properly served on a party if it is served on his solicitor. For this purpose the solicitor must have been specifically appointed to accept and agree to accept service for the particular transaction. The mere fact that one knew that a certain individual had used a certain solicitor in the past (e.g. for a conveyancing transaction) would not entitle one to serve documents on that person by posting them to his solicitor.

When serving documents on a nominated solicitor the writ for service is served together with the original writ and the acknowledgement of service. The defendant's solicitor will send the acknowledgement back to the court in the usual way, but he will also endorse on the original writ that he accpts service on behalf of the defendant and return this to the plaintiff's solicitor.

6.6.1.4 Substituted service

If it has proved impossible for the plaintiff to effect service in accordance with any of the above rules, he may apply to the Master or District Judge for an order that the document be served by some other means. This is increasingly rare in view of the provision for postal service but was of great use when personal service was essential and the defendant was thought to be evading service. In such cases one could apply for an order for substituted service by any appropriate method, e.g. by inserting details of the writ in the legal notices column of some newspaper, or even by announcing the content of the writ outside the defendant's premises over a loudspeaker. This method is not likely to be required in a routine case now.

6.6.1.5 Deemed service

It should be noted that even if none of the above methods has been properly used, provided an acknowledgement of service is *in fact* lodged the writ is deemed to have been properly served. Thus if, contrary to proper practice in a case where the defendant's address was unknown, the writ had been sent to his parents' house, and it had in fact been collected and he had returned the copy of the acknowledgement of service to the court, service would be deemed to have been properly effected.

6.6.2 SERVICE ON A LIMITED COMPANY

In the case of a limited company, service is effected by leaving the documents at, or by posting them to, the registered office of the limited company (see the *Companies Act 1985, s. 725*). If they are posted there is a slight difference from the rules for postal service which apply in the case of an individual. As will be recalled, in the case of an individual service is deemed to be effected on the seventh day after posting. In the case of companies, however, documents are deemed to arrive 'in the ordinary course of post' and this is taken to mean that service is presumed to be effected:

(a) if first class post is used, on the second working day after posting; and

(b) if second class post is used, on the fourth working day after posting.

If the documents are physically taken to the registered office, however, service is deemed to be effective immediately. Any proper officer of the limited company may complete and return the acknowledgement of service, but thereafter a limited company must employ a solicitor in proceedings in the High Court.

6.6.3 SERVICE ON PARTNERSHIPS

Where partners are sued in the name of their firm, the following methods of service are available:

(a) Personal or postal service on any partner.

(b) Postal service by ordinary first class post to the principal place of business. In this case service is deemed to be effected on the seventh day after posting.

(c) Personal service at the principal place of business on the person appearing to have control or management of the business (who need not be a partner as such), in which case service is deemed to be effected immediately.

If partners are individually named on the writ they should be served as individuals.

6.6.4 PROOF OF SERVICE

Service is proved either by a defendant returning the acknowledgement of service to the court, or by the production of the original writ duly endorsed with a solicitor's signature to the effect that he accepts service on behalf of a client. If neither of these two methods is appropriate then it is necessary to provide an affidavit of service, i.e. an affidavit sworn by the person who effected service, whether personal service or the actual act of posting the envelope containing the writ to the defendant.

6.6.5 PERSONAL INJURY CASES

The method of service most likely in a personal injury case is probably now service on a nominated solicitor. In such a case an insurance company or the MIB is likely to be involved. Some, for no good reason, still insist that service should be effected personally upon their insured, the defendant, but since they will immediately then instruct a solicitor to act, it is considerably more simple if that solicitor is nominated to accept service of proceedings.

As indicated earlier, the service of a writ will usually mean that the matter will no longer be dealt with by the claims representatives of the insurance companies but will be passed over to be dealt with by their solicitors. Exceptionally, however, if it is desired to serve the writ merely to ensure that the limitation period does not expire and that the time for interest commences to run, it may be possible to agree that service of the writ will not interrupt the course of negotiations with the insurance company. Some solicitors consider that it is often possible to get a better negotiated settlement from an insurance company representative than from the insurance company's solicitors. This belief is often misplaced but may occasionally be justified. (See **4.5.4**.)

6.6.6 SERVICE OF DOCUMENTS OTHER THAN THE WRIT

Once the action has commenced, service of other documents, e.g. pleadings, interlocutory applications or court orders, is achieved by posting them to the solicitor on the record for the opponent. If the opponent is a litigant in person, although such documents may be served in the ordinary course of post on the person concerned, in the case of extremely important matters, e.g. a summons for an early appointment for summary judgment, it may be deemed prudent to arrange for personal service for the sake of avoiding any doubt about the effectiveness of postal service.

6.6.7 SERVICE BY FAX

By *RSC Ord. 65, r. 5*, documents may be served by facsimile copy. This does not apply to the writ itself, however, since in such a case a copy bearing the court seal must physically be delivered to the defendant. With regard to all other documents, however, such as pleadings, summonses, notices and copies of court orders, service by fax will be sufficient provided that:

(a) all parties to the action act by solicitors, and service by fax is at the business address of the solicitor of the party being served;

(b) the solicitor of that party has indicated in writing a willingness to accept service by fax (indicating a fax number on one's headed notepaper is deemed to be an indication of such willingness unless there is a specific indication to the contrary); and

(c) a copy of the document is served by post at the same time.

6.7 The Acknowledgement of Service

When the writ is received by the defendant a form of acknowledgement of service will be served with it. The defendant has 14 days after service of the writ (including the day of service) in which to acknowledge service.

There are in effect four things for the defendant to consider when completing the acknowledgement of service:

6.7.1 THE DEFENDANT'S NAME

The defendant must write his full name in the appropriate box.

6.7.2 INTENTION TO DEFEND

The form invites the defendant to say whether he intends to contest the proceedings, that is to defend them. There are in fact three boxes inviting the defendant to say whether he intends to contest the whole of the plaintiff's claim; part of the plaintiff's claim; or none of the plaintiff's claim and he is then required to tick the relevant box. If he ticks the box indicating that he does not intend to defend any of the plaintiff's claim the plaintiff will be entitled immediately to proceed to obtain judgment under *Ord. 13* (see **17.1**). If the defendant completes either of the other boxes then he has given notice of intention to defend either the whole claim or part of it and thereafter the action will proceed as described later (see **7.1**).

6.7.3 STAY OF EXECUTION

Suppose that a defendant who is being sued knows that he has no grounds upon which to defend but simply cannot afford to pay the amount claimed immediately? (This is appropriate only in the case of claims for a debt or liquidated demand.) The defendant may legitimately fear that if he merely indicates that he does not propose to defend then the plaintiff will immediately obtain judgment against him and seek to enforce it by execution, i.e. a procedure by which the sheriff's officers may come to the defendant's home and remove his furniture and personal possessions (see **23.2.1** for a full description of this). If the defendant does not propose to defend but merely wishes to be heard on the method of payment of the debt or liquidated demand, he may tick the box indicating that he does not propose to contest the proceedings and then tick the box in paragraph number (3) stating that he does intend to apply for a stay of execution. He then returns the acknowledgement of service to the court.

The effect of this is that whilst the plaintiff will be entitled to obtain judgment immediately, he will not be entitled to enforce the judgment by execution for a further 14 days. Within that period of 14 days the defendant must make an application by summons to the court, supported by an affidavit which discloses his full income, assets, and liabilities. The summons will be served on the plaintiff and there will then be a hearing at which the Master or District Judge will consider what relief, if any, should be given to the defendant against the prospect of immediate enforcement. He may, having taken all relevant matters into account, decide to allow payment of the total of the judgment debt by instalments, or he may make provisions for payment of the amount forthwith if the judgment debtor has assets readily available which would permit this.

6.7.4 TRANSFER OF ACTION

Where a writ was issued from a District Registry and the endorsement relating to where the course of action arose has not been completed and the defendant does not reside or carry on business in the district, then it is open to the defendant to apply by completing the box for the action to be transferred either to the Central Office in London or to a District Registry chosen by him. There will need to be a subsequent hearing (which will take place in the District Registry where the writ was issued) as to where it would be fairest to have the action proceed. The court will have to consider the balance of convenience in the case, which will involve considering not just the parties' preferences but also the whereabouts of any potential witnesses, and therefore their convenience in attending court when the matter comes to trial.

6.7.5 RETURNING THE ACKNOWLEDGEMENT OF SERVICE

The defendant must return the completed acknowledgement of service direct to the court. The form must be returned so that it effectively arrives at the court within the 14-day period which includes the day of service. Posting it within the period will not suffice, it is the date of receipt by the court which counts. For the consequences of failing to return the document in time, see **17.1**.

Once the document has been returned the court will make a photocopy of it and send it to the plaintiff or, if there is more than one plaintiff, to each of them.

6.8 Example Writ

This chapter concludes with a copy of a writ which would be used in a claim for a liquidated sum such as a debt. It will be observed that the statement of claim is endorsed on the writ and is set out rather in the form of an invoice, simply contending that goods have been supplied, referring to the contract for the supply of them and claiming the price of the goods and interest due under the contract. Note that the claim for interest is expressed both as a lump sum due at the date of issue of the writ and as a daily rate thereafter so that the defendant knows the precise amount he owes on any given day. The statement of claim has to be signed on the writ in such a case, although normally statements of claim, when served as a separate document, do not have to be signed.

The amount for fixed costs shown in the endorsement on the writ are taken from the figures in *Appendix 3* to *RSC Ord. 62*. The endorsement indicates to the defendant that if he pays the whole amount due together with the sum for fixed costs within 14 days, there will be no further action in the matter and the plaintiff cannot claim any higher sum for costs. The writ also carries the endorsement reciting that the cause of action arose in Middlemarch, and thus the defendant cannot apply, even had he wished to do so, to transfer the action to London or some other District Registry.

COURT FEES ONLY

Writ indorsed with Statement of Claim [Liquidated Demand] (O.6, r. 1)

IN THE HIGH COURT OF JUSTICE

19 97.—Z .—No. 1081

Queen's Bench Division

[Middlemarch **District Registry]**

Between Zoo Supplies Limited Plaintiff

AND

John Oates Defendant

(1) Insert name

To the Defendant (1) John Oates

(2) Insert address

of (2) The Old Barn, Middlemarch, Loamshire.

This Writ of Summons has been issued against you by the above-named Plaintiff in respect of the claim set out on the back.

Within 14 days after the service of this Writ on you, counting the day of service, you must either satisfy the claim or return to the Court Office mentioned below the accompanying **Acknowledgment of Service** stating therein whether you intend to contest these proceedings.

If you fail to satisfy the claim or to return the Acknowledgment within the time stated, or if you return the Acknowledgment without stating therein an intention to contest the proceedings, the Plaintiff may proceed with the action and judgment may be entered against you forthwith without further notice.

(3) Complete and delete as necessary

Issued from the (3) ~~[Central Office] [Admiralty and Commercial Registry]~~
[Middlemarch District Registry] of the High Court
this 12th day of May 19 97

NOTE:—This Writ may not be served later than 4 calendar months *(or, if leave is required to effect service out of the jurisdiction, 6 months)* beginning with that date unless renewed by order of the Court.

IMPORTANT

Directions for Acknowledgment of Service are given with the accompanying form.

Statement of Claim

The Plaintiff's claim is for the sum of £20,000 being the price of animals sold and delivered to the Defendant by the Plaintiffs pursuant to a contract made the 12th day of February 1996 between the Plaintiffs and the Defendant, and for interest on the said price at the rate of 20% per annum pursuant to clause 7 of the said contract from the date of delivery.

Particulars

To animals supplied to the Defendant on 5th May 1996

One Giant Tasmanian Wombat	5,000
One Siberian Tiger	5,000
One Zambian Gorilla	10,000
	£20,000

And the Plaintiffs claim:

(1) The said sum of £20,000

(2) Interest pursuant to the said contract at the rate of 20 per centum per annum equivalent to a sum of £4,000 for the period from 12th May 1996 to issue herein

(3) Interest as above from the date hereof at the rate of £10.95 daily until judgment or earlier payment.

(Signed) Lydgate QC

If, within the time for returning the Acknowledgment of Service, the Defendant pays the amount claimed and £ 239.25 for costs and, if the Plaintiff obtains an order for substituted service, the additional sum of £ 47.75, further proceedings will be stayed. The money must be paid to the Plaintiff, its Solicitor or Agent.

(1) If this Writ was issued out of a District Registry, this indorsement as to place where the cause of action arose should be completed.

(2) Delete as necessary.

(3) Insert name of place.

(4) For phraseology of this indorsement where the Plaintiff sues in person, see *Supreme Court Practice*, vol. 2, para 1.

([1]) [([2]) [The cause] [One of the causes] of action in respect of which the Plaintiff claims relief in this action arose wholly or in part at ([3]) Middlemarch in the district of the District Registry named overleaf.]

([4]) **This Writ** was issued by Lydgate and Co

of 23 Railway Cuttings, Middlemarch

[Agent for

of]

Solicitors for the said Plaintiff whose address ([2]) [is] [are] registered office is at 1 Main Street Middlemarch Loamshire.

Solicitor's Reference RL/CA Tel. No: 014571 06060

oyez The Solicitors' Law Stationery Society Ltd., Oyez House, 27 Crimscott Street, London SE1 5TS 3.90 F16762 5044027

High Court A2A

Chap 7

Early Stages of Action & PLEADINGS

Pleadings

Must show all the facts which party is relying upon & hopes to establish to the satisfaction of the Ct.

Purpose: define the issues in the case. At trial can't allege facts that were not pleaded.

Pleadings served direct b/t parties.

- P's Pleadings = "Statement of Claim" Sets out the factual allegations relied on to establish his cause of action & the remedy he seeks.
- D's Pleadings = "Defence" Meets the factual allegations made.
- Counterclaim
  Where D, as well as defending the S of C served by P, has any cause of action of his own vs P. Need have no factual connection c P's cause of action
  ↓
  P must then serve a defence to the CC within 14 days
  Failure → D can obtain J vs P in default of defence to CC
- Reply
  P serves a reply (within 14 days after receipt of defence) to ans. any factual allegations raised in the defence (rare) ∵ P deemed to take issue c any matter raised in the defence.

Close of Pleadings

14 days after service of the last pleadings → bench mark for fixing when certain other things ought to happen.

Debt Action:

P serves writ c S of C

D must ack. within 14 days + indicate intention to defend

Then serve defence to SoC (within 28 days of receipt of writ)

ie why D is not liable to pay debt.
[defective goods + not of merchantable Q]

Extensions often granted to allow D time to draft defence.

Failure to serve defence in time → Judgment in default.

Contents of Pleadings

This is who we are
This is what happened
This is what I want

By PLAINTIFF:

1. Heading of the action
2. Title
3. Numbered paras setting out the factual basis of the claim
4. Text in 3rd P + refer to parties as 'P' or 'D'
   Numbers in figs not words
5. Claim for interest
6. Prayer summarising the claim
7. 'Served' / 'Dated'
8. Details of Sol

Do NOT include:

1. Evidence (ie how a party proposes to prove the facts) except ref. to relevant convictions.
2. Law (except where defence is limitation period)
3. Irrelevant material
4. Anticipation of defences which might be raised (eg do not admit not wearing seat belt until they bring it up)
5. Offensive material
6. Your own name (unless you are a barrister or a Sol c rights of audience in HC)

Statement of Claim for Debt

- Give particulars of the debt + goods supplied.
- Set out details of the sum claimed
- "Prayer" c ref to relief or remedy claimed

[Not nec to claim costs in the writ – since Ct always has discretion to award costs. • If fixed costs endorsement is approp → should be completed]

Interest (p131)

Incl in S of C c ref to contractual term under which int is claimed.

If no term → Stat provision SCA1981 s35A

For Liquidated sum compute:

1) Lump sum due on debt upto date of service of pleading
2) Daily rate for day after service of S of C → date of judgment (or earlier payment).

Compute figs as at date of issue of writ (assume writ will be served forthwith)

The Defence

Deal c every matter in S of C – those not dealt c deemed to be admitted.

- Admitting the matter → established b/t parties
- Not admit → not established: P must call evidence to prove at trial; But D may not contest the matter in Q (ie may not have any info at present)
- Denying → denies P's version & goes on to give his own version of the matter. Then goes on to list the matters he relies upon to prove this.

Matters which must be specif pleaded:

- contrib neg.
- Limitation period
- Illegality
- Want of jurisdiction

Counterclaim

Exactly like a S of C – same reqts.

Attacking an Opponents Pleadings

- Further + Better Particulars

Party drafting pleadings must strike a fine balance b/t giving a proper account of facts & leave a certain amt of room for manoeuvre should other matters come to light.

Purpose of F+BP – genuine desire to get info
└ Cut down room to manoeuvre

Failure to comply c reqt:

Apply to District Judge by summons at any stage – usually left until summons for directions hearing.

Particulars not normally ordered before a defence is served.

When F+BP are received → 1 or both parties may need to amend their pleadings.

Status: not strictly pleadings → request does not delay time for next pleading to be sent. But they form part of the bundle for trial.

Where summons issued for Order for F+BF → Order on costs = "Costs in the Cause" unless pleadings so defective it was unreasonable to refuse vol. supply.

- Striking out Pleadings

RSC Ord 18 r 19

- discloses no reasonable cause of action (or defence)
- scandalous, frivolous or vexatious
- may prejudice, embarrass or delay the fair trial of the action
- abuse of the process of the Ct

SEVEN

THE EARLY STAGES OF AN ACTION COMMENCED BY WRIT

7.1 Pleadings Generally

We have so far seen the stages involved in issuing the writ, serving it and returning the acknowledgment of service to the court. We now consider how the action will proceed from that point. What will happen next will depend in part upon whether the claim was one for a debt or liquidated demand, or one for damages. If the case involves a debt or liquidated demand, then the form of writ appropriate to that is likely to have been used, i.e. the statement of claim will be endorsed on the back of the writ. If, however, the case involves a claim for unliquidated damages, then a general endorsement of the nature of the claim will have been inserted on the writ. This necessitates the later service of a separate statement of claim.

The two most important pleadings are the respective statements of each party's case. The plaintiff's is called the 'statement of claim' and the defendant's is called the 'defence'. In the plaintiff's statement of claim he sets out the factual allegations relied on to establish his cause of action and the remedy he seeks. The defendant's defence meets the factual allegations made. Both forms of pleadings are discussed in further detail at **7.2.1** and **7.2.2.**

7.1.1 WHERE THE CASE INVOLVES A DEBT OR LIQUIDATED DEMAND

In the case of suing for a debt or liquidated demand, therefore, the plaintiff need serve no further document apart from the writ. The defendant will have to acknowledge receipt of the writ within 14 days and indicate his intention to defend; thereafter he must serve a defence to the statement of claim which was endorsed on the writ. He must serve this further document, the defence, no later than 28 days from the date on which he received the writ itself. Service is effected directly upon the plaintiff and there is no requirement to send a copy to the court. Therefore, if the plaintiff has sued for non-payment of a debt, the defendant will have to state precisely why he contends that he is not liable to pay the debt, for example because the goods were wholly defective and not of merchantable quality. We shall return to the kind of matters which a defendant needs to raise in his defence in due course.

7.1.2 WHERE THE CASE INVOLVES PERSONAL INJURIES

If the action is one for personal injuries and the claim is for an unliquidated demand, then the writ will not itself contain the statement of claim. A separate document will need to be prepared which sets out all the factual allegations on which the plaintiff bases his claim; an indication of the type of harm he has suffered; and some indication of the relief he seeks, i.e. general and special damages.

In this case, when the defendant receives the writ and acknowledgement of service he should return the acknowledgement of service to the court within 14 days. Thereafter the plaintiff has a further 14 days in which to serve the statement of claim, and it is when this is received that the defendant's 14 days for service of his defence commences. It may well be that the writ has only been served for the sake of protecting the plaintiff in regard to the limitation period, or for the sake of starting interest running. The parties may in such a case agree that they will continue to negotiate and that the statement of claim need not be served for a specified time, or at all until the defendant insists that it should and puts the plaintiff on notice that he must serve it. Alternatively, the plaintiff may wish to progress the action. In such a case he would normally not have served the writ until he had his statement of claim ready prepared so that he could serve it within the further brief period allowed under the rules. If his statement of claim was not ready he would have to ask the defendant to grant him an extension of time for service and, if this was not given voluntarily, apply to the court by way of a 'time summons' for an order extending his time for taking this step. It is even more likely that the defendant will be hard pressed to serve his defence within 14 days of receipt of the statement of claim.

One must remember that the plaintiff may take his time over the issue and service of the writ, subject only to the limitation period. The defendant may thus suddenly receive a very detailed document to which he must comprehensively respond, and with only a fortnight in which to to do so. The solicitor for the defendant may need to re-interview his client and perhaps other witnesses, and thereafter usually send instructions for counsel to draft the defence. Counsel rarely takes less than a fortnight to draft documents. In such a case the defendant's solicitor will usually ask the plaintiff's solicitor for an extension of time for service of the defence. It is normal professional courtesy to allow at least one reasonable extension to a defendant in such circumstances, perhaps of, say, a month. The plaintiff's solicitors sometimes contend that the defendants, having rejected liability throughout, presumably have done so only after obtaining information on the exact happening of the accident, and therefore that they should be in a position to serve their defence very promptly. Nonetheless, extensions are normally given, if only because one would inevitably be allowed by the court if the necessity arose to apply there.

If the defendant's solicitors require further extensions, which is not uncommon because of delay in getting the draft defence back from counsel's chambers, the plaintiff's solicitors may agree to a further extension, or application may need to be made to the court. If an application to the court is required it is made by issuing a so-called 'time summons', which will usually be given a hearing date within a couple of days. The District Judge will almost inevitably allow at least one further extension. Costs will normally be awarded against the party needing the extension.

7.2 Types of Pleadings

The pleadings in civil litigation are the documents in which each party formally states his case. Each pleading must show all the facts which the party is relying upon and hopes to establish to the satisfaction of the court at trial. The purpose of the pleading is to define the issues in the case. Thus at the trial it is not open to a party to allege facts which are not referred to within the pleadings. To do that would be to take the opposite party by surprise and to indicate that much of the process hitherto might have proceeded upon a false basis.

There are four main types of pleadings:

7.2.1 THE STATEMENT OF CLAIM

This is the plaintiff's statement of the facts and matters on which he relies in establishing the cause of action in respect of which the writ was issued. As indicated in **7.1**, in a case of any complexity the statement of claim will be a separate document from the writ, but in an action for a liquidated demand, especially a debt the statement of claim may be endorsed upon the writ itself.

If the statement of claim is a separate pleading it will be served not later than 14 days after the giving of notice of intention to defend. If the plaintiff fails to serve his statement of claim within this time it may lead to an application by the defendant for the action to be dismissed. In view of this, usually a plaintiff's solicitor will already have the statement of claim prepared in draft ready for service by the time he serves the writ itself. Indeed, some solicitors for convenience serve the statement of claim at the same time as the writ, even though it is a separate document and not endorsed upon the writ. In such a case the defendant has 28 days in which to serve his defence.

7.2.2 DEFENCE

The defence is the defendant's first pleading and must be served within 14 days of service of the statement of claim, or within 28 days after service of the writ whichever is the later. As we have seen, this may put the defendant in some difficulties. The plaintiff can choose his own moment to draft, issue and serve the writ, and draft and serve the statement of claim on the defendant. The defendant may then have to reply to very detailed allegations within 14 days. As mentioned in **7.1.2** extensions are commonly granted to allow the defendant time for drafting his defence. If an extension was not allowed, failure to serve a defence in time may lead to judgment being given in default (see **17.1**).

7.2.3 COUNTERCLAIM

If the defendant, as well as defending the statement of claim served by the plaintiff, has any cause of action of his own against the plaintiff, he may add a counterclaim to his defence. As was explained at **6.1.3.2** this counterclaim need have no factual connection with the plaintiff's cause of action.

Where a counterclaim is added to the defendant's defence this operates as a statement of claim made against the plaintiff. The plaintiff must himself then serve a defence to the counterclaim within a further 14 days, and failure to do so will lead to the defendant being in a position to obtain judgment against the plaintiff in default of defence to counterclaim.

It has already been indicated (see **6.1.3.2**) that it is open to the defendant to add new parties to defend his counterclaim along with the plaintiff. Where that happens it is not sufficient for the defendant simply to serve the counterclaim on the new parties. A counterclaim in that case must be issued at court like a writ and the court seal be impressed upon it. It must then be served upon any new parties with a copy of a form of acknowledgement of service so that they may indicate their intentions in relation to this counterclaim.

7.2.4 REPLY

The plaintiff may serve a reply if he wishes to answer any factual allegations raised in the defence. It is seldom compulsory to serve a reply because the plaintiff is deemed to take issue with any matter raised in the defence. A reply should be served within 14 days after receipt of the defence.

7.3 Close of Pleadings

Pleadings are deemed to be closed 14 days after service of the last pleading in the case. The close of pleadings has no significance in itself but it is used as the time for fixing when certain other things ought to happen in the case, to which we shall come later.

Pleadings should be served direct between the parties in the High Court and copies are not sent to the Central Office or District Registry. Accordingly, the High Court has no idea whether the parties have or have not complied with time limits, which is is a specific illustration of the general point that the High Court remains essentially passive in relation to the conduct of cases before it. Thus if the parties have agreed to grant each other mutual extensions for serving pleadings, even for some years, the High Court will not take any action in regard to the matter.

Having noted the above, that proceedings in the High Court still remain essentially under the control of the parties, it is only right to point out that there have been a number of recent steps tending firmly in the direction of 'court control'. The most important of these has been a *Practice Direction (Civil Litigation: Case Management)* [1995] 1 WLR 262 by the Lord Chief Justice which is directed to trial judges of High Court actions indicating ways in which they may exercise their discretion, whatever the parties wish to do, to control the trials before them in various ways, in particular by setting restrictions on the length of speeches and examination-in-chief and cross-examination. At the time of writing these provisions are relatively untried and they are directed in essence at the conduct of the trial rather than at the interlocutory stages, but it is certain that further Practice Directions will, in due course, be issued which will have the effect of requiring the court to impose a fairly strict timetable on most forms of action in the High Court, as already exists to some degree in the county court (see **Chapters 20 and 21**).

7.4 The Contents of Pleadings

7.4.1 GENERAL

Pleadings are formal documents which must contain the heading taken from the writ. That is to say, each must contain the name of the court, the Division, the year and action number, the District Registry where the action is proceeding, the title of the action, i.e. the name and address of the parties, the title of the pleading and the name and address for service of the party who is serving it, together with the date on which it is served. The statement of claim should also indicate the date on which the writ was issued. In addition, if the pleading was drafted by counsel, it should have his name typed at the foot.

The pleading should be drafted in numbered paragraphs for ease of reference, and within these paragraphs there must be set out in so-called 'summary form' the material facts on which the party pleading relies for his claim or defence. The pleading must be as brief as the nature of the claim permits and should not contain matters of evidence, i.e. it should not say *how* a party proposes to prove the facts which he is pleading, nor should matters of law usually be pleaded. Evidence is a matter for the trial and law is something which the court will be deemed to know. However, certain things must appear in the pleading apart from the facts alleged. These are as follows:

7.4.1.1 Special damages

Until 1990, it was customary to include a full computation of special damages up to the date when the pleading was served. That computation would usually have shown in a comprehensible form the precise amounts claimed as constituent parts of special damages and not merely the total figures. Thus, in a personal injury case involving loss of earnings, it was customary to show the computation based on the net figure for loss of earnings over the weeks since the accident, exclusive of tax and national insurance.

The position now is that, by a rule change in 1990 (*Ord. 18, r. 12(1A)*), a plaintiff is specifically required to serve with his statement of claim a statement of special damages claimed. This will now be served as a separate document. The definition given in the rule of 'a statement of the special damages claimed', makes it clear that it is not only special damages up to the date of service of the statement of claim that must be dealt with, but also what is in reality a part of general damages, namely an estimate of future expenses and losses, including loss of earnings and pension rights. Where possible, therefore, a plaintiff will have to make these computations involving projections of future loss so that the rule may be complied with. Thus the defendant ought to be fully informed of the exact figures involved in the case at an early stage.

That, anyway, is the purpose of the rule. In many cases, however, it will be difficult for the plaintiff to give very much by way of worthwhile figures, at least for future loss of earnings and loss of pension rights. If, for example, in a large and complex case the plaintiff has got the action off to a prompt start by issue and service of writ and statement of claim, then clearly any estimate of future loss of earnings, coming at a time when it is unclear when, or even whether, the plaintiff will return to work, and if so in what capacity, is likely to be vague. In such a situation there is provision permitting the plaintiff not to supply such documents, and then either he or the defendant can apply to the court to give directions about the matter. It will often be convenient for the defendant to agree that it is pointless at such an early stage to attempt to provide detailed information. Much the same applies to the case of service of medical reports with the statement of claim, to which reference is made below.

It should also be noted that the plaintiff, shortly before trial, if the case goes that far, must serve amended computations of special damages and future loss of earnings on the defendant. The parties are then obliged to attempt to agree the precise figures so that a great deal of judicial time is not wasted with arguments about computations. See **14.3**.

7.4.1.2 Interest

The question of interest on damages has been referred to earlier (see **1.3** and **1.6**). The claim for interest must be included in the statement of claim and there must be a reference to the contractual term under which interest is claimed, if that is the case, or, if not, to the statutory provision providing for interest, e.g. the *Supreme Court Act 1981, s. 35A*. Moreover, in the case of interest on a liquidated sum, there must be two different computations of interest, first a lump sum due on the debt up to the date of service of the pleading and, secondly, a daily rate from the day after the service of the statement of claim continuing until the date of judgment or earlier payment. In cases where the statement of claim is endorsed on the writ itself, as will commonly be the case in debt actions, these figures must be computed as at the date of issue of the writ, it being assumed that in such a case the writ will be served forthwith.

An example of a writ with a suitably computed endorsement of interest appears at **6.8**. It will be observed that that writ shows the computation of interest under a contract at the rate of 20 per cent in the event of non-payment of sums due under the contract.

Where there is no contractual provision for interest, as mentioned above, interest may be claimed under the court's discretion by virtue of s. 35A of the *Supreme Court Act 1981* (or, in a county court case, the *County Courts Act 1984, s. 69*). By these provisions, if the plaintiff is willing to limit his claim to a rate of interest equivalent to the rate of interest awarded on judgment debts (i.e. currently 8 per cent per annum) then he should show a computation of the interest due at this rate as a lump sum up to the date of issue and a daily rate thereafter. This is tactically wise because:

(a) it allows a defendant to know exactly what his liability is on any given day if he is minded to settle the action;

(b) it may allow the plaintiff, if the defendant does not give notice to defend, to obtain judgment in default. Under Ord. 13 this judgment will be final, i.e. the sum for which judgment is given will include interest due, so obviating the need for any hearing to assess interest (see **17.1**).

In such cases, if the plaintiff is happy with interest at 8 per cent per annum, which at the time of writing would represent a modest rate of interest equivalent to, or slightly better than the return on common forms of investment, he may accept that. If for any reason the plaintiff wished to argue that he should receive interest at a higher rate, then he should not show a computation of the amount claimed but just claim interest pursuant to *s. 35A* of the *1981 Act* generally, since there will inevitably have to be a hearing at court to assess such interest.

In a claim for an unliquidated sum, i.e. damages, no computation of a lump sum due or a daily rate can be provided, because even though in a personal injury case the rates of interest that the court will allow on each constituent part of the claim for damages are known, the final amount which the court will award as damages is not known. It is sufficient to claim interest in general terms referring to the statute. It is important to note that in every case a plaintiff must allege his entitlement to interest on damages in the body of the pleading and claim it at the end of the pleading in the so-called 'prayer', i.e. the statement of the precise remedies which the plaintiff seeks. In a claim for damages, therefore, the statement of claim might end as follows:

> In respect of damages due to him the plaintiff is entitled to interest pursuant to s. 35A of the Supreme Court Act 1981 for such periods and at such rates as to the court shall seem just.
> And the plaintiff claims:
> 1. Damages.
> 2. Under paragraph 7 hereof interest pursuant to the said statute for such periods and at such rates as to the court shall seem just.

7.4.1.3 Matters of law

Although, as indicated in **7.4.1** matters of law normally need not be pleaded, there are some few cases where it is essential to do so. An example is where the defendant wishes to rely on the Limitation Acts in his defence.

7.4.1.4 Matters of evidence

It was explained in **7.4.1** that matters of evidence need not be pleaded in a statement of claim or defence. It is a common error when drafting pleadings to include matters of evidence, e.g. to recite what witnesses will say, or to make *contentions* about matters of fact rather than merely stating the facts. The only important exception to this general rule that evidence need not be pleaded is under *RSC Ord. 18, r. 7A,* which implements *s. 11* of the *Civil Evidence Act 1968*. This important provision is discussed in greater detail at **9.5.1** but for the moment a brief explanation will assist. Where a previous, relevant conviction in a criminal court is to be put in evidence under *s. 11* of the *Civil Evidence Act 1968,* it must be specifically included in the pleading of the party seeking to rely on it.

Quite often the matter which constitutes the tort, and thus the cause of action in the civil case, will also be a crime. A simple example is the crime of driving a vehicle without due care and attention. In such a case any criminal proceedings taken by the police are likely to come to court relatively swiftly, whereas a civil action arising out of the same incident will come on much later. Accordingly, at the time a solicitor is drafting a pleading in the civil action the criminal proceedings generally will be over. If the defendant has already been convicted his conviction can be referred to in the civil action. The effect of proving the conviction in the civil action is to reverse the burden of proof about the matter, i.e. the defendant, if he has been convicted of careless driving, will have the burden of showing that he was wrongly convicted and that he was not driving carelessly at the time. But for this provision, of course, the burden of proof would be upon the plaintiff to prove every fact in issue. This is therefore a great help to the plaintiff.

In order to plead the conviction against the defendant, the following particulars must be stated:

(a) The precise offence for which the other party was convicted and the date of hearing.

(b) The name of the court which convicted.

(c) The issue in the proceedings to which the conviction is relevant.

This last matter is often one that causes some difficulty. Where the tort is the very same thing as the crime for which there has been a conviction, e.g. a single act of careless driving, there is no problem. The criminal conviction is clearly relevant to the tort. There are greater difficulties, however, in the case of crimes of strict liability which need not necessarily connote any negligence on the part of the defendant. Thus if, for instance, the defendant's brakes fail and an accident is caused, he may be convicted of the strict liability offence of using a vehicle with defective brakes but it does not follow that he has been negligent. He may, for instance, have had the vehicle recently serviced and the failure of the brakes may be due to some quite unforeseeable cause. On the other hand, if he has not in fact had the brakes checked for a very long time, arguably his failure adequately to maintain the vehicle is good evidence of negligence.

A party confronted with a pleading in which reference is made to a past conviction may respond to it in one of four ways:

(a) He may *admit* the conviction and its relevance.

(b) He may *deny* the fact of conviction, e.g. say that the plaintiff has got it wrong and that he was acquitted rather than convicted, or that someone of a similar name was convicted. (This would, of course, be very rare because a prudent plaintiff's solicitor would naturally have obtained a certificate of conviction from the criminal court before drafting the pleading.)

(c) He may allege that the conviction was *erroneous*, i.e. he was convicted by the magistrates' court against the weight of the evidence, or perhaps even that he pleaded guilty in ignorance of some fact which would have been a good defence. (To establish this may not be so difficult as might be imagined. A High Court judge trying an action for negligence will form a considerably more expert and demanding tribunal than three lay justices, who are sometimes tempted to believe that if an accident occurs at all this demonstrates that it must be as a result of an error of judgment on the part of some person. It is useful to stress that a magistrates' court is not concerned with trying relative degrees of negligence anyway. It may be that in many road traffic accidents both drivers have some degree of responsibility but the police prefer merely to prosecute the one who appears the more obviously blameworthy. For this reason the finding of carelessness is not in itself conclusive either of the fact that liability was 100 per cent attributable to the defendant, or indeed that he was liable at all.)

(d) He may contend that the conviction is *irrelevant*, i.e. that whilst he admits that he was properly convicted he contends that the offence is not relevant to the cause of the civil action. (A good example of this would be in the case of conviction for a strict liability offence not necessarily connoting negligence, as previously described.)

7.4.1.5 Documents referred to in pleadings

Where a document needs to be referred to or relied upon in a pleading (e.g. the provisions of a written contract), the wording of the document should be summarised where material. If the whole document will need to be referred to in detail at trial, it is usual to say in the pleadings that that will occur and meanwhile to indicate only an outline of the relevant part of the document.

7.4.2 THE STATEMENT OF CLAIM

7.4.2.1 A claim for debt

As we have seen from the examples given above, a claim for a debt or liquidated sum often does no more than set out details of the sum claimed, rather as in the form of an invoice. Having given particulars of the debt and goods supplied there is then a 'prayer', i.e. a reference to the relief or remedy claimed. It is usually preceded by the words: 'And the plaintiff claims . . .' and then the nature of the relief sought (i.e. the claim for the debt and interest). It is not necessary to claim costs in the writ since the court always has discretion to award costs. If the fixed costs endorsement is appropriate, however, that should be completed (see **6.3.2.2**).

7.4.2.2 A personal injury claim

The statement of claim will be drafted so as to contain the following matters:

(a) A brief account of how the accident occurred.

(b) An allegation that the accident was cased by the negligence of the defendant.

(c) Particulars of the negligence alleged. This is usually a set of alternative or cumulative allegations detailing the deficiencies in the defendant's conduct which allegedly amount to a breach of his duty to the plaintiff, e.g.:

The defendant was negligent in that he:

(a) drove too fast;

(b) failed to stop;

(c) failed to keep a proper look-out;

(d) failed to observe a road traffic sign;

(e) failed to observe the approach of the plaintiff;

(f) failed to sound his horn;

(g) failed to heed the warning given by the plaintiff;

(h) in all the circumstances failed so to manage his vehicle as to avoid collision with the vehicle of the plaintiff.

It is usual to plead as many variants as possible of the defendant's negligence so that one is not restricted unduly at trial. It might be, for example, that the plaintiff has no idea whether particular (e) above is true – it might be the case that the defendant was watching the plaintiff closely throughout and just made an error of judgment in steering. The final particular, (h), is a somewhat compendious allegation commonly inserted to cover any kind of error by the defendant.

One common mistake made by beginners when drafting a pleading is to meet a potential defence before it is made, e.g. 'The plaintiff who was at all material times wearing a seat belt and driving well within the speed limit on the correct side of the road . . .' This is never required.

(d) There will then be particulars of injury. Here some brief details of the plaintiff's injury and medical condition are set out, usually in language taken from the medical report. This is so even though a medical report ought in principle to be served with the statement of claim (see **7.4.2.3** below). The plaintiff's date of birth should also be given.

(e) If the particulars of special damages can be very easily worked out and occupy, say, less than a page, it is usual to set out that computation as part of the pleading itself. As indicated above under *RSC Ord. 18, r. 12(1A)*, a plaintiff is required to serve with or in his statement of claim a statement of the special damages claimed, and that the definition given to *special damages* in that connection includes what are in fact, in strict terminology, some elements of *general damages*, in particular an estimate of future expenses and losses including loss of earnings and pension rights. If the computation is complex or lengthy, it should be served as a separate document at the same time as the statement of claim. The computation should be as exact as it is possible to give, showing net figures after the incidence of tax on the claim.

(f) If provisional damages are to be claimed then that must be pleaded, though no great detail need be given.

(g) There should be a claim to interest made in a separate paragraph in the body of the pleading and referring to *s. 35A* of the *Supreme Court Act 1981*.

(h) Lastly is the 'prayer', where the plaintiff states the relief or remedy he seeks. In a personal injuries case that will consist of a claim in general terms to damages and interest pursuant to statute, as described in the examples given previously.

7.4.2.3 Service of medical report with statement of claim

Under a rule change in 1990 (*RSC Ord. 18, r. 12(1A)*), in every case in which a claim for personal injuries is made there is a prima facie requirement that the plaintiff should serve with his statement of claim a medical report, by which is meant a report substantiating all the personal injuries alleged in the statement of claim which the plaintiff proposes to adduce in evidence as part of his case at trial. If the plaintiff intends to comply with this rule, therefore, he will need to obtain medical reports before issue of the writ to ensure that they are readily available. Normally this would be done anyway in a substantial claim so that the necessary particulars of injury could be inserted in the pleading. The importance of this rule, however, is that in principle, if the plaintiff serves the medical report (and it should be borne in mind that more than one report may be necessary since all the personal injuries should be substantiated, so that in a complex case there may be reports from more than one type of specialist), the defendant will be put in full possession of the plaintiff's medical evidence. If the defendant then obtains his own medical report on the plaintiff (there being no provision requiring him to disclose it forthwith to the plaintiff), he will, paradoxically, be better informed about the plaintiff's medical condition than the plaintiff is. Accordingly the defendant, especially if fully worked out computations of special damages have also been provided (see **7.4.1.1** above) ought to be in the position to make a well calculated payment into court at an early stage (see **16.1**).

There is a further provision as to what is to happen if the plaintiff does not comply with this rule. The plaintiff may if he wishes apply to the court for a direction that he need not comply with the rule but may serve his medical report later, or perhaps may withhold it until mutual exchange is possible (see **12.4**). Alternatively, the defendant may apply to *stay* (that is, bring to a halt) the plaintiff's action. The new requirements to serve a fully worked computation of special damages and the medical report, whilst a striking development in the general direction of 'cards on the table' litigation which may encourage early settlement in many cases, are also provisions which are capable of working to the plaintiff's tactical disadvantage, as he has to disclose his hand while the defendant is entitled to keep his secret.

7.4.2.4 Statements of claim in a contract case

Assuming that the matter to be litigated is more than simply a debt, then much will depend upon the exact facts on which the cause of action is based, but in the main an action in contract, or some other commercial action, will involve the statement of claim including the following:

(a) A statement of who the parties are, what their relationship is to each other and any relevant facts prior to the cause of action arising.

(b) An indication of the relationship out of which the cause of action arises, e.g. details of the contract, the setting out or summarising of any relevant terms and giving relevant dates.

(c) The cause of action will then be indicated with full particulars, e.g. the breach of the contract on which the action is based.

(d) Then particulars will be given in much the same way as particulars of negligence in the personal injury claim at **7.4.2.2** above. They will set out the factual basis on which it is alleged there is a breach of contract.

(e) There will then be a statement that because of the breach the plaintiff has suffered loss and damage, and there will then be a paragraph or two setting out particulars of damage together with any figures where a precise quantification is possible. In addition, the basic facts relevant to any type of loss or damage (e.g. distress, inconvenience, loss of business reputation, etc.) for which the plaintiff wishes to claim, but which cannot have a precise figure put on them, will be given.

(f) There will then be a claim for interest, if appropriate.

(g) There will then be a prayer to all the remedies sought, including, where necessary, damages, an injunction, interest and sometimes a claim for costs (although this is strictly unnecessary since the court always has a discretion to award costs).

(h) If an injunction is asked for it is sometimes suggested that the wording of the final injunction sought should be included in the statement of claim.

7.4.3 THE DEFENCE

We have so far mainly considered drafting a statement of claim. We now turn to some specific aspects of drafting a defence. A defendant in his defence must deal with every matter contained in the statement of claim, and those with which he does not deal he is deemed to admit. It is usual, therefore, for the defendant to go through the plaintiff's statement of claim paragraph by numbered paragraph, replying to each point raised in one of the three following ways:

(a) *Admitting* the matter.

(b) *Not admitting* the matter.

(c) *Denying* the matter.

7.4.3.1 Admitting

Where the defendant *admits* some particular matter he relieves the plaintiff of the burden of proving the matter at the trial. It is taken to be established between them. Thus if, for example, paragraph (1) of the plaintiff's statement of claim merely alleged that an accident occurred on a certain road at a certain time, the defendant would probably admit in his defence that this was so (whilst going on to deny the plaintiff's subsequent claims in which he contended that the cause of the action was the defendant's negligence).

7.4.3.2 Not admitting

Alternatively, the defendant may *not admit* some particular allegation. Where he does not admit some allegation it means that he will not allow the plaintiff to take it as established at trial. The plaintiff must call evidence to prove strictly the matter not admitted. However, it does not necessarily imply that the defendant will contest the matter in question. A good example is an allegation in the statement of claim in a personal injury case that the plaintiff has suffered certain injuries, or some loss of earnings. In either case, a defendant may be inclined not to admit these matters. This merely means that he has no information of his own at present about the matters, and he invites the plaintiff formally to prove them by proper evidence at the trial.

7.4.3.3 Denying

Lastly, the defendant may *deny* (or *traverse*) allegations of fact made by the plaintiff. Where this happens the defendant not only denies the version given by the plaintiff but goes on to give his own version of the matter, e.g. to say that not only does he deny that the accident occurred due to his negligence, but that in fact the accident occurred because of the plaintiff's negligence. He then goes on to list the matters he relies upon to prove this.

7.4.3.4 Matters which must be specifically pleaded in a defence

The following matters must be specifically pleaded if the defendant wishes to rely on them:

(a) *Contributory negligence*

This must be specifically pleaded by way of partial defence to a plaintiff's claim. In the absence of such a plea a trial judge is not entitled to find that the plaintiff's negligence has contributed to the accident.

(b) *Limitation period*

The court will not of its own motion take a *Limitation Act* point. As indicated in **6.5.2**, the court will not prevent the plaintiff from issuing a writ outside the limitation period. *RSC Ord. 18, r. 8(1)* provides that in such a case the defendant must plead a *Limitation Act* defence. If the matter is clear-cut, this will normally be followed by an application by the defendant to strike out the statement of claim and dismiss the action. If matters are not so clear-cut, perhaps because there is some doubt about the precise date upon which the cause of action arose, or particularly in a personal injury case where the date of *knowledge* of the plaintiff might be arguable, then matters may well be left to be argued at trial because otherwise there may be considerable duplication of issues.

(c) *Illegality*

A defence that a contract is illegal and thus should not be enforced must be specifically pleaded. However, despite this rule (unlike the question of limitation), if the question of illegality is brought to the attention of the court the judge may take the point although neither of the litigants does.

(d) *Want of jurisdiction*

This defence should also be specifically pleaded if it is relied upon.

(e) *Res ipsa loquitur?*

This need *not* in fact be pleaded. As a leading case puts it, 'it is no more than a common sense approach, not limited by technical rules, to the assessment of the effect of evidence'. (See further, **8.5.3.2.**)

7.4.4 COUNTERCLAIMS

A counterclaim by a defendant stands exactly like a statement of claim. It is therefore subject to precisely the same requirements and technical rules of pleading applicable to a statement of claim. Likewise, a defence to the counterclaim is subject to the same rules as a defence to a statement of claim.

7.5 Attacking an Opponent's Pleading

When a pleading is received from an opponent in which he should have set out his case in full, it may be that either of two aggressive actions may be taken in relation to it. In the first case, if a party is dissatisfied with the amount of detail and particularity given in the pleading because it remains uncertain what is the exact case that is alleged, that party can ask for further details to be supplied, and if they are not supplied the party can apply to the court for them. In the second case, it may be that on receipt of the pleading it seems that there is improper material in it, to the extent where a party can apply to the court to strike out part, or sometimes the whole, of the pleading. If successful in the latter application and the whole pleading is struck out, then, if it is the statement of claim, the case will be brought to an end in favour of the defendant; and if it is the defence, the same will occur in favour of the plaintiff.

7.5.1 FURTHER AND BETTER PARTICULARS

7.5.1.1 Requirement for further and better particulars

A pleading must not be too vague or too general. It must indicate to the opponent the case to be brought against him. There is, nonetheless, a difficulty in pleading a case with excessive precision. Since a party will be tied at trial to the version given, should the evidence adduced at trial differ in any way which might in effect constitute a new allegation, then either the claim will be disallowed because it has not been properly pleaded, or there will at least be a need to amend the pleading at trial, with the almost certain offer of an adjournment to the opposing party to consider his position at the cost of the party in default. Accordingly, a party drafting a pleading must strike a fine balance between giving a proper account of the facts on his version and leaving a certain amount of room for manoeuvre should other matters come to light or the evidence come out in an unexpected way.

Where a party is faced by a pleading that he contends is too vague or general for him truly to see the case which he is called upon to face, he may attempt to have it struck out or to cut down the opposing party's room for manoeuvre by seeking *particulars*, or 'further and better particulars' as they are generally known. *RSC Ord. 18, r. 12(3)* provides that:

> *The court may order a party to serve on any other party particulars of any claim, defence or other matter stated in his pleading . . . or a statement of the nature of the case on which he relies, and the order may be made on such terms as the court thinks just.*

7.5.1.2 Function of further and better particulars

The function of further and better particulars is said to be:

(a) to carry into operation the overriding principle that litigation should be conducted fairly and openly without surprises;

(b) to inform the other side of the nature of the case they have to meet, as distinguished from the mode in which it is to be proved;

(c) to prevent the other side from being taken unawares and to enable them to know what evidence ought to be prepared for trial;

(d) to limit the generality of pleadings and to define the issues to be tried and for which discovery is required.

7.5.1.3 Procedure

The technicalities of pleading were formerly of extreme importance, cases often turning on whether a matter was correctly pleaded or not. It is fair to say that with the exception of one or two particular areas of litigation (especially defamation), pleading is a technical art of somewhat less importance now, in the main due to the provisions which exist for the compulsory exchange of witness statements between the parties substantially in advance of trial. Although witness statements have, of course, nothing to do with pleadings as such, where a party's witness statements have been exchanged it will be harder for an opponent to allege that because some fact has not been properly pleaded he is actually prejudiced in how he has prepared to present his case for trial. Nonetheless, the art of tying an opponent down to a more precise version by an appropriate request for further and better particulars will be a very useful part of the litigant's armoury for a long time to come. It is therefore appropriate to consider some instances of how and when this might arise.

Example Suppose, for example, that a statement of claim merely alleged that the defendant 'drove contrary to the provisions of the Highway Code'. In view of the numerous provisions of the Highway Code it will be far from clear what precisely the plaintiff's case is on this matter. A defendant's request for further and better particulars might therefore say:

> Of paragraph 3 of the plaintiff's statement of claim and the allegation that the defendant drove contrary to the Highway Code state precisely to which provisions of the Highway Code the plaintiff refers.

The document, which is drafted like, and which looks exactly like, a pleading, is then sent with a letter to the other party with a request that he should provide the further and better particulars. The party of whom the request is made ought to comply with the request if it is reasonable, but if he fails or positively refuses to do so an application may then be made by the person seeking the further and better particulars to the District Judge by summons. No affidavit in support is necessary. At the hearing the District Judge will consider whether the further and better particulars are required for the proper progress of the action. One matter which is *not* relevant to this decision is whether the party seeking the particulars already has the information requested. It is sometimes contended in a response to a request for further particulars that 'the plaintiff already has the information', or 'the facts are already known to the plaintiff who was present at the time'. This is irrelevant. It may be that this is indeed the case, but the issue is not *what the plaintiff knows*. The point is that the plaintiff is entitled to know precisely what version of the facts the *defendant is going to allege* at trial, and therefore the response that he already knows the details of how the incident arose is no answer.

The application for further and better particulars may be made by summons at any stage but is usually left until the summons for directions hearing (if any). Particulars are not normally ordered before a defence is served, however, and a defendant faced with an ambiguous statement of claim will have to serve the defence to what is alleged in the plaintiff's pleading whilst at the same time serving a request for further and better particulars of the statement of claim. When the further and better particulars are received it may be that one or both parties will need to amend their pleadings.

7.5.1.4 Answering a request for further and better particulars

Where a party is answering a request for further and better particulars, either voluntarily or pursuant to an order of the District Judge, then the answer must now be set out in a particular way. The original request for further and better particulars is set out with the other party's response to each matter immediately beneath the paragraph in which it is requested. This contributes greatly to the coherence of the answers given unlike the previous practice in which the answers were set out in a separate document from the request for particulars so that one might need to refer to several different documents at once. An example of a typical request and response would therefore be as follows:

Request

1. Of paragraph 3 of the plaintiff's statement of claim and the allegation that the defendants operated an unsafe system of work state with particularity each and every fact relied on in support of that allegation.

Plaintiff's response

The plaintiff will contend that the defendants operated an unsafe system of work in the following particulars:

1. By failing to ensure that all relevant employees had proper training in the use of the model X123 mechanical hoist operated by the defendants at their premises.

2. By continuing to employ one Kevin Hardcastle notwithstanding that the said Kevin Hardcastle had been involved in previous incidents of horseplay on the equipment as a result of which other employees had narrowly escaped injury in the months of June and August immediately preceding the incident giving rise to this cause of action.

3. By failing to supply the work force with steel-capped industrial boots.

4. By failing to ensure that there were sufficient employees on duty in the workshop so as to ensure that the lifting processes could be carried out properly. The maker's specification for the said X123 hoist recommends that no fewer than four employees be engaged in its operation but the defendants at all relevant times employed only three persons in the said workshop.

5. Given that the three workmen in the workshop at the time of the incident giving rise to the cause of action were respectively aged 18, 17 and 16 failing to ensure that the said workers were supervised by a more senior employee.

7.5.1.5 The status of further and better particulars

It ought to be noted that although they have the appearance of pleadings, further and better particulars are not in themselves strictly pleadings, so that a request for them does not delay the time for the next pleading to be sent. However, they are pleadings in the limited sense that they do set out matters which ought to have been included in the original pleadings, and thus when the documents in the case are collected for the trial judge as we shall see at **14.4**, the request for further and better particulars with the answers to the request will be contained in the bundle prepared for him.

7.5.1.6 Costs

Where a summons seeking an order for further and better particulars of a pleading is issued, the general order on costs that will be made is 'costs in the cause' unless the pleading is so manifestly defective that it was unreasonable for the party serving it to refuse voluntarily to supply the particulars required.

7.5.2 SUMMARY

A request for further and better particulars from an opponent may be seen as having two possible purposes. The first is a genuine desire on the part of the person seeking particulars to obtain information, as in the case of the reference to the Highway Code in **7.5.1.3** above. Thus, if a party simply is left in the dark as to what the alleged facts are by the original pleading, a request for further and better particulars would be appropriate. The second possible purpose would be to attempt to tie the other party down to a more specific version of events with a view to eliminating the opponent's scope for manoeuvre at trial. Requesting further and better particulars may often, therefore, be part of the tactical manoeuvring of the parties.

We turn from a request for further and better particulars to what is a much more direct attack on a party's pleading.

7.5.3 STRIKING OUT PLEADINGS

Under *RSC Ord. 18, r. 19*, one party can apply to the court for an order striking out all or part of an opponent's pleading on one of the following grounds:

7.5.3.1 'That the pleading discloses no reasonable cause of action or, as the case may be, defence'

An example would be a statement of claim which alleged negligence by a judge in the exercise of his judicial office, which it will be appreciated is not actionable in English law.

It is difficult to imagine that a professionally drafted pleading would never amount to a *defence* but one could well imagine how the situation might arise where a layman drafts his own pleading. Thus, for instance, if in a debt claim the defendant served what purported to be a defence on the plaintiff, merely saying that he was unable to pay the debt at present, since this is not of course a defence in law the plaintiff would be entitled to apply to strike it out.

7.5.3.2 'That the pleading is scandalous, frivolous or vexatious'

It is a fact of life that some people like to use the law courts for the purpose of causing difficulty or embarrassment to persons who have upset them, and have little serious aim of obtaining redress for a genuine grievance. Habitual petty litigants may be ruled by the court to be 'vexatious', and a vexatious litigant generally needs the leave of the court before issuing further writs. Here we are concerned with someone who is litigating in order to fulfil some collateral purpose, probably to embarrass his opponent. If the pleading is manifestly frivolous or vexatious it will be struck out.

'Scandalous' would imply some matter introduced into a pleading for a purpose that is clearly irrelevant to the cause of action. Thus it may well be the case that in defamation proceedings allegations of a highly scandalous nature are quite properly made. However, in defamation that is often the essence of the case, especially where the defence is justification. If similar allegations were made in the course of a pleading in a debt or personal injury case, however, the court would strike out the pleading or the relevant part of the pleading.

7.5.3.3 'It may prejudice, embarrass or delay the fair trial of the action'

In this context 'embarrass' is used in the sense of 'leave the other party totally unaware of what is being alleged'. Therefore, where a pleading gives no assistance in progressing the case it may be struck out on this ground.

7.5.3.4 'The pleading is otherwise an abuse of the process of the court'

This is something of a catch all provision and there are very few modern cases illustrating the use of this ground when none of the others was appropriate. Generally applications to the court will be made under one or other of the three previous grounds.

7.5.3.5 Procedure

One applies to strike out all or part of one's opponent's pleading by summons to the Master or District Judge, and preferably very soon after the pleading has first been served. If the whole pleading is ordered to be struck out then, if it is the statement of claim, since there will now be no valid statement of claim from the moment it is struck out, the defendant may apply to dismiss the action for want of prosecution. If it is the defence that is ordered to be struck out, judgment for the plaintiff in default of defence may be given forthwith.

7.6 Amending the Writ and Pleadings

It might be imagined that by the time negotiations had broken down and a party was ready to serve a writ, that that party would have a fairly comprehensive factual picture of how the incident in question arose and of his cause of action and the facts necessary to plead in support of it. Certainly it might be imagined that a party would know who his opponents were to be. In a surprising number of cases, however, vital information may come to light only after, sometimes long after, a writ has been issued and served. In this section we consider the steps that need to be taken where it becomes necessary to amend a writ and subsequent pleadings.

7.6.1 AMENDMENT AS TO PARTIES

7.6.1.1 Identifying the proper parties

It may become apparent only after proceedings have been issued either that they have been issued against the wrong person, or, more probably, that there should be a second or further defendant in addition to the present one. An example of how this could arise would be if a pedestrian were knocked down by a motor vehicle which mounted the pavement. It might be thought that he had a very straightforward cause of action. It might not become apparent until proceedings had been issued against the motorist that the nature of the motorist's defence would be that he was forced to swerve onto the pavement to take avoiding action because some other motorist pulled out in front of him, and that in the circumstances he contends he was not negligent. In this situation the plaintiff, on discovering this information, would be well advised to think carefully about adding the other driver as a second defendant. It would certainly be rash to apply to amend by dropping the first driver entirely, because it might be found at trial that the allegations made in his defence were entirely groundless. There is little to lose however, as we shall see, by applying to amend the writ and subsequent statement of claim to add the second defendant.

A feature commonly encountered in employment cases, and which initially always surprises, is that a quite remarkable number of people are not entirely sure who their employers are, or were, at the relevant time, nor even, especially in the building industry, whether they were in fact employees at all rather than independent contractors. This problem is particularly prevalent in industrial disease cases where the cause of action may have occurred decades ago. Even in cases of persons employed by large companies there may need to be some investigatory work initially to find out which particular one of an interlocking group of companies was the true employer. This is pre-eminently so if there have been recent mergers, acquisitions or hiving off in a large group. If in due course it comes out that the true employer is someone other than the present defendant, the plaintiff will need to consider amendment.

In a contract case it is obviously more rare not to know whom a plaintiff should be suing at the outset since it is generally fairly clear with whom he has contracted. The situation could arise, however, in the case of, say, some electrical item which was sold to the plaintiff and exploded on first being switched on causing injury. The plaintiff would have an obvious cause of action against the shop owner who sold the item, but let us suppose that after proceeding with the litigation for some little time doubts began to emerge about the solvency of the shop owner and his ability to satisfy a large claim for damages. It might be that on further consideration it was concluded that there might also be a cause of action under the Consumer Protection Act 1987 against the manufacturer of the defective item, and in those circumstances it might well be wise to add him as a second defendant.

7.6.1.2 Application to amend the writ

If the writ has already been served at the stage where the need to amend it to add a party arises, application has to be made to the court for leave to do so. Application is made by an ordinary summons to the Master or District Judge. There is no need to file an affidavit with the summons, but a copy of the proposed amendment is lodged at court and served with the summons on the opposing party. It is not, of course, necessary at this stage to serve notice of this application on the party whom it is intended to add as a second defendant. That party is not involved in the action until leave to amend is given.

If the need to amend to add another party actually became apparent after the writ had been issued but before it had been served, then the writ can be amended without the leave of the court.

7.6.1.3 Consequent amendment of the statement of claim

If the writ has already been served at the time when amendment is needed, it may well be that the statement of claim has also been served. Since the statement of claim will make allegations only against the original defendant, there will of course be a need to amend the statement of claim too, to add the new party and to make the relevant allegations against him.

7.6.1.4 Other steps to be considered when amending the writ

Where a new defendant is added there are at least two other important tactical steps to consider.

First, if one is adding a new defendant in a road traffic case it will be wise to serve notice of one's intention to proceed by letter on the insurance company of the proposed new defendant in advance of the hearing for leave to amend. This is to gain protection under *s. 152* of the *Road Traffic Act 1988* (see **4.1.6**). For these purposes proceedings are *commenced* against the new defendant on the date when leave to amend the writ is given.

Secondly, the possible necessity to apply to the Legal Aid Board to amend one's legal aid certificate should not be overlooked. Legal aid certificates are not granted in general terms, e.g. 'to take all steps necessary to obtain damages for X', they are issued in very specific terms, e.g. 'to take proceedings against Y for damages for personal injury'. If, therefore, it is wished to add a second defendant, it will be necessary to obtain amendment to the legal aid certificate. This can generally be achieved simply by writing to the area office, setting out the background circumstances and explaining why the amendment is required. When the amended certificate is received a copy should be filed at court and notice of the amendment given to the other parties involved.

7.6.2 AMENDMENT AS TO CAUSE OF ACTION

Precisely the same rules about the necessity to seek the leave of the court apply where the plaintiff wishes to alter or add a new cause of action. If, for example, a writ had been issued alleging negligence against a defendant, and it then came to the plaintiff's attention that the circumstances might amount to both nuisance and negligence, then the plaintiff could apply to the court to add the second cause of action. He would have to obtain leave in precisely the manner described in **7.6.1.2**. If the statement of claim had been served it would need to be amended also.

7.6.3 MINOR AMENDMENTS

The two amendments just considered, that of adding a new party and that of adding a new cause of action, are clearly amendments of very considerable substance. It may well be, however, that as a case develops new information comes to light which makes it apparent that extra or alternative allegations of fact ought to be added to a party's pleadings for completeness. It would be rare for such matters of fact to need to be contained in the writ as well as the statement of claim, but the rule is the same in either case.

If new or alternative allegations of fact need to be put in the writ or pleading, the writ or pleading may be amended once without the leave of the court so long as this happens before the close of pleading stage is reached. If the amendment is required after this stage, however, or if in any case it is a second or later amendment, the leave of the court is needed unless all other parties consent to the amendment. Where leave is needed it is obtained in precisely the same way as described above, by issuing a summons seeking leave, lodging a copy of the proposed amendment with the summons and serving a copy thereof on the opposing party. It is not uncommon to leave amendment of this kind to the stage of the summons for directions which is considered at **13.1**.

Example Suppose that in the case of a road traffic accident the plaintiff is alleging that the defendant was negligent in that he:

(a) failed to allow a proper distance between himself and the vehicle in front;

(b) failed to brake in time;

(c) failed to keep a proper look-out.

Suppose subsequently that an order for discovery of documents is obtained and that when the vehicle's maintenance records are revealed they show that the defendant had failed to have the vehicle serviced for many months. In that case the plaintiff might want to add a fourth and alternative allegation, namely that the vehicle's brakes were defective. To do so, since close of pleadings would already have occurred, he would apply to the court by summons for leave to amend the statement of claim, lodging with the court a copy of the proposed amendment to his pleading.

7.6.4 AMENDMENT BY CONSENT

It should be noted that pleadings may always be amended with the consent of all other parties to the action. If, therefore, at whatever time the pleading needs to be amended, everyone else consents, there is no need to apply to the court for leave.

When considering the question of consent to amendment the matter of costs ought also to be dealt with. The usual principles are described at **7.6.5.1** below.

7.6.5 OTHER CONSIDERATIONS

Before passing on from the topic of amendment it is important to deal with the following miscellaneous matters:

7.6.5.1 The policy of the court

The policy of the court on applications for amendment is extremely liberal. The court does not view itself as an institution for disciplining the parties so an amendment, no matter how foolish or negligent the original oversight may have been, will generally be allowed **'on terms'**. The terms will be that the party who requires the amendment must pay the costs of any other party who incurs costs in consequence of it. Suppose, therefore, that the plaintiff does wish to amend his statement of claim. The defendant will be awarded the costs 'in any event', covering both the expense of attending the summons before the District Judge and of carrying out any consequential amendments to his own pleadings which are needed to answer the new allegations made by the plaintiff.

7.6.5.2 The method of amendment

Amendments are carried out by inserting the new words *in red* on a retyped copy of the original writ or pleading. Any paragraphs which are now to be erased from the pleading must remain typed in and legible but are struck through once *in red*. It may be important, for example, at the subsequent trial to establish just what the original allegations were, even though these are no longer part of the plaintiff's case.

Amendment takes effect from the date on which the original writ was issued and/or the pleading served. In other words, the writ is deemed always to have been in its final form, no matter how many amendments have in fact been made to it. Further amendments after the first are to be made in *green* ink, and thereafter in *violet*, and then in *yellow*.

7.6.5.3 Consequential amendments

As has already been indicated, where a party is given leave to amend his pleadings the opposing party must also be given leave to amend his to cope with any new matters that are pleaded. The costs of these consequential amendments will inevitably be ordered against the party who required the original amendment unless some special factor is present.

Each newly amended pleading must, of course, be re-served unless the court gives leave to dispense with re-service, e.g. because the amendment has been allowed in precisely the form of the document lodged with the summons for leave to amend and therefore the opposite parties will already have copies of the intended amendment.

Where the court gives leave to amend, the amended writ or pleading should have typed on it in *red* 'Amended this . . . day of . . . 1997 pursuant to the order of District Judge Jones.'

7.7 Interlocutory Applications

In actions commenced by writ, interlocutory applications for some procedural, or sometimes substantive, order can be made. We have already briefly mentioned several such applications, in particular a time summons where a party requires an extension of the basic time allowed under the rules for taking steps such as serving a pleading (**7.1.2**); further and better particulars of pleading where one's opponent has declined to give those particulars voluntarily (**7.5.1.3**); striking out all or part of the pleading, e.g. on the grounds that it is vexatious (**7.5.3**); for leave to amend (**7.6**); and for the renewal of a writ by extending its validity to allow further attempts at service on an evasive defendant (**6.5.2**).

Interlocutory applications can be made in the following ways:

7.7.1 *EX PARTE* APPLICATIONS

This means an application made by one party without the opponent being notified and thus enabled to attend the court to be heard on, and perhaps contest, that application. Although this appears to involve a breach of the principles of natural justice, there are in fact relatively few instances of things which may be done by *ex parte* application. One example which we have already seen is where the plaintiff applies to renew the writ and extend its validity before service (**6.5.2**). In such a case an *ex parte* procedure is appropriate because the defendant has not as yet been served with the proceedings and is therefore not technically a party. Other examples are purely administrative steps where the opponent has not himself complied with court procedures, such as an application for judgment in default of intention to defend under *RSC Ord. 13* (see **17.1**) and applications for various methods of enforcement of judgment after the end of the trial. In addition, there are urgent cases where a remedy needs to be applied for in great haste and possibly with some element of secrecy, e.g. an urgent injunction, examples of which are considered below at **7.8.1.1**.

7.7.2 BY *INTER PARTES* SUMMONS

This is by far the most common method of making interlocutory applications in both Queen's Bench and Chancery Divisions. A **summons** is really nothing more than a method of fixing an appointment before a Master or District Judge and notifying one's opponent of the requirement to attend at that appointment and of the nature of the application that is being made. A summons of this kind, as distinct from an *originating summons* described at **24.1** is usually called an '**ordinary summons**' or 'a **summons in the action**'.

To issue a summons two blank forms need to be obtained from law stationers (naturally solicitors carry stocks of these in their offices), or alternatively, and now more commonly, a draft precedent held on a word processor will be adapted. The form of summons is completed at the top with the 'heading in the action', which recites the court, action number and the details of plaintiff and defendant. The text of the summons then instructs the opponent to attend at the offices of the court on a date, which at the moment is left blank, and then describes the order of the court that is being applied for. Those words are completed by the person who wishes to issue the summons (e.g. with a request for an order that the defendant gives further and better particulars of his defence, or that the plaintiff have leave to amend his statement of claim, etc.).

Having completed the forms of summons, they are then taken to the Central Office of the High Court in London or to the District Registry outside London. There a clerk will look at the summons at the counter and ask for an estimate of the length of hearing. For a very simple procedural summons 10 minutes will usually suffice. For more substantial applications it may be that up to half a day, or even longer, needs to be allotted. Suppose, therefore, that one gives the estimated length of hearing as 20 minutes; the court will then look at the nature of the summons. If there is something genuinely urgent about it there may be an attempt to fit it into the District Judge's diary in the immediate future, but otherwise the **first vacant hearing** time of sufficient length will be allotted. When this will be varies, depending in part on the time of year and the locality, but for relatively routine summonses it would certainly be rare to obtain a hearing date within a month of the date of the issue of the summons, and often considerably longer delays will occur in some parts of the country.

When this date is inserted on the summons the court seal is put on the two copies of the summons. The court fee (currently £30) for the issue of the summons must be paid. In London neither of the copies is retained because there is no court file but simply a record of the appointment. Outside London, one copy is retained in the court file and the other given back to the applicant. This procedure is called 'issuing' or 'taking out' a summons, and the date of hearing which has now been given by the court is called the 'return day' of the summons. A photoc [illegible] summons is then prepared by the party who has issued it to be served by post o[illegible]ent.

The pr[illegible] far described relates to the more simple and purely procedural kind of summo[illegible] as for further and better particulars, for leave to amend, and the like. Even in those [illegible] a copy of a relevant document has to be left with the court outside London, e.g. a cc[illegible] further and better particulars sought, or of the proposed amendment. For other ki[illegible]mmons which involve something of more substance, it is sometimes necessar[illegible]pplicant to file evidence at the time. An example of this is a summons seeking [illegible]idgment under *RSC Ord. 14* (described at **17.2**). The evidence to be filed is in the fo[illegible] an *affidavit*.

7.7.2.1 Evidence by affidavit

The court does in fact have the power to hear witnesses in interlocutory applications but oral testimony is very much the exception to the rule. If evidence is required it is almost always given by sworn statement called an *affidavit*. The rules of court usually prescribe whether or not an affidavit is required, although sometimes the rules make no mention of the matter and it is simply a question of custom or practice that an affidavit is required. Usually the editorial notes to the relevant rule in the 'White Book' indicate whether or not an affidavit in support is expected.

7.7.2.2 Form of affidavits

The form of affidavits is prescribed by *RSC Ord. 41* and by *Practice Direction (Evidence: Affidavits)* [1983] 1 WLR 922. These provide that:

(a) An affidavit must be entitled with the heading in the action save that where there is more than one plaintiff only the first need be named with the words 'and others', etc.

(b) Every affidavit must be expressed in the first person and must state the place of residence of the deponent (that is the person who swears it), his occupation and whether he is a party or employed by a party. However, if the deponent is giving evidence in a professional or an occupational capacity, the affidavit may state the work address of the deponent.

(c) The affidavit should therefore commence with the words: 'I John Smith of the Old Barn Middlemarch in the County of Loamshire, managing director, make oath and say as follows . . .'.

(d) Thereafter the affidavit must recite the evidence of the party in numbered paragraphs. In interlocutory proceedings affidavits may contain statements of information or belief (i.e. hearsay) so long as the sources and grounds thereof are given. Affidavits should not, however, include propositions of law, nor, e.g., opinions from counsel.

(e) Every affidavit must be bound up in book form with both sides of the paper being used and the paper numbered consecutively. Dates, sums and other numbers must be expressly in figures not words.

(f) The *jurat* (that is the attestation clause sworn before a solicitor) must be completed. A solicitor may not swear his own client nor his opponent in litigation to an affidavit. The *jurat* should not appear on a page on its own.

(g) An affidavit to be used in proceedings must at the top right hand corner of the first page and also on the back sheet have written in dark blue or black ink:

(i) The party on whose behalf it is filed.

(ii) The initials and surname of the deponent.

(iii) The number of the affidavit in relation to that deponent in the action so far.

(iv) The date when sworn (in figures), e.g. 2nd dft: J Smith: 3rd: 20.1.97.

(h) Any document to be used in connection with an affidavit must be exhibited to it and identified by a certificate of the person before whom the affidavit is sworn. Affidavits should be identified by the initials of the deponent and numbered consecutively, e.g. 'JSD 1'. If exhibits are not in the form of written statements but of physical objects, such as video films or cassettes, they must still be appropriately marked and connected to the affidavit.

Certain kinds of affidavit, especially for summary judgment or for an interim payment, must by the relevant rules contain specified information and if they do not they will be technically defective. However, for other kinds of affidavit there are no specific requirements as to contents. The affidavit will be drafted by the applicant's solicitor to give a simple factual statement in reasonably formal English in numbered paragraphs of the background of the matter and the nature of the application. In principle an affidavit should be sworn by the party concerned where possible, but increasingly it is common for the solicitor to swear it himself.

7.7.2.3 Exhibits

We have referred at point (h) above to cases where sometimes evidence which does not conveniently fit into an affidavit must be brought to court. For example, the person swearing an affidavit may wish to refer to invoices or business records which because of their length cannot conveniently be set out in the text of the affidavit. Also, in some cases it may be necessary to refer to physical objects such as a video cassette (e.g. in a case alleging video piracy). In such a case it is normal to 'exhibit' the document or object referred to in the affidavit by giving it a number comprising the initials of the person swearing the affidavit and the number of the exhibit as referred to above. The exhibit is marked by the solicitor and is then either pinned to, or kept with the affidavit.

7.7.2.4 Service of the summons

When the summons has been issued, a copy of it and of any other document, e.g. an affidavit, or draft of the further and better particulars sought, has to be served on all the other parties. For most forms of summonses only two *clear days'* notice is required. The term 'clear days' means that both the day of service of the summons and the date of hearing are left out of account. Thus if one has a hearing date on a Friday, the summons must be served no later than the preceding Tuesday so that there are two 'clear' days, namely the Wednesday and Thursday between the two. For other more important kinds of summonses different time periods are prescribed. Thus an application for an interim payment must be served with at least 10 clear days' notice; applications for summary judgment likewise must be served not less than 10 clear days before the hearing.

7.7.3 THE HEARING

At the hearing in London there is no court file and the applicant will need to bring the copy of the summons and any relevant documents to be placed before the Master at the time, who will read them there and then. Outside London there is a copy in the file and the District Judge will usually have had the opportunity to read the relevant documents, and thus to know the nature of the application before him.

These applications are dealt with in *chambers* which is usually a small private room set out in the shape of a 'T' with the District Judge sitting at the head of the 'T' and the parties sitting facing each other along the body. It is customary for the person whose application it is to introduce himself and his opponent to the District Judge and then to indicate the nature of the application, describing the type of case and its background and introducing the application which he proposes to make; summarising any necessary points of law practice or evidence; and asking for an order in the form which he seeks. The opponent is then given the right of reply and he can say what he wishes to say, drawing in his turn the District Judge's attention to any points of evidence or other authorities which are said to be material. Thereafter usually the applicant is given a further right of reply and the District Judge will then generally announce his decision on the point at issue. In cases of length or difficulty, the District Judge may need a few minutes to consider his decision and will ask the parties to leave the room while he reads the necessary documents again and perhaps refers to authorities. The parties will then be brought back into the room and he will announce his decision, often in the form of a formal judgment which the parties will then copy down as he pronounces it. Very occasionally, in cases of extreme complexity, the District Judge may reserve his decision to consider overnight, or for some longer period, in which case the decision will be communicated to the parties either at an adjourned hearing or in written form through the post.

7.7.4 TIME SUMMONSES

One particular kind of application previously mentioned is the 'time summons' (see **7.1.2**) in which a party seeks an extension of the time available for some stage in proceedings, most commonly the defendant seeking an extension of time in which to serve his defence. This kind of summons is usually given great priority in listing, time summonses often being listed at the start of the day's business as an extra item and allocated only five minutes for each.

Such summonses normally only have to be served with 24 hours' notice to the other party affected. No affidavit is required. As indicated at **7.1.2** above, the policy of the courts is fairly liberal, so that however long the applying party has already had, at least a further seven days is likely to be allowed.

The costs of an application for an extension of time are almost always ordered to be borne by the party applying for it, though even that principle is subject to the discretion of the court.

7.8 Application for Interlocutory Injunctions

We have already considered at length the principles for the grant of interlocutory injunctions (see **1.7.4**). It is worth setting out separately here some aspects of the procedure for applying for such injunctions, though, chiefly because there are some slight variations from the normal procedures for applying for other interlocutory orders, but in particular because this is the only main instance of interlocutory relief which needs to be sought from a judge rather than a Master or District Judge. We consider the procedure on application in the High Court, though the procedure is the same, with minor variations, in the county court.

7.8.1 *EX PARTE* INJUNCTIONS

7.8.1.1 In general

We have already considered (**7.7.1**) the possibility that an injunction will need to be applied for on an *ex parte* basis, either because of great urgency or sometimes because secrecy is required in order to restrain some action by an unscrupulous defendant by which the defendant might seek to frustrate an application if he had notice of it.

Application for such injunctions can be made even before a writ is issued provided an undertaking is made to issue the writ promptly. Indeed, in exceptional circumstances such an application may be made without any documents being to hand, and may even be granted over the telephone by the judge at home (see, for example, the facts of *Allen* v *Jambo Holdings Ltd* [1980] 1 WLR 1252). Naturally, in such a case a solicitor, and counsel if counsel is used, will be called upon to justify his position, and if there is any element of impropriety or oppressive conduct in the adoption of these unusual procedures, there will be serious consequences. In urgent cases where a judge is needed at night or weekends, there is a telephone number at the Royal Courts of Justice through which contact may be made. Outside London, local Law Societies also hold an emergency local contact number.

7.8.1.2 In the Queen's Bench Division

In the Queen's Bench Division in London application is made at either 10.00 a.m. or 2.00 p.m. Regard must be had to *Practice Direction (Judge in Chambers: Revised Procedure)* [1996] WLR 1432. The necessary papers, which include a copy of the writ if issued and any pleadings served, together with an affidavit sworn by the plaintiff and his solicitor setting out all the relevant facts and giving the appropriate undertakings (see **7.7.2.1**), must be lodged by 3.00 p.m. on the day preceding the application, or, if very urgent, the papers must be produced half an hour before the appointment together with a certificate from counsel as to the urgency of the matter.

7.8.1.3 In the Chancery Division

In the Chancery Division applications are heard at 10.30 a.m. and 2.00 p.m. Regard must be had to *Practice Direction (Chancery Division: Motions Procedure)* [1980] 1 WLR 751. Applications are heard in open court and should be notified to the clerk to the motions judge or the clerk of the lists. Papers should be lodged not later than 12 noon on the working day before the date for which notice of motion has been given.

7.8.1.4 Outside London

Outside London local practice will vary. In the Queen's Bench Division the same documents will be lodged and the clerk of the lists will give a hearing date in a matter of urgency before a Queen's Bench Division judge, usually before he commences his day's list. In the Chancery Division an urgent motion will be listed. If outside London no Chancery judge is available, it may be necessary to transfer that hearing to London. Alternatively, sometimes the Lord Chancellor is prepared to appoint a circuit judge to sit as a High Court judge for the relevant purposes at short notice under *s. 9* of the *Supreme Court Act 1981*.

7.8.1.5 Duration of the injunction

Since this is an *ex parte* procedure, if the judge is satisfied with the documents and argument put to him he is likely to grant the injunction. Usually, however, this will be granted only for a very short period (typically about five days) with leave to apply to continue the injunction *inter partes* until trial. In the Chancery Division the duration of the *ex parte* injunction is until the next appropriate motion day for which the defendant can properly be given notice. Everything depends, however, on the circumstances of the case and the court may name a date for expiry of the *ex parte* injunction thus requiring the plaintiff positively to take action to extend it.

7.8.2 *INTER PARTES* INJUNCTIONS

If there is no extreme urgency or need for secrecy justifying an *ex parte* injunction, or indeed if there has already been an *ex parte* injunction for a short time, application will need to be made for an *inter partes* injunction. The procedure for this is as follows:

7.8.2.1 In the Queen's Bench Division

In the Queen's Bench Division a summons must be issued returnable before a High Court judge and served with two clear days' notice. The court may abridge this time for good reason, although only the judge who hears the application may do that. The application to abridge is made at the hearing of the summons itself.

The documents which need to be lodged include a copy of the writ, any pleadings, the summons itself and a full affidavit in support explaining the basis on which the injunction is required and giving the relevant undertakings. The summons must be endorsed with an estimate of the length of hearing and all the documents are to be served with the appropriate period of notice.

The hearing is in private before the judge and a solicitor thus has rights of audience, although counsel is normally employed. Oral evidence is highly exceptional, the matter being dealt with on the affidavits. The judge will then consider whether to grant or refuse the injunction on the principles described previously at **1.7.4**.

7.8.2.2 In the Chancery Division

In the Chancery Division application is by notice of motion and the hearing is in open court. Again, there must be two clear days' notice at least. In London there are motions days every day, but outside London there may be difficulty in obtaining a very early hearing, especially if the hearing is likely to take some time and to evoke opposition. It may again be necessary to make representations, either for the transfer of this stage of the action to London or for the appointment of a special judge to hear it.

The documents to be filed include two copies of the writ; two copies of the notice of motion; and a certificate of counsel for the applicant giving the estimated length of hearing. The fact that counsel needs to be employed in a Chancery Division action and the fact that it is heard in open court (unless one can convince the judge that it is appropriate for special reasons to be dealt with *in camera*, e.g. because matters of commercial confidentiality are involved), may in themselves be reasons why (where there is a choice) an action should be started in the Queen's Bench Division rather than in the Chancery Division.

Local listing practice in the Chancery Division varies to some extent but normally motions will only be heard in the ordinary 'motions day' if the party applying for the injunction certifies that the hearing will take less than two hours. A quite remarkable number of parties feel able to certify that their motions will last one hour and 59 minutes! If this estimate cannot legitimately be given, then there is likely to be a longer delay until a full day or half day's hearing can be arranged just for this one case. In that case the court may be more willing to grant an *ex parte* injunction to preserve the status quo until the full hearing.

7.9 Drawing up Orders

The Queen's Bench Division remains entirely passive throughout the conduct of civil proceedings. It does nothing of its own motion to ensure that time limits are complied with, it does not call the parties before it at any stage, it does nothing to assist the parties with the service of proceedings, and indeed it does nothing to enforce its own judgments until one or other of the procedures for enforcement is specifically applied for by the successful party. A particular aspect of this passivity is that the Queen's Bench Division does not draw up its own orders. Thus it is up to the party who has succeeded on some interlocutory application, or indeed after the trial itself, to draw up the order of the court and to attend court with two copies of it. The forms of the order are then checked against the minute made by the District Judge or Master at the time of hearing of the interlocutory application. If they are approved, the copy orders are sealed and one copy handed back to the applicant who can now photocopy it and send it to the other party.

In principle, the Chancery Division does draw up its own orders, though there are local variations. In some District Registries the successful party is directed to draft the order and submit it to the court for approval. In London the practice is that orders are drawn up in Chancery Chambers (i.e. by court staff at the Royal Courts of Justice) and a draft submitted to the parties for their agreement in cases of complexity. In some District Registries this has remained the practice as well.

7.10 Example Writ, Statement of Claim and Defence

We have already illustrated a writ used in an action for a contract debt at **6.8**. In the case of a personal injury claim the front of the writ would be completed in precisely the same manner. On the reverse of the writ, however, there would be the following differences:

(a) Instead of there being a fully pleaded statement of claim there would be a brief 'general endorsement' stating simply that the plaintiff claimed damages in respect of the negligence of the defendant at a defined time and place but giving no more details.

(b) There would then be the endorsement certifying that the value of the claim was in excess of £50,000 in the words set out at **5.3.3.5** and this would be signed by the plaintiff's solicitor.

(c) There would not be a 'fixed costs endorsement' because in the case of a claim for unliquidated damages, fixed costs are obviously not appropriate and the plaintiff will be entitled to full taxed costs if successful.

(d) Given the seriousness of the injury the plaintiff's solicitor would pay a court fee of £500 as the amount involved is actually likely to exceed £100,000 (see **6.4.1**).

We now set out an example of a writ issued in respect of damages sustained in a road traffic accident followed by a statement of claim and defence.

Interlocutory Applications

- Failure to give notice of int to defend → P may enter J in default of notice of intention to defend
- Failure to serve a defence → J in default of defence
- Failure to serve defence to CC → D may enter J on the CC in default

Other default in time limits → other party can issue a summons to enforce the time limit.
[Eg P fails to serve S of C within 14 days → D issues an interloc Summons to seek an order that UNLESS P serves S of C within 14 days of order claim will be struck out.]
Equivalent power in hands of P.

Costs
Offending party must meet the costs of the application "in any event."

Ext of Time by agreement & Time Summons
If agreement can't be reached, time summons may be issued for an order of Ct to extend time:
- always reasonable to grant one extention
- Can get "unless order" on subsequent application ie unless they comply they won't be able to bring/defend action.

Other applications (interloc)
- F & B P of pleadings
- Strike out all or part of pleadings
- Leave to amend.
- Renewal of a writ

Ex-parte Applications
By 1 party s̄ notice to other eg renewal of writ (no 2nd P) or where other party has not complied c̄ Ct procedures.

By Inter Partes Summons
= apt before DJ c̄ notice to opponent to attend & notice of application being made.

Procedure:
Fill form c̄ "heading in the action" (152 Ct, action No, details of P & P)
Text of summons instructs opponent to attend on a date (left blank)
Then describe Order being applied for (fill in)
↓
Take forms of summons to Central Office of HC (in Lond) or District Reg (out of Lond)
Provide estimate of length of hearing → get an apt
↓
Date inserted on summons
Ct seal on both copies
Pay fee of £30 for issue of Summs
Copy given to applicant = "issuing"
Date of apt = "return date"
↓
Serve copy by post on opponent
For some summons (substantive matters) file afidavit c̄ evidence

Drawing up Orders
QBD is passive.
Successful party on interloc application must draw up the Order of the Ct
→ attend Ct c̄ 2 copies of it
→ approved, sealed & 1 copy handed back to applicant
↓
copy & send to other party.

COURT FEES ONLY

Writ of Summons [Unliquidated Demand] (O.6,r.1)

IN THE HIGH COURT OF JUSTICE 1997– E.–No. 1313

Queen's Bench Division

[Middlemarch **District Registry]**

Between

Mary Ann Evans **Plaintiff**

AND

George Eliot **Defendant**

(1) Insert name — **To the Defendant** (¹) George Eliot

(2) Insert address — of (²) 7 Vincy Place, Middlemarch, Loamshire

This Writ of Summons has been issued against you by the above-named Plaintiff in respect of the claim set out on the back.

Within 14 days after the service of this Writ on you, counting the day of service, you must either satisfy the claim or return to the Court Office mentioned below the accompanying **Acknowledgment of Service** stating therein whether you intend to contest these proceedings.

If you fail to satisfy the claim or to return the Acknowledgment within the time stated, or if you return the Acknowledgment without stating therein an intention to contest the proceedings, the Plaintiff may proceed with the action and judgment may be entered against you forthwith without further notice.

(3) Complete and delete as necessary — Issued from the (³) [~~Central Office~~] [~~Admiralty and Commercial Registry~~] [Middlemarch District Registry] of the High Court this 12th day of May 1997

NOTE:—This Writ may not be served later than 4 calendar months *(or, if leave is required to effect service out of the jurisdiction, 6 months)* beginning with that date unless renewed by order of the Court.

IMPORTANT

Directions for Acknowledgment of Service are given with the accompanying form.

Notice:
→ 2 CLEAR days (excl day of service & date of hearing)
For Interim Payment/ Summary J: 10 clear days

The Plaintiff's claim is for damages for personal injuries and consequential loss caused by the negligence of the Defendant in the course of driving a motor car, registration number C418 AND on Stoney Road, Middlemarch, Loamshire on 3rd January 1997

This writ includes a claim for personal injury but may be commenced in the High Court because the value of the action for the purposes of Article 5 of the High Court and County Courts Jurisdiction Order 1991 exceeds £50,000.

Dorothea Brooke & Co

---

(1) If this Writ was issued out of a District Registry, this indorsement as to place where the action arose should be completed.
(2) Delete as necessary
(3) Insert name of place.
(4) For phraseology of this indorsement where the Plaintiff sues in person, see *Supreme Court Practice*, vol. 2, para 1.

(1) [(2) [The cause] [One of the causes] of action in respect of which the Plaintiff claim relief in this action arose wholly or in part at (3) Middlemarch in the district of the District Registry named overleaf.]

(4)This Writ was issued by Dorothea Brooke and Co

of 9 Railway Cuttings, Middlemarch, Loamshire

[Agent for]

of

Solicitor for the said Plaintiff whose address (2) [is] [are]

South Farm, Arbury, Loamshire.

Solicitor's Reference DB/7310 Tel. No: 014571 06060

oyez The Solicitors' Law Stationery Society Ltd., Oyez House, 27 Crimscott Street, London SE1 5TS 4 90 F16781

High Court A1 5044019

IN THE HIGH COURT OF JUSTICE **1997-E-No. 1313**

Queen's Bench Division

Middlemarch District Registry

(Writ issued 12 May 1997.)

BETWEEN Mary Ann Evans Plaintiff

and

George Eliot Defendant

Statement of Claim

1. On 3rd January 1997 the Plaintiff was a passenger in the Defendant's motor car registration number C418 AND which was being driven by the Defendant along Stoney Road, Middlemarch when the said car left the road and collided with a concrete bus stop post.

2. The said collision was caused by the negligence of the Defendant.

Particulars of Negligence

The Defendant was negligent in that he

(a) drove too fast
(b) failed to keep any, or any adequate lookout
(c) drove the said car, or allowed the same to travel off the carriageway of the said road onto the pavement adjacent thereto and into collision with the said bus stop
(d) drove when his ability to do so was impaired by the consumption of alcohol
(e) failed to slow down, brake, steer or otherwise manoeuvre the said car so as to avoid the said collision which by the exercise of proper driving skill and care he could have avoided.

3. The Plaintiff will rely on the happening of the said accident as evidence in itself of the negligence of the Defendant.

4. The Plaintiff will rely on the conviction of the Defendant at Middlemarch Magistrates' Court on 2 May 1997 on a charge of driving a motor vehicle whilst having a concentration of alcohol in the blood in excess of the prescribed limit as relevant to the issue of negligence.

5. By reason of the said collision the Plaintiff whose date of birth is 3rd September 1955 sustained pain and injury loss and damage.

Particulars of Injury

The Plaintiff sustained a closed fracture of the midshaft of the left humerus and a compound fracture of the left forearm with considerable damage to the soft tissue. The left forearm developed gas gangrene necessitating amputation at the level of the elbow and subsequently at five inches above the elbow joint. She also sustained facial laceration and crushing of the upper lip, the loss of two teeth and injury to the right eye. Full particulars are set out in the medical reports respectively of Mr Charles Ramadhin dated 6 May 1997; and Dr John Valentine dated 13 May 1997 served herewith.

By reason of the said personal injuries the Plaintiff has suffered pain, discomfort and severe nervous shock, and has been considerably disabled by the amputation. She works as a freelance engineering systems designer and is considerably handicapped in such work despite the fitting of a prosthesis. She will be unable to cope with site visits and in office work has great difficulty in coping with the management of instruments. Although she regularly worked up to 60 hours a week before the date of the said collision she is now able to manage only 30 hours. Her chances of advancement in her profession have been severely curtailed. She may be unable to fulfil contracts and thus may cease to be able to work on a freelance basis. She has been seriously disabled in the labour market and will always be at risk in this respect. A Schedule of Special Damages is served herewith pursuant to Ord. 18, r. 12(1A).

6. In respect of damages awarded to her the Plaintiff is entitled to interest pursuant to section 35A of the Supreme Court Act 1981 for such period and at such rates as to the Court shall seem just.

And the Plaintiff claims

(1) Damages
(2) Under paragraph 6 hereof interest pursuant to the said statute for such period and at such rates as to the Court shall seem just.

Margaret Tulliver.

Served this 12th day of July 1997 by Dorothea Brooke and Co. of 9 Railway Cuttings, Middlemarch Loamshire. Solicitors for the Plaintiff.

7.10.1 STATEMENT OF CLAIM

From the statement of claim, it will be observed that the action is brought by a passenger in a car which collided with a concrete bus stop. Her statement of claim alleges negligence in failing to manage the vehicle so as to avoid the collision. It will be observed that five different aspects of negligence are pleaded. In all probability the plaintiff was not keeping a very close eye on her driver's manoeuvring and would be unable to say precisely what he did wrong, whether actually going too fast, taking his eyes off the road, or simply miscalculating a bend. By pleading every possible alternative, together with the catch all allegation at paragraph 2(e), the plaintiff would seem to have covered every possibility.

In paragraph 3 the plaintiff indicates that she is relying on the maxim *res ipsa loquitur*. In fact it is not necessary to plead this since *res ipsa loquitur* is merely a way of looking at evidence, but it is very common to do so in accidents when no other vehicle is involved. In reality it adds little to the pleading.

At paragraph 4 it will be noted the plaintiff is in the fortunate position of being able to rely on a conviction of the defendant. Had this conviction been for careless or dangerous driving, the plaintiff would have been in an extremely strong position. The conviction unfortunately was for having excess alcohol in the blood, and whilst this is of course a much more serious offence than careless driving, it is less useful as a means of demonstrating negligence because it is self-evident that a driver may in fact drive competently notwithstanding having drunk to excess. It is certainly worth pleading, however, and will be a relevant extra factor at trial in the assessment of the whole of the defendant's driving conduct.

Thereafter the statement of claim gives particulars of injury and of the ways in which the plaintiff's career will be affected. It indicates that a full set of medical reports is served with the statement of claim, as the rules now require, and also that a schedule of special damages is supplied. The method of drafting this schedule varies. Some solicitors continue to put in the text of the statement of claim itself 'one off' items of special damages such as damaged clothing, private medical treatment and the like, while serving a separate schedule dealing with loss of earnings, future loss of earnings, loss of pension rights, etc. as required by *Ord. 18, r. 12(1A)*. We will assume that in this instance this plaintiff has put all her particulars of special damage, including the smaller items, in that schedule.

The statement of claim concludes with a claim to interest and the 'prayer' seeking damages and interest on those damages.

On the face of it what happened looks as though it is an open and shut case and the defendant has little hope of escaping liability. However, even in such cases it is common, by imaginative pleading, for defendants to keep several options alive for negotiating purposes.

7.10.2 DEFENCE

IN THE HIGH COURT OF JUSTICE **1997-E-No. 1313**

Queen's Bench Division

Middlemarch District Registry

BETWEEN Mary Ann Evans Plaintiff

and

George Eliot Defendant

Defence

1. Paragraph 1 of the Statement of Claim is admitted.

2. No further admissions are made as to any of the allegations contained in the Statement of Claim and in particular it is denied that the Defendant was negligent either as alleged or at all or that the said accident was caused thereby.

3. No admissions are made as to the extent of the alleged injury loss or damage or as to the causation thereof.

4. Further or in the alternative, the said accident was not due to any negligence on the part of the Defendant but was caused by the sudden and unexpected deflation of the rear nearside tyre of the said vehicle which resulted in the Defendant being temporarily deprived of his ability properly to control the said vehicle.

5. Further or in the alternative the Defendant denies the relevance of his conviction referred to in paragraph 4 of the Statement of Claim and if (which is denied) the said accident was in any way due to alcohol which the Defendant had consumed the Defendant will contend that the Plaintiff in accepting a lift in the said vehicle at a time when she knew that the Defendant had taken drink was herself guilty of negligence in that she allowed herself to be carried in the said vehicle at a time when she knew that the Defendant had taken drink and that his ability properly to control the said vehicle might be thereby impaired.

6. Further or in the further alternative, if, (which is denied) the Defendant's ability properly to control the said vehicle was in any way impaired by drink either as alleged or at all, the Defendant will contend that the Plaintiff in accepting a lift at a time when she well knew that the Defendant had consumed alcohol voluntarily consented to the risk of injury occurring by reason of any accident which might be attributable to the drink which the Defendant had consumed and impliedly agreed to waive all claims arising out of such matters.

7. Further or in the further alternative such injury (if any) as the Plaintiff sustained in consequence of the said accident was caused wholly or in part by her own negligence in failing to make any, or any proper, use of the seat belt with which the said vehicle was equipped.

Adam Bede

Served this 15th day of July 1997 by Deronda and Co. of 10 King St, Middlemarch, Solicitors for the Defendant.

7.10.3 THE DEFENCE

In the defence it will be observed that the defendant agrees that an accident occurred, but denies negligence in any respect. The defendant makes no admissions as to the extent of the injuries suffered by the plaintiff or damage because, of course, the defendant has no direct proof of these matters at this stage.

The defendant then goes on to make the best of what is obviously a fairly weak case, since he collided with a bus stop with no other vehicle involved, by four different allegations.

First, in paragraph 4, the defendant raises so-called 'inevitable accident' as a defence, saying that the vehicle left the road because of a sudden tyre burst. If this can be shown then the defendant will escape liability, there being no 'fault', and the plaintiff, notwithstanding her terrible injuries, will receive no compensation. Even if this tyre burst is demonstrated (the burden of proof being on the defendant), it may of course still be possible for the judge to conclude that the defendant's consumption of alcohol affected his ability to manage the skid into which the vehicle went.

In paragraph 5 the defendant denies the *relevance* of his conviction, in other words suggests that his ability to manage the car was not affected by the alcohol which he implicitly agrees he had consumed. This denial requires the plaintiff to establish relevance. In some instances, if something wholly irrelevant was contended by a plaintiff, a defendant would be well advised to issue a summons to strike out the offending allegation from the statement of claim and have that matter determined by a District Judge before trial. Thus, for example, if the plaintiff pleaded some ancient, unconnected conviction, perhaps as a way of attempting to show that the defendant was habitually a bad driver, that would be the case. In the present instance, however, the matter of relevance would be left for the judge at trial to decide. On the face of it it is unlikely that the judge will find that there is *no* relevance in the fact that the defendant had drunk to excess.

The defendant then goes on to raise the contributory negligence of the plaintiff in allowing herself to be carried by a driver whom she knew to have drunk to excess. The case law establishes that in such an instance there may well be a substantial discount on damages (perhaps up to 25 per cent) to reflect the plaintiff's degree of blameworthiness for her injuries.

In the subsequent paragraph the allegation is put still more strongly. The defendant is here alleging *volenti non fit injuria*, which is of course, unlike contributory negligence, a complete defence. The suggestion is that the plaintiff voluntarily consented to waive any claims arising out of negligence in driving affected by drink. The case law does not indicate that the defendant will be likely to succeed with this allegation. Indeed, in some cases, even on relatively extreme facts, the courts have not held that a plaintiff voluntarily waived any claim by reason of accepting a lift from a drunken driver. The *Road Traffic Act 1988, s. 149*, appears to negative any possibility of a defence of *volenti*. The position is not, however, totally clear and the suggestion has even been made that, on gross enough facts, a passenger could be deemed to be aiding and abetting a very drunk driver to drive. The maxim *ex turpi causa non oritur actio* may even be called in aid. Such a possibility was recognised in the case of *Pitts* v *Hunt* [1991] 1 QB 24 where a pillion passenger was injured by the negligence of the motor cyclist, both being very drunk and the driver being to the defendant's knowledge unlicensed and uninsured and, moreover, deliberately encouraged by the plaintiff to drive dangerously. (In the actual case on which this case study is based, the plaintiff contended that she had no idea that the defendant had been drinking because, although they had both been at a party, they had been in separate rooms throughout the evening and she had assumed that the defendant had moderated his drinking in view of the fact that he would later be driving.)

Lastly, the defendant seeks further reduction for contributory negligence by the allegation that the plaintiff was not wearing a seat belt. As is also well-known, on the case law, this may likewise lead to a reduction in damages for up to 25 per cent, provided that the plaintiff's injuries would in fact have been reduced or avoided by the wearing of a seat belt.

By the end of the defence therefore, the defendant has at least succeeded in putting into issue enough allegations to make it quite certain that the plaintiff will not be able to obtain summary judgment. In addition, there are now sufficient 'balls in the air' for the plaintiff's lawyers to be left with some considerable uncertainty about the outcome of the case, so that the defendant at least has something to negotiate with in what is obviously, given the plaintiff's future career impairment, a very large claim indeed.

(In fact the plaintiff's solicitors in the actual case were able by the delivery of a request for further and better particulars of the defence and interrogatories, to establish that the defendant had not kept the tyre which had allegedly burst, and thus were going to be unable to establish that at trial. The evidence, moreover, that the plaintiff had been in a separate room from the defendant at the party was very strong, thus taking away any suggestion of *volenti non fit injuria*; in addition the defendant appeared to have had only four or five pints of beer and was well used to drink, and thus although over the limit, there were no indications in his behaviour that he had drunk to excess. Also the impact which caused the most damage was from the side, the car having swerved into the bus stop, and although the plaintiff was, foolishly, not wearing a seat belt, most of the injuries would not have been saved by such a seat belt and in negotiation no discount was given for contributory negligence for failure to wear a seat belt.)

7.11 High Court and County Court Compared

Scrutiny of these documents illustrates how small the differences are between county court and High Court procedure. Whilst the county court summons itself is rather different in appearance to a High Court writ it contains almost precisely the same information. It would be supplemented by a pleading which in the county court is called *particulars of claim*, but which would be identical in drafting to the statement of claim shown here save that the reference to the *Supeme Court Act 1981, s. 35A*, would be replaced by a reference to the *County Courts Act 1984, s. 69*. The defence likewise would be identical, pleadings being every bit as formal in terms of layout and contents in the county court as in the High Court. County court pleadings however, conclude with the words 'dated the — day of —' rather than 'served the — day of —' as appears on High Court pleadings.

General

SGS 2

Stat Criteria + Procedural Reqts.

a) Opinion evid S3(2) CEA 1972: actually a fact
p195 Inadmissible unless from an Expert
Cusurp function of Judge

b) Evid of Conviction:
p187 → to adduce it as evid
need to ----
Effect: reverse burden of proof.

c) HS + informal admissions

p181
d) Relevance – must be rel

e) Speculation → No
can't draw conclusion

Analyse W statement + identify evidence in respect of which objection may be taken

Look for:

1. HS → weight. Eg In a W statemt "he said to me ---- "
If W can't attend → statemt is 1st H HS
+ any admission within it may be 2nd H HS → ↓ wt
2. Opinion – Expert
↳ or factual narrative/perceived fact
Comply c̄ procedure re S2 Notice
3. Relevance
↳ to issue
4. Speculation
5. Informal admission
→ adduce as HS
6. Conviction → procedure to adduce conviction? Effect (p187)
→ reverse burden of proof
7. Offensive – "a maniac"
Must be relevant to case – S11 CEA
→ admissible if pleaded

Evid for Children can be used (p171)
S96 Ch Act 1989

Model Ans Specific Points

Para 2 'I am still in touch'
– delete (irrelevant)

Para 4 'I was impressed c̄
– irrelevant (delete)

"He said -- no one had explained"
Do these 2 sentences contain 1st hand HS which is admissible under S1 CEA 1995, although weight of evid will fall to be assessed by ref to all the Circs + in particular the stat. criteria?
Possible it is not HS ∵ we are not attempting to prove the truth of what is said?

Para 5 "I think – unfair" – irrelevant. Del
"I have seen ---- before" Opinion or fact. If opin delete

"They should have showed..."
Opinion or fact. If op delete.

"Clearwater are notorious..."
irrelevant: +/or inadmissible speculation. Delete

Procedural steps re W statements

1) Final draft in Correct format + contain no inadmissible evid.
2) Maker should sign + date it
3) Procedure for exchange
4) Time scales for exch
5) Will any HS notice accompany the statemt on exch?

EIGHT

CIVIL EVIDENCE (1)

The law of evidence is notoriously a difficult and technical subject. It has reached its present confused state by piecemeal statutory reforms and tinkerings grafted on to a base of common law principles. In a few respects the law of civil evidence is almost the same as that of criminal evidence but the overwhelming majority of the rules are now radically different. One of the main purposes of the law of evidence is to prevent the trier of fact hearing evidence which he or she would be incompetent to assess properly. This is still a dominant feature of the rules of criminal evidence in the light of the supposed naïvety of the average jury. That principle, however, may have little relevance in the ordinary civil case where the trial is conducted by a High Court or circuit judge well able, in principle, to sift the evidence and discard what is unreliable, however superficially attractive. For that, amongst other reasons, there has been some slackening in the former strictness of the rules of evidence in relation to civil proceedings. This has led to the more widespread acceptance of, for example, hearsay evidence, (that trend reaching its zenith in the *Civil Evidence Act 1995*), and evidence of opinion in civil cases. In addition, although no legal authority states this, every practitioner in the civil courts will confirm that advocates are less ready to take purely technical points of admissibility and that a great deal of evidence which might well technically fall foul of one or other rule of admissibility is often admitted without challenge or comment.

In the next four chapters we shall be considering the rules of civil evidence in a straightforward and practical way including giving consideration to the precise stages in a civil case at which matters of evidence may arise and in particular how the evidence in a civil case should be handled.

8.1 Introduction

The essence of the law of evidence is that it regulates what material may or may not be put before the person who is trying the facts, i.e. in an ordinary civil case the circuit judge or High Court judge. It also regulates the manner in which those facts may be proved.

To succeed in a case, the party who wishes to establish his case (usually, but not invariably, the plaintiff) must prove 'the facts in issue'. In most cases the 'facts in issue' can be determined by looking at the substantive law and at the pleadings, the whole point of which is to set out the factual case on which each party relies. So in a straightforward civil case the plaintiff must prove that the defendant owed him a duty, breached that duty, and caused him foreseeable damage flowing from it; or that the defendant had a contractual relationship with him which the defendant breached and as a result of which the plaintiff suffered loss.

8.2 Types of Evidence

8.2.1 IN GENERAL

The kinds of evidence which may be adduced are usually divided into four categories:

(a) *Testimony*

This is an assertion by a witness in court, which in civil cases must in principle be on oath, of what he has himself perceived by one or more of his five senses.

(b) *Hearsay*

Hearsay is 'a statement other than one made by a person while giving oral evidence in proceedings and tendered as evidence of the truth of the fact stated'. Hearsay was in fact inadmissible in civil proceedings until the *Civil Evidence Act 1968* which came into force in 1969. Thereafter there was an awkward regime permitting hearsay in certain circumstances but rejecting it in others. Matters have been greatly simplified and clarified by the coming into force of the *Civil Evidence Act 1995* which has the simple effect of making all hearsay admissible in civil proceedings (though see **9.3** for criteria to be applied by the court and practical considerations).

(c) *Documents*

Documents may be produced for inspection by the court. These may be either hearsay documents (for example a witness statement), or a piece of real evidence (see (d) below). Thus, for example, the very contract, or will or lease may be proved in court to show the court what the terms of the relevant document were where that is relevant to the litigation. Similarly, public documents such as marriage certificates or certificates of conviction may be used in this way.

(d) *Real evidence*

This includes producing actual objects to the court, such as the very piece of machinery which caused an injury, or the shoes that the plaintiff was wearing when he slipped on a factory floor. It may also include going out of court to a 'view' of a material place, as in the famous case of *Tito* v *Waddell (No. 2)* [1977] Ch 106 where, in a dispute to do with mining rights on Ocean Island in the South Pacific, the judge, accompanied by lawyers from both sides, adjourned for several days to visit the island in question.

8.2.2 DIRECT OR CIRCUMSTANTIAL EVIDENCE

There are alternative ways of classifying evidence. A more relevant way is perhaps to consider whether each piece of evidence is either *direct* or *circumstantial*.

8.2.2.1 Direct evidence

Direct evidence is evidence in the form usually of the testimony of the witness who has perceived a relevant fact (e.g. an eye-witness who saw exactly how an accident occurred). Similarly, if the terms of a lease are disputed, the production of the actual executed and stamped lease is direct evidence.

8.2.2.2 Circumstantial evidence

This is evidence which does not directly establish a fact but is still admissible in order to enable the court to decide whether or not it did exist. Circumstantial evidence usually assists by enabling the trier of fact to make some deduction from generalisations, often about ordinary matters of human behaviour. So, for example, if the dispute concerns whether an individual, B, visiting his dangerously ill elderly relative T in hospital, used undue influence to get the latter to change his will to B's advantage, evidence that B's business was in grave financial difficulties at the time might be a relevant piece of circumstantial evidence. The reason is obvious, that persons in financial difficulties may be forced to go to unusual lengths to attempt to extricate themselves, and that the coincidence of the two events is of significance. On the other hand, this is just a generalisation about human behaviour and the conclusion that B *did* employ undue influence is far from inevitable.

Naturally a prolonged examination of circumstantial evidence can lead to side tracks, and it is part of the function of the judge to control the relevance of testimony in the trial before him.

8.2.3 THE FACTS IN ISSUE

The facts in issue are what the plaintiff needs to prove to succeed. It must be borne in mind that the facts in issue are not just those facts relevant to liability. Even though he may establish liability pure and simple, as for example that the defendant breached his contract, or caused a road accident in which he was injured, the plaintiff always needs to go on to prove the damage which he claims to have suffered and that this flowed from the breach of contract or tort. For example, notwithstanding that a plaintiff can adduce sufficient evidence to prove that the defendant collided with his car, it might be the defendant's contention that, although he is liable for vehicle damage, the impact was so minimal that the personal injuries claimed by the plaintiff do not flow from it and are either the result of some pre-existing condition, or that the plaintiff is malingering. In such a case the plaintiff will have to call expert evidence about medical matters and also prove under the strict rules of admissibility each and every pecuniary item for which he is claiming by reference to loss of earnings, past and future, the cost of private medical treatment or nursing care, the cost of his mother travelling to visit him in hospital from the other end of the country and so on, as the case may be. As much time (or more) may be given over in some civil trials to questions of quantum as to questions of liability, and it is easy to overlook the fact that the rules of evidence are the same for matters of quantum.

8.3 The Burden of Proof

As indicated in 8.2.3, in principle a party has the obligation of proving those facts which he needs to establish for success in his case. It is necessary to subdivide the term 'burden of proof' into two elements, the legal burden and the evidential burden.

8.3.1 THE LEGAL BURDEN

The legal burden of proof is borne by the person who asserts a fact. This is normally the plaintiff. Much may depend upon the pleadings, however. A defendant who merely does not admit the plaintiff's case is not positively asserting anything of his own and therefore does not have the burden of proving alternative versions of how an accident came about. On the other hand, if the defendant goes so far as to assert contributory negligence, then he is making a positive allegation against the plaintiff and it is then for him to prove that contributory negligence.

The incidence of the legal burden is usually made clear by the pleadings. It must be borne in mind, however, that in some cases the incidence of a legal burden may be fixed by statute, e.g. where under the *Consumer Credit Act 1974* a debtor alleges that a credit bargain is extortionate, the burden of proof is switched to the creditor to prove the contrary (*Consumer Credit Act 1974, s. 171(7)*). Similarly, the terms of a contract may also fix where the burden is to fall in litigation under the contract. This is quite common, for example, in insurance contracts and international trade contracts.

Outside the run of routine litigation it is often difficult to know on which party a burden falls. Sometimes the courts have placed the legal burden on one party because the other party would have had to prove a negative state of affairs and it is difficult to prove a negative. A good example is the following case which, although it is the case that went the furthest in the judicial system, could hardly be called a leading case in the sense that it enunciates any clear principle.

***Joseph Constantine Steamship Line Ltd* v *Imperial Smelting Corp.* [1942] AC 154**

The appellants were shipowners who had chartered a cargo ship to the respondents. Immediately before the charter was about to start there was a great explosion on board the ship, such that the charter could not proceed and the contract was frustrated. There was no evidence at all about the cause of the explosion. A question arose as to whether it was for the charterers, in their claim for damages against the shipowners for failure to provide a ship, to prove that the explosion had occurred because of the shipowners' negligence, or whether it was for the shipowners to prove absence of negligence on their part. As there was no evidence at all about the cause of the explosion, whichever party bore the burden of proof was bound to lose. The House of Lords held that it was not for the shipowners to prove that the explosion was *not* due to their negligence or default because of the difficulty of proving a negative state of affairs. Thus the defence of frustration succeeded.

8.3.2 THE EVIDENTIAL BURDEN

The evidential burden is the obligation to bring sufficient evidence on the facts in issue to justify, as a possibility, a favourable finding on that issue by the ultimate trier of fact. Whether this burden has been discharged is decided during the course of the trial by the judge. The evidential burden for this reason is sometimes known as 'the burden of passing the judge'.

This term is much more relevant in a criminal context where there is a judge deciding on matters of law and evidence and a jury deciding on matters of fact. It leads to the position in criminal trials that a judge may decide that the evidential burden has not been discharged by the prosecution, and he may then stop the case in favour of the defence without it reaching the jury. In civil cases, which are tried without a jury, the position still arises in principle at the end of the plaintiff's case. If by that stage the plaintiff's case is so weakened that there is no case for the defendant to meet, the judge may be asked to rule on a submission that there is no case for the defendant to be called upon to answer. If he so rules then the case is over.

8.4 The Standard of Proof

8.4.1 PROOF ON A PREPONDERANCE OF PROBABILITIES

In civil cases the standard of proof is proof 'on a preponderance of probabilities', which in ordinary English simply means that the plaintiff must prove that it is *more likely than not* that his version of the facts is right.

In simple terms it might be thought that this means a plaintiff need only prove matters to 51 per cent probability. In fact a wealth of case law has introduced a great deal of confusion into this area. The courts have often considered whether the conduct alleged against the defendant was in some way so reprehensible that it would be right to throw upon the plaintiff a burden of proof to a higher standard, perhaps even to the equivalent of the criminal standard, i.e. proof beyond reasonable doubt. Examples are where it is alleged that the defendant's director made a fraudulent misrepresentation (*Hornal* v *Neuberger Products Ltd* [1957] 1 QB 247); and a serious allegation of medical negligence (*Whitehouse* v *Jordan* [1980] 1 All ER 650), where Denning MR and Lawton LJ considered that allegations of medical negligence were of such a serious nature in view of the doctor's future career and public confidence in the medical profession, that such allegations should be proved to a higher standard. These observations were expressly disapproved when the case reached the House of Lords, however. The best view is probably that of the High Court of Australia in *Rejfek* v *McElroy* (1965) 112 CLR 517 at pp. 521–2 which was approved by Edmund Davies LJ in *Bastable* v *Bastable* [1968] 1 WLR 1684:

> *The difference between the criminal standard of proof and the civil standard of proof is no mere matter of words: it is a matter of critical substance. No matter how grave the fact which is to be found in a civil case, the mind has only to be reasonably satisfied and has not with respect to any matter in issue in such a proceeding to attain that degree of certainty which is indispensable to the support of a conviction upon a criminal charge.*

The matter ought finally to have been decided by a case where the allegation was one of murder in a civil context:

Re Dellow's Will Trusts **[1964] 1 WLR 451**

D, the testator, left his whole estate to his wife with gifts over should she not survive. D suffered cerebral thrombosis and was disabled. He was cared for by his wife who eventually became acutely depressed. Both were found in a gas-filled room having taken sleeping tablets. The issue was whether Mrs Dellow killed herself and the testator, or whether it had been a genuine suicide pact. If she had killed the testator his estate would pass to the subject of his gifts over, whereas if she had not killed him and it had been a genuine suicide pact, his estate would have passed to her and through her to her own beneficiaries. It was held that even though the crime alleged in the civil proceedings was murder, the standard of proof did not reach the very high standard required by the criminal law. On the evidence the only reasonable conclusion was that Mrs Dellow did kill her husband, and the court so found.

Despite this clear outcome a number of cases since have confused the position. For example, *Bahai* v *Rashidian* [1985] 1 WLR 1337, where it was suggested that an allegation of serious misconduct against a solicitor in a civil case involved a higher standard of proof; *Re G (A Minor) (Child Abuse: Standard of Proof)* [1987] 1 WLR 1461, where it suggested that a higher degree of probability was required to satisfy the court that a father had sexually abused his child; and *Miles* v *Cain* (1989) *The Guardian*, 16 December 1989 where a civil action for sexual assault was brought against a defendant whom the police had refused to prosecute. At the trial by judge alone, although the judge purported to direct himself on corroboration as if it were a criminal case, he found in favour of the plaintiff. The Court of Appeal found that the judge's sympathy for the plaintiff had coloured his view and that a higher degree of probability was required to prove that a defendant in a civil action had committed serious criminal assaults.

The best view of these cases is that there is only one standard, namely proof on a balance of probabilities. It is therefore wrong to say that the more serious the allegation the higher the degree of probability that is required. It is better to say that the more serious the allegation the more cogent is the evidence required to overcome the inherent improbability of what is alleged and thus to prove it.

8.4.2 WHAT IF THE COURT IS UNDECIDED?

It might be imagined that at the conclusion of the High Court or county court trial a judge would be reluctant to admit that, despite having heard the evidence of at least two persons and possibly many more, he was unable to make up his mind between the truth of the versions of the opposing parties. In fact there is a surprising number of cases where that has occurred. In *Morris* v *London Iron and Steel Co. Ltd* [1988] QB 493, the Court of Appeal held that although judges and tribunals of fact should make findings of fact in relation to matters before them if they could, in exceptional cases they would be obliged by their judicial duty, having considered all the evidence, to say that they did not know where the truth lay. In such exceptional cases they should decide the issues on the basis of whether the party having the burden of proof had discharged it, without attempting to make findings of fact which they could not in conscience make.

Examples of cases which in the end turn on the burden of proof because the judge could not decide whom to believe, are *T. (H)* v *T. (E)* [1971] 1 WLR 429; and *Wauchope* v *Mordecai* [1970] 1 WLR 317. In both these cases the judge, admitting that he could not decide between the truth of the respective versions, allowed matters to be decided by reference to the burden of proof, so that in each instance the party who bore the burden of proof lost.

8.5 Methods of Proof

The facts in issue must normally be proved by admissible evidence. This usually takes the form of a witness testifying on oath as to matters which he has himself perceived. It may also, as we mentioned in **8.2.1**, involve actual documents being put before the court because their very contents are in issue, e.g. the terms of a lease or will, or a document being produced as admissible hearsay evidence in those instances where this is permissible, or an object being brought to court for the judge to see.

There are four examples of situations, however, where a court may treat matters as established without evidence being brought to court at all. These instances are:

(a) Facts of which *judicial notice* is taken.

(b) Facts which are *formally admitted* by a party.

(c) Facts which are the subject of a *presumption.*

(d) Facts which may be *inferred.*

8.5.1 JUDICIAL NOTICE

Facts which will be judicially noticed are those which are incapable of dispute, either because they are so notorious or because they are readily ascertainable by reference to a proper source. When a court takes judicial notice it declares that it will find that a fact exists even though no evidence has been called to establish it. For example:

(a) That a fortnight is too short a period for human gestation (*R* v *Luffe* (1807) 8 East 193).

(b) That a defamatory postcard is likely to be read by anyone (*Huth* v *Huth* [1915] 3 KB 32).

(c) That criminals have unhappy lives (*Burn* v *Edman* [1970] 2 QB 541).

A judge may also act upon facts which he has ascertained from sources to which it is proper for him to refer. For example:

(a) Where a certificate is received from the Secretary of State on a matter of foreign policy, e.g. the recognition of a foreign sovereign, or whether a state of war exists (*Duff Development Co. Ltd* v *Government of Kelantan* [1924] AC 797).

(b) Matters of historical fact, e.g. *Read* v *Bishop of Lincoln* [1892] AC 644, a case to do with the historic basis of a church practice.

(c) Custom and professional practice, e.g. the practice of conveyancers, shipping customs and commercial customs.

8.5.2 FORMAL ADMISSIONS

Facts may be formally admitted in civil cases by a party before trial. The opposite party is then relieved of the obligation of proving the matters admitted which are taken to be established without formal evidence. Such admissions may be made by any document, e.g. letters between the parties, a response to interrogatories, but more normally are admitted either:

(a) in the pleadings; or

(b) in response to a 'notice to admit facts'.

8.5.2.1 In the pleadings

Example The plaintiff pleads the existence of an oral contract and says that a certain term is imported into the contract, because of previous dealings between the parties. In his defence the defendant admits the existence of previous contracts containing the disputed term but goes on to say that the term was expressly varied here by subsequent agreement. The effect of this is thus to relieve the plaintiff of the obligation of proving the preliminary facts to do with the existence of other contracts and the term that was imported into them. The dispute now centres entirely on the question of whether and how the term was expressly varied in the present case.

8.5.2.2 In response to a 'notice to admit facts'

Under *RSC Ord. 27, rr. 1–5*, or *CCR Ord. 20, rr. 9–10*, a party who wishes his opponent to admit some fact without the need to call a witness at trial to prove it, may serve on his opponent a 'notice to admit facts' which specifies the fact required to be admitted. A party may use this procedure if for any reason he wishes to avoid calling a witness, for example in order to save time and costs. Examples are where the fact appears to be uncontroversial and the witness will be expensive to call because he will demand an expert witness fee, or perhaps will have to be brought from abroad. In addition, it may be useful to use this method to get the opposing party to admit facts which it would be very time-consuming to prove.

Such notices may in principle be served at any time up to 21 days after setting down in the High Court, and 14 days before trial in the county court. A party who receives such a notice may then either:

(a) Admit the fact. This means that the other party is relieved from calling evidence about the fact at trial and it is taken as established. Thus the first party has succeeded in his object.

(b) Not admit the fact. In this case the first party must call the necessary evidence properly to prove the facts at trial. However, if the first party *succeeds* in proving the facts at trial, then whoever wins the case at trial on the main issue, by virtue of *RSC Ord. 62, r. 6(7)*, the costs of proving the facts shall be paid by the party who refuses to admit them unless the court otherwise orders.

Thus the sanction for a party failing to admit the fact that he should have admitted is a penalty in costs. Of course, if the party who serves the notice to admit *fails* to prove the facts at trial the notice is of no effect whatever on costs.

Example The plaintiff is injured in a road accident caused by a collision at a crossroads. The plaintiff is self-employed, and in the period while he is injured he loses some particularly profitable work which he would otherwise have had. It will, however, take a lot of time and expense at trial to prove the existence of these contracts and the precise net amounts which they would have brought him, and the evidence on this aspect, including evidence of an accountant, might take some days. Accordingly, the plaintiff serves a notice to admit the amounts which he would have lost during his period of incapacity. The defendant does not accept the notice to admit facts and the plaintiff is obliged to call all the relevant evidence at trial. The judge finds that the plaintiff has established the exact amount of his loss but finds for the defendant on *liability*, i.e. that the accident was caused by the plaintiff himself. Although the plaintiff will therefore inevitably be ordered to pay the defendant's costs of everything else in the trial, the judge, by the operation of this rule, will order that the defendant pays the plaintiff's costs of the evidence on these items of quantum on the basis that the defendant should reasonably have admitted them.

On the same facts, if the judge had not accepted all the evidence but had found, for example, that the plaintiff's actual loss in the period was rather less than he had claimed, then the notice to admit facts would have been of no effect and the costs of the evidence would have followed the event.

The use of a notice to admit facts at the relevant time is of great importance. Recent rule changes have made the possibility of a costs order still more Draconian in the event of a party not accepting a reasonable notice to admit facts. The rules currently provide that the judge may make a separate finding on this matter in the course of the trial and order the costs to be payable forthwith, a rule which is no doubt only rarely exercised since preliminary findings actually in the course of a trial are not usually appropriate. Nevertheless, the courts are continuing to stress the importance of the parties doing their best to make the trial as brief and efficient as possible by agreeing all matters about which reasonable agreement is possible. A notice to admit facts should not, of course, be abused. There is little point in serving a notice to admit facts on the defendant requiring him to admit some fact so central that the whole of liability and quantum flows from it. If the defendant is continuing to defend then no response will be received. Nor should one behave unreasonably in general with regard to such notices. In the above example it would have been wrong for the plaintiff to have served his notice to admit facts before he had himself given full discovery of the documentary evidence relevant to the claims which he was advancing so that the defendant could have a reasonable chance to consider it.

8.5.3 PRESUMPTIONS

Certain matters may be presumed by the court to exist without formal proof. This means that a person challenging the existence of a certain state of affairs has the burden of disproving it rather than vice versa, no matter which of them is plaintiff and which defendant. An example is the well-known presumption of legitimacy, e.g. that a child born during the existence of a marriage is presumed to be legitimate so that a party wishing to dispute that fact has the burden of proving it; another example is the presumption of regularity in official matters, expressed in the latin maxim *omnia praesumuntur rite esse acta*. This means that there is a presumption, unless the contrary is proved, that public officials have been properly appointed and public acts properly carried out.

It must be noted, however, that neither of the presumptions mentioned above are irrebuttable. They are merely what a court will take to be the case if there is no evidence sufficient to overturn the presumption. Thus if, for example, the whole point of a case is that it is alleged that a certain public official was not properly appointed so that some act done by him is a nullity, provided the person making this allegation can prove it on a balance of probabilities, the presumption will be displaced. In the case of the presumption of legitimacy, this is expressed in *s. 26* of the *Family Law Reform Act 1969*, which provides that:

> *Any presumption of law as to the legitimacy . . . of any person may in any civil proceedings be rebutted by evidence which shows that it is more probable than not that that person is illegitimate.*

There are two main presumptions which may be of importance in civil cases. These are:

(a) the presumption of death; and

(b) *res ipsa loquitur.*

8.5.3.1 The presumption of death

(a) *The common-law rule*

The common-law rule is that if the following matters are shown, then there is a presumption that a person is dead.

(i) That there is no acceptable evidence that the person has been alive during a continuous period of seven years or more by the time the case reaches court.

(ii) That there are persons who would have been likely to hear from him had he been alive, and they have not.

(iii) That such enquiries as are appropriate in the circumstances have been made without success.

***Chard* v *Chard* [1956] P 259**

The issue in this case was whether Mr Chard's first wife, who was last heard of in 1917, would or would not have been alive in 1933. She had indicated to Chard in 1917, at which time he was about to start a lengthy prison sentence, that she would not be around when he came out and had no intention that the marriage should continue. The court concluded that as it was unlikely that she would have contacted Chard, there could be no presumption that she had died by the relevant date.

(b) *The statutory presumption*

Some statutes make provision for a 'presumption' of death, in particular the *Matrimonial Causes Act 1973, s. 19(3),* which provides that a decree of presumption of death shall be granted where for a period of seven years or more the other party to the marriage has been continually absent from the petitioner and the petitioner has no reason to believe that the other party has been living within that time. It should be noted that here there is no requirement for actual positive enquiries, and therefore the test is less strict than at common law.

(c) *Date of death and the commorientes rule*

The presumption of death is satisfactory for establishing the *fact* of death where this is important, for example for distributing the estates of deceased persons. In the absence of additional evidence, however, there will be no presumption that the deceased was dead on *any particular date* during the period of absence. All that the court will find is that the deceased is dead at the date of the legal proceedings.

The establishment of the exact date of death, where this is necessary, for example, to show in which order beneficiaries died under a will, or at what stage income for life under a trust terminates, is a matter of factual evidence. This may obviously cause great difficulties in practice where the person in question is simply missing. In that case the action will turn on who has the burden of showing that the missing person was alive on any particular date; see *Re Phené's Trusts* (1870) LR 5 Ch App 139 and *Re Aldersey, Gibson* v *Hall* [1905] 2 Ch 181.

It should be observed that the *Law of Property Act 1925, s. 184,* may affect the position. This is the so-called 'commorientes' rule and provides:

> *In all cases where . . . two or more person have died in circumstances rendering it uncertain which of them survived the other or others, such deaths shall (subject to any order of the court), for all purposes affecting the title to property, be presumed to have occurred in order of seniority, and accordingly the younger shall be deemed to have survived the elder.*

It should be noted that this is not confined to 'common disaster' cases such as where all the occupants of the house are killed simultaneously by a German bomb, as in *Hickman* v *Peacey* [1945] AC 304. It applies also if, for example, a husband is on a ship which is lost without trace and the wife dies during an operation whilst the ship is missing. Note also that the Act does not apply as between husband and wife on intestacy.

8.5.3.2 *Res ipsa loquitur*

This provides a presumption of negligence where the whole activity is under the management of the defendant and the accident is such as in the ordinary course of things does not happen if those who have the management of the activity use proper care. Thus, in the absence of explanation by the defendants, there is a presumption that the accident arose from negligence, and the effect of this is to shift the burden of proof onto the defendants once the primary facts are established. See *Scott* v *The London and St Katherine Docks Co.* (1865) 3 Hurl & C 596, 159 ER 665 where, while S was passing through the defendant's dock, a bag of sugar fell on him from a crane and injured him. In the normal course of things the plaintiff would have had the burden of proof on all issues of fact, and thus would have had to put his finger on precisely which employee loading the hoist from which the sugar fell had been negligent and in what way. The operation of the presumption, however, once the primary fact was proved, shifted the burden to the defendant to show positively that there was an absence of negligence.

The results of the many decided cases on this presumption leave it extremely unclear precisely what elements of the burden of proof are discharged by its operation. The clearest statement is said to be *Barkway* v *South Wales Transport Co. Ltd* [1948] 2 All ER 460, in the judgment of Asquith LJ at p. 471. On this view where the maxim applies it is for the defendant to do more than show an equally possible non-negligent explanation – he must show positively that the cause did *not* connote negligence. This case was considered in *Henderson* v *Henry E. Jenkins & Sons* [1970] AC 282, which, although a House of Lords case, puts the matter in a somewhat less clear way.

This presumption of law, if it is one, is now of considerably less importance in practical litigation. The presumption does not need to be pleaded, and recent cases have tended to play down its importance. It was said in one case, for example, that it is 'merely a way of helping to evaluate evidence . . . not bound by technical rules' and in another case that it would never have been considered to be a rule of law at all if it had not been expressed in Latin.

8.5.4 INFERENCES OF FACT

These are merely examples of the court being prepared to draw commonsense conclusions from primary facts without subjecting the matter to the need for formal proof. They should thus be contrasted with the question of presumptions, or the strict rules of evidence as indicated above.

An example of an inference of fact is when a judge, in arriving at his decision on negligence, draws conclusions as to what the 'reasonable man' ought to have done in the situation which confronted the defendant. This very non-specific way of establishing matters is inadequately analysed in most evidence textbooks, and it passes without mention in many judgments where judges draw these kind of conclusions. So, for example, in *R* v *Thompson* [1918] AC 221, a case to do with an allegation of homosexual conduct involving young boys, the court treated it as a matter of common sense that where indecent photographs of young boys were found in the home of the accused he was likely to be a homosexual with such leanings. Similarly, if, say, a five-year-old non-swimmer were washed overboard 500 miles from land, the court would draw an inference of death without needing to wait seven years for the common-law presumption of death to operate (see **8.5.3.1**).

When analysing the relevant facts in a civil case it is always vital to bear in mind how many of the primary facts need to be established before the court can be called upon to make reasonable inferences.

8.6 Competence and Compellability

A witness is *competent* if he can lawfully be called to give evidence; *compellable* if he can be made to give evidence even if he is unwilling to do so.

8.6.1 THE GENERAL RULE

The general rule is that all persons in civil cases are competent to give evidence and all competent persons are also compellable. One can compel a witness to attend court and to answer questions by a subpoena in the High Court, or by a witness summons in the county court. Failure to attend court is a contempt and will result in arrest. Similarly, if having come to court the witness refuses to answer questions, this will again be a contempt leading to criminal penalties. A witness may claim *privilege* not to answer certain questions in certain situations, which will be further discussed in the later section on privilege at **10.2**. Subject to that, however, a witness, once called, must cooperate fully in the proceedings.

The rule concerning competence and compellability extends to the opposing party and his/her spouse. Thus if one finds that one's opponent is not proposing to testify, it is perfectly in order to subpoena him to compel him to testify.

8.6.2 EVIDENCE ON OATH

In civil cases oral evidence must in general be given on oath. (This is not entirely logical, for in the situations where hearsay evidence is admitted, e.g. under the *Civil Evidence Act 1995*, evidence in the form of written statements may be put in, and this evidence does not have to be in the form of an affidavit (a sworn statement) but can simply be a witness statement.) The only substantial exception to the rule that all evidence must be sworn is that of children (see **8.6.3** below).

With that important exception, therefore (and a handful of more esoteric ones such as the Sovereign, heads of foreign states, diplomats, etc.), all other persons are competent and compellable and must testify on oath or by affirmation.

8.6.3 CHILDREN

In civil cases, by virtue of *s. 96* of the *Children Act 1989*, children may now give *unsworn* evidence if they are possessed of sufficient intelligence to justify the reception of the evidence and understand the duty of speaking the truth. There will therefore be an initial test by the judge to see how intelligent the child is, and no matter how basically intelligent it is, what its state of awareness is in relation to the proceedings generally and the particular need to speak the truth.

A judge will test a child for its competence by asking it questions, naturally in a friendly and sympathetic manner, in open court. It is impossible to say, from the case law, that there is any hard and fast age at which a child is too young to testify. All the relevant cases deal with criminal evidence, and although previously it had been held undesirable to call a child as young as five years old, later cases have held that at present the public generally have confidence in the evidence of children and that, provided proper precautions are taken by adequately testing the intelligence and awareness of the child, the evidence of a child may be just as reliable as that of an adult. See in particular *R* v *Wright* (1987) 90 Cr App R 91 and *R* v *Z* [1990] 2 QB 355.

8.7 Testimony

The general rule is, as mentioned at **8.6.2**, that all evidence must be given on oath or by a witness who has made an affirmation. The law is governed by the *Oaths Act 1978*. The oath will be administered to Christians or Jews unless the witness objects. A solemn affirmation may be administered instead if the witness is not a believer or taking an oath is contrary to his religion, or if it is impracticable to administer the oath in a manner appropriate to a witness's religion. What matters in these cases is whether the witness agrees that the form of oath or affirmation is binding on his conscience.

Evidence at trial proceeds in three stages – examination-in-chief, cross-examination and re-examination which we shall now consider in turn.

8.7.1 EXAMINATION-IN-CHIEF

The purpose of examination-in-chief is for the advocate calling the witness to obtain evidence to support his client's case. Inevitably, therefore, an advocate will only call witnesses whom he anticipates will provide helpful evidence. The Practice Direction made by the Lord Chief Justice on 25 January 1995 (for the full text see **14.6.4** below), now provides that in the High Court anyway, examination-in-chief is likely to be restricted. Under a procedure described at **12.3** below, in most civil actions the statements of the parties and their witnesses will now be exchanged in advance. The Practice Direction referred to above indicates that in general the judge should take steps to shorten the trial by dispensing with examination-in-chief altogether, and thus requiring each witness merely to swear as to the truth of his previously exchanged written statement and then be tendered for cross-examination.

To the writer's knowledge some judges dislike this procedure, believing that to see a witness telling his own story in his own words in the course of examination-in-chief is very helpful in getting the full facts and in testing the witness's credibility. To the extent, therefore, that judges of this persuasion find reasons not to apply the Practice Direction strictly, there will continue to be evidence-in-chief in civil trials. Recent case law in fact supports the suggestion that the Practice Direction should not be inflexibly applied and that there will be cases where, if there is an important conflict of evidence, the trial judge should use his unfettered discretion to require a witness to give evidence-in-chief orally. See in particular *Cole* v *Kivells (a firm), The Times*, 2 May 1997 (CA).

In examination-in-chief the general rule is that *leading questions* may not be used. A leading question is one which:

(a) assumes the existence of disputed facts as to which the witness is to testify; or

(b) suggests the required answer.

These are improper because constant reiteration of facts which are really in dispute may influence the trier of fact to regard them as established, or because they coach the witness. Thus questions which generally require only the answer 'Yes' or 'No' are often improperly leading. Leading questions may be permitted in respect of formal or introductory matter, or by agreement.

It is necessary to consider three separate topics in relation to one's own witnesses's examination-in-chief, namely:

(a) refreshing the memory;

(b) previous consistent statements by the witness;

(c) unfavourable and hostile witnesses.

8.7.1.1 Refreshing the memory

The witness may refresh his or her memory *out of court* whether outside the courtroom immediately before the trial, or at home previously – from any document. Thus it is perfectly proper to post a witness his witness statement, perhaps made some years previously, shortly before a civil trial. According to the criminal case of *Owen* v *Edwards* (1983) 77 Cr App R 191, in such a case there is a duty to inform one's opponent that the memory refreshing has occurred and the opponent has the right to see the statement in question. This is of less importance now that the exchange of witness statements in advance is the norm in civil cases. A witness may also refresh his memory from a document outside the courtroom, and be permitted to withdraw to do so, even after he has begun to give evidence, in a proper case. See *R* v *Da Silva* [1990] 1 WLR 31.

In court a witness may refresh his or her memory in the witness-box by reference to a document that that witness has made or verified, provided the following conditions are satisfied:

(a) The document must have been made at substantially the same time as the occurrence of the events about which the witness is testifying. This is a question of fact on which case law is inconsistent. Certainly a delay of a few hours will be in order, but longer delays will be fatal.

(b) The document must have been made by the witness himself, or supervised or verified by him immediately afterwards. See, for example, *Burrough* v *Martin* (1809) 2 Camp 112, 170 ER 1098, where a captain who had inspected his ship's log throughout the voyage was allowed to refresh his memory from it although the entries had been made by the mate.

(c) The document must be produced in court for inspection by the opposing advocate, and the judge may also see it. If opposing counsel cross-examines on the parts which have been used to refresh the memory, that does not make the document 'evidence' in itself so that it does not become a separate piece of testimony as to the facts; however, if the opposing counsel cross-examines on other parts of the document he makes it evidence and the document may then be put before the judge who may take note of the whole of its contents notwithstanding that the document may contain hearsay since that will now generally be admissible by virtue of the *Civil Evidence Act 1995, s. 6(4).*

The effect of this is not of any great consequence. It simply means that a separate piece of testimony is in principle provided by the witness's statement in addition to the witness's verbal evidence. A judge is not likely to find that it adds greatly to the picture, however, since both pieces of evidence come from the same witness and the consistency shown may be consistency in a lie, as well as in the truth.

8.7.1.2 Previous consistent statements

The general rule is that a witness may not be asked in chief whether the witness has previously made a statement consistent with his testimony. The reason is that such evidence is in the main pointless. To show that a witness told a consistent story may as easily prove consistency in a lie as consistency in the truth, and it adds little to the trier of fact's overall picture of the disputed facts. See *R* v *Roberts* [1942] 1 All ER 187.

The important exception to this rule in civil cases is where a previous consistent statement is admitted to rebut an allegation of recent fabrication by the witness. If it is alleged by the cross-examiner that a witness's story has been recently concocted, then a previous statement concerning the same matter becomes admissible. This is especially the case if the allegation is directly that the witness has collaborated with one of the parties to falsify his evidence. To bring in this rule it is not enough merely to attack the truth of the witness's evidence; there must be a question of time involved, in the nature of 'When did you invent this version?'.

The best illustration in a criminal context is the case of *R* v *Oyesiku* (1971) 56 Cr App R 240. The accused was charged with assaulting a policeman. After he had been arrested his wife went to see the family solicitor and described what had occurred, which was to the effect that it was the police who had been the assailants. At the time she made this statement the wife had not been able to see her husband in the cells. At trial the wife was cross-examined to the effect that she had collaborated with her husband to make up her untruthful version. The Court of Appeal held that it would have been proper for the solicitor to have been called to prove that the wife had given him a statement at a time when she could not possibly have colluded with her husband.

In fact this principle most often arises during *re-examination* after the allegation has been put in cross-examination, but it is nontheless convenient to deal with it here.

Where a previous consistent statement is put in evidence to demonstrate this, by virtue of *s. 6* of the *Civil Evidence Act 1995*, such a statement is evidence of the facts to be taken into account by the trial judge. It obviously has a particular usefulness if the timing of the previous statement demonstrates that the allegation of fabrication cannot be right.

8.7.1.3 Unfavourable and hostile witnesses

Solicitors in preparing cases take a statement from each witness. This is written down and (if the solicitor is prudent) signed by the witness. This obviates a witness denying that he made a certain statement, or made a statement in a particular way. This statement is called a 'proof of evidence'. A witness whose evidence in court is on the general lines of his statement is said to be 'coming up to proof'. The following paragraphs deal with the situation where a party's own witness lets him down and thus does not 'come up to proof'.

(a) *The general common-law rule*

The general rule at common law is that a party may not impeach his own witness, i.e. he cannot call evidence from another source to show that his own witness is mistaken, forgetful or lying. All he can do is call other witnesses, if he has them, and hope that they will be more favourable and that the judge will prefer those witnesses. Neither at common law can a party cross-examine his own witness or attack his own witness's character.

(b) *Types of unhelpful witnesses*

There are two kinds of such witnesses:

(i) An *unfavourable* witness is one who is not 'coming up to proof' and fails to prove some fact in issue or proves the opposite fact. Unfavourable witnesses cannot be cross-examined, attacked as to credit or have their previous inconsistent written statements put to them to show their lack of credibility. Unfavourable witnesses may be unfavourable because of lapse of time since the incident so that they are forgetful, or are mistaken or foolish. It is when an advocate is confronted with such an unfavourable witness that the bar on leading questions bites the hardest. Often, if the advocate could just prompt his witness with a key phrase it might unlock that witness's memory, but he cannot in principle do this.

(ii) A *hostile* witness is one 'not desirous of telling the truth at the instance of the party calling him'. Thus where an advocate in examining in chief one of his own witnesses finds that that witness appears hostile, he should proceed to ask the judge to allow him to treat the witness as hostile. Whether a witness is hostile may in principle be detected by the judge from the witness's demeanour, since hostile witnesses often exhibit a truculent or an awkward attitude, but the witness's previous written statement may also be shown to the judge so that he can see how glaring the inconsistency is from what was written before. The judge must then consider whether the witness is indeed simply foolish, or mistaken or forgetful, or whether he is actually hostile. If the judge allows the witness to be treated as hostile, at common law cross-examination of a party's own witness is then permitted, e.g. by leading questions to test the memory and perception of the witness and by putting the witness's previous inconsistent statement to him.

(c) *Statute*

A statute now governs the matter, namely the *Criminal Procedure Act 1865, s. 3*, which, despite its title, applies equally to civil proceedings. The statute in effect duplicates the common law. The section reads:

> *A party producing a witness shall not be allowed to impeach his credit by general evidence of bad character, but he may in case the witness shall, in the opinion of the judge, prove adverse, contradict him by other evidence, or by leave of the judge, prove that he has made at other times a statement inconsistent with his present testimony; but before such last mentioned proof can be given the circumstances of the supposed statement, sufficient to designate the particular occasion, must be mentioned to the witness, and he must be asked whether or not he has made such statement.*

Thus the procedure is to invite a hostile witness to consider whether he has ever made a previous statement and, if he denies it, to show it to him and ask him for his explanation of the inconsistency. Thereupon the matter is governed by a further statute, the *Civil Evidence Act 1995, s. 6(3)* which provides that where a previous inconsistent or contradictory statement is put in evidence under *s. 3* of the *1865 Act*, 'the statement shall by virtue of this subsection be admissible as evidence of any facts stated therein of which direct oral evidence by [the witness] would be admissible'. The net effect of this, therefore, is that the trial judge can choose between the two versions and decide which to believe. He can thus take into account any reasons for the change of heart by the witness such as, for example, the suggestion of a grudge having arisen between the parties, or other forms of bias.

diff fr crim

8.7.2 CROSS-EXAMINATION

All witnesses are liable to be cross-examined. All parties have a right to cross-examine any witness not called by them. Therefore, if there are several defendants and third parties, each has a right to cross-examine the plaintiff's witnesses and each others'.

There are two objectives in such cross-examinations, namely:

(a) to elicit information about the facts in issue favourable to the party cross-examining;

(b) to test the truthfulness of, and where necessary cast doubt upon, the evidence given in chief by the witness.

When conducting cross-examination it is an advocate's duty:

(a) to challenge every part of a witness's evidence which is in conflict with his own case;

(b) to put his own case to the witness in so far as the witness is able to say anything relevant about it;

(c) to put to a witness any allegation against the witness which it is proper to put.

If an advocate fails to challenge the evidence-in-chief on any point he may be held to have accepted it and not later be able to call witnesses to contradict it, or to comment upon it adversely in closing speech.

In cross-examination leading questions may be asked, and indeed are the norm, since the advocate is often putting his own version of the facts to the witness and inviting his agreement. A judge will control cross-examination and disallow questions which become improper, vexatious or oppressive. The usual exclusionary rules of evidence apply to evidence sought to be obtained by cross-examination as much as to evidence-in-chief, so that, for example, the rule against hearsay applies.

When framing cross-examination it is vital to bear in mind the objectives mentioned earlier and to ensure that each question, or series of questions, is not merely a ramble around peripheral matters but is directed, however lengthily and persistently, to one or other of the prime objectives of furthering one's own client's case by obtaining evidence from the witness in its favour, or to undo previous adverse evidence from that witness.

The two most important topics in the practice of cross-examination concern:

(a) previous inconsistent statements; and

(b) cross-examination and collateral issues.

8.7.2.1 Previous inconsistent statements

We have already considered the problem of prior inconsistent statements by *one's own witness* and the effect of *s. 3* of the *Criminal Procedure Act 1865* (see **8.7.1.3**). We are now dealing with the situation where an advocate knows that his opponent's witness has made a previous statement inconsistent with his evidence-in-chief, and the procedure by which one can put this inconsistent statement to him.

The relevant sections are *ss. 4* and *5* of the *Criminal Procedure Act 1865*, both of which apply in civil as well as criminal proceedings.

(a) *Section 4*

This applies to oral previous statements. If a witness is asked during cross-examination about a former statement made by him which is inconsistent with his present testimony, then if he does not admit having made such a statement proof may be given that he did in fact make it by calling a witness who heard him say the words in question. However, before that can be done there must be two other steps, namely:

(i) the circumstances in which the alleged statement was made must be put to the witness, and

(ii) he must then be asked whether he made such a statement.

(b) *Section 5*

This applies where the previous statement is in writing. A witness can be cross-examined about such a statement without the statement actually being shown to the witness; but if the cross-examiner actually intends to contradict the witness by using the witness statement, he must draw the witness's attention to those parts he intends to use to contradict the witness. Accordingly, if the witness retracts his evidence-in-chief and agrees with his former statement, there may be no need to use the statement itself.

A cross-examiner is not obliged to put the statement in evidence (remembering that to do so makes the whole statement available to the judge and that there may be matters in it that the cross-examiner would prefer him not to see), and this is so even if he shows it to the witness because that is not 'putting it in evidence'. However, the cross-examiner *must* go on to put the statement in evidence if he wishes to use it as a contradictory statement.

The usual procedure is that counsel asks the witness to read the statement to himself and asks him if he wishes to adhere to what he has said in examination-in-chief. If the witness says 'No', counsel has achieved his object. If he says 'Yes', then counsel will need to decide whether and how to use the statement.

The concluding words of *s. 5* are confusing in the civil context where there is no jury. The section concludes:

> *Provided always, that it shall be competent for the judge, at any time during the trial, to require the production of the writing for his inspection, and he may thereupon make such use of it for the purposes of the trial as he may think fit.*

From this it would appear that a judge has the right to demand a statement even where counsel does not propose to put it in evidence. Case law in a criminal context, however, would indicate that a judge would never take this direction without the consent of counsel using the statement.

(c) *The use of the statement when admitted*

By virtue of *s. 6(1)* of the *Civil Evidence Act 1995*, a contradictory previous statement is evidence of the facts in question. It is thus within the judge's power to choose which of the two contradictory versions he prefers to believe. Often the wisest course would be for the judge to conclude that the witness before him is a liar and to disregard the whole of his evidence. It may in some circumstances, however, be right for the judge to prefer the previous statement to the oral evidence, or the latter if an explanation of the change of mind is forthcoming.

8.7.2.2 Cross-examination on collateral issues

As noted earlier, cross-examination should be directed either to the issues in the case or to collateral issues. When it is directed to the issues in the case, what is asked is up to counsel and there is an opportunity for counsel to call evidence in contradiction or rebuttal of what a witness says. There are, however, special rules relating to cross-examination on *collateral* issues, designed to stop a multiplicity of side tracks being pursued in the interests of saving time.

(a) *The credit of the witness*

The most important collateral issue is the credit of the witness. That is, the question of the extent to which the witness's evidence is trustworthy. The general rule is that a witness's answers in relation to the *issues in the case* can be contradicted by further evidence but that answers relevant *only to the witness's credit* are final.

It must be acknowledged that in marginal cases this is a difficult rule to apply. An illustration from the criminal context was the old rule (now modified by statute) that in a rape case one could ask the victim whether she had previously had consensual intercourse with the accused and, if she denied it, call evidence to rebut her denial. However, if one went on to ask her whether she had had intercourse with other men and she denied it, no evidence in rebuttal could be called. The reasoning was said to be that the first instance went to the issue (i.e. the likelihood of consent) and the second just to credit (promiscuous reputation), but the dividing line as far as relevance is concerned is highly artificial.

(b) *Exceptions to the general rule*

There are several exceptions to the general rule that answers by a witness as to his credit are final. In the following cases evidence in rebuttal is allowed:

(i) *Evidence of the physical or mental condition of the witness such as to show he is unreliable*

If it is alleged that the witness suffers from some medical condition such that his evidence ought not to be believed and he denies suffering from that condition, evidence of the condition may be called. Thus, for example, if it is suggested that a witness could not possibly have seen a certain incident at the distance claimed because he is chronically short-sighted and he does not wear spectacles; or that the witness suffers a hysterical personality and is prone to fantasise then such evidence becomes admissible (see *Toohey* v *Metropolitan Police Commissioner* [1965] AC 595).

(ii) *Bias or partiality*

If it is alleged that a witness is biased against a party or partial in a party's favour and the witness denies it, then it may be proper to put in evidence circumstances from which the bias or partiality is said to have arisen. Thus in the case of *R* v *Shaw* (1888) 16 Cox CC 503, where the accused was charged with forgery, the main witness against him was one P who said that he had seen the accused committing the forgery. P was asked whether he did not have a grudge against the accused arising out of an incident some two years before, and he denied this. The defence were then allowed to call a witness to whom P had sworn he would get even with the accused because of the grudge.

(iii) *Previous convictions*

By virtue of the *Criminal Procedure Act 1865, s. 6*, the witness may be questioned as to whether he has been convicted of any crime. If he denies it it is in order for the cross-examining party to prove such conviction.

In civil cases this rule is subject to the provisions of the *Rehabilitation of Offenders Act 1974. Section 4(1)* of that Act forbids the questioning of a person about 'spent' convictions. Convictions become 'spent' under the Act by reference not to the offence charged but to the kind of sentence passed, with certain kinds of sentence becoming 'spent' very quickly and more serious kinds of penalty never becoming spent. Subject to that, however, one can in principle put convictions of any kind to a witness no matter how irrelevant in truth to his credit. It would obviously be fruitless, though, to put to a witness, say, convictions for past driving offences and the like. Convictions for offences denoting lack of credibility are the most useful, such as perjury, criminal deception, etc. It is also permissible to put to a witness the question of how he pleaded at his trial for the past offence, since it is clearly relevant to credit to show, if it is the case, that he pleaded not guilty but was nonetheless convicted having been disbelieved by the jury.

(iv) *Evidence of general reputation for untruthfulness*

This is an ancient common-law rule which provides that after a witness has given evidence the cross-examiner can call evidence to swear that the first witness has a general reputation as a liar and that his evidence should not be believed. This is an exception of limited use in ordinary litigation and it is not sufficient to call a witness simply to say that he would disbelieve the first witness. General reputation in the locality is what matters. See *R* v *Richardson* [1969] 1 QB 299.

8.7.3 RE-EXAMINATION

In re-examination of one's own witnesses, leading questions may not be asked. Questions should be confined to matters which have arisen out of cross-examination, and thus re-examination cannot be used to supplement defects in an advocate's own examination-in-chief except where these had been touched on in cross-examination.

A new matter may only be introduced with the leave of the judge, and leave will not easily be given, primarily because if new matter is introduced the cross-examiner must then be given another opportunity to cross-examine and so the trial will become somewhat undisciplined.

Re-examination is usually an attempt to salvage evidence which has been shaken in cross-examination. It involves counsel asking his own witness, obviously in a more sympathetic manner than that shown by the cross-examiner, to explain or clarify any ambiguities or confusion brought out in cross-examination.

8.7.4 EVIDENCE IN REBUTTAL

All the evidence which the plaintiff intends to call should be before the court by the end of his own case. New evidence can only be called after the defence case with leave of the judge, and he will only give leave if the evidence relates to a matter which could not reasonably be foreseen. A clear example is *R* v *Day* [1940] 1 All ER 402.

In this case the accused was charged with forgery. The prosecution called their evidence and the defence gave evidence denying the forgery. Thereafter the prosecuting counsel applied for leave to call a handwriting expert. The judge permitted this. On appeal the conviction was quashed. The evidence was wrongly admitted as it did not relate to a matter arising unexpectedly; it should have been clear to the prosecution from the outset that they would have needed a handwriting expert. There had thus been a material irregularity.

It seems, however, that a trial judge has a wide discretion to allow the plaintiff to call further evidence after the close of his case. Such evidence may be allowed, for example, to make good a purely formal omission, as in *R* v *Francis* [1990] 1 WLR 1264 where the prosecution were allowed to recall an inspector in charge of an identification parade to tell the court that it was the appellant who had been identified, that detail having been omitted in error in examination-in-chief.

It is fair to say that in routine civil trials somewhat more latitude is allowed about these matters generally than in criminal cases.

8.7.5 THE JUDGE'S RIGHT TO CALL WITNESSES

It is usually considered an essential part of the adversarial process that the parties themselves decide which witnesses they wish to call and what questions to ask. There is a good deal of case law in a criminal context about the occasions when a judge, without the consent of either party, may call and examine witnesses. In a civil context, however, the general rule is that the judge can call witnesses if he has the consent of all parties.

Such a situation is now unlikely to occur because of *RSC Ord. 38, r. 2A*, by virtue of which in normal litigation the witness statements of all witnesses must be exchanged well in advance of trial. However, that does not oblige any party to call the witnesses whose statements have been exchanged, and if the party chooses not to do so then the opposing parties cannot use the witness's statement. It is hard to envisage, therefore, why a judge would wish to call any such witness and, if he were to do so, why a party who had previously been unwilling for that witness to testify on his behalf should now consent that he should do so.

The judge has a discretion whether or not to permit the parties to cross-examine any witness whom he himself calls, though it will normally be appropriate for him to allow this (although he may restrict it to the subject matter of the witness's testimony).

Hearsay Evidence

Notice: s2(2) Civil Evid Act 1995 specifies manner & time. (RSC Ord 38 r21)
Content see p183
Timing .... see p183

Step 1.
Is evidence to be given in Ct of an oral or written statement made out of Ct? (in the present proceedings)

Step 2
Why are we calling the evid? Is it
1. To prove that the actual words were said or written → not HS
2. To prove the state of mind of the maker of the statement → not HS
3. To prove the effect of the words used on someone else → not HS
4. To prove that the words used were true ⇒ HS

Informal admissions = HS

Step 3
Is it 1st Hand or 2nd Hand HS
Eye Witness W tells X "he overtook on the bend"
Suppose X then tells Y of the statement
• Call W to give oral evid → direct evid
• Put in W's witness statement instead → 1st H HS
• Call X to give oral evid → 1st H HS
• Put in X's witness statement instead → 2nd H HS
• Call Y to give oral evid → 2nd H HS
• Put in Y's witness statement instead → 3rd H HS

Step 4
Comply c̄ procedure re notice & particulars of HS evid.
S2 CEA 1995 provides that notice must be given to your opponent of the intention to adduce HS evid & that on request by the opponent, particulars of that evid. must be given.
If HS in W statement: HS notice should be served at the same time as exch. of W statements. Otherwise it must be served within 28 days of setting down for trial in HC Ct & at least 28 days before trial in CC).
If particulars not given or notice not provided → weight ↓

Step 5
Consider S5 criteria for weight p184
Wt of HS evid always less than that of direct oral evid.
But
A W statement constituting 3rd Hand HS made by a W c̄ an interest in the outcome of the proceed. & some time after the event will carry less wt than
A W statement constituting 1st H HS only made shortly after the event by a reliable indep. W who is unable to give oral evid ∵ he is in Chile

Exam:
S4 CEA
1) Mention each criterion
2) Apply it to facts
3) Consider effect on weight
⇓
Conclusion
"Wt of evid should not be too badly affected"
"On balance admission is likely to carry little wt unless ..."
See p194

Statement of W → 1st H HS
Informal admission within it → 2nd H HS

NINE

CIVIL EVIDENCE (2): THE CIVIL EVIDENCE ACTS 1995 AND 1968

9.1 Hearsay and the Civil Evidence Act 1995

9.1.1 THE RULE AGAINST HEARSAY

The rule against hearsay was said to be the great rule of evidence underlying much of the common law. The definition of 'hearsay' is the same for civil as for criminal cases although the rule forbidding hearsay is of virtually no significance in civil proceedings following the *1995 Civil Evidence Act* ('The 1995 Act').

The definition of hearsay, which was commonly given in major text books, has in fact now been adopted in statutory form and provides *s. 1(2)* of the *1995 Act* in the following words:

> *'hearsay' means a statement made otherwise than by a person while giving oral evidence in the proceedings which is tendered as evidence of the matters stated.*

Hearsay is thus what most laymen would know to be hearsay, that is where a witness attempts to tell the court what he was told by someone else before the proceedings. Hearsay also includes such things as a written statement (such as a witness statement) to be put before the court as evidence of the facts stated in it, and even includes a witness telling a court what he himself may have said on previous occasions. It is important to understand that it is not always hearsay when a witness wishes to repeat something to the court which has been said to him outside court, or a document of some kind is put before the court. It will not be hearsay at all if it is not 'tendered as evidence of the matters stated'. Thus for example if D says to A that P is a thief and P gets to hear of this, in the defamation proceedings which he might bring against D, he can call A to give evidence of what D said. The point is not to show that the words were *true*, but merely to show that they were *uttered* to demonstrate publication, an essential element in defamation. Likewise, if a document is put before the court not to prove the truth of the contents of what is stated in it but, for example, to demonstrate that it is a forgery or merely to show what terms a contract, or will, or lease contained, that also will not be hearsay.

Until 1996 the relevant statute was *Part 1* of the *Civil Evidence Act 1968*. This part of the *1968 Act* has now been repealed by the coming into force of the *1995 Act*. The *1968 Act* provided, putting it simply, that hearsay would not be admissible in civil proceedings except under the provisions of the *1968 Act* which in itself was complex, and had attached to it a similarly complex scheme of procedural rules, all of which were subject to the court's discretions to permit, or not permit hearsay in given circumstances and subject to various criteria. The *1968*

Act was said to be very unpopular with practitioners and gave rise to a great deal of case law to do with the definition of various technical terms used in the Act. None of this now matters, the whole of the first part of the *1968 Act* having been swept away by the *1995 Act*. Although the 1995 Act was uncontroversial, because of the length of the consultation period concerning the rules which were to implement it, and other matters, it did not in fact come into effect until 1st February 1997 and indeed only applies to actions which have not reached the stage at which directions concerning evidence of trial had not already been given by that date. For some time therefore, practitioners will need to be aware of the scheme of the 1968 Act but that will gradually become redundant over the course of 1997/98.

9.1.2 THE DEATH OF THE RULE AGAINST HEARSAY

Section 1(1) provides the simple and revolutionary statement that 'in civil proceedings evidence shall not be excluded on the ground that it is hearsay'.

The effect of this is simple and clear. *All* hearsay is now admissible in English civil proceedings. Moreover, there is no discretion in the court to refuse to admit it, or to consider its weight or usefulness at the stage of admissibility. It simply *must be* admitted before the court and the judge has no discretion to stop it unless the piece of evidence which is hearsay also infringes some quite separate rule (for example, that it is inadmissible evidence of opinion from a layman who is not entitled to give the evidence in question).

Hearsay is therefore generally admissible and s. *1(2)(b)* goes on to say that that simple rule includes hearsay of *any degree* and therefore hearsay evidence may be put before the court no matter how many intermediaries it goes through, even though the number of intermediaries may make the end result highly unreliable (as in a Chinese whispers' scenario where witness W tells the court what he was told by A who had heard it from B who originally heard it from C who had heard it from D). On the question of *admissibility*, the number of intermediaries is irrelevant though that may be highly relevant when the court comes to decide what *weight* it will attach to the evidence.

9.2 Safeguards in Relation to Hearsay Evidence

Section 2 of the Act provides necessary safeguards, because clearly hearsay evidence, if put before the court by surprise, would be capable of causing great injustice. First, one obviously cannot cross-examine an absent witness to test his truthfulness, and secondly one would have been given no opportunity of investigating the nature of the hearsay in question, for example, by attempting to interview the witness who does not come to court and perhaps calling other evidence to contradict what the hearsay evidence will say. Accordingly, s. 2 provides that a person who wishes to use hearsay evidence must give appropriate notice of that fact and particulars relating to the evidence which are 'reasonable and practicable in the circumstances' so as to enable the opponent who receives the notice 'to deal with any matters arising from its being hearsay'.

This means that if a party, say P, is intending to use hearsay evidence at trial, he must give ample notice of his intentions to D so that D can decide whether he wishes to trace the absent witness and call him as a witness himself, or have him interviewed to check that he really did say the words attributed to him. Although there will be many cases when hearsay involves a witness repeating an oral statement it is probable that the most common use of hearsay evidence will be where one party wishes simply to put in evidence in court a written statement from an absent witness without calling that person. This will be the main example considered in the rest of the text.

9.2.1 PROCEDURAL RULES

Section 2(2) specifies that rules are to be made providing for the manner and time at which this notice is to be given. Those rules have now been made (RSC Ord. 38, r. 21; CCR Ord. 20,

r. 14). No form of notice is actually prescribed by the rules, but the rules say that the notice concerned must state that it is a hearsay notice; identify the hearsay evidence; identify the person who made the statement which is to be given in evidence; and state why that person is not to be called to give oral evidence; and if the hearsay evidence is contained in a witness statement, refer to the part of the witness statement where it is set out. A single hearsay notice may deal with the hearsay evidence of more than one witness.

Section 2(3) goes on to provide that the parties can agree between themselves to waive the notice requirement, which is only an instance of the general principle that the parties in a civil case can, by agreement, waive any of the Rules of Evidence if they wish.

9.2.2 THE SANCTION FOR DISREGARDING PROCEDURAL RULES

The issue then remaining is, what is the sanction on a party who has failed contrary to the rules, to give the appropriate notice and advance information? Since *s. 1(1)* is in absolute terms and *requires* the court to receive the hearsay evidence, it would not be an appropriate sanction for the trial judge to say that he proposed to punish the party who had not given the appropriate notice by forbidding the use of evidence. The sanction expressed in *s. 2(4)* is that the court may 'consider the exercise of its powers with respect to the course of proceedings and costs'. In other words, if surprise hearsay evidence is introduced, it may offer the other party an adjournment so that he can consider how to collect evidence to meet the hearsay on terms that the offending party who has failed to give the notice pays all the costs of the wasted day in court. In addition, the court may take account of the failure to give notice 'as a matter adversely affecting the weight to be given the evidence'. Therefore the judge in effect has a sanction by saying that he will penalise the failure to abide by the rules, whether that resulted from a simple oversight or deliberate sharp practice, by simply disbelieving the piece of evidence put in.

9.2.3 WHERE, DESPITE HAVING GIVEN NOTICE, A PARTY DOES NOT USE THE HEARSAY STATEMENT

Section 3 provides that the Rules of court (which are to be formulated) shall provide that if a party has indicated in advance that he intends to use hearsay evidence, any other party may call the absent witness with the leave of the court and, having called him to court, contrary to the usual rules, may cross-examine him as if he were a witness called by the party who initially indicated an intention to use his evidence in hearsay form. Therefore the decision whether or not to use such evidence must be taken after careful consideration because if one indicates a general intention to use such evidence but does not then do so the other party may call a witness whose evidence, or indeed possibly whose very existence, was unknown to him initially. This will therefore be an important practical and tactical consideration.

The rules provide that when one party seeks the leave of the court to subpoena the other side's hearsay witness, which will be done by summons to a District Judge, the court may give directions as to how and when the witness is to testify. Usually one imagines that the court will provide that the witness who is now called under subpoena, will be made to testify during the course of the evidence called by the party who originally gave the hearsay notice since he remains, in reality, that party's witness.

9.3 Section 4: The Weight to be Attached to the Statement

Section 4 is a vitally important section because, as we have seen, *s. 1(1)* provides simply that all hearsay is admissible before the court. *Section 4*, however, sets out a number of *essential criteria* to which the court may have regard in deciding whether it will believe the truth of the hearsay adduced. The opening words of *s. 4(1)* provide that the court can have regard to 'any circumstances from which any inference can reasonably be drawn as to the reliability or otherwise of the evidence'. This clearly means that the court must have regard to all the common sense features which might tend to make hearsay evidence less reliable than credible oral testimony before the court. Apart from this general statement, the rest of the section provides some particular matters to which the court will have to have regard. *Subsection (2)* goes on to say that in particular, regard can be had to:

(a) Whether it would have been reasonable and practicable for the party by whom the evidence was adduced to have produced the maker of the original statement as a witness;

(b) whether the original statement was made contemporaneously with the occurrence or existence of the matter stated;

(c) whether the evidence involves multiple hearsay;

(d) whether any person involved had any motive to conceal or misrepresent matters;

(e) whether the original statement was an edited account or was made in collaboration with another or for a particular purpose;

(f) whether the circumstances in which the evidence is adduced as hearsay are such as to suggest an attempt to prevent proper evaluation of its weight.

9.3.1 THE COURT'S DUTY TO ASSESS THE HEARSAY

In considering these matters the court will therefore want to know why no attempt has been made to produce the original maker of the out-of-court statement to give oral evidence, and if no satisfactory explanation of the witness's absence, e.g. illness, death, absence abroad or other genuine unavailability is advanced, the court may well draw adverse inferences. Likewise, the court will want to see how *contemporaneous* the hearsay statement was with the matters to which the statement was directed. As is well known, witnesses' memories fade very fast indeed, even about quite striking incidents, and therefore if a written statement was taken from a witness, say three days after an incident, and one party wishes to use the statement rather than calling the witness at trial, that statement will have a great deal more weight than one that was taken perhaps a year or more afterwards. Possibly the central features will still be remembered, but witnesses are unlikely then to remember the peripheral details which often help to set the whole picture, for example, if a witness has seen a dramatic road traffic accident although he may remember what happened to the vehicles at the centre of the action, he may not be able to remember such matters as the width of the road, angle of the junction, how other vehicles were parked, or the lighting or traffic conditions.

On the matter of *multiple hearsay*, it is again self-evident that hearsay at one remove has less risk of being unreliable than hearsay which has been repeated in turn through many mouths before reaching the court and this is simply a matter of common sense. Similarly, if any person involved had a *motive to conceal or misrepresent*, because, for instance, they have a close bond to one or other party to the litigation, or perhaps even some active grudge against a party in the litigation, then due weight will be given to that feature. Thus self-evidently, if there has been a road accident a hearsay statement from a disinterested passerby is a more valuable piece of evidence than a hearsay statement from a passenger in one of the vehicles, passengers being notoriously inclined to side with their own driver in relation to disputes about responsibility for an accident. Thus if the form of the hearsay were to be a witness statement tendered on behalf of the defendant, in those circumstances, if the statement came from a bystander the court would naturally give it more weight than if it came from the defendant's passenger.

If the statement which is to be used is in some way an *edited or collaborative account* it will have less immediate value than one person's own statement in his own words. For example, if what is put forward is an edited account of proceedings before a committee of inquiry, and describes the conclusions they came to about, say, whether commercial fraud had occurred in the activities of a company's management, that will be much less valuable than full factual accounts from each of the people at the committee meeting who may in turn be able to contribute hard facts.

Finally, and here there is clearly some overlap with the first of the criteria, the court will have regard to whether the circumstances indicate an *attempt to prevent proper evaluation* of the evidence by it being tendered in hearsay form rather than by bringing the person who knows the facts at first hand to court. Again a close examination of the reasons for the claimed unavailability of the original witness will be undertaken and if the court is not satisfied as to the genuineness of this unavailability, it will have due regard to that feature in deciding what weight if any to attach to the evidence.

The result of the court having to have regard to all these criteria is that, if it is possible, it will be better in the majority of cases to call the witness to give oral evidence so that he can be suitably cross-examined and the court will have the opportunity of judging his manner and demeanour to assist in assessing his credibility. Using evidence in hearsay form will therefore only be the norm for either relatively uncontroversial evidence, or evidence which is impossible, or perhaps simply inconvenient or too expensive to call. A party would need to consider very carefully whether the advantages of getting in the evidence unchallenged because the absent person cannot be cross-examined is not far outweighed by the fact that the court may then attach little weight to it.

9.3.2 COMPETENCE OF THE ABSENT WITNESS, AND ATTACKING HIS EVIDENCE

Section 5 can be more briefly dealt with. It provides, which is simply a matter of common sense, that one cannot get round the rules as to competence of witnesses by purporting to submit their evidence in a hearsay statement, so that if the court has reason to believe that the statement is from a child, or someone suffering a mental handicap, it will have to investigate the competence of the original witness who is the source from which the evidence comes.

Moreover, there is the further provision in *s. 5(2)* which is both common sense and common fairness that since, if hearsay evidence is to be admitted, the opponent is deprived of the opportunity of cross-examining the absent witness to test his evidence, that opponent may adduce any evidence about the credibility of the absent witness that he could have used in cross-examining him had he been present. Thus he may in particular prove that there was a previous inconsistent statement which says something different from that which is in the hearsay statement now adduced, or that the absent witness has a reason for being biased in favour of the party who is using his evidence or has a grudge against the opposite party, or had previous convictions for perjury, or as the case may be. The evidence which one can adduce under this section includes everything on which it would have been proper to cross-examine the absent witness had he been present.

Where one wishes to attack an absent witness's credibility, notice of that intention must be given within 28 days of receipt of the 'hearsay notice' previously referred to. No precise form of notice is prescribed by the rules.

In order to demonstrate the format of a notice and counter-notice indicating intention to attack credibility, examples are given at the end of this chapter.

9.4 Section 6: Use of Previous Statements of Witnesses

Section 6 provides that if a party has given notice in advance that he intends to use the hearsay statement of a witness, but at trial actually calls that witness, the hearsay statement cannot be used without the leave of the court except for the specific purpose of rebutting a suggestion that the evidence has been fabricated. The purpose of this is simply to save court time by the unnecessary proliferation of multiple accounts of the same thing from the same witness. It is of little evidential value, if a witness is actually called and gives oral evidence then to introduce his previous written statement. This is discussed fully in the context of oral evidence of witnesses at **8.7.1.2**. The rules as to putting previous inconsistent statements of a witness to him, whether he is a hostile or an opposition witness, are preserved by the rest of *s. 6*. These matters are discussed fully in relation to witnesses who appear at court at **8.7.2.1**. Thus one can still, as before, use the previous statement to discredit either a hostile witness whom you yourself have called but who lets you down, or opposing witnesses who have said something inconsistent in a previous statement.

Section 6(4) provides that nothing in the Act is to change the Rules relating to refreshing of memory, so that witnesses may still refer to statements for that purpose without them becoming part of the evidence. This topic is discussed at **8.7.1.1**.

9.5 The Effect of the 1995 Act on Various Common Law Rules

Section 7 of the Act is a lengthy and confusingly worded section which preserves various common law rules about the admissibility of certain specific kinds of hearsay evidence which were themselves preserved in the *1968 Act*. The most important of these is to provide that evidence of informal admissions made by a party is still admissible. An example of an informal admission would be where, say, one driver gets out of his car after a collision and apologises for causing the accident. Evidence of that admission could be given at trial whether by the other driver or by a passerby who overheard it. It is beyond the scope of this text to discuss the precise historic and technical reasons as to why such a specific provision might have been thought by the draftsman of the *1995 Act* to be required, since one could easily have said that the general provision in *s. 1(1)* as to the admissibility of **all** hearsay would have covered the position. Putting it simply, *s. 9* of the *Civil Evidence Act 1968* expressly preserved certain common law rules and it might have been thought that the repeal of the *1968 Act* might have the effect of repealing those rules unless they were restated explicitly in the *1995 Act*. None is of any great practical significance in everyday litigation and all would certainly have been encompassed in the general terms of *s. 1(1)*.

9.6 Sections 8 and 9: Technical Methods of Proof and Definitions

Sections 8 and 9 are extremely useful, supplemented by *s. 13* and together they provide definitions of certain terms and provisions for means of proving the statements.

Section 8 provides that if a statement is contained in a document it can be proved either by production of the document, a copy or a copy of the copy and it is up to the court to decide how the document needs to be authenticated. This useful provision means the death of the old so-called 'best evidence' rule, which at its zenith forbade the reception into evidence of a copy of a document if the original was still in existence. Now carbon copies, photocopies, or printouts, authenticated in such manner as the court may direct, are admissible. Moreover *s. 9* goes on to provide that if a document is part of 'the records of a business or public authority' it can be received in evidence without further proof so that there is no need to call a witness to describe the contents and attest to the authenticity of it. In such cases documents are taken to be part of the proper records of a business or public authority if there is a certificate (which could easily be endorsed on the document itself) certifying that it is a true copy of the record signed by an officer of the business or authority. *Section 9(4)* goes on to provide that the word 'record' means a record in whatever form and thus this could include manuscript entries in a ledger, the contents of computer databases, or copies of accounts. The words 'public authority' are said to include any public or statutory undertaking, any

Government department, and any person holding office under the Crown. The word 'business' is rather oddly defined to include 'any activity regularly carried on over a period of time whether for profit or not by anybody (whether corporate or not) or by an individual'. This is a very wide definition indeed and would include all manner of activities which surely would not be viewed as 'businesses' by most people. For example, personal records of an obsessive train spotter, bird watcher or collector of statistical material about sporting events and the like would no doubt qualify as 'business records' for these purposes under the definition.

9.7 Miscellaneous

Section 13 makes it clear that the provisions of the Act extend beyond mere statements of fact in hearsay form to include statements of opinion. Of course these will only be admissible where the original witness would have been entitled to give a statement of opinion to the court — principally where that witness is an expert in the field concerned.

Section 10 of the Act to which reference has already been made, provides for admissibility in evidence of the Ogden Tables which will have the effect of permitting the court to use higher multipliers in personal injury litigation when computing loss of earnings and continuing care claims (see **1.2.2.3** for discussion).

The Act concludes with various further definitions and provisions for amendment and repeal of other statutes including *Part 1* of the *Civil Evidence Act 1968* and some sections of the *Civil Evidence Act 1972*.

9.8 Part II of the Civil Evidence Act 1968

9.8.1 *SECTION 11*: ADMISSIBILITY OF PREVIOUS CONVICTIONS

We now turn to the second part of the *Civil Evidence Act 1968* which deals with miscellaneous matters, and particularly to *s. 11*. We have already come across this section in the context of pleadings (see **7.4.1.4**). The law used to be that a party's conviction for criminal offences was not admissible in civil proceedings. This was so even where the conviction appeared directly relevant to the civil suit, i.e. arose out of the same facts. For example, suppose that a collision occurred between vehicles driven by P and D. The police eventually prosecuted only D who was convicted of the offence of careless driving. Before the coming into force of *s. 11* of the *Civil Evidence Act 1968*, in subsequent civil proceedings between P and D, no reference at all to D's conviction for careless driving could be made, even though the issue in the trial, negligence, is almost exactly the same as the issue which has already been judged in the criminal proceedings, i.e. carelessness. Now, however, by *s. 11* of the Act:

> *In any civil proceedings the fact that a person has been convicted of an offence by a court in the United Kingdom is admissible to prove, where relevant, that he committed that offence and he shall be taken to have committed it unless the contrary is proved.*

An early case which very neatly demonstrates the working of the section on reversing the burden of proof is as follows:

***Wauchope* v *Mordecai* [1970] 1 WLR 317**

The plaintiff was riding his bicycle when the driver of a parked car opened the door suddenly, knocking the plaintiff off. The defendant was prosecuted before the magistrates' court on the charge of opening a door in such a way as to cause injury and was convicted. The plaintiff then brought an action in the county court and sought to treat the conviction as admissible evidence. The judge did not know that the *Civil Evidence Act 1968* had now come into force.

He ignored the conviction altogether and said it was irrelevant. He came to the conclusion on the facts that he could not be sure whom to believe – the plaintiff, who claimed that the car door had opened suddenly, or the defendant, who claimed that he had opened the car door long before the plaintiff reached it and that the plaintiff must have been day dreaming. The judge decided that as he was not sure whom to believe, the whole decision rested on the burden of proof. Accordingly, the plaintiff had not discharged that burden, and he gave judgment to the defendant. On appeal, the Court of Appeal gave judgment for the plaintiff. The effect of *s. 11* (which was in force) was to make the evidence of conviction admissible and to reverse the burden of proof, so that it was now up to the defendant to show that he had *not* opened the door in such a way as to cause injury. Since the judge had decided matters by reference to the burden of proof, this should have meant that the plaintiff would succeed.

9.8.1.1 The relevance of the conviction

The clearest use of *s. 11* is where the crime and the subsequent civil action are based on the very same facts, e.g. an error of judgment whilst driving. An example is given in **9.5.1** above where, after a collision between P and D, the police prosecute only D who is in due course convicted in the magistrates' court of the offence of driving without due care and attention. In the subsequent civil proceedings between the parties, the conviction can be used by P against D and will have the effect of reversing the burden of proof on the issue. In other words, it will now be for D to prove positively, on a balance of probabilities, that he was wrongly convicted, i.e. that he did not drive carelessly at the time of the incident. Here, with the interchange of the words 'careless' and 'negligent', it can be said that the issue in the civil proceedings is precisely the same as that in the criminal proceedings, in so far as it relates to D's conduct.

There is a more difficult case where the crime is not precisely the same as the tort but may or may not be relevant to it. Suppose, for example, that there is a collision between P and D caused by D's brakes failing. D is subsequently charged with, and convicted of, the offence of using a vehicle with defective brakes. There is no doubt that in factual terms, D's vehicle caused the accident, but the question is what use this conviction is to the plaintiff. For this offence there is strict liability, and therefore if the brakes were in fact defective, this is sufficient to ground a criminal conviction. In the tort of negligence, however, there is no such strict liability, and what must be shown in every case is that there was a breach of the duty of care viewed in terms of the conduct of the reasonable man. Accordingly, one might envisage two different situations. In the first, D does not have his vehicle serviced for many months, even after the need for such servicing becomes apparent. He continues driving the vehicle even after it has become obvious to him that the brakes are very weak indeed, and finally the brakes fail, leading to the collision. If all these facts could be proved there is no doubt that negligence is established and therefore that D will be liable in tort to P. Imagine, however, a situation in which D is scrupulous about having his vehicle properly serviced, and in fact has had the vehicle serviced only an hour before the accident occurs. The braking system was thoroughly overhauled and checked but a mechanic at the servicing garage failed to fit some part properly, with the effect that the brakes fail the first time they are applied at speed, leading to the accident. In this situation, D is certainly still guilty of the criminal offence, which is one of strict liability. There is, however, no element at all of lack of reasonableness in his conduct this time. Therefore, under these circumstances, the conviction would be of no use in proving D's negligence. Any action by P in these circumstances would be better brought against the negligent garage.

Consequently, with offences of strict liability, and which relate to the condition of the vehicle rather than to the manner of its driving, one cannot always immediately see whether a conviction will or will not be relevant. Suppose, for instance, that a vehicle is driven with windscreen wipers which do not work. The criminal offence of driving a vehicle without effective windscreen wipers is certainly established. If an accident occurs to that vehicle, however, then clearly the state of the windscreen wipers is quite irrelevant to the causation of the accident, unless it happens to be raining at the time so that the driver's vision is substantially impaired. If the accident occurs during dry weather, then it is neither here nor there that the windscreen wipers were deficient. In each individual case, therefore, unless the tort is the very same thing as the crime, e.g. cases of dangerous or careless driving, one must look closely at the circumstances to decide how relevant the conviction is.

9.8.1.2 The effect of the conviction

It is important to note that where such a conviction is pleaded, it is not by any means conclusive proof that the person committed the crime concerned. It merely reverses the burden of proof on the issue and requires the convicted person to prove that his conviction was wrong.

This is by no means impossible. Although in principle one would be trying to show that a conviction reached on the standard of proof appropriate in a criminal case, i.e. beyond reasonable doubt, was wrong, there may well be a reason why this is possible. In the case of driving offences particularly, such offences are prosecuted in the magistrates' court. Many people may actually plead guilty by post to relatively trivial driving offences, or may not choose, or be able to have legal representation when answering such charges because some magistrates' courts have a policy of not granting legal aid for driving offences. Where there is a collision between vehicles, the same incident in criminal terms may be the relatively trivial offence of careless driving, but in the civil action in the High Court, sums of tens of thousands of pounds may be involved. The degree of legal expertise brought to bear on the civil action by the solicitors and barristers on each side and the High Court judge, may lead to a very different conclusion from that reached by three lay magistrates who have received a plea of guilty by letter, made mainly because the person concerned could not afford legal representation or the time off work to attend court, and who thought that conviction was inevitable because of police evidence against him.

9.8.1.3 Procedural requirements for the use of *s. 11*

Section 11 of the *Civil Evidence Act 1968* is implemented by *RSC Ord. 18, r. 7A,* which provides that a party wishing to rely on a conviction must state in his pleading full particulars of it and the issue to which it is said to be relevant. When the other party receives such a pleading, then, by *Ord. 18, r. 7A(3),* he may:

(a) *deny* the conviction itself (e.g. say that it does not in fact relate to him); or

(b) allege that the conviction was *erroneous* (e.g. say that he pleaded guilty in ignorance of some fact which could have constituted a defence, or was otherwise wrongly convicted); or

(c) deny that the conviction is *relevant* to any issue, (e.g. say that although convicted of using a vehicle with a defective tyre, the state of the tyre did not contribute in any way to the accident).

The use of the section and the operation of *Ord. 18, r. 7A,* are illustrated in the following example:

Example Vehicles driven by P and D are involved in a collision. Subsequently the police prosecute D for three offences, on each of which he is convicted:

(a) driving the vehicle without due care and attention;

(b) driving a vehicle with two defective tyres;

(c) driving a vehicle whilst uninsured.

The plaintiff's solicitors will obtain a certificate of conviction from the magistrates' court and will then insert in the plaintiff's statement of claim (not the writ itself) details of the relevant convictions. They will plead convictions only for the offences of driving without due care and attention and driving with defective tyres. Obviously, whilst it may be relevant to the source from which compensation comes, lack of insurance does not in itself contribute to how an accident occurs, and therefore they will not plead this third offence.

In his defence, the defendant may well meet this plea by alleging:

(a) The conviction for driving without due care and attention was erroneous in that he was convicted against the weight of the evidence by the magistrates.

In that case, the burden of proving this is on the defendant on the civil standard of proof, and it will now be for him to establish at the subsequent trial, on the balance of probabilities, that he was not driving carelessly. Accordingly, if the judge is undecided about the matter, i.e. he cannot make his mind up which version to believe of how the accident occurred, he must find in favour of the plaintiff, because the defendant now bears the burden of proof on this issue. If it were not for the operation of *s. 11*, then in that situation he would have to decide in favour of the defendant because it is normally for the plaintiff to prove every element of his claim. Therefore the effect of *s. 11* is simply to reverse the normal burden of proof.

(b) With regard to the plea concerning the conviction for driving with defective tyres, the defendant may admit the conviction and that it was correct, but go on to deny that the conviction is in any way relevant to how the incident occurred, e.g. he may say that the incident arose because of a head-on collision when neither party had the time to brake. Accordingly, the state of the tyres is factually quite irrelevant to how the incident came about. It will then be for the plaintiff to establish the relevance of this matter.

9.8.1.4 Further points

For completeness, it is worth pointing out that if two motorists are involved in an accident and the police prosecute only one of them who is convicted of driving without due care, then that conviction can be used by the other driver; this does not mean, however, that the driver who was not prosecuted (or was acquitted) must necessarily be held totally free from any liability in tort. The prosecution are not concerned with degrees of blame, only with assessing whether there is sufficient evidence to establish guilt to a criminal standard of proof. Motorists charged with careless driving often try to show that some other driver was partly to blame, but this is no defence to the criminal charge. It may, however, be very important in the civil action because of the effect of a finding of contributory negligence by the plaintiff. Thus the fact that the police chose not to charge one party is no evidence at all that he bore no proportion of responsibility, and it is open to the other party to seek to show:

(a) that his own conviction was wrong;

(b) that the other party was wholly to blame for the accident; or

(c) even if he cannot establish (a) and (b), that the other party was at least contributorily negligent.

9.8.2 *SECTION 13*: DEFAMATION PROCEEDINGS AND CONVICTIONS

Section 13 of the *1968 Act* provides that for a defamation action a conviction is conclusive evidence that a person committed the offence concerned. This is designed to remedy the difficulties and abuse of a series of cases in the mid-1960s in which convicted criminals, long after their appeals had been dismissed, tried to re-open their cases by civil proceedings. An example is the well-known case of *Hinds* v *Sparks* [1964] Crim LR 717, in which a convicted robber successfully sued the former chief of the Flying Squad who had serialised his memoirs in a Sunday newspaper. In the course of these he discussed the plaintiff's guilt of a certain armed robbery. The plaintiff's libel action was successful, because at that time the defendant could not rely on the plaintiff's conviction. Such a situation could not now happen in the light of *s. 13*.

9.8.3 FINDINGS IN CIVIL CASES

We have so far dealt with the result of a conviction in criminal proceedings in subsequent civil actions. It should be noted that findings in *civil cases* are outside the *1968 Act* and the general law is:

(a) If the previous case is between the *same parties*, a judgment will create an estoppel between them preventing them denying the facts as found.

(b) If the previous case is between *different parties*, then the finding of the first court is inadmissible in later proceedings.

Example A lorry driven by D leaves the road and crashes into a bus queue, injuring several people. Each issues a separate writ. The case of P1 comes to court, the lorry driver is found to be negligent and damages are awarded. However, when the case of P2 comes to court P2 cannot rely on the previous finding of negligence. He has to prove negligence again. Similarly, if the previous action had ended in a verdict for the defendant on a finding of no negligence, this would not have been of any use to the defendant either in the second action.

9.8.4 RELEVANCE OF OTHER CONDUCT

The concept of relevance has been discussed at a number of places in the text. In the context of discovery reference should be made to **12.1.4**; in the context of the relevance of convictions reference should be made to **7.4.1.4** as well as to **9.5.1.3** above. To be **relevant** a piece of evidence must be logically probative of something bearing on the dispute in question. Thus for example while one can certainly plead, say, all convictions arising out of a given road accident which caused injury to the plaintiff which may demonstrate bad driving by the defendant, one is not permitted to plead the whole of the defendant's record of driving convictions on other (or indeed subsequent) occasions simply to demonstrate that in general terms he is a bad driver. The court would conclude that however gross the driving record it would not be legally relevant to show negligence on the occasion in question. There is however a principle of the law of evidence, much more relevant in criminal cases known as the *'similar fact'* principle whereby if one is able to show that a party has engaged in very similar conduct on another occasion, the court might be persuaded to conclude that notwithstanding that the occasion may have been months or years before the incident with which the litigation is concerned, the conduct by the other party is in some way relevant. Moreover the conduct by the other party does not have to have ended in a criminal conviction, and one may just wish to show similar behaviour in a commercial context. It is unlikely that this principle would ever be relevant in the context of road traffic accidents though it might conceivably be relevant in, say, factory accidents in order to show a continuing pattern of an unsafe system of work by the employer especially if the machinery or process in question was the same as that which led to the present incident. Here convictions under the *Factories Act 1961* or more recently under the *Health and Safety at Work Act 1974* might well be of assistance to an injured plaintiff. It is in the commercial sphere however that evidence of past behaviour is more likely to be relevant and if the court concludes that what the other party did on some previous occasion is of sufficient similarity to the conduct now alleged, it may allow evidence of that other incident. So in the leading case of *Mood Music Publishing Co. Ltd* v *de Wolfe Ltd* [1976] Ch 119 the plaintiffs, a songwriter and his publishers, believed that the defendants had published a song which very closely copied one of the plaintiff's works. The defendants contended that it was a coincidence but the plaintiffs had reason to believe that the defendants habitually engaged in this kind of activity. Accordingly, they employed someone to approach the defendants pretending to be a songwriter who had recorded a piece of music from the radio in the USA and who asked the defendants if they would help him by making a slight re-arrangement of it so that he could pass it off as his own work. When the defendants willingly agreed to this course of conduct the plaintiffs wished to use evidence of their general unscrupulousness in the original proceedings concerning the pirated song and the court held that this was a sufficiently similar course of action on the part of the defendants as to have genuine probative value in the present action.

9.8.5 MISCELLANEOUS FURTHER MATTERS

There are miscellaneous further matters contained in the concluding sections of the *Civil Evidence Act 1968*. Only one is of much general significance, the privilege against self-incrimination. *Section 14(1)* of the Act expressly preserves the right of a person in civil proceedings to refuse to answer any question on the grounds that to do so might expose that person or his or her spouse to criminal proceedings in the UK. Where such a claim to privilege is taken, either at the stage of discovery of documents, or at the trial, it will be for the trial judge to assess whether there is a realistic risk of prosecution. See **10.2.1.1**.

9.8.6 EXAMPLES OF A HEARSAY NOTICE AND COUNTER-NOTICE

In the High Court of Justice **1997-G-1234**
Queen's Bench Division
Middlemarch District Registry

Between:	**Mandy Gill**	**Plaintiff**
	and	
	Caroline Hoyle	**Defendant**

<u>Notice of Desire to Adduce Hearsay Statement</u>

Take Notice that at the trial of this action the Plaintiff desires to give in evidence the statement made in the following document, namely the witness statement of Ruth Davenport dated 1st November 1997 a copy of which is annexed hereto.

And Further take notice that the particulars relating to the said statement are as follows:

(a) It was made by the said Ruth Davenport
(b) The said Ruth Davenport may not be called to give evidence at the trial because she is a construction works manager currently working on the construction of a new airport at Kuala Lumpur, Malaysia which project will last until late 1998. It is not possible to fix the trial to coincide with her annual leave because she has not decided when this leave will be nor even whether she will return to the UK during it.

Dated 20th November 1997

To: The Defendant

Dorothea Brooke & Co
Solicitors for the Plaintiff

In the Hig[illegible] Justice 1997-G-1234
Queen's B[illegible]on
Middlema[illegible] Registry

Between:	**Mandy Gill**	**Plaintiff**
	and	
	Caroline Hoyle	**Defendant**

Notice of Intention to Attack Credibility of Absent Witness

Take Notice that at the trial of this action the Defendant intends to attack the credibility of Ruth Davenport, in respect of whom the Plaintiff has given notice of intention to adduce hearsay evidence in the following respects:-

(a) The Defendant contends that Ruth Davenport is the sister-in-law of the Plaintiff

(b) Shortly after the accident giving rise to this cause of action Ruth Davenport gave a statement to the Defendant's insurers in substantially different terms from the description of the accident contained in the witness statement of Ruth Davenport.

Dated 8th December 1997

To: The Plaintiff

Lydgate & Co
Solicitors for the Defendant

HEARSAY

W sees the accident → W's oral evid of what he saw

Assuming W was competent, evid won't be HS. W's written statement cannot be adduced as well as W's oral evid (a "previous consistent statement") ̄s leave of Ct (unless t rebut a suggestion of recent fabrication (S6(2)). If leave is given the weight of the statement must be considered under S4

W sees the accident → W's written statement in place of W's oral evid

W sees the accident → W tells X what he saw. X's oral evid

The evid relied on is HS

Was W competent to give direct oral evid?

NO → Same evidence in HS form is not admissible (S5(1))

YES → Same evid in HS form is admissible (S1)

Was notice of intention to rely on HS evid given to opponent (S2(1)(a)) and particulars if requested? (S2(1)(b))

NO → Did the parties agree that notice need not be given or did the opponent waive the failure t give notice? S2(3)

NO → Ct may consider adjournment, costs & the effect of this failure on weight (S2(4))

YES → Did the opponent obtain an order t call W for cross-exam? (S3)

NO → W not called to give oral evid. at all → Opponent can call evid to attack W's credibility (S5(2)(a)) or refer t previous inconsistent statements (S5(2)(b)). If the HS is given by way of X's oral evid, X can also be cross-examined

YES → Opponent can cross-examine W as if the HS was W's evid in chief & in the course of that X-exam. attack W's credibility & refer to any previous inconsistent statements made by W (S6(3)) [relate to competence]

Consider (& both sides may make reps as to) the weight of the HS evid (S4)

(Also see p181)

Model Ans: Ss2–6 CEA Implications
X's statement will be relied on at trial in his absence as 1st H HS.

S2 Give notice t def of our intention
This is documentary HS → serve notice not less than 28 days after setting down.
On receipt D's Sol may require particulars relating t evid & is reasonable & practicable in the circs for the purpose of enabling them t deal ̄c any matters arising fr it being HS. eg where, when, how, t whom etc statement was made

S3 D can apply t Ct for Ord t call X t cross-exc. Can he be found? If order made under S3 written S treated as evid in chief (apply within 28 days of HS notice)

S4 In considering Wt Ct will consider any circs fr which an adverse inference of reliability can be drawn. In particular - - - -

S5 If X not competent (mental, physical) at time of S → can't be admitted. ~~If not~~ Subject t attack on credibility → show previous inconsistent statement

→ If no suggestion of lack of competence → credibility should not be an issue

Where Y gives oral testimony of what X said:
S2 Notice needed when S by Y is exchanged
S4 apply criteria

S6 Can't use written S if X giving oral testimony – unless (̄c leave of Ct) t rebut suggestion of recent fabrication

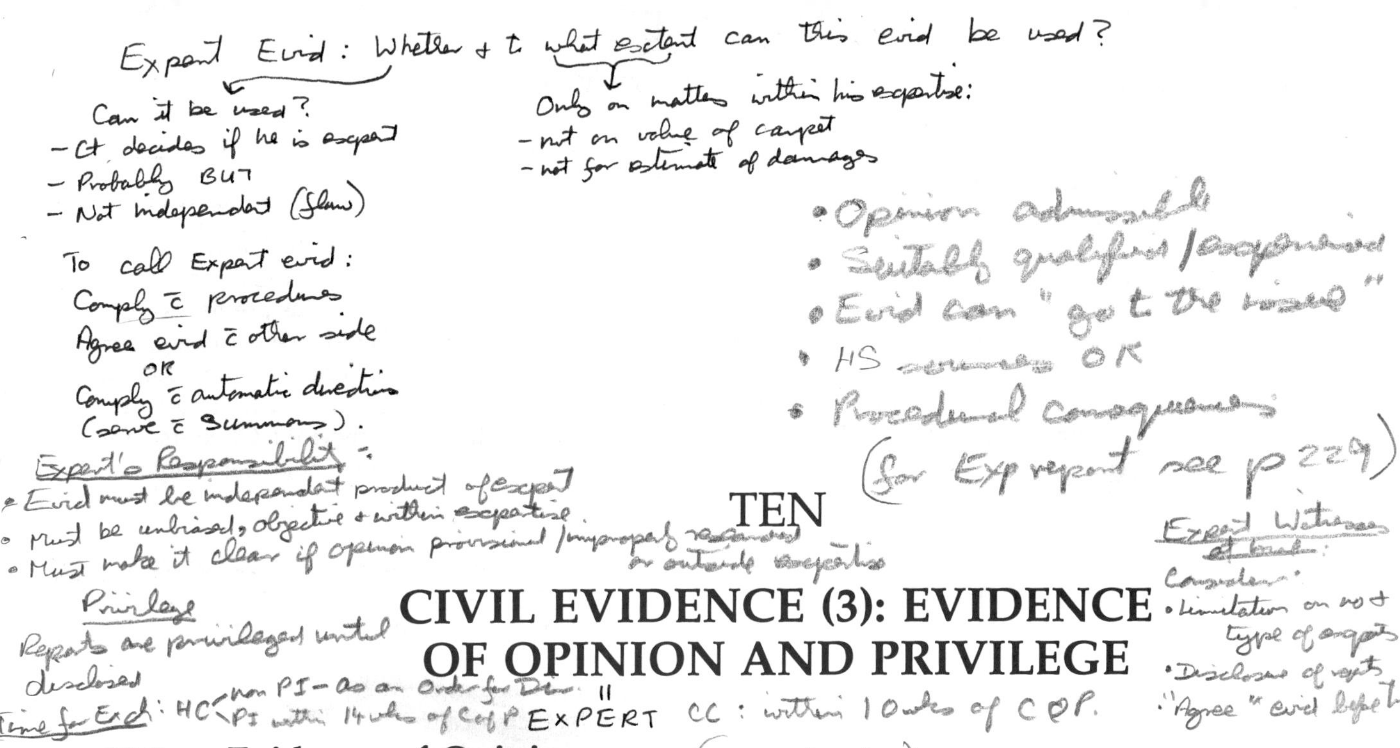

TEN

CIVIL EVIDENCE (3): EVIDENCE OF OPINION AND PRIVILEGE

10.1 Evidence of Opinion

10.1.1 THE GENERAL RULE

The general rule is that a witness may only testify as to matters actually observed by him and may not give his *opinion* about those matters. The drawing of inferences from narrated facts is the whole function of the trier of fact, i.e., in a civil case, the judge.

The distinction between fact and opinion is easy enough to see in cases at both ends of the spectrum. Thus a statement that A was driving on the wrong side of the road is clearly fact; that he was driving negligently is opinion; but statements of how fast someone was driving or, say, as to identity of handwriting are clearly both.

In civil cases in the modern era there is a considerable relaxation of the rule that a witness may not testify as to matters of opinion. Where it is impossible to separate facts from inferences based on them, the law usually permits the witness to narrate both. This is sanctioned by *s. 3(2)* of the *Civil Evidence Act 1972*, which states:

> *It is hereby declared that where a person is called as a witness in any civil proceedings, a statement of opinion by him on any relevant matter on which he is not qualified to give expert evidence, if made as a way of conveying relevant facts personally perceived by him, is admissible as evidence of what he perceived.*

The effect of this is that where a witness gives evidence in what is really a compendious way of narrating individual facts, there should be no difficulty. Thus if a witness wishes to say 'X was drunk', whilst this is a matter of opinion, since the witness could certainly narrate the individual facts on which it is based, e.g. he could say that X staggered, his breath smelt of drink, his speech was slurred, his eyes were glazed, etc., the compendious way of stating this is permitted.

10.1.2 EXPERT WITNESSES

To the general rule prohibiting evidence of bare opinion there is one exception, namely the case of expert witnesses. The most important modern use of experts is that of medical witnesses in personal injury litigation. Other frequent instances are the evidence of consultant engineers, handwriting experts, valuers, and increasingly the evidence of forensic accountants who in the context of, for example, personal injury, loss of future earnings, commercial frauds or tax matters testify about matters involving complex computations.

10.1.2.1 Competence of expert witnesses

It is for the court to accept that a witness is an expert, i.e. to rule on whether he has undergone a sufficient course of study, or is of sufficient experience to qualify. Such evidence is always introduced by a statement of qualifications, although no formal qualifications are necessarily required depending on the nature of the activity about which expert evidence is to be given. Thus, for example, an experienced car mechanic, even one who did not have any formal certificate or diploma, would certainly be an acceptable witness about some matter to do with motor vehicles, e.g. as to whether a given vehicle had been adequately serviced. Of course, for more complex mechanical matters the evidence of a qualified consulting engineer would be preferable.

It is always desirable to ensure that one's choice of expert witnesses is such that the court will feel confident in relying on their evidence. So, for example, in personal injury litigation the judge will become used to seeing the same handful of medical consultants, part of whose practices involve a substantial amount of medico-legal work, i.e. the examining of plaintiffs, the preparation of medical reports and the giving of evidence in court cases in respect of such matters as the likely period or degree of incapacity. In each locality there will be a handful of such experts having a substantial medico-legal practice on whom solicitors, and judges can rely for full and disinterested opinion evidence, even if in any given case there may be a radical difference between the plaintiff's and the defendant's experts. For material on choice of experts see **11.4**.

10.1.2.2 The ambit of expert opinion evidence

In criminal cases there remains a rule that an expert should not be asked his opinion about the very matter which it is for the jury to decide. In civil cases, however, that rule has now gone, because by *s. 3(1)* of the *Civil Evidence Act 1972* an expert may give his opinion *'on any relevant matter on which he is qualified to give expert evidence'*. In this section 'relevant matter' includes an issue in the proceedings (*s. 3(3)*).

It therefore follows that an expert may testify about the very matter in question. For example, in a medical negligence case an expert witness may testify as to whether, in his belief, the defendant doctor was negligent in the carrying out of some medical procedure or diagnosis.

10.1.2.3 The content of expert evidence and hearsay

An expert need not have personal knowledge of every relevant matter within the field of his expertise. Once someone qualifies as an expert he is entitled to base his testimony on academic books, or articles, professional publications, research data, etc. from the experiments of others. See, for example, *H* v *Schering Chemicals Ltd* [1983] 1 WLR 143.

In a civil action for damages against a drug company, it was held that an expert witness could properly refer to learned articles, findings of research in his field, etc., and the court would regard references to reputable authority within the expert's field of expertise as supporting any inferences which the expert drew in the case in question. The fact that he was in essence relying on hearsay did not disqualify him from testifying on the relevant matter.

10.1.2.4 Procedural rules governing expert evidence

By virtue of *RSC Ord. 38, r. 36* and *CCR Ord. 20, r. 27*, the calling of expert evidence at trial is subject to procedural rules which we consider in greater detail at **12.4.2**. In general these require full prior disclosure of expert evidence between the parties by exchange well in advance of trial of written reports, in the interests of saving time and costs at the trial. This requirement assists with efficiency and fairness, so that each side is well aware of what the other side's experts will say and each can in turn obtain his own expert witness's comments upon the opinion of the opposing experts. Thus counsel on each side is fully armed at trial with the material on which to cross-examine the opposing expert witness. In the case of such experts' reports, they are usually exchanged by letter between the solicitors with a view to agreement.

It should be noted that this rule requiring prior disclosure applies even to a party to an action who wishes to give expert evidence on his own behalf, and also to 'in-house' experts giving evidence on behalf of their employers, as well as to independent experts. Medical negligence cases, which had previously been considered in a special category, are within the usual rules for disclosure now following the decision in *Naylor* v *Preston Area Health Authority* [1987] 1 WLR 958 reversing the previous law.

10.2 Privilege

In general, public policy favours the open and frank conduct of legal proceedings. This means one should be able to ask any question at trial and insist upon an answer, and that any material document should be made available to all parties and to the court for inspection. This cannot be an absolute rule, however. There are conflicting interests which must be balanced, and in some circumstances facts or documents which may appear relevant to the fair conduct of a given piece of litigation may be withheld, either in the public interest, or in the exercise of private privilege, i.e. a rule which protects certain kinds of private communication from disclosure. It is now appropriate to consider the doctrine of privilege under its two main heads, ~~printed~~ privilege and public interest privilege.

10.2.1 PRIVATE PRIVILEGE

10.2.1.1 Self-incrimination

The *Civil Evidence Act 1968, s. 14,* provides that no witness can be required in civil proceedings to answer any question or produce any document or thing if to do so would expose that person or that person's spouse to proceedings for any criminal offence in the UK.

Thus in a civil case a witness cannot be compelled to answer any question which would, in the opinion of the judge, have a tendency to expose that witness to a criminal charge.

There is an important exception to this privilege under *s. 72* of the *Supreme Court Act 1981,* which provides that a person shall not be excused from answering relevant questions on the grounds of potential self-incrimination in certain kinds of proceedings, in particular infringement of rights pertaining to intellectual property or passing off.

10.2.1.2 Legal professional privilege

Privilege arises in a civil case at two stages. One is, of course, the trial itself, and if privilege is properly claimed it entitles a witness to decline to answer certain questions or produce certain documents to the court. The other stage is discovery and inspection, where in pre-trial procedures each party is required to admit the existence of and show to each other all relevant documents. This procedure must be carried out with complete honesty so that a party must show to his opponent all relevant documents, even if one of them is utterly conclusive of liability against the party who has it. The exception to this principle is where a party can claim a privilege for a certain document or class of document, in which case, whilst the existence of the document in general terms must be revealed, the contents need not.

Example A plaintiff in a case arising out of a road accident, when his vehicle collided with that of the defendant at unmarked crossroads, obtains a statement from an eye-witness which blames him (the plaintiff) for the accident. The plaintiff is obliged to reveal that he has the statement, though he need not name the witness nor show the statement to his opponent because it is privileged.

In civil proceedings, communications, oral or written, can be withheld from evidence and inspection by an opponent before trial, if the communication:

(a) was to enable the client to obtain legal advice; or

(b) was made with reference to actual or contemplated litigation; or

(c) was written 'without prejudice'.

10.2.1.3 Lawyer-client communications

The privilege applies whether the communication relates to litigation or not – the important point is said to be that anyone taking legal advice is asking about legal rights which may have to be enforced by litigation, however unlikely litigation may seem. The communication must arise out of the lawyer client relationship in some way, so that casual conversations between friends who also happen to be solicitor and client are not within the privilege. The privilege extends to all forms of communication, written, oral, telex, etc.

10.2.1.4 Communications with third parties for the purpose of actual or contemplated litigation

For this privilege to apply there must be a definite prospect of litigation but it is not necessary that the action should have started, or even that the cause of action should have arisen. The communication must have been made, or the document brought into existence, for the purpose of enabling the legal adviser to act or advise with regard to litigation. The most common examples of the privilege are therefore advice from counsel to solicitor on conduct of the action; and statements taken from witnesses, or experts' reports obtained by the solicitor for litigation.

10.2.1.5 Documents having a dual purpose

The main problem that has arisen and been the subject of much case law concerns a document which has come into being for more than one purpose. Suppose, for example, that after a factory accident a witness fills in an accident report form for his employer which may partially be for the safety officer to consider improvements to factory procedures. If the injured person sues, is this report privileged, i.e. in the course of discovery can the plaintiff see it in advance?

In *Waugh* v *British Railways Board* [1980] AC 521, a report prepared for an internal enquiry after a fatal rail accident, headed 'For the information of the Board's Solicitor', was basically prepared:

(a) so that the enquiry could establish future safety measures, and

(b) to enable the Board's solicitor to advise for the purpose of the litigation that was bound to ensue.

The Board resisted discovery on the grounds of legal privilege.

The House of Lords held that public interest in the proper administration of justice required disclosure of such a vital item of evidence, thus privilege could only be claimed where the preparation for the purpose of litigation was shown to be 'the dominant purpose' for the preparation of the report. It was always open to a court to investigate which was the dominant purpose. It was not conclusive that the document purported on the face of it to have been prepared for such a purpose. On the facts, as the document appeared to have two equal purposes the document was not privileged and had to be disclosed.

10.2.1.6 Without prejudice communications

No privilege attaches to communications *between* the parties or their advisers. Thus letters written by the other side can always be produced in evidence, e.g. to establish admissions or to use for cross-examination on the basis of inconsistency in versions of facts given. The exception to this is the case of 'without prejudice' correspondence.

Where correspondence is entered into with a view to attempting to settle a dispute, whether or not actual litigation has yet begun, letters are often marked 'without prejudice' or contain those words within the text. The use of these words confers a joint privilege on both writer and recipient so that the letters may not be put in evidence without both parties' consent. Frequently admissions, or partial admissions, are made in such correspondence in an effort to compromise, which is why the privilege is required to protect the person making the admission or other tactical concession. There may also be without prejudice meetings or telephone conversations in which what is said is privileged and may not be repeated.

So long as correspondence is directed at a bona fide attempt to compromise an action, it is not in fact necessary that the words 'without prejudice' be marked on the correspondence at all. Likewise, the mere marking of correspondence with the words 'without prejudice' will not protect it if it is not in fact bona fide written for the purpose of negotiations. Thus to mark a letter 'without prejudice' would not protect it if it was in fact defamatory.

Although, therefore, it is not strictly necessary to employ the words 'without prejudice', it is better, and likely to save potential disputes as to the status of the correspondence, always to use those words where that is the intention. Exceptionally, if a person wishes to keep open the right to refer to matters in court despite the letter being written in an attempt to negotiate a compromise, he must stipulate expressly that the correspondence is 'open' for this purpose.

The dangers of being unclear about this are well demonstrated by the case of *Dixons Stores Group Ltd* v *Thames Television PLC* [1993] 1 All ER 349 where, in substantial litigation, long-running correspondence between the parties' solicitors which had been at times on a without prejudice basis and at other times open, left the parties unclear about whether certain letters which they had exchanged were without prejudice or not, an issue which had to go as far as the Court of Appeal to be resolved.

The privilege conferred by the without prejudice status of the correspondence is discharged when the correspondence does lead to an agreement. Thus if, say, D writes to P offering to pay £10,000 in full and final settlement, marking the letter 'without prejudice', and P then writes to D accepting the offer, this has the effect of 'opening' the correspondence so that if D does not pay the money P may sue on the agreement contained in the letters.

10.2.1.7 Exceptions to the rule

Even though legal professional privilege prima facie applies, the general principle may be affected by the following exceptions:

(a) Waiver by the client – the privilege belongs to the client not the solicitor, and thus a client may waive it.

(b) Communications to facilitate crime or fraud (see *R* v *Cox* (1884) 14 QBD 153). A document which is prepared to facilitate fraud does not attract legal professional privilege. If a lawyer participates in the fraud he ceases to act as a lawyer. If he is himself innocent of any fraud, the privilege is still lost if the clients have the criminal purpose, for example as in the case of *Cox*, where they sought advice about fraudulently backdating a document.

10.2.1.8 Inadvertent disclosure of privileged documents

A difficult question is, is the privilege lost if the privileged document falls into the hands of someone else, e.g. one's opponent, by accident? The rule is that where this happens, in principle the privilege is usually lost and the opponent can use the document. Thus if an opponent produces the privileged document or a copy of it at trial, nothing can be done to prevent this. However, if one finds out *in advance* that an opponent has such a document, it may be possible to obtain an injunction to prevent the use of the privileged document by that opponent.

The precise working out of the principle is unclear, in particular because it seems from other authorities on improperly obtained evidence generally (see **10.3**) that there is little discretion in the trial judge to prevent the use of improperly obtained evidence at trial. Thus whether or not an injunction can be obtained depends upon whether the party whose privilege is about to be breached realises in time that the other party has the document so that a separate action can be launched for an injunction. In *Goddard* v *Nationwide Building Society* [1987] QB 670, where the plaintiffs contended that a note in the hands of the defendant was privileged and applied for an injunction restraining the defendant from using it, the Court of Appeal granted the injunction requiring the defendant to deliver up the note and restraining him from disclosure or making any use of the information contained therein. A similar result occurred in *English and American Insurance Co. Ltd* v *Herbert Smith & Co.* (1987) *The Times*, 22 January 1987, where a barrister's clerk mistakenly returned documents to the wrong solicitor. The court again held that it was undesirable that the security that one normally had in obtaining legal advice should be threatened by mischance and granted an injunction restraining the use of the material thus obtained.

Everything, however, depends on the facts. Thus in two cases to do with the inadvertent disclosure of part of expert evidence – *Webster* v *James Chapman & Co.* [1989] 3 All ER 939 and *Kenning* v *Eve Construction Ltd* [1989] 1 WLR 1189 – the court refused the injunctions, holding in each case, however, that there had been a duty on the party part of whose privileged report had inadvertently been disclosed to disclose it honestly in any event and therefore the actions were respectively dismissed. This proviso must, however, be read in the context of the rules relating to full disclosure of opinion evidence.

This matter is now dealt with by *principle 16.07* of the *Solicitors' Practice Rules* in the following terms:

> *Where it is obvious that privileged documents have been mistakenly disclosed to a solicitor on discovery or otherwise, the solicitor should immediately cease to read the documents, inform the other side and return the documents. Before informing the other side the solicitor should consider whether to obtain instructions from the client, and if deciding to do so, should advise the client that the court will probably grant an injunction to prevent the overt use of any information gleaned from the documents and that both the client and the solicitor might find costs awarded against them in respect of such an injunction.*

That rule must be read subject to the decision of the Court of Appeal in *Pizzey* v *Ford Motor Co. Ltd* (1993) *The Times*, 12 March 1993. In that case the defendant's solicitor received medical reports which were unfavourable and had been disclosed to her by accident by the plaintiff's solicitors. At the time of reading them the defendant's solicitor reasonably believed that the plaintiff's solicitor had waived the privilege in them and it was not until the reports had been fully read that their adverse nature was revealed. The Court of Appeal held that where a solicitor had behaved honestly and reasonably in continuing to read a document which was clearly privileged in the belief that privilege had been waived, no injunction would be granted restraining the defendant from using the privileged documents at trial.

That principle was affirmed in the important case of *IBM Corp.* v *Phoenix International (Computers) Ltd* [1995] 1 All ER 413. In that case the Court of Appeal held, whilst affirming

Pizzey v *Ford* on its facts, that the crucial test was whether a hypothetical solicitor would, on a balance of probabilities, have realised that privilege had not been waived. In the *IBM* case the court reached a different conclusion on the facts from that in *Pizzey* v *Ford*, holding that a reasonable solicitor would have concluded that the documents had been disclosed by mistake in view of the surrounding circumstances.

The suggestion that a solicitor ought to take his client's instructions before deciding what to do was criticised as positively wrong in law in the case of *Ablitt* v *Mills & Reeve (A Firm) and Another* (1995) *The Times*, 25 October 1995. The solicitors for the defendant had received some documents disclosed inadvertently by the plaintiff and took their insurance client's instructions on what use to make of these documents instead of simply returning them unread. The court was highly critical of the wording of the Practice Rule and awarded the plaintiff an injunction against the defendant's solicitors forbidding them to act any further for the defendant in the litigation, thus compelling the defendant to change his solicitors. The court observed that a competent solicitor acting honourably ought not in such circumstances to be obliged to take his client's instructions first.

10.2.1.9 Privilege and other professions

There is no professional privilege for other professions in general, even those such as accountants who may give quasi legal advice. There are, however, certain quasi exceptions two examples of which are:

(a) By virtue of the *Copyright Designs and Patents Act 1988, ss. 280* and *284,* in civil proceedings a privilege may be claimed in respect of communications between a person and his patent agent or trademark agent made for the purpose of pending or contemplating proceedings.

(b) By s. *10* of the *Contempt of Court Act 1981*:

No court may require a person to disclose, nor is any person guilty of contempt of court for refusing to disclose, the source of information contained in a publication for which he is responsible, unless it be established to the satisfaction of the court that disclosure is necessary in the interests of justice or national security or for the prevention of disorder or crime.

This thus creates a limited privilege in respect of sources of journalists and others, reversing previous case law which had held that journalists had no privilege whatsoever to refuse to answer relevant questions.

10.2.2 PUBLIC INTEREST PRIVILEGE

Where evidence is excluded because of some public interest in withholding it which outweighs the usual public interest in open litigation, it is usually called 'public interest privilege', or 'public interest immunity'. The right to claim the privilege is by no means restricted to the government or the Crown – it may be claimed by bodies such as local authorities, quangos, the police and the like.

10.2.2.1 The principle

The principle is that whoever makes the claim to privilege, the court may demand to see the document and will then rule on whether the greater public interest lies in open and frank disclosure in litigation or in confidentiality. So in *Burmah Oil Co. Ltd* v *Bank of England* [1980] AC 1090, discovery was sought of various memoranda of meetings attended by government ministers, and other documents which would have revealed the inner workings of high level government. The House of Lords held that it was going too far to lay down that no document in any particular category should ever in any circumstances be produced, even when they were high level documents to do with government. The nature of the litigation and the apparent importance to it of the documents in question might in extreme cases demand production even of the most sensitive communications at the highest level (see, for example, *Nixon* v *US* 418 US 683 (1974) relating to the disclosure of Presidential papers). The courts will always bear in mind that it is in the public interest that justice should be done and should be publicly recognised as having been done.

The House of Lords in *Burmah Oil Co. Ltd* v *Bank of England* subsequently found that certain of the documents in question were likely to reveal the attitude of the Bank of England to the transactions the subject of the litigation, and therefore under *RSC Ord. 24* these could be inspected. Once the House of Lords had inspected them, however, the House held that the documents did not contain material which was 'necessary for fairly disposing of the case' and on that ground upheld the objection to disclosure, i.e. on the basis that disclosure would not have assisted the party seeking it.

As the speeches in this important case and many others make clear, the court is essentially engaged in a balancing exercise between the claimed public interest, giving due weight to the ministers' views, and the desirability of open litigation. The court must always have regard to *RSC Ord. 24,* which provides:

> *No order for the production of any documents for inspection or to the court shall be made . . . unless the court is of the opinion that the order is necessary either for disposing fairly of the cause or matter or for saving costs.*

Thus it will be pointless for a plaintiff to attempt to gain documents on a fishing expedition where he has no idea whether the contents will or will not assist him.

10.2.2.2 Types of document covered by public interest privilege

It is quite impossible to attempt closely to categorise the types of public document where exclusion is likely to be ordered. Most confusingly, even cases involving essentially the same type of document have ended in conflicting decisions. This is most apparent in a series of cases which dealt with the problem of enquiries into police conduct under *s. 49* of the *Police Act 1964*. The question later arose in each case as to whether the statements given for the purpose of complaints against the police should be liable to disclosure in civil proceedings, e.g. proceedings brought by persons alleging false imprisonment or wrongful arrest. It was difficult to see any coherent line arising from the case law and differently constituted Courts of Appeal took different decisions on relatively similar facts. See for example *Peach* v *Metropolitan Police Commission* [1986] QB 1064; *Neilson* v *Laughane* [1981] QB 736; *R* v *Metropolitan Police Commissioner, ex parte Hart-Leverton* [1990] COD 240; *Evans* v *Chief Constable of Surrey* [1988] QB 588; *Makanjuola* v *Metropolitan Police Commissioner* [1992] 3 All ER 617 (a particularly strange case because the complainant sought disclosure of *her own* earlier statement but it was still refused). The specific problem in those cases was eventually resolved by the House of Lords ruling authoritatively on the matter in the recent case of *R* v *Chief Constable for West Midlands Constabulary, ex parte Wiley* [1994] 1 All ER 702. However, further difficulty has been caused by the Court of Appeal case of *Taylor* v *Anderton* [1995] 1 WLR 447 where the Court of Appeal held that investigating officers' reports, as distinct from police complaints statements, would be accorded public interest immunity.

These cases indicate the difficulty that the court will often have in deciding on a matter of public interest immunity and whether it can properly override a certificate from the relevant Secretary of State. The capacity for public interest immunity to be abused by Ministers of the Crown or, in effect, their civil servants, is obvious and is what of course led to the Scott enquiry into the circumstances in which, having given approval for the export of armaments to Iraq, several Ministers of the Crown successively signed public interest immunity certificates when relevant documents were called for by defendants who were prosecuted for being involved in those self-same exports.

10.2.2.3 The court's decision on where the public interest lies

The decision as to where the public interest lies is in the end one for the court. It has been held in some recent cases that the court may even take the point of public interest immunity where it is not claimed by either of the parties.

For an indication of how nicely balanced the point may be, the following two cases can be compared:

***D* v *NSPCC* [1978] AC 171**

The NSPCC sought help from members of the public in giving information concerning child abuse and offered a guarantee of confidentiality. A malicious informant falsely told the NSPCC that the plaintiff's daughter had been ill treated. In due course the plaintiff brought an action for damages against the society alleging negligence, contending that insufficient care had been exercised in investigating the complaint before sending an inspector to see the child. The plaintiff sought discovery of the identity of the malicious informant. The House of Lords held that the identity should not be disclosed because the public interest required that people with genuine suspicions of child abuse should feel free to communicate those suspicions without being put in fear of defamation proceedings. That was so even though the effect of the ruling in the present case was to protect a malicious person.

***Campbell* v *Tameside Metropolitan Borough Council* [1982] QB 1065**

The plaintiff was a schoolteacher who had been attacked in the class by a violent pupil. She brought an action against the Education Authority contending that it should have known that the pupil had a violent disposition and that he should have been educated in a special unit. She sought preliminary discovery of reports maintained by the Authority which were believed to contain material which would have demonstrated the Authority's knowledge of the pupil's tendencies. The Court of Appeal held that in the present case, whilst there was some merit in the defendant's argument that the writing up of teachers' and educational psychologists' reports on children might be made less candid if the writers thought they might be used in subsequent litigation, this should be overriden by the need for open litigation.

This case indicates that the burden of justifying non disclosure is always upon the party seeking it and not the converse. The more low level the document is the more difficult will it be to justify withholding it.

10.3 Improperly Obtained Evidence

The rule in civil cases in essence is that evidence, if relevant, is admissible no matter how it was obtained. Thus even in the case of a privileged document, if it is obtained by, say, subterfuge, or even theft, the document can be used in court. However, the court does have the power to prevent abuse of process of the court, which it sometimes interprets so as to prevent the party using in some way or adducing in court a document wrongly obtained, or improperly using a document properly obtained. In the case of such disclosure, everything appears to depend upon whether the party whose document it was gets wind of the situation in advance of trial. If so, and a request for the return of the document and an undertaking that it will not be used is refused, then on the general principles previously discussed it would appear that a separate action will lie for an injunction requiring the return of the document. If, however, the document is simply produced at trial in the instant case, it will then be too late to seek an injunction.

The law in this area remains unsettled. In *Riddick* v *Thames Board Mills Ltd* [1977] QB 881, in proceedings between the plaintiff and the defendant concerning the plaintiff's employment, a memorandum was revealed which contained passages which were allegedly defamatory of the plaintiff. It was held that a party was entitled to be protected against the improper use of materials disclosed on discovery for purposes other than the litigation for which they were disclosed. Accordingly, the plaintiff was not entitled to use the memorandum as the basis for an action in defamation. (For further discussion of this case see **12.1.9**.)

This case appears to assume that the court has a discretion to exclude evidence on grounds of policy, as does the case of *ITC Film Distributors* v *Video Exchange Ltd* [1982] Ch 436. There, the defendant, during the trial of an action for breach of copyright, obtained by a trick certain papers which the plaintiff's solicitors had brought to court for the trial. Since the papers were undoubtedly relevant and apparently admissible the defendant sought to put them in evidence. Warner J held that despite the general rule that the court had no power to exclude relevant evidence, the public interest in the due administration of justice required the parties to be free to bring papers into court without fear that they might be filched during the trial. This consideration outweighed even the competing public interest that the court should receive all available evidence. The matter was one of public policy.

In this case the misconduct in obtaining the papers might also have amounted to contempt of court. It is not clear whether Warner J was ruling the evidence inadmissible (which it was surely not), or creating a new discretion to exclude in such cases. In the subsequent case of *Goddard* v *Nationwide Building Society* [1987] QB 670 (discussed at **10.2.1.3**), Nourse LJ indicated clearly that Warner J's decision should not be regarded as one under some inherent discretion but as one based on public policy.

ELEVEN

CIVIL EVIDENCE (4): PREPARATION OF CIVIL EVIDENCE

11.1 Practical Considerations: Introduction

As has often been observed, except for those rare cases where the entire case is on admitted facts and the dispute turns on a matter of law or construction of documents, it is not sufficient to have a good case. A party must always consider at every stage whether he has sufficient admissible evidence to prove his case, and this is relevant not just to issues of liability but to every matter of quantum.

Litigation solicitors commonly carry a heavier case load than they can efficiently and thoroughly deal with. In addition, there is the psychological point that solicitors know perfectly well that a very high proportion of cases are settled before trial. Moreover, despite the accuracy and precision with which difficult issues of quantum may have been worked out, e.g. by collecting expert accountancy evidence of tax computations so as to arrive at a very specific figure for loss of future earnings, solicitors also know perfectly well that in negotiations to settle claims, even very late in the day where figures of a very specific kind have been produced, often cases are settled by round lump sum figure agreements with individual items being rounded up or down in a global package. Thus a solicitor may often be left with a sense of frustration that hours or days of work have been done to very little end purpose. In personal injury cases particularly, plaintiffs' solicitors will often say that if defendants' solicitors, or more commonly their insurance clients, had taken the case by the scruff of the neck seriously at a much earlier stage and talked in sensible figures instead of attempting to wear a plaintiff down with inadequate offers and a process of attrition, a great deal of time and costs could be saved.

All these things are true. Nonetheless, a plaintiff's solicitor who has the case settled just before trial, even at the court room door, does have the modest satisfaction of knowing that every hour of his time properly charged for will be paid by the defendants, and to that extent the defendants have penalised themselves for intransigence or slowness. Moreover, if a solicitor has prepared his own case meticulously to argue every single point of quantum, then in negotiations with a defendant's solicitor who clearly has not prepared matters with the same thoroughness, the latter will inevitably be at a considerable disadvantage. In the context of such matters as future loss of earnings, it is not enough now for the defendant's solicitor simply to make the plaintiff prove every element and challenge it in the round. *Practice Direction (Damages: Personal Injury Actions)* [1984] 1 WLR 1127 provides (see **14.3** for full discussion) that shortly before trial a plaintiff must serve worked computations of all special damages (including elements of future loss) upon a defendant, who must then respond with his own counter-proposals or indicate specifically how he proposes to challenge the figures produced by the plaintiff.

There are thus very substantial tactical advantages in approaching every case as though it fell within that handful of cases which go all the way to trial and in which no compromise will take place. By keeping thoroughly on top of every element of detail in the case from start to finish, a solicitor immeasurably increases his own confidence in the outcome and his negotiating position with defendants. Moreover, it is wrong to consider that this is providing some 'Rolls Royce' version of litigation as opposed to what is the norm. To approach litigation in this way *should be* the norm and is what every client consulting a solicitor in a litigation matter is entitled to expect.

The face of civil litigation has been radically changed in the recent past by *RSC Ord. 38, r. 2A* and *CCR Ord. 20, r. 12A*. These rules will be discussed in detail subsequently, but in brief they provide that parties, unless there are special reasons to the contrary, must serve on each other well before trial statements of *all* their evidence, both those of witnesses of fact and of experts. Thus both parties should be fully armed with knowledge of the other party's case, there should be no element of 'trial by ambush' and the litigation will proceed in the light rather than in the dark. In the light of this we now discuss specific practical considerations.

11.2 Evidence of Facts

11.2.1 INTERVIEWING POTENTIAL WITNESSES OF FACT

It is vitally important to interview potential witnesses of fact as soon as possible after receiving instructions. Any delay in obtaining this evidence will substantially impair its quality. Even where a witness has seen a very spectacular incident, e.g. a very bad road accident, memory of vital details soon fades, such as approximate distances from the kerb, the line of manoeuvre taken by one of the vehicles, the number of other vehicles in the vicinity, the lighting conditions and so on. It is therefore important to interview all material witnesses as soon as possible. Moreover, to avoid duplication of effort, they should be interviewed as thoroughly as possible to obtain comprehensive statements. Formerly, a well-recognised technique was to obtain brief details from witnesses indicating the general tenor of their evidence. Then, if the case happened not to be one of the overwhelming majority which settled, a further and more detailed proof would be obtained closer to trial. This is undesirable anyway, but now, since rules provide for exchange of witness statements before trial, it is vital that a thorough and comprehensive proof of evidence is taken so that work is not duplicated and that original, early statements can be used.

Having taken the statement one must of course remain alive to what the witness has said throughout the litigation. For example, when the defence is received it may be that there are matters in it on which the witness has not commented but on which he should be given the chance to give his version. Important new facts may emerge. At that time the witness may be re-interviewed, with the defence or other document reciting new facts to hand.

The statement should initially be taken as earlier described (**4.1.2.2**) in as full a form as possible. Thus it may include hearsay, opinion, speculation, or indeed details of a previous similar instance, e.g. after a factory accident where a description of previous incidents might show continuing lack of regard for employees' safety. This information is for the purpose of the plaintiff's solicitor being able to consider lines of enquiry and other sources of information. It therefore forms a vital function in the early stages of investigation. However, in the witness statements which are to be exchanged and put before the judge at trial, inadmissible material such as opinion must not appear. Solicitors are usually perfectly competent to judge what is or is not admissible, but in cases of difficulty counsel's opinion on evidence may be taken before exchange, and indeed in exceptional cases counsel may assist in drafting the witness statement. The final form of statement for exchange, taken from the witness's original full proof of evidence, needs to be prepared in typed and paragraphed form and then sent to the witness for signature in preparation for exchange.

11.2.2 STATEMENTS FROM THE CLIENT

Obviously a very thorough statement from the client should be taken at the outset. It is in the nature of things, however, that a client's case may develop as the litigation rolls on. This is especially so if there is any continuing element in quantum, especially in personal injury cases. It must be remembered that a client's statement must also be exchanged at the relevant time and it is vital that this be as comprehensive as possible. The initial statement, as with that of other witnesses, should include any material, even if legally inadmissible, which might assist.

The eventual statement for exchange must not contain such inadmissible material, but should nonetheless, especially in personal injury cases, deal thoroughly with every aspect of quantum as well as liability, and in this regard it is as well to have a checklist put to a client. Although round sum figures may well be awarded for such matters as 'loss of amenity', so that, for example, one plaintiff who has suffered a common type of injury, say a broken ankle, is prima facie likely to obtain much the same as every other plaintiff, these figures can be adjusted to take into account specific aspects of a person's interests or lifestyle. Thus if one can substantiate that the plaintiff is a very keen sportsman so that his enjoyment of life has been considerably impaired by the injury, as opposed to someone who had a sedentary hobby, that may be reflected in damages. Similarly in the case of more serious or permanent injuries, it is always important for the plaintiff to describe his whole lifestyle to show how he is now affected. For example, if he commonly did a lot of DIY, painting and decorating, or looked after his own large garden, then the fact that he is no longer able to do these things will be reflected in monetary terms in reimbursement for the outside assistance which he has to employ. Too often these things used to be glossed over in a proof of evidence, leaving the client to expand on them at trial. That will no longer be satisfactory since a client must set out his evidence on *every* material matter.

Likewise, a client should describe with some particularity any injuries or pain he is suffering, even if he might tend to make light of it. If he continues to suffer sleepless nights or throbbing pains, then these should be reflected in his statement and he should not be encouraged to adopt a stoic attitude towards them. The same applies in other kinds of litigation, e.g. about commercial or contractual matters. A plaintiff's statement should always carefully detail every element of quantum as well as matters relevant to liability because if he does not put these matters in his statement for exchange he may either be refused the right to give any evidence about them at all later; or possibly an adjournment may be awarded to the opposing party to call evidence to meet the client's allegations, and the cost of that adjournment will inevitably be paid by the plaintiff.

11.2.3 STATEMENTS FROM THE DEFENDANT OR DEFENCE WITNESSES

If acting for the defendant taking statements from the defendant or defence witnesses requires quite as much skill, although in the nature of things one has to make less of the running. In particular, it will not usually be relevant for defence witnesses at this stage to comment on matters of quantum, although if, for example the case concerns an accident at work then evidence about such matters as the plaintiff's pay and future prospects will clearly be within the competence of the personnel department.

Again, it is as well to obtain a thorough proof of evidence at an early stage, notwithstanding that the hard factual information on which it might be based remains readily available. For example, the plaintiff's immediate superior may have particular views about the plaintiff's actual competence as a worker. It is as well to have these committed to paper as soon as possible in case, for example, the superior leaves, dies, or in some way becomes disenchanted with the firm, e.g. by himself being refused a promotion or being made redundant so that his view of the plaintiff might materially improve!

11.2.4 WITNESS STATEMENTS AND THE RULES OF EVIDENCE

In **12.3.3** some aspects of the drafting of witness statements for exchange are considered.

It may be that witness statements can be agreed between the parties. This applies not only to witness statements which are wholly uncontroversial, but possibly to at least some parts of the more contentious evidence too. This will have the useful effect of limiting the issues at trial.

11.2.5 WITNESSES OF FACT: SUMMARY

(a) It is generally best if witnesses of fact attend to give oral evidence at trial if they are available. A judge prefers to see a witness, even though the observation of demeanour is generally recognised as being a highly fallible guide to finding the truth. Thus if a party has a witness, whether as to liability or to quantum, it is as well to call the witness unless his statement has been agreed in advance.

(b) If the witness is uncontroversial, or unavailable for some good reason then one can serve a copy of his evidence on the defendant and put the hearsay statement in at trial. It must always be remembered that the trial judge will apply the criteria in *s. 4* of the *Civil Evidence Act 1995* in deciding on what weight he will attach to the evidence of the absent witness. He will in particular ask questions as to why the witness has not attended and may draw adverse inferences from absence.

(c) Affidavit evidence. By *RSC Ord. 38, r. 2*, it is provided that the court may at or before the trial of an action begun by writ, order that the affidavit of any witness may be read at trial if in the circumstances of the case it thinks it reasonable so to order.

Despite this provision it is very rare to have affidavit evidence at trials of routine actions in the Queen's Bench Division, or the County Court. If the witness is for any reason unavailable then more normally one would invoke the *Civil Evidence Act 1995* procedures, which are more convenient in that the statement for use does not have to be sworn, nor is any court order required in respect of it.

(d) Notices to admit facts. We have already considered the nature of admissions procured by a notice to admit facts (see **8.5.2.2**). This is a useful alternative means of proving facts which are expensive or inconvenient to prove by oral evidence. It may be that the statements of one or several witnesses can be wholly dispensed with by the timely service of a notice to admit facts which achieves a successful response.

11.3 Documentary Evidence

11.3.1 THE AUTHENTICITY OF DOCUMENTS

When producing documents to a court it is necessary to demonstrate their authenticity. In the case of one's own documents there are two provisions:

(a) In all actions begun by writ there is a procedure known as discovery of documents, which will be discussed in more detail at **12.1**. At that time it is necessary to serve on your opponent a list of documents which you have in your possession relevant to the action. In relation to documents in that list, *RSC Ord. 27, r. 4*, provides that an opponent receiving such a list is deemed to admit the *authenticity* of the documents in the list unless within 21 days after inspection of the documents he serves a notice stating that he does not admit the authenticity of the document in question and requires it to be proved at trial. Thereafter, the document is to be taken as authentic. If the opposing party does not admit the authenticity of any such document, but its authenticity is established at trial, then the costs of proving authenticity fall on the party who wrongly objected.

In the case of documents which for any reason do not form part of the list of documents on discovery there is a second provision.

(b) By *RSC Ord. 27, r. 5* (*CCR Ord. 20, r. 3*):

> *. . . a party to a cause or matter may within 21 days after the cause or matter is set down for trial* [county court 14 days before the trial] *serve on any other party a notice requiring him to admit the authenticity of the documents specified in the notice.*

Thereafter the party on whom the notice is served, if he wishes to challenge the authenticity of the document, must within 21 days (seven in the county court) serve on the first party a notice stating that he does not admit the authenticity of the document and requires it to be proved at trial. Failure to serve this notice is deemed to be an admission of the authenticity of the document.

The effect of this provision has to do with admitting the *authenticity* of documents and not the *content*. It simply saves the time of the trial, and the cost of witnesses being called to prove authenticity. Suppose, for example, that it is possible that the terms of a lease executed 15 years ago are material. If it were contended that it was not authentic then a good deal of time or trouble might be spent in tracing the witnesses to the attesting parties, the solicitor who was responsible for the transaction, etc. By this procedure that is avoided, or at least the onus is thrown on the party who wishes to dispute the authenticity. This should be contrasted with the procedure under notices to admit the facts, in the case of which passivity by the person receiving the notice indicates that he *does not* admit the facts (see **8.5.2.2**). In the present case the party wishing to dispute authenticity of documents must *positively* serve the notice referred to.

As in the case of notices to admit facts, a party disputing authenticity of document will be called upon to pay the costs of proving the document at trial if it is proved to be authentic, whatever the outcome of the trial in the normal course of things (*RSC Ord. 62, r. 6(8)*). It should be noted that where a list of documents is served on discovery, the receiving party is deemed to be on notice to admit the authenticity of any documents in that list unless a notice of objection is served.

11.3.2 PROVING DOCUMENTS

Suppose, however, that a party needs to prove his own document because its authenticity is not admitted. If the document is available it may be produced and is then the best evidence of its contents. If its authenticity is not admitted, however, then that will have to be proved by oral evidence, i.e. by the persons who executed it, possibly those who witnessed it, or the solicitor on whose instructions it was prepared. Suppose, though, that it is not available. In that situation secondary evidence of the contents may in certain circumstances be given. For example handwritten copies may be used, photocopies, or simply a verbal account given of what the document contained. Secondary evidence may be given in the following situations:

(a) Where the original can be proved to be lost despite a proper search.

(b) Where it is impossible to produce the original because, for example, it is privileged in the hands of some other party, or held outside the jurisdiction.

(c) Where another party has been served with a notice under *RSC Ord. 27, r. 5(4)*, which provides:

> *. . . a party to a cause or matter may serve on any other party a notice requiring him to produce the documents specified in the notice at the trial of the cause or matter.*

Where, despite having received this notice, the other party does not comply, then secondary evidence of the contents may be given and the court may draw any proper inference from a refusal to produce by the party.

11.3.3 SUMMARY OF THE RULES ON DOCUMENTARY EVIDENCE

(a) A party should normally list all the documents which he has which are relevant to the action in his list of documents. Unless the opponent then specifically objects to the authenticity of any given document its authenticity is taken as established.

(b) In the case of any other document which has not been listed in the list at discovery, where a party wishes to produce it in evidence, it is appropriate to serve notice to admit under *RSC Ord. 27, r. 5 (CCR Ord. 20, r. 3)*.

(c) Where another party has the document one should serve a notice to produce under *RSC Ord. 27, r. 4(3) (CCR Ord. 20, r. 3)*.

(d) Where a non-party has the document the procedure is to serve a subpoena *duces tecum* which compels that witness to attend court and to produce the specified document (see **14.2.3.3**). The equivalent in the county court is called a witness summons.

11.4 Expert Evidence

We have already considered in general how to go about choosing and obtaining expert evidence. We shall in due course consider the precise requirements for the exchange of expert evidence in the form of written reports well in advance of trial (see **12.4**).

11.4.1 EVIDENCE RELATING TO LIABILITY

In this category would be included evidence from experts such as consulting engineers about factory machinery or how a road accident might have occurred, road accident reconstruction specialists and the like. Such reports are likely to be obtained at an early stage, possibly with some urgency, as, for example, where it is desired to examine the defendant's vehicle after a road accident.

Once having obtained that evidence it should be kept under review as with all other forms of evidence, bearing in mind that it will need to be exchanged with the opponent well before trial under *RSC Ord. 38, r. 36* (see **12.4.2**). Thus when the defendant's evidence is received or when any new matter is discovered, the same expert should be consulted to give his views on the opposition's report or on the new development. If this leads to a supplemental report of significance that should be disclosed to the opponent. If, however, the expert merely comments on some matters within the opponent's expert's report, e.g. suggesting that report relies on an outdated approach, or that the statistical evidence is more ambiguous than the opposing expert concedes, then that kind of information may be simply used as a tool for the cross-examiner when facing the opposing expert in court.

11.4.2 EXPERT EVIDENCE ON QUANTUM

This is likely to be provided by medical specialists in personal injury cases; by valuers, auctioneers, accountants and the like in other cases. In the case of serious personal injuries a forensic accountant's evidence will be needed to deal with such matters as loss of future earnings and the tax consequences thereof, and various alternative permutations of the plaintiff's career prospects; loss of pension rights or other financial benefits; or the loss of earnings of a self-employed plaintiff. In addition, more esoteric specialists may include those to describe the nature and cost of a nursing care regime; an architect to describe what alterations need to be made to a disabled plaintiff's house and the like.

As the evidence of these experts relates to quantum, there will not be quite the same urgency to obtain it in most cases. In the case of business disputes, however, evidence of losses arising out of commercial difficulties may need to be collected with just as much speed and precision as evidence on liability.

Such evidence, even more than that on liability, will need to be constantly updated. For example, in a major personal injury case the plaintiff may need to be examined by three or four different types of medical specialists, each of whose reports need to be updated every year between accident and trial. Moreover, once all the reports are exchanged it is vital to have one's own expert look at the opposing expert's report to see whether an agreement is possible, e.g. whether the two specialists are in fact saying the same thing albeit it in a different language, or whether the area of disagreement is so trivial that a compromise form of wording could be adopted.

11.4.3 MEETINGS OF EXPERTS

As we shall see in more detail at **12.4.7** the court has power to direct that experts meet to discuss the case in an attempt to agree a form of report (or at least to identify those areas on which no agreement is possible). Experts may indeed carry out a joint examination for this purpose, e.g. of a plaintiff in a personal injury case, or a piece of equipment or machinery. Specialists who are commonly consulted for litigation inevitably get to know each other well and are likely to be on good personal terms. When brought face to face it may be that their approach is more conciliatory than it was when they were merely swapping conflicting reports through the post. At the very least it may be possible to agree on some of the points in dispute, leaving the rest outstanding for the trial.

11.4.4 EXPERTS' FEES

When consulting any expert it is important to have regard to the likely level of fee to be charged. In routine cases fees are relatively standard for medical reports and engineers' reports. Other more esoteric forms of specialist (especially forensic accountants) may charge fees which vary considerably, and it is important to attempt to agree the fees in advance (and in a legal aid case to obtain prior authority to incur them). It may be necessary to attempt to agree with the specialist that only fees recoverable on taxation will be payable. The plaintiff's express agreement to bear any shortfall on the fees recovered on taxation in appropriate cases may need to be obtained.

11.4.5 CONCLUSION

As will be considered in more detail at **12.5**, a bundle of experts' reports and of witness statements exchanged under *RSC Ord. 38, r. 2A*, must be prepared for use of the trial judge and lodged at court in advance of the trial. At this time it must also be very clearly indicated which parts of which statements or reports are agreed so that the judge can apply his mind in advance to the areas remaining in contention.

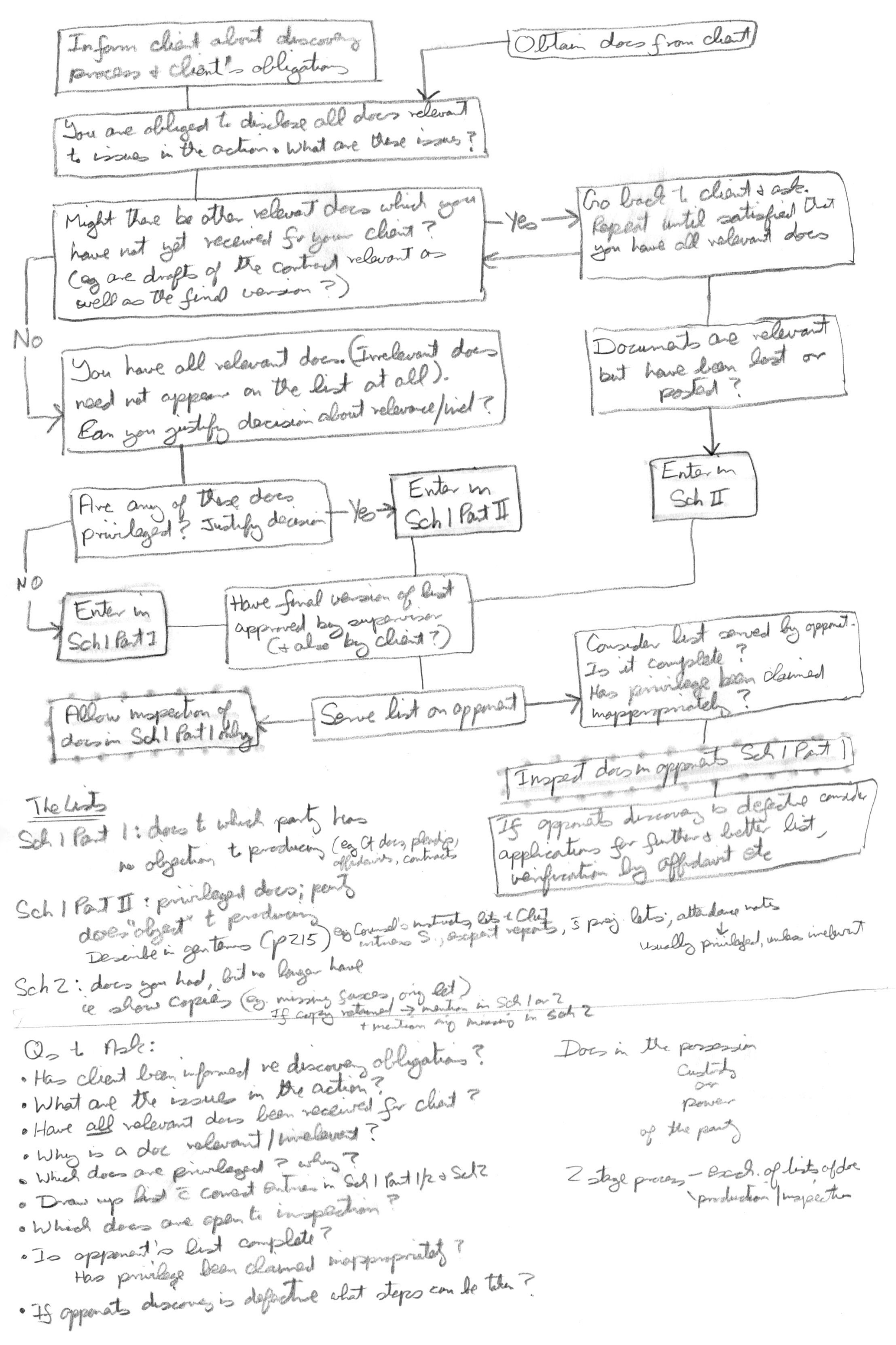
Inform client about discovery process & client's obligations
Obtain docs from client
You are obliged to disclose all docs relevant to issues in the action. What are these issues?
Might there be other relevant docs which you have not yet received for your client? (eg are drafts of the contract relevant as well as the final version?)
Yes
Go back to client & ask. Repeat until satisfied that you have all relevant docs
No
You have all relevant docs. (Irrelevant docs need not appear on the list at all). Can you justify decision about relevance/irrel?
Documents are relevant but have been lost or posted?
Enter in Sch II
Are any of these docs privileged? Justify decision
Yes
Enter in Sch I Part II
NO
Enter in Sch I Part I
Have final version of list approved by supervisor (& also by client?)
Consider list served by opponent. Is it complete? Has privilege been claimed inappropriately?
Allow inspection of docs in Sch I Part I only
Serve list on opponent
Inspect docs in opponent's Sch I Part I
If opponent's discovery is defective consider applications for further & better list, verification by affidavit etc
The Lists
Sch I Part I: docs to which party has no objection to producing (eg Ct docs, pleadings, affidavits, contracts)
Sch I Part II: privileged docs; party does "object" to producing. Describe in gen terms (p215) eg Counsel's instructions, lets & Chief witness S, expert reports, s̄ prej lets, attendance notes
usually privileged, unless irrelevant
Sch 2: docs you had, but no longer have ie show copies (eg. missing faxes, orig let)
If copy retained → mention in Sch I or 2 + mention any missing in Sch 2
Qs to Ask:
• Has client been informed re discovery obligations?
• What are the issues in the action?
• Have all relevant docs been received for client?
• Why is a doc relevant / irrelevant?
• Which docs are privileged? why?
• Draw up list c̄ correct entries in Sch I Part 1/2 & Sch 2
• Which docs are open to inspection?
• Is opponent's list complete? Has privilege been claimed inappropriately?
• If opponent's discovery is defective what steps can be taken?
Docs in the possession custody or power of the party
2 stage process — exch. of lists of docs
production / inspection

TWELVE

CIVIL EVIDENCE IN THE COURSE OF PROCEEDINGS

12.1 Discovery and Inspection

Discovery and inspection is the stage of an action at which one party reveals to the other what relevant documents are or have been in his possession, custody or power, and provides an opportunity for that other party to inspect and take copies of those documents which the first party has and in respect of which he is not entitled to refuse inspection. A party will be entitled to refuse inspection of documents only where he claims they are irrelevant, or where he claims there is some privilege attaching to them.

12.1.1 THE PRINCIPLES AND NATURE OF DISCOVERY

The principles of discovery are said to be:

(a) to assist the parties in clarifying the issues and evaluating the strengths of their respective cases; and

(b) to enable the parties to see what matters remain in contention.

It is important to note that the term 'discovery' therefore strictly means revealing the existence of documents, and the term 'inspection' means allowing the opposite party to look at those documents. However, somewhat confusingly, the term 'discovery' is sometimes used of the whole process, i.e. of both discovery and inspection, and a non-technical word 'disclosure' is also sometimes used in respect of either stage or both.

We have already considered briefly the nature of discovery in the context of pre-action discovery in a personal injury case (see **4.1.4**). The essence of discovery proper is that it is the stage of an action at which a party is compelled honestly to reveal documents in his possession which are relevant to the case. Documents are relevant if they 'relate to any matter in question in the proceedings'. Thus they are relevant if they relate to either liability or quantum and, most importantly, whether they assist or are detrimental to the case of the party who has them.

At the stage when discovery is reached a party is obliged to carry it out truthfully and comprehensively. The ethics of negotiating in litigation generally permit the advocate to argue as fiercely as he can in favour of his client's case and attempt to obtain as advantageous a settlement of the litigation as possible. However, at the time of discovery it is absolutely vital that the procedure is carried out completely honestly. Viewed ethically this leads to somewhat odd conclusions. For example, if an advocate has in his possession a document which is harmful to his client's case, indeed conclusive of the issues against that client, and the document is not protected by privilege, then he is obliged to reveal it to the other side in the process of discovery. Thus although he may have attempted to negotiate as aggressively as possible up to that point, if the document is conclusive the case is as good as over from the time when the other side are made aware of the document. However, what if the item of evidence is the kind of document which is privileged? Suppose, for instance, that there is a collision between vehicles driven by P and D. Acting for P you manage to trace an independent eye-witness who gives a very convincing description of the incident in which he totally blames P. You also find that D is unaware of the existence of this eye-witness. A witness statement is a document which is privileged. Accordingly, a party need not show this document to the opposite side, nor reveal the name and address of the witness concerned, nor subsequently call that witness at trial. P can therefore go to trial hoping that his version will be believed as against D, but knowing that the only truly independent observer exonerates D from blame. This is perfectly consistent with the ethics of litigation.

Let us take an example which illustrates the converse situation. Suppose, for example, that there is litigation over whether or not a certain type of engine supplied to the plaintiff is or is not adequate for certain jobs and the plaintiff is suing the defendant and alleging that there is a serious design fault in that engine. There is a number of memoranda from the defendant company's design engineers going back some months before the engine was put on the market, expressing grave reservations about its capacity to do certain jobs and pointing to the very defects in design for which the plaintiff contends. It is perfectly proper to negotiate hard on a defendant's behalf and attempt to settle the claim as cheaply as possible, or even to convince the plaintiff to withdraw his action. However, when one reaches the stage of discovery, since these documents are not privileged, when inspection takes place they must be revealed to the plaintiff. At that stage clearly the defendant's case would look hopeless. Discovery must then be carried out honestly despite the adverse nature of these documents.

12.1.2 TIME FOR DISCOVERY

In most actions begun by writ the parties must make so-called 'general discovery', i.e. disclose to each other the documents which they have in their possession, custody or power which are relevant to the action. Under *RSC Ord. 24, r. 2*, within 14 days after the close of the pleadings the plaintiff and defendant must exchange lists of all the relevant documents which have been or are still in their possession, custody or power.

The lists of documents must in principle be in the prescribed form which is described in **12.1.3**. In fact if there are very few documents and the nature of them is obvious, it may be agreed to list them in some more informal way, e.g. by letter, but it is generally best to adhere to the rules and insist on discovery in the appropriate form.

12.1.3 THE FORM OF THE LIST

The list of documents contains three separate sections: **Schedule I, Part I**, which is a list of documents which a party has in his possession and does not object to producing; **Schedule I, Part II**, listing documents which a party has and which he does object to producing, together with a statement of the grounds of his objection; and **Schedule II**, which lists documents which a party once had in his possession which are relevant to the action but which he no longer has.

An example of one document of each kind would be, in Schedule I, Part I, correspondence between the parties forming the basis of a contract; in Schedule I, Part II, a witness statement; in Schedule II, the original of some letter which had been sent to another person which was relevant to the action (the carbon copy of that letter being a document listed in Schedule I, Part I as still being in the party's possession).

In addition, at the end of the list there must be a statement of the time and place at which the documents in Schedule I, Part I will be made available for inspection, which must be in principle within seven days after the exchange of the lists. It is usual for solicitors to complete this statement by saying that a party will give inspection at any reasonable time on reasonable notice at the office of his solicitor. Unless the documents are very bulky, inspection generally takes place, by convention, by the defendant's solicitor attending at the plaintiff's solicitor's office with his documents so that mutual inspection can be carried out at one and the same time with saving of costs.

As an alternative to attending an opponent's office to inspect the documents physically, by virtue of *RSC Ord. 24, r. 11A*, a party may simply require the opponent to supply photocopies of the documents in his list which are considered to be of relevance. Accordingly, there is only very much point in attending a physical inspection if it is suspected that there may be something worth seeing in the very fabric of the document which may not reproduce on photocopying, or perhaps if the documents disclosed on discovery are very voluminous indeed so that a great deal of expense would be occasioned by simply asking for photocopies of them all.

12.1.4 RELEVANCE

Discovery must be made of documents which are ***relevant***. The question of relevance is not usually a difficult one. It includes documents which have to do with the subject matter of the action and also those which 'contain information which may enable the party either to advance his own case or to damage that of his adversary. Any document which may fairly lead him to a train of inquiry which may have either of these two consequences must be disclosed' (*Compagnie Financière et Commerciale du Pacifique* v *Peruvian Guano Co.* (1882) 11 QBD 55).

Thus, for example, in *Board* v *Thomas Hedley & Co. Ltd* [1951] 2 All ER 431, where an action was brought in negligence against the manufacturers of a washing powder alleging that dermatitis had been contracted from its use, the manufacturers (who had resisted doing so) were eventually ordered to give discovery of all other complaints of personal injuries made by persons who had used the product in the relevant period.

12.1.5 WHAT DOCUMENTS ARE PRIVILEGED?

Documents in Schedule I, Part II of the list are those which attract privilege. The subject of privilege has been considered more fully in **10.2**. In routine litigation one will only be concerned with documents which attract private privilege, and that is in particular communications between a solicitor and his client about any matter at all and communications between the solicitor and any other person in connection with the litigation. Examples of the latter would be statements obtained from eye-witnesses; expert witness reports; notes from, advice from, and instructions sent to counsel and so on.

Where a party's documents are within this head of privilege it is common to list them in Schedule I, Part II in a vague and uninformative way so that the opposite party is aware only in the most general terms of the nature of the document and, in the case of witness statements, is provided with no details about the date and the name and address of the maker. For example, a common way of completing Schedule I, Part II is to say 'instructions to and advice and notes from counsel; witness statements, expert witness reports and other documents prepared solely for the purpose of the litigation'.

We have so far discussed so-called automatic discovery. It is fair to say that this provision under *RSC Ord. 24, r. 2* is one of those most commonly ignored in practice, and many solicitors wait until the summons for directions to obtain an order for discovery, even though such is strictly speaking superfluous and they would have been entitled to discovery automatically as the rules provide. We now turn to the topic of orders for discovery.

12.1.6 ORDERS FOR DISCOVERY

Automatic discovery is not always applicable. There are several exceptions, the most important two of which are in third party proceedings (see **18.1**) and in the case of claims for damages for personal injuries arising out of an accident on land.

Automatic discovery in the case of a personal injury action arising out of an accident on land does not have to be as full as in other cases. In such a case:

(a) the defendant does not have to make any discovery at all; and

(b) discovery by the plaintiff is limited to documents relating to any special damages claimed (e.g. details of loss of earnings, tax rebates received, receipts for private medical treatment, etc.).

This apparently strange rule is simply a matter of expedience which recognises reality. In most such cases the defendant will not in fact have any documents which are relevant to the action. Nor will the plaintiff have any documents other than those relevant to special damages. This rule merely recognises routine situations, however. If it does in fact occur to one or other party that the opponent has some document which is important and is worth seeing, then an application can be made to the court to vary this prima facie rule and to ask for an order for discovery.

Where there is no automatic discovery or no full automatic discovery, as in the case of a road accident as we have discussed, a party may apply to the court on summons for an order for discovery. No affidavit in support is necessary. This matter is often left until the taking out of a summons for directions, which is a stage we consider at **13.1**. At the hearing of the summons a party may ask for either *general* discovery, whereby the opponent must list all relevant documents, or *particular* discovery, whereby a party can be ordered to list documents or a class of documents in a particular category. If a party is applying for particular discovery, he must show at the hearing of the summons the nature of the documents which it is believed the opponent has and why they are relevant to the case.

12.1.7 DISPUTES CONCERNING DISCOVERY

12.1.7.1 Disputes concerning the applicability of privilege

If one party has claimed privilege for a document and the other party disagrees that the document has that status, then naturally the matter can be determined by the court. Application should be made to the District Judge on summons (no affidavit is strictly speaking required) asking him to order that the document in respect of which privilege is claimed be disclosed for inspection. The party claiming privilege will then attend the hearing and a ruling can be obtained on the status of the document in question.

12.1.7.2 What if it is believed that an opponent has not made full and honest discovery?

In such a case there are three alternatives, though they all amount to much the same thing:

(a) The party can apply to his opponent, and if refused apply to the court by summons, for a *further and better list* of documents in a case where it appears from the list supplied, or the documents referred to in it or admissions made in the pleadings of the party concerned that there must be other relevant documents. Thus if, for example, the plaintiff discloses balance sheets of a business in his list of documents and the defendant wishes to see the accounts and working books of the firm from which these were compiled, this would be the appropriate procedure.

(b) *Particular* discovery (often also called *specific* discovery). A party may apply to the court for an order requiring another party to make an affidavit specifying a class of document or an individual document which that party believes he is withholding.

(c) Lastly, a party can apply to have the list already served confirmed on *affidavit*. The list completed and exchanged between the parties is not of course on oath. If a party believes there has been improper withholding of documents, he can go a stage further in bringing home the consequences of dishonest discovery by asking for an order that his opponent gives discovery on affidavit in which the opponent must make a sworn statement that the documents revealed by him are the only relevant ones. The consequences of swearing that affidavit falsely are obvious.

In respect of any of these three methods of attacking the completeness of an opponent's list, naturally it would be both courteous and cost efficient to write first to the opponent pointing out that you believe that the list is incomplete and that there are other material documents and indicating the nature of them. Only if there is then a refusal will the matter be taken further by way of summons to the District Judge.

12.1.8 NON-COMPLIANCE WITH AUTOMATIC DISCOVERY AND/OR AN ORDER FOR DISCOVERY

The procedure to be adopted in such cases is a good example of what should be done in the event of non-compliance by an opponent with *any* procedural requirement. First, application should be made back to the District Judge by summons for an order that the party in default comply either with the provisions of the rules on automatic discovery, or with the specific order for discovery which has been made earlier and is now ignored. The consequences will be that the party in default will inevitably be criticised by the District Judge and be required to pay the costs of the wasted hearing in any event. In addition, where a rule of court or specific order has been disobeyed, the party in default may have what is called an 'unless' order made against him. The nature of this order is that the court directs that the party carry out whatever step it is in respect of which he has made default within a further short period, typically seven or 14 days and that 'unless' he does so, if he is the plaintiff, his action is dismissed, or if he is the defendant his defence is struck out and judgment entered for the plaintiff. In either case this drastic sanction brings about the end of the action.

Moreover, either in addition to or in substitution for the previous remedy, by virtue of *RSC Ord. 24, r. 16*, there may be an application made by summons to a judge in open court to commit the party in default (and even if he is to blame, the party's solicitor) for contempt if discovery is not properly made as required. The judge will generally make a suspended order for committal which will only come into effect if the party in contempt does not purge his contempt by giving discovery properly within a very short further period. If there is failure to do so, the committal becomes operative and the party in default will be taken to prison.

12.1.9 MISUSE OF MATERIAL OBTAINED ON DISCOVERY

We have already briefly considered this in the section on privilege (see **10.2**). In principle, since one is required to complete discovery with absolute honesty, highly confidential documents may be disclosed. In order to protect a party who discloses those documents there is a principle that a party who obtains discovery from another party may use the documents so disclosed only for the purpose of conducting his own case in the present matter, and there is an implied undertaking by him not to use his knowledge of those documents for collateral purposes. Thus, for example, an action for defamation based on a document obtained in other proceedings, will ordinarily be stayed as an abuse of process of the court (*Riddick* v *Thames Board Mills Ltd* [1977] QB 881).

Where a party attempts to misuse documents obtained in litigation for other purposes, he may be restrained by an injunction. In addition such misuse of documents may be treated as a contempt of court. There is, however, a new principle contained in *RSC Ord. 24, r. 14A*, which provides that the implied undertaking not to use a document obtained on discovery for any purposes other than those of the present action, ceases to apply where that document has been read to, or by, the court or referred to in open court, unless the court otherwise orders. This happens because once the document is used in open court it comes into the public domain and its confidential nature no longer exists.

12.1.10 DISCOVERY AND INSPECTION AGAINST A NON-PARTY

It will be recalled that there was a procedure for obtaining discovery of a vital document even before the issue of a writ under *RSC Ord. 24, r. 7A*, in a personal injury case (see **4.1.4**). Although, subject to some few exceptions which are beyond the scope of this text, discovery can in general only be ordered as between opponents in an existing action, there is in a personal injury case a power to order a person who is not a party to the action to give discovery of some relevant document to one or other of the parties in the action. To take a very straightforward example, suppose that there is an action for damages for personal injuries for a plaintiff. The plaintiff's claim to future loss of earnings depends on obtaining a good deal of information from his present employers, and the employers are proving difficult about providing this information. If every avenue of reasonable approach has failed, then under the second limb of *RSC Ord. 24, r. 7A*, in a personal injury case only, either of the parties may apply as against a non-party (here the employer) for discovery and inspection of a relevant class of documents (here wages records and details of career structure of the plaintiff).

This method of application is by summons in the action. However, for the purpose of this single application only, the party against whom non-party discovery is sought must be added as a further defendant to the summons. (There is no need to amend the other documents of course.) The summons is then served on both the party against whom the application is made and on all other present parties to the action, and the court will, if the documents are indeed relevant for the progress of the action, make the order against the non-party.

There is a general provision that the non-party may obtain an order for his costs both in attending the application and in carrying out the court order, so that a person who had no actual interest in the litigation between the other parties is not prejudiced by having to perhaps spend time going through extensive employment records to obtain the necessary information.

It is obviously anomalous that this useful provision should only exist in personal injury proceedings. The court, in its inherent jurisdiction, has in fact now found a way round this restriction in the recent case of *Khanna* v *Lovell White Durrant (a firm)* [1995] 1 WLR 121. In this case the court held that it had a general power to allow the issue of a *subpoena duces tecum* compelling a witness to attend and bring documents with them at some date earlier than the trial itself. Thus a party can compel someone who is not a party to produce documents earlier than on the day of the trial. This is obviously a sensible provision because in both personal injury and non-personal injury cases it might well be inconvenient to have a person producing detailed evidence, especially in financial matters, only on the morning of the trial itself. Its production to the parties at an early stage would allow them to prepare proper computations, for example, in loss of income or loss of profits cases, which would obviously shorten the trial and make it more efficient by allowing financial evidence to be agreed.

We have so far dealt only with discovery of documents, but it is appropriate for completeness at this stage to deal with one further aspect, namely inspection of *property* in the possession of a non-party under *RSC Ord. 29, r. 7A*.

12.1.11 INSPECTION OF PROPERTY

Just as in the case of non-party discovery, once an action involving personal injury has commenced discovery can be ordered of any property in the possession of a non-party. Thus, in a personal injury case only, where some non-party has a thing which is either the subject matter of the action or as to which any question may arise, application may be made for an order that that person allow inspection, etc. of the thing in question. Thus, for example, if the vehicle which is alleged to have caused an accident has now been sold to a scrap yard, a summons can be taken out asking for an order obliging the owner of the scrap yard to allow inspection of the vehicle in question.

The procedure is exactly the same as in the case of non-party discovery, namely that a summons in the action is issued naming the non-party as an additional defendant for the purpose of this application only. An affidavit is required from the applicant's solicitor indicating the full basis for the application. There is a corresponding presumption that the costs of the application and of carrying out any order made will be payable to the non-party by the person requiring it.

We have now dealt with the basic provisions for discovery and inspection, but a number of other matters relevant to this general area ought now to be mentioned.

12.2 Interrogatories

We have just considered *RSC Ord. 24* (discovery). This has to do with the obligation to disclose material evidence in documentary form to an opponent unless a party can claim privilege against doing so. *Order 26* of the *Rules of the Supreme Court* has to do with *interrogatories,* which is a linked part of the process of discovery (indeed the old title for it was 'Discovery by Interrogatories').

12.2.1 NATURE OF INTERROGATORIES

The essential nature of interrogatories is that a list of questions is delivered to the opponent which the opponent may be required to answer on oath by affidavit. The point of interrogatories is usually to secure some kind of admission of a fact, or evidence of a relevant fact. There may be other ways of achieving this with less difficulty, e.g. by a request for further and better particulars of a pleading or a notice to admit facts. In addition, now that exchange of witness statements is the norm (see **12.3.2**), it may that interrogatories are often unnecessary.

Until 1990, interrogatories in routine actions were relatively rare because leave of the District Judge or Master was always necessary before interrogatories could be administered to opponents. With effect from 1990, however, new rules in *RSC Ord. 26* provided for the first time for the administering of interrogatories between the parties direct, without the party who sought to administer them needing leave of the court to do so.

12.2.2 THE PROCEDURE

Where a party wishes to serve interrogatories on his opponent, a list of questions is served which ends with a note specifying a period of time (which must be not less than 28 days from the date of service of the interrogatories) within which the interrogatories are to be answered. If the party to be interrogated is not an individual (e.g. a limited company) then the name of the individual by whom the interrogatories are to be answered must be included in the notice.

Interrogatories may be served without an order of the court on up to two occasions. However, a party served with interrogatories who contends that they are unnecessary or oppressive, or that some of them are within that category, may apply to the court for the interrogatories to be varied or withdrawn; and at that application the court may make any order that it thinks fit. That application is made by summons to the Master or District Judge.

It may be, therefore, that in most cases interrogatories which are unexceptionable will be served and answered direct without the intervention of the court. If there is a dispute by the recipient of the interrogatories as to their propriety, however, there will be a hearing, and at that time the relevant criterion for the District Judge in deciding whether the interrogatories are proper is whether the interrogatories are necessary either:

(a) for disposing fairly of the cause or matter; or

(b) for saving costs. (*RSC Ord. 26, r. 1.*)

The rule thus provides that interrogatories will only be allowed where they are of assistance in disposing fairly of a case, and therefore the court will always take into account offers of alternative methods of supplying the necessary information, e.g. by open letter, further and better particulars or in the course of exchange of witness statements.

12.2.3 ESTABLISHING THE ADMISSIBILITY OF INTERROGATORIES

In deciding whether interrogatories are of assistance in disposing of the matter, the relevant principle is that if the interrogatory has sufficient bearing on the question in issue or might form a step in establishing liability it should be admitted. In other words, interrogatories are admissible which go to support the applicant's case, or impeach or destroy his opponents. However, 'fishing interrogatories' will not be permitted. A fishing interrogatory is one which is speculative and delivered in the vague hope of finding an item of information which will support the interrogator's case.

Applying this principle is very difficult because one legitimate use of interrogatories is, of course, to discover facts which the party administering does not know, or at least to confirm facts which he only strongly suspects. Sadly, many of the authorities cited in the notes to *RSC Ord. 26* are very old, a significant majority of them being in fact from before the First World War, and the principles remain unclear even to experienced litigators. The following principles may be relevant, however:

(a) Interrogatories will not be allowed where it is plain that no admission can be obtained, e.g. where the interrogatory in effect asks the opposite party to concede the plaintiff's case.

(b) Interrogatories will not generally be allowed to secure an admission of facts solely within the knowledge of the party administering the interrogatories.

(c) Interrogatories will not generally be allowed for the purpose of securing an admission of something which is a matter of opinion.

(d) Oppressive interrogatories will not be allowed (though the test for what is oppressive is obscure).

(e) Interrogatories will not be allowed with a view to limiting the opponent's case if there is some other way of doing this, e.g. by a request for further and better particulars.

(f) Interrogatories as to *evidence* as opposed to *facts* will not be allowed. The distinction between facts and the evidence to prove them may be one of some difficulty, as mentioned earlier in the section on pleadings.

(g) Interrogatories relating solely to the *credit* of a witness as opposed to *facts* will not be allowed.

(h) In the recent case of *Hall* v *Selvaco Ltd* (1996) *The Times*, 27 March 1996 the court observed that 'interrogatories must not be regarded as a source of ammunition to be routinely discharged as part of an interlocutory bombardment preceding the main battle' and held that in a personal injury case it was inappropriate to order interrogatories before exchange of witness statements or receipt of answers to a request for further and better particulars.

12.2.4 SUMMARY

Interrogatories were relatively rarely used before 1990. From 1990 they became extremely popular, with parties in even the most routine of cases commonly sending detailed questionnaires to each other to obtain evidence on oath with a view to cutting down the areas of dispute at trial. The popularity of interrogatories may have been significantly reduced, however, by the rule making mandatory the exchange of statements of witnesses of fact which came into force in November 1992. As a result of this rule, parties should go to trial significantly better informed about each other's cases than previously, and it is incumbent on parties to disclose the evidence about their cases in the very fullest form since any omissions will not be capable of remedy at trial.

The answers obtained on oath to interrogatories may of course be put in evidence at trial, either as direct evidence of a fact, to refute a previous inconsistent statement by that witness, or as the case may be.

12.3 Exchange of Witness Statements

12.3.1 INTRODUCTION

Until relatively recently it could be said that the dominant features of English civil procedure were that all evidence would be oral and that each party would be able to run his case in the way that he preferred (and in particular that each party would be able substantially to keep his case secret from his opponent until trial). It was actually considered that advantages of surprise at trial might assist the court in finding the truth.

Judicial and other criticism has led over the past 15 years to an almost complete *volte face* on this principle, so that now a good deal of the evidence at trial is written rather than oral and that in almost all instances there should be minimal elements of surprise in a civil trial, each party being made fully aware of the other party's case not just in the form of pleadings but by orders for exchange of written statements of oral evidence before trial. This has been the case in respect of *expert evidence* (see **12.4**) for many years. In the case of *witnesses of fact*, a rule has existed for some time in the more specialised courts – in particular the Commercial Court, the Official Referee's Court (which deals mainly with construction disputes) and in the Chancery Division – requiring each party to exchange the written statements of those witnesses of fact whom the parties wish to call at trial well in advance of trial. That provision was extended to the Queen's Bench Division and the county court in 1988, but it provided only that the court *could make* such an order if it was so inclined or the parties were in agreement. In November 1992, however, the relevant rule, *RSC Ord. 38, r. 2A*, was redrafted to provide that an order for the exchange of witness statements is virtually mandatory.

12.3.2 THE PROCEDURE UNDER *RSC ORDER 38, RULE 2A*

Order 38, r. 2A provides:

> *The powers of the court under this rule shall be exercised for the purpose of disposing fairly and expeditiously of the cause or matter before it and saving costs, having regard to all the circumstances of the case, including, but not limited to,*

> *(a) The extent to which the facts are in dispute or have been admitted.*
>
> *(b) The extent to which the issues of fact are defined by the pleadings.*
>
> *(c) The extent to which information has been or is likely to be provided by further and better particulars, answers to interrogatories or otherwise.*
>
> *. . . the court shall direct every party to serve on other parties within 14 weeks [10 weeks in County Court] . . . written statements of the oral evidence which the party intends to adduce on any issues of fact to be decided at trial.*

Corresponding provisions to this are inserted in automatic directions applicable to personal injury cases in *RSC Ord. 25, r. 8(1)* and in county court automatic directions in *CCR Ord. 17, r. 11(3)*, with a corresponding presumption in the county court at pre-trial review in those cases where there are no automatic directions. See **21.3**.

The objects of this rule are to enable the parties to identify the real issues in dispute; to end 'trial by ambush'; to make more effective cross-examination; to increase the likelihood of facts being admitted and encourage early settlement.

We have already discussed (in particular in the sections on early preparation and on evidence), the effect that this provision has. It means that a 'cards on the table' approach is now almost inevitable, because even if both parties are in agreement that they do not want prior disclosure of evidence, the rule in effect virtually compels it by requiring that the court 'shall' make such an order. This will have a great effect on how parties conduct litigation because it will require the taking of very thorough witness statements at an early stage with a view to exchange.

12.3.3 PRACTICAL CONSIDERATIONS

The following points should be noted:

12.3.3.1 Proper drafting of witness statements

The witness statements for exchange must be formally drafted. They must be in numbered paragraphs and must be signed by the witness unless there is good reason (e.g. the witness died before he could sign). In addition, there must be a statement in the text by the witness that the contents of the statement are true to the best of his knowledge and belief.

12.3.3.2 Identification of relevant documents

Any documents referred to in the witness statement must be properly identified.

12.3.3.3 Presumption of simultaneous exchange

There is a presumption that the witness statements will be exchanged simultaneously. In other words, the court will fix a day for mutual exchange and the parties will be expected to comply with that. It should be borne in mind that there would be significant advantages in one of the parties being allowed to serve his statements subsequent to receipt of his opponent's because he would have the opportunity to adapt his witness's evidence to deal with points which might take him by surprise in that evidence. This is the reason why simultaneous exchange will be the norm, and only very exceptionally will sequential exchange be permitted.

If one party is not ready for exchange on the appropriate day he should give his opponent early intimation of the fact. There is a specific provision in the Rules that it is not open to the parties between themselves to vary the day imposed by the court and to grant each other extensions of time and, thus, an application to the court is necessary in every case where one of the parties cannot comply with the date for exchange ordered. The court will be relatively liberal in permitting the parties to fix a new timetable within reason, so long as it is not too close to the date of trial so that there will be difficulty caused with the possible need for adjournment of the trial. The principles are set out in the case of *The Mortgage Corporation* v *Sandoes, The Times*, 27 December 1996 (although that case concerned the county court where a slightly different rule applies).

12.3.3.4 The statement as evidence in chief

A judge may direct that the statement served, or part of it, stand as evidence in chief, that is to say that the witness will simply take the witness-box and confirm on oath that his statement is true. This may have the useful effect of shortening trials but is not inevitably to be accepted in every case. The act of drawing evidence from a witness may provide useful indications as to his credibility. However, *Practice Direction (Civil Litigation: Case Management)*, issued by the Lord Chief Justice on 25 January 1995, the full text of which is set out at **14.6.4**, indicates that in the High Court at least there will be a very strong presumption that the statement is to be used as evidence-in-chief.

12.3.3.5 Where the maker is not called as a witness

If a party who has served a witness statement does not then call the witness concerned, no other party may put the statement in evidence. This is therefore a valuable safeguard. It should be borne in mind, however, that the serving of the witness statement may indicate lines of enquiry for an opponent of which he had not previously been aware, and therefore great care will be needed in assessing the evidence as to whether it is worth exchanging.

If a witness has given a statement and it is not intended to call the witness at all, and a party knows that at the earlier stage, then nothing compels exchange of the witness statement. The statement is privileged and remains so. It is only witness statements from witnesses who are *to be called at trial* which matter and where a party is required as a condition of calling the witness to waive the privilege and disclose the statement.

12.3.3.6 Contents of statements

Nothing in *RSC Ord. 38, r. 2A*, makes inadmissible evidence admissible, and consequently the statements must be drafted with great care for two different reasons. First, they must contain only matter which is acceptable under the rules of evidence and thus inadmissible opinion, or speculation must be edited out of them. Since the coming into force of the *Civil Evidence Act 1995* however, it will be permissible for the statements to contain hearsay (see **9.1**). Secondly, however, it must be borne in mind that the statement must be absolutely thorough and must contain everything which one would have hoped for in evidence in chief from that witness. In particular, in regard to personal injury cases, it is often overlooked that witnesses will need to deal thoroughly with all aspects of quantum as well as with the establishing of liability; and this is particularly true of the plaintiff's own statement since the rule of course extends to statements of the parties. Thus a plaintiff will have to describe comprehensively the way in which the accident has affected his life, not merely in terms of the more obvious matters such as loss of future earnings, but in terms of more marginal things which may nonetheless have a significant financial value attributable to them, such as loss of amenity in being deprived of the opportunity to practise a favourite sport or hobby. Witnesses must likewise give full statements in relation to quantum, e.g. members of the family who can confirm that a plaintiff's life has been significantly affected by his inability to follow a favourite hobby.

12.3.3.7 Failure to exchange witness statements

If a party fails to comply with a direction for the exchange of witness statements he will not be entitled to adduce that evidence without leave of the court. This means that not only will he not be able to call a witness at all unless the witness's statement has been exchanged, but also, if a material matter has been omitted from the statement, the court is likely to stop the witness testifying about that matter at trial. Alternatively, if the subject matter is of great importance, the court may allow an adjournment, but this will inevitably be at the expense of the party needing it, or his solicitor. Every care should therefore be taken to ensure that all witnesses deal thoroughly with all relevant matters.

12.3.3.8 Where a witness statement cannot be obtained

If a party is unable to obtain a witness statement in writing from an intended witness, the court may direct the party wishing to adduce that witness's evidence to provide the other party with the name of the witness and a statement of the nature of the evidence intended to be adduced. This is thus a useful provision for the rare case where someone cannot obtain a witness statement because the witness is uncooperative.

Normally it is very unwise to call witnesses from whom one has not obtained full cooperation and a statement, but just occasionally there is no alternative. A commonly encountered example is that of a truculent workmate of the plaintiff who saw an accident but insists he does not wish to get involved but where, if the plaintiff wishes to risk it and subpoena the witness, one may expect him to tell the truth. That this is tactically undesirable is obvious, and unfortunately the plaintiff will have to give the game away that the witness is potentially uncooperative by being unable to supply a copy of his statement. The rule may provide a useful backstop for extreme cases, however.

12.3.3.9 Practical problems associated with timely exchange

There are clearly practical problems in the rule. If new material arises after the exchange of statements, or if on seeing an opponent's statement a crucial, forgotten matter is recalled, a party will have to apply to the court for permission to serve a supplemental or an amended statement. In cases of bona fide oversight this may well be allowed, but inevitably the witness's credibility about the forgotten matter will be impaired and this is something which will have to be faced. For this reason it can only be stressed again that statements in the most thorough form should be prepared.

In cases of difficulty, extra matter, even if superfluous, should be inserted from an abundance of caution. The statements should, of course, be drafted by the solicitor, perhaps in difficult cases in collaboration with counsel, who may need to be consulted on tactical or evidential matters. Counsel may indeed wish to assist in drafting statements to ensure that they comply with the rules of evidence and, perhaps, that there are no hostages to fortune given in the materials supplied to the opponent.

12.3.4 SUMMARY

As has been observed before, the fact that an order under *Ord. 38, r. 2A* is inevitable may have an effect on the number of applications for further and better particulars or interrogatories, which may now be virtually superfluous in view of the full disclosure of each party's evidence to the other, well in advance of trial. It is inevitably the case that settlement is likely to be encouraged in the light of this full disclosure.

As will be described later (**12.5**), copies of the statements exchanged have to be lodged at court for the use of the trial judge in advance of trial, together with an indication of the extent to which the contents of those reports are agreed. The opponent's statements when obtained should of course be discussed with your own client and relevant witnesses, and then you will need scrupulously to go through them to see to what extent that is non-controversial or agreed matter.

12.4 Expert Evidence

12.4.1 LIMITATIONS ON THE USE OF EXPERT WITNESSES

So far as ordinary witnesses are concerned, no restrictions whatsoever are placed upon the right of the parties to call as many witnesses as they like no matter how repetitive. In the case of expert witnesses, however, there is more specific provision under *RSC Ord. 38, rr. 35–44*, which constitute a code in relation to expert evidence.

In the first place, a party's right to call any expert evidence he chooses has been restricted so that he can only do so with the leave of the court or by agreement between the parties, or subject to compliance with the direction of the court that he should disclose before the trial the substance of such expert evidence to all other parties.

Secondly, the court will in any event limit the number of experts who may be called. In the normal situation the court will allow no more than one expert to be called by each party on the subject matter of each specialism. In a case involving serious personal injuries this may nonetheless mean that each party may call several expert witnesses, but each one will be in respect of a different aspect of the plaintiff's injuries.

Thirdly, the right of a party to withhold disclosure of his own expert evidence until trial has been modified by the provision that he may be required to make such disclosure before trial as a condition precedent to using the evidence at trial by calling the witness.

These rules make a significant advance in the direction of more open pre-trial proceedings so as to enable the parties to prepare and present their respective cases on the basis of the full facts rather than proceeding half in the dark. This is an example of the progress towards more open trial generally, of which the rule relating to the exchange of witness statements (*Ord. 38, r. 2A*) is a further significant example.

The objects intended to be achieved by the rules are described as including the following:

(a) To assist the parties to reach a settlement on a fair basis in the light rather than in the dark in relation to expert evidence.

(b) To avoid surprise at the trial.

(c) To secure agreed experts' reports, thus obviating the need for the attendance of experts at the trial.

(d) To shorten the evidence at the trial by identifying the matters of expert opinion which are really in dispute.

(e) To enable the experts themselves to prepare their evidence on those matters more thoroughly and helpfully.

In these ways the rules are designed to improve the conduct and quality of civil trials by reducing costs, delay and the unnecessary attendance at the trial of experts where there is no significant disagreement between them. Inevitably also, the rules lead to the settlement of a greater proportion of matters since parties no longer go to trial completely in the dark about each other's cases.

12.4.2 DISCLOSURE OF EXPERTS' REPORTS

A party who is calling expert evidence, whether on liability or quantum, needs to consider well in advance how he is to approach the trial. The rules as to disclosure make no difference whatsoever to the substantive law of privilege. An expert's report obtained for the purpose of litigation is still a privileged document, and thus nothing can *make* a party disclose it. So if a party's expert evidence is unhelpful to his case (for example, where a medical specialist to whom a client was sent suggested that the client would make a very quick recovery from the accident and a second more helpful report is obtained from a second consultant) there is no need to disclose the contents of the first report or to call the first expert at trial. Only in relation to the second helpful report is there likely to be prior disclosure.

In relation to expert evidence, therefore, there are the following possibilities:

(a) The court can be asked to give leave for the expert to be called at trial without disclosure of his report in advance. It is highly unlikely, save in the most unusual circumstances, that such an order would be made given the very strong presumption in favour of disclosure and the current atmosphere of openness and frankness in litigation.

(b) Alternatively, all parties may agree that they will call their expert evidence at trial without prior disclosure. This second approach, although possible in theory, would be extremely rare in practice. There is very little to be gained by adopting it, and it would be extremely likely that the trial judge would be displeased that no prior disclosure had been undertaken if the trial was significantly lengthened by this, as would appear probable.

(c) Instead of (a) or (b) above, a party can ask for a direction from the court in advance of the trial (usually at the summons for directions), in which case that direction will almost inevitably be for prior disclosure of the expert evidence on which he wishes to rely at trial; or, in a personal injury case, a party can comply with the automatic directions which similarly provide for such disclosure.

If there is a hearing about the matter at summons for directions or otherwise, the Master or District Judge will prima facie wish to make a direction in similar terms to the provisions currently found in the automatic directions (see **13.2**). That is that each party disclose to the other the substance of his expert evidence in the form of a written report within a specified time. The principle contained in *RSC Ord. 38, r. 36*, is that, unless the court considers that there is sufficient reason for not doing so, it *shall* direct that the substance of the evidence be disclosed in the form of a written report or reports to such other parties and within such periods as the court may specify.

In other words, there is a very clear onus on the person who seeks an order that there should not be prior disclosure of expert evidence to satisfy the court as to what exceptional circumstances there are which justify this.

We shall now further consider the question of expert evidence in the light of this ultimate probability that there will be an order for it to be disclosed in advance.

12.4.3 COMMISSIONING EXPERTS' REPORTS

If anything in the case is likely to require expert evidence the plaintiff will, at a very early stage, have commissioned his own expert's report. In the case of a commercial contract action that may well be a report on the subject matter of the action, e.g. some mechanical equipment, a building or other structure, or an accountant's or auditor's report. In the case of personal injuries there may be a requirement for reports on liability, such as an engineer's report, and on quantum such as medical reports or accountant's reports about loss of earnings. For present purposes we concentrate on the case of the medical report in personal injuries litigation since most of the relevant case law deals with that situation.

12.4.4 MEDICAL REPORTS IN PERSONAL INJURIES LITIGATION

12.4.4.1 Initial report for the plaintiff

The plaintiff will have obtained an early report of some kind, bearing in mind that a medical report substantiating the injuries must be served with the statement of claim. That report need not necessarily be the report from the plaintiff's final choice of medico-legal expert, and it may well be that a brief report from the hospital casualty officer will suffice for service with the statement of claim. Inevitably, however, the plaintiff will eventually want to collect full medical evidence about his condition.

12.4.4.2 The defendant's medical report

The defendant will soon also want his own medical report carried out if the case is one of any substance. The plaintiff must allow him the facilities for this, and if the plaintiff refuses then the court will *stay* the plaintiff's action until he consents. See *Edmeades* v *Thames Board Mills Ltd* [1969] 2 QB 67. It is possible, however, to insist on reasonable conditions being imposed as the price of granting facilities for a medical examination. Suitable conditions might be the following:

(a) That the defendant immediately pays the expenses of the plaintiff in travelling to attend the examination and any loss of earnings.

(b) That if for any reason the plaintiff is particularly nervous, especially in the case of a child, a friend or relative be present.

(c) That only the defendant's specialist will be present and no other person (e.g. a representative of the insurance company).

(d) The defendant's doctor will only examine injuries caused in the accident and will not attempt to discuss the circumstances of the accident with the plaintiff.

Those are the only conditions which will normally be upheld without difficulty in the case of dispute. Other more doubtful conditions which plaintiffs sometimes attempt to impose are:

(e) That the defendant must immediately disclose the contents of the report to the plaintiff's solicitors. This condition would not have been acceptable until relatively recently. There is now a possible argument, however, that since the plaintiff's solicitors have to disclose their own medical report on service of the statement of claim, there ought to be reciprocity (since there is actually no provision that the defendant must disclose his report with his defence and he is in principle entitled to wait to disclose it until the stage fixed by automatic directions which is described more fully at **13.2**, but which comes relatively late in the case). There is, therefore, some justification in arguing for this condition since the defendant will in fact be better informed at this stage than will the plaintiff's own solicitors about the plaintiff's injuries because the defendant will have his own medical report as well as that of the plaintiff. In particular, this will enable him to make a relatively well informed payment into court which may have serious tactical consequences for the plaintiff, see **16.1**. It remains to be seen, however, whether such a condition will be upheld as reasonable by the courts. To the writer's knowledge individual District Judges have upheld a condition in terms that the defendant decides within 14 days whether he wishes to rely on the report at trial and, if so, directing him to disclose it forthwith. Everything will depend on the facts of individual cases.

(f) The plaintiff will not be allowed to reject the defendant's choice of doctor unless the facts are very extreme. Suggestions that a certain defendant's doctor is hostile, aggressive and only ever acts for defendants' insurance companies *might* ground an objection, and there is a note in the 'White Book' which suggests that it may be prudent for the defendant to offer a choice of specialists, though little case law supports this view.

(g) A condition that the defendant's doctor can only examine the injuries in the presence of the plaintiff's doctor. This would not usually be upheld unless the facts were exceptional.

12.4.4.3 Practical matters

The plaintiff should be warned in advance of the examination that the defendant's doctor does not stand in a normal doctor-patient relationship with him and that there will be no requirement of confidentiality. He should be warned not to discuss any aspect of the causes of the accident. Although in principle medical witnesses should be disinterested and objective, it is the experience of all personal injury solicitors that medical witnesses may appear relatively partial (though for further discussion of this see **12.4.5.2** below).

12.4.4.4 Cooperation with the defendant's doctor

The plaintiff must, of course, cooperate with the defendant's doctor to a reasonable extent. He must do exercises if required for the purpose of testing and observation, e.g. leg lifting, bending etc. If the defendant's doctor wishes to carry out tests on the plaintiff, then the extent to which he should be permitted to do so will vary with the facts of each case. It will be important for the court to balance the plaintiff's right to privacy and not to have intrusions on his body with the defendant's right to defend himself in the litigation. Painful or dangerous procedures or tests will not be considered reasonable (*Prescott* v *Bulldog Tools Ltd* [1981] 3 All ER 869).

12.4.4.5 Updating the evidence

Naturally the plaintiff's own medical evidence will be updated at frequent intervals, perhaps as often as every six months as the case progresses. The defendant is likewise entitled to update his medical evidence at reasonable intervals, and indeed to have the plaintiff examined by a specialist in each of the specialisms concerned. This may involve the plaintiff submitting to numerous medical examinations over the course of each year during the litigation.

12.4.4.6 Voluntary disclosure

In many situations the parties undertake voluntary early disclosure of their reports. If a report is wholly favourable to a plaintiff (for example, if it says that a plaintiff is clearly badly injured and that no firm prognosis can be achieved for a year or more), there is little harm in forwarding this to the defendant (or even his insurers) at an early stage before the writ is issued. In such situations often the defendant will voluntarily disclose his own reports as a reciprocal courtesy, especially given the ultimate probability that disclosure will be ordered by the court. If proceedings are issued, as we have seen, the plaintiff will have to serve a medical report of some kind with his statement of claim.

12.4.5 THE CONTENTS OF EXPERTS' REPORTS

12.4.5.1 In general

Experts' reports should fully summarise the issues involved and then give as firm a view as possible on the question posed to the expert, whether it be as to liability for causation of an accident, prognosis for a plaintiff's return to work, the impact of tax on a plaintiff's loss of earnings or whatever. Reports should allude specifically to any professional publications or research data on which the expert relies.

12.4.5.2 The responsibilities of expert witnesses

As indicated above, experts' reports often appear far from impartial and sometimes tend very definitely to favour the case of the party instructing the expert. Sometimes matters would even be taken to the length of a party receiving a draft expert's report containing his provisional views and then submitting this to counsel for redrafting in a more favourable light. This practice was deprecated by the House of Lords in the important case of *Whitehouse* v *Jordan* [1981] 1 WLR 246, where counsel in fact deleted relevant aspects of the expert's preliminary view in the final draft of the report. Nevertheless, the practice continued, to the extent that some experts would submit a report for disclosure wholly favourable to the party instructing them together with (on a separate piece of paper) a so-called 'confidential conclusion', often pointing to the diametrically opposite view. Something like this happened in the case of *Kenning* v *Eve Construction Ltd* [1989] 1 WLR 1189, where the defendant's expert's report for disclosure contained a view highly adverse to the plaintiff's case but was accompanied by a further report indicating that in all probability the plaintiff's case was soundly based, although wrongly pleaded. By accident the confidential conclusion was disclosed as well as the main body of the report. The court concluded that reports in such form were improper and that it was incumbent upon an expert to give his full, honest view.

That view was subject to some further discussion in other cases particularly *Derby & Co. Ltd* v *Weldon (No. 9)* (1990) *The Times*, 9 November 1990, but the position is now clarified by the leading case *National Justice Compania Naviera SA* v *Prudential Assurance Co. Ltd* [1993] 2 Lloyd's Rep 68 which lays down the principles on which expert witnesses should testify and emphasises their responsibilities as follows:

(a) Expert evidence presented to a court should be and should be seen to be the independent product of the expert, uninfluenced as to form or content by the exigences of litigation.

(b) Independent assistance should be provided to the court by way of objective, unbiased opinion regarding matters within the expertise of the expert witness. An expert witness should never assume the role of advocate.

(c) Facts or assumptions upon which the opinion was based should be stated together with material facts which could detract from the concluded opinion.

(d) An expert witness should make it clear when a question or an issue falls outside his expertise.

(e) If the opinion was not properly researched because it was considered that insufficient data were available, then that has to be stated with an indication that the opinion is provisional. If the witness cannot assert that the report contains the truth, the whole truth and nothing but the truth, then that qualification should be stated on the report.

(f) If after exchange of reports an expert witness changes his mind on a material matter, the change of view should be communicated to the other side and, where appropriate, to the court.

(g) Photographs, plans, survey reports and other documents referred to in the expert evidence must be provided to the other side at the same time as the exchange of reports.

These matters should therefore be carefully borne in mind when instructing an expert and using his report. The common practice of certain specialists, especially in orthopaedic injury cases, being either 'plaintiffs' men' or 'defendants' men', and almost always coming down firmly in matters of any doubt in favour of the party who instructs them is likely now to cease.

Experts who only ever testify for either plaintiffs or defendants are likely to forfeit all credibility in the eyes of trial judges and their evidence will come to be seen as of little objective value. Experts who are prepared to act equally for either side and always reach a measured conclusion sustainable under cross-examination are much more likely now to attain the respect of judges and thus to be of greater use to the parties who instruct them.

12.4.6 REVIEWING OPPOSING EXPERTS' REPORTS

As has been briefly discussed earlier, having obtained an expert's report a party should use that expert to review and comment on the reports obtained from the opponent throughout the litigation. This will be an essential guide for counsel in preparing cross-examination of the opposing expert before trial. Thus at all stages the opponent's expert's engineers, medical or accountants reports, as the case may be, should be sent to one's own specialist asking for his comments on them, and whether, if the terminology appears different, his evidence could be said to tally with the opposing report.

If the experts are in truth agreed and the reports can be put together in an agreed bundle for the trial judge then neither expert needs to be called. Although the reports are of course hearsay, there is no need to go through the strict provisions and formalities of serving them in the form required for witness statements. If there continues to be disagreement, then notice will need to be given that the opponent's expert's report is not accepted and that a party will be calling his own expert.

12.4.7 ORDER FOR MEETINGS OF EXPERTS

By *RSC Ord. 38, r. 38,* it is provided that the court may in any case direct that there be a meeting on 'without prejudice' terms of such experts as the court may specify for the purpose of identifying those parts of their evidence which are in issue. After such meeting the experts may prepare a joint statement indicating those parts of their evidence on which they are in agreement or not.

This useful provision allows the court to order what was in many cases undertaken as a matter of good practice between the parties anyway. If the case is one of personal injuries, the plaintiff's and defendant's specialists may even carry out a joint examination of the plaintiff and prepare a joint report identifying their precise differences.

12.5 Documents for Trial

Under the rules now relating to the preparation of the bundle of documents for trial (*RSC Ord. 34*), a bundle is to be prepared comprising the witness statements which have been exchanged together with the experts' reports which have been disclosed, with an indication of the extent to which the contents of the documents are agreed. Thus a judge will, well before the trial, have access to those reports and will be able thoroughly to familiarise himself with the relevant issues in contention. See **14.6**.

The question of preparation and management of documents for trial in the High Court, and especially in lengthy trials, will now be significantly affected by the Lord Chief Justice's *Practice Direction (Civil Litigation: Case Management)* dated 25 January 1995, the full contents of which are set out at **14.6.4**.

A strict compliance with that Practice Direction is likely to be required in all High Court cases in future and thus the documents must be prepared in meticulous form in readiness for the trial judge.

THIRTEEN

DIRECTIONS

The directions stage of an action occurs in the High Court after close of pleadings. It is the culmination of the preparatory stage of a civil action. In this chapter we first consider the High Court directions stage as it is relevant in a contract or commercial action, and then go on to consider a personal injuries case, because there are significant differences between the two.

13.1 Summons for Directions in the High Court

As has been stressed in discussing the procedures so far described, the Queen's Bench Division of the High Court remains passive throughout the course of the proceedings. With the exception of the writ which is issued at court and the acknowledgement of service which must be returned to the court before a copy is sent out to the plaintiff, all further proceedings pass between the parties directly. Pleadings are served directly and no copy is sent to the court; and unless one party or other requires an order for something which his opponent is unwilling to give voluntarily, there is no need in an ordinary case for either party to make applications to the court.

The first time the parties come before the court and the court takes some initiative in controlling the future running of the case is the directions stage. It might be expected from looking at the time specified for the early steps in the 'White Book', that this stage would be reached about two months after the writ has been issued and served. This is only rarely the case, however. Even in the most vigorously fought case, the parties' solicitors usually remain on sufficiently good professional terms mutually to grant reasonable extensions of time, e.g. for serving pleadings. In personal injury cases, it would invariably be wise and in the plaintiff's best interest to wait until his medical condition has stabilised before pressing on to trial, and in contract cases the desire to proceed quickly must be balanced against the need to ensure that one is ready for each subsequent stage and has collected all the necessary evidence, and thus delays are often inevitable.

Before looking at the procedure at a summons for directions, it should be noted that in some cases the directions stage is pre-empted when the District Judge treats as a summons for directions a summons issued for some other purpose, e.g. an application for summary judgment (see **17.2**), or for an interim payment (see **16.5**); and in personal injury actions, the summons for directions is usually unnecessary because *automatic directions* apply (see **13.2**).

13.1.1 PROCEDURE

Order 25 of the *Rules of the Supreme Court* requires the plaintiff to take out a summons for directions within one month after the close of pleadings. This is done by completing a standard printed form available from law stationers, or increasingly by preparing one from a precedent held on a word processor. Both forms list the directions most commonly sought together with some blanks in which any extra or further directions not accommodated in the main text can be inserted.

The plaintiff indicates on the summons for directions the directions which he is seeking by crossing out the *numbers* of those paragraphs (not the whole paragraph) which he is *not* seeking, and by filling in the relevant details in those which he requires. It is common for the plaintiff to indicate by letter to the defendant what directions he proposes to seek and to ask if the defendant has any objection, or if there is likely to be anything contentious at the summons for directions. This is so that an appropriate length of hearing may be obtained, because if there are serious contentious issues the usual short appointment of 15 minutes or so will be inadequate.

Two copies of the summons for directions are taken to the court office and a hearing date will be allocated, giving the length of hearing which has been estimated by the plaintiff or by the parties by consent. As indicated above, this is usually a fairly short appointment. It is necessary at this stage to lodge at the court office, with the court copy of the summons for directions, copies of the pleadings, and this is the first time the court receives these documents. A copy is then served on the defendant.

13.1.2 WHERE THE PLAINTIFF FAILS TO ISSUE THE SUMMONS FOR DIRECTIONS

If the plaintiff does not issue a summons for directions, what the defendant does then is very much a matter of tactics. If the defendant wishes to appear positive and aggressive he can himself issue the summons for directions, thus indicating his confidence in his position and his desire to press on to trial to have the matter resolved. More normally, however, a defendant does nothing. He will hope that the plaintiff lets the action 'go to sleep' for long enough to give him the opportunity of applying to have it dismissed for want of prosecution. Most of the case law on want of prosecution (a topic which is dealt with at **17.9** below) shows that the stage of an action at which a dilatory plaintiff fails to progress the case properly is the summons for directions, and for that reason the case law on dismissal for want of prosecution is set out in the text of the 'White Book' after *Ord. 25*, even though as a topic dismissal of want of prosecution has nothing to do with the summons for directions itself.

As we shall see at **17.9** below, in the High Court a quite remarkable length of inactivity is required before the defendant is to have any hope of successfully applying to have a case struck out for want of prosecution, but, nonetheless, as the Law Reports show, it does happen in a considerable number of cases.

13.1.3 FORM OF THE SUMMONS FOR DIRECTIONS

The summons has the heading in the action and the plaintiff should then deal with each of the numbered paragraphs. The full form is illustrated at **13.5** below.

13.1.3.1 Paragraph 1: Consolidation

Consolidation of two or more actions into one may be sought where either there is some common question of law or fact in each case, or the rights to relief claimed in each arose out of the same transaction or series of transactions, or where consolidation is desirable for some other reason. This topic is discussed in more detail at **6.2**.

13.1.3.2 Paragraph 2: Trial by Official Referee

Either party can apply for trial by Official Referee. The Official Referee is a judge who has a specialist jurisdiction, particularly in matters to do with disputes involving technical evidence especially in the construction industry. This paragraph is rarely required because matters involving such disputes are usually commenced in the Official Referee's court in the first place.

13.1.3.3 **Paragraph 3: Transfer to the county court**

This may arise because one of the parties requests it, but the District Judge will, in any event, consider it himself (see **5.3.2**).

13.1.3.4 **Paragraphs 4 and 5: Amendments**

This is one matter which the District Judge will consider. Unless there is something manifestly inadequate in the pleadings which will need correction, it is most unusual for a District Judge to take the initiative in suggesting amendment if it has not previously occurred to the parties.

13.1.3.5 **Paragraph 6: Further and better particulars**

These will usually have been requested by letter. If no, or no adequate, further and better particulars have been given, it is usual to delay asking for an order until the summons for directions.

13.1.3.6 **Paragraphs 7 and 8: Discovery and inspection**

This should take place before the summons for direction is heard. It is included in the prescribed form of summons for use in the exceptional cases which do not require automatic discovery, or where the parties have failed for tactical reasons or simple slackness to complete automatic discovery and inspection under *RSC Ord. 24, r. 2*.

13.1.3.7 **Paragraph 9: Retention, preservation and inspection of property**

This paragraph is rarely required for the simple reason that the summons for directions comes too late for this to be material. If there was any need to ensure that property was preserved until trial, it would usually have been essential for the party who required such retention, etc. to have applied by summons before this stage, and indeed possibly before the writ itself was issued under *RSC Ord. 29, r. 7A*.

13.1.3.8 **Paragraph 10: Expert evidence**

This is the paragraph which deals with expert evidence, both in terms of requiring prior disclosure and in limiting the number of expert witnesses. This topic is discussed at **12.4**.

13.1.3.9 **Paragraph 11: Exchange of witness statements**

Paragraph 11 provides a direction for exchange of the statements of witnesses of fact together with an exchange date and a requirement that the statements so exchanged be lodged with the court on setting down.

13.1.3.10 **Paragraph 12: Other directions**

This paragraph is left blank for any other out of the ordinary directions to be applied for. This might be used for application for any of the other procedural orders which we have discussed elsewhere in the text, e.g. for leave to administer further interrogatories. If the requirement is for numerous further directions so that they cannot be accommodated within the prescribed form, a separate sheet may be attached.

13.1.3.11 Paragraph 13: Directions for trial

An order will be made for the trial centre which is the most convenient for witnesses, parties, counsel and the solicitors, although the District Judge may also consider the most convenient place for the court itself, e.g. where the case has hitherto been proceeding in a District Registry which is equidistant between two or three trial centres and it is known to the District Judge that the lists are much shorter at one rather than another so that the case can be called on much more quickly at one particular trial centre.

The mode of trial will need to be ordered. This is almost inevitably going to be by 'judge alone', the use of the civil jury now being restricted to cases of defamation, false imprisonment, malicious prosecution and those involving allegations of fraud. A listing category must also be given. Category A cases are of great substance, difficulty or public importance, Category B cases are cases of substance or difficulty, Category C cases are all other cases. It is usual to ask for the case to be listed as Category B. If the case was not one of substance or difficulty, it would in any event be likely to be transferred to the county court, and thus 'Category C' is virtually redundant in the High Court.

The parties are required to give an estimate of the length of trial. Even allowing for time saved by the 'cards on the table' approach in modern litigation, there is still a tendency for the inexperienced to underestimate how long a trial will take, bearing in mind how relatively short is the judicial day. This estimate of length is not of great importance, however, because it will be supplemented by a much more up-to-date estimate at a later stage when the case is being prepared for trial; and at that stage it will be known how much is agreed between the parties and thus by how much the potential trial can be shortened. Counsel is usually involved in assisting to estimate length of trial.

A period must be fixed within which the case shall be set down for trial. Setting down is the formal stage at which the documents are lodged at court in readiness for the case to be called on. It is usual to fix this period as quite a lengthy one, thus ensuring that the parties have the opportunity to be thoroughly prepared. Indeed, if the summons for directions has come about very swiftly and the parties still need to collect a good deal of evidence and perhaps continue negotiations, it may be that the order will be that it be set down within a year, or even longer. The form of summons indicates the possibility of having the case listed with and tried either after or before another case. That would be appropriate where, for example, there are several plaintiffs who have chosen to sue on separate writs and not to ask for the actions to be consolidated, so that a great deal of time will be saved if the matters are dealt with, albeit separately, by the same judge who will thus build up a good deal of familiarity with the background circumstances.

13.1.3.12 Paragraph 14: Costs

The sample form assumes that the order for costs will be 'in the cause'.

13.1.4 THE DEFENDANT'S NOTICE UNDER THE SUMMONS FOR DIRECTIONS

As we noted above, the parties will often correspond to see whether they can agree on the directions to be sought. If that has not happened, or if there has been no agreement, then when the defendant receives his copy of the summons for directions notifying him of the date of the hearing he may, if he considers that there are directions required in the case for which no provision is made on the plaintiff's summons, himself make application for those which he requires by filing at court and serving on the plaintiff the 'defendant's notice for directions'. A copy of this notice is served on the plaintiff and all other parties no later than seven days before the hearing.

13.1.5 THE HEARING OF THE SUMMONS

13.1.5.1 In general

The summons for directions is intended to provide an opportunity for a 'stocktaking exercise'. The District Judge considers the case for the first time: he looks back over the progress which the parties have made and gives directions for any further preparation necessary; and looks forward to the trial, giving directions on evidential matters and on the time, place and mode of trial.

RSC Ord. 25, r. 6, expressly provides that, although no affidavit is used at the hearing of a summons for directions in the normal case:

> *. . . it shall be the duty of the parties to the action and their advisers to give all such information and produce all such documents on any hearing of the summons [for directions] as the court may reasonably require for the purpose of enabling it properly to deal with the summons.*

The parties therefore are expected to attend by responsible representatives who are thoroughly familiar with the case, the documents and the file. All relevant documents should be available in case they are needed, and the person attending should be ready to make decisions, including offering possible compromises on procedural matters to assist in the 'thorough stocktaking' which the summons for direction should represent. Latterly the courts have been in general much more pro-active about requiring the parties to knock their cases into shape for efficient and expeditious trial, and the former, rather passive attitude, whereby the District Judge would not readily go outside the terms of the orders already requested by the parties, is encountered in fewer cases.

13.1.5.2 Matters for the District Judge or Master to consider

In addition to the directions sought by each party, the Master or District Judge is required to consider certain matters of his own initiative, in particular:

(a) *Transfer to the county court*

One party, usually the plaintiff, is required to file a statement of value in practice form PF. 204 and serve it on all the other parties not later than the day before the hearing of the summons for directions (in London this is simply produced at the summons itself). In the event of non-compliance, the court will order the action to be transferred to a county court. At the hearing, the plaintiff may be called upon to justify the statement of value which he has lodged and give further information. The District Judge may have to consider the four criteria (financial substance, importance, complexity and speed of trial) in order to determine as follows:

(i) if the plaintiff's estimated value of his claim is less than £25,000, whether the presumption in favour of transfer to the county court is rebutted;

(ii) even if the plaintiff's estimated value of his claim is £50,000 or more, whether the presumption against transfer to the county court is rebutted;

(iii) if the plaintiff's estimated value of his claim is between £25,000 and £50,000, or if the claim has no quantifiable value, which is the most suitable court to hear the case.

(b) *Whether an order should be made for different questions or issues to be tried at different places or by different modes of trial, and whether one or more questions or issues should be tried before the others*

By virtue of *RSC Ord. 33, r. 4(2)*, the court should of its own motion consider this in every case. In its most common form this order for a 'split trial' will be made where the issues of liability and damages are quite severable and it will be efficient for the court to try liability early, and first, leaving quantum to be determined later. The kind of case in which this would be most appropriate is usually a personal injury action where a summons for direction is a rarity, but there are other kinds of case also where this will be useful. Taking a personal injury case as an example, however, the reason why such an order is particularly appropriate in that case is that the issues of liability and quantum are completely separate. Thus, suppose that a plaintiff in a road accident has sustained serious injuries which will not stabilise for some years. If the parties press on to trial while the memories of the witnesses of fact about the accident itself are fresh, they could get a decision on liability very quickly. If that decision was in favour of the plaintiff there could then be a very large interim payment and the full trial of the quantum of his claim could be left until later. If the decision was in favour of the defendant, then all the extremely expensive work of collecting evidence of quantum from specialists, forensic accountants and the like will be superfluous, and thus a very efficient outcome has been achieved. Indeed, once the decision is given on liability so that the whole dispute focuses on quantum, there would be an increasing likelihood of the matter being settled without further recourse to the court. Such an order can never be made, however, where the issues of quantum and liability are totally intertwined, as, for example, in some kinds of commercial case where the defendant's activity has been improper and has caused the plaintiff substantial loss, the extent of which depends in part on an assessment of the precise scope of the defendant's actions.

(c) *Whether the writ endorsement and pleadings are in proper form or ought to be amended.*

(d) *Whether directions should be given concerning medical or other expert evidence*

This must now be considered by the court unless both parties are determined to go to trial without disclosure of expert evidence, which would be highly unusual. This is discussed more fully at **12.4**. The court will both require disclosure and limit the number of experts to be called in the usual case.

(e) *Whether to make a variety of directions concerning the presentation of evidence at the trial,* including evidence by affidavit, and directions concerning the method by which particular facts may be proved, e.g. the use of plans and photographs.

(f) *What directions, if any, should be given as to the contents of the court bundle of documents to be prepared for use at trial under RSC Ord. 34, r. 10, and whether that bundle should include a skeleton argument*

(See further, **14.6**.)

(g) *Whether the parties have made all proper agreements and admissions*

It is important for the District Judge to see whether he is able to secure any agreements or admissions between the parties and to record them, or to record the parties, refusal to make reasonable agreements and admissions, with a view to saving time at trial. This ought to be very useful if some clear issue arises. Usually, however, the parties will be reluctant to make formal admissions which they have not already considered making in the pleadings or otherwise.

(h) *Order 38, r. 3*

This useful rule provides that the court shall consider whether *'evidence of any particular fact shall be given at the trial in such manner as may be directed'*. See **9.3.6**.

(i) *Agreement of plans, photographs, models and working models (RSC Ord. 38, r. 5)*

In principle, where a party wishes to use a plan, photograph (including video film), model or working model the court will order that at least 10 days before the commencement of the trial (preferably earlier) the other parties be given the opportunity to inspect the plan etc. and to agree its submission without it being formally proved. This avoids the necessity to call witnesses to swear that the plan etc. corresponds precisely to the dimensions of the original, and saves time at trial. The court is almost certain to make an order for prior disclosure of such things even if the thing in question is a video film which is said to demonstrate that the plaintiff is malingering (*Khan* v *Armaguard Ltd* (1994) *The Times*, 4 March 1994).

13.1.6 THE ORDER FOR DIRECTIONS

Immediately after the hearing, the plaintiff should draw up the order for directions and produce it to the court office for sealing together with a copy. A copy of the order should then be served on any defendant who failed to attend the hearing. In practice, in routine cases, the parties agree the directions to be sought and the plaintiff applies for a consent order for directions by leaving an order in the appropriate form endorsed with the consent of both parties, for consideration by the District Judge. Before making such a consent order, the District Judge will require to see the pleadings and will of his own motion consider what further or other directions are appropriate, e.g. to transfer the case to the county court.

13.2 Automatic Directions in the High Court

We have so far considered the basic summons for directions which ought to come about in most actions begun by writ. There is, however, an exception which applies in personal injury actions. In personal injury actions (other than medical negligence cases) 'automatic directions' apply (*RSC Ord. 25, r. 8*). In personal injury actions when pleadings have closed, the following directions take effect automatically:

13.2.1 DISCOVERY AND INSPECTION

There shall be discovery of documents within 14 days and inspection within seven days thereafter, save that where liability is admitted or the action arises out of a road traffic accident, discovery shall be limited to disclosure by the plaintiff of any documents relating to special damage.

13.2.2 EXPERT EVIDENCE

Where any party intends to place reliance at the trial on expert evidence, he shall within 14 weeks disclose the substance of that evidence to the other parties in the form of a written report, which shall be agreed if possible. If they are not agreed, the parties are at liberty to call as witnesses the experts whose reports have been disclosed, but the number of experts each party may call is limited to two medical experts and one expert of any other kind.

If more than one party intends to adduce expert evidence, the reports shall be disclosed by mutual exchange, medical for medical, and non-medical for non-medical, within the 14 weeks provided, or as soon thereafter as the reports on each side are available. A plaintiff need not produce a further medical report unless he is intending to rely upon expert medical evidence going beyond the report which was served with the statement of claim. But if a further medical report is served he must, in principle, also produce an up-to-date statement of special damages claimed. In fact in many cases the parties dispense with this requirement because full worked schedules and counter schedules have to be produced shortly before the trial and it is often considered unnecessary to produce an interim further document at the stage of disclosure of medical evidence.

13.2.3 OTHER ORAL EVIDENCE

A party intending to adduce any other (i.e. non-expert) oral evidence must, within 14 weeks, serve on the other parties written statements of all such oral evidence (as to the form and content of these statements, see **12.3**).

13.2.4 OTHER EVIDENCE

Photographs, sketch plans, and the contents of any police accident book shall be receivable in evidence at the trial and shall be agreed if possible.

13.2.5 PLACE OF TRIAL

The action shall be tried at the trial centre for the place in which the action is proceeding, or at such other trial centre as the parties may agree in writing.

13.2.6 MODE OF TRIAL

The action shall be tried by a judge alone as a case of substance or difficulty (Category B) and shall be set down within six months. When the action is set down the court may direct a hearing to determine whether the action should be transferred to the county court.

13.2.7 LENGTH OF TRIAL

The court shall be notified on setting down of the estimated length of trial.

13.2.8 THE APPROPRIATENESS OF AUTOMATIC DIRECTIONS

The reason for automatic directions applying only to personal injury cases, is a reflection of the fact that these were the directions found to be routinely used in personal injury cases. Making them take effect automatically saves a good deal of District Judges' time (and litigants' money) as the parties do not normally require a hearing, and they need not come before the court until the trial itself. It must be stressed, however, that these automatic directions are not peremptory in the sense that they *must* apply in *every* case. If one party considers that the automatic directions, or any one of them, are not suitable for his case, or if he wants further or other directions not contained in the automatic directions, then he can ignore the automatic directions and apply for a summons for directions as if the case were not a personal injury action. Both parties would then attend before the District Judge to consider applications for specific directions sought in the summons for directions.

If the parties are agreed about which of the automatic directions are appropriate, but one or other requires some further directions, then each party should conform to the automatic directions in the usual way, whilst issuing a separate summons for directions seeking the further specific directions that they think are appropriate.

13.3 Split Trials in Personal Injury Cases

We mentioned in **13.1.5.2** the possibility of direction concerning split trials. *Order 33, r. 4(2A)* provides that in an action for personal injuries the court may at any stage of the proceedings, and of its own motion, make an order for the issue of liability to be tried before any issue or question concerning damages. If, as described in **13.2.8** above, a summons for directions has been issued because the parties to a personal injuries action require other directions than those contained in the automatic directions, then clearly this will be an opportunity for the court to consider ordering split trials. But if the automatic directions apply, it is only after setting down, when the District Judge looks at the papers, that he will consider whether it is appropriate to order that liability will be tried first and separately from quantum.

If such an order is made, each party has 14 days in which to object. If either or both of the parties object, there will be a hearing for the District Judge to consider the objections. Unfortunately by the time of setting down it is often too late for there to be much saving of costs by an order for split trials because the parties will already have collected a good deal of evidence, and probably be ready for trial, on the question of quantum as well.

13.4 Overview of the Case So Far

The summons for directions is meant to be the end of the preparatory stage of the case. Parties should have been alert to ask the court for any directions that they are likely to require at the summons for directions stage. If a party has to apply later for some direction which he ought to have realised would be required at the directions stage, such as leave to amend pleadings, that party is most likely to be ordered to pay the costs of the further hearing which his oversight has rendered necessary, whatever the outcome of his application. By this stage all the pleadings should be in order and have been served; each party should have prepared, or know very well, what he is going to require tactically and practically to prove his case; and each should be preparing for the final stages of mutual disclosure of evidence of facts and expert evidence. If the parties have, wrongly, failed to carry out discovery before the directions stage, it may of course be that discovery reveals new lines of enquiry which in themselves require further directions from the court. This is why automatic discovery really should be undertaken between the parties before directions are obtained.

The coming about of the directions stage, which may well be the first occasion on which the parties' solicitors have seen each other face to face, is often an opportunity for negotiations. The procedural path which the case is likely to take will by now have become clear and the consequences of pressing on to trial for both parties in terms of costs to be risked ought to become somewhat easier to quantify. The need to get one's evidence in order for the next stage also concentrates the mind powerfully on the consequences of losing at trial. From now on we shall be considering the practical and tactical matters which the parties need to undertake in order to get their cases absolutely ready for trial, and the procedures by which the case is eventually brought into the list for hearing before a judge.

13.5 Comparison with the County Court

We have in the last few chapters been considering the rules relating to the law of evidence and practical matters to do with the collection and presentation of that evidence both at trial and in the various interlocutory stages, for example, discovery of documents, interrogatories, and the rules relating to exchange of expert evidence and evidence of witnesses of fact. In all those matters there is virtually no difference between High Court and county court procedure save in regard to peripheral details such as the timing of certain stages and the time limits applicable. In regard to the direction stage which we have just dealt with in the High Court there is a corresponding procedure in the county court which again is only marginally different. In the county court there is a form of automatic directions which is applicable in the vast majority of cases, and not simply in personal injury actions. Automatic directions in the county court set out a fairly strict procedural timetable to be followed by the parties in relation to a number of matters with which we have now dealt, in particular, the exchange of witness statements, exchange of expert evidence, discovery and inspection generally, and the time for setting down for trial. These matters are dealt with later at **21.2**. There are certain classes of action in the county court where automatic directions do not apply and these are also discussed later at **21.2.4**. In those situations there is a 'pre-trial review' which is the exact counterpart of the High Court summons for directions, where a District Judge will consider progress in the case and make procedural orders fixing what is to be done on a prescribed timetable which will take the case from the pre-trial review to the eventual trial.

13.6 The Form of Summons for Directions

IN THE HIGH COURT OF JUSTICE 1997-L-3110

QUEEN'S BENCH DIVISION

Between GEORGE LEWIS Plaintiff

AND

ROBERT BLACKWELL Defendant

SUMMONS FOR DIRECTIONS PURSUANT TO Ord. 25

Let all parties attend the Master in Chambers in Room No. Royal Courts of Justice, Strand, London WC2A 2LL, on day, the day of 19 , at o'clock in the noon on the hearing of an application for directions in this action:

1. This action be consolidated with action(s) 19 , , No. , and 19 , , No. and that this action [action 19 No.] be the leading action.
2. The action be transferred to an official referee, and that the costs of this application be costs in the cause.
3. The action be transferred to County Court under section 40 of the County Courts Act 1984, and that the costs of the action, including this application be in the discretion of the County Court.
4. The plaintiff have leave to amend the writ of summons as shown by the document initialled by the Master and that service of the writ and the defendant's acknowledgment of service do stand and that the costs incurred and thrown away by the amendment be the defendant's costs in any event.
5. The plaintiff have leave to amend the statement of claim [or the defendant have leave to amend the defence (and counterclaim) or the plaintiff have leave to amend the reply (and defence to counterclaim)] as shown in the document initialled by the Master, and to re-serve the amended pleading within days and that the opposite party have leave to serve an amended consequential pleading, if so advised, within days thereafter and that the costs of and occasioned and thrown away by the amendments be the defendant's [or the plaintiff's] in any event.
6. The plaintiff serve on the defendant or the defendant serve on the plaintiff within days the further and better particulars of his pleading specified in the document initialled by the Master.
7. The plaintiff within days serve on the defendant and the defendant within days serve on the plaintiff a list of documents [and file an affidavit verifying such list] [limited to the documents relating to the special damages claimed or as may be].
8. There be inspection of the documents within days of the service of the lists [and filing of the affidavits].
9. The plaintiff [defendant] retain and preserve pending the trial of the action [and upon days notice give inspection of] [the subject matter of the action] to the defendant [plaintiff] and to his legal advisers (and experts).
10. A (Agreement)
All parties having agreed as to the adducing of expert (medical) evidence (of accountants/ engineers/surveyors/) and as to the disclosure to each other of the substance thereof, they have leave to call expert evidence of limited to witnesses for each party.

B (Leave conditional on disclosure)
All parties do have leave to adduce oral expert (medical) evidence (of accountants/engineers/surveyors/) on condition as regards the plaintiff (defendant) that he discloses the substance of the evidence on which he intends to rely within and as regards the defendant (plaintiff) that he discloses the substance of the evidence on which he intends to rely within the like period (thereafter), such evidence to be limited to that of witnesses the substance of whose evidence has been so disclosed and to witnesses for each party, second or subsequent reports to be exchanged within of receipt of the report of the other party.

C (Leave not conditional on disclosure)
All parties do have leave without previously disclosing the substance thereof to adduce oral expert (medical) evidence (of accountants/engineers/surveyors/) limited to witnesses for each party.

11. That signed statements of witnesses of fact be cross-served by the day of 19 copies to be lodged with the court together with the pleadings upon setting down for trial.

12. [Set out any other directions intended to be applied for]

13. Trial Place Mode
Listing category: A or B or C. Estimated length
To be set down within days [and to be listed with and tried immediately after (before) action 19 , , No.].

14. The Costs of this application be costs in the cause.

Dated the day of 19
To Messrs. of
This summons was issued by

Solicitors for the defendant(s)

Solicitors for the Plaintiff(s).

Preparing for Trial (Sr CGS)

1. Pre-trial Disclosure of Expert Evid (see p 195; 244; 253)

2. Witnesses of fact who will be attendg trial to give evid
   - each W statements within time limits in directions
   - Draft in "own" words & signed; check for inadmissible evid; Incl HS → HS Notice RSC Ord 38 r 21

3. Witnesses of fact who will not be attendg trial to give evid
   - Contents of statements
   - Exchange
   - HS notices → give on exch or within 28 days of settg down

4. Final Preparations for Trial
   - Evidence must be in order & issues // parties prop identified:
   - seek Counsel's advice
   - make sure it is up-to-date
   - agree as many evidential pts as poss
   - make sure witnesses who are able to attend Ct will attend (subpoena)
   - Serve HS notices re those witnesses who are unable to attend

Main procedural steps:

Case must be set down for Trial

HC – lodge bundle of docs c̄ Ct incl pleadings etc (p248

Date by which trial must be set down given in the directions. or

HC – automatic dir: 6 mths for Cl of P

After settg down, actual hearing date must be fixed. Follow Practice Dir of 25 Jan '95 at p250-51

SGS12

Check Witness Statements < Format / Evidential issues

Format

Name/address/description rel to party

---- will say ----

Separate paras / double spaced

Chronological Order

In own words / first person

Identify any docs referred (before Trial cross ref to Trial Bundle)

Statement that "true to best of knowledge & belief —"

Date

Signed

Content

No inadmissible evid:

Opinion, speculation, irrelevant evid of character, privileged info, no anticipation of defence

⇓

- Stands as evid in chief
- Litigation privilege → when statement exchanged loses privilege
- Exchange simultaneously in accordance c̄ directions given
- If HS within statement → give S2 Notice
- Statement itself NOT HS unless W doesn't attend Ct.

(What are the outstandg issues?)

After exchange of W Statements

1. Witness Statements
   Ask for particulars of HS evid
   Try to trace maker of statement
   Subpoena W – keep updated re trial date
2. Experts
   Formal memo of agreement
3. Counsel
   Get advice on evidence
4. Set down for Trial
   P does this
   In accordance c̄ directions
   If 2 CC? (→ statement of value)
5. Ct bundles
   Prepare
   Agree c̄ other side
   Approve by Counsel
6. Counsel
   Brief – ask to attend Ct
   (+ instructions to do other things eg draft)
   Pre-trial Conf.
7. Advise Client
   Costs
   Prospects of success → settlement
8. Final
   Pre-trial check list
   Liaise c̄ Ct Office → date
   Lodge bundles – 2 days before

FOURTEEN

PREPARING FOR TRIAL

In this chapter we consider the procedural steps necessary to get the case before a judge in a given courtroom at a given time with everybody present and ready. In addition, we discuss the tactical and procedural steps that a party needs to take to ensure that he is ready for trial and that his case is prepared as well as it may possibly be.

14.1 Complying with the Order for Directions

After the hearing of the summons for directions the order should normally be drawn up and sealed at court, since it should be included in the documents put before the trial judge. It should be served on opposing parties, though this is really only of much significance in the case of parties who did not attend the hearing of the summons. That order for directions should, of course, be thoroughly complied with, if possible, by the dates fixed for each stage.

If an extension of time is found to be needed at this late stage there is usually reasonable cooperation between the parties, although there is really little reason why extensions of time should be needed. Thus, for example, the court will fix a date by which witness statements and experts' reports are to be exchanged, and as this is likely to be several weeks after the hearing of the summons for directions, there is really little reason why the parties should not be ready to comply with the dates given.

We now consider the necessary events in approximately the order in which one should give one's mind to them.

14.2 Evidence

The importance of ensuring that a party can prove his case by admissible evidence has been constantly stressed. After the summons for directions it is customary, in cases of any weight at all, to ask counsel formally to advise on evidence.

Counsel will be the person presenting the case at trial, and even if he has advised on the merits of the case once or more often, it is usual to send the papers back to him at this relatively late stage for him to consider just what appears to be outstanding, in the light of what has been conceded or agreed so far, and what evidence he thinks appropriate to prove each given point outstanding, and by what method. A full set of instructions should thus be drafted for counsel explaining all the outstanding matters, the progress of the case so far, and asking for his advice in a series of specific questions. The solicitor himself should go through the relevant matters and give his own views on the points at issue. Copies of all relevant documents should be enclosed. It may also be necessary to indicate to counsel matters that do not appear in documentary form, e.g. the contents of telephone negotiations with an opponent. Counsel will review the evidence in the whole case on both liability and quantum, thus the instruction should deal fully with matters of medical evidence, details of loss of earnings and other special damages.

It is usually appropriate to ask for counsel's advice in written form rather than at a conference, although it is also customary to have a conference with counsel at a slightly later stage, to which we shall come in due course.

When advice is received from counsel it should, of course, be implemented immediately. In the light of counsel's advice, all or any of the following matters may be relevant.

14.2.1 EXPERT EVIDENCE

The expert evidence should be thoroughly updated to as close as possible to the eventual trial date in a case where there is any change in circumstances, e.g. in a case where the plaintiff is suffering serious and lasting injuries. At this late stage the whole of the medical evidence should be sent to the client's own specialist, and an appointment arranged for the client to see him again. The specialist should be asked for a summary of his full view in the case together with, perhaps separately, a commentary on his views of the opposing experts' reports. The purpose of this is to have both a document appropriate for disclosure to the opponent and for use by the trial judge; and a separate document to enable counsel effectively to cross-examine the opposing expert. As we have noted at **12.4.5**, the document to be disclosed to the opponent must be an honest summary of the expert's full views and he should be asked for his impartial conclusions.

If an order has been made, or the parties have agreed, for a meeting of experts to examine the object of their disagreement (or the plaintiff himself if it is a personal injury case), this should be arranged. The experts should be asked to write a joint report indicating what is and is not agreed. It is fruitful in some fields of litigation, though possibly not in personal injury cases, to then go on to arrange a negotiation meeting straight after the experts' meeting, with the experts being present.

14.2.2 WITNESSES OF FACT

Almost inevitably now there will be an order for the exchange of statements of the witnesses of fact. These should be prepared in the formal way described at **12.3.3**, that is in numbered paragraphs and signed. As noted earlier, they should contain only matter which is admissible under the rules of evidence, and thus it may be that in cases of difficulty counsel's advice is needed about the drafting of these statements both for evidential and, indeed, tactical reasons. It will be remembered that these statements should be as full as possible because the witness will be restricted to what is said in these statements in evidence in chief.

A date for exchange should be agreed between the parties if the court did not order a fixed exchange day, to ensure that one party does not obtain an unfair advantage by seeing his opponent's statements first. This is particularly important in automatic directions cases where the automatic directions just fix a time within which exchange is to be effected. Telephone contact should be made to establish a fixed date.

14.2.3 METHODS OF ADDUCING EVIDENCE

Next, it must be considered how the evidence will be brought before the court. There are three main methods:

14.2.3.1 Hearsay evidence

As was noted earlier the *Civil Evidence Act 1995* permits the parties to adduce hearsay evidence and the court has no discretion to exclude it although regard must also be had to the fact that under *s. 4* of the *1995 Act*, detailed criteria are provided by which the judge may determine the weight which he should attach to the evidence, so that in most cases it will inevitably be preferable to call the witness if the witness is available, rather than relying on hearsay evidence. Notice must be given in accordance with Rules of court in advance, of the intention to adduce hearsay evidence and regard should be had to this important procedural provision.

14.2.3.2 Notice to admit facts

This is a useful alternative to calling witnesses to give oral evidence, particularly in cases where the evidence in question will be inconvenient or expensive to adduce. The nature and purpose of the notice to admit facts has been described earlier at **8.5.2.2**.

A notice to admit facts must be thoroughly drafted to cover with precision the points on which agreement is sought. The notice should be served no later than 21 days after setting down for trial. The consequence, as we have seen, is that if the opposite party fails to admit a fact which he should have admitted, he will bear the costs of proving the fact at trial whatever the outcome of the trial.

14.2.3.3 Witnesses

It is wise to subpoena all lay witnesses, even members of the plaintiff's family or close friends who have guaranteed their cooperation in attending trial. It is always disappointing to find that witnesses may well put their own selfish concerns (such as going on holiday) before a party's justifiable entitlement to insist that they turn up to testify at trial. Witnesses should be told that this subpoena does not represent any slight on their reliability but is merely a matter of formality. The reason for doing this is that if a subpoena has not been served and a key witness does not attend at trial, then either the judge may not permit an adjournment at all (in which case the action may well be lost), or, if he does permit an adjournment, it will inevitably be at the cost of the party requesting it. On the other hand, if a subpoena has been served the judge will agree that there is no fault in the party requiring the adjournment and it will therefore usually be allowed without penalty.

There are two kinds of subpoena:

(a) A *subpoena ad testificandum* requires a witness to attend court for the purpose of giving verbal testimony. This would thus be appropriate to ensure the attendance of an eye-witness.

(b) A *subpoena duces tecum* is issued for a witness who is required to attend court to produce and prove the authenticity of some document or thing. Accordingly, if the client's employer is required to attend and bring wages and salary records with him, a *subpoena duces tecum* will be served.

The method of obtaining a subpoena is to attend at the High Court District Registry with a *praecipe*, which is simply a form of request for a subpoena, and the completed form. The court will then seal the subpoena.

A subpoena must be served within 12 weeks of issue and, if possible, no later than four days before the trial of the action. The form of subpoena simply indicates whom the action is between and tells the witness concerned to attend the court to testify at that action, but it cannot say *when* the action will take place because this is not generally known at the time when the subpoena is issued. The subpoena should be served personally with conduct money, that is a sum sufficient to cover the witness's expenses and subsistence in attending the hearing. The witness should be told orally that he will not lose earnings by attending court because these will be reimbursed in due course, but they do not have to be paid in advance.

When the case is finally listed for trial and the hearing date is known, the subpoena is 'activated' by the solicitor contacting the witness personally or by telephone and informing him that the hearing date has now been fixed and that he must regard the subpoena as binding upon him to attend at court on the day concerned.

14.2.3.4 Subpoenas and expert witnesses

It is now increasingly common to subpoena an expert witness. Popular expert witnesses may become double or treble booked for their various commitments and the service of a subpoena is often helpful to them to allow them to break other appointments. Doctors in particular are often protected by ferocious receptionists who will claim that a certain date is out of the question because of other commitments. The service of the subpoena can magically make these commitments evaporate.

14.2.4 BUNDLES OF DOCUMENTS

For the avoidance of delay and expense, as much as possible of the documentary evidence should be 'agreed' between the parties. In this sense 'agreed' has the special meaning of 'agreed as authentic and relevant to the trial'. It does not indicate that the *contents* of such documents are 'agreed'. It thus has a very different meaning from the context in which the word is used of medical reports, where the term 'agreed' means 'agreed as to substance and truth'.

> **Example** It may be that there has been a great deal of correspondence between the parties about their dispute before solicitors were ever instructed, for instance correspondence to do with the disputed terms of a commercial contract and whether or not one of the parties has carried it out properly. In this correspondence each party asserts, increasingly strongly, the justice of their own position and their complaints about the other party's conduct. This correspondence will be highly relevant at trial to show what was being said at the earlier stages and how the argument developed. It must therefore be put before the court; but it does not, of course, follow that each party 'agrees' with the contents of what is asserted in the other party's half of the correspondence. In this sense, therefore, the correspondence is 'agreed' as being authentic and relevant but certainly not agreed as to the substance.

As we discuss at **14.8**, the Rules of court actually require the parties to correspond shortly before trial in an attempt to agree this bundle of documents. It is far better, however, for the parties to attempt to agree these matters well before the stage suggested in the rule described below (*Ord. 34, r. 10*) in order to ensure that they are thoroughly prepared well in advance. The parties should correspond sometime between the end of discovery and the stage of setting down for trial in order to ensure that they are in agreement about what documents are relevant for the judge's use at the trial. It is quite inadequate to turn up at trial with loose files of copy documents. The bundles must be properly prepared in ring binder files, and duly paginated and indexed. In most trials it will be necessary to prepare at least seven identical bundles for each party's solicitors and counsel, and a copy to be put before witnesses for comment, as well as one for the judge.

14.2.5 PRODUCTION OF ORIGINAL DOCUMENTS

If a party is in possession of an original document, then that original should be produced at trial. As we have seen at **11.3**, such a document's inclusion in a list of documents on discovery requires the other party to give positive notice if he does not admit its authenticity, and thus the dispute about that matter can be determined before the trial. If the opposing party possesses the document, notice to produce the document should be given. If there is non-compliance with that notice the other party may prove the contents of the document by secondary means, e.g. carbon copies, photostats, or even a verbal account of what it contained.

If somebody other than one of the parties is in possession of an original document, a *subpoena duces tecum* should be served on that person (see **14.2.3.3**). It will be recalled that in a personal injury case one would have had the power to inspect the document by a proper application under *RSC Ord. 24, r. 7A*, requiring non-party discovery, after proceedings had commenced. The use of *Ord. 24, r. 7A* merely advances the stage of seeing the document by one step, since a party can in any kind of case serve a *subpoena duces tecum*. If in a personal injury case after inspection the document proves to be relevant, a *subpoena duces tecum* will still be required to ensure that the person owning the document brings it to trial.

14.3 Special Damages in Personal Injury Cases

In personal injury cases a considerable amount of the judge's time is likely to be taken up with investigations of very complex figures. In order to cut down so far as possible the amount of the judge's time taken up at trial with investigating difficult arithmetical matters, the plaintiff must comply with *Practice Direction (Damages: Personal Injury Actions)* [1984] 1 WLR 1127.

This note provides that in a personal injury action in which the damages claimed include a claim for loss of earnings, loss of earning capacity, medical or other expenses relating to or including the cost of care, attention, accommodation or appliances or loss of pension rights, particulars (in the form of a Schedule if appropriate) must be prepared shortly before trial and served on the defendant. The defendant must within seven days thereafter, inform the plaintiff whether, and to what extent, each item claimed is agreed, or the reason it has not been agreed, and any counter proposals. These counter proposals must be set out as formally as the plaintiff's proposals, giving the corresponding alternative calculations.

> **Example** A plaintiff's claim includes a suggestion that he will be unable to work again in his administrative job because of a head injury causing personality change and inability to concentrate. His solicitor has put forward a calculation of the plaintiff's future loss of earnings on the basis that he would shortly have been promoted to manager by his employers, but conceding that in five years' time he will be fit to return to unskilled work in some form. The defendants put forward a counter argument with figures contending that the plaintiff would not in fact have been promoted to manager, and thus that his future loss of earnings should be computed on his present salary alone; and that he will be fit to return to some form of work in only two years' time.

The reason for this provision is, of course, to attempt to narrow down the area of dispute and clarify the precise figures and the reasons for any objection to them.

The time for service of these particulars in London is seven days after the case appears in the warned list (see **14.5** below). Outside London it is upon setting down (and outside London the defendant has 14 days to reply rather than seven – although both in and outside London rather longer than this is likely to be required and to be allowed between the parties). If there is a fixed date for trial the time for service of these particulars is 28 days before trial with 14 days to respond.

We now turn to the formal requirements of setting down.

14.4 Setting Down for Trial

14.4.1 THE DOCUMENTS REQUIRED

By *RSC Ord. 34, r. 3*, it is provided that:

(1) In order to set down for trial an action which is to be tried before a judge, the party setting it down must, subject to any order of the court to the contrary, deliver to the proper officer, by post or otherwise, a request that the action be set down for trial at the place determined in accordance with automatic directions or by order of the court and lodge two bundles consisting of one copy of each of the following documents—

(a) the writ,

(b) the pleadings (including any affidavits ordered to stand as pleadings),

(c) any request or order for particulars and the particulars given, and any interrogatories and answers thereto,

(d) all orders made in the action except only any order relating only to time,

(e) in proceedings to which article 7(1) of the High Court and County Courts Jurisdiction Order 1991 applies, a statement of the value of the action,

(f) a note agreed by the parties or, failing agreement, a note by each party giving (in the following order)—

(i) an estimate of the length of the trial,

(ii) the list in which the action is to be included,

(g) the requisite legal aid documents, if any.

These documents are required because the court does not keep a court file as such, and even though, if there is a summons for directions, copies of pleadings will have been lodged before the Master or District Judge these are likely to have been handed back at the end of the directions hearing.

Bundles containing these documents must be prepared, which are by custom bound up in the lefthand margin with green tape. Top copies or good photocopies must be supplied. The bundles are bound up in chronological order, save that orders or requests for further and better particulars and the particulars supplied in response to them are bound up after the pleading to which they relate so that there is a convenient coherent narrative. The phrase 'requisite legal aid documents' means merely the notices of issue of legal aid. The original certificate will have been filed at court.

The two bundles should be taken to:

(a) in the Queen's Bench Division at the Royal Courts of Justice, the Head Clerk of the Crown Office;

(b) in a Chancery action to be tried at the Royal Courts of Justice, the Cause Clerk in Chancery Chambers;

(c) in an action to be tried outside London, the District Registry for the district comprising the place of trial (which may be different from the District Registry where the case has hitherto been proceeding).

Outside London there is a further document required to be lodged when setting down for trial. This is pursuant to *Practice Direction (Trial out of London)* [1987] 1 WLR 1322. This document:

(a) confirms that the order made on the summons for directions has been complied with, or states in what respect it has or has not;

(b) states to what extent medical reports have been agreed;

(c) states to what extent plans and photographs have been agreed;

(d) gives an agreed estimated length of trial;

(e) gives full details of the party's solicitors, agents and intended counsel, including their addresses and telephone numbers.

14.4.2 FEE

On setting down there is a further fee paid to the court (currently £150).

14.4.3 TIME

If the plaintiff fails to set down for trial the defendant may take this action. The time within which an action should be set down for trial will have been fixed by the order for direction, or in automatic directions cases, as we have seen at **13.2.6**, is six months.

14.4.4 NATURE OF SETTING DOWN FOR TRIAL

It should not be imagined that setting a case down for trial means that the case will be listed for immediate hearing by a judge. Setting down for trial may very well be far in advance of the actual hearing.

In addition to the formalities on setting down, it should be noted that there is a checklist to be completed by the parties and supplied to the court no later than two months before the date of hearing pursuant to the *Practice Direction: Civil Litigation: Case Management* [1995] 1 WLR 262 (for further details see **14.6.4** below).

When the bundles are lodged at court on setting down, the court will look at the certificate of value supplied and consider for the last time the possibility of transfer to the county court. If the Master or District Judge is minded to order transfer to the county court, he will give notice to the parties who may then object and request an oral hearing so that the matter may be canvassed. Likewise, the question of split trials will be considered by the Master or District Judge in automatic directions cases, although, as we have previously observed (**13.1.5.2**), by the time the setting down stage is reached the savings obtained by an order for split trials may be less relevant because the parties will have collected most of their evidence on quantum as well as liability. Such orders are therefore rare.

If further interlocutory applications are needed after setting down they are usually made to the District Registry of the trial centre, rather than to the District Registry where the case has proceeded hitherto, if they are different.

14.5 Listing

14.5.1 IN GENERAL

In London there are several different lists. An example is the 'short cause list', which is available where a solicitor can certify that the case will last no longer than four hours. Relatively few cases which have got as far as trial can genuinely be listed as certain to take such a short time. Outside London there is only one list.

The case will then move up the lists. The speed at which it does this is very much a local matter and may change considerably from time to time. Much will depend upon the length and complexity of the case, and the rate at which cases above it in the list are settled or withdrawn. Cases do, however, move up the list a little haphazardly. Clearly it is easier to find a space in the court's time for a case estimated to last one day than one estimated to last three months.

A particular problem with the somewhat unpredictable way in which cases will come into the list is that one may find difficulty in ensuring the attendance of all witnesses, e.g. if the case is coming on in a popular holiday period such as July. Equally, one may find the counsel of first choice is unavailable. A way of avoiding this difficulty is to apply for a fixed date.

14.5.2 FIXED DATES

An application for a fixed date, or an application that a date be given *before which* an action is *not* to be heard (e.g. where someone will not be available for some months), must be made within seven days of setting down outside London and 28 days within London. This should be lodged at the trial centre by the parties jointly, or by one of the parties on seven days' notice to every other party stating fully the matters relied on.

The price of obtaining a fixed date unfortunately is likely to be that the date fixed will be considerably later than the date on which the case would otherwise have come into the lists. It may nonetheless be desirable to obtain a fixed date if there may be problems with securing the attendance of some particular witness, or obtaining a particular counsel.

14.5.3 THE WARNED LIST

The procedure by which a case is finally listed has some local variations. In London, even if a fixed date for trial has not been applied for, solicitors are usually very keen to ensure their case does not become a 'floater', which means that it may be called on at less than a day's notice with considerable consequences of inconvenience in dropping all other business so as to prepare and contact one's witnesses, etc. It is usually possible to ensure that at least the day on which the case will start is fixed with three or four days' notice. Outside London, usually a preliminary warned list is sent out in advance indicating that a certain case will begin to come into the list in three weeks' time. At that stage it is possible to object on the basis of unavailability of witnesses or any other good reason. If you do object the case will reappear in a warned list at some subsequent date. Bona fide objections can be put forward again. If the same thing happens a third time, however, you will need to provide very cogent evidence of the difficulties you have in meeting the date, and mere matters of convenience will not weigh heavily with the Listing Officer. If no objection is taken, then in the week preceding the week of the trial you may be given some indication of the exact date in the following week on which your case will start.

You will often be disappointed to see that there are three or four cases listed for the same day before the same judge even though your own case might have been estimated to last two or three days. This is a very real problem which has to be taken into account in advising a nervous client. Even if everyone is prepared for the day in court, often the day is vacated (i.e. postponed) late on because the preceding case has run over. Cases are often listed in numbers far in excess of those with which the court can deal, in the certainty that some will be compromised late on or even at the courtroom door. Indeed, the disappointment thus engendered can in itself be a powerful incentive to the client to accept a so-called 'courtroom door' offer whereby defendants marginally increase the last offer on the table.

If parties do turn up in vain for a hearing which cannot proceed, costs mount without either party being at fault. It by no means follows that the case will proceed on the following day. Often the case is relisted for some weeks later.

14.6 'The Court Bundle'

14.6.1 CONTENTS

We have so far considered the documents which need to be provided on setting down for trial (see **14.4.1**). Under a recent and very important rule change there is a further bundle of documents which has to be supplied immediately before trial. This bundle is intended to be read by the trial judge, who will now be extremely well informed of the issues in the case. Until this practice came in in 1992, all that a judge would have had to read before trial would be the copy pleadings and sometimes experts' reports if they were agreed. This amendment to the rules provides that each party will have to cooperate in an effort to agree a bundle to be called 'the court bundle'. The relevant text of *RSC Ord. 34, r. 10*, is as follows:

(1) *At least 14 days before the date fixed for the trial or, in the case of an action entered in any running list, within three weeks of the defendant's receiving notice of such entry, the defendant shall identify to the plaintiff those documents central to his case which he wishes included in the bundle to be provided under paragraph (2).*

(2) *At least two clear days before the date fixed for the trial the plaintiff shall lodge two bundles consisting of one copy of each of the following documents—*

(a) *witness statements which have been exchanged, and experts' reports which have been disclosed, together with an indication of whether the contents of such documents are agreed.*

(b) *those documents which the defendant wishes to have included in the bundle and those central to the plaintiff's case, and*

(c) *where a direction has been given under Order 25, rule 3(2), a note agreed by the parties or, failing agreement, a note by each party giving (in the following order)—*

(i) *a summary of the issues involved,*

(ii) *a summary of any propositions of law to be advanced together with a list of the authorities to be cited, and*

(iii) *a chronology of relevant events.*

(3) *Nothing in this rule shall—*

(a) *prevent the Court from giving, whether before or after the documents have been lodged, such further or different directions as to the documents to be lodged as may, in the circumstances, be appropriate; or*

(b) *prevent the making of an order for the transfer of the action to a County Court.*

Thus the bundle of documents to be agreed following discovery between the parties will be lodged at court to be seen by the judge in advance of the case. As we have already observed the procedure to agree this bundle should really be put in motion well before the date suggested in *Ord. 34, r. 10*. In addition he will have all the pleadings and other things in the bundles which have to be lodged on setting down for trial (see **14.4**), witness statements which have been exchanged and experts' reports, together with an indication of whether the contents of these documents are agreed.

The rule thus requires the parties to cooperate closely in identifying precisely the extent to which reports are and are not agreed, and the same in respect of statements of witnesses of fact. It may be that counsel will have to be involved in this because, since witnesses may well express matters in different words, it may not be absolutely clear-cut that, for example, paragraph 7 of the plaintiff's statement does correspond *exactly* with paragraph 27 of the defendant's. In case of any difference of nuance of meaning, it is no doubt safest not to identify the relevant matter as agreed.

14.6.2 THE SKELETON ARGUMENT

Attention should be given to *RSC Ord. 34, r. 10(2)(c)*, which is set out above. This is something which should be considered at the summons for directions. It will be very helpful in a case of any complexity and follows a practice long adopted in the specialist Commercial Court in London and in the Divisional Court on the hearing of judicial review applications requiring the parties to lodge a 'skeleton argument' identifying the true issues involved and the propositions of law to be advanced, together with a list of authorities to be cited and, in cases of difficulty, a chronology of relevant events.

These hardly matter, of course, in a straightforward road accident case. In cases of any complexity, however (especially in commercial disputes), a detailed chronology — for example, reciting the different stages of changes of shareholding or directorships in a web of interlocking companies — can be invaluable in enabling a judge clearly to see the issues. Naturally counsel's assistance will be called upon for him to identify the issues involved and the propositions of law and the authorities which he proposes to cite, and so if any such order has been made at the summons for directions one will have to stay closely in touch with counsel about this at the relevant stage.

14.6.3 SUMMARY

The effect of lodging this bundle, then, is that the judge will be very well informed of the issues before trial if he has had time to read all the documents. The thoroughness with which a judge can prepare himself may indeed enable him to dispense with opening speeches in the case, a subject to which we will return in the context of the trial in the following chapter.

14.6.4 PRACTICE DIRECTION (CIVIL LITIGATION: CASE MANAGEMENT)

On the 25 January 1995, the Lord Chief Justice and the Vice Chancellor of the Chancery Division, in conjunction, issued a *Practice Direction* entitled *Civil Litigation: Case Management* reported at [1995] 1 WLR 262. This Practice Direction, the full text of which is set out below, is intended to be a significant further step in the direction of 'court control' of civil litigation, at least in so far as the trial itself is concerned. It commences by stressing the need to reduce costs and delay, in particular at the time of trial, but also, by implication, at preliminary stages. Thus, for example, in para. 2 the indication is that the court should seek to limit discovery to what is really necessary. The Practice Direction is aimed at trial judges in the High Court and at the moment does not apply to the County Court nor indeed is there any specific way in which it can be said to apply to District Judges or Masters dealing with interlocutory stages in High Court actions. Thus although the Practice Direction boldly states 'the court would accordingly exercise its discretion to limit discovery' it is not entirely clear how, by a Practice Direction, the substantive law on discovery, relevance and privilege can in fact be changed, nor how this can be achieved in the matter of discovery, at least at the trial by which stage of course all issues in relation to discovery should be well settled. No doubt the intention is that District Judges and Masters, dealing with issues of discovery, should give their attention to the spirit of the Practice Direction. In addition the parties are instructed to concentrate their minds particularly on the need to plead only what is relevant and to attempt to reduce or eliminate disputes between experts and concentrate on the main issues.

The full Practice Direction is supplemented by a check list to be supplied by the parties no later than two months before the date of hearing. The full text of the Practice Direction and the check list is as follows:

1. *The paramount importance of reducing the cost and delay of civil litigation makes it necessary for judges sitting at first instance to assert greater control over the preparation for and conduct of hearings than has hitherto been customary. Failure by practitioners to conduct cases economically will be visited by appropriate orders for costs, including wasted costs orders.*

2. *The court will accordingly exercise its discretion to limit (a) discovery; (b) the length of oral submissions; (c) the time allowed for the examination and cross-examination of witnesses; (d) the issues on which it wishes to be addressed; (e) readings aloud from documents and authorities.*

3. *Unless otherwise ordered, every witness statement shall stand as the evidence in chief of the witness concerned.*

4. *RSC, Ord. 18, r. 7 (facts, not evidence, to be pleaded) will be strictly enforced. In advance of trial parties should use their best endeavours to agree which are the issues or the main issues, and it is their duty so far as possible to reduce or eliminate the expert issues.*

5. *RSC, Ord. 34, r. 10(2)(a) to (c) (the court bundle) will also be strictly enforced. Documents for use in court should be in A4 format where possible, contained in suitably secured bundles, and lodged with the court at least two clear days before the hearing of an application or a trial. Each bundle should be paginated, indexed, wholly legible, and arranged chronologically and contained in a ring binder or a lever-arch file. Where documents are copied unnecessarily or bundled incompetently the cost will be disallowed.*

6. *In cases estimated to last for more than 10 days a pre-trial review should be applied for or in default may be appointed by the court. It should when practicable be conducted by the trial judge between eight and four weeks before the date of trial and should be attended by the advocates who are to represent the parties at trial.*

7. *Unless the court otherwise orders, there must be lodged with the listing officer (or equivalent) on behalf of each party no later than two months before the date of trial a completed pre-trial check-list in the form annexed to this practice direction.*

8. *Not less than three clear days before the hearing of an action or application each party should lodge with the court (with copies to other parties) a skeleton argument concisely summarising that party's submissions in relation to each of the issues, and citing the main authorities relied upon which may be attached. Skeleton arguments should be as brief as the nature of the issues allows, and should not without leave of the court exceed 20 pages of double-spaced A4 paper.*

9. *The opening speech should be succinct. At its conclusion other parties may be invited briefly to amplify their skeleton arguments. In a heavy case the court may in conjunction with final speeches require written submissions, including the findings of fact for which each party contends.*

10. *This direction applies to all lists in the Queen's Bench and Chancery Division, except where other directions specifically apply.*

LORD TAYLOR OF GOSFORTH C.J.
SIR RICHARD SCOTT V.-C.

24 January 1995

PRE-TRIAL CHECK-LIST

[Short title of action, folio number]
[Trial date]
[Party lodging check-list]
[Name of solicitor]
[Name(s) of counsel for trial (if known)]

Setting down
1. Has the action been set down?

Pleadings
2. (a) Do you intend to make any amendment to your pleading? (b) If so, when?

Interrogatories
3. (a) Are any interrogatories outstanding? (b) If so, when served and upon whom?

Evidence
4. (a) Have all orders in relation to expert, factual and hearsay evidence been complied with? If not, specify what remains outstanding. (b) Do you intend to serve/seek leave to serve/any further report or statement? If so, when and what report or statement? (c) Have all other orders in relation to oral evidence been complied with? (d) Do you require any further leave or orders in relation to evidence? If so, please specify and say when will you apply.

5. (a) What witnesses of fact do you intend to call? [Names] (b) What expert witnesses do you intend to call? [Names] (c) Will any witness require an interpreter? If so, which?

Documents
6. (a) Have all orders in relation to discovery been complied with? (b) If not, what orders are outstanding? (c) Do you intend to apply for any further orders relating to discovery? (d) If so, what and when?

7. Will you not later than seven days before trial have prepared agreed paginated bundles of fully legible documents for the use of counsel and the court?

Pre-trial review
8. (a) Has a pre-trial review been ordered? (b) If so, when is it to take place? (c) If not, would it be useful to have one?

Note: This check-list has now been added to the Queen's Bench Masters' Practice Forms as No. PF77.

14.7 Using Counsel

14.7.1 INTRODUCTION

As the case approaches its final stage it will become clearer whether or not it is indeed going to be seriously defended. Of course, insisting on the strength of your defence and leaving offers or further offers until very late in the day is an obvious tactic in negotiations. A defendant must weigh up the mounting costs of this 'last ditch' bluff against his knowledge of the probably rising anxiety of a plaintiff whose (in personal injury cases, and sometimes in business disputes) whole quality of future life will depend on the outcome. As we have already remarked, this is what gives defendants a tremendous psychological advantage in personal injury cases since the real defendant, being a large insurance company, does not have anything like as personal a stake in the outcome of such cases. Nonetheless, the defendant's insurer's solicitors will have to consider to what degree the costs are rising in proportion to the amount at stake in the action itself.

In very large actions substantial amounts can be risked on bluffing until the very last stage in order to take advantage of any faltering in the plaintiff's determination. In more modest actions the costs of going to trial represent a very considerable proportion of the global costs of settlement, and therefore defendants are likely to put in their true final offer somewhat earlier. As we have seen, payments into court can still be made, and take effect, even very late in a case; and although by then the point of a gamble is rather less pressing on a plaintiff, if the trial is likely to be long, or expensive in terms of the number of expert witnesses, any payment in is not a matter lightly to be disregarded. Negotiations direct between the parties may therefore become particularly intense in the immediate pre-trial stage.

It may be that after a meeting of experts a joint meeting will be arranged. It may even be the case that counsel is involved in these meetings. Even if counsel is not formally involved there may be some interchanges between him and his opposite number in the immediate pre-trial stage about the way in which the case is to be formally presented for convenience between them, and at which possible offers of settlement could be discussed. This may be particularly important if, as is unfortunately sometimes the case, the solicitors for the plaintiff and defendant have fallen out personally and are no longer taking a detached view of the case, so that the interposition of a more objective viewpoint helps the true issues to emerge. The negotiation position may also change because of new evidence coming out very late in the case. The exchange of witness statements in particular may be an important point at which one or other party sees that his case is somewhat weaker than he has supposed. Similarly, the precision with which a plaintiff can prepare and serve a Schedule of Special Damage may make the defendant see that the apparently outrageous figures being claimed in earlier negotiations can perhaps be substantiated at trial by hard factual evidence.

When negotiating for a plaintiff at a late stage, it is naturally imperative to give the impression that he is now happy to press on with the trial and let the court decide. Any degree of hesitancy is likely to be seized on by the defendant. In the case of a defendant, then, ideally a payment into court which is relatively close to the likely award should have been made at the earliest stage, thus putting the plaintiff at risk for as much as possible in the way of continuing costs. If new evidence has emerged which makes the plaintiff's claim seem stronger or bigger than had previously been thought, it is as well to make a further payment in late on if the defendant hopes to get out of the action without the costs of trial. An alternative, albeit brinkmanship, tactic (as is well known) is to wait to make that final offer at the courtroom door, when the plaintiff's nervousness at the ordeal of giving evidence, as well as at the gamble involved, may be at its peak.

14.7.2 CONFERENCE WITH COUNSEL

It will commonly be the case that a conference with counsel will be arranged not long before the trial. Usually, in civil litigation, a client will not have seen his own barrister until this late stage, all other matters having passed between barrister and solicitor in written form. If the facts remain seriously in dispute on either liability or quantum, it is common to arrange a conference with the client present. The barrister will probe the contested parts of his client's story, suggesting to him the way in which he will be cross-examined about it and looking for his response to likely questions. He may want to explain to the plaintiff why he gave written advice at earlier stages to refuse offers or payments into court, and answer questions from the client about the possible difficulties to be faced and the prospects of success.

Quite often such a conference is in two parts, the first with the client present and the second with the solicitor alone, the client having been told there are legal matters to be discussed which would bore him. Once the client has left the barrister may then give the solicitor further advice about the client's prospects, e.g. if the client, under close questioning, has seemed to be evasive, or clearly gaping holes or improbabilities have appeared in his account of what happened. It may be that in the light of seeing how the client has performed as a witness, even in the limited context of a conference in a private room, the barrister will firmly urge the solicitor to accept some offer that has been made, or to see whether any improved offer can be obtained before the delivery of briefs for trial.

14.7.3 CONFERENCES WITH EXPERT WITNESSES

Until 1995 barristers were not permitted to see witnesses of fact before trial in order, supposedly, to preserve their detachment. Following a change in the rules of Professional Conduct, barristers are now permitted to see witnesses of fact, although cases in which barristers will request to see witnesses of fact before the trial will probably remain rare until a settled practice is established at the Bar. Barristers have, however, always been permitted to see expert witnesses and it may well be helpful to arrange a conference with expert witnesses if there are substantial disputes concerning expert evidence.

The consultant in the case normally attends the barrister's chambers for the conference, although increasingly such conferences can take place in the solicitor's offices where sometimes the accommodation is rather better. The purpose of the conference is for counsel to ask detailed questions about the experts' views, e.g. in a personal injury case about the prognosis of the plaintiff, or to seek clarification of the matters in the consultant's or his opponent's report and ask for ammunition from the consultant about lines of cross-examination to take with the opposing expert.

14.7.4 BRIEFING COUNSEL

14.7.4.1 Delivering the brief

The solicitor should prepare a brief for the counsel who has been involved in the case hitherto. A brief should generally be delivered not so late that counsel cannot prepare the case thoroughly, nor so early that the brief cannot take account of new developments, e.g. offers made at a late stage. When a solicitor chooses to deliver a brief is very much a matter of feel but in a High Court action at least a fortnight before the date of trial is thought to be the minimum. Counsel's clerk should be contacted earlier than this, however, to be told to expect the brief; he may then be involved in using his powers of persuasion with the listing officer to ensure that the case comes into the list at a time convenient for the counsel concerned. The other side should be notified that one is about to deliver a brief because the brief fee becomes payable upon its delivery, even if the case is settled immediately thereafter. This is therefore a powerful final incentive to the opposing party to consider settling since a very heavy disbursement is about to be incurred on the plaintiff's side for which the defendant will be liable if he loses or settles later. In fact, despite this rule, if the case is settled shortly after delivery of the brief and before counsel has commenced work on it, it may be possible to negotiate a reduction in the brief fee with counsel's clerk.

14.7.4.2 Contents of the brief

One thing a brief should not be is brief. A solicitor should not trust to the fact that a barrister is already familiar with the case from having drafted pleadings or given advice in connection with it. A good brief should set out in coherent, chronological order a discussion of all relevant issues of fact, evidence and law, and supply good copies of all necessary documents including proofs of evidence, computations of special damages, the writ, pleadings, procedural orders, accounts of negotiations with the opponents and so on.

Counsel should be given a copy of the court bundle in the same order and, with proper pagination and indexing so as to correspond with the bundle which the judge will have for ease of cross-reference in opening speech, cross-examination, or argument.

The brief should deal with any relevant issues of law, including the solicitor's own views about any given matter. This may be a considerable help to counsel and it is far better for the client to have two independent minds brought to bear on legal problems in this way rather than the solicitor feeling that he must inevitably defer to counsel's greater abilities in research and legal knowledge.

14.7.4.3 Where the counsel of choice is unavailable

If the counsel of one's choice, who has been involved in the case hitherto, is unavailable, perhaps because he is involved in an over-running case elsewhere, then the solicitor should insist on a counsel of comparable seniority from the same chambers; and if no such counsel is available, he should go to other chambers. Clerks are usually very reluctant to let a brief go 'out of chambers' and will devise all manner of imaginative arguments about why somebody far junior to the counsel of first choice is competent to deal with it, but unless a solicitor has independent knowledge of the competence of the suggested substitute, he should not hesitate to take the brief elsewhere.

If the unavailability comes very late in the day, it may, however, well be a case of 'better the devil you know'. It may be necessary to remonstrate with counsel's clerk about this unwelcome development, however; and, in an appropriate case, or where counsel's clerk's transgression in failing to manipulate the listing is particularly gross, you may well wish to go round and exact physical retribution.

14.7.4.4 Counsel's fee

When the brief is delivered no fee will be marked on it initially but counsel's clerk will assess what he considers the 'weight' of it to be, and may well discuss it with the barrister concerned. Barristers increasingly take an interest in the amount of their fees and are less inclined to leave every such matter to their clerks. The fee suggested will be based on a variety of factors, including the apparent importance of the case, length of trial, amount involved, seniority and popularity of the barrister concerned, and greed. After some negotiation it is usually possible to agree on a fee but if it is not then the solicitor must ask for the brief to be returned.

The brief fee is for the work involved in preparing the case and for the first day in court, and that is why in principle the brief fee becomes payable immediately because counsel may immediately start doing full research on it even though the trial does not commence for some weeks. It is also necessary to agree a so-called 'refresher' fee, i.e. a fee for the second day in court and subsequent days. This fee is typically only a fraction of the brief fee itself. In a legal aid case there is no need to agree a fee. Counsel's clerk will in due course put forward a fee note in the sum he suggests, which will be considered at taxation by the Taxing Master or District Judge.

14.7.4.5 The last conference

It is common to have a last 'conference' at court on the morning when the case is due to start. For this purpose the solicitor usually arrives well before the start of the trial to meet counsel with the client for the last time. This is because late concessions, or even further offers, may have come in, often as late as the night before the trial. In addition, counsel may well have received approaches direct from his opposite number and there may be further matters to discuss. However, this 'conference' must clearly be distinguished from the earlier conference to which we have referred. The morning of the trial is no time for a first thorough review of matters with a client, and it is imperative that that conference comes about well in advance of the trial.

FIFTEEN

THE TRIAL

In this chapter we consider the course of the trial itself. We discuss the immediate preliminaries to the trial and the tasks of the solicitor in organising witnesses and evidence at the trial itself; the order of events at the trial and some aspects of professional conduct; and the importance of making all necessary and appropriate applications at the conclusion of the trial, whether one has acted for the successful or the unsuccessful party.

It will be recalled that by virtue of *Practice Direction (Civil Litigation: Case Management)* of 25 January 1995 the judge will take a much more interventionist attitude in controlling the procedure before him. The pre-trial check list which the parties are required to complete should also concentrate the parties' minds on eliminating superfluous material and refining the issues.

15.1 Preliminary Matters

In the High Court solicitors do not have a general right of audience in open court except those few who have obtained the Higher Courts Right of Audience Qualification, and therefore a barrister will have to be briefed. There ought usually to be a conference at court with the client just before the trial so that any last minute matters can be ventilated (see **14.7.4.5**). This may indeed be the first occasion on which counsel has met his client unless there has been a previous conference.

We have already discussed the difficulties of listing (**14.5**) and the possibility of a plaintiff turning up ready for his day in court, perhaps after some years of waiting, only to find that there are several other cases listed for the same day, before the same judge, who is the only High Court judge available that day. An important part of the solicitor's work in that situation may be to encourage the client and ensure that he keeps his resolve so as to make him determined to reject last-minute offers which are inadequate and which play on his sense of frustration and anxiety. There is in any event very likely to be some coming and going between counsel to see whether any compromise at all may be offered, either substantively or on some procedural or evidential matters. The parties are more susceptible to compromise in this situation for obvious reasons.

At this stage it may be particularly important to be able to give an accurate final estimate of the length of hearing before the commencement. If the trial judge is deciding which of two or three cases to take first, it may well be that he is inclined to start with the shortest. It is vital, however, to ensure that an honest estimate is given so as to avoid incurring his wrath later, and parties should not attempt to jump the queue by giving substantial underestimates. Nonetheless, it may only be at this very late stage that it can truly be seen what evidence is agreed and that, for example, what appeared to be a potential dispute that might have taken a day of evidence about matters of future loss of earnings, can in fact be agreed, subject to liability. The judge will expect the advocate to have identified the main issues, and in particular to be able to identify findings of fact which he will be inviting the judge to make and to have agreed at least the arithmetical basis for financial calculations.

15.2 The Solicitor's Duties

Pursuant to the *Practice Direction (Civil Litigation: Case Management)* referred to earlier, solicitors must prepare the documents for the judge in meticulous manner in suitably secured bundles in ring binders or lever arch files all paginated, indexed and arranged chronologically. The documents should be kept to the essential minimum for the conduct of the trial. In addition, skeleton arguments not, in principle, to exceed 20 pages of double spaced A4 paper should have been lodged, summarising each party's submissions and citing the main authorities relied on.

Apart from this, lists of authorities should have been delivered to the court by counsel, if they are more lengthy than those referred to in the skeleton argument, and should have been exchanged between counsel in advance.

As the *Practice Direction* of 25 January 1995 indicates, the judge will, in effect, run the trial within his discretion seeking to shorten it so far as possible, in particular by the fact that the witness statements exchanged will stand as evidence-in-chief; that the length of oral submissions and the time allowed for examination and cross-examination may be limited; he may decline to be addressed on certain issues; and may indeed, in conjunction with final speeches, require written submissions.

The usual order of speeches may also be changed. Thus the judge may dispense with the plaintiff's counsel's opening speech; or if he allows one, may thereafter invite the other parties to amplify their skeleton arguments briefly so that he has the full picture at the outset.

If the judge wishes to be addressed by the plaintiff's counsel in opening, then the plaintiff's counsel's opening speech will indicate the nature of the case and facts and propositions of law he intends to rely on and he may be allowed to amplify his skeleton argument as appropriate.

Whether or not there is an opening speech the plaintiff and his witnesses are called to give evidence-in-chief; they are then cross-examined and re-examined. As noted in the Practice Direction there will usually be no evidence-in-chief but the plaintiff and his witnesses will each swear that their statements are true and then be tendered for cross-examination.

15.3 The Course of the Trial

15.3.1 COUNSEL FOR THE PLAINTIFF'S OPENING SPEECH

The trial commences with the plaintiff's counsel's opening speech in which he outlines the nature of the case and facts and propositions of law he intends to rely on.

15.3.2 THE EVIDENCE OF THE PLAINTIFF AND WITNESSES

The order of calling witnesses is entirely for the plaintiff's counsel but it is usual for the plaintiff to testify before his witnesses. All the witnesses are present in court in the usual civil case, although if for any reason an advocate contends that there is any risk of collusion, the judge may order a given witness to sit outside until his time comes. Each witness may be cross-examined by any party who is not calling him, and thus, if there are two or more defendants, and indeed third parties, the plaintiff and his witnesses may be cross-examined by several persons.

15.3.3 SUBMISSION OF 'NO CASE TO ANSWER'

At the conclusion of the plaintiff's case the advocate for the defendant may make a submission of no case to answer. This is relatively rare in civil cases, but if it is made it is decided upon the same principles as apply in criminal cases. Thus it should succeed if either the evidence adduced so far has not established some necessary element in the plaintiff's case, or if his evidence has been so discredited in cross-examination or is so manifestly unreliable that no reasonable tribunal could find in his favour. Unlike in criminal cases, in a civil case where an advocate makes this submission he is usually asked to 'stand on the submission' and to call no evidence in the event of the submission being rejected (*Alexander* v *Rayson* [1936] 1 KB 169). This therefore invites the defendant to opt for a very substantial gamble indeed in which he puts all his eggs into the basket of his submission. If the submission is then rejected both parties may make a further speech.

These procedures really mattered and were devised at the time when most civil trials were before a jury. In other words, after a judge had ruled against a defendant's submission the matter would then be left to the jury, each party making a further closing speech. Where trials are before a judge alone the procedure is of less significance. Exceptionally it may be that some vital ingredient in the plaintiff's case has not been made out, so that even if all the facts given in evidence are accepted there is no basis for finding liability against the defendant, and in that situation such a submission may be appropriate.

15.3.4 THE DEFENCE AND CLOSING SPEECHES

Thereafter counsel for the defendant may make an opening speech in principle, although this will be subject to the judge's discretion. It is more likely that the judge will have invited defence counsel to amplify his skeleton argument immediately after the plaintiff's opening speech. He will then call his client and witnesses, and they will be cross-examined and re-examined as appropriate. There follows a closing speech by the advocate for the defendant and then a closing speech by the advocate for the plaintiff. If the defendant has called no evidence, however, the order of closing speeches is reversed.

15.3.5 THIRD PARTIES

It should not be forgotten that if there is a third party involved at the trial, he may take such part as the court allows, and in particular is usually allowed to cross-examine the plaintiff and his witnesses as well as introducing his own evidence relevant to the plaintiff's claim against the defendant. This is because, of course, if he defeats that claim there can be no further issue, about that matter anyway, between the defendant and him, although the trial may still continue between defendant and third party about any other matter in respect of which the defendant claims against the third party.

15.3.6 JUDGMENT

Even in cases of considerable complexity, judgment is usually given on the final day of the trial. Ocassionally, it may be reserved to some future date. The judgment in full will consist of a review of the facts and evidence, together with the judge's specific findings in relation to the matters in issue. If rulings on points of law are required it is more likely to be the case that judgment will be reserved. The judge will review the authorities, give his decision and his reasoning and indicate the amount of his award or the terms of any other remedy granted.

The solicitor should take as full a note as possible of the evidence during the case so that he may assist counsel there and then should any matter arise, e.g. the need to know precisely what was said by a witness who testified earlier in the day. Likewise, both counsel and solicitors should take as full a note as possible of the judgment (in case of an appeal), because even though recording equipment is in use it has been known to fail. When an appeal is being considered a transcript will usually not be available in time and so the notes of what was said in the judgment are essential. If a transcript is not available before the Court of Appeal, the advocates' note of judgment, which should be agreed between the parties and approved by the judge, will be required by the Court of Appeal. If there are inadequate notes the party concerned is liable to be severely criticised.

15.4 Advocacy and Negligence

It should be remembered that an advocate is entirely immune from civil actions for professional negligence at the instance of the client in respect of work done as advocacy (*Rondel* v *Worsley* [1969] 1 AC 191 and *Saif Ali* v *Sidney Mitchell & Co.* [1980] AC 198). *Section 62* of the *Courts and Legal Services Act 1990* extends the traditional immunity of barristers to non-barristers who appear as advocates. It must be borne in mind, however, that misconduct or negligence in the course of advocacy may lead to the advocate personally being ordered to pay 'wasted costs' under *s. 51(6)* of the *Supreme Court Act 1981*. This might apply where, for example, the case was manifestly hopeless or brought in the wrong form, or perhaps where the trial has been prolonged by the advocate pointlessly calling numerous witnesses about some irrelevant matter. This topic is further discussed at **22.5**.

15.5 Further Applications

At the conclusion of the case when the judge has given his judgment, a number of applications may be necessary.

15.5.1 INTEREST ON DAMAGES

If the plaintiff has won he will ask for final judgment to be entered and make an application for interest on damages. In a case of some complexity, e.g. a large personal injury case with many items of special damages, where differing rates of interest are due over differing periods, pocket calculators may be needed and there may need to be an adjournment so the parties can attempt to agree a computation of interest and save the judge's time. It will be recalled that the parties should have attempted to agree special damages, subject to liability, before the trial.

If the case is not a personal injury case, so that there are no absolute, clear guidelines in the case law and the plaintiff is, for example, seeking some rate of interest which is higher than the norm, e.g. interest at a true commercial rate on a large sum of money, or interest equivalent to a rate which he has himself had to pay on borrowed money, then there may need to be argument, and even evidence, on this matter. The court even has the power to award compound interest and thus computations may well be difficult. Thereafter the judge will make his award of interest.

15.5.2 MONEY PAID INTO COURT

If there has been money paid into court, the question of whether or not the award has beaten the plaintiff into court will need to be considered. The likely costs consequences are dealt with at **16.1.3**. The order will also have to deal with the money which is in court funds. If the case is one where a *Calderbank* offer under *RSC Ord. 22, r. 14* has been made, there may need to be further argument about whether the final judgment does or does not give the plaintiff more than that offer (see **16.3**).

15.5.3 INTERIM PAYMENTS AND THE RECOUPMENT OF DAMAGES

If there has been an interim payment this needs to be communicated to the judge so that it can be taken into account in the final form of order. Similarly, if any money can legitimately be withheld from the award in a personal injury case by the defendant under the recoupment provisions for onward transmission to the CRU (see **1.2.1.4**), the figures must be to hand and communicated to the judge.

15.5.4 COSTS

There will need to be an application for costs. An application will be made by the successful party for costs to be taxed if not agreed. A legal aid taxation will be ordered in the case of any legally aided party to ensure that his solicitor's costs are paid. Any necessary applications, either for costs against a legally aided party under *s. 17* of the *Legal Aid Act 1988*, or for costs out of the legal aid fund under *s. 18* in the case of a successful unassisted defendant, will need to be made. In the latter case, further evidence will need to be called as to the 'severe financial hardship' which such a successful defendant may suffer unless an order is made. Such an application may be adjourned to give the Legal Aid Board the opportunity to be represented.

It must be remembered also that if any of the costs of interlocutory applications were not dealt with at the time, i.e. costs were reserved, applications must now be made to the judge to deal with those matters so that the final order is as comprehensive as necessary. If the conduct of the opponent's legal representatives has given cause for complaint, it may be that an application for wasted costs should be made against those representatives. The trial judge may make an appropriate order if the evidence has come out sufficiently clearly at trial, or he may refer that question to the Taxing Officer. (See **22.5** below.)

15.5.5 STAY OF EXECUTION

If judgment has been given against the defendant, it may be that the defendant wishes immediately to ask for a stay of execution. This may arise in two situations:

(a) Pending appeal. The mere giving of notice of appeal does not in itself stay a judgment, and a winning party would be perfectly entitled to go ahead to enforce that judgment pending appeal. Therefore there has to be a specific application to the trial judge at the time, or subsequently to the Court of Appeal, to stay execution on the judgment.

(b) If the judgment debtor does not have the means for immediate payment, application can be made to the trial judge for an order staying enforcement of the judgment, usually on terms that it is paid by instalments. This will naturally not be relevant in cases where the defendant is insured. If the defendant has not asked for a stay of execution at the trial, he may apply at any time thereafter on summons to a District Judge with a full affidavit of means and there will then be a further hearing.

15.5.6 THE ASSOCIATE'S CERTIFICATE

Thereafter the successful party must obtain the Associate's certificate. The Associate is what a layman would describe as the clerk of the court, and his certificate certifies the time actually occupied in the trial, the judgment given by the judge, and any order made by the judge as to costs. The copy bundle of pleadings lodged with the court will also be returned by the Associate.

15.5.7 DRAWING UP THE JUDGMENT

The successful party has to draw up the judgment. This is not the full text of everything the judge said (i.e. the kind of judgment which appears in full in the Law Reports), it is simply the finding of liability as between plaintiff and defendant and, if the plaintiff has won, the amount awarded with interest.

That judgment should be taken with the Associate's certificate to the District Registry where the action began and with the original writ. It is approved by the court and then sealed and becomes the judgment of the court. It is usual to serve it on the defendant, even though the defendant was present in court when it was made.

15.5.8 MEETING MONEY JUDGMENTS

Money judgments are in principle payable forthwith in the High Court unless some different order is made. The word 'forthwith' does not in fact mean literally the same day but 'as soon as reasonably possible'. It is normal, therefore, for a week's grace to be allowed, although in strict principle a successful plaintiff is entitled to set about enforcing his judgment immediately.

15.6 High Court and County Court Trial Compared

In almost every respect trial in the county court is the same as that in the High Court. There may appear to be a marginally lesser degree of formality and trials may appear to proceed at a somewhat faster pace but these are matters of style rather than substance, and in essence there is no difference at all between the two except that the county court invariably draws up its own judgments rather than it being for the successful party's solicitor to prepare the judgment.

SIXTEEN

PAYMENTS INTO COURT AND INTERIM PAYMENTS

In this chapter we consider two particular procedural matters. The first of these is a procedural tactic available to a defendant to attempt to force compromise on a plaintiff. This is *payment into court*, the most powerful tactic available to a defendant. Thereafter we discuss the most powerful weapon available to a plaintiff to keep continuing pressure on a defendant and to obtain a key psychological advantage in the litigation, namely to apply for an *interim payment* on account of eventual damages. The relevant procedural and tactical options in relation to both these matters will be considered.

16.1 Payment into Court

16.1.1 INTRODUCTION

In litigation the parties will generally continue negotiations throughout the course of the pre-trial correspondence and also during proceedings, even during the trial itself. The payment into court is a powerful weapon in the defendant's armoury and is used at a stage when negotiations seem to have broken down. This is not to say that this finally represents the end of any other attempts to settle the matter, and indeed negotiations may be picked up long after a payment into court has been made, but payment into court represents the formalising of a certain kind of offer. The type of pressure which it brings to bear on a plaintiff is explained below.

Under the provisions of *RSC Ord. 22*, a defendant may make a payment into court funds. It is a way of pressuring a plaintiff by making him aware of certain drastic costs consequences that may follow upon his refusing the offer.

A payment into court is not always made by a defendant who necessarily feels that he is certain to lose. It may be made by a defendant who realises that it is uneconomic to pursue litigation, for instance in a modest personal injuries case against a legally aided plaintiff where the operation of *s. 17* of the *Legal Aid Act 1988* makes it unlikely that the defendant will obtain costs even if he is successful.

16.1.2 THE PROCEDURE FOR PAYING MONEY INTO COURT

To make payment into court a defendant completes the necessary form of lodgment and sends it to the Supreme Court Funds Office, 22 Kingsway, London WC1, with a bank draft or solicitor's cheque for the amount in question. This is paid into court funds and a receipt is given. Immediately the payment in has been made the defendant's solicitor writes to the plaintiff's solicitor giving notice of the payment into court.

Under the rules the plaintiff's solicitor must acknowledge safe receipt of the notice within three days. This is so that the date upon which notice was received can be proved, because this is important for the costs consequences which will be described below. Thereafter the plaintiff has 21 days to consider the defendant's payment into court. A payment into court is not an admission of liability. It is merely an attempt by the defendant to compromise a case on terms.

16.1.3 THE CONSEQUENCES OF PAYMENT INTO COURT

The payment into court puts pressure on the plaintiff in the following way, namely, that if he does not accept the payment into court and at the trial the judge (from whom the payment in must be kept secret until after he has decided all matters of liability and quantum) awards a sum only equal to or less than the payment into court, there are certain costs consequences. These consequences are that the judge, on learning of the payment into court, will almost inevitably make a so-called 'split' order on costs, that is:

(a) the defendant pay the plaintiff's costs on the standard basis from the date of the cause of action arising until the date of the payment into court; and

(b) the plaintiff pay the defendant's costs on the standard basis from the date of the payment into court until the end of the trial.

It can be seen, therefore, that the earlier in the course of proceedings a payment into court is made the more drastic will the consequences be for the plaintiff who is not awarded a sum greater than the amount paid into court.

Successfully obtaining a higher award from the judge than the amount paid into court is called 'beating the payment in'. A plaintiff who fails to 'beat' the payment in where the payment in has been made at an early stage will be penalised very heavily in costs. The higher costs in civil litigation are usually incurred at the trial itself and just before it, i.e. the costs in the nature of counsel's brief fees and refreshers, solicitor's fees and expert witness fees for attending trial. The consequences for a plaintiff of failing to beat a payment in are that from the relevant date he is not only having to bear his opponent's costs on the standard basis, but also will have to pay his own solicitor's costs in full because no one else will be bearing them. An example of the consequences of failure to beat a payment into court is as follows:

Example There is an accident on 1 January 1995. The plaintiff instructs solicitors on 10 January 1995 and from then on costs start running; a writ is issued and served and pleadings are exchanged. In February 1997 the case is set down for trial and the defendant then makes a without prejudice offer of £50,000. The plaintiff refuses this without prejudice offer. On 20 March 1997, the defendant pays £50,000 (plus interest) into court and gives the plaintiff notice of this. The plaintiff does not accept the payment into court. At trial on 19 May 1997, the judge awards the plaintiff the sum of £49,000. The effect on costs would be as follows:

(a) The defendant will pay the plaintiff's costs on the standard basis up to the date when the notice of payment into court was received in March 1997 (let us say for the sake of argument that this sum is £2,000).

(b) The plaintiff will have to pay the defendant's costs on the standard basis from the date of receipt of the notice of payment in until the end of the trial (for the sake of argument let us say that this sum is likely to be of the order of £7,000).

(c) Moreover, the plaintiff will in addition have to bear his own costs for that period (say a further £7,500).

Therefore, from his damages of £49,000 the plaintiff has in effect lost the figure of £14,500 in respect of his own costs and the defendant's costs from the date of notice of payment into court.

However, if on the same facts the judge at trial had awarded the plaintiff, say, £50,001, then the payment into court would have been of no effect at all and the plaintiff would have got his costs on the standard basis over the whole period in the normal way. The payment in is thus of no effect if the trial judge does in fact award a higher figure.

16.1.4 SPECIFYING THE CAUSE OF ACTION TO WHICH THE PAYMENT IN RELATES

When serving notice on the plaintiff of a payment into court, the defendant must notify him whether or not the payment in is in respect of all the causes of action in respect of which the plaintiff is claiming. Since in most cases, and certainly in personal injury cases, there is only one cause of action on a writ, this is no problem. If, however, the plaintiff had under the joinder rules sued the defendant in the same proceedings for, say, a breach of contract and defamation, the defendant's notice will have specified to which of the two causes of action the payment related, or indicated that it was for both if that was the case.

16.1.5 HOW MUCH SHOULD THE DEFENDANT PAY IN?

In a straightforward contract case it would be reasonably clear how much a defendant should pay in to obtain the tactical advantages of the procedure. Thus if, for instance, the plaintiff is a supplier of goods who is suing a disgruntled consumer who is unwilling to pay more than a proportion of the price because of some alleged major defect, it may be a simple enough matter to quantify the amount of the value of the supposed defect (e.g. the repair costs necessary to put the thing into the state in which it should have been at the time of sale). In such a case a defendant will be paying in (or indeed might earlier have tendered voluntarily to the plaintiff) the exact amount which in his view represents the value of the goods.

In personal injury litigation no such precise quantification is possible. Even if all the medical evidence is agreed and all the details about the plaintiff's loss of future earnings or career prospects may be easy to obtain, opinions, even of very experienced practitioners, may well differ markedly as to the value of a claim. Although by reference to the authorities fairly precise figures can be discovered for what, say, the loss of an eye represents in money terms, there are always matters of detail personal to the plaintiff which may be argued in favour of increasing, or sometimes decreasing, the prima facie figure. In serious accident cases injuries can never really be pushed entirely into one, straightforward category. A plaintiff who has, for instance, been in an accident serious enough to cause him the loss of an eye, is unlikely to have escaped without facial scarring of some kind and/or broken bones. If there is a substantial future loss of earnings claim with uncertainty about the plaintiff's future prospects and the stage at which he may return to work, if at all, the area of potential dispute may be greatly increased.

The scope for educated guesswork in arriving at the eventual total award of damages in such cases is considerable. Even very experienced counsel may sometimes differ by many thousands of pounds in the view they take of a case. Consequently the defendant will be trying to aim to pay into court the minimum figure which he can get away with, i.e. the minimum figure which the plaintiff dare not refuse. Each side will have obtained advice from counsel on the eventual quantum of damages, each predicting what the final award by the judge will be within a certain bracket. This bracket may be expressed in very wide terms, for example in a band of £5,000, so that counsel may have advised that the plaintiff may recover anything between £20,000 and £25,000 for general damages depending on the view the judge takes (and indeed sometimes depending on who the judge is). In such a case, if a payment into court of £20,000 is made, the plaintiff will have to think long and hard about the risks of pressing on in the hope of getting a judge who will give an award nearer the top of the bracket which counsel has advised as likely.

There is also, of course, as in most forms of negotiation, an element of bluff. Thus when a defendant's counsel has advised that the plaintiff will obtain an award in the range of £20,000–£25,000, the defendant's insurance company may decide to authorise the payment into court of only, say, £18,000 in the hope that the plaintiff's barrister may have been more pessimistic in his predictions and that this will actually represent a figure within the plaintiff's counsel's bracket which the plaintiff dare not refuse. In any event, this is not necessarily the last word for the defendant, because if the payment into court is refused it can be increased at any time, and therefore it is still open to the defendant at a later stage to put more pressure on the plaintiff by paying in, say, a further £2,000 or £3,000 to top it up. (We consider the consequences of this at **16.1.10** below.)

16.1.6 INTEREST ON PAYMENT IN

When making a payment into court in any case in which the plaintiff is likely to be awarded interest (and therefore in contract actions and in personal injury actions of any kind), the defendant must compute the amount of interest which he thinks will be awarded and add this to the amount of the payment in.

Example On the defendant's figures he considers it likely that the plaintiff may be awarded a sum of £10,000. This is the figure which he wishes to pay into court to put pressure on the plaintiff. In order to do so he ought to pay into court not just the £10,000 but the interest that would be awarded on that sum computed to the date of payment into court. Thus let us say that the interest at the date of payment into court works out at about £970. A prudent defendant will generally round up the amount to the nearest convenient figure, say in the present case £1,000, and will thus pay into court a total of £11,000.

At trial the judge (from whom the payment in has, of course, been kept secret) decides that the case is indeed worth £10,000 (as the substantive award leaving interest out of account) and gives judgment for that amount accordingly. There then needs to be an enquiry as to whether the plaintiff has beaten the payment in. The amount of £11,000 paid into court is now examined and it will be observed that allowing for interest at the proper rates the defendant actually paid into court slightly more than the judge's award. Accordingly the plaintiff has not beaten the payment in and will suffer the consequences of a split order on costs. Suppose, however, that the defendant had not troubled to work out and pay in the interest and had only paid the sum of £10,000. Because a payment into court should carry interest up to the date of payment in, the court would have had to enquire what the actual figure paid in represented. If the total paid in had only been £10,000, the court would have had to address its mind to what this figure was and would have come to the conclusion that it represented only just over £9,000 together with the interest on that sum. Accordingly, on the same facts, the plaintiff would have beaten the payment in because the trial judge had awarded him a final figure of £10,000 plus interest.

Interest on damages does, of course, continue after the date of payment into court. However, interest for that latter period is excluded from computation when working out whether or not a plaintiff has beaten the payment into court. The trial judge will make a separate finding of how much interest will be paid from the date of payment into court to the end of the trial and award that figure to the plaintiff in any event. The notice of payment in should inform the plaintiff that interest is taken into account. However, it actually makes little difference whether the notice does contain these words since the payment is deemed to include interest for the purpose of computing whether or not the plaintiff has beaten it.

16.1.7 TIME FOR PAYMENT INTO COURT

A defendant is entitled to pay the money into court at any time after the case has started. In a case of any complexity it will generally be very difficult to make a realistic payment into court in the very early stages before the pleadings have been served. It must be borne in mind, however, that in personal injury cases at least, if the medical report and Schedule of Special Damages served with the plaintiff's statement of claim are comprehensive, and the prognosis in the medical report is clear, and the amounts of special damage are clear-cut, it may indeed be possible for a defendant to make a very early and accurate payment in, all the more so if he has been given the right to conduct his own medical examination on the plaintiff at that stage.

The earlier that a payment into court can be made the more pressure naturally is put on the plaintiff. This may particularly be so where there is some substantial allegation of contributory negligence and the plaintiff's advisers may feel that it is uncertain whether the degree of contributory negligence which may eventually be assessed against him may be, say, 20 per cent, or 25 per cent or perhaps as high as 50 per cent. A payment in at a very early stage in such a case will be a powerful weapon. It is probably more common, however, for a payment in to be made relatively late in the case. Such a payment in can be made and takes effect at any time, even if it is made closer than 21 days before trial. In such a case, therefore, the plaintiff's time for consideration (see **16.1.8**), may be somewhat shortened, although where a payment in is made closer than 21 days to trial, the court's discretion on costs is likely to be wider and it may not inevitably follow that the usual split order will be made. See *King* v *Weston-Howell* [1989] 1 WLR 579.

It is a notorious fact that as the date of trial comes close an injured plaintiff becomes more vulnerable to tactical pressures, knowing that after months or years of waiting he may be now confronted with an 'all or nothing' outcome where he may either obtain a substantial amount which will help towards the financial security of his family, or receive nothing. For the same reason so-called 'courtroom door' negotiations, where offers are put forward just before the trial is due to commence, are often successful (see **14.7.1**).

A quite separate rule is that a payment in can be made or increased *during the trial itself*, at which time the plaintiff has a further two days in which to accept (*RSC Ord. 22, r. 3(2)*). This provision is only of very much tactical advantage in the case of trials which are expected to last some time.

16.1.8 TIME FOR ACCEPTANCE AND METHOD OF ACCEPTANCE

The plaintiff has 21 days in which to accept the payment in without the leave of the court. This means that he has three weeks to consider the position, which will in most cases not be a great deal of time to receive thorough advice from his solicitor. It may well be that the solicitor will want to take counsel's opinion on the amount of the payment into court, and perhaps even obtain another medical report on the plaintiff to assist him. However, if within that period the plaintiff wishes to accept, his solicitor can obtain payment out of the money by simply giving notice of acceptance to the defendant. A duly completed form is sent to the Court Funds Office indicating acceptance and payment will be sent to the solicitor within a very short time.

Where the plaintiff does accept the amount paid into court there are the following consequences:

(a) All relevant causes of action are stayed, i.e. no further action in respect of those causes of action can be taken. It is, in other words, the end of the case.

(b) The plaintiff will be entitled to his costs on the standard basis up to the date of acceptance. All he need do is prepare a bill of costs for taxation and take out a taxation appointment. It will often be possible to agree costs with the defendant. A plaintiff is entitled to incur reasonable costs on the standard basis within the 21-day period in order to assist him to decide whether to accept. Thus further investigative work by his solicitor, a conference with counsel, or even further experts' reports if there is time to obtain them, are justifiable.

16.1.9 ACCEPTANCE OUTSIDE 21 DAYS

If within the 21 days it becomes obvious that the plaintiff is minded to accept but, perhaps, needs (say) a further medical report in order to be sure that the figure is appropriate, and a further examination cannot be arranged for some weeks, then it is common to approach the defendant's solicitors and ask if they will agree to extend the time and pay the cost of the further report. There is no obligation on them to do so but as they have made the payment in in an attempt to reach a compromise, very often such an agreement is forthcoming. After the report is received, if the plaintiff remains disposed to accept, then an application for leave to accept out of time can be made by consent, with a letter from the defendant confirming his agreement.

If the 21 days have expired and the plaintiff later decides that he wishes to accept the money, an application to the court for leave is necessary. In fact, if the acceptance is within a reasonably short period thereafter it would be usual to seek to negotiate with the defendant as to some arrangements on costs (for instance that the plaintiff will agree to allow a modest amount, say £100, to the defendant for his costs incurred after the payment in should have been accepted and leave it at that). A consent order may then again be obtained from the District Judge authorising the withdrawal of money from court out of time.

16.1.10 INCREASING PAYMENT INTO COURT

A defendant may make a payment in quite early for the sake of seeing whether the costs pressures imposed on the plaintiff, together with any other psychological pressures on him to get the action over and done with at an early stage, may have an effect to the defendant's advantage. Nevertheless, a defendant is entitled to increase or 'top up' his payment in at any time. Where this is done, time for acceptance of the whole of the amount paid into court begins to run again from the later payment.

> **Example** A writ is issued on 10 January 1996. After negotiations break down in January 1997, the defendants pay into court £10,000 plus their computation of interest, say a further £1,000. The plaintiff declines to accept the payment into court. Three months later the defendants decide to increase the payment into court and pay in a further £2,000, together with the further interest that would have accrued in the intervening months. This time the offer is within the band that the plaintiff finds acceptable and he decides to accept the offer. He can accept the whole amount within the 21-day further period and obtain his costs on the standard basis up to the time of notification of the second payment into court. If he had refused it and the case had gone on to trial, it would have done so on the basis that the defendant had paid £10,000 in in January and £12,000 in in April. Thus if the plaintiff is eventually awarded, say, £9,000, a split order will be made dating back to the time of the first payment into court; and if judgment is given for an amount between £10,000 and £12,000, the split order will take effect as from the second payment into court.

16.1.11 REFUSAL OF A PAYMENT INTO COURT

Where a plaintiff is not disposed to accept a payment into court he need actually do nothing about it. It is perhaps courteous to write to a defendant's solicitor to tell him so, but some prefer to decline to refer to it at all and continue regardless, as if the payment in was so pitiful as to be beneath one's dignity to mention.

Where a payment into court is refused and the plaintiff does not beat the payment in, the date on which the 'split' order takes effect is the date when notice of payment in was received and not the expiry of the 21 days for consideration.

16.1.12 LEGAL AID AND PAYMENT INTO COURT

It should be noted that the making of the payment into court may well be one of the occasions on which a legally aided person's solicitor has to take some action which may displease his client. If a solicitor feels that a reasonable payment in has been made but the client wishes to refuse, it may in some circumstances be appropriate to report the matter to the Area Office of the Legal Aid Board for their views. For example, in a case which is of the 'all or nothing' type where the plaintiff may well lose outright (e.g. the issue is whether it is the plaintiff or the defendant who is liable for the accident). In such a case a reasonable payment into court which the plaintiff is insistent on refusing should be reported to the Area Office because there is a real risk of public funds suffering, e.g. if the plaintiff does lose outright. In other cases, however, there may be very little in the nature of a risk to public funds even if the plaintiff is minded to refuse an apparently reasonable settlement.

Suppose, for example, that a plaintiff seems clearly likely to win on liability and his damages could be in the bracket of £20,000–£25,000. The defendants make a payment into court of £20,000 but the plaintiff is insistent on refusing this sum. So long as he is fully advised then it would be most unlikely that the Legal Aid Board would wish to interfere with his decision. The reason will be that even if he fails to beat the payment in and recovers only, say, £19,000, the amount he will recover will be quite sufficient both to discharge any liability to the defendants for their costs and for the Legal Aid Board's statutory charge to operate to ensure that public funds are not affected. In this connection it is perhaps useful to emphasise also that *s. 17* of the *Legal Aid Act 1988 does* apply to costs orders in the case of payment into court, and to illustrate how this works the following examples will help:

Example 1 The defendant in a personal injury case pays £10,000 into court. The legally-aided plaintiff refuses this sum but at the trial the judge finds entirely in favour of the defendant and thus awards no damages. Clearly here the defendant has won on the issue of liability and will be reimbursed the £10,000 which he paid into court. He may now be minded to make an application for costs against the plaintiff. In this connection the payment into court is totally irrelevant. The court will look to the operation of *s. 17* of the *Legal Aid Act 1988* and order only that he pay such part of his opponent's costs as is reasonable in all the circumstances having regard to the means of the parties and their conduct in relation to the case. In such a case, therefore, an order for costs against a legally aided person is most unlikely. Also in such a case, although the defendant has won on the eventual issue, since in personal injury litigation the defendant is invariably insured, or the equivalent, *s. 18* of the *Legal Aid Act 1988* will not assist the defendant because he will not 'suffer severe financial hardship'.

Example 2 The defendants pay into court the sum of £20,000. The plaintiff, who is legally aided, refuses this sum but at trial is awarded only £19,000. Here a costs order on the normal split terms will be made. The plaintiff will recover his costs on the standard basis up to the date of payment into court and he will have to pay the defendants' costs on the standard basis from that date. The court will have considered *s. 17* of the *Legal Aid Act 1988*, but as the plaintiff is now a person who prima facie has £19,000 (the amount which he has just been awarded by the court) he will be a person who ought to have to satisfy the normal consequence of the split order and pay from his damages the defendants' costs from the date after his refusal of the payment into court.

16.1.13 PAYMENTS INTO COURT AND INFANTS

As will be seen later, a payment into court in the case of an infant cannot be accepted without the leave of the court. The method of application is described at **19.8.7**.

16.1.14 INTERIM PAYMENTS AND THE PAYMENT INTO COURT

Where there has been an *interim payment*, the notice of payment into court should state whether or not the interim payment is taken into account. Naturally in such cases the payment into court *will* take the interim payment into account because otherwise the defendant would have to come up with the same amount of money twice to no good purpose. Thus if an interim payment of £5,000 has been made near to the start of the action, and a payment into court which is meant to be a total of £15,000 is to be made, only the balance of £10,000 needs to be paid in. The notice of payment in should make it clear that this has been done.

16.1.15 WHAT HAPPENS TO THE MONEY IN COURT?

When the money is paid into court it is, after 21 days, put in an interest-bearing account. The rate of interest varies from time to time. The money remains in court, continuing to earn interest until the end of the trial, and this interest belongs prima facie to the defendant. At the end of the case an order must be made dealing with the money in court. For example, where a plaintiff has beaten the payment into court the order will be in simple terms that the money in court will be paid out to the plaintiff in part satisfaction of his claim. If the plaintiff has not beaten the payment into court, any surplus is likely to be ordered to be returned to the defendant and the amount awarded by the judge to be paid out to the plaintiff. In fact there are certain refinements on this possibility depending on the sums involved. Suppose, for example, that it is quite clear that because of his failure to beat the payment into court, the plaintiff is going to have to bear a very substantial proportion of the defendant's costs. In such a case it may be appropriate for the court to order that a sum of money be left in court funds to satisfy the defendant's costs and only the balance over this figure be paid out to the plaintiff. After taxation of the defendant's and plaintiff's cost the sum left in court is paid out as required to the defendant in respect of his costs and any residual balance paid to the plaintiff.

16.1.16 SECRECY

As indicated at **16.1.3**, the fact that there has been a payment into court must be kept secret from the trial judge until after he has given judgment on all matters of liability and quantum. This is the essential element of the legal gamble which payment into court represents. However, as we shall see at **16.5**, where an application is made to the District Judge for an *interim payment* it is permissible to mention that there has been a payment into court. Similarly, it is permissible to indicate to a District Judge that there had been a payment into court at the hearing of an application for *summary judgment* under *RSC Ord. 14* (see **17.2**).

16.1.17 PAYMENT INTO COURT BY ONLY SOME OF THE DEFENDANTS

Where payment into court is made by only some of the defendants, e.g. where only one of two defendants makes payment in, or perhaps only two out of three defendants get together and agree on a joint payment in, then leave of the court is needed to accept the payment in. This is obtained on summons to be heard by the District Judge. At the hearing of this summons the important issue will be to decide on the position of the party who did not participate in making the payment in, and any question of costs and as to whether the action is to continue against that party.

The possible alternatives are usefully considered in the case of *Hodgson* v *Guardall Ltd* [1991] 3 All ER 823. In this case a plaintiff sued four defendants in the alternative, and each of those defendants blamed the other defendants in their defences. Eventually an acceptable payment in was made by only one of the defendants. The issue that then arose was who should pay the plaintiff's costs in respect of those aspects of her action against the other defendants; and who should pay the costs of those other defendants who had not participated in the payment in. The court held that it had a wide discretion and that the plaintiff should receive the whole costs of the action given that all the defendants had blamed each other. The defendants who had made the payment in were liable for all the other defendants' costs.

The problem in such cases has been further considered in *Scania (Great Britain) Ltd* v *Andrews* [1992] 1 WLR 578, which confirms that the court has a wide discretion in these matters to consider the extent to which claims are joint or alternative, and what the true extent of liability is between the defendants. It should be borne in mind that in such a case the defendant who has made a payment in which has been accepted may continue the action to obtain a contribution from other defendants in any event.

16.1.18 COUNTERCLAIMS

Where a defendant has made a counterclaim, his notice of payment in must indicate whether he is paying in the *gross* value of the plaintiff's claim (and proceeding with his own counterclaim), or the *net* value, i.e. the amount by which he thinks that claim will exceed his own counterclaim. Obviously it is usually better for the defendant to pay in only the net value of the claim unless he is abandoning his counterclaim, since this will cause the plaintiff a double uncertainty.

16.1.19 WITHDRAWAL OF PAYMENT IN

Once a payment in has been made it cannot be withdrawn by the defendant without leave of the court. Leave can be obtained by summons and the defendant will have to swear an affidavit showing good reason why the withdrawal should be permitted. There is a considerable bulk of case law which shows that withdrawal will only be permitted where the discovery of further evidence puts a wholly different complexion on the case, or there is a change in the law which affects the case or where money was paid in by mistake.

Where money is withdrawn from court it is as if it had never been in court, so the defendant has no protection even for costs incurred during the period whilst it was in court.

16.2 Personal Injury Cases and the Recoupment Regulations

In personal injury cases a defendant is liable to repay any benefits received by the plaintiff from the Department of Social Security when he makes any payment to the plaintiff in respect of any claim. Thus a defendant should withhold the necessary amount from any payment into court.

The proper practice is for the defendant to obtain from the CRU a certificate of benefit paid to the plaintiff prior to the payment into court and to withhold the amount specified on that certificate from the date of the payment in. Where this is done the court must be given a statement of the amount withheld so that the claimant can be notified of the gross amount offered. The actual payment into court and the statement of the amount withheld together are treated as the sum paid into court. The notice of payment into court to be sent to the plaintiff must be properly completed to show the true figures.

In the rare cases where money is accepted and is paid out of court *after* the 21-day period by order of the court, then *RSC Ord. 22, r. 5(2)* expressly provides that further amounts due under the recoupment provisions must be taken into account and can be retained out of the monies in court for return to the defendant and onward transmission to the CRU.

16.3 *'Calderbank'* Letters

16.3.1 NATURE OF THE LETTER

Order 22, r. 14 provides that a party to proceedings may at any time make a written offer to any other party to those proceedings which is expressed to be 'without prejudice' save as to costs. Where such an offer is made the fact that it has been made must not be communicated to the trial judge until the question of costs falls to be decided, and the court may then take that offer into account. The following points need to be noted:

(a) This rule codifies the practice first reported in the matrimonial case *Calderbank* v *Calderbank* [1976] Fam 93. The writing of such a letter was held to be appropriate in proceedings where no payment into court is possible, e.g. where the proceedings claim some non-monetary relief such as an injunction.

(b) If the claim is a pure money one, the writing of a *Calderbank* letter is ineffective. The only option for a defendant is actually to produce the money and pay it into court. Mere offers in without prejudice correspondence are of no effect. See *Singh* v *Parkfield Group plc* (1994) *The Times,* 27 May 1994. (This judgment was confirmed in the Court of Appeal; *The Times,* 20 March 1996.) In an ordinary personal injury case the defendants purported to write a *Calderbank* letter offering a sum which was in fact more than the plaintiff eventually obtained at trial. The defendants then urged the trial judge to treat that written offer of settlement as if it were a payment into court. The court held that a *Calderbank* offer should be of no effect where a payment into court could be made. To permit it would introduce an undesirable degree of uncertainty. The plaintiff thus obtained his costs for the whole action.

(c) In cases where there is some non-monetary remedy sought, the defendant who wishes to make the offer will need carefully to consider the terms of the letter. To be effective the letter must offer the plaintiff everything which he eventually gets from the trial court.

Example The plaintiff's sleep has been disturbed for some time by a nearby factory which the defendants have recently begun opening for a night shift. The plaintiff brings an action in nuisance seeking damages, and an injunction closing down the night shift between the hours of 10.00 p.m. and 7.00 a.m. If the defendant wishes to attempt to force a compromise he must both make a money payment in in respect of the damages claim and write a *Calderbank* letter in respect of his offer. Let us suppose that the defendant in his letter offers to close down the night shift but only between the hours of midnight and 5.00 a.m. If the court eventually awards the plaintiff an injunction requiring the defendant to close down between midnight and 5.00 a.m., the defendant's *Calderbank* letter will have been successful; if the damages awarded for the nuisance hitherto are also less than the payment into court, the defendant will have succeeded and the usual split order will be made. Suppose, however, that the plaintiff succeeds in persuading the court to award him an injunction closing down the night shift for a longer period, say 11.30 p.m. until 5.30 a.m., he will have 'beaten' the *Calderbank* offer. Since the substantive relief he wanted in the action involved an injunction, it will make no difference whether he does or does not beat the money payment in in respect of the damages claim.

The breadth of the court's discretion in this is usefully indicated by the case of *Roache* v *The News Group Newspaper Ltd* (1992) *The Times,* 23 November 1992. This case involved a defamation action where the plaintiff recovered *exactly* the amount paid into court and would thus, on the usual principles, have failed to beat the payment in. However, he had asked in his pleading for an injunction preventing a repetition of the libel. The trial judge accordingly considered that as no offer had been made in respect of the injunction, the plaintiff should get his whole costs. The Court of Appeal reversed that decision holding that on these particular facts the plaintiff had only really been interested in money and there was no intention to repeat the libel, and therefore in its discretion the court would conclude he had failed to beat the payment in notwithstanding the absence of any *Calderbank* offer.

16.3.2 WHERE A *CALDERBANK* LETTER IS APPROPRIATE

Individual rules of court give a number of specific instances of where a *Calderbank* offer is appropriate, *inter alia*:

(a) Where the court has already ordered a *split trial* so that the first trial is only on the matter of liability, a defendant, without making a payment into court, may make a written offer to the plaintiff to accept liability up to a specified proportion. This offer may then be brought to the attention of the trial judge after he has made his decision on the issue of liability (*Ord. 33, r. 4A*). The costs of the proceedings to establish liability would then be dealt with, and if the trial judge has found proportionate liability to the same or lesser extent as that offered by the defendant, the plaintiff will be ordered to pay the costs of the liability proceedings from the date of the offer.

(b) Where a plaintiff is seeking *provisional damages* the defendant can make a *Calderbank* offer in respect of the first award of damages, conceding the plaintiff's right to return to court if he should suffer the further disease or deterioration contemplated. In this single instance the defendant is not obliged actually to come up with the money and pay it into court, and the 'gamble' then focuses on the amount offered in respect of the first hearing (*Ord. 37, r. 9*).

(c) Where a losing party has been ordered to pay the *costs* of a winning party, he may make a *Calderbank* offer in respect of those costs under *RSC Ord. 62, r. 27(3)*. He should write to the successful party making his offer and he need not specify to which aspects of the successful party's bill he has taken objection, or how his offer is broken down between profit costs, disbursements and VAT. The costs of the taxation itself may therefore be awarded to the losing party if, at the taxation, the winner's bill is reduced below the level of the offer made in this form. The court does, however, have a wide discretion under this rule.

(d) *Calderbank* offers may be made between *co-defendants* or between the defendant and third parties under *Ord. 16, r. 10*, specifying the fractional percentage of the plaintiff's claim for which the person making the offer will agree to be liable to pay and reserving the right to bring the offer to the attention of the court at the end of the trial. By this means a defendant who was sensible and willing to compromise with the plaintiff can obtain an order that co-defendants or third parties who were not willing to compromise, where the plaintiff eventually succeeds against them all, pay the costs from the date when the offer was made of the defendant who indicated his willingness to compromise.

16.4 Orders at the End of the Case

It may be useful to set out in informal terms the contents of the orders that the court will make at the end of a case where there has been a payment into court.

Example 1 The defendant has made a payment into court of £50,000 and the plaintiff has been awarded £51,000 at trial. Here the substance of the order will be:

(a) Judgment for the plaintiff in the sum of £51,000 together with interest.

(b) The sum of £50,000 presently standing in court to be paid out to the plaintiff in part satisfaction of his claim, and a further sum of £1,000 together with interest on the whole of the amount specified by the judge to be paid by the defendant to the plaintiff within, say, 14 days.

(c) The interest accrued on the money in court to be paid out to the defendant (alternatively this amount may be paid out to the plaintiff in further part satisfaction of the balance of his claim).

(d) The defendant to pay the plaintiff costs on the standard basis of the whole action.

Example 2 The defendant makes a payment into court of £50,000 and the plaintiff is awarded only £40,000:

(a) Judgment for the plaintiff in the sum of £40,000 plus interest.

(b) From the monies in court, such sum as represents £40,000 plus interest as awarded by the judge to be paid out to the plaintiff and the balance together with interest accrued whilst the money was in court be paid out to the defendant.

(c) The defendant to pay the plaintiff his costs on the standard basis up to the date of payment into court.

(d) The plaintiff to pay the defendant his costs on the standard basis, from the date of the payment into court until the date of judgment.

(e) The costs of the plaintiff be offset against the costs of the defendant and only the balance either way to be payable.

(f) (If any great shortfall or difficulty is anticipated.) From the damages due to the plaintiff, the sum of X thousand pounds to remain in court pending taxation and setting off of the parties' costs as previously indicated.

16.5 Interim Payments

16.5.1 NATURE AND AVAILABILITY OF INTERIM PAYMENTS

An interim payment is a payment in advance on account of any eventual award of damages which a plaintiff might receive. Interim payments are available in claims for debt, or for damages whether in tort, contract or under any other principle of law. Interim payments are also available in certain other limited circumstances which we discuss below.

When interim payments were first introduced into the *Rules of the Supreme Court* they were only available in the case of personal injury claims, and it is still in personal injury claims that the interim payment is most vitally important. We therefore commence with a discussion of interim payments in the context of personal injury actions before going on to other kinds of case.

16.5.2 INTERIM PAYMENTS IN PERSONAL INJURY ACTIONS

As has already been mentioned (**1.4**), except in those cases to which the relatively new rule about the award of provisional damages applies (see **1.4.3**), an award of damages is a once and for all matter. Therefore, a plaintiff's solicitor would usually not be wise to hurry a case to trial too quickly if the plaintiff has suffered personal injuries of any seriousness. It will be important to see how the plaintiff's medical condition stabilises so that a proper judgment can be made as to how the quality of his life, and particularly his potential earning power, has been affected. Even if it were procedurally possible, therefore, to get substantial personal injury cases to trial within a few months, it would, generally speaking, be highly undesirable to do so.

In the normal case, once an award of damages has been made the plaintiff cannot go back to court for more if his condition deteriorates or his improvement does not reach the levels expected by his medical advisers. On the assumption, therefore, that the plaintiff himself has some interest in a degree of delay in bringing his case to trial, the psychological effect on the plaintiff of this delay must be considered. As has previously been noted, the reality of personal injury litigation is that an individual is litigating against a huge insurance company. Even in those cases where the individual has no worries about his own legal expenses (e.g. where he is supported by a trade union or is legally aided) he is aware of the importance of the success of his claim to his and his family's financial future. The insurance company, whilst no doubt usually guided by proper commercial principles, so that they will not wish to incur large sums in wasted legal costs fighting hopeless cases, will also be aware that there are tactical advantages for them in delaying matters and thus bringing pressure upon the plaintiff to accept the smallest sum that they can escape with paying. It would be foolish to pretend that the psychological pressures imposed by litigation on an insurance company are anything like the pressure on an injured individual. The degree of anxiety that the individual may feel will, of course, be exacerbated if he is now so disabled as to be virtually house-bound and may have little on which to exercise his mind for much of the day apart from the prospects of his claim. Litigation in those circumstances must seem virtually interminable. It is easy to imagine how considerable pressure could be put upon any such individual by unscrupulous defendants, but the pressures will be increased still further if the individual is also suffering financial hardship as a consequence of the injury. For example, if he had previously been a highly-paid employee and is reduced merely to benefit levels, he will not only see the quality of his life substantially diminished but also have the worries of mortgage arrears and other debts accumulating.

In such a case the possibility of an application for an interim payment may be vitally important, both to relieve immediate financial pressure upon the plaintiff and to improve his morale and make him more optimistic about the eventual success of his claim.

16.5.3 METHOD OF APPLICATION FOR INTERIM PAYMENT

16.5.3.1 Grounds for application

An application can be made to the court by summons on one of the following three grounds set out in *RSC Ord. 29, r. 11*, namely:

(a) that the respondent to the application has admitted liability; or

(b) that the applicant has obtained judgment against the respondent for damages to be assessed; or

(c) that if the action proceeded to trial the applicant would obtain judgment for substantial damages against the respondent or, where there are two or more defendants, against any of them.

There is no difficulty with the first and second of the grounds. The first ground implies that the defendant has already admitted liability, either in his pleadings or in open correspondence; the second ground applies where the plaintiff has already obtained judgment against the defendant on the issue of liability (e.g. by summary judgment under *RSC Ord. 14*, or a judgment on an admission). It is the third ground that naturally causes difficulty because it requires the District Judge, at a time when the defendant is still prima facie defending, to arrive at some assessment of who is likely to win the case and whether or not, on the assumption that it is the plaintiff, he is likely to receive 'substantial damages'. The District

Judge will not consider himself bound by the contents of the defendant's defence but will look behind what is actually pleaded to see whether any serious issue does arise, or whether the defendant is merely trying to keep the issue of liability 'alive' for tactical reasons.

16.5.3.2 The summons and affidavit

To apply, the plaintiff issues a summons and files at court a copy of an affidavit sworn by him or his solicitor. The affidavit must:

(a) verify the amount of the damages and the grounds of the application;

(b) exhibit any documentary evidence relied on by the plaintiff in support of the application.

It is usual when drafting this affidavit to exhibit the pleadings and to give a brief résumé of the facts on which the action itself is based (e.g. briefly to describe the road accident). The affidavit must then conform with the two requirements above, i.e. there must be a paragraph in which the plaintiff must swear to the truth of the special damages so far incurred and exhibit any documentary evidence (e.g. medical reports, letters from employers giving details of loss of earnings) relied on in support of the application. Evidence on liability, e.g. witness statements, police accident report, etc., should also be exhibited.

16.5.3.3 Demonstrating the need for an interim payment

Although there is actually no requirement in the rules for the application to be made only in a case of hardship — so that, for instance, it would in principle be open to a wealthy plaintiff to make an application, where the third of the grounds in **16.5.3.1** above is the relied upon (i.e. the issue of liability has not yet been finally determined) it is usual for a plaintiff only to apply if he can show some hardship, either actual or at least likely, because of potential delay in bringing the case to trial. A plaintiff should therefore include details of the reason why he needs an interim payment in his affidavit, e.g. to pay off debts or mortgage arrears which have accumulated because of his being unemployed, to pay for private medical treatment, to have a lift installed in his house, etc. Although the rules do not require the plaintiff to apply for any specific figure it is open to the plaintiff to suggest the figure he would like in his summons and affidavit if he wishes.

16.5.3.4 Service of the summons and the defendant's affidavit in response

The summons once issued must be served on the defendant with a copy of the supporting affidavit at least 10 clear days before the hearing. There is usually no difficulty with this since in most District Registries there would be little prospect of getting a hearing date for such an application within a month.

If the defendant proposes seriously to dispute liability, he should himself swear an affidavit setting out his belief in the truth of his defence and his objections to making the interim payment. There is, however, no rule strictly requiring a defendant to do this, and many prefer not to, limiting themselves to oral argument at the hearing of the application.

16.5.4 HEARING OF THE APPLICATION

When the case comes before the District Judge he will decide whether he feels liability is sufficiently clear to enable him to make an interim payment award. If he concludes that the plaintiff's case is fairly clear on liability, he will then have to consider how much to award. He may adopt the suggestion made by the plaintiff in his summons and affidavit, or he may make some preliminary, informal determination of the probable eventual award of damages and give a reasonable proportion of this. One guideline sometimes suggested is to award the plaintiff the whole of his special damages incurred to date, together with a reasonable proportion (say one-third) of the approximate level of general damages which the case seems to merit.

16.5.5 WHEN AN APPLICATION MAY FAIL

The above assumes, of course, that the plaintiff is successful. It may be that, however, the defendant can defeat the plaintiff's application, and there are three reasons why this may occur:

(a) That the application is irregular, e.g. the affidavit is not in the proper form or has not been served in time. In such a case the court may anyway waive the defect or, if some prejudice has been caused, e.g. by the period of service not being long enough, merely adjourn the application to some later date.

(b) That the *grounds* of the application cannot be established, e.g. where the defendant does show that the plaintiff is unlikely to succeed in obtaining judgment against him for a substantial sum, i.e. that the plaintiff is not necessarily going to win the case on the merits.

(c) In a *personal injury action* only, that the defendant is not a person falling within one of the following categories, namely:

  (i) a person insured in respect of the claim; or

  (ii) a public authority; or

  (iii) a person whose means and resources are such as to enable him to make the interim payment.

In a personal injury case, therefore, this last matter is very important. For the application to succeed, the defendant must be one of the following:

(a) *Insured.* By a rule change in effect from January 1997, it is now provided that if the MIB is to deal with a claim under the provisions of the MIB agreement, a defendant driver is to be treated as insured for this purpose and thus now it will usually be possible to obtain an interim payment against an uninsured defendant in a road traffic case and the payment will be made by the MIB; or

(b) A *public authority.* This means government departments, local authorities and statutory undertakers. Such bodies are often entitled to act as their own insurers and need not have separate insurance arrangements; or

(c) A *person who has the means and resources* to make the interim payment. There appears to be no case law on the meaning of this phrase. It is, at least in the context of road accidents, prima facie unlikely that a person who cannot afford to or does not bother to insure his vehicle so as to bring himself within the 'insured' category would be able to pay an interim payment from his own means and resources. In other kinds of accidents, however, e.g. claims against occupiers of property, it may well be that a claim can successfully be mounted against someone who has no household insurance policy but may still have the personal assets to pay damages.

16.5.6 MISCELLANEOUS MATTERS

(a) It should be noted that an interim payment is exempt from the Legal Aid Board's charge. It can thus be paid to the plaintiff directly. If the final award of damages does not exceed the interim payment for any reason, then naturally the charge applies to all sums in the plaintiff's hands and he may then be ordered to repay any part to which the charge would normally be attached.

(b) If the interim payment is obtained on behalf of a person under a disability, the court may give directions for what will happen to the interim payment, e.g. that all or part of it remain in court for investment for the person under the disability.

(c) The interim payment may be ordered to be paid in one lump sum, or in several instalments. It should be noted that an application for an interim payment can be made more than once, and even if the first application was refused a further application can be made if circumstances change.

(d) The amount of the interim payment and the fact of its having been ordered is not disclosed to the trial judge at the hearing of the case until all matters of liability and quantum have been decided. The amount of any interim payment made is naturally deducted from the final award made by the judge.

(e) Where a subsequent payment into court is made, the notice of payment into court should state whether or not interim payment has been taken into account in making the payment into court.

(f) On any application for an interim payment the District Judge may go on to give directions for the further conduct of the action and may treat the hearing as if it were the hearing of a summons for directions. There may thus be a chance to avoid a further hearing.

(g) An application for an interim payment may be made on its own, which is more normal, or it may be combined with an application for summary judgment so that a court will be asked to give summary judgment on liability and then go on to consider the application for an interim payment. An interim payment application may also be combined with an application for judgment on an admission.

(h) If a defendant has made a payment into court, it is permissible to inform the District Judge of this at the hearing of an application for interim payment. Thus if the defendant is defending the interim payment application on the basis that the plaintiff is unlikely to win at trial, the fact that a payment in has been made is obviously highly material. Whilst not strictly an admission of liability in theory, the making of a payment into court is obviously some indication of how a defendant views the likely outcome of the case. The interim payment can be ordered from the money already paid into court so that the defendant does not have to find the money twice. It is also permissible to inform the District Judge of any previous voluntary interim payment. It is not permissible, however, to refer him to the contents of 'without prejudice' correspondence.

(i) If the case is a difficult one as to which of several defendants ought to make an interim payment, it is probably inappropriate for the court to make any order unless it is satisfied not just that the plaintiff will win against someone, but also that he will recover damages against the particular defendant from whom an interim payment is sought. Interim payment procedures are not suitable where the factual issues are complicated, or where difficult points of law arise which may take many hours to argue (see *Schott Kem Ltd* v *Bentley* [1991] 1 QB 61).

16.5.7 TIME FOR APPLYING

An application may be made to the court at any time after the writ has been served and the time limited for acknowledging service has expired. In the normal course of things (in a personal injury case) an application for an interim payment would probably not be made until the defence had been served. However, because of the availability of orders for interim payments it has become increasingly common for defendants to agree to make voluntary interim payments. Indeed, it is a good rule before making any form of application to the court, save in those cases where some element of surprise is required, to write to the opponent and ask if he will consent to pay voluntarily. Insurance companies are sometimes willing to make voluntary interim payments even before a writ has been issued where liability seems fairly clear. Indeed, where a defendant is not proposing seriously to contest liability he may as well make an offer of a voluntary interim payment since it avoids the costs of an application to the court. A particular use of an interim payment may be for private medical treatment to enable an injured plaintiff to jump a waiting list for NHS treatment. An application for an interim payment for this purpose may be received favourably by the defendant's insurers if they think it may hasten the plaintiff's recovery and return to work.

A solicitor should always be alert to the possibility of making an application for an interim payment in every personal injury case, both as a means of improving the morale of his own client and of keeping some tactical pressure on the opponent. He should not wait for a client to point out that he is suffering severe hardship before enquiring as to whether this might be the case and whether an interim payment might be beneficial.

16.5.8 CASES OTHER THAN PERSONAL INJURY CASES

Although the illustrations given above all concern a personal injury case, as indicated in **16.5.1**, an interim payment may be awarded in any case where a claim is made for debt or damages. An interim payment may also be awarded in the following situations in cases other than those involving a debt or damages.

16.5.8.1 Where the plaintiff has obtained an order for an account to be taken as between himself and the defendant

This applies in the situation where it is clear that there will be some liability between defendant and plaintiff but the drawing up of accounts needs to be undertaken to establish the precise amount. This is common, for example, where partnerships have been dissolved and one partner is clearly owed a substantial amount from the remaining partners but the final figure cannot be known for some time. An interim payment can be awarded in such cases.

16.5.8.2 In claims for possession of land

Where the plaintiff's action includes a claim for possession of land, and if the action proceeds to trial, the defendant is bound to be held liable to pay the plaintiff a sum of money in respect of his use and occupation of the land during the currency of the action. Even if the defendant wins the action, the plaintiff can be awarded an interim payment equivalent to rent.

This arises where the plaintiff is undeniably the owner of land and the issue is whether he is entitled to possession of it from a defendant who is in occupation. It commonly comes about where a landlord and tenant are in dispute about holding over at the end of a tenancy, or whether the basis of occupation is a tenancy or merely a licence, or whether some breach of covenant has been waived by the landlord. The defendant will not vacate the land until the end of the action but it is unsafe for the landlord to accept any money equivalent to rent because by doing so he may be held to have waived his objections to past breach of covenant, or to have acknowledged the legitimacy of the defendant's occupation. In such a case, pending the final determination of the lawfulness of the defendant's occupancy, an application for an interim payment can be made and the court will order the defendant to pay the plaintiff a sum equivalent to rent until trial. It should be noted that in such a case it is probably unsafe for the plaintiff to accept *voluntary* interim payments since this may be deemed to be waiving breaches of covenant, and application to the court should be made in every such case.

16.5.8.3 In other cases where the plaintiff would obtain judgment against the defendant for a substantial sum of money apart from damages or costs

This could arise, for example, in a claim for a *quantum meruit*, especially in claims to do with building work. In such a case the court may feel satisfied that even though the defendant has raised a defence, the plaintiff will obtain judgment at trial for a substantial sum and an interim payment may then be awarded at this stage. Often an application for summary judgment is a useful alternative.

In contract and commercial cases, applications for interim payments are very commonly used as a tactical manoeuvre, and especially to improve the plaintiff's cash flow. In contract cases there may well be some element of financial hardship as well, especially if the plaintiff is a small businessman. It must be borne in mind also, however, that in contract and commercial cases, if the grounds are sufficiently clear-cut to enable a party to obtain an interim payment, they are often sufficiently clear-cut to enable him to obtain summary judgment on liability under *RSC Ord. 14* (see **17.2**). Such applications are thus somewhat less common than in personal injury cases.

A good deal of recent case law emphasises that complex commercial and contractual disputes are not really suitable cases for the court to be called on to decide interim payment applications. This is especially so where there are multiple parties, or difficult points of law which may take many days of the court's time to resolve. See particularly *British and Commonwealth Holdings plc* v *Quadrex Holdings Inc.* [1989] QB 842 and the *Schott Kem Ltd* case referred to at **16.5.6**.

16.5.9 COSTS OF THE APPLICATION

Who is to receive the costs of the application will depend upon many factors. Usually an order for costs in the cause is appropriate, there being no final determination of liability. Nonetheless, the court retains its full discretion. Thus where, for example, a plaintiff has refused a proper and generous offer of a voluntary interim payment and pressed on for more, it may be that the defendant will be awarded the costs of the interim payment application. Similarly, if the defendant in a clear case has refused to offer any interim payment whatsoever but there may be some eventual risk to the plaintiff on costs generally, e.g. if there has been a previous payment into court, then an appropriate order might well be for plaintiff's costs in any event.

16.5.10 APPEAL

Appeal from the decision of the Master or District Judge is to a judge in chambers without leave within the usual time limit (see **26.1.1**). Although a Master or District Judge has an unlimited financial jurisdiction in such cases, sometimes if the amount involved is very large or there are points of some complexity, application is made to a High Court judge in the first instance.

16.5.11 ENFORCEMENT

If an interim award is not paid voluntarily within the appropriate time, enforcement proceedings may be commenced by any appropriate method pursuant to *RSC Ord. 45* (see **23.2**) and the interim award may also found insolvency proceedings.

16.6 High Court and County Court Compared

In relation to both payment into court and interim payment, the essence of the practical and tactical aspects is absolutely identical. In particular now that very substantial personal injury cases are commonly brought in the county court, interim payment applications are much more frequent than they were before 1991 and the considerations relevant to payments into court likewise occur very frequently in county court cases from the most modest right up to very substantial claims. There are minor differences of detail in respect of the documentation required on payment into court in the county court and these will be dealt with in **Chapters 20** and **21**.

SEVENTEEN

TERMINATION WITHOUT TRIAL

We have so far followed the course of an action through from commencement to trial, considering various general matters along the way including practical, tactical and evidential questions. The case that goes to trial is one of only a tiny minority, however. The vast majority of civil actions do not reach trial for a number of reasons, some of which we briefly considered earlier, e.g. stay of the action on acceptance by the plaintiff of a payment into court (see **16.1**). There are several ways in which an action can be brought to a premature end with considerable savings in costs and time. We deal first with procedures by which the plaintiff can bring a case swiftly to an end to his advantage, and then consider some procedures in which the case ends to the defendant's advantage.

Before going on it is important to consider the meaning of the terms 'final judgment' and 'interlocutory judgment'. 'Final judgment' refers to a situation where judgment is complete in respect of all matters, i.e. it covers both liability and amount. 'Interlocutory judgment' refers to a judgment which is final as to some question, e.g. usually the liability of the defendant, but leaves other matters to be worked out subsequently, e.g. assessment of damages.

17.1 Judgment in Default of Notice of Intention to Defend (*RSC Ord. 13*)

17.1.1 PROCEDURE

When a writ is served upon a defendant he has 14 days from the date of effective service to return the acknowledgement of service to the court. *Order 13* of the *Rules of the Supreme Court* applies both where the defendant fails to return the acknowledgement of service to the court *at all*, and where the defendant does return the acknowledgement of service to the court but has indicated on it that he does not *intend to defend* the case. In both cases, the plaintiff can bring matters to an abrupt end without the need for any hearing at all.

The plaintiff's solicitor, either upon receiving an acknowledgement of service indicating that the defendant has acknowledged service but does not intend to defend, or after the effective 14-day period has expired and the acknowledgement of service has not been returned, may obtain judgment at the court counter. As will be recalled (**7.9**), the High Court does not draw up its own orders. Thus the plaintiff must prepare two copies of the form of judgment which he requires. These are produced at the court counter with the original writ. If the acknowledgement of service has been returned, then proof of service will not be required; but if the acknowledgement has not been returned, then before judgment will be entered proof of service will be required, i.e. an affidavit of service made by the person who personally delivered the writ or actually posted the writ to the defendant. On production of the original writ and proof of service, the counter staff will enter judgment immediately. The copies of the judgment are sealed by the court and one copy is returned to the plaintiff's solicitor.

This procedure does not apply where the remedy sought is an injunction because in that case there must, of course, be a hearing before a judge. It is mainly applicable in money actions.

17.1.2 THE FORM OF JUDGMENT

The form of judgment will differ depending upon whether the claim was for a liquidated sum or for damages. If it was for a liquidated sum, e.g. a debt, then the judgment will be *final*, which means that when drafting the judgment, the solicitor will have inserted the amount of the sum claimed and the computation of interest where this has been pleaded. As will be recalled, if interest is due under contract, then the statement of claim endorsed on the writ should show the amount outstanding for interest at the date of issue of the writ, together with a daily rate for interest thereafter. If there is no contractual provision for interest, provided the plaintiff is content with a rate of interest equivalent to the interest rate prevailing upon judgment debt (currently 8 per cent per annum) then that rate may be claimed without investigation by the court. The judgment will state the precise amount for which it has been granted, and allows the plaintiff to enforce the judgment against the defendant immediately. In a liquidated sum case the plaintiff will obtain fixed costs in the amount shown on the writ, and thus there need be no further hearing of any kind and the case is over for all purposes except enforcement.

In the exceptional case where the plaintiff — perhaps because of the large amount involved, or because of some argument that he has himself had to borrow the sum owed from a bank at a higher rate of interest pending payment — wishes to press for a higher rate of interest on the debt, he will obtain judgment only on liability and immediately issue a summons for interest to be assessed by a District Judge at a subsequent hearing. At the hearing of the summons, at which the defendant will be given the opportunity to attend, the question of the appropriate rate of interest can be argued and the matter finalised then and there.

In a damages case where the plaintiff is not claiming a liquidated sum, the form of judgment will be *interlocutory*, i.e. final as to liability only. It will be necessary to apply on summons for a hearing before the District Judge at which damages will be assessed. Sometimes the plaintiff may wish to issue this summons for a hearing for a damages assessment immediately. In a personal injuries case, however, if the plaintiff's medical injuries are such that it is better to wait until his condition has stabilised, there may be a long delay before the assessment of damages.

The advantage to the plaintiff of obtaining early judgment on liability is that it provides an opportunity to apply for an interim payment on account of damages (see **16.5**). However, in most forms of personal injury litigation, whether road accident or factory accidents, the defendant's insurers will be prompt to appoint solicitors to deal with the writ. Even if their case on liability is apparently hopeless, very few insurance companies will let default judgment be entered at this early stage, choosing to keep some argument on liability open for as long as possible for negotiation purposes. Thus default judgment under *RSC Ord. 13* is rarely possible.

If default judgment is given for damages to be assessed, then at the subsequent summons for assessment of damages, the District Judge will award the plaintiff taxed costs. It should be borne in mind that at that subsequent hearing for assessment of damages, a very lengthy appointment may be needed, indeed one which may last some days if the evidence on quantum is very complex. Although the District Judge has unlimited jurisdiction in terms of amount, in very substantial cases it is common to refer this assessment to a High Court judge.

17.1.3 SETTING ASIDE JUDGMENT

If a judgment has been obtained under *RSC Ord. 13*, the defendant can apply for it to be set aside. The court will set judgment aside in two situations (*Ord. 13, r. 9*):

(a) In the case of procedural irregularity as, for example, where although the plaintiff in good faith served the writ by post, the defendant went away for a month's holiday on the very day on which the writ was posted to him, thus returning to find judgment had been entered in his absence. In such a situation the defendant should apply on summons to set the judgment aside so that he may defend the case. No affidavit is necessary in such a case and the judgment will be set aside as of right; since no party is in any way to blame, the usual order will then be for costs in the cause and the case will go on as defended.

(b) Where the defendant is at fault, for example where he received the writ properly but delayed seeking legal advice for too long after receiving it. In such a situation he may still apply to set the judgment aside, but this time he will need to file an affidavit explaining his reasons for delay and disclosing some arguable defence on the merits. It will then be within the discretion of the District Judge whether to allow judgment to be set aside. If it is set aside, inevitably the court will impose some terms, at least that the defendant at fault pay the 'costs thrown away' in the plaintiff's favour, i.e. the costs of entering the judgment fruitlessly and of attending court to argue against it being set aside. Other terms may also be imposed, e.g. for the defendant to pay money into court as security.

17.1.4 OTHER PRACTICAL POINTS

(a) The plaintiff is entitled to proceed immediately to enforce his judgment where it is final. There is no need for the judgment to be served on the defendant, and accordingly it is common for the plaintiff to take the necessary documents for immediate enforcement (e.g. for the issue of a writ of *fieri facias*, see **23.2.1**) down to court at the same time as the document for obtaining judgment.

(b) If there is more than one defendant then the plaintiff is entitled to proceed with his action against other defendants even if he has signed judgment against one of them under *RSC Ord. 13*. Judgment obtained against one defendant is no bar to proceeding against another in most cases.

(c) If, having entered judgment in a case involving postal service of the writ, the writ is later returned via the Post Office to the plaintiff, then by *RSC Ord. 13, r. 7*, the plaintiff has the obligation to apply to set aside his own judgment and to ask the court for directions.

17.2 Summary Judgment (*RSC Ord. 14*)

17.2.1 INTRODUCTION

As we have remarked before, it might be imagined from collectively adding together the time limits for the various stages of High Court procedure, that an action could proceed from issue of the writ to trial in a matter of a few months. Even in the most straightforward case, however, that might well be optimistic. The pressure on court time is such that even in the rare cases where both parties comply strictly with all time limits and are keen to cooperate in getting the case to trial as soon as possible, trial within a year of commencement would be unusual. In some parts of the country the period would be considerably longer even than that. In cases where either party does not wish to cooperate, or has any reason to spin things out by seeking extensions or by delaying tactics of any kind, the period will inevitably be much longer again.

In some kinds of action, especially in actions for debts, a defendant who is unscrupulous, or merely impecunious, could in effect obtain credit for lengthy periods by delaying payment until proceedings were issued, and thereafter by putting in an entirely spurious defence and spinning things out until trial. Pleadings are not on oath and therefore a defendant would commit no crime or contempt of court by putting in a spurious defence, provided he abandons it as soon as the trial starts, or just before trial, and does not attempt to substantiate it. Of course the costs of this further delay will inevitably be large, and the person adopting these tactics will be ordered to pay costs and interest, but even these may not be sufficient disincentives to an unscrupulous person to defer payment of debts. Indeed it is not only unscrupulous people who are driven to these tactics. The defendant may himself be in business and be owed many bad debts and have serious cash flow problems. Only by deferring payments of major debts, for example to his trade suppliers, for as long as possible may he be able to hope to stay in business. Thus he may be tempted to prevaricate and delay matters to the point where a writ is issued, and even beyond, by advancing spurious defences in order to obtain many more months' grace.

The procedure which we are about to describe is what in effect prevents these tactics from succeeding.

17.2.2 THE PURPOSE OF SUMMARY JUDGMENT

The purpose of *RSC Ord. 14* is to enable early judgment to be obtained in cases where the defendant has no hope of success and any defence raised will merely have the effect of delaying judgment. The following procedure applies to all actions begun by writ, with a few exceptions (e.g. defamation, malicious prosecution), but its main use is in contract actions, particularly debt cases. In many other cases, e.g. negligence actions, and especially road accident cases, *Ord. 14* would not be appropriate since the defendant will often be able to put up a defence which is arguable, even if it is not ultimately successful.

Example

The plaintiff is a trade supplier suing a customer for debts. He instructs his solicitor to issue and serve the writ as soon as the letter before action has received no response. As is normal in this kind of case, the statement of claim is endorsed on the back of the writ (i.e. it is the 'liquidated demand' form of writ). No separate statement of claim is therefore required. The plaintiff is surprised and annoyed to find when the acknowledgement of service is returned to the court and a copy sent to his solicitor, that the defendant has ticked the box indicating that he intends to defend the action. The plaintiff believes that there is no possible defence to the action because the goods were supplied months before and no complaint has been received about their quality, nor have any letters demanding payment received any reply. He therefore instructs his solicitor to do everything possible to bring matters to a speedy conclusion. The solicitor will therefore apply for summary judgment.

17.2.3 TIME FOR APPLICATION

If no acknowledgement of service is returned at all, or the acknowledgement of service indicates that there is no intention to defend, then the plaintiff will enter judgment under *RSC Ord. 13* as discussed at **17.1.1**. Where the acknowledgement of service indicates an intention to defend, however, and the statement of claim has already been served (as we have seen, this will usually be endorsed on the writ), the plaintiff will apply immediately for summary judgment. He does not need to await service of the defence, nor indeed does service of the defence (if the defendant has got it in immediately) preclude a plaintiff from applying for summary judgment if he concludes that the defence is spurious. However, where the plaintiff does apply for summary judgment the effect of this is to extend the time of service of the defence until after the hearing of the summons.

17.2.4 METHOD OF APPLICATION

Application is made to the District Judge by summons seeking summary judgment and supported by an affidavit. The affidavit must:

(a) verify the facts upon which the claim is based (usually by repeating that the contents of the statement of claim are true);

(b) state the deponent's belief that there is no defence to the claim.

These are the mandatory requirements for the affidavit and, if it is sworn by the plaintiff personally, are all that there need be. If, however, the affidavit is sworn by someone acting on the plaintiff's behalf (for example where the affidavit is sworn by the plaintiff's solicitor, or where the plaintiff is a limited company and the affidavit is sworn by a director or manager), that person must also swear that he is duly authorised by the plaintiff to make the affidavit. If there is some fact in the affidavit not known personally by the deponent, then he must identify the source of his information or belief.

Once a summons has been issued and the original affidavit lodged at the District Registry, a copy of the summons and affidavit must be served on the defendant. Service must be not less than 10 clear days before the hearing date of the summons. A notice included in the summons warns the defendant that, if he wishes to oppose the application, he should serve on the applicant a copy of any affidavit he intends to use at least three days before the hearing date of the summons. The defendant should now consider his position carefully. The effect of the requirement that he serve an affidavit is that he must put any defence which he intended to serve on oath. Even the most unscrupulous defendant will usually think twice before committing perjury about the validity of his defence in an affidavit. If the defendant fails to serve the affidavit in time but, as is quite common, produces it at the hearing, the plaintiff may either require an adjournment to enable him to consider the affidavit, or press on and deal with any allegations made in it. If an affidavit is supplied by the defendant which contains allegations which the plaintiff needs to meet by serving a further affidavit, he may do so, but by this stage it may become clear that there is a genuine dispute on the facts. Where that is the case, the summary judgment procedure is not appropriate (see **17.2.5**). If the defendant does produce an affidavit late so that an adjournment is required, he will be required to pay the costs caused by the adjournment.

17.2.5 THE HEARING OF THE SUMMONS

The matter is governed by *RSC Ord. 14, r. 3*, which provides:

> *Unless on the hearing of an application [for summary judgment] either the court dismisses the application or the defendant satisfies the court with respect to the claim . . . to which the application relates that there is an issue or question in dispute which ought to be tried or that there ought for some other reason to be a trial of that claim . . . the court may give such judgment for the plaintiff . . . as may be just.*

At the hearing of the plaintiff's application, the District Judge will consider the plaintiff's affidavit and any affidavit filed by the defendant and, after hearing argument, may make one of the following four orders:

17.2.5.1 Judgment for the plaintiff

The defendant must satisfy the District Judge that there is an issue or question that ought to be tried, or that there ought for some other reason to be a trial of the plaintiff's claim. Unless the defendant manages to do this (and the burden of proof is on him) the District Judge will give judgment for the plaintiff. Even if the defendant has insisted on affidavit that he has a defence, the District Judge will give judgment for the plaintiff if he is not satisfied as to its bona fides.

The important case of *National Westminster Bank plc* v *Daniels* [1993] 1 WLR 1453 establishes that a District Judge is entitled to look behind the affidavit to what seems to be the true position, and if in the light of other evidence, for example contemporaneous documents, the defence seems quite implausible, then notwithstanding that the defendant has deposed to it on oath, the District Judge may give judgment for the plaintiff.

The test is whether there is some ***arguable issue*** which ought to be tried before a judge in open court, after all proper interlocutory stages such as discovery have been undertaken to assist the court to get at the truth. If there is such an issue, then summary judgment is inappropriate. The fact that the District Judge does not give judgment for the plaintiff at this stage in no way pre-empts the final decision. It may be that after full trial the plaintiff wins conclusively on the issue of liability and the defendant is totally discredited, or his arguments shown to be flawed. That does not imply, however, that the District Judge in any sense 'got it wrong' when refusing an application for summary judgment. The issue at the summary judgment stage is simply 'is there a triable issue'.

If the claim is for a liquidated amount, the District Judge may give *final* judgment for the sum claimed and interest thereon and make an order for costs. On a claim for unliquidated damages, the District Judge will give judgment on *liability* only and (unless the assessment of damages is very straightforward) adjourn the question of assessment of damages to a future hearing when detailed evidence on quantum can be presented.

If the defendant does not attend the hearing and has not acknowledged service of the summons, the plaintiff will be required to prove service of the summons. Any judgment given against a defendant who does not attend the hearing may be set aside, or varied on such terms as the court think fit.

17.2.5.2 Unconditional leave to defend

Unconditional leave to defend must be given whenever the defendant raises a triable defence (e.g. a serious question of law or fact), or for some other reason satisfies the District Judge that there ought to be a trial. The plaintiff's application for summary judgment fails and the matter will proceed to trial.

Such a decision does not necessarily imply any criticism of the plaintiff's conduct of the case. It is usually that he has taken an over-optimistic view of the question of whether or not there is some triable issue. Indeed it may not be until this stage, when the defendant puts his case on affidavit, that the plaintiff is fully aware of exactly what the alleged defence will be.

In deciding these matters the District Judge is entitled to look behind an affidavit within reason and see what the substance of the case really is. A defendant will be expected to give full particulars of his defence and a mere general denial will not do. Likewise, if a point of law is raised, the facts forming the basis of it must be set out with some particularity. Two other matters need to be considered:

(a) *Counterclaims and third parties*

If a defendant wishes to make a counterclaim in the action the court has a wide discretion. If the claim and counterclaim are related, the plaintiff may be given judgment but subject to a stay of execution pending trial of the counterclaim, or at least subject to stay of execution up to the potential amount of the counterclaim. If the counterclaim arises out of quite separate transactions, so that there is no connection between claim and counterclaim, the usual order is for judgment of the plaintiff with costs without any stay pending the trial of the counterclaim. If the action is more complex than that, because the defendant wishes to bring in some third party, that is not in itself a reason not to give summary judgment, but everything will depend upon the facts and the degree of the third party's alleged involvement.

(b) *'Some other reason' for trial*

These words in *RSC Ord. 14, r. 3*, allow the District Judge to give unconditional leave to defend where there may not be a defence as such but where there is some other reason which makes it inappropriate to bring the case to a conclusion at this stage. This might be the case, for example, where the interests of some other person might be affected by summary judgment.

17.2.5.3 Conditional leave to defend

Where there is some kind of defence put forward but the District Judge doubts the good faith of the defendant, or is almost certain that the defence raised is bound to fail, then he may give leave to defend but only upon some condition. The most common condition is the payment by the defendant into court funds of the whole or part of the sum in dispute. In other words, in such a case the District Judge is looking to the defendant to establish his good faith and to demonstrate that his reason for defending is not simply that he cannot afford to pay the sum claimed. The payment into court of this sum should not, of course, be confused with 'payment into court' in the other sense of an offer from defendant to plaintiff. It is not open to the plaintiff in this instance to take the sum out of court in purported acceptance. The payment into court is simply in the nature of a security.

17.2.5.4 Dismissal of the summons

The District Judge may dismiss the summons if the case is not within *RSC Ord. 14* (e.g. a defamation case, to which *Ord. 14* does not apply), or if it appears that the plaintiff's application is in bad faith, i.e. he knew that the defendant would be entitled to leave to defend. Unlike the two previous orders, where no criticism of the plaintiff's conduct is implied in the refusal of the application and the usual costs order is 'costs in the cause', if an order is made *dismissing* the summons, the plaintiff will usually be ordered to pay costs in any event, and in some cases to pay them forthwith. No directions for trial can be given in this case. The action will then proceed as normal with the defendant serving his defence before both parties undertake all the usual interlocutory stages.

17.2.5.5 Directions for trial

Where either conditional or unconditional leave to defend is given, the District Judge is required to give directions for the trial of the action as if the hearing were a summons for directions, in the hope that this may avoid the need for a summons for directions later. Directions may be given, for example, for serving a defence (as the defence may not have been served since the application for summary judgment extends the time for service of the defence), for discovery or for any other interlocutory matter. When giving directions the court will order a statement of value to be lodged by the plaintiff and served on all other parties within a specified time (usually seven days). If this statement is not lodged, the action will be transferred to the county court.

This is a useful provision which may save a further attendance before the court. Unfortunately in some cases it comes about too early for the parties really to know what directions they are eventually likely to need, and thus there will, in any event, have to be a subsequent hearing of a summons for directions.

It should be noted that if summary judgment has been given on liability only, directions may well be needed before there can be a hearing of the assessment of damages. Thus there may need to be directions in relation to discovery, expert evidence and the like. In personal injury actions, although summary judgment in such cases is rare, an application for summary judgment is sometimes combined with an application for an interim payment, the latter being heard immediately after summary judgment is given.

17.2.6 *ORDER 14* AND NEGLIGENCE ACTIONS

As indicated in **17.2.1** above, the most common use of summary judgment under *RSC Ord. 14* is in contract debt cases. Quite apart from those cases where it specifically does not apply by the terms of *Ord. 14* (e.g. defamation cases), there are other kinds of cases where it is extremely rare. Road accident cases are one such kind, simply because if a defendant is minded to attempt to defend and wishes to make, as is common, allegations of negligence (or at least contributory negligence) against the plaintiff, it is generally very difficult for the District Judge to say that there is no triable issue without an exhaustive investigation of the facts for which an *Ord. 14* hearing is inappropriate. Thus *Ord. 14* is rare in all negligence actions and very rare in road accident cases. Exceptionally, if the defendant has already been convicted of a relevant criminal offence (e.g. dangerous driving) in relation to the incident, a court may sometimes be persuaded to grant summary judgment.

A case study on summary judgment with commentary appears at the end of this chapter.

17.3 Disposal of a Case on a Point of Law (*RSC Ord. 14A*)

Order 14A of the *Rules of the Supreme Court* came into force in 1991 and should be read in conjunction with *RSC Ord. 14*. It is not confined to applications for summary judgment but may arise at a number of interlocutory stages, including applications to strike out pleadings. It is restricted to questions of law or construction of documents and enables the court *summarily* to determine such issues. It is an addition to the court's powers, enabling a District Judge to decide that the issue in a case turns on the construction of a document; that the question is suitable for determination without a full trial, and that such a determination will finally decide the case; and that he can determine the question of construction for himself. Rather than merely deciding that there is a triable issue and giving the defendant leave to defend, the District Judge can try the issue itself.

Order 14A can be used in the following circumstances:

(a) Where the defendant has given notice of intention to defend.

(b) The question of law or construction of the document is suitable for determination without a full trial of the action.

(c) Such determination will be final (subject only to appeal).

(d) The parties have had an opportunity of being heard on the question of law or construction, *or* have consented to an order or judgment being made on such determination.

Obviously, where issues of fact and legal issues are interwoven it will be inappropriate for the plaintiff to rely on this order in an attempt to dispose of the case. For the rule properly to apply the question of law or construction must be suitable for determination without a full trial, and thus must not involve substantial disputes of evidence.

There does not need to be a formal application, and such an application may be made orally in the course of other interlocutory applications. Whilst in principle it may therefore be possible to take one's opponent by surprise with such an application, clearly in a case of any difficulty oral applications are only likely to be permitted where both parties consent. If a summons is issued it must state in very precise terms what the question of law or construction is.

At the time of writing this provision seemed relatively little used and there is only a modest amount of case law cited in the notes to the order. One example is *WG Clark (Properties) Ltd v Dupre Properties Ltd* [1992] Ch 297 where during the course of the hearing of an application to strike out a statement of claim as disclosing no reasonable cause of action under *Ord. 18, r. 19*, the parties consented to the court exercising its powers under *Ord. 14A* to determine a question of law which had arisen on the Landlord and Tenant issue which underlay the action. Although no formal application is required and *Ord. 14A* can be referred to in the course of other interlocutory applications, e.g. to strike out pleadings, or under *Ord. 14* itself, it is usually considered best specifically to refer to *Ord. 14A* in the summons as an alternative ground of procedure, so that one's opponent will not be taken by surprise.

17.4 Judgment in Default of Defence (*RSC Ord. 19*)

Applications for early judgment under *RSC Ord. 19* are less common than under either *Ord. 13* or *Ord. 14*. This applies where a defendant has given notice of intention to defend the case and the plaintiff has served his statement of claim but the defendant has not then served a defence either within 14 days of receiving the statement of claim, or within 28 days of receiving the writ, whichever is the later, or within any further period of extension granted by the plaintiff.

When the time for service of the defence has expired the plaintiff may apply for judgment in default of defence. As in the case of *Ord. 13* applications (see **17.1.1**), no hearing is necessary. The plaintiff simply prepares two forms of judgment and takes them to court with the original writ. There is no need for an affidavit of service of the statement of claim, but there is an endorsement on the forms of judgment under *Ord. 19* in which the plaintiff confirms that the time for service of the defence, taking into account any extensions, has expired. The forms of judgment are sealed at the court counter and the plaintiff may then proceed to enforce the judgment as in the case of *Ord. 13* judgments. If the action is for a liquidated sum, judgment will be final on liability and quantum; if it is for an unliquidated sum, there will be a need for a later hearing to assess damages.

17.5 Summary Proceedings for the Possession of Land (*RSC Ord. 113*)

Order 113 of the *Rules of the Supreme Court* provides a means for a plaintiff to apply for possession of land against persons who are unlikely to have any defence, e.g. squatters, 'travellers' and licensees of land whose licences have been terminated. The procedure is a draconian one and can be used to obtain very early judgment against occupiers even where the names of the latter are not known to the plaintiff. The order once obtained can be executed very swiftly by a writ of possession by the sheriff.

17.5.1 COMMENCEMENT OF PROCEEDINGS

The proceedings are commenced by a special form of originating summons to which an acknowledgement of service is not required, supported by an affidavit stating:

(a) the plaintiff's interest in the land;

(b) the circumstances in which the land has been occupied without licence or consent and in which the claim for possession arises; and (where appropriate)

(c) that the plaintiff does not know the name of any person occupying the land who is not named on the summons.

The plaintiff does not need to go to any trouble to ascertain the names of all, or any, of the occupiers of the land in question. Even though the plaintiff may believe that he does know the names of all the occupants, it is usually prudent to add a claim against 'persons unknown' and to swear in the affidavit that there may be such other persons whose names he does not know. Otherwise the effect of any order made may be limited to those defendants named, and this may be unwise for obvious practical reasons.

17.5.2 METHOD OF SERVICE OF THE SUMMONS

The method of service depends on whether any defendant has been named on the summons. A sealed copy of the summons and a copy of the affidavit must be served on named defendants, either personally or by leaving them at or sending them to the premises, or in such other manner as the court may direct. Where the defendants are also 'persons unknown', then (in addition to service on any named defendant where necessary) the copy summons and affidavit are served by fixing them to the main door or other obvious part of the premises and, if practicable, inserting further copies through the door in a 'sealed transparent envelope' addressed to 'the occupiers'. If the premises are land not including a building, then service of the summons is by placing stakes in the ground in conspicuous parts of the occupied land, to each of which is affixed a sealed transparent envelope containing the necessary documents.

17.5.3 THE HEARING

On the issue of the summons an appointment is given for a hearing before the District Judge to take place at least five days after the expected date of service in the case of residential property, and two days in the case of other land. It is possible in an urgent case to obtain an expedited hearing even more swiftly than this, by applying *ex parte* at or after the summons has been issued.

The hearing of the summons is a summary trial and the District Judge *must* make an order for possession if the plaintiff proves his case. The defendant cannot prevent summary judgment merely by raising a triable issue, but he may raise a substantial defence, possibly requiring oral evidence, which will make the case not suitable for summary trial. In such a case the court should give directions for a full trial.

If the plaintiff succeeds, the judgment is in a special form, providing that the plaintiff 'do recover possession'. The judgment is enforceable against all occupiers of the premises, even those who may have entered into possession after the action commenced. As an exception to the general rule, an *Ord. 113* judgment can be enforced without first notifying all the occupiers of the land and (if the plaintiff applies within three months of the making of the order) without first obtaining the leave of the court. Enforcement is by the sheriff. The plaintiff should be in a position to make the premises secure after the sheriff has evicted the occupiers, to avoid further unlawful occupation.

17.5.4 ANOTHER PRACTICAL POSSIBILITY

The plaintiff may, if the premises are residential, seek the assistance of the police under *s. 7* of the *Criminal Law Act 1977*, since a trespasser onto such premises is guilty of an offence if he fails to leave them on being required to do so by the displaced occupier. There is a power of arrest by a police constable in uniform.

In addition, under *s. 61* of the *Criminal Justice and Public Order Act 1994*, the police have new powers to remove trespassers from land, in particular where either damage has been caused to the land or to property on the land or threatening, abusive or insulting words or behaviour have been used by any of those people towards the occupier of the land, or the persons in question have between them six or more vehicles on the land. This latter provision will often allow the police to assist by clearing travellers or the like.

At the time of writing it is said that many Chief Constables are unhappy with using their powers to remove 'new age travellers' as they consider that this falls properly within the civil jurisdiction and that local authorities should apply to the civil courts. Such matters are within the discretion of Chief Constables and nothing can be done to compel them to take such action although they are much more likely to do so if there is evidence of criminal damage or the risk of violence. Nonetheless when acting for a client a useful first stage might be to see if the police will assist, which will save time, costs and be more effective.

17.6 Compromise

A solicitor has authority to compromise a claim on behalf of a client once an action has begun: counsel has power to compromise during the trial. However, these powers should never be relied on: the client's express authority to compromise the claim should be obtained in each case. Because, as indicated earlier, negotiations proceed throughout the course of the litigation, an acceptable resolution may be achieved at any time. Provided there is agreement as to costs (either that they will be agreed or taxed in default of agreement), the claim may be resolved by the defendant simply making a payment of the agreed amount to the plaintiff.

If the parties conclude a compromise, any rights of action they had will be replaced by rights under the contract of compromise. Where all matters are agreed there is no need to do more than notify the court of the agreement by letter. If some court order is required to implement the agreement, there is provision under *RSC Ord. 42, r. 5A* for obtaining consent orders from the court without attendance by sending in the text of the order required with the consent of both parties endorsed. There is then no need to attend court.

17.6.1 TOMLIN ORDERS

If the terms of the compromise provide for something other than a simple payment of money, a stay in the form of a Tomlin order might be made, i.e. a stay of the action on terms set out in a schedule to the order, with liberty to restore if necessary for the purpose of carrying such terms into effect. This method of compromise is commonly used where there are complex terms to be carried out, for example where a defendant undertakes to do certain scheduled work, for example, building repairs, and the plaintiff then undertakes to pay for it at certain agreed rates. This kind of compromise is inappropriate for recital in a formal court judgment because the court would not have the mechanism to carry out and enforce the terms given their complexity.

A Tomlin order is not the same as a money judgment, even where it requires payment of a sum of money, thus it cannot be enforced without further application to the court and does not carry interest unless provided for in the order. If any costs are to be taxed, the order should deal with costs, providing for taxation if that is what is agreed between the parties.

17.6.2 COMPROMISE OF THE CLAIM OF A PERSON UNDER A DISABILITY

In any action in which money is claimed by or on behalf of a minor or mental patient, no settlement, compromise or payment, and no acceptance of a payment into court is valid without the approval of the court. The procedure for obtaining such approval is set out in **19.8.7**.

If no action has been commenced because the claim is too small to merit the cost of court proceedings, however simple, the defendant's insurers may make a payment direct to the parent or guardian in return for an indemnity by them should proceedings on the claim be commenced in the future.

17.7 Discontinuance and Withdrawal (*RSC Ord. 21*)

17.7.1 DISCONTINUANCE BY THE PLAINTIFF

A plaintiff may find himself in the position of having started proceedings, only to find that he has overstated his case, or has sued the wrong defendant or cannot now produce the evidence required to prove his case. If he wishes to discontinue the action this can be done simply by serving notice on the defendant. The plaintiff will naturally be responsible for the defendant's costs incurred in the matter.

Once 14 days have elapsed after the service of the defence the plaintiff can discontinue only with leave of the court. This requirement is imposed to prevent a discontinuance which would unfairly prejudice the defendant, and the court will thus exercise a supervisory jurisdiction over the terms on which withdrawal will be permitted, e.g. it may need to consider wasted costs orders against an impecunious plaintiff's solicitor. See **22.5**.

17.7.2 WITHDRAWAL OF DEFENCE

Naturally a defendant is entitled to withdraw his defence in whole or in part at any time. Thereupon the plaintiff may apply for judgment immediately under *RSC Ord. 19* (see **17.4**) and there will follow an assessment of damages if that is required, and an order for taxation of costs.

17.8 Judgment on Admission (*RSC Ord. 27*)

If the defendant makes a clear admission of liability either in his pleadings or in open correspondence, then the plaintiff may apply to the court on summons for judgment to be given on liability. The advantage of this is that it brings the case to an end so far as liability is concerned and allows the plaintiff to apply immediately for an interim payment if this is appropriate to the case.

It must be noted that before an application can be made the admission must clearly be one of liability. A mere offer in open correspondence to compensate the plaintiff for his injuries does not amount to an admission of liability, since it may be that the offer could be interpreted as being one of an *ex gratia* payment.

It should also be clearly noted that it may not be enough in a negligence claim for the defendant to admit liability in negligence for the accident. The reason is that an admission of negligence alone is not sufficient and there must also be an admission that the plaintiff suffered injuries flowing from the negligence. See *Blundell* v *Rimmer* [1971] 1 WLR 123; and *Parrott* v *Jackson* (1996) *The Times*, 14 February 1996.

17.9 Dismissal for Want of Prosecution

17.9.1 INTRODUCTION

We have so far considered the opportunities which a plaintiff may have to bring matters to a speedy conclusion in his own favour, or occasionally to end the case by withdrawing his action. There are several rules under which the defendants can take the initiative and apply for dismissal of the action for want of prosecution. This may come about typically where the plaintiff fails to serve a statement of claim (*RSC Ord. 18, r. 1*); where the plaintiff fails to take out a summons for directions (*RSC Ord. 25, rr. 1* and 2); or where the plaintiff fails to set down the action for trial within the time fixed by the order for directions (*RSC Ord. 34, r. 2*). The court also has an inherent jurisdiction to dismiss the action for want of prosecution wherever the plaintiff is in breach of a time period imposed by an order of the court. Unlike such stages as judgment in default of defence, a dismissal for want of prosecution is never granted automatically on the plaintiff's failure to obey a rule or order, and it will always require a summons by the defendant for that purpose.

The text relevant to this subject in the *Supreme Court Practice* appears at *Ord. 25, r. 1*, which generally deals with the summons for directions. In itself, however, dismissal for want of prosecution has nothing to do with the summons for directions as such. It is simply that that is one of the two most common times (together with failure to set down) when a plaintiff foolishly lets an action 'go to sleep', thus enabling the defendant to make his application.

17.9.2 METHOD OF APPLICATION

Frequently in such cases there will be a delay of more than a year since the plaintiff took the previous step in proceedings. There is a special rule which deals with this matter (*RSC Ord. 3, r. 6*), which provides that a party who wishes to take a further step in the action after more than a year's delay must give to every other party not less than one month's notice of his intention to proceed. Thus the usual way in which this situation arises is where the plaintiff, having allowed a substantial period to elapse, now wishes to get on with the action either by issuing the summons for directions, setting down for trial, or by some other procedural application. He thus needs to give the defendant a month's notice of his intention to proceed under *RSC Ord. 3, r. 6*. That will be the trigger for the defendant, who has been, so to speak, lying in wait, to put in motion his own summons to dismiss for want of prosecution. No affidavit is required, strictly speaking, in support of the application but it is more prudent for a defendant to provide an affidavit, and it is now almost invariably the practice to do so.

Two distinct grounds have developed for dismissal for want of prosecution. These are considered in detail below.

17.9.3 GROUND FOR DISMISSAL (1): DELAY AND PREJUDICE

A defendant may apply for an action to be dismissed for want of prosecution where:

(a) the plaintiff has been guilty of inordinate and inexcusable delay; and

(b) such delay has given rise to substantial risk that it will not be possible to have a fair trial of the issues in the case, or is likely to cause or have caused serious prejudice to the defendant; and

(c) the limitation period has expired.

It is now important to consider the elements.

17.9.3.1 'Inordinate and inexcusable delay'

By this phrase is meant delay materially longer than the time usually recognised by the profession and courts as an acceptable period. The courts are increasingly ready to construe 'inordinate' as being rather less than it was deemed to be in cases decided some time ago. The word 'inexcusable' must be looked at primarily from a defendant's point of view, making reasonable allowances for, say, the illness of the plaintiff, accident or any agreement. The fact that the plaintiff's solicitors are to blame will not make the delay 'excusable'. In considering the period the court will look at the whole period since the cause of action arose. Thus a plaintiff who has left it until the last few days of the limitation period to issue his writ and then been guilty of substantial further delay will have the whole period taken into account.

17.9.3.2 'Prejudice to the defendant'

This is a matter of fact and degree which will vary from case to case. Thus if witnesses' memories are likely to fade, or witnesses have become unavailable and oral evidence is essential, this may be relatively easy to demonstrate. It will be otherwise if the type of action is a well-documented commercial action.

Prejudice must be looked at in the wider context and may involve matters which have nothing to do with the litigation so, for example, in *Biss* v *Lambeth Southwark & Lewisham Health Authority (Teaching)* [1978] 1 WLR 382, it was held that prejudice caused to a professional man by having matters hanging over his head for a long time may be relevant, although in that case the facts were extreme ($11\frac{1}{2}$ years' delay). Similarly, prejudice to the defendant's business interests may be sufficient (*Department of Transport* v *Chris Smaller (Transport) Ltd* [1989] AC 1197); or economic prejudice, as where a defendant's insurance arrangements have changed in the interim (*Ancliff* v *Gloucester Health Authority* [1992] 1 WLR 1044 and *Gascoine* v *Harrison* (1992) *The Times*, 30 July 1992).

17.9.3.3 'Expiry of limitation period'

The limitation period must have expired because otherwise, since the substantive law guarantees the plaintiff the right to issue a writ, the plaintiff could issue a further writ and it would be pointless to strike out the action.

17.9.3.4 Acquiescence by the defendant

If the defendant has positively acquiesced, e.g. by continuing the negotiations, or even by giving indefinite extensions of time, then he may not apply to dismiss successfully. However, acquiescence must be distinguished from the defendant's right merely to 'let sleeping dogs lie' and not to take any action continually to press the plaintiff. A defendant is perfectly entitled to lay quiet until a sufficient period has elapsed or the plaintiff seeks to take another step.

In the past, a defendant whose conduct amounted to any form of estoppel, for example, leading the plaintiff to incur expenditure in the reasonable belief that the action would proceed to trial, could not succeed with an application to strike out – see *County and District Properties Ltd* v *Lyell* [1991] 1 WLR 683. That case, however, was expressly disapproved by the House of Lords in *Roebuck* v *Mungovin* [1994] 2 WLR 290 in which it was held that there is no general principle that acquiescence in delay, even where the plaintiff has been led on by the defendant to spend further money on proceedings, will in every case create an estoppel. This is merely one factor to be taken into account with others in determining what the outcome of such acquiescence should be.

It follows that a defendant will not be absolutely estopped from applying to strike out by, for example, permitting the plaintiff facilities for a factory inspection, corresponding about further expert evidence, permitting the plaintiff facilities to view a video or the like. These are merely factors to be weighed in the overall exercise of the court's discretion.

17.9.3.5 Remedies against others

Neither the fact that the plaintiff has a remedy against his solicitor nor the existence of legal aid makes any difference to the position. If there is no real prejudice to the defendant he will not get the action struck out merely because the plaintiff could then sue his negligent solicitor. This is in the main because a plaintiff suing his own solicitor for negligence is in a less advantageous position than a plaintiff suing the primary wrongdoer because, *inter alia*, his own former solicitors will obviously know weaknesses in his case.

A brief case study illustrates the possibility of an application to strike out for want of prosecution at the end of this chapter.

17.9.4 GROUND FOR DISMISSAL (2): ABUSE OF PROCESS

A quite separate ground for dismissal of an action occurs where there is deliberate default in complying with a peremptory order of the court, or conduct amounting to an abuse of process of the court. In this context a 'peremptory order' is one which makes it clear to the party who is the subject of the order that exact compliance is required with no further argument within a stated time, such as an 'unless' order.

The clearest example of this principle is the leading case of *Wallersteiner* v *Moir* [1974] 1 WLR 991. In this case a 'gagging' writ alleging defamation was issued by the plaintiff in an attempt to stifle criticism of his business conduct in company meetings. He had no serious intention to pursue defamation proceedings and hoped that the effect of being able to claim that the matter was *sub judice* would stifle such criticism for some time. The court in such a case is willing to strike the action out as being an abuse of process of the court after a relatively brief delay where the improper motive can be shown, and it is irrelevant that the limitation period has not expired. In these circumstances any attempt by the plaintiff to issue a second writ would lead to the second action also being dismissed as an abuse of process.

17.10 Stay of Action

A stay of an action does not in itself bring an action to an end, although once a stay has been put upon an action, after a substantial further period of time has elapsed a defendant can then apply to strike out the action for want of prosecution (see **17.9**).

The court has a wide discretion to stay proceedings. A stay may be removed and the action recommenced where the person in default of some step that has been ordered is now willing to comply with the previous order of the court. A good example would be the case where the plaintiff was unwilling to undergo medical examination by the defendant's choice of doctor. Whilst the court has no power to order the plaintiff to undergo such examination, it does have the power to stay the action until the plaintiff consents. Thus if the plaintiff never consents the action will be stayed indefinitely, and after a further period has elapsed the defendant will apply to strike the action out for want of prosecution.

The *Rules of the Supreme Court* make several other references to proceedings being 'stayed'. In many cases the 'stay' is virtually equivalent to the action being over, as, for example, where a plaintiff accepts money paid into court in full and final settlement.

17.11 High Court and County Court Compared

All the foregoing methods of terminating a case before trial apply equally in the county court. The only substantial difference is that in the county court there is no stage of returning an acknowledgment of service and the defendant is required to file a defence within 14 days. It therefore follows that the possibilities under *RSC Ord. 13* and *Ord. 19* which exist in the High Court are telescoped together into one in the county court. If a defendant fails to file a defence the plaintiff will bring the matter to an end with a default judgment then and there. If the claim is for a liquidated sum that judgment will be final; if it is for damages then the judgment will be final as to liability leaving damages to be assessed at a later hearing before a District Judge. See the relevant parts of **Chapters 20** and **21**.

17.12 Summary Judgment: Case Study

The writ shown as an illustration of a claim for a liquidated demand is set out at **6.8**. As will be observed, that represents a claim for a substantial amount of money together with interest pursuant to a contract in respect of the sale of wild animals for a private zoo. Let us assume that the defendant returned his acknowledgement of service indicating that he proposed to defend and that the plaintiffs, after receiving proper advice, instructed their solicitors to proceed to try to obtain summary judgment. A summons would be prepared for issue in the Middlemarch District Registry and an affidavit drafted to be sworn by somebody on behalf of the plaintiff company (here Darryl Hall, the Managing Director of the company).

That affidavit does not deal with the merits of the contract, it merely recites that an invoice has been delivered and not paid. The summons and affidavit are taken to the District Registry and a hearing date given, usually about a month ahead. The original affidavit is retained at the District Registry and a copy of the summons and a photocopy affidavit will then be served on the defendant's solicitors.

An affidavit in reply is sworn by the defendant who strenuously disputes liability for the reason given, namely the fact that the animals, when supplied, were subject to a contagious disease and, indeed, that he intends to make a substantial counterclaim for another of his animals which caught this disease.

In the light of the information in this further affidavit, the plaintiffs' solicitors would be well advised to reconsider the matter with their clients. If it is true that these allegations were made in a letter from the defendant in August 1996, then it seems that the plaintiffs did know that there was a potential defence to the action. In the circumstances it is probably improper to have attempted to obtain summary judgment. A prudent solicitor would advise his client that there is a real risk of the summons being dismissed with an order for the defendant's costs. This is not because the defendant is bound to win the action; it may be that the veterinary surgeon, Ms Wilson, can be discredited and her diagnosis of the animals' condition attacked. It may indeed be that the bear referred to in paragraph 8 infected the purchased animals rather than vice versa. Nonetheless, it is clear that there is an arguable defence and a substantial factual dispute, and in the circumstances the plaintiffs would probably be well advised to consider withdrawing the summons since the outcome of the hearing seems inevitable.

The only cautionary note is that it seems strange that no written report has been obtained from Ms Wilson to be exhibited to the affidavit of Mr Oates; and that, if he had a substantial counterclaim which became obvious as long ago as September 1996, it is perhaps odd that he has taken no initiative to institute his own proceedings. These may be important matters of credibility at trial, but the outcome of the summary judgment application seems doomed. However spurious he thought the claim made in the letter of August 1996, Mr Hall was foolish not to have drawn it to the company's solicitors' attention in order to obtain proper advice.

IN THE HIGH COURT OF JUSTICE **1997-Z No. 1081**
Queen's Bench Division
Middlemarch District Registry

Between ZOO SUPPLIES LTD Plaintiff

and

JOHN OATES Defendant

Let all Parties concerned attend the District Judge at the Office of the District Registry situate at 7 Quay Street Middlemarch on Monday, the 23rd day of June 1997 at 2.30 o'clock in the afternoon on the hearing of an application on the part of the Plaintiff for final judgment in this action against the Defendant for the amount claimed in the statement of claim with interest, if any, and costs.

Take Notice that a party intending to oppose this application or to apply for a stay of execution should send to the opposite party or his solicitor, to reach him not less than three days before the date above-mentioned, a copy of any affidavit intended to be used.

Dated the 30th day of May 1997

To Messrs Casaubon and Co
3 High Street
Middlemarch

Solicitor for the Defendant

This Summons was taken out by
Lydgate and Co
23 Railway Cuttings,
Middlemarch

Solicitor for the Plaintiff

Plaintiff: D Hall: 1st: 28.5.1997

IN THE HIGH COURT OF JUSTICE **1997-Z-No 1084**
Queen's Bench Division
Middlemarch District Registry

Between Zoo Supplies Limited Plaintiff

and

John Oates Defendant

I, Darryl Hall of 11 Philadelphia Terrace, Middlemarch, the Managing Director of the Plaintiffs make oath and say as follows:-

1. The Defendant John Oates is and was at the commencement of this action, justly and truly indebted to the above-named Plaintiffs in the sum of £24,000 for the supply of animals and interest thereon.
2. It is within my own knowledge that the said debt was incurred and is still due and owing.
3. I verily believe that there is no defence to this action.
4. I am duly authorised by the Plaintiffs to make this affidavit.

Sworn at 14 Bulstrode Place
Middlemarch in the County
of Loamshire

D Hall

the 28th day of May 1997

Susan Brown

Before me A Solicitor.

Defendant: J Oates: 1st: 10.6.1997

IN THE HIGH COURT OF JUSTICE **1997-Z No. 1081**
Queen's Bench Division
Middlemarch District Registry

Between ZOO SUPPLIES LTD Plaintiff

and

JOHN OATES Defendant

I, John Oates of The Old Barn, Middlemarch in the County of Loamshire make oath and say as follows:-

1. I am the Defendant in this case and I have read the affidavit of Darryl Hall sworn the 28th day of May 1997.
2. I am a farmer by occupation and on part of my farm I keep a small private zoo for my own interest. It is not open to the public although I usually permit parties of school children to visit the zoo without charge. I have regularly expanded the zoo over the last ten years and have a large collection of unusual mammals. Until the transaction which is the subject of this litigation I have always obtained my animals from a large firm in London.
3. In January 1996 I received a brochure from the Plaintiffs and decided to purchase the three animals referred to in the Statement of Claim herein. To this end I entered into a contract in February 1996 with the Plaintiffs.
4. In clause 5 of the said contract a stipulation appears in the following terms:

   'The Vendors will supply the said animals in good health and shall produce to the purchaser a certificate of good health from a veterinary surgeon in respect of each animal.'
5. The animals were delivered on 5th May 1996 and a certificate of good health was supplied signed by one Howard Leese who is described on the certificate as a veterinary surgeon.
6. Less than a week after the said delivery I was informed by my mammal keeper that all three animals were looking ill and that the wombat had not eaten for three days. I subsequently instructed a veterinary surgeon who specialises in illnesses affecting exotic animals one Ann Wilson. She diagnosed that all three of the animals were suffering from Tarrant's Syndrome, a rare virus the effect of which is to render an animal very lethargic and which leads eventually to a coma and death. She informed me that this condition was very contagious. All three animals died in the month of July 1996 from this syndrome. I am informed by Ann Wilson that this condition lies dormant for 12–15 weeks before the symptoms manifest themselves and therefore that the animals must have been carrying the virus at the time of delivery.
7. I informed the Plaintiffs of these facts by letter dated 4th August 1996 and that I was intending to withhold payment.
8. Further to the above in August 1996 the rarest and most valuable animal in my zoo, a Javanese Jumping Bear manifested the symptoms of Tarrant's Syndrome from which it died in September 1996. It could only have contracted the disease from the three animals supplied by the Plaintiffs. I wish to make a counterclaim against the Plaintiffs for the value of the bear and for the distress this has caused me. I value the bear at £20,000.
9. In the premises I ask this Honourable Court for leave to defend this action.

Sworn at 15 High Street
Middlemarch in the County of Loamshire
the 10th day of June 1997

Before me

A practising solicitor.

17.13 Dismissal for Want of Prosecution: Case Study

Below there appears a copy of an affidavit such as would be used in connection with an application to dismiss an action for want of prosecution.

The background facts are set out in the affidavit which is sworn by a partner in the firm of solicitors acting for the defendants. The affidavit describes what is obviously gross delay by any standards, with total inactivity since March 1989 and the limitation period clearly having expired in 1991.

Substantial delay alone is not sufficient and the defendants' solicitor has tried, in his affidavit, to explain how his clients' case is prejudiced. This comes about in two respects, namely (a) that two witnesses are now unavailable for trial and (b) that he was not allowed facilities for a medical examination of the plaintiff closer to the time of the accident, so that his ability to argue the case on quantum might be seriously prejudiced.

It will be observed that this application has been triggered, as is quite common, by the plaintiff having changed solicitors (her original solicitors having been quite clearly negligent) and by the new solicitors attempting to get the action started again. They have perhaps been a little foolish simply to give notice of change of solicitors and notice of intention to proceed to setting down without offering the defendants facilities for medical examination. Had they done that, and had the defendants taken them up on it, it might well be that the defendants could be deemed to have waived their objection to the delay.

Even on these gross facts, it is by no means certain that the defendants will succeed. If they have taken good witness statements from missing witnesses they can use those statements under the *Civil Evidence Act 1995*. Much will depend upon how badly prejudiced they are by their inability to have a contemporaneous medical examination of the plaintiff. Depending on the thoroughness of the witness statements, this application is perhaps relatively evenly balanced.

Defendant: J Dunn: 1st: 2.5.1997

IN THE HIGH COURT OF JUSTICE **1989-A-No. 0315**

Queen's Bench Division

Middlemarch District Registry

Between FARIDA ALI Plaintiff

and

AMALGAMATED ENGINEERING LIMITED Defendants

AFFIDAVIT IN SUPPORT OF APPLICATION
TO STRIKE OUT FOR WANT OF PROSECUTION

I, John Dunn a partner in the firm of Vincy and Co solicitors of Bank Chambers Middlemarch in the County of Loamshire make oath and say as follows:-

1. I am a partner in the firm of Vincy and Co who are instructed by the O-So-Safe Insurance Co plc the insurers of the defendants in this case and I am duly authorised by them to make this affidavit.

2. This is an action for personal injuries arising out of an alleged accident on the defendants' premises on the 3rd May 1988 as a result of which the plaintiff alleges that she sustained

serious injuries. A writ was issued on the 12th January 1989 and served on me on the 15th January 1989; a statement of claim was served on the 5th February 1989; my defence was served on the 3rd March 1989. In the letter which accompanied my defence I asked the plaintiff's solicitors for facilities for medical examination of the plaintiff but I have received no reply nor any other correspondence from them since that time.

3. In order to prepare for this case in 1989 I interviewed the two most relevant witnesses of fact namely one Henry Cross a foreman at the defendants' factory premises; and Peter Smith who witnessed the plaintiff lying on the ground shortly after the alleged accident.

4. In September 1993 the said Henry Cross died in a road traffic accident; in February 1994 the said Peter Smith emigrated to New Zealand. I have obtained this information from a next-door neighbour of Peter Smith but although I have made exhaustive enquiries I have been unable to discover the precise address in New Zealand to which Peter Smith moved. I exhibit hereto and mark J.D.1 a bundle consisting of two reports from enquiry agents one in Middlemarch and one in Auckland New Zealand made respectively by Peter Green; and Jeremy Spencer; and which reveal that it has proved impossible to trace the said Peter Smith despite exhaustive efforts.

5. On 30 April 1997 I received a letter from Messrs Garth and Co which I exhibit hereto and mark J.D.2. This letter indicates that they have been instructed on behalf of the plaintiff in place of her former solicitors; gives me Notice of Change of solicitor; and purports to give notice under RSC Ord. 3, r. 6 that in a month's time they propose to set this action down for trial and requesting me meanwhile to agree two medical reports on the plaintiff which they attach to their letter.

6. I respectfully submit that after more than 7 years of inactivity in this case the defendants' position and their ability to defend the action is seriously prejudiced by the absence of the two key witnesses to the alleged incident; by the failure of the plaintiff to afford me opportunities for medical examinations closer to the time of the accident; and moreover I contend that I will be prejudiced by my inability to obtain or check information about the plaintiff's loss of earnings since the time of the accident.

7. In the premises I ask this Honourable Court to strike out the plaintiff's claim for want of prosecution.

Sworn at 10 High St Middlemarch
in the County of Loamshire
this 2nd day of May 1997
before me.

J. Dunn

L. Evans

* Note: Exhibits not supplied.

EIGHTEEN

PROCEDURAL COMPLICATIONS

Thus far we have, in the main, been considering straightforward actions between an individual plaintiff and an individual defendant, having made appropriate allowances at the relevant points for the possibility of other parties being involved. In the next two chapters these possibilities will be more thoroughly considered.

In this chapter we consider the situations where a defendant wishes to blame some other person and the current trend to 'group' actions in the case of large numbers of parties (usually plaintiffs in personal injury claims) who are all affected by the same act of the defendant. In **Chapter 19**, we go on to consider differences in rules and tactics where there are special kinds of litigants other than ordinary individuals.

For the first time, in this chapter, we consider both High Court and county court procedure side by side to avoid unnecessary duplication in the later chapters.

18.1 Third Party Proceedings

18.1.1 INTRODUCTION

It will be remembered from the earlier discussion of joinder of parties (see **6.1**) that it is not open to a *defendant* to join any other person as co-defendant. Third party proceedings provide a procedure whereby a defendant may have an issue which is in some way relevant to the plaintiff's claim against him tried as between himself and some other person (*RSC Ord. 16*). In such a case it would always be open to the defendant, as an alternative, to issue his own writ against this other person. Third party proceedings, however, have the advantages, first, of preventing a multiplicity of actions and enabling the court to settle disputes between all parties in one action and, secondly, of preventing the same question being tried twice with possibly different results. There is also a considerable saving in costs.

A claim may therefore be brought by a defendant against the third party. We consider the kind of claims that can be made at **18.1.2**. It is important to note at this stage, however, that there is no direct connection between the plaintiff and the third party. The plaintiff has brought an action against the defendant and against him only, and what happens between defendant and third party is irrelevant to the plaintiff. Thus, if it transpires that the plaintiff has sued the wrong person, he cannot obtain judgment against the third party instead of the defendant unless he has previously taken certain action which we discuss at **18.1.4.5**.

18.1.2 TYPES OF CLAIM

A defendant may by *third party notice* make a claim against a person who is not already a party to the action for:

(a) a contribution or indemnity; or

(b) any relief or remedy relating to or connected with the original subject matter of the action and substantially the same as some relief or remedy claimed by the plaintiff; or

(c) any question or issue arising out of the plaintiff's claim to be determined not only as between the plaintiff and the defendant, but also as between either or both of them and a person not already a party to the action.

We now consider how these might arise.

18.1.2.1 Claim for a contribution

To take a straightforward case, suppose that P has been knocked down by a vehicle driven by D. D contends that he was not the only one responsible for the accident and that another car driven by T contributed to the cause of it. He may therefore join T as a third party. The consequence will be that although D will remain liable for any damages awarded to the plaintiff, he may, having paid those damages, be able to obtain a contribution if the court concludes that T did bear a share of responsibility for the accident. Of course, if in a negligence case D claimed that T had *wholly* caused the accident, this would provide a complete defence for D and, if the court found that this was so, D would be exonerated from any liability. The consequence of this would be that, as there is no direct relationship between the plaintiff and T, the plaintiff would recover no damages and (indeed) be left to pay D's costs. The action that the plaintiff should take to cope with this possibility is discussed at **18.1.4.5** below.

18.1.2.2 Claim for indemnity

An example of this would be a case where a consumer sues a retailer for damages in respect of the supply of an item which is not of merchantable quality. The retailer may have a contract with the manufacturer which provides the retailer with indemnity in such cases. The retailer may, of course, defend the action on the merits, perhaps alleging that the item was not defective when it left the shop but broke because of rough treatment by the plaintiff, or that the damages claimed do not flow naturally from the alleged defect, but the point of issuing third party proceedings will be that if he fails in these allegations he may recover an indemnity from the manufacturer.

In fact, in such a situation what would happen would be that the retailer would more or less drop out of the proceedings. Although strictly liable in the law of sale of goods for the supply of the defective item, if it was indeed impossible for him to check the quality of the item before selling it (e.g. canned goods) any claim which the plaintiff does have against the retailer will probably lead to a full indemnity from the third party to the latter. The third party might as well negotiate directly with the plaintiff for settlement of the action. A common development is for the third party to offer to take over the conduct of the defendant's defence of the action.

18.1.2.3 Other relief

Possibilities (b) and (c) in **18.1.2** may be considered together. They allow the defendant in general to introduce in the action an issue which has some connection with the situation out of which the plaintiff's claim against the defendant arose. An example of this is a case where P, a pedestrian, is knocked down by a vehicle driven by D, and D's car goes on to strike a wall and D is injured. D contends that the accident may have been caused or contributed to by another vehicle driven by T. He will issue third party proceedings against T seeking a contribution towards any damages he is found liable to pay P, and in addition damages for his own personal injury.

18.1.3 HOW ARE THIRD PARTY PROCEEDINGS COMMENCED?

18.1.3.1 Third party notice

A third party notice in the prescribed form may be issued at court at any time after notice of intention to defend has been given. Provided the notice is issued before the defence is served, no leave of the court is necessary. The defendant's solicitor takes down to the court the necessary copies of a third party notice in the prescribed form for sealing. The third party notice stands as if it were a writ and brief statement of claim indicating to the third party the substance of the defendant's claim against him.

18.1.3.2 Leave of the court required where the defence has been served

It will be recalled that the defendant has only 14 days from service of the statement of claim in which to serve his defence. However, given that there will usually have been some pre-action negotiations, the need to issue a third party notice should have already become apparent. It may well be possible, therefore, to issue the third party notice before serving the defence. If, however, it has not proved possible, or the possibility of a right of action or the identity of the third party has only become known to the defendant at some later stage, then the leave of the court must be obtained. This is sought by an *ex parte* application to the Master or District Judge. The plaintiff is not involved at this stage. An affidavit is sworn, usually by the defendant's solicitor. The affidavit must state:

(a) the nature of the claim made by the plaintiff against the defendant in the action;

(b) the stage which proceedings in the main action have reached;

(c) the nature of the claim made by the defendant applying for leave to issue the third party notice and the facts on which the proposed third party notice is based; and

(d) the name and address of the proposed third party.

The defendant's solicitor takes the affidavit to the court and leaves it with three copies of the third party notice to be placed before the Master or District Judge. There is no hearing. The Master or District Judge will in due course read the affidavit and, if it seems to him an appropriate case for third party proceedings, he will give leave for the third party notices to be issued. The defendant then collects them from the court. One notice is sealed as the original, a copy is sealed for service on the third party by the defendant and another copy is sealed for retention by the court. There is no need in the Queen's Bench Division to draw up the order giving leave to issue third party proceedings.

If the affidavit is not wholly convincing, or the case is one of some difficulty, the Master or District Judge may instead of dealing with the matter *ex parte* direct that a summons be issued and that both parties to the existing action (i.e. defendant and plaintiff) be called before him to make their representations on the propriety or otherwise of third party proceedings in the instant case.

18.1.3.3 Service of the third party notice

When the third party notice has been issued it must be served on the third party in the same way as a writ is served (see **6.6**). Copies of the writ and pleadings in the main action (i.e. that between plaintiff and defendant) must also be served, together with a form of acknowledgement of service. The form of acknowledgement of service is basically the same as that served with the writ itself, with slight modifications, e.g. the change of 'defendant' to 'third party'.

18.1.3.4 Acknowledgement of service

The third party when served must acknowledge the third party notice in the same way in which a defendant must acknowledge a writ, by returning the acknowledgement of service duly completed to the court within 14 days indicating whether he proposes to defend the third party proceedings against the defendant, or to contend that the defendant is not liable to the plaintiff.

If he does not return this acknowledgement of service, although the defendant cannot enter judgment in default against the third party, the third party is now deemed to admit any claim stated in the notice and will be bound by any judgment in the action, and will not in principle be permitted to play any further part in the proceedings.

18.1.4 THE COURSE OF THIRD PARTY PROCEEDINGS

It should be apparent, even from reading this brief account, that proceedings involving third parties become procedurally 'messy', and therefore the rules of court provide that at a very early stage there should be a sort of tidying-up operation when all the parties are called before the court. The rules provide that as soon as possible after the third party's acknowledging service and giving notice of intention to defend, the **defendant must take out a summons for third party directions**. The summons is issued in the usual way and a hearing date obtained from the court, and the summons will then be served by the defendant on both the plaintiff and the third party. It will be noted that there has not hitherto been any requirement for the service of formal pleadings between the defendant and the third party, and the third party need take no further steps after returning the acknowledgement of service until he attends the hearing of the summons for third party directions.

There is a number of orders which the court will consider making when all the parties are before the court. The most important ones are as follows:

18.1.4.1 Dismissal of the application for directions

The District Judge may dismiss the application for directions with the result of terminating the third party proceedings. He will do this where, for example, it does not appear to him that the case is an appropriate one for third party proceedings or where third party proceedings may cause unacceptable delay and difficulty in the substantive action between the plaintiff and the defendant.

18.1.4.2 Judgment for the defendant

If the liability of the third party to the defendant is established (e.g. if there is clearly a contract for indemnity of the defendant), the District Judge may order judgment to be entered for the defendant against the third party.

18.1.4.3 Directions for trial

The judge may order any claim, question or issue to be tried in such manner as the court may direct as between plaintiff and defendant and third party.

18.1.4.4 Allowing the third party to defend the plaintiff's claim

The third party may be given liberty to defend the plaintiff's claim, either alone or jointly with the defendant. Such a situation has already been envisaged at **18.1.2.2**, e.g. a claim against a retailer who has a contract for indemnity by the manufacturer. The manufacturer may take over the retailer's defence letting the retailer drop out (with an appropriate order for costs). The manufacturer may then avail himself of any defences which would have been available to the defendant retailer, e.g. he may say that the goods were not in fact defective.

18.1.4.5 Adding the third party as a defendant

The District Judge may make an order adding the third party as a defendant where the plaintiff applies for this and wishes to raise a claim directly against the third party, e.g. in the case of the motor accident referred to at **18.1.2.1** above, where it now appears that T may have been negligent either as well as, or instead of D.

18.1.4.6 Third party pleadings

Third party pleadings may be ordered, that is the service of pleadings between defendant and third party, because the statement of facts which appears on the third party notice itself is rather brief and it may be appropriate for this to be supplemented by a fully pleaded statement of claim to which the third party should respond in a formal third party defence.

18.1.4.7 Discovery and other procedural orders

Thereafter the judge may give orders for discovery between the third party and the defendant, or the third party and the plaintiff. In addition, he may make any other proper procedural orders which would be normal on a summons for directions, e.g. for exchange of witness statements, mutual disclosure of expert evidence, and the like. There are no automatic directions in third party proceedings even where these involve personal injuries, and thus directions are necessary in every case.

18.1.4.8 Trial of the third party issue

The District Judge may give directions for trial of the third party issue. The common order is to direct that the third party be at liberty to appear at the trial of the action, and take such part as the judge shall direct and be bound by the result of the trial. It should be noted here that proceedings between the defendant and third party can go on even after those between plaintiff and defendant are stayed.

18.1.4.9 Summary

When giving these directions the court will have in mind the interests of all the parties, and special care will be taken to see that the plaintiff is not subject to injustice and delay by unnecessarily allowing third parties to be involved. The usual order giving directions for the progress of the action allows the third party to attend at the trial of the plaintiff's claim against the defendant and to oppose the plaintiff's claim so far as he personally might be affected by it, and for this purpose to call oral or documentary evidence and himself to cross-examine the plaintiff's witnesses.

18.1.5 THIRD PARTY PROCEEDINGS IN A PERSONAL INJURIES ACTION

Here we consider the way in which the matter will most commonly arise in a personal injury case and what steps might be taken tactically by either party.

18.1.5.1 The defendant

Let us first suppose that the plaintiff's vehicle has been in collision with the defendant's vehicle and that both parties have suffered personal injuries. The plaintiff contends that the defendant's negligence was the cause of the accident and issues a writ against him. The defendant may not only defend but, if he contends that the plaintiff was to blame, also counterclaim for his own vehicle damage and personal injuries. No other parties are involved.

A more complicated situation would arise if a pedestrian plaintiff is injured by a vehicle driven by D. He sues D. D, however, contends that the accident was actually caused by another vehicle driven by T, which suddenly swerved out in front of him causing him to take evasive action in the agony of the moment. D is therefore in the position of claiming that he is completely innocent. Here D may take one of two courses, namely:

(a) He may simply blame T in his defence and leave it at that. There is no need to issue third party proceedings. If at trial his defence is accepted, i.e. it is found that the accident was in fact caused by T, then the plaintiff's claim will fail against D. T is not involved at all and the plaintiff will in principle have to pay the defendant's costs. It must be said, however, that merely to do this and put the allegation in his pleading as a form of defence would be an act of very great confidence on the part of D. He would run the risk of bearing the whole of the plaintiff's damages in such a case even if he were found to be only 1 per cent to blame for the accident. Putting his defence in that way without taking any further action would therefore generally be considered extremely rash.

(b) Consequently, in addition to blaming T in his defence, the defendant will normally go on to issue third party proceedings against T. This will particularly be the case if D has himself suffered some damage in the accident for which he can hardly blame the pedestrian plaintiff, e.g. where, having hit the pedestrian plaintiff, he then hits a tree nearby. He will accordingly in such a situation issue third party proceedings claiming both a contribution towards any damages for which he is found liable to the plaintiff and his own damages. If the court found that T was in fact 90 per cent to blame, whilst D would initially have to pay the whole of the plaintiff's damages he could recover a 90 per cent contribution from T, and also 90 per cent of the amount appropriate for his own damages, if any.

18.1.5.2 The plaintiff

In the first case, where the defendant merely blames T in his pleading but does not issue a third party notice, it will of course be prudent for the plaintiff to apply for leave to amend the writ to add T as a second defendant. In this he can hardly lose in terms of costs because, at the end of the trial, should he succeed against either of the defendants the costs order to be made is likely to be a *Bullock* or *Sanderson* order, i.e. one which has the effect of requiring the losing defendant to pay the costs of everyone (see **6.1.4**). It can hardly be contended that he was unreasonable in adding T as a defendant where the suggestion of T's liability came from D himself.

In the second situation, where D has issued third party proceedings, it may again be considered prudent to join T as a second defendant. Although P only has to show that D was 1 per cent to blame for the accident to recover the whole of his damages, if there is any suggestion that somebody else may have caused or contributed to the happening of the accident it would be a safer course for him to join that person. It might be that P would fail outright at the trial against D, in which case he would end up paying D's costs and, of course, bearing his own. By that stage it might be too late to issue separate proceedings against T because the limitation period might have expired. Moreover, even if P was in time to issue separate proceedings against T, it would by no means follow that he would win against T at a trial before a different court. It must be remembered that the findings of courts in civil cases are not binding in any other case unless the parties before the second court are the same as those in respect of whom judgment has already been delivered in the first case. Therefore, the fact that the first judge considered T had caused the accident would not bind the second one to come to the same conclusion, and if he concluded that D had caused the accident P might again fail outright. It is therefore greatly to P's advantage to avoid any possible risk of this and achieve a saving in costs and time by joining everybody involved at the appropriate stage.

The obvious time for the plaintiff to apply for this order adding the third party as second defendant is at the stage of the summons for third party directions when all parties are conveniently before the court and the plaintiff will issue his own summons returnable on the same occasion. It should be remembered that the plaintiff will need to apply for leave to amend his writ and pleadings and ought, before the hearing, to have been prudent enough to have already written a letter protecting himself under *s. 152* of the *Road Traffic Act 1988*, and to have obtained the prior authority of the Legal Aid Board to amend any legal aid certificate to add a reference to the proposed second defendant.

18.1.6 CONTRACT AND COMMERCIAL CASES

We have considered the procedural options above and given the example of third party proceedings in a personal injury case. Much the same applies, however, to sale of goods or other commercial cases. Thus, for example, if a plaintiff has suffered from the purchase of defective goods which have perhaps caused damage or injury (such as a defective electrical item which causes a fire on use, with or without personal injury consequences), the plaintiff will normally sue the retailer. The retailer may well blame the manufacturer, but the plaintiff need not be concerned with this since he has the advantage of a virtual strict liability claim under the *Sale of Goods Act 1979*.

If he were so minded, if the retailer joined in the manufacturer by third party proceedings, the plaintiff might well be able to make a claim against that manufacturer under the *Consumer Protection Act 1987*, and thus might amend his writ and pleadings to join in the manufacturer as a second defendant. Since he would appear to have an unanswerable claim against the retailer, however, unless of course, some defence on the facts could be mounted (such as that the plaintiff had tampered with the wiring of the electrical item before use), there would be little point in the plaintiff joining in the manufacturer except where he might doubt the solvency of the retailer to meet any claim for damages. Unless that is the position, therefore, the plaintiff would probably not concern himself to amend to join the manufacturer as second defendant.

The procedural path which the action would take would inevitably be that the manufacturer would take over the conduct of the retailer's defence, giving him an indemnity for all costs incurred hitherto and agreeing to meet any damages awarded to the plaintiff. It would then be open to him to mount any factual or legal defences available to the defendant against the plaintiff.

18.1.7 CAN ONE DEFENDANT USE THIRD PARTY PROCEEDINGS AGAINST ANOTHER DEFENDANT?

For completeness it ought to be said that if P had commenced proceedings against D1 and D2, D1 would not need to issue third party proceedings merely to allege D2's part in the accident. In such a situation the courts have a wide power to apportion liability under the *Civil Liability (Contribution) Act 1978* for any damages found due to the plaintiff. However, in the situation where a defendant, in addition to defending the plaintiff's claim, has a claim *of his own* against a co-defendant (e.g. when P and D1 have both been injured in an accident and D1 wishes to claim against D2), he must issue third party proceedings of his own against the co-defendant. In that situation he may, without the leave of the court, issue a third party notice. A summons for third party directions will follow and there will be a similar tidying up operation to that described in **18.1.4** above, with the court addressing its mind both to the action by the plaintiff against the defendants and what is in effect the action by the first defendant against the second defendant.

18.2 Security for Costs

18.2.1 THE IMPECUNIOUS PLAINTIFF

In ordinary litigation, there is no protection for a defendant who is being sued by a plaintiff, however unmeritorious the claim, unless it is so unmeritorious that he can have the whole claim dismissed or struck out at some early stage. Thus, for example, it would be open to an impecunious plaintiff to harass a defendant with expensive and time-consuming proceedings knowing that even though he loses at trial, the defendant is unlikely to be able to recover the costs awarded to him because of the plaintiff's impecuniosity. Unfortunately in the majority of cases defendants who are harassed in this way will have little recourse, although if the facts are extreme it may be possible to obtain a 'wasted costs' order against the impecunious plaintiff's solicitors on the basis that they have assisted him in pursuing utterly groundless litigation. One such case which ended in this way was *Tolstoy-Miloslavasy* v *Aldington, The Times*, 27 December 1995, where the court concluded that the impecunious plaintiff's solicitors had improperly assisted him to bring a quite hopeless action for the purpose of harassing the defendant and ordered that a substantial proportion of the costs be paid by the plaintiff's solicitors personally.

To the general rule therefore that there is likely to be little recourse in the ordinary case for a defendant who wins against an impecunious plaintiff, there is one major exception. This is a rule which provides that in certain circumstances the court can order that a plaintiff, as the price of continuing with his action, gives 'security for costs' usually by paying a substantial sum into court funds as a guarantee that he will be able to meet any costs order eventually made against him.

18.2.2 THE FOUR 'SUSPECT' CATEGORIES OF PLAINTIFFS

In the High Court, the rule provides that if it appears to the court that the plaintiff is in one of four 'suspect' categories, the court can 'having regard to all the circumstances of the case if it thinks it just to do so order the plaintiff to give such security for the defendant's costs of the action . . . as it thinks just'. (RSC Ord. 23, r. 1.)

There are thus two separate tests, the first to show that the plaintiff falls within one of the 'suspect' categories and the second which allows the court to exercise its discretion, once the plaintiff is shown to be in one of those categories, to order security for costs. It must be stressed therefore that the remedy is *discretionary* and may not be awarded even though the plaintiff falls within one of the four categories.

In the High Court the categories are as follows:

(a) where the plaintiff is *ordinarily resident out of the jurisdiction*; or

(b) where the plaintiff is suing in a *nominal capacity* for the benefit of some other person and there is reason to believe that he will be unable to pay the defendant's costs if ordered to do so; or

(c) where the plaintiff's *address is not stated* in the writ or incorrectly stated; or

(d) where the plaintiff has *changed his address* during the course of the proceedings with a view to evading the consequences of the litigation.

The categories are exhaustive. It is no use showing merely that a plaintiff is impecunious, unless he also fits one of these categories. There is for example no prospect of obtaining an order that a plaintiff should have to give security for costs merely because he is on the verge of bankruptcy. Neither can one obtain such an order against a legally aided plaintiff within the jurisdiction.

In the corresponding county court rule there is only one category specified by the rule (*CCR Ord. 13, r. 8*) and that is the case where the plaintiff is ordinarily resident outside England and Wales.

18.2.2.1 **'Ordinarily resident out of the jurisdiction'**

The rationale of this part of the rule is obviously based on the difficulty of enforcing a costs order against someone who is outside the jurisdiction and presumably has no assets within it. The question of 'ordinarily resident' is to be determined on a common sense basis and it may not correspond to the concept of domicile in other matters, for example tax or family law. If a plaintiff works most of the year abroad, but has clear roots in this country, he may not be 'ordinarily resident' out of the jurisdiction. In any event, if he retains assets within the jurisdiction which could be used to enforce a costs order, for example a house or business interests, then it may be that although he may be deemed to be ordinarily resident out of the jurisdiction, the court would not make a security for costs order.

The problem of plaintiffs resident within the European Union has led to a great deal of case law. It was alleged that it is inappropriate to make a security for costs order against a plaintiff who resides elsewhere in the European Union because to do so would be improperly discriminatory and contrary to Article 7 of the EEC Treaty. That point has now been upheld in the case of *Fitzgerald and Others* v *Williams and Others* [1996] 2 All ER 117 which held that to require a European Union based plaintiff to give security for costs simply on the grounds of residence is improperly discriminatory. The court did reserve consideration of the position as to whether, if there was clear evidence that procedures in the plaintiff's home country were ineffective to enforce an English judgment for costs, notwithstanding the existence within Europe of conventions concerning mutual enforcement of judgements, that might be a ground to permit the court to order security for costs.

18.2.2.2 **'Nominal plaintiff'**

A plaintiff who sues in a representative capacity, such as a next friend is *not* a nominal plaintiff. The test is whether the plaintiff retains a general interest in the outcome of the litigation. If he does then he is not 'nominal' and no security for costs order can be made. An interesting case demonstrating this is *Envis* v *Thakker, The Times,* 2 May 1995 where the plaintiff was nearly insolvent and intended to use the proceeds of the litigation to distribute amongst his creditors to avoid bankruptcy. The court held that as he had an interest in the outcome of the litigation, he did not become a 'nominal' plaintiff even though he himself would not keep any of the fruits of the litigation.

18.2.2.3 **The plaintiff's address**

There is no modern case law of importance on the other two categories which have to do with plaintiffs who do not give their honest address in the writ or change their address with the objective of avoiding the consequences of litigation. If these factors could be established then it would be obvious that security for costs should be given in such cases.

18.2.3 ARE THERE ANY OTHER 'SUSPECT' CATEGORIES?

It must be noted that this order can only be made in favour of the defendant against a plaintiff. It can never be made against a defendant. However, a defendant who brings a counter-claim is in the position of a plaintiff in relation to that counter-claim and an order for security for costs in relation to the counter-claim part of the proceedings can be made. Recent case law has otherwise tended to show that the categories given are exhaustive. Thus in *Condliffe* v *Hislop and Another, The Times,* 3 November 1995 the court refused an application by a defendant in a libel action for an impecunious plaintiff to give security for costs merely on the grounds that the plaintiff's action was being financed by a wealthy relative.

18.2.4 SECURITY FOR COSTS UNDER OTHER STATUTES

Order 23, r. 3 expressly preserves the power of the court to order security for costs where some other rule permits it. Of these, by far the most important in practice is *s. 726(1)* of the *Companies Act 1985*. This provides:

> *Where in England and Wales a limited company is plaintiff in an action or other legal proceeding, the court having jurisdiction in the matter may, if it appears by credible testimony that there is reason to believe that the company will be unable to pay the defendant's costs if successful in his defence, require sufficient security to be given for those costs, and may stay all proceedings until the security is given.*

As will be observed from the wording, this is a wider power than exists under *Ord. 23* and is commonly used to stifle claims by small limited companies. Limited companies of small or modest size, ranging from small family businesses to much larger companies which employ several hundred people, are often put in a difficult position by this statutory provision. The reason is that hitherto, quite understandably, they will have caused their accounts to be drawn up with the major objective of avoiding tax. Thus if, for example, very large profits would have been shown just before their financial year end, they may well decide to use much of those profits to buy additional stock, upgrade company vehicles and the like so as, quite legitimately, to avoid tax. When they come to sue someone those accounts will be obtained by the defendant and may be ruthlessly used against them to show that they are not very profitable and therefore unlikely to be able to bear a large costs order should they lose the litigation.

A device adopted quite recently to evade this problem was for a company to assign its right of action to one of its directors or shareholders so that he could be substituted as a plaintiff. The courts, somewhat surprisingly, upheld the lawfulness of this device, even when part of the reason was to allow the director to obtain legal aid to sue (legal aid of course not being available to a company). As a device for escaping the rigours of *s. 726* it will continue to be successful, but as a means of a director obtaining legal aid it is likely to be less useful in future following the introduction of *regulation 33A* of the *Civil Legal Aid (General) Regulations 1989* in June 1996 which provides that a legal aid application may be refused if it appears that it is based on a cause of action which was assigned by a limited company with the object of allowing the action to be commenced or continued with the benefit of a legal aid certificate.

18.2.5 FOREIGN COMPANIES

It will be recalled from the case law on *Ord. 23* above that the courts have held that it was improperly discriminatory to require a European Union based plaintiff to give security for costs where an English plaintiff would not have been so ordered. In the case of limited companies registered abroad, however, the same considerations do not apply. In *Chequepoint SARL* v *McLelland, The Times*, 18 June 1996, the court concluded that it was not improperly discriminatory against a French company to require them to give security for costs where in similar circumstances an English company would have been required to give such security under *s. 726* of the *Companies Act*. The point was that it was not that the plaintiff was abroad that mattered, it was that the plaintiff was a limited company.

18.2.6 DISCRETION OF THE COURT UNDER *SECTION 726* OF THE *COMPANIES ACT 1985*

The court's discretion under *s. 726* is very wide and general. The most important case is probably *Sir Lindsay Parkinson & Co. Ltd* v *Triplan Ltd* [1973] QB 609, which set out the tests for the exercise for the court's discretion. These tests will also be relevant in many applications under *Ord. 23* not involving companies.

The tests are:

(a) whether the plaintiff's claim is bona fide;

(b) what are the plaintiff's prospects of success (although the court stressed that an application for security for costs must not be used to go into the full merits of the claim in any depth);

(c) whether the defendant has made any admissions;

(d) whether there has been a substantial payment into court or open offer;

(e) whether, even if a plaintiff is outside the jurisdiction, he retains substantial property within it against which an order for costs could be enforced;

(f) whether the application is being used oppressively, for example to stifle a genuine claim;

(g) whether the plaintiff's impecuniosity has been brought about by any conduct of the defendant, such as a delay in payment. This is a very important ground in practice especially in litigation in a commercial context. It is sometimes the case unfortunately that, for example, a major building contractor withholds payment from a sub-contractor on spurious grounds. Such sub-contractors may be working whole time for the main contractor and if they are not paid, may have no monies to pay their own workforce or even to continue in business. Withholding payment can therefore be used quite unscrupulously as a weapon to cause a sub-contractor to re-negotiate on more favourable terms or to drop other claims or as the case may be. Should the sub-contractor, possibly after months of pressing and attempting to get the outstanding payment have no other option but to sue, then the main contractor may use the sub-contractor's lack of means as a reason to apply for security for costs. The court will, so far as it can without excessive investigation of the background facts, be alert to see that this tactic should not succeed. An interesting case reviewing these possibilities in the context of limited companies is *Keary Developments Ltd* v *Tarmac Construction Ltd* [1995] 3 All ER 534.

(h) finally, the court will examine the stage of the proceedings at which the application has been made. To make this application credibly the defendant should apply quite early in the proceedings and the later application is made, the less likely it is that the court will order security.

18.2.7 WHAT IF THE COURT IS MINDED TO ORDER SECURITY?

If the court decides to order security for costs it will fix the amount. This is usually intended to be a fairly realistic estimate of the costs and is often fixed to be an estimate up to a certain stage of the action after which the defendant may re-apply for a further order for security for the costs of the rest of the action if the litigation goes on. Where the defendant is ordered to give security for costs and is unable to do so, the action will be *stayed* until he does and if he does not produce the money in the relatively early future, the action will then be struck out on the defendant's application. The method of giving security is most usually payment into court of a defined sum to await the outcome of the litigation. Other less common methods are for security to be given by insurance bond, or sometimes part of the money to be paid into a joint account in the names of the party's solicitors or, exceptionally, for the plaintiff's solicitor to give an undertaking to pay the costs of the action if unsuccessful. This latter is not unknown, but is very rare and a solicitor before giving it should of course ensure that he is unequivocally in funds from his client, otherwise he will be personally at risk for the costs.

18.2.8 SUMMARY

Applications for security for costs can therefore be made by a defendant who is sued by a plaintiff in one of the four suspect categories under *Ord. 23* in the High Court, or who simply resides abroad if it is a county court action. In addition, an application can be made against a limited company which is a plaintiff where there is evidence to show the company may be unable to satisfy a substantial order for costs. Application is made by summons and affidavit and the affidavit must carefully demonstrate the background circumstances and, e.g., exhibit the last set of accounts for the plaintiff company. It should also give an estimate of the costs which will be incurred if the case goes on up to a certain stage, usually the stage of setting down for trial and a draft bill should preferably be produced to demonstrate what these costs are likely to be.

Although unusual in personal injuries litigation, this is a vitally important tactical aspect of commercial litigation which has given rise to a remarkable amount of case law in the last decade.

18.3 'Class' or 'Group' Actions

It has become increasingly common in recent years for actions to be commenced with numerous plaintiffs involved. The terms 'class action' or 'group action' are often used in respect of such cases, but it is important to distinguish the two.

18.3.1 CLASS ACTIONS

Properly speaking, the term 'class action' should only be used in a case where all the plaintiffs have exactly the same rights based on the same facts. In its strict use, therefore, it should only be used of actions brought, for example, by a group of beneficiaries against a trustee for breach of trust, or perhaps in some cases of shareholders' actions against a company. It is in fact a misnomer to use it of the much more common situation where there are multiple plaintiffs in a personal injury claim, and in such cases the term 'group action' is better.

18.3.2 GROUP ACTIONS

Such cases commonly come about in one or other of the following situations:

(a) 'Instant' disaster claims arising out of a common cause of action such as an aircraft, shipping or train accident, or a major fire, or a failure in crowd control, e.g. the Zeebrugge shipping disaster, or the Hillsborough football disaster.

(b) Claims arising out of defects in pharmaceutical products such as the 'Benzodiazepine' litigation, where some thousands of plaintiffs alleged harmful side effects and addiction arising from their use of various tranquilliser drugs.

(c) Claims arising out of environmental pollution causing disease.

(d) Claims against local authorities by children in their care who have suffered abuse of one kind or another due to the misconduct of employees of the local authority.

18.3.3 PROCEDURE

In this text a full discussion of the very great practical and procedural problems associated with these types of actions is inappropriate. Anyone involved in this kind of litigation should acquire a copy of a publication from the Lord Chancellor's Department, *Guide for Use in Group Actions* (£1.50).

The applicable rules are *RSC Ord. 15, rr. 4, 5, 6* and *17*, and *RSC Ord. 4, r. 9(1)*. These rules state as follows:

Order 15
4.—*(1) Subject to rule 5(1), two or more persons may be joined together in one action as plaintiffs or as defendants with the leave of the court or where—*

(a) if separate actions were brought by or against each of them, as the case may be, some common question of law or fact would arise in all the actions, and

(b) all rights to relief claimed in the action (whether they are joint, several or alternative) are in respect of or arise out of the same transaction or series of transactions.

5.—(1) If claims in respect of two or more causes of action are included by a plaintiff in the same action or by a defendant in a counterclaim, or if two or more plaintiffs or defendants are parties to the same action, and it appears to the court that the joinder of causes of action or of parties, as the case may be, may embarrass or delay the trial or is otherwise inconvenient, the court may order separate trials or make such order as may be expedient.

6.—(1) No cause or matter shall be defeated by reason of the misjoinder or non-joinder of any party; and the court may in any cause or matter determine the issues or questions in dispute so far as they affect the rights and interests of the persons who are parties to the cause or matter.

17. The court may give the conduct of any action, inquiry or other proceeding to such person as it thinks fit.

Order 4

9.—(1) Where two or more causes or matters are pending in the same division and it appears to the court—

(a) that some common question of law or fact arises in both or all of them, or

(b) that the rights to relief claimed therein are in respect of or arise out of the same transaction or series of transactions, or

(c) that for some other reason it is desirable to make an order under this paragraph,
the court may order those causes or matters to be consolidated on such terms as it thinks just or may order them to be tried at the same time or one immediately after another or may order any of them to be stayed until after the determination of any other of them.

18.3.4 PRACTICAL DIFFICULTIES

The practical problems of this kind of litigation are enormous. Even in the 'instant' disaster case, although perhaps the issue of breach of duty and causation will be identical for each plaintiff, the differences in quantum of damage, and even possibly of contributory negligence, may be extreme. Thus, to take the case of the Hillsborough litigation, whilst at its worst there were numerous victims who suffered fatal accidents, equally there were others on the fringe of the disturbance who suffered quite minor injuries such as broken fingers; in addition, some spectators suffered no physical injuries but sustained nervous shock, whether by viewing directly within the ground, or on television. The extremely difficult questions of liability for nervous shock went, as is well known, to the House of Lords in the case of *Alcock* v *Chief Constable of South Yorkshire* [1992] 1 AC 310.

In pharmaceutical product cases such as the tranquiliser cases the issues are even more complex. There will be patients of different susceptibilities who have taken different quantities of the drug (or possibly in combinations of different tranquilliser drugs, sometimes made by different manufacturers) over very different periods of time and who may well have desisted from taking tranquillisers for certain stages during that time. Moreover, the issues of liability in such cases are increased because the question of relevant scientific knowledge or degree of proper pre-testing may vary from drug to drug and manufacturer to manufacturer. Thus this apparently simple issue of negligence may be very different in respect of each plaintiff on different facts. In addition, there may be different side effects and different issues of limitation in respect of each plaintiff.

18.3.5 COMMENCING A GROUP ACTION

In most such disaster cases notice is given through the legal press and elsewhere that the court considers it desirable that a 'group' should be constituted. In such a case there is usually service of a 'Master' statement of claim, with each individual plaintiff serving separate schedules of special damage; discovery by the defendants is carried out once only to the solicitors for the steering group of the lead cases. (Of course each individual plaintiff will have to carry out discovery separately of the factors relevant to quantum.)

After the group is finalised certain lead cases are selected to come forward as test cases. The very need to set up such 'groups' in itself causes enormous complications. Thus in *AB* v *John Wyeth & Brother Ltd* (1992) *The Times*, 20 October 1992, the court had to consider the 'Benzodiazepine' litigation referred to at **18.3.2** above. For such litigation to be manageable as a group there will have to be cut-off dates after which other interested plaintiffs will not be allowed to join the lead group. If it were not so, plaintiffs who have come forward early would be severely prejudiced by having to proceed only at the pace of the slowest to come forward. In these cases the court issues Practice Directions, usually reserving all actions concerned with the same defendants to a given Master or judge for the interlocutory stages. That is what happened in the 'Benzodiazepine' litigation where the judge in control, Ian Kennedy J, imposed cut-off dates after which persons should not be eligible to join in the group litigation. Those cut-off dates were in fact extended on several occasions, eventually to 31 August 1992, but even so many hundreds more persons came forward attempting to join the group after that date. The Court of Appeal upheld the judge in his refusal to permit others to join in the actions, holding that a cut-off date was essential for the expeditious monitoring of large group claims. It must be borne in mind that that does not in itself destroy the claims of those who come forward later. It is simply that they will have to proceed alone, or form a later group, subject to the problem of limitation periods and, of course, of obtaining legal aid to join the group. (It may well be, for example, that the legal aid authorities would consider that it was unreasonable conduct to fail to come forward in time to join the first group, and legal aid may be harder to obtain for those who have not been sufficiently alert or cooperative to do so, provided that their symptoms became known in time.)

The lead actions chosen after the control of the interlocutory stages will go forward to try the primary facts. The problem is that, strictly speaking, such lead actions do not bind the parties unless they have positively agreed in advance that the decision is to bind them. Although, however, that is the legal position it is certainly possible that, if the lead action is properly constituted, represents a good example of the problem, and is thoroughly and competently litigated, but the lead plaintiff loses, any other litigants in the group reliant on legal aid will have their legal aid withdrawn as being unable to show a reasonable chance of success dependent on the outcome of the lead action. In that way some practical effect will be given to the lead case.

Costs sharing orders which provide that the costs will be shared in certain proportions can be made in order to make the group action more effective. There are serious complications in this, of course, where some plaintiffs have legal aid and some do not.

18.3.6 CONCLUSION

The precise practicalities of the conduct of group litigation remain to be explored by the courts, such procedures still being in their infancy, although the lead cases in some such actions have in fact come to trial. The procedure is no doubt at its most effective in 'instant disaster' cases, where it may be possible to establish fully and finally that the defendants are liable because of some clear finding of fact (e.g. pilot error in an aircraft), which will then leave each member of the group separately and later to establish quantum, a great deal of costs having been saved at the stage of establishing liability. In pharmaceutical litigation, as indicated above, the problems are much more complex, since issues of causation may differ in respect of each individual plaintiff as well as issues of quantum.

Such group actions are becoming more and more common, and most practising solicitors will have clients at some stage for whom they need to consider whether or not a group action is appropriate. The courts have consistently stressed that 'modern case management techniques' should be used as far as possible in such cases, and that the so-called 'sporting theory of litigation' (according to which it is up to each plaintiff to make the best he can of all the tactical advantages available to him whatever the position of other plaintiffs) has no place in such a scenario. Failure properly to join a group and proceed appropriately may well be treated as culpable in terms of wasted costs orders being made against solicitors. By way of illustration, a copy of the Practice Direction relating to the 'Yorkshire Water' litigation is set out below. Such directions are now increasingly in fairly common form:

1. *This practice note applies generally to the 'Yorkshire water litigation', that is any action in which a party, whether by claim or counterclaim, alleges that he or she has suffered personal injuries in the form of the disease cryptosporidiosis as a result of consuming water supplied from the Barmby Water Treatment Works, Barmby, North Yorkshire between the dates of December 1989 and May 1990.*

2. *All interlocutory proceedings in any such actions will, so far as is possible, be heard at the High Court of Justice, Queen's Bench Division, Bristol District Registry by His Honour Judge Fallon QC and not by other judges, Masters or District Judges, save for minor or consent matters (as directed by His Honour Judge Fallon QC).*

3. *The listing on interlocutory proceedings in these actions before his Judge Fallon QC will be facilitated if all 'Yorkshire water litigation' cases which are not presently proceeding in the Bristol District Registry are transferred there, even if the amount claimed is less than £50,000. Such claims will be deemed to meet the criteria specified in Art. 7(5) of the High Court and County Courts Jurisdiction Order 1991.*

4. *Solicitors should make any necessary applications for transfer promptly and are reminded that by Rules of the Supreme Court (Amendment No. 3) 1991 there has been substituted for Ord. 4, r. 5(4) a rule enabling the court of its own motion to make orders transferring cases from the Royal Courts of Justice to a district registry and from one district registry to another. This rule does not apply to cases proceeding in the county courts but, as already indicated, it is appropriate that such cases should also be ordered to be transferred to the Bristol District Registry, in exercise of the powers conferred by s. 42 of the County Courts Act 1984.*

5. *Any delay or increase in costs occasioned by unjustified failure to comply with this practice note may be treated as culpable.*

NINETEEN

SPECIAL KINDS OF LITIGANTS

In this chapter we consider the rules and practical considerations relevant to special kinds of litigants. For ease of reference we will deal with the position in relation to each of them in both High Court and county court actions.

19.1 Limited Companies

19.1.1 LEGAL PERSONALITY

A limited company is a legal person and may bring and defend proceedings in both High Court and county court. In the High Court a limited company must act by a solicitor, except that where the limited company is a defendant any proper officer of the company may acknowledge service on behalf of the company. This is in view of the relatively short time span of 14 days permitted for acknowledgement of service. Thereafter, however, a limited company must employ a solicitor in the High Court and any action taken without a solicitor will be a nullity. In the county court a limited company can act for itself without employing a solicitor and there are no particular complications in such a case.

19.1.2 SERVICE OF DOCUMENTS

A writ may be served on a company under *s. 725* of the *Companies Act 1985* by sending it by post to the registered office of the company. Unless the contrary is shown, the date of service will be presumed to be, if posted by first class mail, the second working day after posting, and if posted by second class mail, the fourth working day after posting. If service is effected by leaving the document at the registered office or putting it through the letter box there, service is deemed to be immediate.

In the county court a summons may be served either at the registered office or at any place of business having some connection with the action.

For documents other than writs, such as pleadings, summonses, affidavits, etc., service will be made on the solicitor on the record.

19.1.3 ENFORCEMENT OF JUDGMENTS

A limited company may enforce a judgment or have one enforced against it. Where judgments or orders are made which require some personal compliance, however, then clearly there is some difficulty. For example, if it is desired to ask interrogatories of a company; or ask a company to attend for oral examination; or even to punish a contempt of court by a company, what is to be done? The answer is that in such cases it is up to the opposite party to select the relevant officer of the company and direct the request for interrogatories or order for oral examination to that person. The same applies in the case of an application to commit for contempt of court. It is clearly appropriate to select the officer of the company most involved with the action, or with the contempt complained of. Although a limited company cannot, of course, be committed to prison, it can in its own right be fined for contempt of court (see **23.3**).

19.2 Overseas Companies

Foreign corporations which establish a place of business in Great Britain must, pursuant to *s. 691* of the *Companies Act 1985*, within a month of the date of establishment, deliver to the registrar of companies for registration, *inter alia*, the names and addresses of one or more persons resident in Great Britain authorised to accept service of process and notices on behalf of the company.

19.3 Corporations other than Limited Companies

Corporations, like limited companies, may sue and be sued in their corporate name. Service may be effected on the Mayor, President, Chairman, Town Clerk, Secretary, Treasurer or other similar officer. Interrogatories, orders for oral examination and applications for committal may be made against any proper person, as in the case of limited companies.

19.4 Trade Unions and Unincorporated Employers' Associations

Pursuant to *ss. 10* and *127* of the *Trade Union and Labour Relations (Consolidation) Act 1992*, these bodies can sue and be sued in their own names.

19.5 Clubs

It is important to distinguish between proprietary clubs and members' clubs. A *proprietary* club (for example a night club, and even if there is a so-called 'membership fee') is simply a business. It may either be a limited company, sole trader or a partnership and be sued accordingly. A *members'* club (for example a sports or social club), however, has no legal personality and cannot generally sue or be sued in its own name. If all the members of a members' club are similarly interested in the dispute, one or more of the members may sue on behalf of all of them in representative proceedings (*RSC Ord. 15, r. 12*). If it is desired to sue a club then it may be necessary to obtain a copy of the rules to ascertain against whom actions should be brought. The proper defendants are usually the trustees or committee of the club.

19.6 Partnerships

19.6.1 COMPARISON WITH LIMITED COMPANIES

Limited companies are of course legal entities. They may, broadly speaking, litigate much as a private individual may litigate, and there are very few special rules appertaining to them. In the case of partnerships, however, there is a considerable procedural problem caused by the difficult status of the entity. A partnership, or firm, is not, as such, a legal entity, and neither is the firm name anything more than a mere expression (although it may for convenience be adopted throughout the litigation).

The particular difficulties caused by partnerships in civil litigation arise in three areas, namely:

(a) how they may sue or be sued;

(b) how they may be served with proceedings; and

(c) how judgments may be enforced.

The provisions of *RSC Ord. 81* provide a comprehensive code relating to these and other particular areas of difficulty. The approximate county court equivalents are in *CCR Ord. 5, r. 9.*

19.6.2 ACTIONS BY AND AGAINST PARTNERSHIP FIRMS WITHIN THE JURISDICTION

Provided that the firm concerned carries on business within the jurisdiction, then:

(a) Two or more persons carrying on such business may issue a writ or originating summons in the name of the firm without setting out the names of all the partners, and may give as the address the place of business of the firm instead of the partners' private addresses.

(b) As defendants, a firm may be sued in the firm name without the necessity for the plaintiff to discover the names of the individual partners, and the firm may be described as of the address at which the business is carried on. A person who sues such partners in their firm name sues them as individuals, just as much as if he had set out all their names and addresses.

(c) If, however, there has been a change in the personnel constituting the firm between the cause of action and the issue of the writ, then suing in the firm name may cause difficulty. In such a situation words should be used to indicate that the action is brought against those persons who were co-partners at the time of accruing of the cause of action. It may be better, if possible, to name such partners. If there has been a dissolution, or partial dissolution, it is important to serve the proceedings individually on the persons who are alleged to have been partners at the time of the accrual of the cause of action.

19.6.3 PRACTICAL POINTS AND SPECIAL CASES

19.6.3.1 A sole trader

A sole trader must sue in his own name, but can be sued in his trade name (*RSC Ord. 81, r. 9; CCR Ord. 5, r. 10*). If the plaintiff suing a sole trader believes that the name of the firm is not the trader's own, he ought to add, after the defendant's name in the title to the writ or summons, the words 'a trading name'.

19.6.3.2 Limited partnerships

Since the rules are silent as to the procedure to be adopted in the case of limited partnerships, service would only be appropriate upon the general partners in such a firm, and not on limited partners. Execution may, however, be made against the limited partners to the extent of the limitation.

19.6.3.3 Disclosure of partners' names

It is sometimes, particularly for plaintiffs wishing to sue a firm, an important matter to identify the partners. This may be crucially important in the question of enforcing judgment against the private assets of partners. It is a particularly difficult question when actions are to be brought, for example, against family businesses, where it is by no means clear to the outside world which members of the family have the status of partners and which are mere employees. The other provisions of the general law, such as the disclosure of partners' names on business notepaper or at their main place of business, are very often ignored in practice. In such situations the rules (*RSC Ord. 81, r. 2; CCR Ord. 5, r. 9*) usefully provide that where a person is either suing or being sued by a firm, he may serve on that firm or its solicitor a notice requiring it or him forthwith to furnish a written statement of the names and places of residence of all the persons who were partners in the firm at the time when the cause of action accrued. If this notice is not complied with, an application may be made to the court by summons for an order that the details should be given.

The application is made to a Master or District Judge. Although it is discretionary, it is difficult to envisage any proper reason for which it could be refused, given the likely motives for non-disclosure. In the case of plaintiff firms, the court may order that proceedings be stayed until such details are given. In the case of defendant firms, an order may be made compelling such disclosure, in the last resort by striking out the defence or committal.

19.6.4 SERVICE OF A WRIT ON A PARTNERSHIP

19.6.4.1 Methods of service

A writ may be served by the following methods (*RSC Ord. 81, r. 3; CCR Ord. 7, r. 13*):

(a) personally, on any one or more of the partners; or

(b) by personal service at the principal place of business of the partnership on any person having at the time of service the control or management of the partnership business there (whether or not such person is a partner); or

(c) by sending a copy of the writ by ordinary first class post to the firm at the principal place of business of the partnership within the jurisdiction.

Where the writ is served by either of the first two methods it is immediately effective. In the case of the third method, it is deemed to be served on the seventh day after the day on which the copy writ was sent to the firm.

In addition to the above methods which are prescribed by the *Rules of the Supreme Court* and *County Court Rules*, the House of Lords held in *Kenneth Allison Ltd* v *A.E. Limehouse & Co.* [1991] 3 WLR 671 that it is open to a partnership to stipulate any other method by which it will accept service of proceedings even outside the relevant rules of court.

19.6.4.2 Affidavit of service

If it is necessary to swear an affidavit of service, then such an affidavit must contain a statement to the effect that:

(a) in the opinion of the deponent (or if the deponent is the plaintiff's solicitor, or his employee, in the opinion of the plaintiff) the copy of the writ, if sent to the firm at the address in question, will have come to the notice of either one of the partners, or of the person having control or management of the partnership business, within seven days; and

(b) the copy of the writ has not been returned marked undelivered.

19.6.4.3 Service of notice of capacity

Where personal service is effected either on a partner or on the apparent manager of the partnership business, a written notice stating whether that person is served as a partner, as a person having control or management of the partnership business, or as both, must be served on that person. If no such notice is served then the person concerned is deemed to be served as a partner.

The effect of this somewhat curious provision is that without such notice service would be invalid if effected only on the person having management or control of the partnership business at its principal place of business, unless that person did happen to be a partner. Therefore, if, for example, one is certain that an individual is a partner, and it is proposed to serve him at work or his private address, there is no need for any notice to accompany the writ. The importance of the provision arises where one is serving the person managing the partnership business and one is unsure of the status of such a person. In such a case the best method is to serve with the writ a notice stating:

> Take notice that the writ served herewith is served on you as the person in control of the business of the defendant firm of XY & Co and also as a partner.

In such a situation, service will be valid even though that person is not a partner, for that person may then acknowledge service and deny partnership. Service will, nonetheless, be effective as against the firm, provided the proper notice is served.

19.6.5 ACKNOWLEDGEMENT OF SERVICE IN THE HIGH COURT

The rules relating to acknowledgement of service seem complex but are in reality quite straightforward. The problems are partly caused by the substantive provisions of partnership law. The position is as follows.

19.6.5.1 Acknowledgement by partners

If persons are sued as partners in the name of their firm, service may not be acknowledged in the name of the firm but must be by the partners individually, although the action will continue in the name of the firm. Thus, an individual partner should acknowledge service individually with the description 'partner in the firm of', or 'trading as', or 'practising as' as in the firm name. Any partner has the right to acknowledge service of the writ.

19.6.5.2 Acknowledgement by a non-partner

If a person denies that he was a partner, he may acknowledge service of the writ, stating in his acknowledgement that he does so as a person served who makes such denial. The acknowledgement of service, however, stands until it is set aside, i.e. judgment in default cannot thereupon be given, but either:

(a) the plaintiff may apply to the court to set the acknowledgement aside on the ground that the defendant was a partner or liable as such, or may leave that question to be determined at a later stage (it may be appropriate to direct that the issue be tried separately, e.g. under *RSC Ord. 33, r. 3*); or

(b) the defendant may apply to the court to set aside the service of the writ on him on the ground that he was not a partner or liable as such at the material time, or may serve a defence denying either liability as a partner or liability of the defendant firm. Thereafter, the court may at any stage order that the question as to the liability of that defendant or of the firm be tried in such a manner, and at such time, as the court directs.

19.6.5.3 Acknowledgement by a person having control or management

Where the writ is served on the person who has control or management of the partnership business at its principal place of business, that person may not acknowledge service in the action unless he is a partner in the firm sued. In other words, although service on the firm is effective on such a person if he is the manager, it is on the basis that he will forthwith bring the writ to the attention of one of the partners who may then acknowledge service. Judgment in default will lie in such a case if no acknowledgement of service is returned. The affidavit of service must comply with the provision mentioned in **19.6.4.2**.

19.6.6 JUDGMENT

Where a firm is sued in the firm name, judgment must be entered against the firm and not against the individual partners. Judgment cannot be entered against one partner separately for default of notice of intention to defend, nor can any judgment be entered in an action against a firm so long as any partner in the firm is defending the action on behalf of the firm.

19.6.7 ENFORCING A JUDGMENT OR ORDER

(See *RSC Ord. 81, r. 5; CCR Ord. 25, r. 9.*)

Execution upon a judgment or order against a firm may be issued:

(a) against the property of the firm within the jurisdiction (this is so whether or not the partners all participated in the proceedings against the firm);

(b) without leave of the court against the private property of any partner who:

   (i) has acknowledged service of the writ as a partner, or

   (ii) having been served as a partner with the writ, failed to acknowledge service of it in the action, or

   (iii) admitted in his pleading that he is a partner, or

   (iv) was adjudged to be a partner;

(c) where a member of the firm was out of the jurisdiction when the writ of summons was issued, execution to enforce the judgment against that person may not be issued unless that person acknowledges service of the writ as a partner, or was served within the jurisdiction as a partner or was, with leave of the court, given under *RSC Ord. 11*, served out of the jurisdiction with the writ as a partner.

The aforementioned are the situations where leave is not required to issue execution against the private property of partners. Leave is required where a judgment or order against a firm has been obtained, and none of the foregoing situations apply. Application is made to the court by summons, and a summons must be served personally on the person against whom the execution is sought. If the person against whom that summons is issued does not dispute liability, the court may order the liability of that person to be tried or determined in any appropriate manner.

Enforcement against an individual partner may be commenced by any of the usual methods (see **23.1**), and, in addition, under *RSC Ord. 81, r. 10,* by making application under *s. 23* of the *Partnership Act 1890* to charge a partner's interest in a partnership. Application is made by summons by the judgment creditor, and the summons must be served on the judgment debtor and on such of his partners as are within the jurisdiction. The summons usually asks for a charge on the defendant's interests in the partnership property and that a receiver be appointed as provided by the rule. The receiver should be named. There should be an affidavit in support of the application, although it is not necessary that in this case the affidavit should state that the defendant has no other property available for execution. If it is anticipated that there will be an attempt to dispose of, or deal with, the interest in the partnership property, an injunction may be applied for *ex parte* on affidavit to restrain the person from doing so pending the hearing of the summons.

19.7 Proceedings By and Against Estates

If a *plaintiff* dies during the course of an action, his personal representatives may apply to the court under *RSC Ord. 15, r. 7*, for an order to carry on the action. There is usually no problem in obtaining such an order. If a *defendant* dies during the course of an action, a plaintiff may apply for an order to carry the proceedings on against the defendant's personal representatives.

If a cause of action survives for the benefit of a deceased person, the action must be brought by all his executors or administrators as parties to the action.

If the deceased was to have been the defendant in an action and the cause of action survives, proceedings may be commenced against his estate. If personal representatives have taken out a grant of representation, they should be named as defendants. If, as is often the case, no person has taken out a grant of representation then a writ may still be issued against 'the personal representatives of AB deceased', without naming them or needing to give an address. Once the writ is issued application should be made *ex parte* by affidavit to the Master or District Judge for an order to carry on the proceedings and for a person to be appointed to represent the estate for the purpose of the proceedings (*RSC Ord. 15, r. 6A*). It is very important that this step be taken, as without it the whole action will become a nullity. If no person comes forward to represent the estate the court will appoint someone. Should the deceased have been the cause of a motor accident this is likely to be a representative of his insurer, or of the MIB; in other cases the Official Solicitor will be appointed.

19.8 Persons Under a Disability

19.8.1 DEFINITION AND STANDING

Under *RSC Ord. 80*, 'persons under a disability' means:

(a) an infant or minor (these terms are interchangeable); or

(b) a patient, i.e. a person who, by reason of mental disorder within the meaning of the *Mental Health Act 1983*, is incapable of managing or administering his property and affairs.

Such persons under disability may not be parties to proceedings in their own name. If plaintiffs, they must sue by an adult called a 'next friend'. If defendants, they must defend proceedings by a 'guardian *ad litem*'. Whether plaintiffs or defendants, all persons under a disability must employ a solicitor in the High Court. However, it is not necessary to employ a solicitor in the county court.

19.8.2 COMMENCEMENT OF PROCEEDINGS

There are certain important differences in the documentation necessary to commence an action for a person under a disability.

19.8.2.1 High Court

In the title to the writ or originating summons in the Queen's Bench Division the name of the next friend appears, e.g. 'John Smith by Mary Smith his mother and next friend'. In the Chancery

Division in the title to the writ or originating summons the infant's name appears alone, although with the words 'an infant' after it; thereafter, in the body of the writ or originating summons the words 'at the suit of John Smith an infant by Mary Smith his mother and next friend' should appear.

In the case of a patient plaintiff, in both Divisions the action is entitled 'AB by CD his next friend' but the word 'patient' does not appear in the title. There is then a statement in the body of the writ, originating summons or statement of claim that the plaintiff is a patient and is suing by his next friend.

A written consent by the next friend (or guardian *ad litem* as the case may be) of the person under disability is given by the person proposing to be such friend or guardian and must be filed when commencing proceedings, together with:

(a) if the person proposing to be such friend or guardian of a person under disability who is a patient is authorised specifically under *Part 7* of the *Mental Health Act 1983* to conduct the proceedings, an office copy of the order or other authorisation in question; and

(b) a certificate by the solicitor for the person under disability certifying that he knows or believes, as the case may be, that the person to whom the certificate relates is an infant or patient, giving (in the case of a patient) the grounds of his knowledge and belief, if necessary annexing any medical opinion relied on, and stating that there is no person authorised (if it is the case) to act for the patient under *Part 7* of the *Mental Health Act 1983* as described above; in addition, unless the next friend or guardian *ad litem* is the Official Solicitor, a statement that the person in question has no interest in the cause or matter in question adverse to that of the person under a disability.

As will be observed, a certain special responsibility is placed upon the solicitor in these circumstances. It is not enough merely for him to act mechanically in the matter in which he is instructed; he must also take certain initiatives. Thus, if he accepts instructions from an adult purporting to be a next friend without at least some enquiry into the facts of the matter to ensure that there is no conflict of interest, he will be acting improperly. So, for example, if a father brings a child who has been injured in a road accident to a solicitor and wishes to act as that child's next friend, and it is apparent that the accident occurred when the father was driving the vehicle in which the infant was the passenger, then even though on the father's version some other driver was responsible, the solicitor must tell the father that some other relative should be appointed as next friend.

19.8.2.2 County court

In the county court it is not necessary that a solicitor be employed. Instead of the written consent to act at the time when the summons and particulars of claim are filed, a written undertaking by the next friend to be liable for the costs of the action must be filed.

19.8.3 POWERS AND DUTIES OF NEXT FRIEND AND GUARDIAN *AD LITEM*

The powers and duties of persons acting as next friend and guardian *ad litem* require them to act in the best interests of the infant in the case. The next friend is meant to be 'an officer of the court to take all measures for the benefit of the infant in the litigation'. The object of having such persons is to supplement the want of capacity in judgment of the person under disability in the conduct of the litigation. For this purpose, the next friend or guardian *ad litem* may make any proper procedural agreements or compromises, e.g. may extend the opponent's time for service of pleadings, agree to dispense with discovery, or even reject a compromise or settlement offered. If, however, a next friend wishes to *accept* a compromise offered, there is a special rule that he must seek the approval of the court before doing so, and we return to this at **19.8.7**.

Despite these powers, the next friend or guardian *ad litem* is not, as such, a party to the proceedings, although he may be liable for costs. The position is that a next friend is personally liable for costs, although he may have an indemnity against the plaintiff under a disability. A guardian *ad litem*, however, is liable for costs only if they are caused by his personal negligence or misconduct.

It is now necessary to consider some practical points which arise during the conduct of litigation on behalf of persons under a disability.

19.8.4 PRACTICAL MATTERS

19.8.4.1 Infant coming of age

If an infant *plaintiff* comes of age, he should file at the Central Office, Chancery Chambers or District Registry a notice that he is of age and that he adopts the action, and the fact will be noted in the cause book or on the cause index cards (where full particulars of current actions are kept). The proceedings should then be entitled 'AB (late an infant but now of full age) plaintiff'.

If an infant *defendant* comes of age, he should file in the action department of the Central Office, Chancery Chambers or in the District Registry a notice that he is of full age and adopts the acknowledgement entered by the guardian *ad litem* on his behalf, and he must serve the notice on all other parties. The notice may be given by the solicitor acting on his behalf. The title to the action will likewise be amended in the same way as in the case of a plaintiff. Thereafter, proceedings will continue as if he had been adult throughout, except that no admission will be implied in any pleadings served whilst he was still an infant.

19.8.4.2 Party becoming a patient

If a party to an action becomes a patient after the action has commenced, application must be made to the court for the appointment of a next friend or guardian *ad litem*. This is largely the responsibility of the solicitor for the party concerned, who should then take the requisite steps to add a next friend or guardian *ad litem*, as the case may be. Where application to the court is made, it is not necessary for the person subsequently appointed to file the additional documents referred to at **19.8.2** as in the case where where a person was under a disability at the commencement of the proceedings.

19.8.4.3 Admissions

No admission is to be implied from the pleading of a person under a disability. Thus, for example, a failure properly to deny any given allegation does not in itself amount to an implied admission of it, contrary to the usual rules of pleading. There is, nevertheless, nothing to prevent an *express* admission in a pleading by an infant.

19.8.5 SERVICE OF DOCUMENTS ON INFANT OR PATIENT

(See *RSC Ord. 80, r. 16; CCR Ord. 10, r. 4.*)

19.8.5.1 Writs and originating process

Originating process and other documents which require personal service on the party affected by them should be served, in the case of an infant who is not also a patient, on his father, mother or guardian, or if he has no father or guardian, on the person with whom he resides or in whose care he is; in the case of a patient, service should be effected on the person (if any) who is authorised under *Part 7* of the *Mental Health Act 1983* to conduct the proceedings in the name of the patient, or if there is no person so authorised, on the person with whom the patient resides or in whose care he is.

The court may, nonetheless, order that a document which has been served on the person under a disability or on some person other than the person prescribed, may be deemed to be duly served.

Accordingly, writs and originating process may be served by any of the methods prescribed, i.e. not only by personal service but by postal service.

19.8.5.2 Service of other documents

Other documents, such as pleadings, procedural orders and interlocutory summonses, may be served on the solicitor on the record in the usual way, or on the next friend or guardian *ad litem* in a county court case if the person is unrepresented.

19.8.5.3 Default of acknowledgement of service

The problem that may arise is if originating process is correctly served, either on someone who has previously indicated that he will act as guardian *ad litem* or on the proper person prescribed, and service is not acknowledged. In such a case judgment in default cannot be signed against the person under a disability, and an application must be made to the court to appoint a guardian *ad litem*.

Application for appointment is made on summons to the Master or District Judge, and should be made after the time limited for acknowledging service or filing a defence in the county court has expired, before any further step is taken. The notice of the application should be served personally on the infant.

19.8.6 CHOICE OF GUARDIAN *AD LITEM*

The choice of a person ought to cause the plaintiff no difficulty. If someone has come forward who is willing to act, then naturally he is likely to have expeditiously returned the acknowledgement of service or filed a defence in the county court. If such a person has come forward, no application to the court need prima facie be made. This procedure is not appropriate for compelling the infant's parent to act as guardian *ad litem* if he or she is unwilling, for in such a case the parent cannot be made to do so.

If a willing person subsequently comes forward it would seem better for them simply to complete the acknowledgement of service and file the other necessary documents previously described. If the infant is insured (e.g. a 16-year-old motor cyclist) and no person comes forward, then the insurance company or the MIB are likely to appoint a guardian *ad litem* since they will be called upon to pay the eventual judgment. If it is not an insurance case and no appropriate person comes forward, then the Official Solicitor is usually approached and will consent to act.

19.8.7 COMPROMISE OF A MONETARY CLAIM FOR A PERSON UNDER A DISABILITY

(See *RSC Ord. 80, rr. 10, 11; CCR Ord. 10, r. 10.*)

The most important difference in the procedure relating to persons who are under a disability is the need for the court's approval in both High Court and county court cases, before any compromise or acceptance of a monetary claim can be made. It ought to be noted that there is no requirement for the court to give its approval where a compromise of a monetary claim is made by a *defendant* under a disability, nor indeed where a compromise of a claim for a non-monetary remedy is made on behalf of an infant. Thus, for example, if an infant seeks some non-monetary remedy such as the return of goods, and a compromise is effected perhaps on terms as to costs, etc., this can be validly approved by the next friend without the need for the court's approval to be sought. If there is some claim involving money as well as other relief, then the court's approval is necessary.

The rule applies whether or not proceedings have begun. If proceedings have not begun but negotiations lead to an acceptable offer to settle an infant's or a patient's claim, application must be made to the court by originating summons or originating application for approval of the compromise. If the action has already commenced, the application is made by summons or application in the action.

19.8.7.1 The rationale

The reasons for these provisions are said to be:

(a) To protect infants and patients from any lack of skill or experience in their legal advisers which might lead to settlement for inadequate sums.

(b) To provide a means by which a defendant may obtain a valid discharge from an infant's or a patient's claim, which would not otherwise bind the plaintiff unless it could have been proved to have been made for his benefit.

(c) To ensure that solicitors acting for infants or patients are paid their proper costs and no more, so as to prevent potential overcharging or supposed willingness by solicitors improperly to accept unfavourable settlements by tempting offers to agree costs.

(d) To ensure that the money recovered on behalf of the infant or patient is properly looked after and well invested by the court, so that he gets the benefits of it rather than his parents.

19.8.7.2 Procedure for approval of compromise or settlement

(a) If the settlement is achieved *before* proceedings have been issued, an appointment before the Master or District Judge should be obtained by the issue of an originating summons or originating application in the county court (bearing in mind in particular rules concerning jurisdiction). Such a summons or application should ask for the approval of the court to the settlement or compromise and for directions for dealing with the money agreed to be paid.

(b) *After* proceedings have begun, application is by summons or application in the action to the Master or District Judge in chambers, unless the compromise occurs during the course of the trial when application may be made to the judge hearing the case without further formalities.

19.8.7.3 Practice

In the Chancery Division application is made in chambers by summons, and an affidavit sworn by the plaintiff's solicitor is filed exhibiting counsel's opinion approving the settlement with other relevant evidence.

In the Queen's Bench Division application is made by summons but no affidavit is required, although if the case is a complex one there is no harm in preparing an affidavit describing the background to the matter.

In the county court no affidavit is required.

19.8.7.4 Practical steps

Where the defendant puts forward a satisfactory offer, or when an adequate payment into court is made, the steps that must be taken are first to ensure that the plaintiff's legal adviser has the necessary evidence on which properly to advise the next friend as to the adequacy of the sum offered. Accordingly, medical evidence and evidence relating to loss of earnings or future loss of earnings ought to be brought up to date, and a further counsel's opinion should be obtained unless there is already a relatively recent one as to quantum. It must be borne in mind that the issue is not necessarily what amount of damages would the plaintiff have obtained at trial if he were wholly successful, but whether the settlement itself is reasonable and is for the benefit of the infant, having regard to all the circumstances including the risk of litigation, the potential delay, the desire of the parties to settle, the disinclination of the plaintiff to go to trial, and the difficulties in establishing liability or in resisting a finding of contributory negligence. If, taking all these matters into account, the plaintiff's legal advisers are minded to recommend compromise and the next friend is agreeable, action should be taken to obtain the court's approval.

If a payment into court has been made, then although in principle the 'consideration period' is only 21 days, there is little doubt that longer would be allowed for the proper consideration of such a payment into court by those advising an infant plaintiff. In such a situation, therefore, the best method of approach would be for the plaintiff's solicitor to write in 'without prejudice' terms to the defendant indicating that the offer is being seriously considered, and requesting positive agreement by the defendant to pay necessary costs in the period of delay, e.g. for obtaining further medical reports or counsel's opinion, even though this takes the plaintiff outside the 21-day period. Thereafter, a summons should be issued immediately seeking approval of the compromise.

It is important that the Master or District Judge should approach the hearing with a fresh mind, so for this reason the summons and any affidavit used should not refer to the actual figure paid into court or offered. Likewise, if counsel's opinion is to be put forward at the hearing, then, if he has referred to the exact figure offered, that figure should be blanked out of the opinion in the copy handed to the Master or District Judge.

It is useful to consider the course of a typical hearing, and to take as an example a personal injury case, although the same considerations *mutatis mutandis* would apply to any other kind of claim for a monetary remedy.

19.8.7.5 The hearing

(a) At the hearing no evidence as such is called. The Master or District Judge should first be told whether there is any dispute on liability. If there is none, he need be told no more about the actual facts of the incident causing the injury. If, however, there is some issue on liability, then the nature of the evidence should be indicated by the plaintiff's solicitor or by both sides. The court should be told what evidence can be adduced and what witnesses are available, and the police report and witness statements, if any, may be produced. If counsel has advised on liability, that opinion should be placed before the Master or District Judge, so as to enable him to assess the plaintiff's chances of success in the action and the possible discount which should be given for contributory negligence, or the risks of litigation. There is no doubt that the Master or District Judge, in the time usually available on such a summons, is unlikely to be able to look further into liability than the plaintiff's own legal advisers, and the circumstances would be exceptional where the Master or District Judge took a strongly different view on liability from them, especially if counsel has also advised. It is important that the defendant's solicitors also attend the hearing so that they may know what is said, if, e.g., approval is refused or some point as to the drafting of the order arises.

(b) The second matter is the quantum of damages. It is crucial that full evidence be provided about the nature and extent of the plaintiff's injuries and their likely effect on health, education, enjoyment of amenities, future earning power and risk on the labour market. Medical reports should be comprehensive and substantially up to date. Full computations and, if necessary, documentary evidence of the items forming special damage, should be produced. If the action is one under the *Fatal Accidents Act 1976*, a great deal more information will need to be provided, about the age, occupation, earnings and prospects of the deceased, the ages of the widow and dependent children, and the amount of the deceased's estate.

(c) By convention, the plaintiff and next friend usually attend such a summons, and this is especially so if the Master or District Judge might wish to see the plaintiff, for example, to see any facial or other cosmetic blemishes or physical disabilities. If the next friend does not attend, his written approval of the settlement should be produced. The plaintiff's solicitor should be able to produce the plaintiff's birth certificate to prove date of birth and full name. Evidence of any change of name must be to hand. If the Master or District Judge is then satisfied by the proposed compromise, he will make the order approving settlement. If he is not satisfied, he may, if the difference is only a modest one, express his misgivings and ask the parties if a short adjournment would be of any use. If so, he may adjourn briefly, even for 10 or 15 minutes, to allow the parties to talk outside the court. Prospects of concluding the matter may then largely depend, in a personal injury case, upon whether the defendant's solicitors have authority to offer more, or can get in touch with their insurance clients with a view to obtaining further instructions. If nothing can be achieved in a short adjournment, or if the disagreement is serious, the Master or District Judge may offer a longer adjournment to some future date. If, however, the defence are adamant that the offer cannot be increased, the summons will be dismissed.

Where the compromise is not approved, the court must go on to give directions as to what is to be done next. If the application is before the issue of proceedings, and thus brought by originating summons, directions will simply be to issue a writ and proceed with the action. If the application is made by summons in an existing action, then what orders can be made will generally depend upon the stage of the proceedings at which the hearing comes about, and the state of preparation of either party. It may be that nothing more needs to be ordered than the usual automatic directions, or it may be that approval is sought after directions have already been given, in which case the only additional direction may be, e.g., an order for a speedy trial.

19.8.7.6 Further practical points

(a) *Patients*

If an action is brought by the next friend of a patient under the sanction or direction of the Court of Protection, the approval of the Court of Protection should be obtained, but this does not absolve the parties from applying to the court where the action is continuing for approval. In such a case, money recovered should be transferred to the patient's account in the Court of Protection. The decision whether or not to approve the settlement is that of the court where the action is proceeding, whatever view has been taken by the Court of Protection. If the Court of Protection has not previously been involved, the Master or District Judge, after approving the terms of the compromise, will order (unless the amount recovered is very small) that the next friend should apply within a stipulated time to the Court of Protection for the appointment of a receiver. The Court of Protection is a part of the court which has a very specialised jurisdiction dealing with aspects of protecting the interests and managing the assets of persons unable to manage their own affairs, in particular mental patients, persons in 'persistent vegatative state', infants with very substantial claims and the like.

(b) *Appeal*

If the settlement is not approved by the Master or District Judge, either party (and presumably both, if both are still eager to settle) may appeal to the judge in chambers.

(c) *The order*

If the settlement is approved, then the order directs by, to whom, and in what amounts the money is to be paid, and how the money is to be applied. The order should be drawn up without delay, so as to avoid possible loss of income. The plaintiff's solicitor should draw up and serve the order promptly, and meanwhile the defendant should put in hand obtaining the requisite cheque so that the money can be brought into court.

19.8.7.7 Control of money recovered by a person under a disability

Directions must be given by the court, and will usually be for the sum be paid into the court to be invested and dealt with there. There may be exceptions. It may be appropriate to release a modest sum of money immediately for something which the infant wants, especially if this is of some educational value, e.g. a school trip abroad, or home computer. If the sum is very modest, it may be appropriate to have the money invested informally out of court, e.g. in the form of saving certificates or a building society deposit account. It is worth indicating here some of the principles involved in the directions that the court will give as to the money:

(a) The basic principle is that the damages should be applied for the purpose for which they were awarded; thus, if damages have been awarded for pain and suffering, injury and future disability but there is as yet no economic loss, neither capital nor income should be used for ordinary maintenance for the child. The fact that a child has recovered damages, say, for a broken limb, does not relieve the parents of their duties to support him, nor any public authority which might have a duty to maintain the child.

(b) If the damages represent the child's loss of support from a deceased parent under the *Fatal Accidents Act 1976*, then income on capital could properly be applied to ordinary maintenance. However, much would depend upon the position of the widowed parent and the global settlement which had been achieved in the action.

(c) In between these possibilities is the middle ground where there may be some element of economic loss which is continuing, e.g. if the child needs special nursing or attendance. As far as possible here, payments may be made out of income.

(d) The same principles apply, *mutatis mutandis* to a patient.

The fund, if it is not to be applied immediately, should be invested as appropriate by the court, and there is no need here to consider the nature of the court's discretion in relation to this.

It ought to be noted that if the parent or next friend wants money from time to time for the welfare, benefit or education of the infant, then an application can be made in a relatively informal way. The procedure to some extent differs locally, but usually application by letter will suffice. The applicant will be called for an interview with the Master or District Judge to explain more precisely the nature of the requirement for the infant (e.g. private medical treatment, school fees, etc.) and the court will give its decision then and there. The court will not of course release the infant's money simply to repay the parent for money which any normal parent would have expended for his or her child, e.g. to pay the infant's share of a foreign holiday which the family would have taken anyway.

19.8.7.8 Costs

As indicated at the outset, one of the alleged justifications referred to in the 'White Book' for requiring the court to investigate and approve settlements effected on behalf of infants, is the perceived risk of the infant's solicitors behaving improperly or unfairly in some way with regard to costs. It will be recalled that there are two bases of costs, the standard basis which is that also applicable to legal aid taxation, and the indemnity basis. It is sometimes possible to arrange in negotiations on behalf of an infant for the defendants to offer payment of costs on the more generous indemnity basis, in addition to their offer for damages. Even if this is not achieved, quite commonly infant plaintiffs' solicitors will waive any further demand for costs from the infant over and above what will be recovered from the defendant on the standard basis.

A solicitor cannot, except by express order of the court, receive more costs than he is allowed on taxation. Accordingly, the court will insist that there is a taxation as between the infant plaintiff and his own solicitor, unless the solicitor does expressly waive any further costs than those which can be obtained against the defendant. Even in such a case, however, there must be a taxation of the *inter partes* bill unless the court is willing to dispense with it. The court may be prepared to allow agreement of costs in the following cases:

(a) If the solicitor satisfies the court that his costs will be met by a trade union or other third party without any recourse at all to the plaintiff infant directly.

(b) If the solicitor undertakes to take no more than is recovered as costs from a defendant. However, in this case, the Master or District Judge will usually require to be told the amount already agreed, so as to ensure that it seems appropriate given the weight of the case, and that there is no great disproportion between the plaintiff's damages and the solicitor's costs. If the plaintiff is legally aided, any such agreement to accept costs paid by the defendant requires the approval of the Legal Aid Board, though this is usually given without difficulty.

TWENTY

COMMENCEMENT OF PROCEEDINGS IN THE COUNTY COURT

We have now considered the course of actions in the High Court, dealing with most of the mainstream procedural permutations. We now turn to the county court and review the main differences between High Court and county court procedures. Before doing so, a brief introduction to the county court, its function, constitution and personnel is necessary.

20.1 Development of County Courts

County courts were established 150 years ago to provide a cheap and simple system with local jurisdiction in very small cases. Regular increases in jurisdiction, and other changes to bring county court procedures and High Court procedures into line, increased the importance of the county court. With the reforms of civil justice in the late 1980s the importance of the county court has grown still further, so that the effect of recent changes has been to make county courts the major forum for the resolution of mainstream civil disputes, leaving the High Court to return to its more specialised role in dealing with cases of complexity and substance.

20.2 Procedure

In considering procedures in the county court we shall in effect review the main differences between those procedures and the ones applicable in the High Court. In many instances the procedure in the county court is virtually identical to that in the High Court, although time limits for taking certain steps are often slightly different, and the times at which certain steps may be taken may also differ. Often, however, the county court rules do not even fully describe the procedures to be followed but merely say that the procedure is as described in the corresponding *Rules of the Supreme Court* for a High Court case.

The principal points of difference from the corresponding High Court rules are the methods by which actions are commenced and defences served; the existence of automatic directions in almost all cases; and the mechanism by which a case comes on for trial. The most important aspect of procedure in the county court which differs from the High Court is the extent of the court's direct involvement in certain of the processes, particularly in the initiation of proceedings, drawing up of most orders and judgments, and convening pre-trial reviews in fixed date actions.

The procedure, despite the apparent similarity of rules, is often less formal than in the High Court. This may be a reflection of the considerably greater use of the county court by litigants in person and the leeway allowed to them by the court staff. Whether this more informal approach will survive the anticipated shift of large volumes of work from the High Court to the county court remains to be seen.

20.2.1 APPLICABILITY OF HIGH COURT PRACTICE

If there is any gap in the *County Court Rules* (*CCR*), then High Court practice applies. This is provided by *s. 76* of the *County Courts Act 1984*, which reads:

> *In any case not expressly provided for by or in pursuance of this Act the general principles of practice in the High Court may be adopted and applied to proceedings in the County Court.*

Moreover, there is a specific rule, *CCR Ord. 13, r. 7*, which lists a number of procedural matters in respect of which the 'provisions of the Rules of the Supreme Court shall apply'. That particular rule refers to a number of important procedural provisions, in particular pre-action discovery and inspection; pre-action detention, preservation and inspection of property; and others.

20.2.2 THE 'GREEN BOOK'

The *County Court Rules* are contained in the *County Court Practice* (known as the 'Green Book') and their purpose is the same as that of the *High Court Rules*, i.e. to facilitate a fair trial by ensuring that cases are properly prepared so as to clarify matters in dispute and avoid surprise.

The Green Book is divided into four main parts. The first part deals with the court's general jurisdiction under the *County Courts Act 1984* and the *County Court Rules 1981*, as subsequently amended. It also takes account of various provisions of the *Rules of the Supreme Court* which apply directly to the county court. There are procedural tables and notes of fees to be paid. This is the section of the book to which one would first look if one wanted to find a specific procedural provision. There is a general index at the very back of the whole book to which one could also refer and then one will be directed to the relevant pages showing the section of the *County Courts Act 1984* and/or the relevant rule. When a statute or rule is consulted then, just as with the *Supreme Court Practice*, after the text there are editorial notes summarising principles from case law. It is probably fair to say that these editorial notes are less full and less useful than the corresponding editorial notes in the *Supreme Court Practice*. In particular there is a remarkable reliance on very old case law.

The second part of the book has to do with the special jurisdiction of the county court under appropriate titles arranged alphabetically. A list of these titles appears in the table of contents at the beginning of part 2. The 'special jurisdiction' of the county court is jurisdiction under individual statutes, for example, sundry *Landlord and Tenant, Housing,* and *Rent Acts, Adoption Acts,* the *Consumer Credit Act 1974* and the like. Relevant parts of these Acts, or in some cases the whole Act, are set out with appropriate editorial notes. There are often cross-references to other books such as *Halsbury's Laws* and standard textbooks on divorce and family matters and the law of landlord and tenant. Information about the court's special jurisdiction is found by looking at the general index at the end of the book or by going directly to the relevant titles which can be located by consulting the table of contents.

Part 3 of the Green Book deals with costs and fees and includes, set out separately, *Ord. 38* of the *County Court Rules* which is the one dealing particularly with costs. There is a full explanation of the principles relating to the award and taxation of costs in the county court and cross-reference to relevant parts of *RSC Ord. 62*.

Finally in the fourth part there are set out numerous prescribed forms for use as precedents and a county court directory showing the courts in alphabetical order with their addresses, telephone numbers and special jurisdictions.

20.3 Constitution and Personnel

20.3.1 CONSTITUTION

The *County Courts Act 1984* governs the constitution of the county court. There are over 300 county courts in England and Wales, and often the same building is used for both the local District Registry of the High Court and the County Court registry. As there are more than twice as many county courts as High Court District Registries, in rural areas in particular, the nearest High Court registry may be a considerable distance away, whereas there should be a county court within relatively easy reach.

20.3.2 PERSONNEL

The equivalent of the High Court District Judge is the county court District Judge. Where the High Court registry and the county court registry occupy the same building, it is likely that the staff will be shared by both, and indeed that the same person will hold the office of District Judge of both.

The jurisdiction of the District Judge is:

(a) to try any action or matter in which the defendant fails to appear at the hearing or admits the claim;

(b) to try any action or matter the value of which does not exceed £5,000;

(c) to try any action in which the mortgagee under a mortgage of land claims possession of the mortgaged land; and

(d) by leave of the Circuit Judge and with the consent of the parties, to try any other action or matter (*CCR Ord. 21, r. 5*).

In addition, the functions of the District Judge are to deal with all interlocutory applications other than those where an injunction is sought; and to deal with arbitrations, which we consider at **21.9** below.

The Circuit Judge is the judge who will hear trials in the county court. In actions in tort and contract his jurisdiction is unlimited. The work of a Circuit Judge is likely to consist of alternately trying county court actions in his circuit (i.e. local group of county courts) and spending periods in the Crown Court sitting on criminal cases. The work of a Circuit Judge may also be carried out by Recorders or Assistant Recorders, appointed from practising solicitors or barristers to sit on a given number of days each year.

The county court, like the High Court District Registry, has a substantial clerical staff under a Chief Clerk to whom all correspondence must be addressed. It should be noted that unlike the High Court, which employs nobody for the service of process or enforcement of judgments, the county court employs bailiffs who are responsible for personal service of documents and for some steps in enforcing judgments.

20.4 Jurisdiction of the County Court

20.4.1 INTRODUCTION

Until 1991, the jurisdiction of the county court was severely limited financially so that, in the main, actions could only be brought in respect of sums involving £5,000 or less. In addition, there had to be a local connection with the cause of action. Both the low limit on jurisdiction and the requirement for a local connection were substantially changed in 1991.

The High Court and County Courts Jurisdiction Order gave the county court an unlimited upper jurisdiction in contract and tort cases. The county court has general jurisdiction, special jurisdiction and, more rarely, jurisdiction by agreement.

20.4.2 GENERAL JURISDICTION

(a) Unlimited financial jurisdiction in contract and tort actions.

(b) In equity cases in general, jurisdiction limited to £30,000.

(c) Effectively, exclusive jurisdiction for personal injury actions where the claim is for less than £50,000.

(d) Unlimited in all actions for the recovery of land.

(e) Injunctions, declarations, orders for specific performance and all equitable orders whether interlocutory or final (but not orders of certiorari, prohibition or mandamus).

(f) Some county courts have Admiralty jurisdiction for claims up to £5,000, or salvage claims where the property saved does not exceed £15,000.

20.4.3 SPECIAL JURISDICTION

(a) A number of statutes give jurisdiction to the county court in particular areas of law, e.g. bankruptcy and marriage breakdown.

(b) In some cases the jurisdiction is exclusive, e.g. regulated agreements and linked transactions under the *Consumer Credit Act 1974*, applications to consider residential security under the *Rent and Housing Acts*, sex discrimination under the *Sex Discrimination Act 1975*.

(c) In others, the jurisdiction is unlimited, e.g. as well as contract and tort and actions for the recovery of land, orders under the *Inheritance (Provision for Family and Dependants) Act 1975*; landlord and tenant applications, e.g. for relief from forfeiture (*Law of Property Act 1925*); and for new business tenancies and compensation for improvements (*Landlord and Tenant Acts 1927* and *1954*).

20.4.4 JURISDICTION BY AGREEMENT

If the parties to an action are agreed that they wish to proceed in the county court and the court does not have jurisdiction, they can usually extend the general jurisdiction by filing a written memorandum to that effect signed by them or their respective legal advisers. This may be done on commencement of the action or later, and the jurisdiction can be conferred for most of those kinds of cases which in the High Court would have been assigned to the Queen's Bench or Chancery Divisions. This power is relatively rarely used.

For example, the county court has no *original* jurisdiction in defamation actions and thus one cannot be started there unless the parties agree to the county court having jurisdiction. However, a defamation action, though started in the High Court, may be transferred to the county court for trial, although this would be unusual.

20.5 Types of Proceedings in the County Court

Whereas, as we have seen, the High Court proceedings are in almost all cases commenced either by writ or by originating summons, in the county court there are several ways of commencing actions. The following are some of the most common.

20.5.1 DEFAULT ACTIONS

These are actions to recover money, whether it is a liquidated claim (i.e. where the amount of the claim is ascertained, such as claims for the price of goods sold) or an unliquidated claim, such as damages in personal injury cases. Default actions may be commenced in any county court and there is no requirement for a local connection with the cause of action (but see below at **20.7.8**).

20.5.2 FIXED DATE ACTIONS

All actions other than those for the recovery of money, such as actions for injunctions, rectification or specific performance, are called 'fixed date actions'. If both money and some other remedy is sought, the action is also a fixed date action.

20.5.3 ORIGINATING APPLICATIONS

Any proceedings which are required to be brought in the county court but for which there is no prescribed procedural rule, are commenced by way of an *originating application*, e.g. an application by a tenant of business premises for a new tenancy under the *Landlord and Tenant Act 1954*. In addition, there are certain specified forms of procedure for which an originating application is required, in particular:

(a) *Summary proceedings for possession of land (CCR Ord. 24, r. 1).*

This is a specialised form of originating application used against squatters in particular. It is almost exactly equivalent in nature and procedure to *RSC Ord. 113*, which we considered at **17.5**.

(b) *Rent actions.*

These are originating applications providing a simple and speedy procedure for a landlord claiming rent from a tenant under *CCR Ord. 24, r. 8*.

20.5.4 PETITIONS

These are used only where expressly required by some Act or rule. They are not relevant to the subject matter of this text, being mainly of use in divorce and bankruptcy proceedings.

20.6 Other Preliminary Matters

Before we consider the commencement of an action, it is worth dealing with some other preliminary matters in order to note similarities and differences between High Court and county court.

20.6.1 PARTIES

20.6.1.1 Limited companies

A limited company does not need to employ a solicitor in the county court; whereas in the High Court, for all stages apart from filing an acknowledgement of service, the services of a solicitor are required (**19.1.1**).

20.6.1.2 Persons under a disability

If the plaintiff is under a disability, although the terminology used is the same for the persons appointed to represent his interests (namely, next friend and guardian *ad litem*), there is no need in the county court for those persons to use the services of a solicitor: they are entitled to act in person.

There is also a change in the documentation to be filed (see **19.8.2**). In the High Court a next friend must file a simple consent to act and a certificate from the solicitor certifying that there is no conflict between the person under a disability and the next friend. In the county court, the next friend delivers either a written undertaking to be responsible for costs, which must be signed before a solicitor or before a properly authorised court official, or an office copy of the written order of the Court of Protection authorising the next friend to conduct the proceedings.

A guardian *ad litem*, when delivering an admission or a defence to the plaintiff's claim in the High Court, must also deliver a certificate stating that he is a fit and proper person to act as such and has no interest in the proceedings adverse to those of the defendant. A guardian *ad litem* in the county court does not have to deliver such a certificate.

20.6.2 JOINDER

The rules relating to joinder are the same as in the High Court (see **6.1**) and nothing further need be said about this.

20.6.3 INTEREST ON DAMAGES

The county court has the power to award interest on damages under *s. 69* of the *County Courts Act 1984*. The rules of pleading are the same as in the High Court, and therefore a plaintiff will plead his claim for interest as follows:

(a) In a claim for an unliquidated demand, he will plead it by reference to *s. 69* of the *County Courts Act 1984* and interest will be awarded on the same principles as in the High Court (see **1.3**).

(b) In a claim under a contract, reference to the term of the contract and contractually fixed rate should be made. The precise figures up to the time of issue of the proceedings, together with the daily rate thereafter, should be stated in the particulars of claim.

(c) If there is no contractually agreed rate but the claim is for a liquidated sum, then, provided the rate claimed is no higher than the rate on judgment debts in the High Court (8 per cent at the time of writing) and precise figures of the amounts due up to the date of issue of proceedings together with the daily rate thereafter are shown in the particulars of claim, the plaintiff will be able to sign judgment if the defendant does not take sufficient steps to defend in the same way as in signing judgment under *RSC Ord. 13* in the High Court (*CCR Ord. 9, r. 6* — see **7.4.1.2** above).

20.6.4 INTEREST ON JUDGMENTS

Judgments obtained in the county court on or after 1 July 1991 for the payment of a sum of money of not less than £5,000, carry interest at the rate for the time specified in *s. 17* of the *Judgments Act 1838* (at the time of writing 8 per cent), i.e. the same rate as in the High Court.

If the judgment creditor applies for *oral examination* or takes proceedings to enforce the judgment in the county court (other than for a *charging order*), the debt ceases to carry interest during the oral examination or enforcement procedure except in cases where the enforcement procedure fails to produce any payment from the debtor. If that is the case, interest continues to accrue as if the enforcement proceedings had never been taken.

The fact that interest ceases to run during enforcement is a crucial disadvantage. Even though 8 per cent per annum may be a relatively modest return, if the debt is, say, £10,000 that would have produced £800 a year in interest. In order to avoid losing this sum where enforcement of judgment takes some time, it is vital to transfer the county court judgment to the High Court for enforcement. This then becomes a High Court judgment and carries interest at 8 per cent until paid in full.

Any county court judgment for more than £1,000 can be transferred to the High Court for enforcement, and thus in the bracket £1,000 to £5,000 there is a particular incentive to transfer it since such judgments do not carry interest at all in the county court. The procedure for transfer is very straightforward under *RSC Ord. 78, r. 2,* and *Practice Direction (County Court Order: Enforcement)* [1991] 1 WLR 695. All that is required is to produce at the High Court District Registry a certificate of judgment of the county court sealed with the county court seal. The case will then be re-allocated a High Court reference number and in effect becomes a High Court case for enforcement purposes.

20.7 Commencement in the County Court

20.7.1 VENUE

Under *CCR Ord. 4, r. 2,* the general rules for venue are:

(a) an action may be commenced in the court in the district in which the defendant or one of the defendants resides or carries on business; or

(b) in the court for the district in which the cause of action wholly or in part arose; or

(c) in the case of default actions, in *any* county court (see below, however, as to the possibility of transfer on filing a defence);

(d) landlord and tenant cases and the like are to be commenced in the court for the district in which the land or any part of it is situated.

It will thus be observed that in actions where money is the only remedy sought, the plaintiff has an absolute right to choice of court, at least for the commencement of proceedings. Where the case will proceed thereafter depends upon the matters referred to below (**20.7.8**).

20.7.2 DEFAULT ACTIONS

Actions are commenced by delivering or posting to the court a *default summons* and the particulars of claim, with an extra copy for the court and one for each defendant, and by paying the fee which is fixed by reference to the amount claimed (*CCR Ord. 3, r. 3*). The nature of these documents is as follows:

20.7.2.1 The summons

This is in one of two forms prescribed by the rules N1 (claim for a fixed amount) or N2 (claim for unliquidated damages). These forms are obtainable from law stationers or from the counter of the county court. As an alternative, a person may fill in another form, a 'Request for Summons', and the county court staff will then draw up the form of summons. County court staff are extremely busy and overworked and most solicitors prefer to prepare their own form of summons. (The forms of summons are illustrated at the end of this chapter.) The default summons is thus the equivalent of a High Court writ.

20.7.2.2 The particulars of claim

This represents a significant difference from the High Court procedure. The particulars of claim are the exact equivalent of the statement of claim which would be used in a High Court action. The same principles of pleading apply: they are to be signed by the plaintiff's solicitors and must state an address for service; if drafted by counsel, counsel's name must be typed at the foot. The essential differences here are that, first, the solicitor needs to prepare the particulars of claim and take them to the court at the very time of issuing the summons. (It will be remembered that in the High Court, whilst a writ could be issued with a short form of statement of claim endorsed on it in a simple case, e.g. a debt, in other cases normally the statement of claim would be a lengthy document prepared for service after the return of the acknowledgement of service giving notice of intention to defend.) Secondly, the particulars of claim are taken *to the court*. (In the High Court if the statement of claim is endorsed on the writ, and since the court keeps a copy of the writ, it would have on file the statement of claim; but in cases where it was not endorsed on the writ there would be no need for the court to see the statement of claim which would be served direct between the parties.)

There are two other matters to note:

(a) If the particulars of claim are very short they may be inserted in the space provided on the form of summons itself. This is only really possible in the case of a simple debt since there is very little space for a full pleading.

(b) It will be recalled that the county court District Judge has the jurisdiction to try any case involving less than £5,000. If more than £5,000 is sought by way of unliquidated damages, it is preferable to certify in the particulars of claim that a sum of more than that figure is being sought, otherwise the District Judge will be assumed to have jurisdiction (*CCR Ord. 6, r. 1A*).

20.7.2.3 Other documents

In addition to the summons and particulars of claim, which are needed in every case, other documents may need to be produced at the time of issue of the summons:

(a) The legal aid certificate, if applicable, and the notice of issue of legal aid for each of the defendants.

(b) In a personal injury case, a medical report substantiating all the personal injuries which it is intended to adduce as part of the plaintiff's case at trial (see **7.4.2.3**).

(c) In personal injury cases, full particulars of special damages, just as in High Court cases (see **7.4.1.1**).

It will be noted that the time at which the medical report and special damage details have to be provided comes even earlier than in the High Court, namely on issue of the proceedings. If for any reason these documents are not available, or the plaintiff proposes to ask the court to disapply the rule in relation to supplying them, e.g. because the limitation period is about to expire, the plaintiff must ask for directions, and then an early preliminary hearing before the District Judge will be arranged so that he can explain the difficulties.

20.7.3 ISSUE AND SERVICE OF PROCEEDINGS

20.7.3.1 Procedure

On issue the court will prepare a *plaint note* and, if not prepared by the plaintiff, a summons, and will attach to the summons a form called an 'Admission Defence and Counterclaim' (Court form N9). The court then serves the summons, form of admission defence and counterclaim (and in personal injury actions and actions involving persons under a disability, the additional documents required) by first class post on each defendant. The summons is (unless the contrary is shown) deemed to have been served on the seventh day after posting. The plaintiff does not receive a sealed copy of the summons from the court, but is given the *plaint note*, which is the equivalent of the original writ in the action and which gives the case number which must now be used on all documents, the date of postal service and is a receipt for the amount of court fee paid.

The court will always effect service by first class post unless the plaintiff's solicitor has asked for the court bailiff to effect personal service, in which case another fee is payable. In addition, the following points should be noted:

(a) The plaintiff's solicitor is always entitled to ask for the documents to be returned to him so that he can effect service. He is likely to do this where some difficulty with service is anticipated, especially in debt cases where it may be that the defendant will contend that he did not receive the documents by post and a good deal of time is wasted in what is an urgent matter. Using the county court bailiff might be thought to avoid this, but in fact the bailiff is overworked and not especially efficient at service. Many solicitors therefore prefer to employ their own process servers in such cases.

(b) In personal injury cases only, a solicitor may serve a defendant by post. In all other cases a solicitor must serve the defendant personally.

(c) Service may also be effected on a nominated solicitor.

(d) In the case of a limited company, service may be effected at any place of business of that company having any connection with the cause of action. It will be recalled that in the High Court documents can only be served on a limited company at its registered office (see **19.1.2**). Here, if, for example, a party has a dispute with the local branch of some supermarket chain, it will be sufficient to serve the summons and particulars of claim at that local branch rather than at the company's registered office.

20.7.3.2 Proof of service

Where service was to have been by the court, the court will either complete a certificate of service, where it has taken place successfully, or a notice of non-service (e.g. where the bailiff has failed to find the defendant). If the summons has been served by the plaintiff's solicitor, whether by post in a personal injuries case or personally, then an affidavit of service by the person effecting service must be filed at court within three days of service. If service is on the defendant's solicitor, that solicitor must give a certificate accepting service and stating his address for service of further documents.

20.7.3.3 Duration of validity of summons

Just as in the case of a writ in the High Court, a summons, whether in a default or in a fixed date action has a 'life' of four months only. If it is not served within that time an application must be made to the court to renew or extend the time in the same way as in the case of a High Court writ (see **6.5**).

20.7.3.4 Summary

The defendant will thus have been served with the summons, the particulars of claim and a form of admission, defence and counterclaim on which to respond to the court. In addition, where appropriate, he will have been served with a notice of issue of legal aid, and a copy of any medical report or statement of special damages in a personal injury case. The way in which the action proceeds will now be determined by the defendant's response (if any) to service of these documents.

20.7.4 THE ADMISSION, DEFENCE AND COUNTERCLAIM

This form (N9) which the defendant receives is different from the High Court form of acknowledgement of service. The admission, defence and counterclaim constitutes both an acknowledgement of service and the defendant's full response for the action whatever that is. The defendant has 14 days from service to complete and return the form to the court office. The form is designed for use by a layman and there is little room in it to set out a properly pleaded defence in the way in which a lawyer would wish to draft it. Thus, if solicitors are instructed for the defendant, they will probably not use the form but will file a properly drafted defence which replies to each paragraph of the plaintiff's particulars of claim in exactly the same formal manner as the High Court defence.

In most claims for damages, and particularly in personal injury claims, the defendant is likely to get immediate legal advice, whether through his insurance company or otherwise. In those cases usually it will be solicitors who will deal with the defence and will file a properly drafted pleading. Here, we first consider the admission defence and counterclaim in a liquidated demand or debt case, where the defendant is much less likely to be legally represented.

20.7.5 DEFENCE AND COUNTERCLAIM

The principles for a counterclaim are precisely the same as in the High Court. Thus if a defendant considers that he has some claim against the plaintiff, whether or not causally linked to the plaintiff's claim against him, he may incorporate it with his defence. In such cases automatic directions take effect, and this will be considered in **Chapter 21**.

20.7.6 LIQUIDATED DEMANDS: ADMISSION AND PAYMENT OF THE AMOUNT CLAIMED

20.7.6.1 Procedure

As in the High Court, it is possible for a defendant to pay direct to a plaintiff the total amount of the claim plus interest and fixed costs to bring an action to an end. The County Court procedure is as follows:

(a) In the case of a liquidated demand, if the whole sum claimed by the plaintiff, including interest and the amount of fixed costs shown on the face of the summons, is paid direct to the plaintiff within 14 days of the service of the summons on the defendant the action is stayed.

(b) If in the case of a liquidated demand the defendant pays the sum in full at any *later* stage (e.g. after delivery of a defence), he should pay the full amount together with his computation of the interest accrued, but *not* the fixed costs because fixed costs are no longer appropriate as after 14 days the plaintiff will be entitled to taxed costs.

This applies to a defendant who admits the claim and has the means immediately to pay it at the outset, and to one who wishes to pay it immediately at some later stage. If the defendant, whilst admitting the claim or some part of it, is not in a position to pay the money to the plaintiff immediately, he should complete the form of admission, defence and counterclaim stating whether he admits the whole or part of the claim and what proposal he makes for method of payment (e.g. as to half of the amount forthwith and the balance by instalments over a year, or the whole by instalments or as the case may be). The court photocopies that form and sends it to the plaintiff. If the plaintiff accepts the defendant's admission as final, he should notify the court by letter and the District Judge will then enter judgment for the sum claimed plus interest and fixed costs.

20.7.6.2 Disposals

Where the plaintiff is dissatisfied with the method of payment offered by the defendant (usually because the instalments offered are too small and thus it would take too long to collect the money), the plaintiff should write to the court giving his comments on the offer and setting out his counter proposals. Thereupon the chief clerk of the court will 'dispose' of the case by fixing an amount which he considers fair on all the evidence of the defendant's means, and also taking into account the plaintiff's legitimate right to have his debt paid promptly. The chief clerk will fix an amount usually for weekly or monthly instalments which he considers fair on all the evidence.

Having notified this provisional decision to the parties, either party then has five days in which to object by letter. If either does object — the defendant because he considers the weekly instalments beyond his means, or the plaintiff because he considers the amounts payable too low — there will be a 'disposal hearing' before the District Judge. At this hearing both parties will attend chambers and there will be a detailed investigation of the defendant's means and an opportunity for the plaintiff to cross-examine the defendant about them. The District Judge will then decide whether to make the provisional disposal final, or whether to vary it in the light of the further representations. The plaintiff is usually entitled to his costs of attending the disposal though a relatively modest fixed sum is allowed.

20.7.6.3 Admission of part of the claim

Under *CCR Ord. 9, r. 3(6)*, if the defendant admits only *part* of the amount claimed, the plaintiff cannot simply accept that amount and continue with the action to recover the balance. He must either notify the court of his acceptance of the sum in full satisfaction of the claim, or notify the court that he does not accept that amount in which case the action goes on as defended and a date for a pre-trial review will be given (see **21.3**). Where there is a clear admission of a separable part of the claim the plaintiff may, of course, be able to go on to get summary judgment, thus ending the dispute about that part of the action so that it only continues in relation to the disputed part. (See further at **20.7.9.2**.)

20.7.7 ADMISSION IN AN ACTION FOR AN UNLIQUIDATED SUM

As in the High Court, where the action is for damages and the defendant admits liability but makes no offer on quantum, the plaintiff may obtain interlocutory judgment with an order for damages to be assessed. Somewhat more unusually, the defendant may actually offer a specific sum, in which case the plaintiff may refuse or accept as in the case of offers related to liquidated demands discussed at **20.7.6** above.

20.7.8 TRANSFER ON FILING OF DEFENCE

As we have seen, the plaintiff has the initial choice of venue in a default summons action. It is possible, however, where a defence is filed, for the action to be transferred to the defendant's 'home court', i.e. the court closest to his home address (*CCR Ord. 9, r. 2(8)*). The rules are:

(a) Where in an action for a *liquidated* sum the defendant files a defence, the action is automatically transferred from the court of commencement to the defendant's home court. Thereafter the plaintiff may make representations, by letter, or by asking for a hearing if he wishes, to the defendant's home court that the action should be transferred back to the court in which he commenced it. The District Judge must then consider under *CCR Ord. 16, r. 1* whether the matter can be more conveniently and fairly heard in that court, and he may exercise his discretion appropriately having also given the defendant an opportunity to make representations.

(b) In the case of an action for an *unliquidated sum*, the filing of a defence will not cause it to be automatically transferred. In that case the defendant, when filing his defence, may lodge an application that the case be transferred to the court more convenient for him and the plaintiff will be given an opportunity to reply to those representations. Though the District Judge has a general discretion under *CCR Ord. 16, r. 1* in such a case, it is suggested that normally the case ought to stay in the court most convenient for the plaintiff, because in damages claims the plaintiff has the job of running the action and therefore his convenience should outweigh that of the defendant.

The question of where the *trial* should take place in such cases may be different again, since the convenience of other persons (including the length of local court lists and the whereabout of witnesses) may need to be considered. In any event, given that there are automatic directions in most cases (see **21.2**), there may not be much difference in the matter of convenience unless a number of interlocutory applications are anticipated.

20.7.9 EARLY JUDGMENT

Here we consider briefly two ways in which early judgment may be obtained in the county court, which correspond almost exactly to High Court provisions previously considered in **Chapter 17**.

20.7.9.1 Judgment in default

If the defendant does not return his form of admission, defence and counterclaim at all within 14 days after service of the summons on him, the plaintiff may enter judgment in default (*CCR Ord. 9, r. 6*).

This is carried out by the plaintiff producing a form at the court counter with the plaint note, and judgment is entered there and then. On a claim for a liquidated sum together with interest properly pleaded, judgment will be final for the amount of the claim, interest and fixed costs. In a claim for unliquidated damages the judgment entered, as in the High Court, will be an interlocutory judgment, i.e. it will deal finally with the question of liability but leave damages and interest thereon to be assessed at a subsequent hearing. In such a case an order will be made for costs to be taxed at that subsequent hearing.

Just as in the High Court, the county court has the power to set aside a default judgment, either as of right where service was in some way imperfect, or on the merits where the defendant, notwithstanding that he is in default, can show some reason why discretion should be exercised in his favour, and that he has some prospect of successfully defending the action.

20.7.9.2 Summary judgment

We have already considered the procedure in the High Court for forestalling an attempt by a defendant to get unmerited delays by serving a spurious defence (**17.2.2**). The same principle applies in the county court, although it comes about at a slightly different time. It will be recalled that in the High Court an application for summary judgment would be triggered by the receipt of the acknowledgement of service in which a defendant had indicated that he proposed to defend. In the county court there is no equivalent to the form of acknowledgement of service and the defendant is actually required to return his defence to the court within 14 days. If the plaintiff considers that the defence is spurious, he may still apply for summary judgment notwithstanding it. The plaintiff applies by notice of application to the District Judge, filing an affidavit in court which is in the same wording as the High Court affidavit except that it needs to add the words 'notwithstanding the purported defence filed' to indicate on oath that the plaintiff does not accept the bona fides of that defence.

Once the application is issued it must be served on the defendant not less than seven clear days before the day fixed for the hearing. At the hearing of the application precisely the same criteria are applied by the District Judge as in a High Court case, so that he must decide whether on the documents before him, including any affidavit in reply filed by the defendant, he thinks that there is a triable issue. He may then give one or other of the four forms of judgment described in the corresponding section on High Court procedure in **17.2.5**. If the defendant is given leave to continue to defend, the court will proceed at that stage with a *pre-trial review* and give appropriate directions for the further conduct of the action.

20.7.10 FIXED DATE ACTIONS

20.7.10.1 Procedure

In a fixed date action the plaintiff prepares the appropriate document, which is a form of summons but in a different form to that used in default actions. In most cases both the summons served on the defendant and the plaint note sent to the plaintiff have a 'fixed date' endorsed which will indicate a date fixed either for the hearing itself or for a pre-trial review. However, if the fixed date action is one of those governed by automatic directions (see **21.2**) no fixed date is given because the automatic directions deal with the procedure for obtaining a hearing date.

The summons is served together with the particulars of claim and a form of admission, defence and counterclaim. Service must be not less than 21 days before the date of the first hearing.

20.7.10.2 Admissions in fixed date actions

If the defendant delivers an admission, the plaintiff can apply before the return day for such judgment as he may be entitled to on the admission. As the application must be on notice to the defendant, and as a date for the pre-trial review will have been given, the plaintiff will wait until that day. (In actions for the recovery of land the delivery of an admission simply limits the defendant's liability for further costs.)

20.7.10.3 Defence in fixed date actions

If the defendant disputes liability he must, within 14 days of service of the summons upon him, deliver to the court a defence (using if he wishes the form supplied), a copy of which the court will send to the plaintiff. Despite this time limit the defendant may serve a defence late at any time before the return day, and may even appear at the hearing to dispute the plaintiff's claim without having delivered *any* defence. In such a case, the defendant would be ordered to pay the costs incurred in consequence of his failure or delay, and the court may at any time before trial order the defendant to deliver a defence or be debarred from defending the action at all. If the particular fixed date action is governed by automatic directions, if the defendant fails to deliver a defence within 14 days the plaintiff can apply for judgment in default (*CCR Ord. 9, r. 4A*).

20.7.11 ORIGINATING APPLICATIONS

Originating applications are the equivalent of what in the High Court is called an originating summons. This subject is dealt with comprehensively in **Chapter 24**. An originating application is used in the county court in preference to a default summons or a fixed date summons where there is in principle one issue to be decided by the court which usually will not raise any great contested issues of fact. Some statutes specifically provide that the method of procedure is to be by originating application (for example, *Part II* of the *Landlord and Tenant Act 1954* prescribes that an orginating application shall be used to determine a business tenant's application for a renewed tenancy). In other cases an originating application is used where the case turns on one single point of law or where the case has to do with construction of the terms of a document.

In originating application cases, a form is prepared and taken or sent to the court. The court then prepares a notice of hearing or date for pre-trial review which is served with the originating application on the respondent. In most cases the respondent has 14 days after service to file an answer with the court, a copy of which the court sends to the applicant. The next stage is then the pre-trial review or hearing. If it is a pre-trial review then directions are given for the parties to file further affidavits or prepare for trial in much the same way as in originating summons cases in the High Court.

20.8 Example County Court Summons

County Court Summons

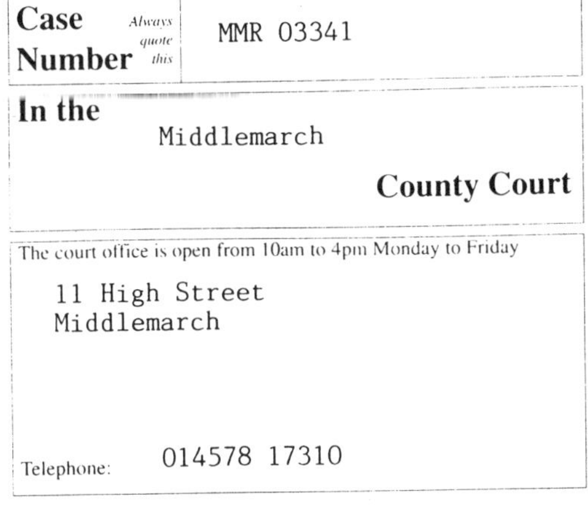
Case Number *Always quote this* MMR 03341

In the Middlemarch County Court

The court office is open from 10am to 4pm Monday to Friday

11 High Street
Middlemarch

Telephone: 014578 17310

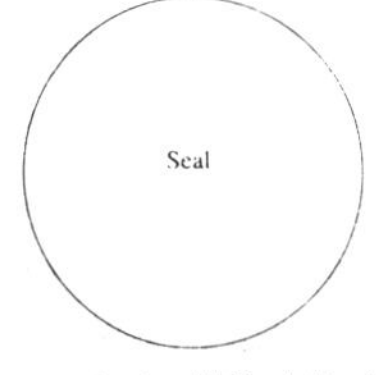

This summons is only valid if sealed by the court
If it is not sealed it should be reported to the court

Keep this summons. You may need to refer to it

(1) Plaintiff's full name address

Robert Arkwright & Co
(a firm)
3 Railway Road
Middlemarch

(2) Address for sending documents and payments *(if not as above)* **Ref/Tel no.**

Vincy & Co
Bank Chambers
Middlemarch

014578 13333 RV/D

(3) Defendant's full name *(eg Mr, Mrs or Miss where known)* **and address Company no.** *(where known)*

Diane Horton
5 Park Road
Middlemarch
Loamshire

What the plaintiff claims from you

Brief description of type of claim: Money owed on invoices and interest

Particulars of the plaintiff's claim against you

Payment for goods sold and delivered and interest pursuant to contract
(see separate particulars)

Signed
Plaintiff or plaintiff's solicitor
(or see enclosed particulars of claim)

Amount claimed	4,720	00
Court fee	70	00
Solicitor's costs	61	00
Total amount	4,851	00
Summons issued on	19.5.'97	

What to do about this summons

You have 21 days from the date of the postmark to reply to this summons
(A limited company served at its registered office has 16 days to reply)
If this summons was delivered by hand, you have 14 days from the date it was delivered to reply

You can

- **dispute the claim**
- **make a claim against the plaintiff**
- **admit the claim and costs in full and offer to pay**
- **admit only part of the claim**
- **pay the total amount shown above**

You must read the information on the back of this form. It will tell you more about what to do.

N1 Default summons (fixed amount) (Order 3, rule 3(2)(b)) (11.95) *Printed by Satellite Press Limited*

If you do nothing	**Judgment may be entered against you without further notice. This will make it difficult for you to get credit.**
If you dispute the claim	Complete the white defence form (N9B) and return it to the court office within the time allowed. The notes on the form explain what you should do. It is not enough to contact the plaintiff by telephone or letter.
If you want to make a claim against the plaintiff (counterclaim)	Complete boxes 5 and 6 on the white defence form (N9B) and return the form to the court office. The notes at box 5 explain what you should do.
If you admit all of the claim and you are asking for time to pay	Fill in the blue admission form (N9A). The notes on the form explain what you should do and where you should send the completed form. You must reply within the time allowed.
If you admit all of the claim and you wish to pay now	**Take or send the money including any interest and costs to the person named at box (2) on the front of the summons.** If there is no address in box (2), send the money to the address in box (1). You should ensure the plaintiff receives the money within the period given for reply. Read 'How to Pay' below.
If you admit only part of the claim	Fill in the white defence form (N9B) saying how much you admit, and why you dispute the balance. Then **either:** Pay the amount admitted as explained in the box above; **or** If you need time to pay fill in the blue admission form (N9A) and return the forms to the court office within the time allowed.

Costs

In addition to the solicitor's costs for issuing the summons, a plaintiff's solicitor is entitled to add further costs if the court enters judgment against you.

Interest on judgments

If judgment is entered against you and is for £5,000 or more the plaintiff may be entitled to interest on the total amount.

Registration of judgments

If the summons results in a judgment against you, your name and address may be entered in the Register of County Court Judgments. **This will make it difficult for you to get credit.** A leaflet giving further information can be obtained from the court.

Further advice

Court staff cannot give you advice on points of law, but you can get help to complete the reply forms and information about court procedures at **any** county court office or Citizens Advice Bureau. The address and telephone number of your local court is listed under 'Courts' in the phone book. When corresponding with the court, please address forms or letters to the Chief Clerk. Always quote the whole of the case number which appears at the top right corner on the front of this form; the court is unable to trace your case without it.

How to Pay

- **PAYMENT(S) MUST BE MADE to the person named at the address for payment quoting their reference and the court case number.**
- **DO NOT bring or send payments to the court. THEY WILL NOT BE ACCEPTED.**
- You should allow **at least** 4 days for your payments to reach the plaintiff or his representative.
- Make sure that you keep records and can account for all payments made. Proof may be required if there is any disagreement. It is not safe to send cash unless you use registered post.
- A leaflet giving further advice about payment can be obtained from the court.
- If you need more information you should contact the plaintiff or his representative.

Certificate of service

To be completed on the court copy only

Served on

By posting on

Officer

Not served on (reasons)

N1 Default summons (fixed amount) (Order 3, rule 3(2)(b)) (11.95)

Printed by Satellite Press Limited

County Court Summons

Case Number *Always quote this*	MMR 03131

In the Middlemarch **County Court**

The court office is open from 10am to 4pm Monday to Friday

11 High Street
Middlemarch

Telephone: 014578 17310

(1) Plaintiff's full name address

John Brooks

7 High Bank
Middlemarch
Loamshire

(2) Address for sending documents and payments *(if not as above)*
Ref/Tel no.

Vincy and Co
Bank Chambers
Middlemarch

014578 13333 RV/D

(3) Defendant's full name *(eg Mr, Mrs or Miss where known)* **and address Company no.** *(where known)*

Lydgate Bakery Company Ltd
1 The Old Mews
Middlemarch

seal

This summons is only valid if sealed by the court
If it is not sealed it should be reported to the court

Keep this summons. You may need to refer to it

What the plaintiff claims from you

Brief description of type of claim: Damages for negligence

Particulars of the plaintiff's claim against you

Damages for personal injuries arising out of the Defendant's employee's negligent driving on 3.5.96 (see accompanying particulars of claim).

My claim is worth £5,000 or less ☐ over £5,000 ☑

Total claim over £3,000 and/or damages for personal injury claims over £1,000

I would like my case decided by trial ☐ arbitration ☐

Signed [signature]
Plaintiff or plaintiff's solicitor
(or see enclosed particulars of claim)

Amount claimed see particulars

Court fee	80	00
Solicitor's costs	To be taxed	
Total amount		

Summons issued on 3.5.97

What to do about this summons

You have 21 days from the date of the postmark to reply to this summons
(A limited company served at its registered office has 16 days to reply)
If this summons was delivered by hand, you have 14 days from the date it was delivered to reply

You can

- **dispute the claim**
- **make a claim against the plaintiff**
- **admit the claim and costs in full and offer to pay**
- **admit only part of the claim**
- **pay the total amount shown above**

You must read the information on the back of this form. It will tell you more about what to do.

N2 Default summons (amount not fixed) (Order 3, rule 3(2)(b)) (11.95) *Printed by Satellite Press Limited*

Please read this page: it will help you deal with the summons

If you dispute all or part of the claim

You may be entitled to help with your legal costs. Ask about the legal aid scheme at any county court office, Citizens Advice Bureau, legal advice centre or firm of solicitors displaying the legal aid sign.

- Say how much you dispute on the enclosed form for defending the claim and return it to the court office within the time allowed. It is not enough to contact the plaintiff by letter or telephone. The court will arrange a hearing and/or will tell you what to do next.
- If you dispute only part of the claim, you should also fill in the part of the form for admitting the claim and either pay the amount admitted to the court or make an offer of payment.
- If the court named on the summons is not your local county court, and/or the court for the area where the reason for the claim arose, you may write to the court named asking for the case to be transferred to the county court of your choice. You must explain your reasons for wanting the transfer. However, if the case is transferred and you later lose the case, you may have to pay more in costs.

How the claim will be dealt with if defended

If the total the plaintiff is claiming is £3,000 or less and/or the claim for damages for personal injury is worth £1,000 or less, it will be dealt with by arbitration (small claims procedure) unless the court decides the case is too difficult to be dealt with in this informal way. Costs and the grounds for setting aside an arbitration award are strictly limited. If the claim is not dealt with by arbitration, costs, including the costs of help from a legal representative, may be allowed.

If the total the plaintiff is claiming is more than £3,000 and/or he or she is claiming more than £1,000 for damages for personal injury, it can still be dealt with by arbitration if you or the plaintiff ask for it and the court approves. If your claim is dealt with by arbitration in these circumstances, costs may be allowed.

If you want to make a claim against the plaintiff

This is called a counterclaim

Fill in the part of the enclosed form headed 'Counterclaim'. If your claim is for more than the plaintiff's claim you may have to pay a fee - the court will let you know. Unless the plaintiff admits your counterclaim there will usually be a hearing. The court will tell you what to do next.

If you admit owing all the claim

- If the claim is for more than £3,000 and/or includes a claim for damages for personal injury for more than £1,000, you may make a payment into court to compensate the plaintiff (see **Payments into Court** box). The figure of £3,000 includes interest claimed under contract but **excludes** costs and interest claimed under section 69 of the County Courts Act1984. Send a notice or letter with your payment, saying that it is in satisfaction of the claim. If the plaintiff accepts the amount paid, he is also entitled to payment of his costs.
- **If you need time to pay,** complete the enclosed form of admission and give details of how you propose to pay the plaintiff. You must reply within the time allowed. If your offer is accepted, the court will send an order telling you how to pay. If it is not accepted, the court will fix a rate of payment based on the details given in your form of admission and the plaintiff's comments. Judgment will be entered and you will be sent an order telling you how and when to pay.
- **If the plaintiff does not accept the amount paid or offered,** the court will fix a hearing to decide how much you must pay to compensate the plaintiff. The court will tell you when the hearing, which you should attend, will take place.

N2 Default summons (amount not fixed) (Order 3, rule 3(2)(b))

If you do nothing

Judgment may be entered against you. This will make it difficult for you to get credit.

General information

Court staff cannot give you advice on points of law, but you can get help to complete the reply forms and information about court procedures at **any** county court office or Citizens Advice Bureau. The address and telephone number of your local court is listed under 'Courts' in the phone book. When corresponding with the court, please address forms or letters to the Chief Clerk. Always quote the whole of the case number which appears at the top right corner on the front of this form; the court is unable to trace your case without it.

Costs

In addition to the solicitor's costs for issuing the summons, you may have more costs to pay if the court enters judgment against you.

Registration of judgments

If the summons results in a judgment against you, your name and address may be entered in the Register of County Court Judgments. **This will make it difficult for you to get credit.** A leaflet giving further information can be obtained from the court.

Interest on judgments

If judgment is entered against you and is for £5,000 or more the plaintiff may be entitled to interest on the full amount.

Payments into Court

You can pay the court by calling at the court office which is open 10am to 4pm Monday to Friday

You may only pay by:

- cash
- banker's or giro draft
- cheque supported by a cheque card
- cheque (unsupported cheques may be accepted, subject to clearance, if the Chief Clerk agrees)

Cheques and drafts must be made payable to HM Paymaster General and crossed.

Please bring this form with you.

By post

You may only pay by:

- postal order
- banker's or giro draft
- cheque (unsupported cheques may be accepted, subject to clearance, if the Chief Clerk agrees)

The payment must be made out to HM Paymaster General and crossed.

This method of payment is at your own risk

And you must:

- pay the postage
- enclose this form
- enclose a self addressed envelope so that the court can return this form with a receipt

The court **cannot** accept stamps or payments by bank and giro credit transfers.

Note: You should carefully check any future forms from the court to see if payments should be made directly to the plaintiff

To be completed on the court copy only

Served on

By posting on

Officer

Not served on (reasons)

TWENTY ONE

COUNTY COURT ACTIONS

Once a plaintiff has formally commenced proceedings against a defendant, the future conduct of the case will depend upon the action taken (or not taken) by the defendant in response to service of the summons, etc. In a default claim, the defendant may admit the claim and come to a satisfactory accommodation with the plaintiff for paying the judgment debt; or the plaintiff may obtain an early judgment. Assuming that the case proceeds, however, we must now consider the directions stage in a county court action; the automatic directions and pre-trial review; interlocutory matters; preparations for trial, and the conduct of the trial.

It should again be emphasised that in many instances the procedure in the county court is virtually identical to that in the High Court, and that the same practical and tactical considerations will apply. Thus the way in which the solicitor will set about the collection of evidence, negotiations, the use of experts and counsel, are all the same.

21.1 General Principles

21.1.1 INTERLOCUTORY APPLICATIONS

Where a party needs to make an interlocutory application, e.g. for further and better particulars, discovery, etc., such applications are said to be made 'on notice'. The form of notice of application (Court form N244) serves exactly the same function as a general summons in a High Court case. It simply provides a way of fixing an appointment before the District Judge and gives an indication to the opponent of the order the applicant seeks.

The normal way to apply for any form of interlocutory application is to take to court two general forms of notice of application, prepared in exactly the same way as an ordinary summons in an action in the High Court, setting out the nature of the order sought. The court will give a hearing date which is inserted on the notice of application. This is then sealed and a copy served in the usual way by post on the defendant's solicitor (*CCR Ord. 13*).

21.1.2 EXTENSIONS OF TIME

The practice is exactly as in the High Court (see **7.1.2**). It may be necessary for the defendant to ask for an extension of time, say, to file a defence. As in the High Court, it is the usual courtesy to grant one reasonable extension. If the extension is not agreed, or one extension has been granted but the plaintiff refuses a second one, the defendant will apply on notice as described above. (*CCR Ord. 13, r. 4.*)

21.1.3 AMENDMENT

The practice and procedure in relation to amendment is similar to that in the High Court but there are some slight differences which reflect the somewhat greater degree of informality in the county court. The position under *CCR Ord. 15* is as follows:

(a) A party who wishes to amend his summons and pleadings to add or substitute any party after the summons has been served, must make an application to the court for leave to do so. The practice at the hearing of that application follows the High Court procedure and the criteria for granting the application are the same, so that in fact amendment is very liberally allowed.

(b) In the case of any other amendment to the pleading, amendment can be made at any time before 'the return day' by simply filing the amended pleading and serving a copy on every other party.

The **'return date'** means the date for the pre-trial review where there is a pre-trial review. If there is no pre-trial review so that the first hearing is the trial itself, then the rule permits amendment without leave at any time up to the close of pleadings.

It should be noted that there is no specific rule, unlike in the High Court, for an amendment which changes the cause of action or adds a new cause of action. This is simply treated like any other amendment. If, however, the claim added is one which cannot be made in a default action (e.g. a claim for an injunction), the action will continue as if it had been commenced as a fixed date action.

(c) At any stage of the proceedings, any party may file an amended pleading endorsed with the consent of every other party to the proceedings.

21.1.4 FURTHER AND BETTER PARTICULARS

The principles on which a party may require further and better particulars are the same as in the High Court (see **7.5.1**). A written request should first be made, and only if this is refused should application be made to the District Judge. Copies of any further and better particulars sought and given must be filed at court since the court keeps a full file of the pleadings. (*CCR Ord. 6, r. 7; Ord. 9, r. 11.*)

21.1.5 STRIKING OUT PLEADINGS

The principles applied in an application to strike out the whole or any part of any pleadings are the same as in the High Court (see **7.5.3**; *CCR Ord. 13, r. 5*).

21.2 Automatic Directions

21.2.1 INTRODUCTION

The directions stage of an action in the county court is usually marked by the coming into operation of the automatic directions, or, in exceptional cases, by the court fixing a pre-trial review. There are some cases, however, which do not have any directions stage, in particular summary proceedings where a swift and efficient remedy is sought in particular cases, e.g. where a dispossessed land owner seeks possession of land from squatters. In those cases there are no provisions for directions at any stage and the first time when the party is before the court is the substantive hearing of the action. Even in such cases, however, if it becomes apparent that the issue is not as simple as it had been thought the District Judge has the power to give directions and adjourn to some later date.

There is a number of cases where automatic directions do not apply and a pre-trial review will be fixed automatically (see *CCR Ord. 17, r. 11*). The most important of these are as follows:

(a) In a debt action where the defendant has made an admission of *part* of the plaintiff's claim and this has not been accepted in full and final settlement.

(b) In cases commenced by originating application in which a pre-trial review is expressly provided for by the rules.

(c) In third party proceedings.

(d) In any other case in which a pre-trial review is required by the District Judge.

21.2.2 TYPES OF AUTOMATIC DIRECTIONS

Whereas the only actions in the High Court where automatic directions apply are personal injury actions (see **13.2**), in the county court (subject to the exceptions referred to above) there are automatic directions in almost all cases. Automatic directions take effect upon the close of pleadings which, as in the High Court, is deemed to be 14 days after the delivery of the defence, or, if a counterclaim is served with the defence, 28 days after the delivery of the defence. The following are the automatic directions in the county court.

21.2.2.1 Automatic directions applying generally

(a) There shall be discovery of documents within 28 days, and inspection within a further seven days. Where liability is admitted, discovery is limited to disclosure of any documents relating to damages.

(b) Except with the leave of the court or where all parties agree:

(i) no expert evidence may be adduced at the trial unless the substance of that evidence has been disclosed to the other parties in the form of a written report within 10 weeks;

(ii) the number of expert witnesses of any kind shall be limited to two;

(iii) a party intending to adduce any other (i.e. non-expert) oral evidence shall within 10 weeks serve on the other parties written statements of all such oral evidence. If more than one party is intending to call non-expert evidence, the written statements must be exchanged simultaneously.

(c) Photographs and sketch plans shall be receivable in evidence at the trial and should be agreed if possible.

(d) Unless the hearing date has already been fixed the plaintiff must within six months ask the court to fix a date. The plaintiff must give an estimate of the length of trial (agreed by all parties if possible) and the number of witnesses. If no request for trial is made within 15 months (of close of pleadings) the action is automatically struck out.

(e) Nothing in the above shall prevent the court from giving of its own motion or on the application of any party such further or different directions or orders as may in the circumstances be appropriate, or prevent the making of an order for the transfer of the proceedings to the High Court or another county court.

21.2.2.2 Automatic directions in personal injury cases

In personal injury cases there are the following additional automatic directions:

(a) In road accident cases discovery is limited to disclosure of any documents relating to damages.

(b) The plaintiff does not have to serve a further medical report if he is going to rely at the trial only on the medical report served with the particulars of claim. If a further medical report is disclosed it must be accompanied by a (updated) statement of special damages claimed.

(c) The number of expert witnesses is limited in any case to two medical experts and one expert of any other kind.

(d) The contents of any police accident report book shall be receivable in evidence at the trial and shall be agreed if possible.

21.2.3 AUTOMATIC STRIKING OUT

It will be seen that many of the directions set out above closely correspond to those available in personal injury cases in the High Court. The most important difference is the Draconian penalty prescribed for a plaintiff in the county court who fails to apply for a hearing date within the prescribed time. In such a case, without any application being necessary by the defendant and with no prior warning to the plaintiff, the court will automatically strike out any action if 15 months have gone by since the close of pleadings (*CCR Ord. 17, r. 11(9)*). At the time of writing many county courts are overlooking this provision, but the increasing computerisation of county court records means that in due course it will become very easy for the court to identify such cases.

It is important to consider whether such a striking out order is final, or whether there will be any possibility to restore an action in such a situation. The rule itself makes no provision for a case being restored, and on the face of it is as final as it sounds. It may be possible, however, to apply to restore such a case under the general authority of *CCR Ord. 13, r. 4*. This provides:

> *(1) Except as otherwise provided, the period within which a person is required or authorised by these rules or by any judgment, order or direction to do any act in any proceedings may be extended or abridged by consent of all the parties or by the court on the application of any party.*
> *(2) Any such period may be extended by the court although the application for extension is not made until after the expiration of the period.*

The uncertainty which had prevailed for two years since the coming into force of the rules concerning automatic striking out has finally been laid to rest by a Court of Appeal case, *Rastin v British Steel plc* [1994] 1 WLR 732.

In this case the Court of Appeal reviewed the jurisdiction to reinstate an action which had been automatically struck out under *Ord. 17, r. 11(9)* of the *County Court Rules 1991* because of the plaintiff's failure to request the fixing of a hearing date.

The court did not proceed simply on the basis of whether the delay had caused prejudice to the defendant. Rather, the court found that *r. 11(9)* was intended to have a Draconian nature in setting a fixed timetable for litigants, particularly plaintiffs, and decided that a county court should not exercise its discretion in favour of reinstatement of an action unless a plaintiff was able to show, as a threshold requirement, that, apart from the non-compliance with the rule about setting down, he had overall conducted his case with reasonable diligence. Only if he discharged that burden would the court go on to consider other matters including the interests of justice generally, prejudice to the defendant and the like.

The Court of Appeal indicated that the time limits were relatively generous. Initially a plaintiff was in fact required to set the action down within six months of the close of pleadings and the 15-month period referred to in the rule was a generous prima facie maximum. The court concluded that an application to extend the time for setting down should be made, if the plaintiff's solicitor was diligent, within the 15-month period so that he still had an opportunity to set down if that application for extension was refused. Where an application was made retrospectively *after* the expiry of the 15 months he would have to satisfy a stricter test. His failure to comply with the rules would never be justifiable but he could, in all the circumstances, persuade the court that it might be excusable if he could show that, had he sought an extension of time before the expiry of the 15 months, it would in all probability have been granted. Everything would depend upon the plaintiff's diligence in the conduct of the case hitherto although that did not mean that there had to be no room to criticise any aspect of his conduct of the case. Any prejudice suffered by the defendant would be a very powerful and usually a conclusive reason for not exercising discretion in the plaintiff's favour.

Though the decision in *Rastin* provides a clear statement of principle and guidelines, a variety of procedural conundra arose as to the possibilities of re-instatement after automatic striking out. In particular, there were difficulties with:

(a) computation of the precise date for commencement of the timetable fixed by automatic directions;

(b) questions of what the position was if the court itself was mistaken in informing the plaintiff of the precise date of commencement of the timetable for automatic directions;

(c) what the position was where there were two or more defendants and when the 15-month time limit expired in such a case;

(d) what was to happen if, negligently, the court did not forward a copy of the defence to the plaintiff so that he was unaware of the timetable's precise starting date;

(e) what the position was where the plaintiff had applied to the court for an extension of the time for setting down but there was no opportunity for that application to be heard until just after the expiry of the 15-month period;

(f) whether, if an action were struck out under the 15-month rule but the plaintiff was still within the primary limitation period, a second action could be commenced, and if so, subject to what terms

and many more.

Applications to re-instate an action that is prima facie struck out are made intially to a District Judge. These are likely to be fully argued, with lengthy affidavits setting out in detail everything that the plaintiff has done, or failed to do, and the reasons or excuses for failure to set down within the 15-month period. Such applications might quite commonly take two hours or more to hear. Whatever the outcome of that application, since clearly a great deal turns on it, either party might then appeal, as they have the right to do, to a Circuit Judge sitting in chambers. Thereafter either party might appeal further to the Court of Appeal.

Even though appeals to the Court of Appeal obviously represent only the tip of the iceberg of such 'satellite litigation' there were said to be well in excess of 1,000 cases pending before the Court of Appeal from summer 1995 onwards. Eventually, a number of test cases dealing with particular areas of principle were taken by the Court of Appeal over the course of several days just before Christmas 1995. The outcomes are reported at [1996] 1 WLR 571. Even that lengthy set of authorities, however, did not conclusively decide some of the many problems arising under automatic striking out. A further set of authoritative judgments has been delivered by the Court of Appeal, presently reported in *The Times*, 2 May 1977, under the title *In re Order 17 rule 11 of the County Court Rules; Bannister* v *SGB plc* and related appeals. Whilst this is further authoritative guidance, it by no means resolves all outstanding matters of difficulty and, despite the legal principles enunciated, there is of course a good deal of room for dispute as to whether the facts of any given case provide a reasonable excuse for missing the 15-month period. The Court of Appeal noted with approval that because of the difficulties of *Ord. 17 r. 11* a number of county courts had decided to issue their own separate sets of rules under local practice directions and these often had the effect of avoiding all the difficulties of automatic striking out by fixing a set date of trial, sometimes in the distant future, immediately upon receipt of a defence and a timetable for both parties to work towards that hearing date.

These resolve a number of the areas of difficulty and establish further guidelines as to when it will be right for the court to permit a plaintiff to re-instate an action even after it has been struck out and provide several glosses on the principles in *Rastin's* case. Extremely important though this is, not only for the profession, given the number of cases which were pending, but also for the solicitors' indemnity fund in view of the potential negligence implications where a plaintiff's solicitor had a case automatically struck out, a full discussion of the various procedural alternatives is beyond the scope of this text. It is however vitally important to note that the court will continue to apply a draconian test of 'due diligence in conduct of the action' to plaintiffs before they are likely to have any chance of having the action re-instated.

It follows that when acting for plaintiffs (and although most of the leading cases appear to be personal injury cases, there are other cases where a plaintiff is likely to get into this kind of trouble), solicitors must ensure that they collect their evidence and are as thoroughly organised as possible before the issue and service of proceedings. This will ensure that they are not taken aback by finding, for example, that the expert witness of their choice can only give them an appointment nearly a year into the future thus putting them badly behind with the automatic directions timetable.

Once an action is issued the key dates must be diarised, preferably on computer as well as manually, and cases kept under constant review. This applies to interlocutory steps such as discovery and exchange of witness statements and experts' reports as well as to the crucial 15-month date. If it is likely that an extension of time is needed, then it is vital to apply well in advance of the expiry of the 15 months and to be able at that stage to show that one has conducted proceedings with appropriate diligence and that the reasons for the delay are sensible and do not denote sloppiness or an oversight on the part of the plaintiff's solicitor.

The best possible advice for coping with the 15-month rule is never to need to be in the position of applying to reinstate an action automatically struck out and always to be on top of time limits to ensure that they are complied with, as difficult as this may be. Some District Judges will give time extensions quite liberally, recognising the harshness of the Rules and also on occasions, it must be said, the impractical nature of the relatively short times in the Rules for dealing with what may be quite complex cases (bearing in mind that personal injury cases involving up to £50,000 are likely to be in the county court). Others provide a much more demanding test and one can never rely on an extension being granted.

21.2.4 DEFAULT IN COMPLYING WITH OTHER PARTS OF THE AUTOMATIC DIRECTIONS

As indicated above, where there has been failure to set down within the 15-month period, the remedy is relatively drastic and reinstatement will only be permitted subject to the criteria in *Rastin*. Another question which has given rise to a great deal of litigation has been the effect of the failure by either party, usually the plaintiff, to comply with the various dates for other steps in the action before setting down, in particular for exchange of witness statements, or experts reports, or discovery. There was again a good deal of case law demonstrating that some individual county courts required very good reason before, for instance, a plaintiff who had failed to serve his witness statements in time would be permitted any extension of time to do so. In one particular case, although on peculiar facts, the Court of Appeal concluded that a plaintiff who had failed to serve certain witness statements at the proper time should not be given permission to serve them late and should not be permitted to call those witnesses at trial. A rather more liberal regime however is now in operation following the leading case of *The Mortgage Corporation* v *Sandoes, The Times*, 27 December 1996 which held that, in general, unless there was great difficulty caused by a party missing a key date within the automatic directions timetable, such that for example there would need to be an adjournment of a pending trial, the parties should be required to cooperate reasonably with each other so as to agree amended timetables for fulfilling any of the other procedural requirements and that a party should not be entitled to take advantage of an opponent's inability to comply exactly with the timetable, so long as no prejudice was caused. If the parties were unable to agree on a revised timetable then an application to the court should be made to fix a different timetable and the court would look sympathetically on such a request.

21.2.5 APPLICATION TO THE COURT FOR DIRECTIONS

Automatic directions are by their nature routine provisions only, intended to cover the run of the mill case in tort and contract which is likely to be ready for trial within about six months of the close of pleadings. It is at this point that both parties should consider whether the automatic directions are, in fact, appropriate for the case, or whether some further or alternative directions should be sought. As in the High Court, if either of the parties does not wish to comply with the automatic directions, or wants further or different directions, then he may apply to the court (*CCR Ord. 17*). There may be a number of reasons why the automatic directions need varying, e.g. further and better particulars of pleadings may be required, or extra time needed within which to obtain and disclose expert evidence, or an order for a split trial required.

If in a particular case some variation is required, the party should first seek to agree it with his opponent. If it can be agreed, a simple application can be made by post or *ex parte* for an order by consent. Only if agreement cannot be reached should an application be made on notice to the District Judge. If, whether by consent or by order after a hearing, a particular direction is made, the automatic directions will still apply but will take effect subject to the further or other directions specifically made.

21.3 Pre-trial Review

As mentioned at **21.2.1** above, *pre-trial reviews* are held in cases where the automatic directions do not apply, in certain cases commenced by originating application, and in cases where the District Judge considers a pre-trial review necessary. In particular, a pre-trial review may be held at the end of an application for summary judgment where leave to defend is given, or where there has been an application for an interim payment, whether an interim payment has been awarded or not. (See *CCR Ord. 17.*)

21.3.1 CONDUCT OF PRE-TRIAL REVIEW

The pre-trial review corresponds to the directions stage in a High Court action. The District Judge is similarly under a duty to consider the course of the proceedings and give all appropriate directions. He must endeavour to secure that the parties make such agreements and admissions as are appropriate. Every party must, so far as is practicable, apply for any direction required on a pre-trial review, so that further interlocutory hearings for directions are not necessary.

A party intending to raise any matter or seek any direction should notify the parties and the court of his intention to do so prior to the hearing date. Often the parties can agree all directions which they consider appropriate, and if this is the case, one party (usually the plaintiff) will draw up an agreed order and send it to the court. Provided the District Judge considers the order to be appropriate in all the circumstances, then he will make the order which will be served by the court.

All the considerations already discussed in the context of the summons for directions will apply. The District Judge is required to give directions as to the date of trial, and in most cases the order made simply duplicates the automatic direction as to date for trial.

21.3.2 NON-APPEARANCE AT THE PRE-TRIAL REVIEW

If the *plaintiff* fails to appear at the pre-trial review the review is usually adjourned and an order for costs made against him, since it is likely in such a case that it has been mere oversight. Where a *defendant* fails to appear then the District Judge has a wide discretion and will assess all aspects of the case. He may strike out the defence and give judgment for the plaintiff. This will only be interlocutory judgment on liability unless the plaintiff is in a position to prove his damages, in which case judgment may then be final. Alternatively, the judge may adjourn the pre-trial review, or give directions for trial in the absence of the defendant depending on the nature of the case, his assessment of the true issues, and any application that the plaintiff makes.

21.4 Interlocutory Applications

We now turn to some of the most commonly used interlocutory matters and applications in order to indicate the extent to which procedures in the county court are substantially the same as, or differ from, those in the High Court.

21.4.1 DISCOVERY (*CCR ORD. 14*)

Discovery means precisely the same as in the High Court. As noted at **21.2.2.1**, the requirement for discovery now forms part of the automatic directions. Discovery is by list which is in the same form as in the High Court; and if there is some dispute over discovery, the matter will be determined by the court in the same way as in the High Court. The court can make orders for particular discovery, determine disputes as to the existence or otherwise of privilege, and make 'unless' orders requiring a party in default to comply if there is some failure to comply with the original order.

In personal injury cases, pre-trial discovery and inspection and non-party discovery and inspection are available under *CCR Ord. 13, r. 7*, just as in the High Court.

21.4.2 INSPECTION, ETC. OF PROPERTY (*CCR ORD. 13, R. 7*)

Pre-action inspection, etc. of property in the possession of an opponent is obtainable in the county court in precisely the same way as in the High Court, as is inspection, etc. of property in the possession of a non-party after issue of proceedings.

21.4.3 INTERIM PAYMENTS (*CCR ORD. 13, R. 12*)

Interim payments may be claimed in the county court in any cases except those referred to arbitration (see **21.9**). The procedure is the same as in the High Court, except that not less than seven days' notice must be given before the hearing (10 days in the High Court). Otherwise the provisions and criteria relevant to an application for interim payments are the same as in the High Court.

It is worth repeating here two matters of particular concern to the plaintiff: first, that whether an interim payment is made voluntarily or under an order of the court, the recoupment of benefit rules will apply (see **1.2.1.4**), and in calculating the amount to ask for the plaintiff should take into account the amount the defendant is likely to deduct to pay to the DSS Compensation Recovery Unit; and, secondly, that if the plaintiff is legally aided, the interim payment is free from the statutory charge and can be paid direct to the plaintiff.

21.4.4 PAYMENT INTO COURT (*CCR ORD. 11*)

The rules applicable in the High Court in relation to payments into court are applicable in the county court (see **16.1**). If the plaintiff declines to accept the money it remains on deposit in the county court, is kept secret from the trial judge until all questions of liability and quantum have been determined, and thereafter orders for costs follow in the same way as in the High Court.

In the county court, as in the High Court, if the plaintiff wishes to accept money paid into court after the 21-day period, he may do so only with leave of the court and after an appropriate order dealing with costs since the date of payment in has been made. The same provisions with regard to recoupment of benefit rules applies in the High Court, so that a notice of payment into court must specify the amount withheld from damages in respect of recoupment of benefits.

21.4.5 *CALDERBANK* OFFERS (*CCR ORD. 11, R. 10*)

The *County Court Rules* make similar provision to the High Court rules in relation to *Calderbank* offers. Where the claim is not one for pure payment of money, the rules provide that effect may be given to any offer made 'without prejudice save as to costs'. Unlike in the High Court, a party making such an offer must file a copy of the offer in court in a sealed envelope which is not to be brought to the attention of the judge until the question of costs falls to be decided.

21.4.6 THIRD PARTY PROCEEDINGS (*CCR ORD. 12*)

The situations in which third party proceedings may be used are the same as in the High Court, i.e. where a defendant wishes to claim against someone who is not a party in the action for any contribution, indemnity or other relief or remedy relating to or connected with the original subject matter of the action. The procedure, however, does differ slightly. In the High Court it is possible for a defendant to issue a third party notice without leave of the court, provided it is done before his defence has been served (in principle no less than 28 days from the date of service of the writ). In the county court the requirement to serve a defence arises much earlier and the provisions are different. No leave to issue the third party notice is required provided a date has not been fixed for a pre-trial review or before pleadings are deemed to be closed. When a third party notice is issued by the defendant the court will give a date for a pre-trial review in the third party proceedings and this will be endorsed on the third party notice itself. This is unlike the High Court procedure where it is up to the third party to file an acknowledgement of service (to which there is no county court equivalent) and only then would the defendant need to issue a summons for third party directions.

The third party notice must be served on the third party together with a copy of the summons and particulars of claim filed. A copy of the third party notice must also be served on the plaintiff. Once a third party notice is issued, the plaintiff is prevented from entering judgment in default and there must be a pre-trial review. The third party should file a defence in court, however, within 14 days of the service of the third party notice. If he defaults the court will order him to file it at the pre-trial review.

In circumstances where leave is necessary the application must be made by the defendant on notice to the plaintiff so that the plaintiff has the opportunity to attend and make his preliminary objections (e.g. that the application is made so late in the day that his own case is prejudiced). At the hearing of that application the court, if it grants leave, will give directions as to service of the third party notice and the further conduct of the proceedings. There will inevitably be a third party pre-trial review at which all parties will then come before the court so that a similar kind of tidying up operation can take place to that already described in relation to the same stage in the High Court (see **18.1.4**). The District Judge will consider, for example, whether the third party should file further pleadings, be added as a defendant, or even take over the defendant's case, as in examples previously given in the section on High Court procedure. If the third party fails to attend the trial, whether or not he has filed a defence, he is deemed to admit the third party claim against him.

21.4.7 COMPROMISE OF CLAIM OF PERSONS UNDER A DISABILITY (*CCR ORD. 10*)

As in the High Court, approval of the court must be given for a settlement of the claim of an infant or a mental patient once proceedings have been commenced in the county court, and the procedure is equivalent to that in the High Court (see **19.8.7**). If approval is sought where proceedings have not been commenced, an originating application will be made.

21.5 Setting Down for Trial

Setting down for trial in the county court is a much less formal process than in the High Court. There is no need to file bundles of documents, as the court file will already contain copies of most of the documents in question and others are filed at a later stage; nor is there need to file a statement as to readiness. The automatic directions simply provide that the plaintiff should apply (a letter will usually be acceptable) giving an estimate of the length of trial and the number of witnesses to be called and paying the fee (currently £50). It is usually courteous to check with the defendant that he has no objection to the application being made because of justifiable unreadiness on his part. There are no 'running lists' of cases awaiting trial as in the High Court, and in the county court all cases are given a fixed date with at least 21 days' notice. Unfortunately this is not in itself a guarantee that a case will be heard on the date on which it is first listed, since often there are more cases listed than the court has time to deal with. If the case has to be adjourned in those circumstances, the court usually makes considerable efforts to ensure that the next date will be effective.

In some cases the court office will fix a date for hearing without waiting for a request to do so. These are:

(a) actions in which the trial date is usually fixed at the time of commencement, such as for recovery of land;

(b) in cases where a pre-trial review is held, where the District Judge is required to fix a date and give notice thereof to the parties immediately upon the completion of the pre-trial review or as soon as practicable thereafter (unless some alternative form direction is made, e.g. a direction duplicating the automatic directions as to fixing date of trial).

21.6 Preparations for Trial in the County Court

21.6.1 INTRODUCTION

There is little to add to the discussions of the appropriate preparations for trial in the High Court. All the same tactical considerations apply. The procedures for serving Civil Evidence Act 1968 notices, notices to admit, the rules relating to expert and non-expert evidence, the desirability to obtain counsel's advice on evidence and so on are all the same.

One difference of terminology which should be noted is that what is called a 'subpoena' in the High Court is called a 'witness summons' in the county court. The party requiring the witness summons files a request for the issue of the summons, and may request that the summons is served by the court bailiff, in which case conduct money must be left at the court to give to the witness when the summons is served. As the date for trial will normally be fixed, it is usually possible for the summons to state where and when the witness is to attend, unlike a High Court subpoena which will usually be served before the trial date is known. The witness summons may specify whether the witness is to give evidence orally, or that he is required to bring some document with him, or both.

21.6.2 LODGING BUNDLES OF DOCUMENTS

As in the High Court, there are rules requiring the plaintiff to prepare and lodge at court copies of all documents intended to be used or referred to at trial by either the plaintiff or the defendant, obliging the defendant to give the plaintiff advance notice of his requirements, and obliging both parties to agree certain documents (witness statements and expert reports) where possible. In the county court the defendant must contact the plaintiff 14 days before the date fixed for the hearing and must identify to the plaintiff those documents which he wishes to be included in the bundle. The plaintiff must then prepare and lodge a paginated and indexed bundle comprising the documents which either party wishes to have before the court. The plaintiff is also required, at least seven days before the trial, to file two further bundles, each containing documents which in a High Court case would be included either in the bundles lodged on setting down, or in the bundles lodged two days before the trial, i.e.:

(a) any request for particulars and particulars given, and any answers to interrogatories;

(b) witness statements which have been exchanged and experts' reports which have been disclosed, together with an indication of whether the contents of such documents are agreed;

(c) if one or more of the parties is legally aided, any notice of issue of certificate served and any notices of amendment.

The District Judge has the same power as in High Court cases to give different directions as to the documents to be lodged.

It should be noted that bundles of documents (including witness statements) do not have to be lodged in cases which are subject neither to automatic directions, nor to directions made at a pre-trial review, e.g. actions for the recovery of land, or other actions or matters which from commencement proceed directly to trial.

21.7 The Trial

21.7.1 REPRESENTATION IN THE COUNTY COURT

The most obvious difference between High Court and county court trials remains the restriction imposed on solicitors' rights of audience in High Court trials. In the county court, solicitors have full and unrestricted rights of audience and may conduct trials as advocates without the necessity of briefing counsel.

21.7.2 CONDUCT OF THE TRIAL

Trial in the county court is broadly the same in terms of order of speeches, etc. as in the High Court. Judges in the county court have the same rights as in the High Court to give directions as to which party should speak first, the order of speeches and, in cases where there is no jury, to dispense with opening speeches altogether. The conduct of county court trials where no directions of the type mentioned above have been made, is the same as previously described in relation to the High Court.

Unlike the High Court, however, the atmosphere in the county court may be relatively informal, and it should be noted that there is no shorthand writer present though the proceedings are recorded. It is important to ensure that a full note of the evidence is taken, particularly if there is likely to be an appeal.

The Lord Chief Justice's *Practice Direction (Civil Litigation: Case Management)* set out at **14.6.4** applies only to High Court trials. There is no doubt, however, that county court judges are likely to have regard to the spirit of it when exercising their discretion to run trials before them with the maximum of efficiency consistent with justice, so that they may, for example, dispense with evidence in chief as in the High Court.

21.7.3 COSTS AND JUDGMENT DEBTS

When the judge has delivered his judgment he will be asked to make an order as to costs. He will specify the relevant scale of costs (see **21.8**), and may certify that on taxation the District Judge will not be bound by the amounts appearing on that scale.

In the county court payment of any sums awarded by the judge is normally to be made within 14 days from the date of the judgment (although the order may specify a different time). It is not uncommon for the losing party to ask the judge to make an order for payment by instalments. He is usually required to go into the witness-box and give details of his means on oath. Whether or not an order is made for payment by instalments, a subsequent application can be made by the judgment debtor (usually to the District Judge) requesting an order varying the method of payment, e.g. asking for payment by instalments or by lesser instalments than previously ordered. Equally, the judgment creditor can re-apply for an increase in the rate of instalments if the debtor's means increase.

21.7.4 DRAWING UP JUDGMENTS

In the High Court it is the successful party who is responsible for drawing up the judgment and entering it in the books of the court. In the county court, strictly it is for the court to draw up the judgment. There are prescribed forms of judgment in the 'Green Book' and, if the order made can be suitably recorded on one of these prescribed forms this will be done by the court staff. If there is no appropriate prescribed form, the court staff will ask the successful party's solicitor to draw up the judgment as he would have to do in a High Court case.

21.8 Costs

21.8.1 THE SCALE OF COSTS

In the High Court, although there is a 'scale of costs' this scale simply relates to the format in which the final bill must be drawn up for taxation (see **22.3.3**). In the county court, however, there are three scales of costs, the importance of which will be considered below.

The relevant material on costs and fees is set out in Part III of the 'Green Book' at the very end. The relevant rule is *Ord. 38*, and this provides in the main that precisely the same interlocutory and final orders for costs are available as in the High Court; that the same basis of taxation applies in most litigation; and that the same discretions are available to the court. However, the costs recoverable from an opponent depend on the scale applicable, and these scales relate to the amount of money recovered by the plaintiff, or, if the defendant is successful, the amount originally claimed in the action by the plaintiff. The scales are as follows:

Exceeding £25 but not exceeding £100	Lower scale
Exceeding £100 but not exceeding £3,000	Scale 1
Exceeding £3,000	Scale 2

21.8.1.1 'Lower scale'

It will be observed that this scale is of minimal significance in litigation. Few persons would try to employ lawyers on a claim involving £100. Where such amounts are recovered the maximum amount recoverable for costs is fixed in *Appendix C* to the *County Court Rules*. As will be imagined, the amounts are decidedly modest.

21.8.1.2 Scale 1

On Scale 1 (claims between £100 and £3,000) the amount recoverable is determined in accordance with *Appendix A* to the *County Court Rules*. This Appendix provides maxima not merely for the whole of the work done by a solicitor in an action, but for many of the individual interlocutory stages. These maxima are far from generous. Thus there may be a considerable shortfall in this form of county court litigation between the amounts recoverable from the losing opponent and those which a client will be obliged to pay on a solicitor and client basis. It is very important to warn a client of this when undertaking county court litigation for under £3,000. The trial judge, and the District Judge at interlocutory stages, and indeed at the taxation of costs, does have the power to authorise the prescribed maxima to be exceeded on good cause being shown.

Although Scale 1 does cover sums of between £100 and £3,000, it will be borne in mind that where the amount involved is less than £3,000 the provisions as to arbitration considered below at **21.9** may well come into play, unless for one of the reasons specified a reference to arbitration is rescinded so that the action remains in the ordinary court system. If the case is referred to arbitration the amounts recoverable will usually be only the modest amount of fixed costs (see **21.9**).

21.8.1.3 Scale 2

On Scale 2 there is no problem, because Scale 2 is expressed to be precisely the same as that applicable in the High Court. Thus, on Scale 2, where sums of over £3,000 are involved, the court has an unlimited discretion on costs and is not bound by any maxima.

21.8.1.4 Discretion of the court as to costs

Where the action is not one for money, e.g. for an injunction, the costs applicable are entirely within the discretion of the court.

21.8.2 FIXED COSTS

There are Appendices to the *County Court Rules* in which various sums are given for fixed costs for county court actions. These are applied at much the same stages at which fixed costs are awarded in High Court cases, in particular in debt or liquidated demand cases which finish very early, whether by judgment in default or summary judgment. The figure given is the figure for solicitors' costs, to which is added the amount of the court fee payable on the county court summons. In such cases this is all that the plaintiff's solicitor will recover. (For High Court procedure, see **22.7**.)

21.9 References to Arbitration

21.9.1 THE 'SMALL CLAIMS PROCEDURE'

So far we have considered the course of a county court action for a debt or damages, or for non-monetary relief. There is, however, a special form which such proceedings may take where the action is brought for a sum of less than £3,000 or, in personal injury cases only,

£1,000 and a defence is filed. In such a case the action is automatically referred to arbitration (*CCR Ord. 19, r. 2*). This is what the layman describes as 'the small claims court', although the court itself is simply the ordinary county court. It would be more accurate to call this the 'small claims procedure'.

Once the defence is received in such a case the District Judge is likely to deal with it by arbitration. The rules do, exceptionally, provide that he may appoint some outside arbitrator to deal with it (e.g. an expert in the field to which the complaint relates) or refer it to the Circuit Judge, but in the overwhelming majority of cases such actions, however technical the subject matter, remain before the District Judge himself.

21.9.2 RESCINDING THE REFERENCE TO ARBITRATION

The District Judge may, either on the application of any party or of his own motion, decide to rescind the reference to arbitration and send the case back into the ordinary court procedure if he is satisfied either:

(a) that a difficult question of law or a question of fact of complexity is involved; or

(b) that a charge of fraud is in issue; or

(c) that the parties are agreed that the dispute should be tried in court; or

(d) that it would be unreasonable for the claim to proceed to arbitration having regard to its subject matter, the size of any counterclaim, circumstances of the parties or the interests of any other person likely to be affected by the award.

21.9.3 PRELIMINARY CONSIDERATION AND THE HEARING

21.9.3.1 Preliminary consideration

The District Judge will consider whether he needs to hold any *preliminary consideration* (which is in the nature of a pre-trial review). If he thinks it unnecessary or undesirable, he will simply appoint a date for the hearing of the arbitration, giving any appropriate direction, e.g. as to discovery or exchange of witness statements.

If there is a preliminary appointment he will give directions appropriately after hearing the representations of the parties.

21.9.3.2 The hearing and costs

At the hearing of the arbitration itself, the procedure is informal and the strict rules of evidence do not apply. The arbitrator may adopt any method of procedure which he considers to be convenient and fair.

In claims involving £3,000 or less no solicitor's charges are allowed as between party and party except:

(a) the costs which were stated on the summons, or which would have been stated on the summons if the claim had been for a liquidated sum;

(b) the costs of enforcing the award;

(c) such further costs as the arbitrator may direct where there has been unreasonable conduct on the part of the opposite party in relation to the proceedings or the claim.

21.9.4 HOW EFFECTIVE IS THE PROCEDURE?

This procedure, then, is meant to be one designed to help resolve disputes, especially consumer-type disputes, between unrepresented litigants. The procedure is informal and will usually be run by the District Judge in a relatively inquisitorial manner, in which he will seek to get at the truth whilst assisting both of the unrepresented parties before him by guiding them as to the facts they might wish to adduce and any matters of law that arise. That anyway is the principle. Unfortunately it remains true that many people will need legal assistance even to get things as far as the reference to arbitration, for example in obtaining preliminary advice about the claim, writing letters in an attempt to resolve matters without litigation, and lodging the summons and particulars of claim and then knowing how to respond, say, to any fixing of a preliminary appointment by the District Judge. (It may be that some of this advice can be given on the Green Form, although the solicitor must not, of course, get on the record in the court proceedings. Nonetheless, he could use the Green Form time for drafting the documents for the plaintiff.)

Whilst the District Judge will do his best at the arbitration to ensure that the truth comes out and that justice is done, a tongue-tied and nervous party may nonetheless be severely handicapped notwithstanding the relaxation of the rules of evidence and the informality of the procedure. This is especially likely to be the case where the plaintiff is a consumer bringing some complaint against a large company which has an in-house legal department, a member of which will most certainly attend the hearing and take all proper tactical and legal points. Unfortunately, the rule prohibiting the District Judge from awarding costs beyond the modest sum of fixed costs stated on the summons means that it will be uneconomic for most plaintiffs in such a situation to employ a lawyer, because the costs of running the action, however efficiently, are likely to outweigh most of the benefit obtained. Unless the District Judge can be persuaded (and success in this is rare) to treat the defendant's conduct in defending the claim at all as unreasonable so as to obtain a greater award of costs (e.g. costs to be taxed in the usual way), then the usual advice to a would-be litigant in such situations is that it is uneconomic to employ a lawyer to pursue the matter.

21.9.5 PERSONAL INJURY CLAIMS AND ARBITRATION

Until January 1996 the limit for arbitration proceedings in all kinds of claims was £1,000 — above that, cases went into the ordinary court system. Despite a good deal of opposition from the legal profession the upper limit for arbitrations was increased to £3,000 with effect from January 1996. The opponents of such an increase contended that sums of £3,000 were very significant amounts to a large part of the population and that because of the 'no costs' rule it would be costly for people to employ lawyers to put their claims whereas especially when faced with large bodies, insurance companies and the like, their opponents would often be legally represented. Moreover, although there is no actual rule forbidding legal aid to be granted in arbitration cases, most area offices will consider it unreasonable simply because as no eventual award of costs will be made, even if the plaintiff is successful, the legal aid fund will be put at too great a risk should the plaintiff lose. Should the plaintiff win then most, if not all, of any award would be swallowed up on repaying the legal aid fund's charge from damages recovered.

There was, however, some success from the lobby that argued against an increase in arbitration limits in the case of personal injury claims where the upper limit was left at £1,000. It seems to have been accepted that even in the case of relatively modest accidents involving, say, a broken finger and a month off work, it would be difficult for most unrepresented plaintiffs adequately to prepare their cases, and obtain the necessary medical and technical evidence. Consequently, if one is prepared to certify that the personal injury element of a claim is worth more than £1,000 there will be no reference to arbitration and the case will continue in the ordinary court system.

21.9.6 OTHER ARBITRATIONS

The rules also permit a District Judge himself to refer other cases to arbitration. In cases of over £3,000 in value it might occur to the parties that it is better to have the matter litigated quickly and informally without the application of the strict rules of evidence. Where both parties consent to this arbitration this may be a useful option. Nonetheless, both parties must ensure that they are properly ready for trial and that the absence of formality does not become a pretext for sloppiness in calling evidence and having the facts available for the arbitrator in the correct form. Where arbitration in a case involving more than £3,000 is agreed between the parties, the District Judge has his full power to award costs in the usual way and is not restricted to the fixed costs on the summons as in the case of arbitrations involving less than that figure.

21.10 Comparison of High Court and County Court Procedures

A procedural chart follows, indicating the main differences between High Court and County Court procedure in the early stages.

Default/Writ Actions: Early Stages
Comparison of County Court and High Court Procedures

STAGE	COUNTY COURT	HIGH COURT
Place of issue	Any county court	RCJ or District Registry
Application by	Request for issue	Producing relevant documents
Form	Summons	Writ
Completed by	Court/Plaintiff	Plaintiff
Plaintiff's receipt	Plaint note	Original of writ
Service by	Court/Plaintiff	Plaintiff
Method of service	By court: 1st Class post — if this fails bailiff. By plaintiff's solicitor: personal service only (except in personal injury cases)	1st class post or insertion in letterbox or personal service
Form accompanying	Admission Defence and Counterclaim	Acknowledgement of Service
Time of response	14 days	14 days
No response by Defendant: Judgment in default	Apply by request	Prove service Lodge form for judgment to be entered
Defendant responds	Admission Defence and Counterclaim or Defence	Acknowledgement of Service stating intention to defend
Plaintiff receives from court	Copy Admission Defence and Counterclaim or Defence	Copy Acknowledgement of service

TWENTY TWO

TAXATION OF COSTS

We considered earlier one of the most important matters at the outset of any piece of litigation (see **2.1**). This is the need to establish firmly with one's own client the basis on which he will be required to pay for a solicitor's time and expertise. In non-litigation cases that is the end of the matter. The client will expect to pay proper charges and these will not be recoverable from anyone else. In litigation, however, there is the extra element that the loser is usually called upon to pay some element of the winner's costs, which may vary from the whole amount down to a relatively small proportion. It is now appropriate to discuss the nature of and procedure for *taxation of costs*, as assessment by the court is called.

22.1 Solicitor and Own Client Basis

Suppose that a client objects to his own solicitor's bill. This could occur where the party has lost the case and therefore is not to receive any other contribution towards his costs; or even where he has won the case and, after receiving the amount due from the opposing party, the client is dissatisfied with the shortfall between that amount and the amount he has had to pay his own solicitor. In that situation a client is entitled to have his own bill *taxed* — in other words, to call upon his solicitor to justify to the court every aspect of the charges made in it.

Where such a challenge is made the solicitor must draw up a formal bill, which might not otherwise be necessary, and obtain an appointment at court to have it taxed. (The method of preparing the bill and the procedure on taxation is discussed below.) At court the taxing officer will consider the bill on what is called the 'solicitor and own client basis'.

This basis provides that where the taxing officer is left in any doubt about the propriety of some item charged for, or the rate at which it is charged, the benefit of that doubt is to be given to the solicitor. In addition, the court has to bear the following points in mind:

(a) In so far as reasonableness is concerned, it is deemed reasonable to incur expenditure on items which the client has expressly or impliedly approved.

(b) Amounts incurred are reasonable if the client also approved these amounts in advance.

(c) It is, however, unreasonable to incur expenditure on unusual items unless the client was specifically warned in advance that those items might not be recoverable on a taxation from the losing party.

The taxing officer will delete or reduce those items which have been unreasonably claimed by the solicitor and an order will then be made that the client pay the balance to the solicitor.

22.2 *Inter Partes* Costs

Here we consider the more important situation of the procedure by which a winner recovers as much as possible of the legal costs from a loser.

22.2.1 THE COMPENSATORY PRINCIPLE

The English theory of damages in tort and contract is compensatory. It aims to put the aggrieved party in exactly the same position as he would have been but for the tort or breach of contract. Where this is a purely financial matter, as in the collection of a debt, the law can do precisely that. Where something not directly expressible in money terms happens, such as the infliction of personal injuries, then the law ensures the payment of financial compensation. The difficult problem is, however, that of the legal costs incurred by the innocent party in enforcing his or her legal rights. In strict theory the loser should be required to pay the whole of the winning party's legal costs, because otherwise the winning party is not in fact put in precisely the same position in which he would have been but for the tort or breach of contract because he will have had to expend some money of his own to enforce his right. In some jurisdictions it is actually the case that the loser must pay the whole of the winner's legal costs. In other jurisdictions, for example the United States, there is usually no order for costs between the parties and the lawyer for the winning party will recover his costs direct from his client often by a contingency fee arrangement.

In England and Wales the provision for the loser to pay the winner's costs is something of a compromise between these two extreme positions. However, it is fair to say that because of the way in which the winner's costs payable by the loser are now assessed, it will often be the case that the winner's costs will in fact be recovered in full if the litigation has been conducted in a reasonable and efficient manner.

22.2.2 CONVENTIONAL AND NEGOTIATED COSTS

In litigation there is no right to costs. Costs are always in the discretion of the court, but certain conventions have been established and will usually be followed. The principal convention is that costs 'follow the event', i.e. that the winner is usually entitled to an order that the loser should pay his costs. This will be the case where the matter has been litigated as far as trial. However, if the parties reach a negotiated settlement at an earlier stage it is usual for the party who is putting forward the compromise to agree to pay the other party's costs. Refusal to make this offer usually leads to a counter-refusal to accept the offer of compromise.

Litigation may, of course, be terminated with no requirement for either party to pay costs to his opponent, for example where a plaintiff sues a defendant who raises a counterclaim of an approximately equivalent amount and after a certain stage both parties realise that the costs of litigating outweigh the possible advantages. Each might agree to withdraw his claim and counterclaim on the basis that each pays his own costs.

22.3 Taxation

22.3.1 INTRODUCTION

As we discuss at **22.3.4.4**, at the end of the case where the loser has been ordered to pay the winner's costs, it will often be the position that the parties will try to agree what this figure should be. Very often this is possible. If, however, the parties cannot agree and the loser thinks that the winner's claim for costs is excessive, there is a further hearing in court where an officer of the court (in London called a Taxing Master and outside London a District Judge) assesses the bill of the winner and determines how much of it the loser should be required to pay. This process is known as 'taxation', though it has nothing to do with the Inland Revenue.

Where this process takes place the *taxing officer*, that is the person assessing the bill, will be trying to determine the amount which it is proper for the loser to have to pay the winner. In the High Court this depends on the basis of taxation that will be used. In the county court it will depend both on the basis of taxation and on the scale of costs fixed in the County Court Rules for the case.

22.3.2 BASES OF TAXATION

There are two bases of taxation:

(a) the standard basis; and

(b) the indemnity basis.

22.3.2.1 The standard basis

Where costs are ordered to be taxed on the standard basis, then, by *RSC Ord. 62, r. 12*:

> *. . . there shall be allowed a reasonable amount in respect of all costs reasonably incurred and any doubts which the taxing officer may have as to whether the costs were reasonably incurred or were reasonable in amount shall be resolved in favour of the paying party.*

The court will thus have to determine whether the sums claimed are for reasonable items (i.e. whether it is proper to charge for those items at all) and whether the amounts claimed for each item are reasonable.

(a) *What kind of items are likely to be attacked?*

It is open to the paying party (the loser) to challenge each and every item. One item to which there is commonly an objection is the amount of time spent interviewing and advising the plaintiff. It is a well-known fact that plaintiffs vary greatly in their degree of patience. Suppose that a plaintiff in a case called into his solicitor's office for a half-hour chat about the case every week over some months or years, even though nothing had happened on the case in the meantime. The solicitor naturally has to charge that amount of time to someone, and he will charge it at first to his own client. However, is it reasonable to require the loser to pay this sum? If the District Judge determines that the number of hours spent in attendance upon the plaintiff is excessive and serves no real purpose in the case, he is likely to disallow any such hours charged for. The outcome, of course, will be that any items disallowed as against the paying party (the loser) will have to be charged by the solicitor to his own client (the winner). Thus a solicitor must always remind a client who is unduly importunate in seeking appointments that he may himself have to pay for excessive time which has been spent to little purpose.

Another item often attacked is the amount of fees paid to counsel for advising throughout the case. Solicitors who are recently qualified (and perhaps do not have a great deal of assistance or supervision in the office) often seek counsel's advice as a case proceeds about matters on which a more experienced solicitor would not need to seek assistance. Thus at various stages counsel may be asked to advise about procedural options, tactics, quantum of damages, and so on. The loser may contend on taxation that a competent solicitor would not have needed to take counsel's advice so often, or at all. If the taxing officer agrees, those items will be struck off the bill.

(b) *The reasonableness of the amount*

Local factors are very important here. District Judges and Taxing Masters are well aware what are proper hourly charging rates for certain kinds of work in the locality, and rates may vary as between, say, London and the north of the country. So, if in routine High Court litigation in the area in question solicitors are being permitted to charge, say, £75 per hour and the present case is a routine one, if the solicitor is claiming £100 per hour his bill will be disallowed or 'taxed down' by a corresponding amount. Thus, if he had claimed that he had spent 20 hours on the client's case in respect of which he was claiming £100 per hour, i.e. £2,000, the District Judge would reduce this claim to the going rate of £75 per hour, i.e. £1,500.

(c) *Application of the standard basis*

The standard basis of taxation is applied in two routine situations:

(i) It is the basis on which the loser is required to pay the winner in ordinary litigation.

(ii) It is the basis on which, hitherto, the legal aid fund has paid an assisted person's solicitor. As to the situation in respect of legal aid certificates granted after 25 February 1994 however see below and **2.5**.

Thus in a routine case which has been efficiently conducted where the winner has legal aid, the legal aid fund charge ought not to take effect. Since the standard basis of taxation is to be applied, the losing party will be required to pay the winner's costs on exactly the same basis as the legal aid fund is required to pay the winner's solicitor's costs. If there is in fact no difference between the two (and usually the taxation process in respect of both will be carried out simultaneously) there is no need for the charge to come into operation; thus not only will the client get his damages untouched by any reduction but any contribution he has had to pay will also be returned to him.

Though this is common it is not inevitably the case. It may be, for example, that the costs of some particular part of the proceedings were not awarded against the other party (see notes on costs on interlocutory applications at **7.7**). Or it may be that a payment into court was rejected and the plaintiff failed to beat the payment into court (see **16.1.3**) so that a considerable proportion of the costs is eventually borne by the legally aided party. Nonetheless, in routine litigation it will now commonly be the case that the legally aided person's solicitor will recover the cost in full from the loser.

Where a legal aid certificate is granted after 25 February 1994 and the fees for the assisted person's solicitor are to be paid only by the legal aid fund (i.e., the plaintiff's solicitor has not recovered costs against any other party) then the *Legal Aid in Civil Proceedings (Remuneration) Regulations 1994* provide for fixed fees for some items of work and prescribed hourly rates for preparation, advocacy, travelling and waiting and attending with counsel (see **2.5**). There will still of course need to be a legal aid taxation and the court will need to be satisfied that, for example, the hours claimed were reasonable in nature and amount, and as to the number of letters properly written. In addition the court will often be asked to give its mind to the potential 'enhancement' whereby in certain cases the hourly rates prescribed can be increased by up to 100 per cent in the county court and up to 200 per cent in the High Court.

22.3.2.2 The indemnity basis

The indemnity basis is a more generous basis and provides that where any doubts about the propriety of charging some item arise in the case, the benefit of the doubt is to be given not to the paying party as in taxation on the standard basis, but to the party who is to receive the amount. This basis is only likely to be awarded where the loser's conduct has in some way been disapproved by the court. In negotiations between parties for settlement, however, it may be possible sometimes to insist on payment of costs on this basis. It is often thought particularly appropriate in the case of settling an action for defamation, and also when acting for an infant plaintiff.

22.3.2.3 Summary

Those are the two bases of taxation between the parties. It must be borne carefully in mind that in many cases they will amount to precisely the same. The difference between them only really bites where the taxing officer has a doubt about an individual item. If he is left in doubt as to the propriety of some part of a bill, then, in the case of the standard basis he exercises the benefit of that doubt in favour of the loser, i.e. he strikes the item off the bill; in taxation on the indemnity basis he exercises the benefit of the doubt in favour of the winner, i.e. he allows the item charged for.

22.3.3 SCALES OF COSTS

In the High Court there is only one scale of costs. This does not provide fixed amounts because in every case the amount to be allowed is within the discretion of the taxing officer; the scale merely dictates the form in which the bill should be drawn up. In the county court, however, there are three scales, the lower two of which provide certain fixed maxima for what is allowed no matter how much time has been expended as we have seen at **21.8**.

22.3.4 ADDITIONAL CONSIDERATIONS

22.3.4.1 Restriction on counsel's fees

The Rules provide that no costs are allowed on taxation in respect of counsel attending an interlocutory application before Master or District Judge, unless the Master or District Judge has certified the attendance as proper in the circumstances. In cases of any importance there is no great difficulty in getting this certificate, which should be applied for at the end of the interlocutory application. If the matter is a substantial one which requires detailed argument, for example an application for summary judgment in a case which is far from clear-cut, or an interim payment, or on complex matters relating to discovery or further and better particulars of pleadings, it is often appropriate to brief counsel, at least in the High Court. If the Master or District Judge at the end of the interlocutory hearing certifies that the application is 'fit for counsel', counsel's fees can be claimed from the opponent at the end of the whole case should the first party succeed. It must be borne in mind, however, that it is not appropriate to brief counsel on purely procedural applications because the certificate that the case was 'fit for counsel' will be refused.

22.3.4.2 Costs on a counterclaim

It must be remembered that a counterclaim need not have any direct relationship to the plaintiff's cause of action. Thus, for example, a plaintiff who sues for defamation may have a counterclaim for a previous debt made against him. If both parties succeed in the action, i.e. the plaintiff succeeds in his claim and the defendant in the counterclaim, then the usual form of order is that the plaintiff obtains costs on the claim and the defendant costs on the counterclaim. It is by no means always the case that these two will offset each other.

The defendant can recover only the costs of his counterclaim and not the costs of unsuccessfully defending the plaintiff's claim. Although it is easy to see if the claim and counterclaim have nothing to do with each other, what aspect of the work done relates to which, it may well be that claim and counterclaim arise out of the same incident (e.g. an accident where both parties are injured and each blames the other). In that case the costs of claim and counterclaim are considerably intermingled. For example, suppose the plaintiff who has suffered moderate injuries sues the defendant for damages arising out of a road traffic accident. The defendant has suffered very serious injuries in the same accident and counterclaims, contending it was the plaintiff's fault. At the trial the judge finds for the plaintiff but with a 25 per cent degree of contributory negligence on the plaintiff's part. In other words, the defendant has succeeded on his counterclaim to a limited extent, although in his case with a finding of 75 per cent contributory negligence. On these facts, if the extent of the plaintiff's injuries lead to an award of damages to him of £10,000, he will now receive £7,500. However, suppose that the defendant (who is seriously injured) would have been awarded £100,000. The finding of 75 per cent contributory negligence means he will actually get £25,000. There is then a difficult issue, i.e. who has won the case overall for the purpose of the issue of costs? The answer is that the court has the power to make a special judgment on the balance between the claim and counterclaim, and to make an appropriate order for costs within its discretion.

It is always important to ensure that you, or counsel, are fully prepared to argue these issues because there is a difficult precedent, *Medway Oil and Storage Co. Ltd* v *Continental Contractors Ltd* [1929] AC 88, which appears to say that in principle an order for costs on a counterclaim, even if arising out of the same facts as the plaintiff's claim, can relate only to costs incurred exclusively for the counterclaim. Thus in the example given above, only the costs of dealing with the defendant's quantum of damages would be allowable to the defendant and the whole costs of litigating the issue of liability would be awarded to the plaintiff. That would clearly wreak injustice and the Court of Appeal in *Millican* v *Tucker* [1980] 1 WLR 640 held that, despite the *Medway Oil* case, it was well within a judge's discretion to order the apportionment of the costs of claim and counterclaim in any appropriate way.

22.3.4.3 Two or more defendants

As we have already discussed at **6.1.4**, where the plaintiff succeeds against only one of several defendants the court has to protect the successful defendant. This is done by an order that the losing defendant in effect pays everybody's costs, either by the mechanism of a *Bullock* order, whereby the plaintiff pays the winning defendant but then recovers those costs from the unsuccessful defendant; or by a *Sanderson* order, where the losing defendant pays the successful defendant's costs direct. It is suggested that a *Sanderson* order is a neater and more appropriate way to bring the litigation to an end, especially in cases where all defendants are insured and so the successful defendant is at no risk as to costs. If there is some doubt about recovering all the costs from the losing defendant, the court will usually make a *Bullock* order so that the successful defendant is protected by having his primary order for costs against the plaintiff.

22.3.4.4 Agreeing costs

At the end of the litigation it is common practice for the loser to offer to agree costs. In such a case the winner's solicitor will prepare a list of the items which he is claiming and the rates at which he wishes to charge, and give some overall indication of the hours spent on the case, in letter form. There will then inevitably be some negotiation, whether by post, telephone or face to face. In the majority of cases a satisfactory agreement is achieved. It should be noted that even where one is acting for a legally aided party it is possible to agree costs with the opponent, provided the first party is willing to accept the sum achieved in full settlement of the costs and no further claim is made to the Legal Aid Board. In such cases the solicitor has to submit details of the costs agreed to the Legal Aid Board so it may confirm that it has no objection, but in a routine case there is no reason why they should have any objection if no claim is made for costs on the fund. If the client has paid a contribution this will then be returned to him as well.

The reasons for agreeing costs are as follows:

(a) The process of taxation is lengthy and time-consuming and one may well wait some months for a taxation hearing.

(b) Drawing up High Court bills, despite recent rules which have simplified the process, is not work which solicitors themselves tend to do. Specialists called costs draftsmen now exist. Larger firms employ their own costs draftsmen in-house for preparing all bills. Medium-sized and smaller firms, however, will not be able to afford a full-time employee simply to do this and will go instead to freelance costs draftsmen who work alone or in partnership providing this service. Freelance costs draftsmen charge on a straight commission basis for drawing up bills of costs based on the total of the bill. This varies but may be between about 5 per cent and 7½ per cent of the bill. Consequently, if a bill of £10,000 is drawn up and the costs drafter is charging 6 per cent for drawing it up, immediately £600 of the solicitor's profit costs have been lost. Moreover, no charge can be made on taxation for drawing up a bill of costs unless there are special circumstances. Therefore this money is simply lost to the solicitor. This provides a powerful incentive for him to save the cost of having the bill formally prepared and to agree costs.

(c) There is a court fee on taxation of costs to be paid by the losing party, which is currently 7½ per cent of the bill. Again, therefore, if a bill comes to £10,000 the losing party will have to pay a court fee of £750 for the taxation process. In addition, the losing party will have to pay costs for the carrying out of the taxation process itself to the winning party. This is all money lost to the losing party and provides a powerful incentive to agree costs.

(d) There is the psychological factor that after lengthy litigation, when the judge pronounces final judgment (subject to any decision to appeal), both sides' solicitors are usually glad to treat the matter as over and turn their minds to the rest of their case load. To prolong a matter by continuing to argue about costs and to wait for what might be a lengthy taxation (involving perhaps a half day in the case of a substantial bill) is unwelcome. The solicitor will have to retain the file as current and remember in detail its contents so as to be able to justify the work done at the taxation, and this is to be regretted in cases which have been to all other purposes laid to rest.

(e) Finality is also in both clients' interests. A winning client will not know his own net liability for costs until the amount which can be recovered from his opponent is ascertained. A losing client will be anxious to know his total liability for damages and costs to his opponent and costs to his solicitor (including those for carrying out the taxation process).

Nevertheless, if agreement is not possible there will have to be a taxation hearing.

22.4 The Taxation Process

22.4.1 FORM OF THE BILL OF COSTS

A bill must be prepared in proper itemised form. The form of the bill is described in *RSC Ord. 62, Appendix 2*. The form of the bill is similar in the county court. That form, and the practice on taxation, is now set out in *Practice Direction (Taxation: Practice)* [1993] 1 WLR 12.

The bill is set out in numbered paragraphs, each describing the work done, the rate charged and any factors which justify the rate. The bill typically has a number of columns on the righthand side in which the items are set out, the column on the far right being the column in which the taxing officer indicates what items he is reducing or deleting.

The bill must commence with a short and succinct narrative indicating the issues, the relevant circumstances, the date when instructions were received and when the matter ended. In addition, the narrative must identify the status of the persons concerned with the legal work (i.e. whether it was the senior partner, trainee solicitor or as the case may be) and state the expense rates claimed for each.

22.4.2 LODGING THE BILL OF COSTS

In principle the bill of costs should be lodged for taxation within three months of the end of the case. This is a relatively short time in fact for the two litigants to consider the possibility of appeal; thereafter to attempt to agree costs; and, when that fails, to have the bill fully prepared by a costs draughtsman. Accordingly, somewhat longer is usually allowed. The bill should be lodged for taxation as soon as possible and the application for leave to tax out of time will be taken as the preliminary point.

The bill when lodged at court must be accompanied by all necessary papers, receipts and vouchers, including instructions to counsel, brief to counsel, copies of the pleadings, copies of correspondence, etc. A copy of the bill must be served on every other party with the notice of the appointment obtained from the court endorsed on it. In the county court the court serves this.

Under the *Practice Direction (Taxation: Practice)* [1993] 1 WLR 12 referred to above, it is no longer sufficient for the party who has lost the litigation and will therefore be paying the winner's bill of costs simply to turn up at the taxation appointment and make his objections then and there. He is now required to serve on the successful party an itemised schedule of the precise objections which he is going to raise, whether as to items in principle, the rates charged, the reasonableness of given disbursements or counsel's fees, or as the case may be. The successful party may lodge with the court and serve his replies to the objections giving more detail and justifying the items concerned or the rates claimed. When reading the file before the taxation hearing the District Judge or Taxing Master will therefore be relatively well informed about the precise areas of disagreement.

Under a recent rule change the successful party who lodges his bill also has to pay half of the potential court fee as a deposit. As will be noted from **22.3.4.4**, the court fee is at a rate of 7.5% on the gross total of the bill and thus a deposit of 3.75% on the gross total of the bill will need to be paid. The successful party will in due course recoup this from the losing party who is eventually liable to pay the whole of the taxing fee.

22.4.3 PROVISIONAL TAXATION

In both High Court and county court it is possible that the taxing officer will consider the bill without attendance by the parties and indicate the amounts he proposes to allow. This is more common in the county court. The provisional certificate gives both parties a chance to accept his taxation without a formal hearing. However, if either party objects then the provisional certificate is of no relevance and a hearing is fixed in the usual way.

22.4.4 THE TAXATION HEARING

At the taxation hearing the taxing officer will go through the bill item by item and listen to objections, either to items in principle or to the amount claimed for individual items. If he accedes to the objection he will then *tax off* or disallow the item, i.e. he will say that the item is not within the standard basis of taxation and therefore must be borne by the winner personally. At the end of the taxation the amount disallowed or taxed off will be totalled up, deducted from the original total of the bill and the final amount is then payable by the losing party.

The taxation process is therefore an adversarial process in which the loser will be attempting to get the winner's bill reduced by as much as possible. In the case of a legal aid taxation, no representative of the legal aid fund attends and the taxing officer conducts the taxation in an inquisitorial manner, his purpose being to protect the legal aid fund by insisting that the legally aided person's solicitor justify the items claimed.

22.4.5 REVIEW

Any party dissatisfied with the decisions made on taxation may request a reconsideration by the original taxing officer by stating his objections by letter. The original taxing officer will then reconsider his decision and notify the parties of the decision made at the reconsideration.

If a party remains dissatisfied, the procedure is to issue a summons for review of the taxation. Three bundles of documents need to be lodged for this, the procedure being that the review is conducted by a judge and two assessors. A further schedule must be prepared setting out the nature of the objections to the amounts allowed on taxation, and there is an opportunity for the opposing party to give his comments on the matters to which objection is taken.

22.5 Personal Liability of Legal Representatives for Costs

By virtue of the *Supreme Court Act 1981, s. 51*:

> (6) *In any proceedings . . . the court may disallow, or (as the case may be) order the legal or other representative concerned to meet, the whole of any wasted costs or such part of them as may be determined. . . .*
>
> (7) *. . . 'wasted costs' means any costs incurred by a party—*
>
> (a) *as a result of any improper, unreasonable or negligent act or omission on the part of any legal or other representative or any employee of such a representative; or*
>
> (b) *which, in the light of any such act or omission occurring after they were incurred, the court considers it is unreasonable to expect that party to pay.*

The procedure to bring these provisions into effect is contained in *RSC Ord. 62, rr. 10, 11 and 28*. The provisions mean that the court may order that where any costs are 'wasted', they may either be disallowed on taxation, i.e. the solicitor will have to bear them himself, or, if the legal costs of one party have been increased by the improper act or omission of his opponent's lawyer, the legal representative of that opponent may be ordered to pay the first party's costs.

This rule is at its most important, although not exclusively applicable, in cases where a party has legal aid and either pursues a hopeless case, or pursues a case in such a way as materially and improperly to increase the costs of his opponent. If the opponent then wins the case he is unable to recover any costs from the legally aided person by virtue of *s. 17* of the *Legal Aid Act 1988* (see **2.3.3**) which limits costs in such cases to those which are reasonable for the assisted person to pay having regard (*inter alia*) to his means. The personal liability rule provides an opportunity to claim those costs from the legally aided person's lawyer — in essence to penalise him for pursuing a hopeless case after the point at which it should have become apparent that it was hopeless, or for pursuing his case in a wasteful and improper manner.

Under the predecessor to the present rule it was usually considered that for this Draconian power to be used against the lawyer personally, conduct of an oppressive or improper nature was required. It is clear that under the new provisions all that is required is simple negligence, and thus a solicitor who is merely sloppy or slow in the conduct of the case, or who misses some point by oversight may be called upon to pay the opponent's costs. Case law shows that the courts are not slow to make this order against solicitors, and even (in an appropriate case) against a barrister where that barrister has advised on or persisted with some course of conduct in a case which is clearly improper. See, in particular, *R* v *Secretary of State for the Home Department, ex parte Abbassi* (1992) *The Times*, 6 April 1992.

Where a party wishes to claim a 'wasted costs order' from his opponent's solicitor or barrister, an application for this can be made at the end of the trial. Alternatively, an application can be made in the course of taxation. The procedure requires the issue of a separate summons, giving the opposing solicitor adequate notice of the case to be met and indicating what the acts or omissions are on which the party applying proposes to rely.

The increased powers available since 1991 for the court to order wasted costs against an opponent's solicitor or counsel personally were taken up with enthusiasm, one might also say with glee, by the legal profession. In many instances such orders were very well merited and a useful reminder to solicitors and counsel that slow or slipshod work could be directly penalised against them irrespective of the outcome of the litigation between the clients. However, in *Ridehalgh* v *Horsefield* [1994] 3 WLR 462, the Court of Appeal held that matters were on the verge of going too far and that the whole field of wasted costs was about to become what it described as 'a satellite form of proceedings'. The Court of Appeal laid down guidelines for making wasted costs orders. The court said that it could not be assumed in every case which was litigated without much prospect of success, or even where an interlocutory stage was prosecuted without much prospect of success, that this was the fault of the lawyers for the litigant, who in most cases would be acting properly on their client's instructions. The threat of wasted costs orders should not deprive the unpopular or unmeritorious litigant of being legally represented. Moreover the benevolent purpose of legal aid might be subverted by an excessive risk of wasted costs orders. Lawyers for legally aided parties felt themselves to be specially at risk from wasted costs orders given that costs orders against their clients directly are unlikely to be enforceable.

It was incumbent on a court which was minded to make a wasted costs order against a solicitor or counsel to give him or her the opportunity on notice to show cause why such an order should not be made and to exercise doubts in favour of the solicitor or counsel concerned.

22.6 '*Calderbank*' Offers and the Costs of Taxation

In general the losing party will have to pay the costs of the taxation even if the winner's bill is reduced by a significant amount. The court does preserve a discretion on this, however. No payment into court is possible in respect of a bill of costs but there is an analogous procedure whereby the party liable to pay costs to the other party may make a so-called '*Calderbank* offer' under *RSC Ord. 62, r. 27(3)*. By this procedure the party who is liable to pay indicates in a without prejudice letter to the successful party what sum he is prepared to pay in respect of costs. There is no requirement on him to break this amount down between profit costs, disbursements and VAT, nor to indicate the precise items which he is challenging, though it would be normal to do so.

The letter must not be drawn to the attention of the taxing officer until the taxation is completed, but once it is completed, if the party who has made the *Calderbank* offer has succeeded in having the winner's bill reduced to a sum equal to or below the figure which he has offered, then the court may make a separate ruling on the costs of the taxation in the light of the fact that a fair offer had been put forward which would have avoided the taxation. The court may order that the party liable to pay the costs should receive the costs of the taxation from the winner, or order that each party should bear its own costs of the taxation; and may make further provision for who is to bear the cost of the taxation fee of 5 per cent of the total bill. The court has a very wide discretion as to what order to make but normally will give effect to the reasonable offer (see *Platt* v *GKN Kwikform Ltd* [1992] 1 WLR 465).

It should be noted that this procedure is not available where the winning party is legally aided because in such cases there has to be a taxation.

22.7 Fixed Costs

It will be recalled that in both High Court and county court a plaintiff is only allowed to claim fixed costs if the case terminates in early judgment or payment (see **6.3.2.2**). Thus:

(a) In the High Court the fixed costs endorsement must be completed on any writ claiming a liquidated sum. If the defendant then pays the amount claimed together with interest as claimed (remembering that interest should be specified and a computation shown) and the amount allowed for fixed costs direct to the plaintiff within 14 days of service of the writ, then those are the only costs which the plaintiff may claim as against the defendant. Thus in such a case the plaintiff will inevitably have to bear a further element of solicitor and own client costs.

(b) If the plaintiff obtains judgment in default of notice of intention to defend, or of defence in the High Court, again there is a specified allowance for fixed costs and these are all that the plaintiff will normally be able to obtain.

(c) In the county court there is similar provision for fixed costs where the action ends by payment of the full amount within 14 days of receipt of the summons direct to the plaintiff or in default of defence.

(d) In summary judgment applications in both High Court and county court, there is a provision for fixed costs to be allowed where the claim is for a liquidated sum such as a debt. Nonetheless despite that prima facie provision the court does have a discretion to award taxed costs. Whether fixed costs or taxed costs will be allowed depends on how the actual hearing for summary judgment went. If the defendant was a litigant in person who turned up merely to put some quite inadequate argument which was easily disposed of, then fixed costs would be likely to be all that was allowed. If on the other hand say, the defendant served a 20-page affidavit attempting to justify why he should be given unconditional leave to defend, and at the hearing was represented by a solicitor, and even counsel, there is no doubt that after a lengthy contested hearing of that kind taxed costs would be awarded and the court would most probably even give a certificate that the application was 'fit for counsel'.

(e) For some kinds of work done at various other stages of an action there is provision in the rules (particularly in *RSC Ord. 62, Appendix 3*) for an amount for fixed costs only. This does not apply to most interlocutory applications in a normal action but does apply to much of what is done after judgment e.g. as to the costs allowable where application is made to enforce a judgment by garnishee, a charging order and so on.

(f) Where there is no specific provision in the rules for fixed costs the assumption is that taxed costs may be ordered, and this is always the case in an unliquidated damages case even where the case ends early, e.g. by judgment in default of acknowledgement of service. This is because in such a case there will inevitably need to be a hearing to assess damages, even though the case is brought to an early end on liability.

22.8 Assessed Costs

22.8.1 APPLICATION FOR ASSESSED COSTS

A party may apply at trial for assessed costs rather than taxed costs under *RSC Ord. 62, r. 13*. This is usually done where the matter has come to a conclusion swiftly with no great complexity. It is particularly appropriate in certain kinds of cases, e.g. especially cases where there is a claim for arrears of rent, or mortgage payments and possession by a landlord or building society mortgagee.

The actual procedure on taxation is time-consuming and long-drawn-out, and with a difficult (or absent) losing party there is little prospect of agreeing costs. Accordingly, a party can ask at trial for costs to be assessed and can suggest figures there and then to the judge. A skeleton bill should be available, though this need only run to a page or so of narrative of the work done.

The figure to be allowed on assessment tends to be rather less than a party would be likely to receive on taxation but it does avoid the cost and delay of taxation and, if it is thought possible that it may be difficult to recover the costs anyway, e.g. in building society repossession cases, it is usually advantageous for a successful plaintiff.

22.8.2 ASSESSMENT OF LEGALLY AIDED PARTY'S COSTS

In addition, the Legal Aid Area Office can assess the costs of a legally aided party in two cases, one of which we have mentioned before, namely where the total amount payable to solicitor and counsel will not exceed £1,000.

Example 1 In a straightforward personal injury case, after full investigation of the evidence at the stage of discovery of documents it becomes obvious to the legally aided plaintiff's solicitor that the case is unlikely to be successful. The plaintiff accepts the advice to discontinue and the defendants agree not to ask for costs (bearing in mind that because of *s. 17* of the *Legal Aid Act 1988* they would have been unlikely to get an order for costs anyway). Instead of going through the process of taxation the plaintiff's solicitor may apply by letter for his costs to be assessed by the Legal Aid Area Office, giving details of the costs appropriately, provided that the sum amounts to less than £1,000.

Example 2 In a case where a legally aided plaintiff has won, or achieved a negotiated settlement, and his opponent is to pay costs, if the solicitor and counsel are willing to accept the amounts offered by the opponent in full settlement the Area Director will assess the reasonableness of the costs offered. See *Civil Legal Aid (General) Regulations 1989, reg. 106.*

As to the hourly rates for which one might contend, it is likely that in respect of legal aid certificates issued after 25 February 1994, the Legal Aid Area Office will have regard to the prescribed rates in the schedule to the *Legal Aid in Civil Proceedings (Remuneration) Regulations 1994* (see **2.5** and **22.3.2.1**).

TWENTY THREE

ENFORCEMENT OF JUDGMENTS

In this chapter we consider how a judgment, once obtained, may be enforced. We discuss the practical considerations, including those relevant to interest on judgments; the alternative means of enforcing a monetary judgment and the kinds of asset which may be taken under each appropriate method; and enforcement of non-monetary judgments, e.g. in injunction cases. We include a brief discussion of cumulative and alternative methods of enforcement of judgments, and insolvency proceedings.

23.1 Practical Considerations

23.1.1 INTRODUCTION

Civil judgments are not enforced automatically by either High Court or county court. This is the case whether the judgment is for payment of a sum of money or for an injunction. Even though in the latter case breach of the injunction is a contempt of court, it is still up to the affected party to instigate proceedings for committal for contempt. In the case of money judgments, failure to pay, or even deliberate refusal to pay, is not a civil contempt. Until the successful party (the *judgment creditor*) instigates one or other of the relevant court procedures to enforce the judgment against the losing party (the *judgment debtor*) the court will take no action.

In the light of the above it is vital to discuss with a plaintiff suing for a sum of money the possible problems at the outset, and to ensure that he appreciates that even success in obtaining a judgment does not necessarily mean that the money, whether it be damages or debt, will be paid in full and promptly. Early enquiries about the status of a potential defendant are often essential to ensure that good money is not thrown after bad in pursuing hopeless debts.

In personal injury cases, and some other cases, the defendant in the main has the advantage of being insured (or having his judgment paid by the MIB). Provided the proper measures have been taken at the outset of the litigation, by way of giving notice either under *s. 152* of the *Road Traffic Act 1988* or by writing the necessary letters to the MIB, there is therefore unlikely to be any problem in enforcing the judgment. It must be borne in mind, however, that there are some kinds of personal injury actions where there may be no insurance, such as where a pedestrian or a cyclist causes a road accident, or where a plaintiff is suing under the *Occupiers' Liability Acts*.

23.1.2 INTEREST ON JUDGMENTS

In the High Court judgments carry interest at 8 per cent per annum. Alternatively, if the action was founded on contract and the contract itself provides for interest to run after judgment, interest will run at the contractual rate whether higher or lower than 8 per cent.

In the county court the matter is governed by the *County Courts (Interest on Judgment Debts) Order 1991*, which provides:

(a) Interest will not run on judgments of less than £5,000.

(b) Interest will run at 8 per cent per annum on judgments of more than £5,000, but it is important to note:

  (i) that where interest is claimed two copies of a certificate must be lodged with any request or application for enforcement, giving details of the amount of interest claimed and the sum on which it is claimed, the dates from and to which interest has accrued, and the rate of interest which has been applied;

  (ii) Where interest is claimed it ceases to run once enforcement of proceedings have been commenced, except where those proceedings fail to produce any payment from the debtor in which case interest continues to accrue as if the proceedings have never been taken. This applies to all methods of enforcement and oral examination with the exception of proceedings under the *Charging Orders Act 1979*.

The unavailability of interest on judgments in the county court for sums of under £5,000 can obviously cause injustice and great annoyance to clients. If a judgment for £4,000 had been obtained in the High Court, interest would run at about £320 per annum. In the county court the same debt depreciates year by year without any provision for interest to compensate. For this reason it is important to remember that county court debts can be registered in the High Court and enforced there as long as they are for a sum of more than £1,000. Once registered in the High Court interest runs as if they were High Court judgments, and therefore a prudent judgment creditor's solicitor will immediately take this step.

Under a recent rule change, where it is intended to enforce a judgment by execution against goods, one may apply to transfer the judgment to the High Court by a simple administrative procedure involving production of a Certificate of Judgment. Where, however, it is intended to enforce the judgment by some other method such as garnishee, one needs to apply to a District Judge on a formal application on notice to the judgment debtor. It would seem, however, that, given the bona fide reason for transfer, namely the availability of interest on the judgment, there is no reason why a District Judge should not grant the application in the usual case.

Above £5,000, interest runs at 8 per cent but subject to the major disadvantage that interest does not run for any period during which enforcement proceedings are being undertaken so long as any money is produced. Consequently, if one takes proceedings for oral examination, followed by attachment of earnings, interest will not run for the total period provided some money is obtained. This is an enormous drawback capable of creating considerable injustice. The only exception is the case of charging orders where interest will continue to run.

23.1.3 OBTAINING INFORMATION ABOUT THE JUDGMENT DEBTOR'S MEANS

As indicated above, it is always preferable to spend some time and trouble at the outset of litigation to ensure that a client appreciates that judgments are not automatically enforced; that you cannot get blood out of a stone; and that there is no realistic possibility of imprisoning a person for a civil debt. If the client is in business, for example a builder's merchant supplying small builders, this is an opportunity to give him general commercial advice about his business procedures, e.g. to ensure that when extending credit to his customers he obtains proper references, full details of the assets and location of the assets of his customers; procures personal guarantees from the directors in the case of customers which are limited companies, and so on. Here, however, we consider the situation where either the litigation has become so long-drawn-out that the information originally obtained is no longer valid; or, perhaps, where the client for reasons of speed instructed you to press on with the litigation immediately without making initial enquiries in the belief that the judgment debtor was a person of some means. There are essentially two different routes by which to proceed:

(a) non-judicial enquiries; and

(b) oral examination.

23.1.3.1 Non-judicial enquiries

It is always open to a person to employ an enquiry agent to obtain a status report on an opponent or a potential opponent in litigation. The court is not involved and this can as easily be done before litigation as after judgment. In such cases private detectives have various means of finding information. Often an enquiry agent will undertake a certain amount of surveillance on an individual, for example by following him to his place of work and then making enquiries there; trying to trace the whereabouts of his bank account and seeking to make enquiries there; seeing whether he owns his own home and, if so, attempting to procure an approximate valuation of it, etc. In the case of run of the mill debts enquiry agents are unlikely to have recourse to the more elaborate options often employed in commercial investigations (e.g. clearing out the contents of a person's dustbin in the hope of finding useful material such as bank statements).

As well as this, in the case of limited companies, company searches may be undertaken which sometimes give some indication of the value of a company and the whereabouts of its assets. On the other hand, the kind of limited company that gets into trouble with bad debts is often the kind which, despite increased penalties, fails to keep the documentation at the Companies Registry up to date, so this avenue may be of only limited use.

23.1.3.2 Oral examination

See *RSC Ord. 48; CCR Ord. 25, r. 3.*

Oral examination involves obtaining a court order that the judgment debtor attends court to be cross-examined as to his means and assets. It is a time-consuming and often frustrating procedure, which should most certainly not be embarked upon in a case where one already has some idea about likely assets so as already to commend one or other method of enforcement. It will take at the very least some hours of a solicitor's time and, for reasons which will be explained below, will often involve travel to some distant court for which only modest amounts will be allowed as *inter partes* costs, leaving one's client with a substantial shortfall of the actual cost involved of implementing this procedure.

(a) *In the High Court*

The judgment creditor's solicitor prepares an affidavit confirming the amount of the judgment and the fact that the judgment creditor is entitled to enforce it; identifying the judgment by giving its date and number; stating the amount remaining unpaid; and giving the address of the debtor and the nearest county court to his home, this is taken to the court together with two copies of the order required. This is an *ex parte* procedure and the documents are left to be read by the District Judge who will then make the order for oral examination.

Unfortunately for the judgment creditor, the practice is that the oral examination of the judgment debtor takes place not at the District Registry of the High Court where the action has been proceeding, but at the county court nearest to the judgment debtor's home. There is likely to be a short delay whilst the District Registry of the High Court where the case has been proceeding obtains a convenient time for the appointment at the county court, especially if the latter is some way away. Thereafter the order can be collected by the judgment creditor and must be served personally on the judgment debtor and conduct money (i.e. travelling costs to and from court) must be tendered.

(b) *In the county court*

The method of application in the county court does not require an affidavit but merely a filing of a written request in the appropriate form for oral examination. Postal service of the order for oral examination is possible provided that a certificate to the effect that postal service will be effective is completed, but most solicitors prefer personal service to avoid difficulties. Again, conduct money must be tendered.

(c) *The hearing*

The form of the order for oral examination instructs the judgment debtor to bring with him relevant documents. Often a first hearing will prove abortive because the judgment debtor does not bring those documents and it is as well to remind him by letter what is required shortly before the oral examination, giving details of the most important class of documents (e.g. bank statements, wage slips, etc.).

The oral examination usually takes place before an officer of the court appointed by the District Judge for that purpose, and only rarely takes place before the District Judge himself. The atmosphere is not very intimidating, the examination taking place in a private room and not in a court. The officer asks questions by reference to a pro forma questionnaire and takes down the answers which are given on oath. The judgment creditor's solicitor then has the right to cross-examine. According to the rules the examination should be 'a cross-examination of the severest kind' and the debtor is obliged to answer all proper questions.

(d) *The un-cooperative debtor*

If the judgment debtor does not attend the hearing there will usually be an adjournment for further service of an amended hearing date. Thereafter the court may embark upon committal proceedings, and sometimes this has the effect of producing the money. If, having attended, the debtor is un-cooperative and will not answer proper questions or produce relevant documents, application must first be made to the District Judge himself for directions. This may in itself lead to an adjournment. If there is further recalcitrance, in principle the judgment debtor may be committed to prison for contempt; this, however, entails a separate application to a judge in open court. This is also rarely fruitful because the judgment debtor will usually be given one further opportunity to purge his contempt by producing the relevant document or answering the relevant question. By this time the judgment creditor will have spent a considerable sum on this abortive process, especially bearing in mind that oral examination is not a method of enforcement but merely a method of obtaining information.

(e) *Costs*

If anything of use is obtained from oral examination then an order for costs will usually be made, and these are often assessed there and then. Usually only relatively modest sums are likely to be awarded which will certainly not cover the full cost to the client of the solicitor's work in attending the oral examination.

23.2 Enforcement of Money Judgments

23.2.1 EXECUTION

23.2.1.1 High Court writ of *fieri facias*

See *RSC Ords 45* and *46*.

Execution is the term describing the process whereby moveable property of a judgment debtor may be seized to be sold at auction to satisfy the judgment debt, legal costs and, indeed, the costs of enforcement. To obtain this the judgment creditor's solicitor takes to the District Registry where the judgment was obtained:

(a) two copies of a writ of *fieri facias* (usually referred to in brief as fi fa);

(b) a *praecipe* (that is a request for the issue of fi fa);

(c) the judgment obtained together with (if the costs have already been taxed by the court, which is unusual) a copy of the taxing officer's certificate;

(d) the court fee.

The procedure is an *ex parte* one and the judgment debtor is not involved. The solicitor simply produces these documents to the clerk at the counter of the District Registry. The fee is taken and one form of the writ of fi fa is sealed and returned.

The judgment creditor then posts the writ to the under sheriff of the county concerned. This is the county where the judgment debtor resides, or alternatively where he has the assets which it is intended to seize. It is customary when sending the writ to the sheriff to give him any information that might be of use to him in knowing what or where to seize, e.g. it might be that a status report has disclosed that the judgment debtor owns a certain car which he parks some distance away from his house.

The sheriff's officers can seize any of the debtor's goods in the county which are sufficient to realise the judgment debt, interest, costs and expenses. Anything moveable may be seized, including cash or security found on the premises. The sheriff's officers have no right to force entry onto residential premises, although they do have that right in the case of commercial premises. They do, however, have their means for ensuring that they are invited in without too much fuss.

In practice, when an under sheriff receives a writ of fi fa he endorses upon it the precise date and time of receipt. The under sheriff is usually a solicitor in private practice who carries out this function and employs sheriff's officers. If he receives different writs from different creditors relating to the same debtor, he is obliged to execute them in the order of receipt, and therefore with this method of execution the first one in may get the whole of the cake. In principle the sheriff's officers go immediately to the debtor's house and seize valuables which they estimate will bring in the necessary amount at public auction. Many sheriff's officers are in full-time business as auctioneers and therefore are well aware of the value of secondhand items at auction. As an alternative to immediate seizure, they may make an inventory of the contents of the house which they propose to seize. This is called 'taking walking possession' and the officers indicate that they will return shortly (four days is a common period) to seize the goods and remove them unless the sum is paid. This is to provide a last chance for the debtor to obtain the money to pay the debt; something that he would usually be well advised to do since the goods at auction will fetch only a fraction of their probable value to the debtor personally. If the sum is not paid the sheriff's officers will return and seize the goods. They will then be auctioned some days later, the intervening period giving the debtor one last chance to pay the debt.

If a party has obtained judgment with costs to be taxed, since taxation of costs is likely to take some months it is common to issue execution immediately in respect of the judgment debt. It can be issued again separately for the costs once taxed.

The sheriff's officers will sell the goods at public auction and retain their own fees out of the sum involved (i.e. the judgment debtor in effect pays their fees — a feature which makes this method of execution particularly appealing). They will then send to the judgment creditor's solicitors the full amount of the debt, interests and costs (if appropriate at this stage), and return to the judgment debtor any excess received after auctioning the goods. The sheriff will retain the monies received for 14 days under *ss. 184* and *346* of the *Insolvency Act 1986*, but thereafter, if no indication of insolvency is received, will remit the monies as previously described to the creditor.

23.2.1.2 Warrant of execution in the county court

In the county court the plaint note and request for a warrant of execution are filed together with a fee. In the county court the warrant of execution is executed by the bailiff of the court, a full-time civil servant. The bailiff in principle does much the same as the sheriff's officers in the High Court, and the procedures are in other respects virtually identical. (See *CCR Ord. 26.*)

23.2.1.3 Execution of county court judgments in the High Court

Where it is intended to enforce a judgment by execution there are now restrictions as follows:

(a) A judgment debt of more than £5,000 can only be enforced by the High Court sheriff. Accordingly, if a party has a county court judgment for this sum it is necessary to register the judgment in the High Court under *RSC Ord. 78* (see also *Practice Direction (County Court Order: Enforcement)* [1991] 1 WLR 695). Under this procedure two copies of a certificate of judgment of the county court must be produced, sealed by that court, and setting out details of the judgment. The High Court will thereupon allocate a reference number, letter and year, and endorse that on the certificate. The case will then be entered in a special register at the High Court. Thereafter the certificate may be treated for enforcement purposes as a High Court judgment and interest at the judgment debt rate runs from the date of the certificate. The title of all subsequent documentation must be such as to reflect the transfer to the High Court, with the addition of the words 'transferred from the County Court by certificate dated . . .'.

(b) Judgments for £1,000 or less can only be enforced by the county court bailiffs. Accordingly, a High Court judgment must be registered in the county court for that purpose.

(c) Between the figures of £1,000 and £5,000, enforcement may be by *either* bailiff or sheriff.

23.2.1.4 Leave to issue execution

It has been assumed in the foregoing that there is no leave required of the court to issue execution and that this can be done at the counter without the formality of any judicial decision by the District Judge to permit it. In fact there is a number of examples, although none is relevant in mainstream litigation, where leave of the court is required before execution can be issued. The most important one is where there is an attachment of earnings order in force (see **23.2.5**). With this exception, however, there are usually no difficulties in attempting several methods of enforcement of judgments simultaneously. The interrelationship between the various methods is discussed at **23.2.7**.

23.2.2 GARNISHEE PROCEEDINGS

This is the appropriate method where the judgment debtor is himself owed money by another person. For example, where the judgment debtor is in business and is owed trade debts by customers; or indeed where anyone has a credit balance in any kind of bank or building society account, since such sums are in principle a statement of a debt owed by the bank or building society to the person concerned. Garnishee proceedings are a method of freezing and seizing such sums in the hands of the person who has them, and thus of bypassing the judgment debtor until it is too late for him to do anything about it.

23.2.2.1 Garnishee orders in the high court

To obtain a garnishee order in the High Court (*RSC Ord. 49*), the judgment creditor's solicitor swears an affidavit in which he identifies the judgment or order that he is seeking to enforce; states the amount remaining unpaid under it at the time of the application; gives the name and last known address of the judgment debtor; and states that to the best of his information the garnishee (i.e. the person who owes money to the judgment debtor) is indebted to the judgment debtor giving the sources of that belief and (if he knows this) the amount owed by the garnishee to the judgment debtor. If the garnishee is a bank or building society then the solicitor should state the branch address and the account number, if known.

This affidavit is the formal application, and with it two copies of an order called 'garnishee order nisi' must be prepared. These are in Practice Form 72 in vol. 2, Appendix A of the 'White Book'. They are taken to the District Registry to be put before the District Judge and the court fee paid. No notice need be given to the judgment debtor. If the District Judge is satisfied with the affidavit he will make the order which can later be collected from the District Registry.

The form of the order is directed not at the judgment debtor but at the garnishee. It instructs the garnishee to do two things:

(a) To attend court at the time and place specified in the order *to show cause* why he should not pay the money which he owes to the judgment debtor directly to the judgment creditor. From these vital words the garnishee order nisi is often called an 'order to show cause'.

(b) Meanwhile, to retain the amount owed or freeze the bank account as the case may be.

This order must be served on the garnishee (and in the case of a bank should be served both at the head office and the bank local branch where the account is). Seven days later a copy should be served on the judgment debtor, who only now becomes aware of what has happened (unless, of course, he has in the meantime tried to draw money from his account which will not be permitted). At least 15 days' notice must be given of the time fixed for the hearing date.

The hearing is before the District Judge in chambers. Garnishees commonly do not bother to attend but simply write in confirming that they will abide by any order made by the court. This is particularly the case with banks who after all have no particular interest in the outcome of such matters. If, however, the garnishee disputes his liability to pay anything to the judgment debtor (i.e. says that there was no such debt or credit balance) then he will need to attend, and at the first hearing the District Judge will then give directions as to how the issue of whether or not the garnishee owes money to the judgment debtor will be determined.

The judgment creditor and usually the judgment debtor will attend the hearing. The judgment creditor will be seeking to persuade the District Judge to make the order nisi into a final order (i.e. one directing that the money which has hitherto been frozen should be paid out to him). The judgment debtor may try to persuade the District Judge that for hardship or other reasons this order ought not to be made. Usually, however, the final order will be made if there are admitted debts from garnishee to judgment debtor. Nevertheless, the making of the order is discretionary, and a common situation where the District Judge will not make the order final is where it comes out that there are other unsecured creditors of the judgment debtor so that making the order would represent an unjust preferment of one creditor over another. This method should therefore be contrasted with execution, where the first in gets the whole cake (see **23.2.1.1**)

If there is no reason to the contrary and the order is made, it will be addressed to the garnishee telling him to pay the money over direct to the judgment creditor within a certain short time. This obviously absolves the garnishee from debts up to the relevant amount owed by him to the judgment debtor. If the garnishee fails to pay the judgment creditor may take enforcement proceedings against him direct.

23.2.2.2 Garnishee orders in the county court

In the county court (*CCR Ord. 30*) application is also made on affidavit. The court will then issue the garnishee order to show cause which is served (usually by the court) in the same manner as if it were a fixed date summons. It is later served on the judgment debtor. Thereafter the procedure is the same. If the garnishee disputes that he does owe money to the judgment debtor, he may require the case to be transferred to the county court nearest to his home or where he carries on business for that issue to be decided there.

23.2.3 CHARGING ORDERS

Charging orders are not strictly speaking a method of enforcing a judgment, but rather a means of obtaining security for it which can subsequently be turned into enforcement by an application for an *order for sale*. Where a judgment debtor owns land (even if he owns it jointly with some other person) a charging order can be obtained on the land. The same applies to various other kinds of assets, in particular stocks and shares, where an equivalent order (called 'a stop' order) may be obtained.

Information as to ownership of land is often obtained via oral examination or through an enquiry agent. Whilst in the case of unregistered land there is no method of being positive as to the ownership of legal estates, in the case of registered land there is now open access to the Land Register. It is thus possible to do an index search in Form 96 and follow that up with an application for office copies of the proprietorship register of any property which it is suspected the judgment debtor owns.

23.2.3.1 In the High Court (*RSC Ord. 50*)

The method of application for a charging order in the High Court is in two stages. An affidavit must be prepared to be sworn by the judgment creditor or his solicitor which:

(a) identifies the judgment and states the amount unpaid at the date of application;

(b) states the name of the judgment debtor;

(c) gives full particulars of the subject matter of the intended charge (i.e. the address of the land concerned);

(d) verifies that the interest to be charged is owned beneficially and not as a trustee by the judgment debtor;

(e) states whether the judgment creditor knows of any other creditors of the judgment debtor.

Two copies of the charging order nisi (again, usually called 'an order to show cause') are prepared and taken to the District Registry. Again, this is an ex parte procedure, and the affidavit is read by the District Judge who will then make the charging order nisi. This has the effect of creating a charge on the land owned by the judgment debtor which takes effect as an equitable charge under hand. It is prudent to register this charge at the Land Charges Registry if the land is unregistered, or protect it by notice or caution at the District Land Registry if the land is registered. This will have the effect of preserving priority for the judgment creditor's charge.

A hearing date is fixed by the charging order which must now be served upon the judgment debtor. It invites him to attend the hearing to show cause why the order should not be made absolute.

At the hearing, as with garnishee orders, the District Judge has a wide discretion as to whether or not to make the charging order absolute. The burden of showing cause why it should not be made absolute is on the judgment debtor. However, since with this form of application it is for the judgment creditor specifically to say whether he knows that there are other creditors, it is always a relevant consideration to ensure that the making of a charging order absolute should not give the judgment creditor presently applying unjust preferment over other creditors in the pipeline. The fact that the land is jointly owned or is, for example, a family home is not really a relevant consideration at this stage, however. It will certainly become so should any application be made to enforce the charging order by order for sale (see **23.2.4**).

Application for a charging order in the High Court can only be made if the sum involved exceeds £5,000. It can be made in the county court, however, even in respect of a High Court judgment, for a debt of any amount.

As indicated above, a charging order is not in itself a method of enforcement; it is a way of obtaining security for a debt and of preserving priority other over subsequent encumbrances. Until recently charging orders could validly be described as a 'slow but sure' way of enforcing a debt. Unfortunately, with the general drop in property values and the advent of 'negative equity', it is by no means as desirable as it once was as a method of enforcement. Interest will run at the judgment debt rate (or at any higher rate stipulated by the contract creating the debt) and it may rapidly be the case that the equity in the property is exhausted unless very prompt application is made to enforce the charging order by order for sale.

23.2.3.2 In the county court (*CCR Ord. 31*)

In the county court the procedure for applying for a charging order is similar to that in the case of application for a garnishee order (see **23.2.2.2**).

23.2.4 ENFORCEMENT OF CHARGING ORDER BY ORDER FOR SALE

To enforce a charging order a separate application must be made to the court for an order for sale (*RSC Ord. 88, r. 5A*). This is made to the Chancery Division, or to the county court in separate proceedings. The method of application is by originating summons supported by an affidavit which must:

(a) identify the charging order sought to be enforced and the subject matter of the charge;

(b) specify the amount in respect of which the charge was imposed and the balance outstanding at the date of the affidavit;

(c) state precisely what is the debtor's title to the property charged;

(d) identify any other encumbrancer on the property charged, stating, so far as is known, the names and addresses of the encumbrancers and the amounts owing to them;

(e) set out the plaintiff's proposals as to the manner of sale of the property charged, together with estimates of the gross price which would be obtained on a sale in that manner and the costs of such a sale; and

(f) if the property consists of land of which the plaintiff seeks possession—

(i) give particulars of every person who to the best of the plaintiff's knowledge is in possession of the property charged or any part of it, and

(ii) state in the case of a dwelling house whether a land charge of Class F, or a notice or caution equivalent to that has been entered.

In the case of an application for order for sale, it is as well to join in every party who has a legal title to the land and at least to serve notice of proceedings on all other adult occupants.

The matter will come before a District Judge in chambers for consideration, and at that time he will have regard to *s. 36(2)* of the *Administration of Justice Act 1970*. This provision is relevant in the case of all applications to enforce legal charges by order for possession or sale, and thus is the one relevant also where building societies attempt to repossess dwelling houses. Under *s. 36(2)* the court may adjourn the proceedings or, on giving judgment or making an order for delivery of possession, may stay or suspend execution of the judgment or postpone the date for delivery of possession for such periods as the court thinks reasonable.

This gives the District Judge a very wide discretion indeed to take into account the interests of anyone presently in the house. Thus if, for example, there is a substantial equity still in the property, the debt is a private one incurred by the husband (especially if the husband has now left the home) and the property is a home for small children, the District Judge is likely to adjourn the application for some months, and thereafter possibly to stay or suspend execution of the judgment or order. On the other hand, an order adjourning the proceedings or suspending execution should only in principle be made if 'the mortgagor is likely within a reasonable time to pay any sums due under the mortgage'. All the circumstances have to be taken into account and the legitimate interests of the judgment creditor must not be overlooked. Thus in *Austin-Fell* v *Austin-Fell* [1990] Fam 172 the court concluded that an abandoned wife's interest in the property should not totally override that of the Midland Bank plc who were legitimately seeking to enforce a civil debt owed by her husband. The effect was that the charge remained on the property not to be enforced until the youngest child left education. It must be pointed out, however, that in such a case, with interest running on the judgment debt for over a decade, unless property prices also improved over that decade, at the end of that time the wife would be likely to receive a much reduced amount in respect of her husband's share of the sale of the property. Such considerations are very important in an era of uncertain property prices.

23.2.4.1 Costs

It will be observed that by the time one has obtained a charging order and thereafter embarked on quite separate proceedings in the Chancery Division seeking an order for sale, a good deal more money will have been spent on costs. It is possible that the bulk of these will be recoverable if the application for sale is successful and there is adequate equity. If matters are more nicely poised, however, in terms of diminishing equity in the house, other potential encumbrances and the use of the property as a family home, it may be that of this method of enforcement seems less desirable. Of course, it is always possible to obtain the charging order with a view to ultimate security whilst not immediately embarking on the further stage of applying for an order for sale.

23.2.5 ATTACHMENT OF EARNINGS

Attachment of earnings is in some respects the least desirable of the methods considered so far. It is available only in the county court (*CCR Ord. 27*), although it is of course possible to transfer a High Court judgment to a county court for enforcement. It is a means of ensuring that regular sums are deducted from a judgment debtor's salary by his employer and remitted direct to the county court for onward transmission to the judgment creditor. The procedure is only desirable in the case of a person with no assets worth charging, garnishing or seizing but who appears to be in regular, well-paid employment and does not have many dependants. If none of these conditions obtains, then attachment of earnings may be a frustrating and long drawn out procedure, notwithstanding that in principle once application for it is made the judgment creditor need take no other positive steps but can leave the court to run the procedure itself, and thus costs can at least be kept modest.

A further drawback of the attachment of earnings procedure is that, whilst it will often run on for many years, interest on the judgment debt ceases under the provisions for interest previously described (see **23.1.2**).

23.2.5.1 Application for attachment of earnings

Application is made on County Court Form N55 to the county court for the district where the debtor resides. This has attached to it a form of reply (N56) which is a questionnaire to the debtor seeking details of his employment, income and financial liabilities. It also invites the debtor to pay the amount due direct to the judgment creditor as a way of avoiding an attachment of earnings order. Some persons in employment may choose to do this because one effect of an attachment of earnings application is to bring their debt to the notice of their employers and this may prove professionally embarrassing.

If the debtor does not pay at once he must return the questionnaire to the court which, in the light of the information given, will make an attachment of earnings order. If the chief clerk of the court feels he has sufficient information, he may make a provisional attachment of earnings order and give notice of it to the creditor and debtor. If neither party objects the provisional order becomes final. However, if either objects in writing within five days of receiving the notice there will be a hearing at which the chief clerk, or the District Judge, considers the matter on hearing oral representations.

If a judgment debtor does not return his questionnaire then he may be committed to prison for up to 14 days; similarly, if he is ordered to attend the hearing for an attachment of earnings application, he may be committed to prison for up to 14 days for non-attendance. In principle the court itself puts these procedures into operation and the judgment creditor need not take any initiatives.

23.2.5.2 Contents of the order

When the court has sufficient information it will make an order specifying two matters. These are:

(a) the normal deduction rate (NDR); and

(b) the protected earnings rate (PER).

The latter is the minimum which the debtor needs to earn to achieve subsistence level for himself and his dependants, if any. Once he has earned that figure in any given week, the excess over that figure up to the maximum of the normal deduction rate will be deducted by his employer for onward transmission to the county court. Thus, in the case of an employee who earns the same sum every week, the deduction at the normal rate will be made regularly by the employer who will then send the money direct to the county court. The employer may also make a modest charge for administrative expenses. If the employee's earnings are seasonal or vary with overtime or bonuses, however, then if in any given week his pay sinks below the protected earnings rate no deductions will be made for forwarding to the county court; if only a slight surplus over the protected earnings rate is earned, then only the surplus will be sent on. There is no provision for making up shortages in subsequent weeks, even if extra bonuses take the earnings substantially above the total of both the protected earnings and the normal deduction rates.

If the order is made it is directed to the employer on whom it is served by the court, together with an explanatory leaflet giving details on how to operate the system.

23.2.6 COSTS OF PREVIOUS ABORTIVE ENFORCEMENT

It is possible to obtain the costs of previous abortive enforcement proceedings. An affidavit must be prepared explaining the circumstances and amounts involved, to be lodged at the appropriate time and the District Judge will then, without a hearing, allow the amount he thinks appropriate. See *Practice Direction (Enforcement Costs: Recovery)* [1991] 1 WLR 1295.

23.2.7 CUMULATIVE OR ALTERNATIVE METHODS OF ENFORCEMENT

When one comes to weigh the different methods of enforcement against each other, much depends on the amount of accurate information to hand. There is in principle no objection to using the aforementioned methods simultaneously or cumulatively, except that a party needs the leave of the court to levy execution whilst an attachment of earnings is in force. Having said that, there would be nothing to stop a judgment creditor taking steps to garnish a bank account, send the sheriff in to execute judgment against moveables such as furniture, a car or trade stock, and obtaining a charging order on premises, all at the same time. Care would have to be taken in the completion of the relevant documents but if, for example, each method in turn appeared likely to raise more than had been anticipated, then it would be a simple matter to desist from the garnishee proceedings once the sheriff informed the judgment creditor of the price obtained at auction; or, if garnishee were achieved first, the sheriff could be instructed to withdraw from possession. Care must be taken in the latter instance, however, to ensure that the judgment creditor is aware that in such circumstances the sheriff will be entitled to his full fees, which can be very substantial and in that instance may not in principle be reclaimed from the judgment debtor.

The advantages of each of the methods are best considered as follows:

(a) The advantage of execution is that it is by far the swiftest method of enforcement. The sheriff is likely to execute the writ within a very short time and, if there are indeed goods worth seizing, a very satisfactory outcome may be obtained. The sheriff may in particular be given the money by the judgment debtor at a very early stage to avoid seizure.

(b) With garnishee proceedings, so long as one is certain that there is sufficient money this is perhaps the neatest method of all. It will take effect relatively quickly and it procures the debt in cash form.

(c) Charging orders, as indicated at **23.2.3.1** are a slow method of obtaining security for a charge. They are at their most effective when there is a large equity in the house or business premises and the judgment debtor is the only owner of the premises. In such a situation enforcement by order for sale will be effective, and since interest continues to run from date of judgment to final receipt of monies this method can be very satisfactory. The method becomes markedly less satisfactory if there is no great equity in the house; the premises are jointly owned with another; or the premises are used as a family home.

(d) Attachment of earnings is the least satisfactory method of enforcement. Interest does not run even though it may take many years to recover the money; if the judgment debtor changes jobs then the procedure may need to be reinstituted each time; and there may well be substantial delays in getting the initial order in the event of non-cooperation, which is only rarely punished by imprisonment despite the terms of the *Attachment of Earnings Act 1971*. On the other hand, with certain kinds of employees this application may bring about payment in full because of their embarrassment at having their employers know about their civil debt; and the draining effect of having potentially substantial slices of one's earnings deducted at source over many years may make a debtor who is able to do so prefer to dispose of the matter by early larger payments.

23.2.8 BANKRUPTCY OF INDIVIDUALS (AND COMPANY LIQUIDATION)

Lastly, we should mention one method of enforcement which is the most successful of all in some cases but which is outside the scope of this text, i.e. bankruptcy. This is very successful against persons whose occupation makes it difficult for them if they have been adjudged bankrupt (e.g. professionals or company directors). As a method of enforcement it can be virtually instantaneous, the preliminary notice sometimes bringing payment in full. If the procedure itself has to be embarked on, though, it has serious defects.

Bankruptcy can only be used in the case of debts over £750; and whereas with other methods the initial outlay in terms of court fees is not great, in the case of bankruptcy the initial outlay is over £300 because a deposit must be left in respect of the Official Receiver's accountancy fees. Another defect is that whereas with other enforcement procedures, especially execution, in principle the first in gets the whole of the cake (and even in the case of garnishee or charging orders, if the judgment creditor does not know of the existence of other creditors it may be that he gets in first and gets the whole), the nature of bankruptcy is to bring all creditors forward. Thus a particular creditor may in the end receive only a modest proportion of the debt owed, depending on the assets available.

23.3 Enforcement of Judgments to Do or Abstain From Doing Any Act

23.3.1 THE ORDER OF COMMITTAL

RSC Ord. 45, r. 5, states:

> *Where—*
>
> *(a) a person required by a judgment or order to do an act within a time specified in the judgment or order refuses or neglects to do it within that time . . . or*
>
> *(b) a person disobeys a judgment or order requiring him to abstain from doing an act,*
>
> *then, . . . the judgment or order may be enforced by . . . an order of committal against that person or, where that person is a body corporate, against any such officer.*

This then is the procedure for enforcing an injunction or undertaking. Where the injunction granted is *prohibitory*, any further act of the kind restrained will give the basis for an application for enforcement by committal; where the injunction is *mandatory* (e.g. to pull down a wall wrongly erected barring a right of way) then it is essential that the order fixes a specific time for doing the positive act. If the order does not fix such a time then a further application to the court must be made for a time to be fixed before application to enforce the injunction by committal can be made.

23.3.2 THE PENAL NOTICE

The order containing the injunction must be endorsed with a penal notice. The wording relevant in the High Court is as follows:

> *Disobedience to this order will be a contempt of court punishable by imprisonment.*

In the county court the equivalent wording is:

> *Take notice that unless you obey the directions contained in this order you will be guilty of contempt of court and will be liable to be committed to prison.*

23.3.3 SERVICE OF THE ORDER

It is usually essential as a prerequisite to enforcement by committal that the order should have been served. The order containing the penal notice must be served personally on the person required to do or abstain from doing the act in question, and service on the solicitor on the record will not usually do. However, an order requiring a person to abstain from doing an act may be enforced notwithstanding that service of the copy of the order had not been effected if the court is satisfied that pending such service the person against whom or against whose property it is sought to enforce the order had notice thereof, either by being present when the order was made or by being notified of the terms of the order, whether by telephone or otherwise. In addition, without prejudice to its general powers the court may dispense with service of a copy of an order under the rules if it thinks it just to do so (*RSC Ord. 45, r. 7(6)*).

Despite this last provision, the courts are usually very assiduous in seeing that there is strict observance of the rules about service because the liberty of the subject is at stake. In a clear case, however, and with a gross breach, e.g. one involving violence, it may be that the court can be prevailed upon to dispense with service.

23.3.4 UNDERTAKINGS

An undertaking given by the defendant to the court is for all purposes as good as an injunction, and indeed is better in the sense that (strictly speaking) there is no need for the undertaking to be incorporated in any court order or served on the defendant. It is preferable, of course, that the undertaking is incorporated in such an order endorsed with a penal notice and served personally, but nonetheless the court has jurisdiction to proceed to enforce an undertaking by committal notwithstanding non-service if satisfied that the person who gave the undertaking is aware of its contents and the consequence of disobedience (*Hussain* v *Hussain* [1986] Fam 134).

23.3.5 PROCEDURE ON AN APPLICATION FOR COMMITTAL

In the High Court application is made in the Division where the case has been proceeding, on notice of motion under *RSC Ord. 52, r. 4*.

The notice of motion must state clearly the grounds of the application and describe the contempt in question. It must be accompanied by a copy of an affidavit in support sworn by someone who has personal knowledge of the matters constituting the alleged contempt. However, the notice itself must contain details of the contempt and it is not enough if the information is contained only in the affidavit.

Notice of motion and the copy affidavit must be personally served on the defendant. If it is sought to commit a director of a limited company, service must be on the company and on the director concerned.

23.3.6 THE HEARING OF THE APPLICATION

Since an application for committal to prison is one involving the liberty of the subject it takes precedence over the rest of the day's business in the High Court. It is for the applicant seeking the committal to show on the criminal standard of proof that the contemnor is guilty. The court will then consider the whole matter.

It is often said that it is the paramount consideration of the court to ensure compliance with its orders, and if some other method than committal to prison can be undertaken then it may be that that will be the preferred outcome. For example, if the injunction requires a person to vacate a certain piece of land it may be that the judgment can be enforced by a writ of possession rather than by committal. It may also be that a contemnor will be allowed to purge his contempt by an apology and an assurance that he has already obeyed, or will immediately obey, the injunction or comply with the undertaking concerned. In those instances the court may well suspend imprisonment or any other penalty it imposes. The court has the power to impose fines of unlimited amounts in addition to committal to prison.

Whereas formerly committal was open-ended within the court's discretion under the *Contempt of Court Act 1981*, committal may be only for a fixed period of up to two years. The order must be scrupulously drawn up. There is a long series of county court cases where orders for committal to prison have been set aside because of sloppiness in drafting the order, in particular as to the facts found by the judge and the nature of the contempt. This should be carefully borne in mind.

As mentioned above, a person committed may in principle make an application to purge his contempt and be discharged. Now that committal is for a fixed term, however, this is unlikely to meet with great success.

23.3.7 PRACTICE AND PROCEDURE IN THE COUNTY COURT

The practice and procedure in the county court is substantially the same as in the High Court, but in the county court a District Judge has powers to commit for contempt in certain circumstances, and to allow discharge from imprisonment (*CCR Ord. 29, r. 3*).

TWENTY FOUR

ORIGINATING SUMMONS PROCEDURE

Most of this text is concerned with county court actions commenced by default summons and High Court actions commenced by writ. There is, however, an alternative form of proceeding, i.e. by originating summons in the High Court (called an originating *application* in the county court).

24.1 Originating Summonses v Writs

We have already briefly considered three common originating summons applications. These were respectively for pre-action discovery of documents in a personal injury case (*RSC Ord. 24, r. 7A*: **4.1.4.1**); pre-action inspection of evidence or objects (*RSC Ord. 29, r. 7A*: **4.1.4.2**); and an application for the court's approval of a compromise for an infant plaintiff where no writ had yet been issued (**19.8.7.2**). These instances are good examples of originating summons procedure, being each concerned with obtaining the court's ruling on one separable matter with no substantial investigation of facts involved. Originating summonses have a wider use than merely the determination of preliminary procedural points, though. An originating summons may be used as a means of obtaining the court's ruling on the merits of a case as a whole.

RSC Ord. 5, r. 4 provides that proceedings may, in principle, be begun either by writ or originating summons as the plaintiff considers appropriate. Thereafter, *RSC Ord. 5, r. 2* provides that certain kinds of actions must be begun by writ, i.e:

(a) in which a claim is made by the plaintiff for any relief or remedy for any tort, other than trespass to land;

(b) in which a claim is made by a plaintiff based on an allegation of fraud;

(c) in which a claim is made by a plaintiff for damages for breach of duty, whether by virtue of a contract or under an Act, or independently of any contract or any such provision, where the damages claimed consist of or include damages in respect of the death of any person or in respect of personal injuries or in respect of damage to property; and

(d) in which a claim is made by a plaintiff in respect of infringement of a patent.

Thus almost all actions in tort, or involving allegations of fraud, or those involving damages for breach of duty, and in particular personal injury or property damage cases and patent cases, must be brought by writ.

What is it that links these categories together? It is something of a generalisation but fair to say that in the main, where a court has to investigate disputed matters of fact or complex situations, the writ action is the best procedure. Writ actions, by their several interlocutory stages, provide the best fact-finding mechanism. Originating summons cases, although this is also a generalisation, are better suited to investigating matters of law or the construction of documents. There are in fact relatively few classes of case which are expressly reserved for originating summonses. *RSC Ord. 5, r. 3* provides that:

> *Proceedings by which an application is to be made to the High Court or a judge thereof under any Act must be begun by originating summons except whereby these rules or by or under any Act the application in question is expressly required or authorised to be made by some other means.*

RSC Ord. 5, r. 4(2) goes on to specify that commencement of an action by originating summons is particularly appropriate for certain kinds of proceedings, namely:

(a) in which the sole or principal question at issue is or is likely to be one of construction of an Act or of any instrument made under an Act or of any deed, will, contract or other document or some other question of law; or

(b) in which there is unlikely to be any substantial dispute of fact.

There is a proviso, however, that if the case seems likely to be one where a plaintiff will be wishing to apply for summary judgment under *Ord. 14* or *Ord. 86*, or there is any other reason to consider the proceedings more appropriate to be begun by writ, the choice is that of the plaintiff.

24.2 The Originating Summons Procedure

24.2.1 FORMS OF ORIGINATING SUMMONS

There are three types of originating summons whose form is specified in vol. 2 of the *Supreme Court Practice*. These are:

(a) The general form (form PF 8), which applies in most cases.

(b) The expedited form (form PF 10), which is to be used where a specific rule permits it (about 20 cases are listed in the *Supreme Court Practice*).

(c) The *ex parte* form (form PF 11), which is to be used where there is no opposing party to be served, for example an application for payment of trust funds out of court.

24.2.2 SERVICE OF THE SUMMONS

The summons is issued just as a writ is issued, by being presented with the appropriate number of copies at the Central Office for Queen's Bench cases, at Chancery Chambers in London for chancery cases, or at a District Registry.

If the summons is in either the general or expedited form it must be served with a form for acknowledging service, which is very similar to that used in writ cases. It has the same validity as a writ, namely four months if it is to be served within the jurisdiction, six months if outside.

24.2.3 CONTENTS OF THE ORIGINATING SUMMONS

By *RSC Ord. 7, r. 3*:

> *Every originating summons must include a statement of the questions on which the plaintiff seeks the determination or direction of the High Court or, as the case may be, a concise statement of the relief or remedy claimed in the proceedings.*

In other words, the originating summons must specify precisely what it is (typically the construction of some document) that is sought by the plaintiff.

24.2.4 AFFIDAVIT EVIDENCE

There are no pleadings as such in originating summons cases because pleadings are a vehicle designed to help the opposing parties get at the truth of *factual* allegations. Instead there is a provision in originating summons cases for affidavits to be filed at court and served. The plaintiff must serve affidavit evidence in relation to the matter at issue and the remedy which he claims within 14 days of the defendant acknowledging service; thereafter each defendant may file an affidavit with the court and serve it on the plaintiff and other defendants (*RSC Ord. 28, r. 1A (4)*). The plaintiff has the opportunity to file and serve further evidence in reply within 14 days.

24.2.5 THE FIRST HEARING

Relatively quickly, then, since there may be no need for any further interlocutory proceedings, the case can be ready for a first hearing. The plaintiff should obtain an appointment for the attendance of the parties before the Master or District Judge for the hearing of the summons within one month of the expiry of the time for serving affidavits. Exceptionally, if the summons is in expedited form, the first appointment is fixed at court when the originating summons is issued.

Notice of the hearing is thereupon served on all defendants who have acknowledged service, not less than four clear days before the date fixed. The plaintiff must specify on his notice of hearing any directions which he proposes to seek at the hearing.

24.2.6 PROCEDURE AT THE FIRST HEARING

At the first hearing the procedure is somewhat in the nature of a summons for directions under *RSC Ord. 25* in a writ action (see **Chapter 13**). It is the duty of the Master or District Judge to consider the state of the case, and in particular whether all necessary parties have been joined or are sufficiently represented. The court may consider whether the evidence is complete; and if it is and the point is a simple one, the Master or District Judge may consider whether the plaintiff is entitled to the order sought and make an appropriate order. If he thinks there are other parties to be joined or the Master or District Judge does not consider the matter within his jurisdiction (e.g. where an injunction or other equitable remedy is sought) then he will go on to give directions, including the possibility of transfer to the county court. These directions may include a requirement for the filing of further evidence, or for the attendance of deponents or for cross-examination, and then the proceedings may be adjourned.

24.2.7 SUBSEQUENT HEARING

If the proceedings are not summarily determined by the Master or District Judge at the first hearing, the summons may be adjourned either generally or to a particular date. An order may be made determining the place and mode of trial and directing the manner of setting down, which will usually be in accordance with the manner prescribed for setting down an action by writ with appropriate modifications, e.g. the filing of bundles of affidavits rather than pleadings.

Thereafter the matter will come on for trial in Chancery Division, Queen's Bench Division or county court, as appropriate.

TWENTY FIVE

ALTERNATIVE DISPUTE RESOLUTION

In this chapter it is not intended to deal with all possible forms of ADR, but to indicate very briefly some of the current dispute resolution processes. All of these processes fall into one of the following categories:

(a) negotiation;

(b) adjudication;

(c) mediation.

25.1 The Emergence of ADR

Recent years have seen the growth of 'Alternative Dispute Resolution' ('ADR') in, for example, family disputes, and more recently in commercial and other civil disputes. The term 'alternative' (as in comedy or medicine) may appear to suggest a non-conformist approach to dispute resolution, but this is not the case. ADR offers a range of additional resources to complement the present litigation system and is seen as widening the scope of available forms and processes rather than displacing litigation. Public expectation and professional attitudes tend to regard litigation as a first rather than a last resort, but the costs, delays and risks of litigation have made the possibilities of other means of resolving disputes attractive. A superficial attraction may be that parties hope even to dispense with lawyers in settling their difficulties, but regrettably, where there is any substance in the claim or any complexity in the law, it is rarely possible for lawyers to be dispensed with. Moreover, if one party thinks that he can act for himself but his opponent has competent legal representation, the party without a lawyer is likely to be at a substantial disadvantage however informally the parties have agreed to resolve their dispute.

In reality most court actions are eventually settled or abandoned. Relatively few cases (in the High Court only about 3 per cent) actually reach trial where a writ has been issued. Given that, it is apparent that at some stages in the litigation process the parties are brought to compromise. Thus it is argued that sensible people ought to be able to find some way of getting to the stage of compromise without having incurred the enormous expense and delays of the ordinary High Court action. Attempts to find alternative methods of resolving disputes can lead to illusory benefits, however. Unless some method is found of ensuring that binding procedural orders can be made on the parties, and that the outcome is also binding, it may be that a great deal of time and expense is wasted in trying alternative methods only to find that the parties need to have recourse to litigation eventually anyway. In addition, if either of the parties is recalcitrant or unscrupulous, formal litigation may be the only proper option for his opponent. In many spheres one of the parties will be of sufficient size and wealth to find the costs of litigation a positive tactical advantage because of its deterrent effect on potential opponents. This seems particularly to be true of some large companies, especially recently privatised monopoly statutory undertakers, who tend to have a most uncompromising attitude to claims made against them from their disgruntled consumers.

25.2 Negotiation

Negotiation is the process of discussing or dealing with a matter with a view to arriving at a mutual agreement, settlement or compromise. It is how we all arrange our affairs with one another in everyday life and in business, by establishing areas of agreement and reconciling areas of disagreement. There are various styles and approaches to negotiation used by solicitors which we have already considered at briefly at **4.5**.

25.3 Adjudication

Adjudication involves a third party making a decision which is binding on the parties, by litigation through the courts or by some other procedure.

25.3.1 LITIGATION

Litigation is the action of carrying on a legal action within the court system. The traditional system provides established court procedures, rules of evidence and the application of substantive law and precedent. The neutral 'decision makers' are the judges, Masters, District Judges and official referees. The decisions made in this process, with which the rest of this book is largely concerned, are final, subject to appeal or review.

Outside the formal court system a variety of tribunals also provide finality in their decisions on the rights of parties, e.g. between individuals as in the case of industrial tribunals; or between an individual and the state as in the case of immigration adjudicators and the Immigration Appeal Tribunal.

25.3.2 ARBITRATION WITHIN THE COURT SYSTEM

Claims within the small claims jurisdiction (currently up to £3,000) are automatically referred to arbitration, although the reference can be rescinded if there are special factors (see **21.9**).

It is also possible for the parties to apply for their case to be dealt with by arbitration, whatever the amount involved. In such a case a District Judge has power to deal with the claim informally and without the usual rules of evidence applying. This possibility, although technically available, is very rarely used in practice. In cases of any substance most parties prefer formality of procedure.

In the High Court it is possible to apply for a judge to deal with matters as an arbitrator (sometimes called an 'umpire') in commercial cases, giving the parties the benefit of commercial understanding, legal and judicial skills and the arbitration type procedure with greater speed and informality. Unfortunately, the listing of cases in the commercial list of the Queen's Bench Division (usually known as the 'Commercial Court') is currently under a great deal of pressure due to lack of available judges, and it would not greatly expedite matters to attempt to use this procedure. Moreover, in such cases all the usual interlocutory procedures are available, such as discovery and inspection, orders for exchange of expert evidence, and even interlocutory injunctions, and thus there may be just as much legal expense and complexity.

25.3.3 ARBITRATION OUTSIDE THE COURT SYSTEM

Arbitration outside the court system usually comes about where in the contract between them the parties have already provided that disputes shall be subject to arbitration. In such a case arbitration is usually subject to the terms of the *Arbitration Acts 1950* and *1979* and to the common law. However it is possible for the parties to an arbitration agreement to exclude many of the rules under the Acts and to substitute their own and to specify in particular what procedure is to be followed and what the powers of the arbitrator shall be.

Except in certain specialist trade or commodity disputes, arbitrations in the UK tend in fact to be conducted along similar lines to litigation procedures, applying the same interlocutory processes, e.g. discovery of documents, and even the formal rules of evidence. Thus such cases are likely to involve substantial delay (although perhaps not quite on the scale of formal litigation) and costs of a similar nature to those in conventional litigation. There is, of course, no legal aid available for arbitration. The powers of an arbitrator to award costs in such cases are usually the same as in court cases. The advantages are that in choosing the arbitrator the parties may select a specialist in the field of the dispute, who may not be a lawyer, and who will proceed at an agreed pace. His availability for considering interlocutory orders is likely to be somewhat greater and more flexible than that of High Court judge or Master. In addition, arbitration is usually conducted in private, which is often preferred by the parties in some kinds of commercial disputes.

If the arbitrator is not a lawyer it is possible for legal issues to be referred to the court during the course of the arbitration for separate decision. Although an arbitrator is usually granted some interlocutory powers, e.g. to direct discovery and exchange of witness statements, he will not have the power to make orders for interlocutory injunctions. In such cases, however, it is possible to apply to the High Court, to ask the High Court for any order which is appropriate and which the arbitrator has no power to make. This intermingling of arbitration and High Court is in itself illustrative of the fact that there may be little cost saving. The usefulness of a specialist adjudicator and the greater speed of the proceedings may, however, be sufficient justification for arbitration. The decision made by the arbitrator is usually binding on all the parties. There is a limited right of appeal on questions of law and occasionally there may be the possibility of judicial review if some wholly inappropriate procedural error has been made.

If the parties have an arbitration clause in the relevant contract, then it will take effect and the court will stay the proceedings forcing the parties back to arbitration. Despite *s. 4* however, the court does have a discretion to allow the court action to proceed, especially where there is a suggestion of fraud or fraudulent conspiracy between some of the parties, or where the case entirely turns on a matter of law. The fact that there is no real defence despite an arbitration clause and that the plaintiff wishes to proceed in court in order to obtain the advantage of summary judgment under *Ord. 14*, may in particular be a reason for allowing an action to proceed despite an arbitration clause (see *Archital Luxfer* v *Dunning (AJ) & Son* [1987] 1 FTLR 372). If there is no arbitration agreement between the parties they may, of course, subsequently to the dispute arising, agree to refer the matter to arbitration. Various associations provide arbitration services, including, e.g., the International Chamber of Commerce, local Chambers of Commerce and the Chartered Institute of Arbitrators. Trade associations also often offer arbitration, e.g. to the purchasers of package holidays which have gone wrong.

25.3.4 EXPERT DETERMINATION

This is a final alternative to arbitration. It occurs where the parties have agreed in the contract that disputes (usually of a scientific or technical nature) arising under the contract may be resolved by a chosen expert nominated in the contract or to be chosen by a method described in the contract. The expert's decision will be final and binding on the parties. Such agreements usually provide that the expert will *not* act as an arbitrator, so that the *Arbitration Acts* will not apply and the expert will not have to follow arbitration rules and procedures, nor will there be any appeal.

25.4 Mediation and Conciliation

25.4.1 MEDIATION

Mediation is a non adjudicatory process by which the parties engage the help of a neutral third party to resolve their dispute by negotiated agreement. Since the mediator has no power to deliver a binding decision or impose it on the parties, this may therefore be a helpful alternative in some kinds of case. The fact that if no agreement is eventually reached acceptable to both parties, either may resort to litigation, means, however, that there may be an unwelcome delay (and indeed extra expense, since both parties are likely to wish to consult their lawyers at certain stages of the process, or even have them directly involved with the mediator). The parties reserve their rights to resolve the matter by adjudication if they cannot do so by mediation.

25.4.2 CONCILIATION

Conciliation is a term often used interchangeably with mediation, but it has a slightly different meaning having been defined as a 'process of engendering common sense, reasonableness and agreement'. It is often viewed as a more general form of third-party intervention of a facilitative nature, whereas mediation is seen as a more specific form of this, involving (as in employer/employee disputes) the mediator playing a significant role in suggesting possible solutions. Conciliation is used in a number of fields, in particular in the case of industrial disputes (by ACAS), and indeed at the start of ordinary industrial tribunal proceedings. Likewise, there are possibilities of conciliation in separation and divorce and children's issues, and sometimes in community issues.

25.5 When Should ADR be Considered?

If ADR is to be an effective complement to litigation, then the circumstances in which it will be appropriate, and those when it will be inappropriate, must be considered. Mediation or other ADR procedures may be preferable to litigation in a wide range of business or personal relationships, particularly if the relationship is a continuing one. This is particularly the case in partnerships or as between company and shareholders. It may also be the case between persons who are frequently in a contractual relationship where they do not wish one dispute to sour what has otherwise been a satisfactory working situation, as between contractor and subcontractor, publisher and writer, and the like. ADR should particularly be considered where the issues between the parties arise from a breakdown in communications, misunderstandings about procedures to be adopted or differences on technical issues, especially in the construction industry. Confidentiality is often a very big advantage and the prospect of mediation, which will not involve lawyers at all and thus lead to a considerable costs saving, is always a consideration. Legal advice is often essential, however, at least at the outset of mediation or conciliation procedures, in order to ensure that the parties clearly understand the extent to which decisions made in the process are likely to be binding, and to what extent concessions made for the purpose of conciliation might be held against them should later formal proceedings need to instigated. Full legal advice may need to be given, for example, about the extent to which acknowledgement of errors in working practices might have further tort or insurance complications and even provide a basis for future liability in unrelated litigation. The difficulty of these subordinate issues is sometimes a powerful feature against alternative dispute resolution, at least between individuals; although in the case of disputes between companies, who will receive thorough and competent initial advice, there may be a great deal to be said for it.

Clearly there are circumstances where alternative dispute resolution is unlikely to be suitable once negotiations have broken down. This will be true of most personal injury litigation and in cases where immediate enforcement of a court order may be necessary, i.e. in almost every case where an injunction is likely to be sought.

TWENTY SIX

APPEALS IN CIVIL PROCEEDINGS

26.1 Appeals from Interlocutory Orders

26.1.1 INTERLOCUTORY ORDERS IN THE HIGH COURT MADE BY MASTER OR DISTRICT JUDGE

Where a District Judge or Master makes an interlocutory order there is generally an appeal as of right. It is not necessary to show any specific error or misuse of discretion by the District Judge or Master and the appeal is by way of complete rehearing. This means that one may introduce new evidence not put before the District Judge or Master; and take new or different points of law from those taken below. Appeal is to a High Court judge sitting in chambers and the notice must be issued within five days from the order being pronounced in the case of a Master, and seven days from the order being pronounced in the case of a District Judge. Solicitors have rights of audience before a judge in chambers.

The effect of this is that no matter how major or minor the interlocutory order appealed from, e.g. whether it is for a substantial interim payment, or merely to grant an extension of time at some stage, the unsuccessful party may appeal. It should be noted, however, that where there has been *a trial* of an issue before a Master or District Judge, and where a Master or District Judge has assessed damages, these orders are treated as final and appeal in that case is direct to the Court of Appeal within four weeks from the order being sealed. In other words, the intervening stage of the judge in chambers is missed out. See *RSC Ord. 37*.

26.1.2 INTERLOCUTORY ORDER MADE BY COUNTY COURT DISTRICT JUDGE

Appeal lies as of right to a county court judge in chambers, which must be made by notice of appeal filed and served on the opposite party within five days.

26.1.3 INTERLOCUTORY ORDERS MADE BY A HIGH COURT JUDGE

In the case of an interlocutory order made by a High Court judge, e.g. for an interlocutory injunction, or the order made after appeal from the District Judge or Master, appeal lies to the Court of Appeal and leave is usually required.

The definition of 'interlocutory order' was until recently unclear. A new section (*s. 60*) has been inserted in the *Supreme Court Act 1981*, which provides that rules of the Supreme Court may prescribe the classes of case in which an appeal to the Court of Appeal will lie only with leave, and such rules may prescribe whether leave may be granted by the Court of Appeal or the court below. The class of case which is now to be considered interlocutory is now comprehensively set out in *RSC Ord. 59, r. 1A*. And this is in turn supplemented by a *Practice*

Direction (Court of Appeal: Procedure) [1995] 1 WLR 1191 in its turn supplemented by a *Practice Statement (Court of Appeal: Procedural Changes)* [1995] 1 WLR 1188. Where leave is required it may be given either by the High Court Judge or on a preliminary application to the Court of Appeal, usually by a single judge of that court.

26.2 Appeals in Arbitration Cases

There is in principle no appeal from a District Judge sitting as arbitrator. However, an application can be made to a county court judge for the arbitrator's award to be set aside on the grounds of:

(a) lack of jurisdiction; or

(b) misconduct; or

(c) material error of law on the face of the record.

26.3 Appeals from Final Orders

26.3.1 FINAL ORDERS BY HIGH COURT JUDGE

In the case of a final order made by a High Court Judge, e.g. the judgment at trial on the merits, appeal lies to the Court of Appeal and no leave is usually required. The time for appeal is four weeks from the order being sealed, and within that time notice of appeal should be served on all opposite parties. Thereafter the notice of appeal should be set down within seven days from the date on which it was served.

26.3.2 FINAL ORDERS BY COUNTY COURT JUDGE

Appeal lies to the Court of Appeal without leave, provided that the amount claimed in the action exceeds certain figures to be fixed from time to time by statutory instrument. At the time of writing these figures are:

(a) in actions in contract and tort, £5,000; and

(b) in equity proceedings, £15,000.

Where the amounts are below those figures then the leave of the trial judge or of the Court of Appeal is required. If no money is in issue (e.g. if everything turns on an application for an injunction) then no leave is in principle required.

26.4 Procedure in the Court of Appeal

26.4.1 INTERLOCUTORY APPEALS

Most interlocutory applications have to do with the exercise of the court's discretion, oral evidence not being in general relevant, although there are some significant exceptions (e.g. injunction applications). In almost all cases the discretion is conferred on the Master or District Judge.

On appeal from a Master or District Judge, a High Court or county court judge exercises his or her own discretion without regard to how it was exercised below and deals with the matter completely afresh. On further appeal to the Court of Appeal, however, that court will not as a rule interfere with the intervening judge's discretion. The Court of Appeal will only substitute its own exercise of discretion in limited circumstances, although it is quite clear from the case law that if the Court of Appeal is minded to change the outcome it will easily find that the case falls within one of the following categories, namely where the judge:

(a) failed to exercise his discretion at all, or exercised his discretion in a way in which no reasonable judge could have exercised it; or

(b) erred in principle or in law;

(c) took into account irrelevant matters; or

(d) misinterpreted the facts or evidence in a manifest way.

26.4.2 APPEALS FROM FINAL ORDERS

RSC Ord. 59, r. 3, indicates that these appeals are also by way of rehearing, but in the usual case there is not in fact any oral evidence. The appellant will open, whether he was plaintiff or defendant below. The evidence of witnesses called at the trial will be considered only from the transcripts or the judge's note of the evidence. The court may hear fresh evidence (but in a civil case only very exceptionally) in relation to:

(a) matters occurring since the date of hearing;

(b) evidence which could not have been obtained with reasonable diligence for use at the hearing, which is reasonably credible and would probably have an important influence on the result of the case (see *Ladd* v *Marshall* [1954] 1 WLR 1489). This evidence will usually be put in the form of affidavit. Exceptionally, cross-examination of the new witness may be allowed.

The Court of Appeal's function when hearing a substantive appeal is to consider whether the judge below has erred and whether that error made a material difference to the outcome. Errors of law or errors of principle will be considered fully by the Court of Appeal when argued. However, the Court of Appeal will usually come to different conclusions on matters of fact, evidence or credibility and the exercise of discretion only in limited circumstances.

26.4.3 THE PROCEDURE ON APPEAL

Reference should be made to the 1995 *Practice Direction* and *Practice Statement* referred to at **26.1.3** above. These Directions in part consolidate the previous position but add new material and now provide a Code of Practice for the bringing of appeals to the Court of Appeal. What follows is a bare outline of the procedure.

(a) If it is a case where leave is required, leave should first be sought from the court below. If leave is refused, application should be made *ex parte* to the Court of Appeal for leave to appeal, which will usually be considered by a single judge. Where the appeal is as of right, notice of appeal must be served on all other parties affected by the appeal within four weeks of the order being made below. Thereafter, within seven days the papers must be lodged in the Civil Appeals Office for setting down and the fee paid.

(b) Application should then be made for a transcript of the shorthand writer's notes of evidence and the full judgment, or for the judge's notes of evidence and reasons for the order.

(c) When the appeal is set down it will be given a reference number. The Civil Appeals Office will then send out a form indicating what further steps must be taken and within what timetable. The form also indicates on what date the appeal will be added to the running list.

(d) Thereafter it is for the appellant to lodge the requisite number of appeal bundles comprising all relevant documents in the case, with the Civil Appeals Office. The appellant's counsel should then certify his estimate of the length of the appeal hearing and provide copies of that estimate to other counsel involved. Other counsel may then lodge their own time estimates if they differ from those of the appellant's counsel.

(e) Shortly before the hearing all counsel must lodge copies of their skeleton arguments with the Civil Appeals Office. These must indicate the chronology of events and the matters to be argued, together with a full list of authorities. In complex cases, as well as the chronology a list of *dramatis personae* should be lodged, e.g. in a commercial case where there are many interlocking companies.

(f) The case will then come into the list for hearing, usually by a two or three judge court.

26.5 Miscellaneous Matters Relevant to Appeal

26.5.1 STAY OF EXECUTION

Initiating an appeal does not automatically stay execution in respect of the judgment or order from which appeal is being made. A stay may be sought generally, either from the court below or the court above. In considering whether an application should be granted the court bears in mind that a successful litigant should not be deprived of the outcome of his litigation. A stay may be granted in particular where the appeal is arguable and the consequences for a defendant are drastic, if it appears to the court that there is some prospect of success in a proper case. The principles are contained in *Linotype-Hell Finance Ltd* v *Baker* [1993] 1 WLR 321, although this case should be read together with *Simonite* v *Sheffield City Council* (1993) *The Times*, 12 January 1993, which suggests caution in granting a stay pending appeal.

26.5.2 COSTS ON APPEAL

The costs order to be made on appeal is within the discretion of the court. In general, a successful appellant will be given his costs 'here and below', meaning that he will obtain his costs on appeal and also costs in respect of the proceedings in the lower court. However, a different order may be made where, e.g.:

(a) the appeal is only partly successful; or

(b) the appeal was successful only on a point not raised in the notice of appeal.

If the respondent wins in the Court of Appeal, he will require a costs order only in respect of the appeal proceedings since he will already have the costs order in the court below. A successful respondent may nonetheless be deprived of his costs where:

(a) he has succeeded on a technicality; or

(b) new points were raised which were not raised at the original hearing.

In many cases there will be both an appeal and cross-appeal, and when deciding on the orders made, e.g. where both are allowed or both are dismissed, the court will have regard in particular to the length of the whole proceedings occasioned by each party's conduct; though it may also bear in mind that a cross-appeal might only have been lodged in response to the original appeal and would not have been brought on its own.

26.5.3 DRAWING UP JUDGMENTS

Judgments of the Court of Appeal are drawn up by the court associate and not by the parties.

INDEX